PHILIP PARKER

Philip Parker was educated at Trinity Hall,
Cambridge. He has travelled widely, including
the whole length of the Roman frontier and
large parts of the Viking World. He is the author
of *The Empire Stops Here: A Journey along the
Frontiers of the Roman World,* published by
Jonathan Cape in 2009.

ALSO BY PHILIP PARKER

The Empire Stops Here:
A Journey along the Frontiers of the Roman
World

PHILIP PARKER

The Northmen's Fury

A History of the Viking World

VINTAGE BOOKS
London

2 4 6 8 10 9 7 5 3 1

Vintage

20 Vauxhall Bridge Road,

London SW1V 2SA

Vintage is part of the Penguin Random House group of companies whose addresses can be found at global.penguinrandomhouse.com

Penguin
Random House
UK

First published in Vintage in 2015

First published in hardback by Jonathan Cape in 2014

Permission to quote from *Ibn Fadlan's Journey to Russia*, translated by Richard Frye (2005), courtesy of Markus Wiener Publishers

www.vintage-books.co.uk

A CIP catalogue record for this book is available from the British Library

ISBN 9780099551843

Typeset by Palimpsest Book Production Ltd, Falkirk, Stirlingshire

Printed and bound by CPI Group (UK) Ltd, Croydon, CR0 4YY

Penguin Random House is committed to a sustainable future for our business, our readers and our planet. This book is made from Forest Stewardship Council® certified paper.

MIX
Paper from
responsible sources
FSC® C018179

To my parents, who saw the beginning of this voyage,
but could not be there at its ending.

Contents

List of Plates

List of Maps

Acknowledgements

This book has been more than three years in the making, and many people have helped me along the way. I would in particular like to thank the team at Jonathan Cape who have done a fantastic job in bringing the book to publication: Dan Franklin, who believed in the idea enough to commission it and to wait with admirable patience for its completion; Caroline McArthur and Clare Bullock for their work in shaping the manuscript and Mandy Greenfield, whose astute copy-editing has immeasurably improved the raw material. Thanks also to Joe Burgis who so ably steered the paperback edition to completion. My gratitude is also due once again to Martin Brown, whose excellent cartography has produced maps that beautifully illustrate the sometimes confusing topography of the Viking World. And of course thanks to my wonderful agent, Gill Coleridge at RCW, and her assistant Cara Jones, whose advice and encouragement have, as ever, proved invaluable to the book.

A host of people assisted me during my various visits to parts of the Scandinavian world, and I am grateful for all the countless friendly welcomes and hospitality I received there. I would particularly like to thank Ragnhild Ljosland, Alexandra Sanmark and all the staff at the Centre for Nordic Studies of the University of the Highlands and Islands at Kirkwall, for enabling me to see so much of Orkney during a highly enjoyable week at their Viking Summer School on the island.

Any faults and omissions must remain the responsibility of the author, but I would like to thank all those who commented on the manuscript at various stages during the writing of the book, in particular Amanda Faber, whose suggestions on the very first draft improved it tremendously. Thanks also to Shane McLeod at the University of Stirling, whose expert eye pointed out many pitfalls and areas where my treatment of the subject had fallen short.

I would also like to thank (very belatedly) Richard Overy, whose generous encouragement set me along the path from editor to writer with my first book *The Empire Stops Here* and so, indirectly, is responsible for this one, too. I would also like to thank the staff at the London Library, a wonderful institution which provided the haven in which most of this book was written.

And finally, my heartfelt thanks go to my partner, Tania, who has had to put up with years of Viking-obsession on my part and my disappearances to far-flung parts of the Scandinavian world, and my daughter, Livia, who is never shy of pointing out the error of illustrations which portray the Vikings wearing horned helmets. Without their love and support, none of this would have been possible.

Note on Names

The spelling of names in a history of the Viking Age presents particular problems. The same person's name may be spelled differently in a number of different sources (Irish, Anglo-Saxon, Icelandic, Greek or even Arabic) and so complete consistency is difficult. In general I have chosen to spell place-names in Scandinavia and western Europe in the form most commonly used in those countries today (save where there is a generally accepted anglicised form, such as Copenhagen, rather than København). Elsewhere, I have generally given the Old Norse form of Viking names, with the exception of dropping the final nominative '-r' (and so I use the form Harald instead of Haraldr) and some simplification of accents and diacriticals. Again, where there are generally accepted anglicised forms, such as Odin and Thor (rather than Óðinn and Þórr), I have used these. Two letters which exist in Old Norse and Icelandic may be unfamiliar to some readers – these are ð, which is equivalent to a 'breathed' th (as in *father*), and Þ, which is the same as an 'unbreathed' th (as in *think*).

Map 1 The Viking World

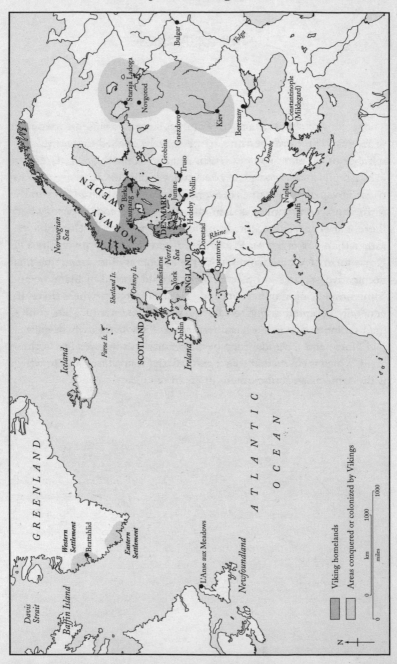

Viking homelands

Areas conquered or colonized by Vikings

Introduction

Then the wolvish Vikings, avid for slaughter, waded to the west across the River Panta. The seafarers hoisted their shields on high and carried them over the gleaming water. Byrhtnoth and his warriors awaited them, ready for battle; he ordered his men to form a phalanx with their shields, and to stand firm against the onslaught of the enemy. Then was the battle, with its chance of glory, about to begin. The time had come for all the doomed men to fall in the fight.

The clamour began; the ravens wheeled and the eagle circled overhead, craving for carrion; there was shouting on earth. They hurled their spears, hard as files, and sent sharp darts flying from their hands. Bow strings were busy, shield parried point. Bitter was the battle. Brave men fell on both sides, youths choking in the dust . . . The brave men stood resolute, rock firm. Each of them hunting for a way to be first in with his spear, winning with his weapons the life of a doomed warrior; the dead sank down to the earth. But the rest stood unshaken and Byrhtnoth spurred them on, inciting each man to fight ferociously who wished to gain glory against the Danes . . . Another seafarer advanced on the earl, meaning to make short work of him and snatch away his treasures – his armour and his rings and his ornamented sword.

Byrhtnoth drew out his sword from its sheath, broad-faced and gleaming, and made to slash at the seafarer's corselet. But his enemy stopped him all too soon, savagely striking Byrhtnoth's arm. The golden-hilted sword dropped from his hand. He could hold it no longer nor wield a weapon of any kind. Then the old warrior raised his men's morale with bold words, calling on his companions to do battle again . . . Then the heathens hewed him down and the two men who stood there supporting him; Aelfnoth and Wulfmaer fell to the dust, both gave their lives in defence of their lord . . . So Aethelred's earl, the prince of those people fell; all his hearth-companions could see for themselves that their lord lay low. Then the proud thanes, with the utmost

bravery, threw themselves once more into the thick of the battle. They all,
without exception, strove to one of two ends – to avenge their lord or to leave
this world.

'The Battle of Maldon Poem', eleventh century[1]

The 'wolvish Vikings' who struck at Maldon in Essex in 991 were the
latest in a succession of Scandinavian warrior pirates who spread terror
throughout Europe and almost overwhelmed the kingdoms in Ireland,
Britain and France that had the misfortune to stand in their way. From
their very first raid 200 years before against the English monastery of
Lindisfarne, these northern pirates inspired fear in contemporary chroniclers, and they have fascinated historians ever since. Their onslaught led
the name of 'Viking' (and its various synonyms) to become a byword
for violence and lawlessness, their pagan religion making it seem to
their victims that the attackers were the agents of divine judgement.
So much so that petrified monks, fearful that their monastic house
might be next on the list of communities sacked by the Norsemen,
were reputed to have prayed for deliverance: *A furore Normannorum nos*
libera, Domine ('From the Northmen's Fury, O Lord, deliver us!').[2]

This book tells the story of the Scandinavian people who, for two
centuries from that first violent onslaught against the monastery of
Lindisfarne in 793, used their mastery of the sea to dominate large
parts of Europe and to colonise lands beyond it. These Vikings were
no mere monochrome warriors, intent solely on bloodthirsty rampage.
They came from a culture of incredible complexity and richness, with
a legacy of vibrant art, a literature rich in sagas and poetry, a society
that produced law-codes and Europe's earliest parliaments. Their
attacks had profound effects on the political development of the countries they raided or settled, while the footprint of their DNA means
that millions of people across the world share Viking ancestry.

How was it that Scandinavia, a land at Europe's far periphery,
suddenly gave birth to a violent migration that almost destroyed the
kingdoms of the Franks and Anglo-Saxons, two of ninth-century
Europe's most advanced cultures? How did the Vikings succeed in
outmanoeuvring their opponents to establish footholds and colonies
across such an astonishingly wide area? Why did the raids peter out
in the eleventh century, and what inheritance did the Vikings bequeath
to the lands they terrorised or settled? These are the questions at the

heart of this book, which begins with an examination of the origins of the Vikings, the very early development of their home countries of Denmark, Norway and Sweden, before looking at their society, their culture and giving an account of the raids, the conquests and a history of the Viking colonies themselves.

Arriving from the sea without warning, the Vikings seemed to their victims to erupt from nowhere. The geographical range of their raids is astonishing. Setting out from their homelands in modern-day Denmark, Norway and Sweden, the raiders moved much more swiftly than their adversaries' land-based forces could match, even sailing up navigable rivers to engage in opportunistic raids on great cities such as London and Paris. Exercising their maritime skills still further, the Vikings sailed east to the southern shores of the Baltic – and then down the great river systems into central Russia, the Ukraine and even to Constantinople (modern Istanbul), the glittering capital of the Byzantine empire. To the west, they ranged as far as the eastern seaboard of Canada, where they landed nearly five centuries before Christopher Columbus 'discovered' America.

Much about the early history of the Viking period remains unclear, our understanding hampered by the lack of written sources. Even the very origin of the term 'Viking' itself is obscure. It was not in fact much used by contemporaries (at least not in the annals that chronicle the first raids), with the Anglo-Saxons in England preferring *Dani* ('Danes'), the Franks *Normanni* ('North-men'), the Irish *Gall* ('Foreigner'), the Byzantines and Arabs opting for variants on *Rus* or *Rhos*, and regular occurrences of the pointedly religious reference *pagani* ('pagans') in the western European annals. The word has been variously associated with the Old Norse *vig*, meaning 'battle', or *vik* ('bay' or 'inlet'), and could also be connected to the Viken, the large bay in Norway's Oslofjord whence many of the raids against England were launched. Less plausible attempts at etymology include *vikja*, meaning 'to move', supposedly derived from the Viking propensity to wander, and even a corruption of *vicus*, the Latin name for the settlement outside a military fort and therefore a reference to the inhabitants who were the 'camp folk'. Contemporary uses of the word 'Viking' are in fact limited to a handful of occurrences in the *Anglo-Saxon Chronicle* in the ninth century, in which, in the form *wicingas*, it refers to small bands of raiders.[3]

Although it is in a sense anachronistic to use the term 'Viking' to refer to the raiders of the eighth and ninth centuries, the word had come into more common usage by the late tenth century to signify pirates, or for a person who had chosen the lifestyle of a maritime freebooter (who was said to have gone 'a Viking'). It is in any case a convenient shorthand for all the various groups who left Scandinavia from the late eighth to the early eleventh centuries, first in search of plunder and then, before long, in pursuit of fresh land on which to settle. There is a further confusion to be had with the terms 'Norse' (or 'Norsemen') and 'Scandinavia', with the former, strictly speaking, referring to the groups who spoke the language known as Old Norse, but equally – as it is a derivation of 'Normanni' – one of the common terms used by chroniclers to refer to the raiders, a perfectly valid term to use. Similarly, although technically today Scandinavia refers to the modern countries of Denmark, Norway and Sweden, the culture which they exported throughout the Viking world was a 'Scandinavian' one, and so for the sake of avoiding repetitive use I have chosen to employ the terms Norse, Viking and Scandinavian almost interchangeably.

In the English-speaking world, the beginning of the Viking Age is almost always set at 793, the year of the attack on Lindisfarne, when these new raiders came so clamorously to the attention of the outside world. From then, for over two centuries, the Viking raids continued almost without pause until around 1000, when many parts of the Viking world began to become Christianised, more settled and the source of far fewer (if any) of the violent sallies against their neighbours that had hitherto characterised them. When, though, did the Viking Age finish? There is no single clear answer to this, and I have chosen to end my account of the Vikings at different dates appropriate to the various areas in which they operated. In England, the Viking Age terminated in the late eleventh century with the final (totally unsuccessful) Scandinavian attempts at conquest, while in Scotland the deeper nature of Norse penetration (particularly in Orkney and Shetland) meant that Norwegian kings could still try to assert their sovereignty there in the 1260s. In Iceland, the Viking Age may be considered concluded when the descendants of the first Viking settlers there gave up their cherished independence to King Håkon of Norway in 1262, while in Greenland I have opted to take the history of the

Viking settlements down to their mysterious disappearance at some point in the mid-fifteenth century. In contrast, in Scandinavia the growth in the power of monarchies there from the start of the twelfth century, when Christianity and stronger royal control emerged (and large-scale raiding ceased), argue for the treatment of Denmark, Sweden and Norway more as mainstream European kingships after that time than as separate Viking phenomena. And finally in Russia by the eleventh century, the principalities that the Vikings had founded there had evolved into states which were more Slavic than Scandinavian and so this, too, marks a convenient point to end that area's 'Viking' history.

The sources by which we know about the Vikings are many and complex, and in general I have chosen to deal with these in the chapter to which they are most relevant. The most important and controversial of these, and the ones that hold the most resonance and sense of immediacy for modern readers, are the sagas, tales of the Viking Age which were (almost all) composed in Iceland in the twelfth and thirteenth centuries. They do, however, very often draw on earlier traditions about the events they recount; the origin of the word 'saga' is in the Old Norse *segja*, 'to speak' or 'to say', indicating clearly the oral nature of these tales in their original form. Although largely in prose (with a certain amount of older 'skaldic' poetry (see p. 7) embedded within) and with deceptively straightforward stories, the sagas are not always easy to use as a basis for constructing a historical narrative. The set known as *konungasögur* ('king's sagas'), which were probably set down in written form in the period 1180–1280, tell us much about the major historical happenings in Norway, Denmark and Sweden, but the larger corpus of family sagas (*Íslendingasögur*), for all their stirring and dramatic stories of murder, revenge and (more rarely) reconciliation, are most concerned with the interactions of particular families and individuals. Though set within a clearly defined historical milieu, they cannot be taken as a literal and detailed depiction of the way things were in Viking-Age Iceland, let alone elsewhere in other Viking lands such as Scotland or Norway. Another group of sagas, including mythical and heroic tales (*fornaldarsögur*) and hagiographical lives of bishops and holy men (*heilagra manna sögur*), draw from folktales in the case of the former, and in the latter are so heavily modelled on lives of saints elsewhere that their use as historical sources is fraught with difficulty.

Although we are dependent for the early phases of the Viking raids on chronicles and histories written by their victims (with the inevitable problems of the sources' general antipathy towards their persecutors), works such as the *Anglo-Saxon Chronicle*, the *Frankish Royal Annals* and the *Russian Primary Chronicle* do provide invaluable accounts of the early Viking period. Other, mainly ecclesiastical writers, such as Adam of Bremen, who wrote a history of the archbishops of Hamburg-Bremen in the twelfth century, also give a great deal of important information about the Vikings (but, again, not from their own perspective). Eventually the Viking world gave rise to its own historical tradition, beginning in Iceland with the works of Saemund Sigfússon, who wrote a history of the Norwegian kings in the early twelfth century, and Ari the Learned who composed the *Íslendingabók* ('The Book of the Icelanders') between 1122 and 1133. Before long the other Viking nations had their historians, most notably the *Gesta Danorum* ('The Deeds of the Danes'), compiled by the Danish clergyman Saxo Grammaticus around 1220, and the *Heimskringla* ('History of the Norwegian Kings'), written by the Icelander Snorri Sturluson (also the author of several sagas) sometime before 1241. With these, we begin to get a genuinely Scandinavian view of Viking history, but it is nonetheless a retrospective one, from a time when the age of the raids was long gone (if not forgotten). A more laconic, yet invaluable (for being contemporary) written testament to the Viking Age comes in the form of runestones, stone monuments inscribed in a Scandinavian alphabet, which most often act as a memorial to dead. Their mention of men who had fought – and often perished – on Viking expeditions abroad (such as a cluster of runestones that remember warriors who fell on the expedition of Yngvar the Widefarer beyond the Caspian around 1040) give them a sense of immediacy that many other sources lack.

A significant part of the corpus of Viking-Age literature comes in the shape of poetry. This falls into two general categories. The first of these are the Eddic poems, which included stories of the gods and heroes and form the largest original body for our knowledge of the Scandinavian pagan belief system. Some of them, such as the *Voluspá*, which sets out the pagan Norse view of the creation, may be of very ancient vintage (although there is an opposing view that these neat collections of stories came about as a reaction to the rise of

Christianity from the tenth century).[4] Skaldic poems (of which around 5,000 verses have survived) often deal instead with historical events, and we frequently have the names of the poets (or skalds)[5] who wrote them, who were more often than not in the retinues of kings or leading chieftains. Composed in a highly alliterative style, the skaldic poems are, to modern eyes, very hard to interpret, making ample use of word-play and riddles in a form called *kennings*. These are circumlocutions that conceal the original meaning, often through several layers of symbolism. Some are relatively straightforward, so that a 'steed of the sea' may refer to a 'ship' or 'sweat of the sword' to 'blood', while others require a knowledge of Viking mythology that a modern reader may lack: hence 'the burden of the dwarves' means 'sky', because the gods are said to have made the world out of the skull of the giant Ymir and to have set four dwarves, one at each of the cardinal points, to support it.

Viking society valued quick wit and action. The *Hávamál* ('The Sayings of the High One'), a collection of aphorisms much in vogue in the early twenty-first century, includes the pithy advice: 'Let the man who opens a door be on the lookout for an enemy beside him' and 'A foolish man who comes among people, had best be silent; for no one knows that he knows nothing, unless he talks too much' and, of more general application, 'Never let a bad man know of your misfortunes.' More resonant of the Viking ethos as a whole, of their search for glory and concern for reputation, is the most famous saying of them all: 'Cattle die, kindred die, we ourselves shall die, but I know one thing that never dies: the reputations of each one dead.'[6]

In their wish to preserve the memories of their deeds, the Vikings succeeded. Perhaps the truth is more complex, more modulated than the reputation the Vikings have established over the centuries. But warriors such as the unknown war-band leaders who attacked Lindisfarne, Eirik the Red who discovered Greenland and Harald Hardrada of Norway, who fell fighting to the last at Stamford Bridge in 1066, would have been most pleased that history remembers them as the men they wished to be – heroic, proud, undaunted by danger – rather than perhaps as the men they really were.

Map 2 The Early Viking Raids in Britain and Ireland

Raids on Ireland, 795–850
Viking longphorts in Ireland
Raids on Britain, 793–850
Area of Viking settlement in Scotland by 850

Shetland

Orkney

CAITHNESS

Hebrides

**ALBA
(SCOTLAND)**

Atlantic Ocean

Iona

North Sea

Lindisfarne
first dated Viking raid, 793

NORTHUMBRIA

*Vikings first overwinter
in Ireland, 840* Derry

Inishmurray Lough Neagh
Bangor

Armagh

Monkwearmouth

CONNACHT
IRISH
Clonmacnoise Slane
Durrow
Irish Sea
Clonfert Clonard Dublin
Founded 841
Glendalough
KINGDOMS Ferns

Inis Patraic
The Skerries

Lindsey

Loch Léin Lismore
Skellig Michael Cork
Waterford

**WELSH
KINGDOMS**

M E R C I A

**EAST
ANGLIA**

London
Minehead
Carhampton
Southampton
W E S S E X
Hingston Down Dorchester
CORNWALL
Portland

Rochester
Romney
Marsh
Sheppey
Thanet

*Viking fleet overwinters
for first time in
England, 850*

English Channel

N

N O R M A N D Y

0   km   100
0   miles   100

I

The Origins of the Vikings

One calm summer's day in 793 the Vikings made their tumultuous entry into the historical record. Raiding ships, which had probably made their way over from western Norway, appeared at the monastery of Lindisfarne on Holy Island off the coast of Northumbria in north-east England and proceeded to sack it. The monks, who had led a life of largely blameless sanctity since the Irish hermit St Aidan founded the house in 635, were powerless as their treasures were hauled back to the raiders' dragon-prowed longships. Any who dared to resist were cut down.

To judge from the reactions to this first Viking attack, the raid was totally unexpected. The accounts of contemporary writers verged on the hysterical. The *Anglo-Saxon Chronicle*,[1] whose pages would document the woeful litany of later raids, comments that 'In this year dire portents appeared over Northumbria and sorely frightened the people. They consisted of immense whirlwinds and flashes of lightning, and fiery dragons were seen flying in the air . . . on 8th June, the ravages of heathen men miserably destroyed God's church on Lindisfarne with plunder and slaughter.' One monkish chronicler, Symeon of Durham (writing in the early twelfth century),[2] described how the Vikings 'devastated everything with pitiless looting, trampled the holy things under their sacrilegious feet, dug up the altars and pillaged all the treasures of the church. Some of the brothers they killed, several they bound with opprobrium and threw out naked, and others they drowned in the sea.'[3]

Our impressions of the Lindisfarne raid have been for ever coloured by the reaction of Alcuin, a leading Northumbrian scholar and churchman who had taken service in the court of the Frankish ruler Charlemagne in 786, and who happened to have been on a visit back home just before the Viking raid. Perhaps it was the closeness of Lindisfarne to his own origins (in York) that made him feel so strongly, for Alcuin wrote no fewer than five letters about the attack, using it as a pretext to condemn the lax morals of his English countrymen, and blaming their waywardness for 'the scourge that has fallen on the church of St Cuthbert'.⁴ Alcuin stressed the barbarity of the Vikings – in his view, the instruments of God's judgement – at the cost of a coherent account of the attack itself. In one letter to King Aethelred of Northumbria he writes, 'Lo, it is nearly 350 years that we and our forefathers have inhabited this lovely island and never before has such terror in Britain as we have now suffered from a pagan race, nor was it thought that such an inroad from the sea could happen.'⁵ Warming to his theme, he adds, 'Behold, the church of St Cuthbert spattered with the blood of the priests of God, despoiled of all its ornaments, a place more venerable than all in Britain is given as a prey to pagan peoples.' He places the blame squarely on the shocking behaviour of his compatriots, who should 'Consider the dress, the way of wearing the hair, the luxurious habits of the princes and people. Look at your trimming of beard and hair, in which you have wished to resemble the pagans.' The pillaging of Lindisfarne clearly fitted Alcuin's agenda of ecclesiastical regeneration, a point he pressed home time and time again in his references to the attack. Chroniclers outside England, however, were not so impressed, and the Lindisfarne raid to which Alcuin returned to again and again in his letters merits scarcely a mention.

There is some evidence that the raid on Lindisfarne may not even have been the very first on the British Isles. The entry in the *Anglo-Saxon Chronicle* for 789 refers to the arrival of three ships off the coast of Dorset during the reign of King Beohrtric of Wessex. The royal reeve rode out to them and asked the crews to come to the royal residence, 'for he did not know what they were'. The newcomers refused and, after an argument, killed him. The twelfth-century writer Aethelweard expanded the account to include further details: that the reeve's name was Beaduheard and that he had been at Dorchester when he heard news of the foreign vessels that had put in at Portland. As Beohrtric's reign is known to have been from 786 to 802, the attack could well have preceded that on Lindisfarne.⁶ The West Saxon chronicler was in no doubt that it did, as he wrote, 'Those were the first ships of Danish men which came to the land of the English.'

The likelihood that there were trading relations between Scandinavia and England in the late eighth century which could, on occasion, turn violent is strengthened by a decree of Offa, ruler of the central English kingdom of Mercia, in 792, in which he called on the men of Kent to defend themselves against 'pagan peoples'. The measure also exempted churches from royal taxation, save where this was needed to guard against 'heathens in roving ships' – a sign that there may have been still earlier raids, which have left no trace in the written record. The tendency of the *Anglo-Saxon Chronicle*, our main source for this period, to concentrate almost exclusively on the deeds of the West Saxon house (and in particular on their fight against the Vikings) also raises the possibility that there were other attacks that did not affect Wessex, and which the *Chronicle*'s compilers therefore omitted.

The initial raid on Lindisfarne was all too soon followed by others. Northumbria, in which the monastery lay, was struck again in 794, and an attack up the Tyne aimed at the monastery at Jarrow was beaten off in 796 (when the crews of the Viking vessels were slain). After that, England enjoyed a slight breathing space. There are diplomas issued by the Mercian kings that mention Viking activity in the years 792–822, but these are not recorded in the *Anglo-Saxon Chronicle*, which gives the date of the next raid as 835 (when the Vikings ravaged Sheppey in Kent).[7]

The Norsemen seem to have found more convenient targets elsewhere. From the west of Norway, the voyage to north-eastern Scotland and the Northern Isles was not a difficult one, and so it is little surprise that the Scottish coastline became an early victim of their attentions. The first recorded raid there (on the Hebrides) came in 794, scarcely a year after the attack on Lindisfarne. Attacks also then commenced in rapid succession against Ireland and Francia (where the monastery of Saint-Philibert at the mouth of the Loire experienced the first attack in 799).

Within twelve months of the attack on the Hebrides, the Vikings had fallen upon the island of Iona off the west coast of Scotland. Their target was the great monastery founded there by the Irish monk Columba in 563 as a centre for the conversion of the pagan tribes of Scotland. By the early eighth century it had become a renowned pilgrimage centre and, inevitably, had grown rich from the donations of legions of pious visitors. Just as predictably, its wealth attracted a steady stream of Viking raiders, who followed the attack of 795 with another in 802, and then a major assault in 806, when sixty-eight of the monks were slaughtered.

Fed up of being the helpless victims of these northern heathens, the brethren decamped the following year to Kells in Ireland with whatever was left of their patrimony of precious relics. A few diehards spurned the Christian doctrine of turning the other cheek and, under the direction of the prior, Blathmac MacFlainn, resolved to win the crown of martyrdom should the raiders return. The Vikings duly obliged and in 825 slaughtered the would-be warrior monks to the last man, inflicting horrible torture on Blathmac and finally killing him for his refusal to tell them where the bones of St Columba – which had been interred in a shrine laden with precious jewels – were buried. The poem that Walafrid Strabo, Abbot of Reichenau in south Germany from 838 to 848, wrote to commemorate St Blathmac's martyrdom recalls the scene vividly: 'the violent cursed host came rushing through the buildings, threating cruel perils to the blessed men, and after slaying with mad savagery the rest of the community, they approached the holy father, to compel him to give up the precious metals wherein lie the bones of St Columba . . . but the saint remained with unarmed hand, and with unshaken purpose of mind, trained to stand against the foe'.[8]

Ireland was not spared the fury of the Northmen for long, and in 795 the *Annals of Ulster* reported, 'The burning of *Rechru* by the pagans and Skye was overwhelmed and laid waste.'[9] Worse was to come, for in 798 *Inis Pátraic* (off the Skerries, around 20 miles north of Dublin) was burnt by the Vikings, who are reported as having smashed the shrine of Do Chonna, the patron saint of the monastery, a clear indication of their scant respect for Christian sacred artefacts. The raids, though still intermittent, spread steadily around the Irish coast. In 807 the Norsemen sacked Inishmurray off the coast of Connacht, but, just as in the north-east of England, opposition began to stiffen and the *Annals of Ulster* record a 'slaughter of the heathens' by the Ulaid in 811, and the following year a Viking defeat at the hands of Cobthach mac Máele Dúin, King of Loch Léin. There is then a decade-long pause in the record of Viking attacks, but by 822 the raiders had reached Cork and in 824 even attacked the very remote monastic house at Skellig, around 8 miles off the coast of Kerry, whose superior, Étgal, they took captive.

The Vikings also conducted a series of raids on the main monasteries of the north-east and east of Ireland, beginning with the wealthy house of Bangor on the Belfast Lough in 823 and 824, where again they offended Christian sensibilities by roughly shaking the bones of the monastery's founder, St Comgall, from his shrine (which, like most such reliquaries, would have been made of precious metal and encrusted with jewels). The 830s brought a steady intensification of the raids, with the first on the great monastery of Armagh in 832 – so lucrative did the Vikings find the spoils they obtained there that they returned no fewer than three times in the space of a month. They then began to penetrate further inland, with attacks in 833 against Derry in the north, Clondalkin near Dublin and the large monastery of Lismore in the south. The following two years saw raids against a string of further monastic houses: Glendalough, Slane, Ferns and Clonmore. Yet these continued to be mostly opportunistic, hit-and-run affairs involving just a few ships, taking advantage of the slowness of Irish reaction, which was exacerbated by political divisions that prevented any concerted defence. Unlike England (and to an extent Scotland), Ireland would not benefit from any real pause in the raids, and within five years the attacks entered a new, much more dangerous phase.

Francia[10] under the Carolingian dynasty (of which Charlemagne was the most illustrious member) was the first area outside Scandinavia to come into contact with the Vikings, as the Frankish conquest of neighbouring Frisia (the area along the North Sea coast of the modern Netherlands and north-west Germany) from the 730s had brought its frontier dangerously close to Denmark and certainly within reach of Danish ships. Only the Saxons lay in between, and a prolonged series of campaigns by Charlemagne from 772 resulted in their final subjugation in 797. Alarmed at the prospect of the Franks pushing even further, possibly into Denmark, the Danish King Godfred sailed with a fleet and a large force of cavalry to Schleswig on the Danish-Saxon border. Mindful of his own safety, he prudently declined a personal meeting with Charlemagne and instead sent envoys, who made an agreement about returning fugitives. Relations between the Franks and Danes, however, deteriorated after Godfred attacked the Slavic Abodrites, a tribe to whom Charlemagne had given a large swathe of conquered Saxon territory when he evacuated the original inhabitants back to Francia.[11]

When the Abodrite chieftain – a Frankish ally – was murdered, probably on Godfred's orders, hostility between Franks and Danes mounted to such an extent that in 810 Charlemagne was about to launch an expedition against Godfred, only to find that he had been pre-empted, by a 'fleet of 200 ships from Nordmannia' that attacked Frisia and 'ravaged all the Frisian islands'.[12] Unlike the raids that had begun the Viking era in England, Scotland and Ireland, this one was on a massive scale and had royal backing.

The Frisians paid a ransom of 100 pounds of silver to be left alone, and further hostilities were averted by Godfred's opportune assassination and replacement by his nephew, Hemming. The Franks, though, continued to meddle in Danish dynastic politics, and Hemming was soon displaced by the sons of Godfred. They in turn faced serious opposition from a claimant to the throne named Harald Klak, but he was forced to take refuge at the court of Louis the Pious (who had succeeded Charlemagne after the great emperor's death in 814). Louis's attempt to restore Harald to the Danish throne (presumably as a Frankish client) provoked a strong reaction from Denmark, and a fleet of some 200 ships descended on the coast of Saxony. Louis's policy appears in the end to have enjoyed some success, as by 819 Harald was back home enjoying the status of co-ruler with Godfred's sons. Not that he exhibited any notable gratitude towards his Frankish benefactors, for in 820 a fleet of thirteen 'pirates from Nordmannia' appeared off the Flanders coast and proceeded to raid as far afield as the Seine and Poitou. After a final sortie against Aquitaine, the freebooters returned home.

Louis now turned to Christianity as a means of tempering Danish belligerence, with the first recorded mission to convert the Danes despatched by Archbishop Ebbo of Rheims about this time. King Harald was induced to accept baptism, which he did at a lavish ceremony in the Frankish royal palace at Ingelheim (with Louis standing as godfather, expressing a kind of spiritual suzerainty over the new convert). Unfortunately the policy unravelled when Harald was once again expelled from Denmark in 827, at which point Horik (one of Godfred's sons) emerged as sole Danish king. Harald was given temporary possession of the county of Rüstringen in eastern Frisia, pending his hoped-for final restoration, although this never happened.

The situation in Francia in the 830s became very complicated. Louis the Pious had to contend with a series of conspiracies against him by leading magnates and his own sons Lothar, Charles the Bald and Louis the German. Then in 833 he faced outright revolt and a temporary deposition when his army deserted him for the rebels at the 'Field of Lies'. Although Louis was reinstated some ten months later, Lothar had already enlisted the support of another Danish chieftain named Harald[13] to engage in raids on Frisia and so weaken his father's position. In 834, a Danish army duly attacked the great trading emporium at Dorestad and destroyed the port, amid huge slaughter. Dorestad was looted again in 835 and suffered yet another attack the following year. King Horik then rather smugly sent envoys to the Frankish court denying any responsibility for the raids and saying that he had apprehended and executed the culprits himself. The situation was still tense in 840 when Louis the Pious died, setting off a bout of political instability that would provide ample opportunity for the Danish Vikings to exploit. France's long vulnerable coastline and the estuaries of the Loire and Seine were ominously exposed, but the real storm had not yet struck.

To their early victims in Francia, England, Scotland and Ireland, the Vikings had seemed to appear without warning. Yet the Norsemen did not emerge from a vacuum. The societies from which they emerged were anything but primitive, and had undergone rapid development in the centuries before the raids began. What was this Scandinavian homeland like from which the raiders erupted in the late eighth century? It was certainly not a homogenous place, either geographically or in terms of development. Its diverse regions had varied histories – differences that were largely ignored by those outsiders who chronicled their early attacks, who were less interested in fine ethnic distinctions than in cataloguing the very real violence being inflicted on them.

Scandinavia's vast length (from the northern tip of Norway to the southernmost point of Jutland is a distance of more than 1,200 miles) embraces a wide variety of landscapes. In the south, Denmark is largely flat, with its principal island, Jutland, being an extension of the north-Germanic plain. Split into two by the Great Belt, which divides this from the other main islands of Zealand and Fyn, the eastern part looked northwards towards the (now Swedish) regions of Skåne and Blekinge. As a consequence those two provinces fell into the sphere of rulers from Denmark for much of the Iron Age and early Middle Ages, and formed part of the first united Danish kingdom in the late ninth and tenth centuries. Denmark's abundant and fertile farmland was generally able to support a greater density of population than the lands further north, though its division into a large number of islands tended to work against efforts at political unity.

On the Scandinavian peninsula itself, a large mountain range running from Finnmark in the north to the vicinity of Stavanger (in Norway) in the south cuts the eastern and western regions from each other. The west looked predominantly to the Atlantic, its heavily indented coastline largely ice-free even in the coldest months, while the east, bounded by the Baltic Sea, suffered harsher winters, in which navigation was obstructed by ice for months at a time. These differences shaped the conditions in which a western kingdom (Norway) emerged separate from an eastern one (Sweden).

Much of the land that was not rendered inaccessible by mountains was heavily wooded.[14] Deciduous forest predominated only in the very south (in Denmark, and the southern tips of Sweden and Norway), while to the north a mixed forest of fir, pine and spruce gave way to the *taiga*, the great pine forest of the north. Communication overland was rendered even more difficult by a landscape riven by waterways and lakes (especially in the case of Sweden and Finland), a feature which, together with the long coastline of Norway and the archipelago-like nature of Denmark, goes a long way to explain the Scandinavians' intimate familiarity with boats as a means of transport.

Throughout the Scandinavian peninsula the most fertile regions lay to the south, in the case of Sweden the area around Lake Mälaren and Uppsala, and in Norway in the vicinity of the Oslofjord, with secondary regions in the south-west (around Rogaland, Sogn and Hordaland),[15] and further north around what is now Trondheim. It is no accident that these areas would form the power bases of the first kings about whom we have any kind of information.

Scandinavia was first settled at the end of the last Ice Age by reindeer-hunters of the Hamburg culture who followed the retreating ice-sheets in search of game. Having reached Skåne around 14,000 years ago, they fanned out across the peninsula with the help of skin boats, and by about 7000 BC had penetrated as far as southern Finland. These early migrants depended entirely on hunting and gathering until agriculture reached Scandinavia around 4000 BC. From then until the onset of the Iron Age around 500 BC, Scandinavian society underwent a gradual increase in wealth, complexity and population. Then there was a crisis, as the cooling of the climate (and increased rainfall), the severing of supply routes for bronze from the south by Celtic groups who were expanding in central Europe and the diversion of luxury goods southwards towards the Mediterranean all put pressure on existing social hierarchies in Scandinavia.

The society that emerged during the Roman Iron Age (AD 1–500) was a much more militarised affair, marked by increasing social inequality. Goods from the Roman empire flowed into Scandinavia, including bronze vessels, glass, jewellery and, most notably, Roman-style weapons. The last probably made their way north with soldiers who had served in Roman auxiliary units and then returned home. There were also signs of increased insecurity, such as the construction of a number of hill forts in southern Norway, Sweden and Finland, the largest of which, at Torsbrugen on Gotland, had a rampart almost 1½ miles long. More telling even than this are the finds of weapon sacrifices in bogs, particularly from the period AD 200–500. Nearly twenty such deposits have been discovered in Jutland alone, the size of the largest – found at Illerup Ådal in north-central Jutland – indicating that armies of several hundred fought and that the swords, daggers and spears of the defeated were then ritually cast into the marshes.

The very first historical information we have about Scandinavia comes from Greek and Roman authors. Pytheas, a Greek traveller and writer from Marseilles, wrote an account of his pioneering voyage through the Atlantic coastal regions of north-western Europe around 300 BC.[16] He mentions a land six days' sail north of Britain called 'Thule', where the inhabitants lived off wild berries because of the 'lack of crops and cattle of more genial lands', although there is a great deal of confusion about whether he was referring to (or had actually visited) Scandinavia (or even Iceland). More definite notice comes from the Roman historian Tacitus, who describes a Roman fleet sent by Augustus in AD 5 to explore the coastline beyond Frisia. It reached the very northern tip of Jutland, and the intelligence gleaned from this expedition (the Romans' one and only sally into the region) is probably responsible for the first mention we have of the word 'Scandinavia'. Appearing again in the *Natural History* of Pliny the Elder (in the second half of the first century AD), this is given in the form *Scadinavia*, which has been taken to mean 'dangerous island' – a possible reference to the rapids around the Kattegat, which posed a serious hazard to navigation.[17]

Around AD 150, the Alexandrian writer Ptolemy gives a list of tribes in Scandinavia, amongst whom he numbers the *Suiones*, a term that may have later transferred to the Swedes, and the *Goutoi*, who may be same as the *Geatas* mentioned in the sixth-century Anglo-Saxon epic of *Beowulf*, and whose name attached itself to one of the major historical divisions of the Swedish kingdom. The Age of Migrations, the era in which *Beowulf* was set, provides a greater depth of literary allusions to Scandinavia, although most of them are frustratingly difficult to decode. Principal among them is the *Getica* of Jordanes; writing in the mid-sixth century, Jordanes lists twenty-eight Scandinavian peoples, including the Gautigoths and Suctidi, and describes Scandinavia as the 'factory of the nations', putting forward for the first time an idea that became popular with later writers: that the Goths had migrated south from Gotland, the Burgundians from Bornholm (or Burgundholm) and the Lombards from an original homeland in Skåne[18] in southern Sweden.

Around the second century AD the archaeological record actually becomes somewhat poorer in Denmark, with the ending of the sacrificing of precious objects in bogs and a change in burial practice to favour cremations over inhumations (meaning that we have less information available from the type of grave-goods interred with the deceased). There is, however, a relative wealth of information from Norway and Sweden, and in the latter there is evidence of a flourishing kingdom based in the general area of Lake Mälaren. It was a period of some prosperity, as evidenced by a series of rich boat graves found to the north of Uppsala at Valsgärde and Vendel (after which the two centuries from 550 to 750 in Sweden are known as the Vendel Period).[19]

Much of what we can glean about the earliest developments in Sweden is contained in the *Ynglinga Saga*, a thirteenth-century reworking of a poem (the *Ynglingatal*) originally composed in the ninth century. It tells the story of the earliest Swedish dynasty, most of whose dealings are lost in the debatable territory between myth and history. The dynasty appears to have been established sometime in the sixth century, dominating an area at the point where waterways from Lake Mälaren met routes leading from the rich fur-yielding areas of the interior. Amongst its early rulers were three kings named Aun, Egil and Athils, the only tangible evidence of whose reigns are three magnificent mounds standing near the twelfth-century Romanesque church of Gamla Uppsala ('Old Uppsala'), which were traditionally known as Odin's Howe, Thor's Howe and Frey's Howe, after the leading members of the Norse pantheon.[20] Now gently grassed over, they sit close to what must have been the major royal and cult centre of the Swedish kings (the eleventh-century writer Adam of Bremen gives a lurid account of the pagan sacrifices that he claimed took place here), but only the collection of finds in the nearby museum gives some sense of the power and wealth of these kings, the nature of whose rule and the precise extent of whose power are now almost impossible to recover.

The Yngling dynasty seems to have suffered more than its fair share of mishaps. A king named Sveigdir became obsessed with the idea that the Aesir, the principal Norse gods, originally lived on Earth in a homeland far to the east of Scandinavia, and he set off in search of them. After a lengthy journey he caught sight of a dwarf on the point of entering a cleft in a rock, who invited the king to follow, claiming that Odin awaited him inside. Determined not to be thwarted in his supernatural quest, Sveigdir complied, the rock closed behind him and the king was never seen again. Another Yngling ruler, Dómaldi, was offered up by his own subjects as a human sacrifice to propitiate the gods in a year when the harvest had failed, while yet another king, Yngvi-Donnar, suffered an agonising, if unclear end, 'racked in pain in Sweden'. Perhaps the most unfortunate was the amusingly nick-named Eystein Fart, who drowned when Skjöld of Varna – a warlock whose lands he had plundered – caused a great wind to arise, which made the yardarm of a passing ship swing wildly and knock the king overboard, where he drowned.[21]

The sway of these early Yngling kings seems to have extended into the Vestfold of Norway, where the great mound burial cemetery at Borre, south-west of Oslo, might well have contained several royal graves. Set among shaded groves of birch and oak, many of the half-dozen remaining mounds have indentations in the top where robbers long ago removed most of the burial hoards. They were first excavated in 1852 after the site had been purchased by the local roads department for use as a quarry. Some of the labourers involved in the project found a bronze saddle, and their efforts to dig it out caused the mound into which they were tunnelling to collapse. The great early Norwegian archaeologist Nicolay Nicolaysen was then called upon to make the first proper investigation. At the time there were nine mounds, but the only one he actually dug into was No. 1, where he found evidence of a ship grave (although just the iron nails had survived, the wood having long ago rotted away).[22] The grave-goods interred with the deceased included three horses, complete with fine trapping and stir-rups, iron cauldrons, and pieces of sundry agricultural equipment and pottery vessels. The site yielded the artefacts that gave the name Borre to one of the early Viking artistic styles,[23] and the cemetery seems to have remained in use until the 800s, making it possible that it contained some of the immediate predecessors of Harald Finehair, who began the process of unifying Norway in the late ninth century.[24]

More concrete evidence of the growing prosperity of Sweden in the centuries before the Viking raids has come from a settlement on the island of Helgö on Lake Mälaren, which acted as an early market site in the fifth to seventh centuries. It housed a large number of warehouses and workshops, which produced jewellery (some of it in gold), glass beads and the antler combs that are a ubiquitous find in later Viking-era sites. The geographical range of this mercantile centre's connections is indicated by the find of a figure of the Buddha from India, part of an episcopal crozier from Ireland and glass items from southern England.[25]

In contrast, for the very earliest Danish history, the sources are not plentiful. We have the legend that Denmark was named for Dan, the son of Ypper, the King of Uppland, who is almost certainly mythical, but the story perhaps preserves distant memories of a Swedish connec-tion with the Danish royal families.[26] Beowulf gives the names of the ruling dynasty as the Scyldings ('the shield men'), and Saxo Grammaticus in his Gesta Danorum ('The Deeds of the Danes') mentions a king called Halfdan (which literally means 'half-Dane'), whose son Hrothgar appears in Beowulf (and who may tentatively be assigned to the end of the fifth century).

Beowulf further tells of the Geatish king Hygelach, who embarks on a campaign against the *Hugas* (or Franks) during which he meets his death. The attack, which might be the first 'Viking' raid on record, is confirmed in the literary record by the Frankish historian Gregory of Tours in his *History of the Franks,* where he describes a raid in 515 by the Danish King Chochilaichus (or Hugilaicus) against the Attuarii, a people of Frisian origin living between the lower Rhine and the Zuider Zee.[27] In the aftermath of the assault, Chochilaichus was ambushed and killed by Theudebert, the son of the Frankish ruler Theodoric. It is not much to go on, but the reference seems to indicate that, centuries before the attack on Lindisfarne, Scandinavians already posed a very real threat to the coastlines of northern Europe.

Our next literary notice for Denmark comes in 714, when the English missionary saint Willibrord is recorded as setting out for the 'wild Danish tribes' and meeting their king, Ongendus, an evangelising campaign that appears to have had very little long-term effect.[28] That these shadowy early Danish kings wielded significant power is suggested by the Danevirke, a complex series of fortifications built to defend the base of the Jutland peninsula from intruders to the south. It was for a long time believed that it was begun by King Godfred in the early ninth century, but dendrochronological analysis in the 1970s yielded dates instead from the 730s, with a cluster around 737, implying a surprisingly high degree of royal authority at this stage. The sense that a centralised kingship was emerging is further reinforced by the digging of the Kanhave Canal across the island of Samsø in 726. With its strategic position between Jutland and Zealand, its construction meant that whoever possessed the canal could dominate shipping through the Danish Belts and so choke off access to the Baltic, if desired.

Although petty chiefdoms in Sweden, Denmark and Norway may have been coalescing into small kingdoms by the late seventh and early eighth centuries, the society that was emerging was still an overwhelmingly rural one (towns of a sort only appeared in the early eighth century and then just on a very small scale).[29] Most people lived on farms, in a type of building traditionally known as a long-house. These could be more than 100 feet long and 15–20 feet wide, generally of timber (or turf where this was not available) with a supporting lattice of twigs plastered with wattle and daub. The walls generally curved slightly outwards, giving a bulging appearance and a passing similarity to the hull of a ship. Inside, timber posts supporting the ceiling divided the building roughly into three along its length, while at one end there was often a byre in which to stall animals during the winter. All along the outside aisles were benches on which the inhabitants sat, ate and slept. In the centre was a large rectangular hearth, which served for heating, for cooking food and provided a central focus for the longhouse. There was very little furniture (apart from wooden chests and the 'high seat', the more elaborate high-backed chair of the head of the household, supported at the side by two larger pieces of wood or 'pillars'), and precious little privacy.

Traditionally, this society was divided into three classes: the Þrael (thralls) or unfree; the karl, a class of free farmers; and the jarl or nobility. Although doubtless an oversimplification, the classic exposition of this threefold division is set out in the Rigsþula, a tenth-century poem,[30] which recounts a journey by the messenger god Heimdall. He visits in turn three farms, belonging to each of the three social classes. In the first (said to be the home of 'Great-Grandfather' and 'Great-Grandmother') he is fed coarse bread, but before he leaves he abuses his host's hospitality by fathering a son with Great-Grandmother, who is called Thrall. This boy in time weds a bride called 'Slave Girl', with whom he has children named for an appropriately servile existence: boys called 'Weatherbeaten, Stableboy, Stout, Sticky, Rough, Badbreath, Stumpy, Fatty, Sluggard, Greyish, Lout and Longlegs'; and daughters known as 'Great-Gabbler, Ragged-hips, Bellows-nose and Bondwoman'. Heimdall next visits 'Grandfather' and 'Grandmother' (the representatives of the karl class), where he again beds his hostess. Grandmother then gives birth to a son 'red and rosy with eyes that twinkled', whom the couple name Karl. This strong lad marries 'Daughter-in-Law' and they have sons with the rather more appealing names of 'Man and Soldier, Thane and Smith, Yeoman, Smoothbeard and Fellow' and daughters called 'Lady, Bride, Sensible, Wise, Wife and Shy'. Heimdall's third visit is to the fine house of 'Father' and 'Mother'. Again the god sires a child on the lady of the house, but this baby is a far nobler infant 'with bright cheeks' and 'eyes piercing as a young serpent'. The child grows up and, with his wife Erna, produces offspring with suitably aristocratic names such as 'Son and

Child, Noble, Heir and Offspring, Kinsman, Lad and Kon the Younger (the last a pun in Old Norse, as *kon ungr* means 'king').

Although firmly at the base of the social hierarchy, the position of slaves in Scandinavian society was not as oppressive as it was in some other European societies; Scandinavian law-codes allowed slaves to be freed and also permitted landowners to declare children they had had by female slaves to be free. The group was always a comparatively small proportion of Viking society (and by the twelfth century had been formally abolished in all areas except Sweden[31]).

Both the status of free and slave was hereditary, although the numbers of the latter could be increased by captives taken during raids (a number that rose significantly during the Viking Age). The slave did suffer legal disabilities, and did not have the same rights as a freeman. As an example, if a slave insulted a freeman and was killed by him, the only fine payable was the value of the slave, while if a man murdered his own slave, no punishment at all was imposed (unless he happened to put the unfortunate thrall to death during Lent, in which case the penalty was banishment).[32]

The bulk of the population fell into the free but non-aristocratic category, with the right to representation at local assemblies or *things* (an institution that spread throughout the Viking world, where matters of public importance were settled and lawsuits were heard). The category included a wide spectrum within its general classification, including labourers and tenants, as well as landowners without aristocratic status. The free were generally described as *bóndi*, a term that refers to a man who ran his own household. The most important subgroup were the *óðalsbóndi*, or 'udal' freemen − a status that, although hedged about with legal complexities, referred to land which the landholder was able to pass on to his descendants (but which he could not legally modify from the family to an outsider without his kinsmen's permission). As social differentiation grew, other categories emerged, notably labourers with no land, and smallholders, whose legal position was substantially the same, but who merited a lower level of compensation in the case of death or injury than did their udal-holding relatives.

Amongst the nobility, the most important of all were known as *jarl* or earl. The usage was restricted to men of the very highest rank, often rivals to the king himself, such as the *jarls* of Hladir, who held sway over a large part of northern Norway from their base in the Trøndelag, and who often divided authority with the king or acted as the proxies or regents of the Danish rulers when they sought to exercise authority over Norway. This aristocratic sector of society, from whom the chief royal retainers and advisers were selected, tended to lose much of its influence by the end of the Viking Age as the power of the kings grew and their own freedom of manoeuvre diminished, and as hereditary fiefdoms gave way to offices in the gift of the monarch.

There was one group who lay outside the mainstream of Norse society, for the simple reason that they were not Norse at all. The Saami, a nomadic Finnic-speaking people, who made their living from hunting, fishing and reindeer-herding, have left us no written accounts of their own and so we are totally reliant on Norse sources and the testimony of archaeology for our knowledge of them.

The Saami are mentioned in a number of Icelandic sagas, as well as the *Landnámabók*, a few poems and a series of later Norwegian laws. They are generally referred to as *finnr* or *finni* and their own name for themselves (*saame*) is used only once in Norse sources. They had clearly lived on the Scandinavian peninsula for a long time, quite possibly pre-dating Norse settlement there. A series of burials called 'inland lake graves', which cluster around small lakes in forested areas, date from the late Iron Age, and the location of these indicate that the Saami's range was far wider than it became later in the Middle Ages, when they were confined to the far north of Norway and Sweden. Early Iron Age graves at Krankmårtenhog in Härjedalen in Sweden include reindeer antler crowns that are set in stone mounds, a sign of the Saami's long-standing relationship with the animals. Indeed, evidence from ship-burials as far south as Tuna in Uppland suggests that some of the deceased had a diet rich in reindeer meat (which is not characteristic of the standard Norse diet of the time).

The Saami were specialist hunters, and the most common form of interaction between Norse and Saami seems to have been the tribute that they paid (or which was traded) in the form of furs (a practice described in some detail by the Norse trader Ohthere, who lived in the Saami areas in the ninth century[33]). It is not clear what the Saami received in return for the marten, otter and other furs they collected

(*Ketil's Saga* mentions butter and pork, but this was surely inadequate inducement[34]), but the exchange was clearly mutually beneficial enough to allow it to continue for centuries.

Although the Saami do seem to have lived primarily in Finnmark, there is evidence of them further south, in the Trøndelag, and even in the south and interior of eastern Norway. The Borgarthing Law, which applied in the east of the country, had several measures to prevent Christians from mixing with the *finnr* and specifically forbade them to travel to the Saami lands to ask for healing or prophecies. The taint of such pagan practices was clearly something that concerned the drafters of the laws. It is, indeed, in their role as masters of magic that the Saami loom largest in the sagas. Gunnhild, the wife of the Norwegian king Eric Bloodaxe, is described in one story as having gone to Finnmark in order to learn witchcraft from the *finnr* (and, true to her later bloodthirsty reputation, has her two teachers brutally slain).

Their shamanic tradition, and their long-standing resistance to Christianity, enhanced the sense of 'otherness' of the Saami for medieval (mostly Christian) Norse writers. There is some indication of violence between the two groups. In 1258, an Icelandic vessel was shipwrecked on the north Norwegian coast, after which the crew were killed, possibly by Saami, and there is one account[35] of an attack by the Saami on the farm of a leading Norwegian chieftain; but, for all the centuries of coexistence between Saami and Norse, this is very slight evidence indeed.

There are far more accounts of peaceful interaction. As well as the trading expeditions that were a regular feature of relations between the two groups, the Saami elite seems to have been sought out as prestigious marriage partners by their Norse counterparts.[36] In *Finnboga Saga*, a Saami woman named Lekny is said to have become the mistress of an Icelandic chieftain; but the most famous example was the alleged marriage between King Harald Finehair of Norway and Snaefrith, the daughter of the Saami king, Svási. Harald was summoned to Svási's turf hut and, though initially reluctant to go, eventually relented. When he got there, Snaefrith poured the royal guest a drink and, on catching sight of her, Harald fell madly in love. Svási rebuffed the Norwegian king's suggestion that he and Snaefrith spend the night together and insisted instead on a formal marriage.[37] It was from this pairing that Harald Hardrada, King of Norway in the mid-eleventh century, claimed descent: as Harald Finehair's and Snaefrith's great-great-grandson, he asserted additional legitimacy for his claim to the throne.

Whether or not the marriage of Snaefrith and Harald actually took place, it shows that the Saami were far from being regarded with disdain in the Norse worldview. The familiarity with which they were seen is further expressed by an oath in the Gulathing Law, which refers to an enemy who will be allowed to have peace as long as 'the falcon flies, the pine grows, rivers flow to the sea, children cry for their mother and the Saami go skiing'. It is a timely reminder that Scandinavian society of the Viking Age was never an exclusively Norse affair.

Viking society as portrayed in the sagas was plagued by perpetual violence, or at least its threat and, in the absence of strong centralised authority to prevent this, means had to be found to contain it, or at least to channel it into socially acceptable manifestations. The story in *Egil's Saga* of how the hero, when only seven, murdered Grim Heggson (by sinking an axe into his brain) in an argument over a ball game[38] is a sign of how almost commonplace such violence was seen to be. In such circumstances men looked to the protection of which-ever local chieftain they saw as best preserving their influence (and lives).

When Viking bands formed for raiding expeditions, the men who made them up would be accustomed to the use of arms – a necessity for their personal protection in unsettled times – even if they had not received any formal training. The most commonly carried weapons were axes, spears and bows and, less frequently (at least for non-elite warriors), swords. These last were generally around 3 feet long with a simple cross-guard and pommel, and with a blunt end that made them more useful for slashing than for cutting. Many swords became famous, with suitably martial names such as *Fótbitr* ('Leg-biter') or *Gramr* ('Fierce'). They were strong swords, forged by a process known as pattern-welding, which involved twisting several blocks of iron together and then welding them, thus producing a characteristic pattern on the final blade.[39] Some became heirlooms passed down through the generations, and a few acquired an almost sacral quality, such as St Olaf's sword, *Hneitir* ('Cutter'), which stayed for three generations in the family of the Swedish Viking who picked it up after the Battle of Stiklestad in 1030.[40]

The axes for which the Vikings became best known were initially small narrow-bladed weapons, simple derivatives of those used by peasants for chopping wood. Only later on did the large broad-bladed version (sometimes called the 'Danish axe') appear, which required two hands to wield it. It was in reality rather impractical, since it needed a lot of space, meaning that its bearer could not shelter within a defensive formation.[41] In its most extreme development it became the 'bearded' axe, with a large downward projection to the blade that must have made it extremely awkward (if rather impressive). For missile weapons, the Vikings preferred spears and bows, although the moral code assumed by the sagas, which stressed the glory of single combat, played down the use of such long-distance projectiles.

As defensive equipment, most men would have possessed a shield, generally around 3 feet in diameter and made of wood with a metal boss that covered the hand-grip and sometimes with edge reinforcement. It was only later on, during the eleventh century, that kite-shaped shields appeared, such as those portrayed on the Bayeux Tapestry.[42] Some warriors may also have had a metal helmet, which was generally conical, occasionally with additional eye protection or a downward-projecting nosepiece (but never with the 'horns' that have become an almost essential feature of non-historical representations of the Vikings).[43] If the average warrior had any armour at all, it was likely to be a padded jacket; shirts of mail armour, composed of interlocking iron rings (which were most effective against slashing weapons), were quite rare and generally within the reach of only the well-off (such as Harald Hardrada, King of Norway, whose mail coat was so long that it looked like a skirt and his men nicknamed it 'Emma').

While most recorded Viking raids, at least in the early years, were freelance affairs carried out by small groups from the same general area, later attacks involved significantly larger forces, often royal armies. The kings always had a household bodyguard, or *hird*, but additional forces could be mustered when needed, principally from the ranks of the free farmers (stiffened by the household retinues of other great lords). In Sweden, a land division known as a *hund* was obliged to provide four boats on demand, while in Denmark a similar unit known as a *herred* had to send forty armed men to the king when requested.[44] It was probably under the auspices of such a muster that the large-scale expeditions of Svein Forkbeard and Cnut against England in the early eleventh century were organised. Smaller raiding parties would be put together on a much more informal basis, and the *here* (the general word in Anglo-Saxon sources for such roving armies) might form, break into several parts and re-form over the course of great campaigns, which could last (in the case of England) for as long as a decade.

Against defenceless targets such as monasteries, Viking tactics were little more than those of armed men against unarmed civilians in any era: threats, menaces and a resort to violence if their demands were not met. When they faced armed opposition, the Vikings generally drew up in a line, with their chieftain or king in the centre surrounded by a *skjaldborg* (or shield-fort), which was very similar in nature to the Anglo-Saxon shield-walls. Fluttering in the breeze would be the leader's banner, the most famous of which was the *Landøyðan* ('Land Waster') of the Norwegian king, Harald Hardrada. After an initial exchange of missile volleys, most engagements devolved into a series of confused clashes as the respective lines pressed against each other. Finally, one side or the other would break, and the bulk of casualties were generally suffered by the defeated side while in flight. Even the approximate numbers of dead and wounded in major engagements is hard to determine (as, indeed, is the size of the armies that fought in them). At the Battle of Ashdown in 871, where Alfred the Great of Wessex defeated a large Viking force, the casualties are said to have been 'many thousands', while at the Battle of Maldon in 991 they are reported to have numbered 'hundreds'. Occasionally we get seemingly more precise figures, such as the 120 Vikings slain at Poole in 896, although this number was probably reached simply by counting twenty warriors for each of the six ships they came in; the sixty-two Englishmen said to have died are probably closer to the truth.[45]

As far as there were any tactics on the battlefield, the Vikings were known to make use of feigned flights and ambushes, while they sometimes adopted a wedge-shaped formation known as the *svínfylking* (or 'swine-order', so named for its resemblance to the shape of a boar's snout), the force of which pushing forward made it easier to penetrate an opponent's shield-wall. One particular group of Viking warriors who completely eschewed any calculated tactics were the *berserker* or berserks, so called from the bear-shirts which they may originally have worn in place of defensive armour (they were also called *ulfhednar* or 'wolf-skins'). Fighting unprotected in this manner was evidently an ancient custom amongst Germanic peoples, as it is mentioned in the first century AD by the Roman historian Tacitus, who refers to a dance with swords and spears performed by naked young men, while a youth wearing only a helmet and belt is shown on a helmet from a seventh-century grave at Valsgärde in Sweden.

In the heat of battle the berserks entered a kind of battle rage, which it was said endowed them with superhuman strength. Working themselves up into a battle-frenzy, they were said to acquire immunity to pain. There is, however, little evidence of real berserks outside the pages of the sagas, and tales of them may simply have been designed to intimidate those facing elite Viking warriors in battle. Tellingly, in Iceland 'berserks' were liable to outlawry and such behaviour in battle (in breaking the battle line) may actually have been counterproductive.[46]

The Viking reputation for ferocity may also be seen as rather relative. Although they did shock the sensibilities of monastic chroniclers by their failure to respect Christian holy sites, few of the allegations against them of murder, kidnap or burning match the actions of the Frankish king Charlemagne, who in 782 massacred 4,500 Saxon pagans in revenge for their revolt against his attempts to force Christianity upon them.[47] The killing of King Edmund of East Anglia by using him as archery target practice and the murder of Archbishop Aelfeah of Canterbury by pelting him with ox bones are indicative of a level of casual violence in Viking society, but not of particular brutality. Far more shocking is the 'blood-eagle', a practice in which the victim's chest was cut open, his ribs split and his lungs pulled out from inside the ribcage and then pinned back to his chest like the wings of an eagle. This excruciating and bloody form of execution is first mentioned in the *Knútsdrápa*, a skaldic poem in praise of King Cnut, composed by Sighvat Þórðarson in the early eleventh century in connection with the death of King Aelle of Northumbria; it may well represent a confusion with descriptions in sagas of eagles hovering over the battlefield eager to gorge on the flesh of the dead.[48]

On a more strategic level, the early ninth-century Viking raids seem to be no more than a particularly acute form of piracy, with little planning other than that derived from knowledge of the richest and least well-defended sites, intelligence often garnered from previous expeditions. As news of attackers' success spread, the booty attracted more raiders in their wake, a process only accelerated by the payment of bribes by Charles the Bald of France in the 850s and by Aethelred the Unready of Wessex around 1000 in a bid to get the Vikings to go away.

One of the most distinctive features of Viking warfare was the advantage that their use of sea transport gave them, enabling a wider range of targets to be reached and allowing a rapid getaway with their plunder once the raid was over. For travel overland, the Vikings equipped themselves with horses to allow them a mobility equivalent to that which they possessed at sea. Their most prolonged campaigns, however, were facilitated by their decision to overwinter, staying the months of harsher weather overseas rather then returning home before the sailing season ended. The overwintering sites they selected became bridgeheads into the territories on which they then preyed. At first these were offshore islands or at least coastal areas partly cut off by rivers from the mainland, such as Noirmoutier in France or the Isle of Sheppey in Kent (where the Vikings first spent the winter in 850). In the spring the Vikings dispersed in smaller raiding groups, making it easier to supply themselves, while at the same time remaining in close enough contact to regroup if any organised force appeared to oppose them. They also made use of existing fortifications (such as the old Roman fort at Chester) and, where these were not available, constructed their own earthwork defences, such as the one they built at Repton in Derbyshire, or those that formed the core of the *longphorts* (fortified naval bases) built by the Vikings in Ireland from the 840s.

The size of Viking raiding parties and armies varied enormously, from the three ships that heralded the start of the Viking Age in England, when they raided Portland in Dorset in the time of Beohrtric of Wessex (ruled 786–802),[49] and the battle mentioned in the *Anglo-Saxon Chronicle* entry for 897,[50] which involved only six ships, to fleets of hundreds of ships recorded in the tenth century. Tellingly, the seventh-century laws of Ine, King of Wessex, stated that any group of men above thirty-five was termed a *here*, the word used for most of the Viking raiding forces, so in many cases these groups may scarcely have merited the term 'army' that is often applied to them.

The *Anglo-Saxon Chronicle* records with some (suspicious) precision the size of twelve fleets during the ninth century, and of these eight are made up of thirty-five vessels or fewer. Depending on the number of men that each ship is adjudged to have been able to take, this yields a maximum force of 1,000–1,750 carried in each fleet. On the Loire in France, a fleet of sixty-seven ships is recorded in 843, and by 853 the raiders were able to deploy 105 vessels there, culminating in the gargantuan force that assaulted Paris in 885–6, which, it was alleged, was made up of 700 ships. Allowing for a maximum capacity of fifty warriors a vessel, this would indicate an army of 35,000 (and even at a more modest thirty men each, the total would still come to 21,000 Vikings), so the fleet's size is almost certainly exaggerated. Enormous figures such as this (or even smaller round numbers like 100 or 200 ships) are probably simply the chroniclers' way of indicating a very large number, without intending any great sense of precision. The 'Great Army' that crossed into England from Francia in 892[51] is said to have had 250 ships, but since the *Anglo-Saxon Chronicle* mentions that it carried its own horses, its real size may have been as small as 1,000 men.[52]

What is clear, however, is that the magnitude of the raids did increase over time, and that the numbers involved almost certainly reached several thousands by the time of the great expeditions to England in the early eleventh century. A large part of the Vikings' success may be attributed to the fact that even where their armies were smaller than this, they managed to keep them together as coherent forces for years at a time, whereas their opponents in Francia, Ireland, Scotland and the Anglo-Saxon kingdoms of England were dependent on small cores of royal retainers supplemented by irregular, often ill-trained levies (such as the Anglo-Saxon *fyrd*), who could not be maintained in the field for long.

Our sources tell us quite a lot about when the Vikings came, where they attacked, how they fought, and even about the nature and development of the societies in which they originated. What they do not tell us is why this society – for so long rather separate from developments in the rest of northern Europe – should have turned so abruptly to overseas raiding, and on such a scale. This is perhaps the key question of the whole Viking Age (together with why, after around 200 years, the attacks then stopped).

One theory is that there was a high population density in the pre-Viking Age, which led to competition over resources and intense warfare within Scandinavia. Finally, with too many men fighting over too few resources, the violence became directed instead at tempting targets abroad. There is some evidence of growth in certain Scandinavian settlements of the late Iron Age, which might corroborate this. There are signs of the expansion of habitation into marshland areas of west Jutland that had previously been avoided, while in western Norway, too, there is some archaeological indication of an increasing population putting stress on available resources.[53]

Other evidence is inconclusive. In Denmark, Adam of Bremen reported of Jutland that 'Hardly a cultivated spot is to be found anywhere, scarcely a fit spot for habitation',[54] while in contrast he described Skåne as 'opulent of crops, rich in merchandise and now full of churches'.[55] Timber from Hedeby and Lund show that the demand for oak (for the construction of ships as well as buildings) led to an increase in the coverage of beech forest during the Viking Age, implying increased demand from a growing population, but this took place after the raids began.[56] The Norman historian Dudo of Saint-Quentin, meanwhile, described a type of lottery which he said the Norsemen practised to help contain overpopulation. Because of the shortage of land, he claimed that the men of leading families would draw lots, and those who lost had to accept exile abroad where they could 'gain themselves countries by fighting where they can live in continued peace'.[57] For Hrolf, one of the losers in the early tenth century, this apparent misfortune turned out to be a blessing, as he went on to become the first Viking ruler of Normandy.

More important perhaps than the 'push' factor of rising population was the 'pull' effect of the general increase in trading links across north-western Europe. The seventh century saw the rapid growth of *emporia*, new trading stations such as Quentovic, near Étaples in northern France (which dates to the early part of the century),[58] Dorestad in Frisia (which was certainly in existence by 716 when it was visited by the Anglo-Saxon St Willibrord on his missionary journey to the Danes) and Hamwic in southern England. From centres such as these, trade networks reached into Denmark and linked into the *emporia* of Ribe on the west coast of Jutland, which seems to have been laid out at least as early as 720, and Haithabu (or Hedeby) on the peninsula's eastern side.[59]

These two towns were among the first significant trading centres in Scandinavia, the others being at Birka on Lake Mälaren in Sweden and Kaupang in southern Norway. Scandinavia had always possessed trade goods that were valued in western and southern Europe (notably amber and furs, the latter most often taken in tribute from Saami tribes in Scandinavia and, later, from Slavs in Russia), but the establishment of markets in Denmark and Sweden immeasurably improved the prospects both for traders bringing goods inwards to those areas and for intra-Scandinavian trade. The Dorestad and Hedeby settlements in particular had extensive trading connections along the coasts of the North Sea and the Baltic, with wine-pottery, querns and glass from the Rhineland appearing among the archaeological finds in both towns. Hedeby would also have acted as a conduit for goods (such as furs) coming from the east, which were then traded south and west into the Carolingian empire. A more sinister trade was in slaves; in the late ninth century the Flemish monk St Rimbert, who was visiting the port, ransomed a Christian nun who had been taken into captivity.[60]

The general increase in trade in north-western Europe, of which the *emporia* are a sign, must have been accompanied by a deepening familiarity with both the geography and the rising wealth of the areas in which the Scandinavian merchants operated. Grave-goods of the era reflect a higher level of imports from western Europe (such as quantities of glass interred in eighth-century Swedish boat graves[61] or the thirty-two silver coins found in Ribe in Denmark, which may have originated in Dorestad). The temptation must have been strong for some visiting Scandinavians to move from peaceful trading to the acquisition of those coveted goods by violent means. That the line between merchant and pirate was easily blurred is indicated by an episode from *Egil's Saga*, where the hero conducts a series of raids in the eastern Baltic and then uses the proceeds of this to engage in peaceful trading in Courland.[62]

The adoption of improved ship technology almost certainly played a key role in the Viking eruption. In many parts of Scandinavia (the archipelago of Denmark, the long, indented coastline of Norway and the many lakes of Sweden) communication was significantly easier by boat than overland across difficult terrain, often wooded or mountainous to the point of impassibility. The earliest surviving vessels from Scandinavia are paddle boats, such as the Hjortspring Boat (from around 300 BC), which is a round-bottomed vessel constructed using the 'clinker-built' method (of overlapping planks or strakes), which would remain the characteristic method of construction in Scandinavia for more than a millennium. By the time of the Nydam Boat (*c.* AD 310–20) significant advances had been made to produce a clinker-built boat that had oar-locks for fifteen pairs of oars, suggesting a crew of at least thirty.[63] It did not, though, have a true keel (which prevents the boat from being pushed sideways by the wind), and this development had to wait until sometime before AD 700, the date of the Kvalsund Boat, which does have one.

None of these pre-Viking vessels made use of sails. It was the adaptation of the shallow-keeled, robust clinker-built rowing boats to operate under wind-power that gave the Vikings of the ninth century the advantage of ships that could move swiftly over long distances, carrying crews of up to 100, which could operate without the need for harbours and were able to penetrate far further up river systems than any of their deeper-draughted rivals could manage.[64] When exactly the Vikings adapted their ships for propulsion by wind-power is unknown, but they had certainly done so by the late eighth century. A seventh-century carving of a ship from Karlby in Denmark seems to show a sailing boat,[65] while picture stones from Gotland from the eighth century portray vessels with sails. The discovery in 2008–10 of two boats near Salme on the Estonian Baltic island of Saaremaa may have pushed the concrete proof for use of sails back into the early eighth century. The second of the boats (known as *Salme II*) contained traces of wood and cloth, which could indicate the presence of a mast and sail. The presence of thirty-three male skeletons (including a sword) stacked neatly in the *Salme II* boat, and of seven other skeletons (again, all male) in the other boat (dating from around 650–700), suggests that they may have been killed while engaged on a raid in the eastern Baltic. In the case of the earlier boat, it might even be that they were part of the raiding expeditions sent out by the Swedish Yngling king Yngvar in the late seventh century.[66] If so it would represent the earliest evidence of Viking-style raiding in the area, over a century before the attack on Lindisfarne. The attraction of the increasing commercial wealth of the *emporia* may have provided the motive for the raids, but the improvements that the Vikings made to their ships gave them the method.

Yet, without an opportunity, the Viking raids would have been mere pinpricks, simple annoyances that would have rated only an occasional mention in the chronicles. The clue to the enduring Viking success lies in the fractured nature of the opposition they faced (just as the barbarian attackers of the Roman empire in the fourth and fifth centuries had not had to overcome the frontier defences at the height of imperial power). In England, the raiders came across a country divided between the kingdoms of Northumbria, Mercia, East Anglia, Wessex and a number of other petty states, which allowed the Viking armies to defeat them piecemeal, leaving in the end only Wessex to conduct a stubborn rearguard resistance. In Scotland, the infant kingdom of Alba was nowhere near powerful enough to expand into – still less to defend – the northern and western Isles, embroiled as it was in the final stages of its struggle to absorb Pictish and residual British-controlled territories into its sphere. In Ireland, the fragmentation of the native kingdoms allowed the Vikings to establish toeholds along the coast, which developed into permanent settlements that took several centuries to eradicate.

In Francia (the area of Roman Gaul that had been conquered by the Franks in the fifth and sixth centuries and approximates to modern France, and which by the ninth century included parts of western Germany, Belgium, the Netherlands, northern Italy and Switzerland), it was the success of the great Charlemagne that brought the Frankish frontier within striking distance of Denmark through his final conquest of Saxony in 797. This, and the weakness of his successors, transformed the inevitable border skirmishes (or perhaps outright Frankish attempts at conquest) that might have ensued into raids which threatened for a time to destroy the integrity of the state (and ultimately did detach Normandy from it). In Russia, the Vikings did not come across organised states, but their desire to trade securely in unsettled conditions led them to found new settlements (or take over existing ones) to defend their business. Even here, where they did ultimately come into contact with more established powers, such as the Byzantine and Khazar empires and the various Islamic powers around the Caspian,[67] the lure of plunder meant that they turned to raids just as damaging as those carried out by their counterparts in western Europe.

Another reason often put forward to explain the beginning of the raids (and particularly for the migrations that accompanied them) is an increase in royal authority (or, as some of the sagas put it, of royal 'tyranny'), which led those seeking to avoid new exactions to move abroad. This is particularly associated in saga tradition with Harald Finehair of Norway, the traditional first unifier of the Norwegian kingdom. The linkage is, however, too neat for the chronology to uphold, since Harald's conquests in Norway are traditionally set in the mid-860s, and they were largely completed by the Battle of Hafrsfjord around 871.[68] Yet the settlement of Iceland had already begun in 874, while much of north-western Europe had already been at the receiving end of intense Viking attacks during the 840s, 850s and 860s. Harald's death in 931 was followed by renewed division of the kingdom, a period that saw no let-up in Viking attacks. The unification of Denmark occurred even later, under Harald Bluetooth from around 958, more than a century and a half after the inception of the Viking attacks, and so the suspicion must be that far from political centralisation being to blame for the raids, it was rather political fragmentation and disorder that bred the conditions in which there were large numbers of warriors ready and able to engage in violent adventures overseas.

In the end, though all of these changes were probably necessary for the onset of the era of Viking raids at the end of the eighth century, none of them on their own were sufficient. The patent success of the early raiders in finding undefended targets must have attracted others, and the treasure they looted provided the funds both to build new ships and to offer enticing rewards for new followers. As the Viking Age progressed, the influx of plunder from the west, of silver from the Islamic lands to the east, and the growing reputation of those who had made their fortunes and reputation as Vikings made raiding seem an attractive career option for young warriors. The beginnings of the establishment of the Scandinavian monarchies in the tenth century was too late to have much of an impact on the raiding, until at last that power grew strong enough to stifle independent war leaders, so that the final 'raids'[69] were in reality royal-sponsored ventures.

Map 3 Viking Francia and Frisia

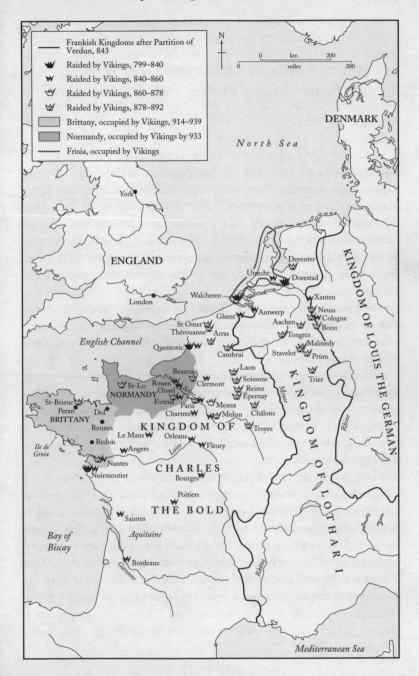

2

From Raids to Settlement: The Vikings in France, Britain and Ireland, 840–950

For around forty years after the initial attacks in England, Scotland, Ireland and France the Viking raids remained isolated affairs, damaging enough to coastal areas, but not representing a mortal threat to the existence of the kingdoms that endured them. It was the growing political instability in Francia from the 830s that allowed the Vikings to establish themselves as more than mere nuisances and to threaten for a time to overturn the whole political order of north-western Europe.

The catalyst was the death of the Frankish king, Louis the Pious, in 840. The succession dispute that ensued pitched three of his sons – Lothar, Louis the German and Charles the Bald – and his nephew, Pippin II, into a bitter struggle that shattered the unity of the Carolingian empire and opened it up to a wave of opportunistic Viking raids. By the time the quarrelsome siblings had patched up an agreement at Verdun in July 843 (which gave the west of the realm to Charles, the area east of the Rhine to Louis and a middle kingdom to Lothar, while ignoring the claims of Pippin II to Aquitaine[1]), the Vikings had already struck.

In the north-east Lothar felt obliged to create a buffer against them by granting the Danish chieftain Harald the island of Walcheren at the mouth of the Scheldt, while in the lands under Charles the Bald's control, Rouen and the monastery of Saint-Wandrille suffered raids in 841, followed by Quentovic – which had already been struck several times between 834 and 838 – and Nantes in 842–3. In the last attack the Vikings descended on the town on the feast day of St John (24 June), beginning an oft-repeated pattern of assaults on cities at times when the Norsemen knew they would be crowded with pilgrims and traders, so increasing the chances of acquiring slaves and easily transportable valuables.

In a foretaste of what was to come, the monks of Saint-Wandrille handed over 26 pounds of silver in exchange for the monastery itself being spared and the ransoming of sixty-eight hostages. If the Franks expected that this tactic would do anything other than attract more raiders, then they found – just as the Anglo-Saxons would a century later – that they were sorely mistaken. The relentless tempo of the raids is echoed in the writings of ecclesiastical chroniclers. Ermentarius of Noirmoutier (whose own monastery was the subject of repeated attacks) summarised the widespread feelings of despair:

> The number of ships increases, the endless flood of Vikings never ceases to grow bigger. Everywhere Christ's people are the victims of massacre, burning and plunder. The Vikings over-run all that lies before them, and none can withstand them . . . Ships past counting voyage up the Seine, and throughout the entire region evil grows strong. Rouen is laid waste, looted and burnt: Paris, Beauvais and Meaux are taken, Melun's stronghold is razed to the ground, Chartres occupied, Evreux and Bayeux looted, and every town invested.[2]

In the half-century between 841 and 892, barely a year passed without a major Viking raid on some portion of Francia, and the attacks came to centre on three main groups, based respectively in the Loire, Seine and Somme, river systems that gave the Norsemen access equally to escaping by sea and to penetrating deep inland to assail towns that hitherto would have felt themselves immune to ship-borne attack.[3] The raids were particularly severe against the western kingdom of Charles the Bald with its long, exposed coastline, while the Frankish defence against the Vikings was weakened both by the chronic feuding between the sons of Louis the Pious and by the occasional tendency of Frankish factions to employ Viking bands as mercenaries. In 857 Pippin II of Aquitaine[4] went so far as to renounce Christianity and join the Loire Vikings, his lack of enthusiasm for his native religion possibly aggravated by his enforced stay in a monastery after his brother Charles had him tonsured in 852.[5] Pippin's apostasy ended badly for him, as in 864 he was captured 'through a trick' by Ranulf, Count of Poitou, handed over to Charles, sentenced to death as a traitor to Christendom and executed. Equally threatening, in 865 the Breton ruler Salomon joined forces with the Danish Viking Hasteinn to attack Maine and Touraine, threatening to open up yet another front against the beleaguered Frankish ruler.[6]

As long as the Viking raids had been confined to coastal communities and monasteries (such as the raid on Saint-Wandrille in 841) they were disruptive enough, but then in 845 the Vikings sailed up the Seine and attacked Paris for the first time. The appearance of this group, led by Ragnar,[7] led to fears that the Franks were being punished for their sins in the same way that God had punished the Israelites. Charles and the Frankish defenders fled in panic to the monastery of Saint-Denis, prompting the Vikings to hang 111 captives in full view of the king. The capital was only saved further depredations by an epidemic of dysentery, which struck down many of the raiders. Nonetheless, Charles was still forced to pay a huge tribute to get the Vikings to move on. The Franks did have the satisfaction of divine vengeance on Ragnar – at least in the eyes of the author of the *Translatio*[8] of Saint-Germain – for he is said to have suffered a terrible death on his return to Denmark, his stomach swelling and bursting open as his diseased guts spilled out, a punishment for his earlier sacking of the monastery of Saint-Germain-des-Prés.

The bribe paid to Ragnar's group in 845 was a colossal 7,000 pounds of silver, but Charles's authority was still sufficiently strong that it took him just three months to raise this vast sum. Although over the next few years the raiders concentrated on Frisia, Brittany and Aquitaine, leaving the central core of Charles's realm untouched, they then returned to the Seine in force, exacting further tributes in 853, 858 and 860. The nature of the raids, too, began to change. In 852, the Vikings overwintered for the first time on the Seine, a development that (just as it would later do in England) marked their permanent entry onto the Frankish political landscape. Their penetration up the Seine also deepened, and in 856 they built a fortified camp at Jeufosse, just 40 miles from Paris, from where they could raid at will into the Vexin (on the river's right bank).

The 860 tribute payment (of 5,000 pounds of silver) was made by Charles to Weland, the leader of a newly arrived Viking band, and was in exchange for besieging (and expelling) yet another Viking force under Björn Ironside, which had based itself on the island of Oissel in the Seine. Björn, with hunger beginning to bite, simply offered Weland an even larger payment (of 6,000 pounds of silver) to be allowed to slip away, an inducement that his duplicitous countryman had no qualms in accepting.[9] The two groups then headed down the Seine and split up to overwinter at various points along the river.

Charles's inaction at these growing threats was in part forced on him by yet another bout of dynastic in-fighting, which began when his son, Louis the Stammerer, revolted in January 862. Finally in 864, emboldened by his success in trapping Weland behind a dam that he had ordered built to block the Vikings' line of retreat and in enforcing the Norse leader's submission and baptism, Charles abandoned his supine policy of waiting for the raiders to come and then buying them off, in favour of a more positive approach. At an assembly held at Pîtres in 864, he ordered stronger measures. Although almost half the decrees issued after the meeting concern currency reforms, one of them forbade the selling of mail-coats, weapons or horses to 'foreigners' (by which he must firmly have had the Vikings in mind), while the most important measure concerning the protection of the realm ordered the whole male population to build defensive works, such as bridges and causeways (and to perform garrison duties by manning them). The intention was to repeat along the length of the Seine the stratagem that had trapped Weland in 862, by constructing fortified bridges that would impede the Vikings' freedom of movement and, it was hoped, stop them from ever getting as far as Paris again. The campaign culminated in the building of the imposing Pont de l'Arche, a bridge at the confluence of the Seine and Eure, protected by two fortresses on either side of the river.

Although the Seine was temporarily rendered more secure by these moves, the Vikings continued their depredations along the Loire and the Somme. The antipathy between Pippin II of Aquitaine and his cousin Charles the Bald heightened the vulnerability of Aquitaine in particular, and the huge loss of life at the Battle of Fontenoy in 841, when his army (combined with that of Lothar) was decisively defeated by Charles, is blamed for weakening the Frankish capacity to resist Viking raiders in the region. As a result, Scandinavian bands had penetrated Garonne and attacked Toulouse as early as 844, while Bordeaux was captured by Norsemen in 848. An already dire situation was then made worse by Pippin II's defection to the Vikings in 857. Pippin's revolt did not prosper, and although the Vikings sacked Angoulême in 863, they suffered heavy losses; and an attack on

Toulouse later that year brought a sharp response from Charles, leading to Pippin's capture.

Even with their convenient local ally removed, the Viking raids in Aquitaine continued until a major Aquitainian counter-attack in 868, when they 'offered prayers to God and St Hilary and boldly attacked the Northmen. They killed some and drove the rest to take flight.'[10] Angoulême was refortified in the same year and thereafter the Vikings largely ceased their activity in the region.

The response to Scandinavian raids in the north-west of Francia was complicated by the existence of the fiercely independent province of Brittany. Raiding there had begun with an attack on Nantes in June 843, and it was probably no coincidence that this coincided with the revolt of Nominoë, who had administered Brittany on behalf of the Carolingians. The attacks then developed much along the same lines as elsewhere, with a series of strikes against monasteries such as Saint-Martin-Tours (in 853). In the same year, Viking loyalty to their own once again displayed itself when Sidroc, whom the Bretons had employed to dispose of another Viking leader, Godfred (who had just sacked Nantes), allowed his prey to slip away to safety at Redon.[11] The Breton position deteriorated after the death of their ruler Salomon in 874, which was followed by a debilitating civil war and an increase in the level of Norse attacks, as once again the Viking raiders exploited the slightest sign of political weakness amongst their victims. The situation grew more severe in the 880s, as the Vikings overran part of the county of Nantes in 886 and then used this as a base to take over most of the rest of Brittany. Only a strong series of counter-attacks by the new Breton duke, Alain I, drove the Vikings out and provided some respite to the beleaguered province. But in 907 he died, and the Breton defences were further weakened by a dispute over his succession, leaving the territory's defenders dangerously divided.

While an agreement in 911 between Charles the Simple and a Viking band led by Rollo (which resulted in the foundation of the Duchy of Normandy[12]) curbed raiding in the core of Francia, it had the unintended consequence that those Norsemen who wished to carry on pillaging turned their intentions instead to Brittany. Finally, in 919, a massive Viking fleet from the Loire launched a full-scale invasion, prompting the flight of most of the Breton nobility. The reality of Viking control was recognised in 921, when Robert of Neustria[13] formally ceded Nantes to Rögnvald, the fleet's leader. It looked as if Brittany, just like Normandy, would become a permanent Viking colony. But after an occupation lasting almost thirty years, the Breton ruling family returned in the shape of Alain I's son, Alain Barbetorte. Having spent the intervening time in England at the court of Athelstan of Wessex, he landed at Dol in 936. The following year he stormed the Viking fortress at Saint-Aignan just outside Nantes, killing many of the Norsemen and causing the survivors to take to their ships and flee down the Loire. When Alain took possession of Nantes soon after, he found it deserted and so neglected by the Vikings that he had to cut through thick weeds to reach the great basilica of St Felix. In 939 at Trans, near Rennes, he defeated the last force of Loire Vikings, putting an end to almost a century of raids against Brittany.

Because Viking rule over Brittany was short-lived, evidence of their occupation is correspondingly slight. There are a number of earthwork forts of probable Viking construction, such as Camp de Péran, near Saint-Brieuc, and another double set of earthworks at Trans, where pottery dating from 920–80 was found. Unlike Normandy (or the English Danelaw), Brittany only has a clutch of place-names identified as being of Scandinavian origin, all containing the element *La Guerche* (from Old Norse *virki*, a fortress).[14]

Far more spectacular, and unparalleled in the rest of France, is the Viking ship burial found eroding from a cliff on the Île de Groix, a few miles off the south Breton coast. Unlike the most important ship burials (a rite in which the deceased body was interred in a ship that was then buried in a mound) found at Gokstad and Oseberg in Norway,[15] the Île de Groix vessel was burnt before being placed in a turf mound. The boat, which was around 40 feet long, contained the remains of two males – one a grown man, the other an adolescent – who were interred together with their weapons, riding gear, some jewellery and a host of other grave-goods before the earth of the 15-foot-high mound was heaped back over the vessel containing them. The burial yielded one unique item, a circular band that probably represents the stern ornament of a ship, the 'tail' of a dragon and the counterpart to the far more numerous finds of dragons' heads for Viking-ship prows.[16] The grave cannot be dated more closely than 900–1000 and the identity of the principal occupant is unknown, although, given the richness of the grave-goods (indicating that its occupant was almost certainly a pagan), it is tempting to suppose that it is one of the leaders of the Viking raids of the 910s that led to the establishment of the fleeting Viking state of Brittany.

In the rest of Francia, Viking activity died down somewhat in the 870s. It was events in England that reignited the Viking threat, when the resounding defeat inflicted on them by Alfred the Great, King of Wessex, at Edington in 878 led to a large number of Norsemen retiring south across the English Channel.[17] They were said also to have been encouraged by hearing of disputes amongst the Franks,[18] a state of affairs caused by the death in rapid succession of Charles the Bald (in 877) and his son Louis the Stammerer (in 879), which led to the division of the kingdom between Louis III and Carloman II. Louis III turned out to be an effective war leader, inflicting a significant defeat on the Vikings at Saucourt in 881, but to the great misfortune of Francia he died in August the next year, when he fell from his horse while chasing after a girl on whom he had amorous designs.

The eastern Frankish kingdom suffered a similar series of dynastic misfortunes when Louis III's son was killed after a fall from one of the palace windows, which meant there was no male heir when Louis died in 882. After Carloman II (the ruler of western Francia) was in turn fatally wounded in 884 in a hunting accident, Charles the Fat (who had succeeded Louis III in 882) inherited both parts of the realm.[19] But it was one in which the Vikings had been marauding almost unopposed for three years, having overwintered in the royal palace at Nijmegen, and having attacked a string of cities, including Cologne, Bonn, Neuss and Aaachen (Charlemagne's old palace, in which the Vikings are said to have stabled their horses).

Having plundered the Rhineland, the Norsemen, led by Godfred and Sigfred, moved ever close to the Frankish royal heartland around Paris. Neither the acceptance of baptism by Godfred nor the payment of a tribute of 2,000 pounds of silver by Charles did much to halt the Danish army's progress. In 884, they sacked Louvain and the following year stormed the Pont de l'Arche, which for all Charles the Bald's fortifications miserably failed to hold them off. By November, they had reached Paris and proceeded to lay siege to it. Nearly a year later, the Vikings had still not succeeded in forcing the defenders to surrender, despite the terrible privations suffered by those trapped inside the city; but neither had the Franks, led by Count Odo, managed to break out of the siege. In the end, unmoved by Odo's desperate pleas to send a relief force, Charles the Fat simply took the way of least resistance and ordered the Parisians to permit the Viking army free passage along the Seine into Burgundy. Charles also agreed to pay the Norsemen 700 pounds of silver, which Odo himself was forced to raise. The damage to the king's reputation was so severe that in 887 he was deposed in favour of Odo, who was seen as the valiant (and betrayed) defender of Paris.

As ruler of the west Frankish kingdom,[20] Odo still had a Viking problem to contend with. In 889 the Vikings once again threatened Paris, but further damage was avoided by the devastating defeat inflicted by the east Frankish king, Arnulf, on a large Viking army at the Dyle near Louvain in 891, and by a famine the following year, which made supplies difficult to obtain. These setbacks persuaded the Viking leader Hasteinn that there were better pickings to be had on the other side of the Channel (together with a tribute payment that he managed to extort from Odo) and he departed for England, where he engaged in a four-year campaign that stretched across the breadth of the country.[21]

Over the next decade, pressure grew on the Seine (particularly with the prospect of Viking-controlled Brittany expanding its borders to absorb more of western France). When a new Viking army arrived under Rollo and began to raid near Chartres in 911, Charles the Simple (who had replaced Odo as king in 898[22]) preferred not to confront them directly, but instead ceded them land on the Seine, which would become the future Duchy of Normandy. In return, Rollo agreed to prevent other Viking bands from raiding Frankish territory.[23]

All along, it had been political weakness and dynastic division that had enabled the Vikings, first to raid with little centralised response, and then to lodge themselves in the Frankish river estuaries. There had always been some localised opposition to them (such as the mustering of ships and warriors by the bishops of Orléans and Chartres in 854, which prevented an attack on the former), but as dynastic divisions and civil war hampered effective royal direction of the defenders, the Vikings easily found alternative targets. That they failed (save in Normandy) to translate this initial success into permanent occupation is a result both of the stiffening of Frankish resistance that began with Charles the Bald's fortification campaigns and of the appearance of

Viking-ruled areas in northern England, Scotland, Ireland and
Normandy, which acted as a siphon for ambitious emigrants who saw
that their compatriots' strength offered easier pickings there.

Apart from Normandy (and to an extent Brittany), the Vikings left
little trace of their activities in France. Most of the monastic houses
they attacked survived and recovered (though Saint-Wandrille was
abandoned between its destruction in 852 and its reoccupation by
Abbot Maynard in the 860s), and displacements of the population
were temporary. Even those towns most badly affected, such as
Quentovic and Dorestad, still survived for a time after the initial Viking
onslaught. Those words of Scandinavian origin that entered the French
language did so via the medium of the Norman-French dialect which
was shaped by a decades-long period of direct Scandinavian colonisation. They include *homard* ('lobster', from the Old Norse *humarr*),
vague ('wave', Old Norse *vágr*) and *quille* ('keel', Old Norse *kjölr*).
Archaeological evidence of the Norse campaigns in Francia is even
sparser, represented in the main by a rich female burial at Pîtres in
Normandy, which included Norse-style brooches, artefacts from the
Viking camp at Péran and the Île de Groix ship burial, and sporadic
finds from elsewhere, including a scattering of axe-heads dropped by
the invaders in various rivers.[24]

The first area of Europe in which the Vikings were able to establish
political control – and which, paradoxically, has often been omitted
almost entirely from accounts of their conquests – was Frisia. Situated
on the North Sea coastline of the modern Netherlands and Germany,
it had gradually been conquered by the Franks over the course of the
eighth century, with the river estuaries and the west being annexed after
the death of the Frisian king, Radbod, in 719. The rest was subsumed
in stages, with most of the east falling into Frankish hands in 734. Finally,
with the conquest of neighbouring Saxony by Charlemagne in 797,
Frankish lands were brought right up to the border with Denmark.

Containing as it did the trading *emporia* of Quentovic and Dorestad,
Frisia was a tempting target for the early Viking raiders. Even harder
to resist was the Carolingian rulers' temptation to destabilise their
new Danish neighbours, which Louis the Pious succumbed to as early
as 814, when he accepted an oath of loyalty from the Danish king,
Harald Klak, who had been expelled the previous year. In 815 Louis

ordered an invasion to restore his new – and, it was hoped, grateful – client to the throne. Although that campaign was abortive, in 819 Frankish pressure resulted in Harald's restoration. Yet just seven years later, Harald travelled to Ingelheim to be baptised – with Louis acting as his godfather, and the Empress Judith acting as sponsor for Harald's wife – and the reaction back home against this over-cosiness with the Franks caused Harald to be chased out of Denmark yet again.

As part of the arrangement for his baptism, Harald had been given the district of Rüstringen, in the far north-east of Frisia, to hold as Louis's client. This effective cession of land to a Danish potentate was an extraordinary event, and marked the beginning of seventy years in which parts (and sometimes the whole) of Frisia were held by a succession of Viking chieftains, with the full legal approval of the Carolingian rulers. While Harald only lasted two years in his benefice before his name disappears from the record, another (and almost certainly different) Harald was in 841 given land around Walcheren by Lothar I (on whose behalf he had raided Frankish lands in the 830s in an attempt to destabilise Lothar's brother, Charles the Bald).[25]

Although the second Harald died in 850, his son Godfred (who had been in Denmark) then proceeded to ravage Frisia, together with his cousin Rorik. The pair's raiding bands seized Dorestad, which Lothar, making the best of a bad situation, gave to Rorik as a benefice. Although the cousins soon returned to Denmark, Rorik came back to Frisia in 855, when he is said to have taken most of it (probably as far south as the Waal and in the east to the borders of the lands of Louis the German).

Rorik held Frisia for at least the next eighteen years. He is last mentioned in the sources in 873 when he visited Louis the German in Aachen to swear him fealty, but it is possible that he remained in power until 882. Frisia enjoyed a surprising period of peace under Rorik and there are only two Viking raids recorded there during the period of his rule: the first in 857 when he was absent in Denmark, and the second in 863 when he was accused of allowing Viking pirates free passage through his lands on their way to raid Xanten. The only hiccup in his reign came in 867, when Rorik was driven from Frisia by a mysterious group referred to as the *Cokingi*. This was a short-lived interlude, however, and by 870 he was back in power and was recorded as holding talks with Charles the Bald in Nijmegen.

By 882, Rorik was almost certainly dead, as his lands were then granted to Godfred, who may well have been another exiled member of the Danish royal family. He received them as part of another expedient deal by Charles the Fat, who chose to make Godfred his client, with possession of Frisia as the inducement, in return for desisting from his devastating campaign of raiding in Francia. Godfred, who was baptised as part of the arrangement, also received the notable prize of a high-born Frankish wife, Gisela, the illegitimate daughter of Lothar II. Godfred became too deeply entangled in Frankish politics, however, and in 885 was involved in a conspiracy with his brother-in-law Hugh, whom he in turn attempted to betray by demanding that Charles the Fat grant him an even larger stretch of land around Koblenz, in return for his continued loyalty. Godfred was summoned to discuss the matter with Duke Henry of Franconia and, as a result of a staged quarrel, was mortally wounded.

For a long time there was no concrete evidence of the seven-decade-long Viking occupation of Frisia with but a single place-name, Assendelft (the older form of whose name, Ascmannedilft, may refer to *Ascmann*, a local north German name for Vikings) and just half a dozen Norse artefacts to show for it. This reinforced the idea of a very ephemeral occupation and certainly gave no sense of actual Viking settlement in Frisia. The discovery of two hoards in 1995–6 and 2001 near Westerklief in Wieringen began to change this pattern. The first hoard weighed 3½ pounds and included arm-rings, ingots and seventy-eight Carolingian pennies, whilst the second, somewhat smaller, find included ninety-five Arabic coins, the largest such find in Europe south of Scandinavia.[26] Another hoard found at Tzimmeringen in 1991 consisted of no fewer than 2,800 coins, and some thirteen coin hoards have now been located dating to the century between 816 and 915.[27] As Viking hoards are not normally found in areas where Scandinavians had not actually settled (why bring such portable wealth if there was no intention to stay?), this may indicate a more permanent presence than was hitherto suspected. Situated in the northern reaches of Frisia, Wieringen might well have acted as a convenient base from which to dominate the Scheldt Valley, just as Walcheren would have allowed the Vikings to exploit the southern part of the province.

The impact of the Scandinavian occupation of Frisia was felt even further afield, in England. The Viking army that attacked York in 867 was said to have been led by Ubba, who is described as *dux Fresciorum* (Duke of the Frisians). It is even possible that his group may have made their way from Frisia after Rorik's expulsion in 867, showing how quickly the ripples of events in one part of the Viking world might reach another. Furthermore, a Viking army that descended on the River Thames in 878 is recorded as having returned to Ghent the following year, and, although this is a little way south of Frisia proper, it does show that Norse command of the southern part of the North Sea coast was becoming a severe problem for Anglo-Saxon rulers (just as it already was for their Frankish counterparts). Some evidence that Frisians may have settled in England is provided by a handful of place-names that include a reference to them, combined with an Old Norse suffix (such as Firsby and Friesthorpe).[28]

Just as there was a pause in Viking raids in France after the initial attacks, so England seems to have experienced a respite in the first quarter of the ninth century. While the concentration of our main sources on events in Wessex in the south may give a false impression of events in the north (where there may well have been attacks), it is equally wrong to argue that the silence of the sources means there were definitely unrecorded Viking incursions. In any case, a series of small-scale raids of the 830s was followed by a more serious attack on Southampton and Portland in 840. The western part of Wessex endured further strikes during the next few years, and in 843 King Aethelwulf (839–858) suffered a defeat near Minehead at the hands of a thirty-five-strong Viking fleet. Despite these setbacks, the English experienced occasional successes, such as the victory by local levies against a Viking fleet on the River Parrett in Somerset in 848, and the Vikings did not threaten to overwhelm the Anglo-Saxon defences.

A dangerous new development occurred in 850. Whereas previously the raiders had retired to their home bases in winter (probably to ports in Ireland for those preying on the west, or to Denmark for those attacking the east coast of England), that year an unprecedent-edly large fleet – the *Anglo-Saxon Chronicle* puts it at 350 ships – arrived and sacked Canterbury and London. Instead of returning home, it overwintered on the Isle of Thanet. Although this army was defeated by Aethelwulf at Acleah,[29] another Viking force appeared and spent the winter of 854/5 on Sheppey, even closer to London. A third Viking

Map 4 Viking England, 865 to 916

Legend:
- → Campaigns of the Great Army, 865–871
- ⇢ Campaigns of Hálfdan and Guthrum, 875–878
- ⊙ The Five Boroughs
- ◇ Other Viking camps
- The Danelaw
- Wessex, *c.* 890
- Conquered by Wessex 890–919
- ⊙ Burhs established, 902–916

0 km 100
0 miles 100

Alt Clud/Dumbarton, 878

Bamburgh

Hexham
Corbridge, 918
Carlisle
Tyne

North Sea

Knock Y
Doonee
Kirk
Michael
Cronk Moar
Ballachrink
Balladoole
Isle of Man

Ouse

*captured by Vikings ,866;
capital of Viking
Kingdom of York*

**KINGDOM
OF YORK**

York

Ribble

Anglesey
The Wirral

Irish Sea

possible site of
**Battle of Brunanburh,
937**
Chester

Bakewell
Lincoln
Mablethorpe

Nottingham
Derby
Repton
Leicester
Trent
Grimsthorpe
Stamford
Thorney

Tettenhall, 910

Bridgnorth

Worcester

Tempsford, 917
Thetford

The Holme, 902
Bedford
Milton

Gloucester

Tiddingford

Mersea
Benfleet
Shoebury
Sheppey

Wallingford
*Ashdown,
870*
Chippenham
Bath
*Edington,
878*
Bratton
Warminster
*Reading,
870*
Englefield, 870
Athelney Marshes
Southampton

London
Fulham

KENT

Lympne
Romney Marsh

Hastings

N

Appledore

Wilton, 870
Chichester

Wareham

English Channel

fleet, which had been marauding around the Somme, crossed the English Channel in 860 and went on to sack the Wessex royal capital of Winchester the following year, before being driven off and returning to Francia. A pattern was becoming established, which would repeat itself time after time over the next half-century, of raiders probing the defences of England and then retiring to Francia if Anglo-Saxon resistance became too stubborn.

The Vikings had raised themselves from nuisance to threat, but the danger to Wessex and its neighbours was still far from critical. All that changed in 865 when a 'great army' (micel here in Anglo-Saxon) arrived in England. Unlike its predecessors, it did not simply overwinter, but remained for more than a decade, destroying one by one the armies (and the independence) of the Anglo-Saxon kingdoms. Its sheer size, probably numbering in the thousands rather than the dozens or, at best, hundreds of previous bands, marked a definitive change in the nature of the Viking menace.[30] It was commanded by a pair of warrior brothers: Halfdan the Wide-Embracer and Ivar (or Ingvar) beinlausi ('the Boneless'). The latter is probably the same as the Imair who is recorded as being active in Ireland in the early 860s, so it is probable that at least part of the Great Heathen Army had made its way across the Irish Sea to England. Exactly how Ivar obtained his curious nickname is the subject of much speculation, including the suggestion that he may even have had some kind of condition that rendered his bones brittle (and so may not have been able to walk unaided).[31] Whether or not they were truly the sons of Ragnar Loðbrok ('Hairy Britches'), a legendary Viking who became associated with the Ragnar who attacked Paris in 845, is more doubtful.[32]

Having passed a very profitable season pillaging the towns and monasteries of East Anglia, Ivar and his companions proceeded north. They made their way directly to York, arriving on 1 November, just as the city was packed with notables attending the All Saints' Day services in the cathedral. Those inside included the two Northumbrian kings Aelle and Osberht, who had been too preoccupied by quarrelling with each other to make serious preparations against a Viking attack. As the congregation worshipped, the Viking host stormed into the city. Both Aelle and Osberht managed to evade capture and returned to the city once the foreigners had departed. And so in March

867 the Viking army, which had overwintered at the mouth of the River Tyne, was forced to come back and take York all over again.[33]

This time, Osberht was killed in the fighting, and King Aelle fell into the Vikings' hands and was put to death. Ivar and Halfdan are said to have performed the 'blood-eagle' ritual on him[34] and thus avenged themselves for the death of their father, Ragnar Loðbrok. According to *Ragnar's Saga* he had become jealous at the fame that his sons were winning in Britain, so he sailed over from Denmark and attacked Northumbria, only to be defeated and captured by Aelle. The Viking raider refused to reveal his name, and so the infuriated Northumbrian king had him cast into a pit of venomous snakes. As the serpents crawled over him and injected their deadly venom, Ragnar – in true heroic Viking fashion – sang a rousing death-song, the *Krákumál*: 'We swung our swords so long ago, when we walked in Gautland . . . since then people call me Hairy Britches . . . I stabbed the spear into the earth's loop'. Finally, as the poison overcame him, Ragnar uttered a dying prophecy: 'How the piglets would squeal if they knew the fate of the boar!'

Having installed a puppet ruler, Egbert, in York,[35] in 868 the Vikings descended on Mercia, taking Nottingham, but failing to inflict a decisive defeat on its king, Burgred. They then returned to York for a year, before striking out at East Anglia in 870 and murdering King Edmund. The *Anglo-Saxon Chronicle* confines itself to the brief note that Ivar's band 'had the victory, and killed the king and conquered all the land',[36] but a cult of martyrdom soon grew up around Edmund, and the late-tenth-century *Passio Sancti Edmundi*[37] adds a number of gruesome details. According to this account, Edmund initially escaped Ivar's clutches, but, when offered the chance to surrender, said that he would do so only on the condition that Ivar accepted baptism. Edmund was then captured and, for his insolent insistence on Ivar's conversion, was tied to a tree and used as target practice by the enraged Vikings. He was beheaded and his head discarded; according to legend, a great wolf came to guard the spot where it lay, crying out '*Hic, hic*' ('Here, here') to help those searching for the dead king's remains. When the two parts of Edmund's body were finally collected by the East Anglians, the head miraculously reunited itself with his torso in time for its burial in Bury Abbey.

With Northumbria and East Anglia conquered, the Great Heathen Army next turned its attention to Wessex, which was attacked in the late autumn of 870. A skirmish at Englefield was followed by a decisive Viking victory at Reading on 4 January 871. Four days later, at Ashdown, the Wessex levy (or *fyrd*) drew up in an attempt to stop the Norsemen reaching the crossing of the Thames at Wallingford. Facing the Vikings (led by Halfdan and a new leader, Bagsecg) was King Aethelred of Wessex (865–71) and his younger brother Alfred.

The Battle of Ashdown that followed nearly resulted in an early death for Alfred, as Aethelred was delayed (at prayer, it was said). When the Vikings tried to outflank his diminished shield-wall, Alfred launched his warriors in a premature attack that would have resulted in their being overwhelmed, had his brother not returned in the nick of time. As the battle swirled around a thorn tree that acted as a rallying point, the Vikings were gradually forced back, and when Bacseag was killed, the Norse army broke and fled. Of the slaughter that followed, the *Anglo-Saxon Chronicle* laconically recounts that 'both enemy armies were put to flight, and many thousands were killed'.[38] Halfdan, having lost five *jarls* in the slaughter, retreated to Reading, but soon regrouped and delivered stinging defeats to the Anglo-Saxons at Basing and *Meretun*.[39]

Ashdown was Alfred's first major military engagement and the start of a seven-year period that would establish his myth-encrusted reputation as one of England's doughtiest defenders. It was just as well that he was a leader of real calibre, for he succeeded to the throne on 15 April 871 after Aethelred died (though whether he had been wounded in one of the recent battles or died of natural causes is unknown). The new king faced a potential threat in the shape of Aethelred's young sons, Aethelhelm and Aethelwold, but nobody can have been much in the mood for dynastic squabbling. Even so, there may have been some resistance to Alfred's accession, as his biographer Asser simply notes that he 'undertook the government of the whole kingdom' rather than being crowned king.[40]

By now a new Viking group had arrived in England, called by the *Anglo-Saxon Chronicle* 'The Great Summer Army'. It joined up with Halfdan's army at Reading and the combined force defeated the new King of Wessex at Wilton (in Wiltshire). Faced with the prospect of his tenure on the throne being a very short one indeed, Alfred had little option but to pay Halfdan a hefty tribute to withdraw from Wessex. The respite this gained was only a temporary one, although it still gave Alfred time to marshal his forces for the inevitable new onslaught. In the meantime, the Viking army had to divert to put down a revolt in Northumbria where they expelled King Egbert and Archbishop Wulfhere from York. It was not until the autumn that the Vikings turned southwards again to attack Mercia, whose ruler, Burgred, found that his policy of paying ever greater tributes had merely betrayed his weakness and made his kingdom a more inviting target.

Late in 873 the Viking army arrived at the royal Mercian cult centre at Repton, where they set up their winter base. Burgred was in no position to dislodge them and his support melted away. A broken man, he embarked on a pilgrimage to Rome,[41] in effect abdicating, while the triumphant Guthrum installed 'a foolish king's thegn' named Ceolwulf as a puppet ruler.

Evidence of the Viking army's stay at Repton has been found in the form of a D-shaped earthwork enclosing some 3.6 acres, which they constructed for their overwintering. These defences incorporated within them a Saxon mortuary chapel (previously used for royal Mercian burials) in which the remains of around 260 mostly male skeletons were tightly packed around a single high-status burial and were then covered with a mound of earth and pebbles. Some of the bodies have been radiocarbon-dated to around 700–750 and so may represent members of the monastery attached to the chapel, who had been exhumed and reburied. However, the fact that 45 per cent of the buried male corpses showed evidence of cut wounds to the head suggests that many of them had violent deaths, possibly in battle, and the association with the undoubtedly Viking earthwork makes it most likely that they were warriors who died during the Great Summer Army's campaign. Exactly who the war leader buried in the central grave was is unknown, although he is unlikely to have been as tall as the nine feet reported by Thomas Walker, the labourer who discovered the remains in 1686. Walker gave the skull of the giant skeleton to a certain Mr Bower, the Master of the local school, but sadly it was later lost.[42]

The threat to Wessex was further diluted when the Great Army split in two, with Halfdan taking his men to Northumbria. Having sacked Carlisle, Hexham and the unfortunate monastery at Lindisfarne yet again, in 876 the Vikings are said to have 'shared out the lands of Northumbria, and they proceeded to plough and to support themselves.'[43] It is a crucial development, marking the real start of the Viking settlements in England. Halfdan himself, meanwhile, showed little inclination for farming and launched an expedition against Ireland in 877, which ended in his death in a battle at Strangford Lough in the north-east.[44]

The other section of the Great Army, now commanded by Guthrum, transferred to Cambridge in 875 to prepare for a renewed invasion of Wessex. In autumn that year, he crossed into Alfred's territory and marched all the way to Wareham in Dorset before facing any real opposition. Although he was then besieged by the West Saxon army, the threat of reinforcements from a 120-strong fleet that was making its way east along the coast encouraged Alfred to permit Guthrum to leave his beleaguered encampment on the promise of an oath he made the Norse warlord take on a sacred gold arm-ring. The Vikings had slipped out of Alfred's trap.

Guthrum felt himself no more bound by an oath sworn on a hallowed pagan object than he would have been by a promise made on a Christian relic, and he promptly moved to Exeter, ready to welcome the approaching fleet. This was, unfortunately for the Vikings, wrecked off Swanage with the loss of as many as 3,600 men. With adversity rather than piety weighing most heavily on his mind, Guthrum stuck to the terms of a new agreement and in autumn 877 withdrew his men from Wessex. Then, to Ceolwulf's great discomfiture, but no doubt to Alfred's delight, the Vikings partitioned Mercia, with a portion of the army settling down in the eastern part of the kingdom, just as their compatriots had done in Northumbria. In their settlement lay the origins of the 'Five Boroughs' (Lincoln, Nottingham, Leicester, Derby and Stamford) which formed the core of Viking territory in the Midlands, and the heart of the Danish-occupied portion of England, which came to be known as the Danelaw.[45]

Guthrum, meanwhile, remained encamped around Gloucester, waiting for an opportune moment to renew the attack at Wessex. Alfred had dismissed the *fyrd* for the winter, and while he was celebrating the Christmas feast at the royal estate at Chippenham, presumably secure in the belief that he was safe at least until the following spring, the Viking army crossed the frontier. On Twelfth Night, Guthrum reached Chippenham to find that his quarry, together with the leading men of the royal council, had slipped away. As the *Anglo-Saxon Chronicle* puts it: 'the enemy host came stealthily to Chippenham, and occupied the land of the West Saxons and settled there and drove a great part of the people across the sea, and conquered most of the others, and the people submitted to them – except for King Alfred. He journeyed in difficulties through the woods and fen fastnesses with a small force.'[46]

Alfred was reduced to the state of a fugitive in his own land. His biographer Asser writes of Alfred leading 'an unquiet life among the woodlands of the county of Somerset, in great tribulation; for he had none of the necessaries of life, except what he could forage openly or stealthily by frequent sallies, from the pagans, or even from the Christians who had submitted to the rule of the pagans'.[47] By around Easter, the runaway king was confined to a narrow strip of territory in the Somerset Levels near Athelney – destined, it seemed, to be a mere footnote in the Viking conquest of all England.

Alfred had plenty of time to brood on his predicament. It is from this period that the famous story of his burning of the peasant woman's cakes comes. The king is said to have taken refuge in the cottage of a humble cowherd, whose wife asked him to look after some cakes that were baking over a fire. Preoccupied with the downturn in his fortunes, Alfred distractedly let them burn, resulting in a hearty scolding from the peasant woman, who was blithely unaware of the identity of her absent-minded guest. The story contains an apt pun on the Anglo-Saxon word for lord (which was *hlaf-weard*, 'loaf wielder'), implying that just as Alfred burnt the bread, so he had failed to look after his royal inheritance of Wessex.[48]

The king did not wait passively for Guthrum to hunt him down, and his messengers criss-crossed Wessex seeking to rally support for a counter-attack. The appointed rendezvous for those who chose to join the loyalist cause was 'Ecgbert's Stone', located somewhere between Athelney and Warminster on the Wiltshire–Somerset border. Alfred and his small band emerged from the marshes in May 878 to find a significant force of men from Hampshire, Somerset and Wiltshire already gathered there, perhaps 4,000 strong.[49]

Guthrum had to strike fast to avoid the insurgency gathering strength and moved rapidly south-west from Chippenham to occupy an abandoned Iron Age hill fort at Bratton near Edington. The Wessex *fyrd* advanced up the ridge of a line of chalk-hills to the outer ditches of the defences. There, they formed up into a shield-wall and moved against the Viking formation. After a brutal clash, the scratch Anglo-Saxon army penetrated the Viking line and, as Asser puts it, 'destroyed the Vikings with great slaughter, and pursued those who fled as far as the stronghold, hacking them down'. Those Norsemen who had escaped the rout – Guthrum among them – were trapped in Chippenham and, after a fortnight of increasing privation, 'the pagans, driven by famine, cold, fear, and last of all, by despair, asked for peace on condition that they should give the king as many hostages as he pleased, but should receive none from him in return'.[50] There was an additional stipulation: that Guthrum and thirty of his leading followers must become Christian, with Alfred himself acting as godfather for the Danish king. So, now bearing the baptismal name of Athelstan, Guthrum retired, first to Mercia and then in 879 to East Anglia, where his army too 'settled and shared out the land'.

There were now Danish settlements based in Northumbria, Mercia and East Anglia, and sometime in 879 or 880 Alfred made a formal treaty with Guthrum setting out the boundary between English-controlled territories and those in the Danelaw (the area in which the Vikings held sway). As well as Wessex, the Anglo-Saxon portion included the western part of Mercia, under the supervision of Ealdorman Aethelred (Ceolwulf having recently died). The divide between the two domains lay roughly along the line of the old Roman road of Watling Street ('up the Thames, and then up the Lea and along the Lea to its source, then in a straight line to Bedford, then up the Ouse to the Watling Street'), with London falling within the West Saxon sphere.[51]

Guthrum kept the peace with Wessex for five years, until 885 when he launched a large-scale attack across the frontier, but this was easily beaten back by Alfred. In the meantime, the West Saxon king had scored another coup when Guthfrith, Halfdan's successor as Viking lord of York,[52] also accepted baptism. Alfred did not, however, rest on his diplomatic laurels, well aware that it was Wessex's brittle defences that had made it and the other Anglo-Saxon kingdoms vulnerable to takeover by the Vikings. He ordered the construction of *burhs*, fortified towns and strongholds, planning to establish a network in which no one would be more than 20 miles from such a refuge. They included many places that later prospered as market towns, such as Wallingford, Chichester, Worcester, Bath, Hastings and Southampton, and were funded by a system of taxation later set out in a document called the *Burghal Hidage*.[53] When the scheme was fully in operation, it may have represented a force of some 27,000 men available to defend the towns and fortresses of Wessex.

In 884–5 the new defences were put to the test when a new Viking raiding force arrived from Francia. This group found that the easy pickings experienced by the *micel here* some twenty years before were now a thing of the past, as Alfred's defence-in-depth strategy began to prove its worth. As the Vikings struggled to make progress, he attacked their camp near Rochester, causing many of the foreigners to flee back to Francia. Even so, some of the remainder succeeded in reaching their countryman Guthrum's kingdom of East Anglia[54] and took to coastal raiding.

Alfred now unleashed another of the weapons he had developed to counter the Viking threat, a fleet of English ships that could take on the Norsemen at sea, a medium in which they had until now been the undisputed masters. Asser recounts a sea-battle at the mouth of the Stour where 'all the Vikings were killed and all their ships were captured'. Thirteen Viking ships sank or were taken that day, an astonishing victory for the West Saxons, and a salutary deterrent for any small forces of Vikings who might contemplate a spell of freelance raiding in the old style.

The Viking army that landed in 892 was no small band, however, but the largest force to arrive since the *micel here* itself. It was said to have included 250 ships,[55] which set sail from Boulogne and landed in the estuary of the Lympne (near Romney Marsh in Kent). They captured the *burh* at *Eorpeburnan* (which had not yet been completed)[56] and then established themselves in a new encampment at nearby Appledore. Alfred's situation was further imperilled by the arrival of a fleet of eighty ships under Hasteinn, which sailed up the Thames estuary and set up camp opposite the Isle of Sheppey. If the East Anglian or even the York Vikings had joined in, then, for all Alfred's military and administrative reforms, Wessex might once more have been overwhelmed.

Alfred and his son, Edward the Elder, fought a series of running engagements with the various Viking groups throughout 893, and even persuaded Hasteinn to allow one of his sons to undergo christening, a conversion that – accompanied by the payment of a hefty baptismal bribe – only kept him off the battlefield for a brief few months. Under severe pressure, the main Viking force withdrew across the Midlands and finally overwintered within the walls of the old (and, presumably, by now decrepit) Roman legionary fortress at Chester. Deprived of supplies by the pursuing Wessex *fyrd*'s scorched-earth policy, the Vikings moved on to North Wales, where they attacked their erstwhile ally Anarawd ap Rhodri, King of Gwynedd, before wheeling round again and making their way to Mersca in Essex.

The far stiffer resistance they faced compared to the raids of the 860s had discouraged many in the various Viking fleets, and one large group made its way back across the Channel; a second contingent, led by Sigeferth, crossed the Irish Sea, where it attacked Sihtric Ivarsson, the Viking King of Dublin.[57] Those who remained made an ill-judged sally in 895 against London and ended up being chased by the Wessex *fyrd* across Mercia until they were trapped at Bridgnorth in Shropshire. But this time there was no battle, no climactic conclusion to the four-year campaign, and the Vikings simply agreed to disperse, with some going to East Anglia, others to Northumbria, and a third group (described as those 'who were moneyless') returning to Francia.

The 892 Viking invaders had been seen off with only a fraction of the disruption caused by the Great Army of 864–5, and their attack was not followed by any large-scale incursions. After a small-scale raid against the Isle of Wight, which was seen off by the new English fleet, Alfred then enjoyed three years of comparative peace, until his death in October 899. At fifty years old, he had been at war with the Vikings for more than half his life and, despite all the odds he had faced, he bequeathed to his son Edward a realm more secure than anyone could have imagined twenty years before.

This still left the Danelaw in Viking hands. The term is not, strictly speaking, contemporary, as it first appears in law codes dating from the reign of Aethelred II (978–1016) and by that time referred more to a separate legal jurisdiction within England than a politically independent territory. It was not, moreover, until the reign of Edward the Confessor (1042–66), some forty years later, that the Danelaw's area was defined to comprise East Anglia, the East Midlands (broadly the area known as the Five Boroughs) and Northumbria, some fifteen counties in all, amounting to around one-third of England.[58] Here, Viking rule lasted between thirty and seventy years.

The extent to which there was a particularly Norse imprint on the customs (and the genes) of these areas, and the numbers of Vikings who came to settle there, have been the subject of much debate. A critical contribution to this is the evidence of place-names of Scandinavian origin. There are virtually none to be found south of the Danelaw, and even north of it there is a great deal of variation in the density of Norse toponyms,[59] with particular concentrations in Lincolnshire, Nottinghamshire and Leicestershire. An outlying cluster on the Wirral in Cheshire is explained by settlement by Norwegian Vikings fleeing the fall of Dublin in 902.

The most notable category of Scandinavian place-names in England is the 'Grimston hybrids', which combine English and Scandinavian elements, and which may represent English villages that were acquired by Norsemen; these include names containing the suffix '–thorpe' (as in Grimsthorpe or Mablethorpe), which is probably derived from the Old Norse *thorp*, meaning a secondary settlement; and those ending in the suffix '–by' (such as Grimsby), which comes from the Old Norse *by*, meaning a farmstead.[60] The latter are the most numerous, with more than 850 names ending in '–by' recorded, over half of them in Lincolnshire and Yorkshire.[61] Efforts to determine whether these place-names demonstrate that waves of Scandinavian colonists came to settle the newly conquered lands, or whether they simply came about through the acquisition by a Danish military elite of villages and estates from the Anglo-Saxon nobility they supplanted, are complicated by the fact that some of the name-forms may have appeared as late as the twelfth century. Others could have acquired Danish names at the time of the conquest of England by Cnut in 1015.[62] In most cases, all we can say is that the settlements had Scandinavian name-forms by the time of the Domesday Survey in 1086, which comprehensively listed the landownership of much of England.[63]

The Viking imprint was perhaps most profound in York, a city they ruled for nearly ninety years (from its first capture in 866 to its final loss in 954[64]), establishing a mini-kingdom in the north of England whose links with its counterpart in Dublin looked likely at times to create a Viking realm with the Irish Sea at its heart. The core of the Norse settlement at Coppergate ('Street of the Cupmakers') has yielded a mass of Viking-Age artefacts, preserved in the waterlogged soil near the River Ouse, which leached oxygen and allowed organic material such as leather and wood to survive. These range from the almost ubiquitous bone-combs found in settlements throughout the Viking world, to the world's largest human coprolite (fossilised faeces) and, more precious, assorted swords and jewellery.[65]

Little is known of the very early phase of Viking rule in York. After the expulsion of King Egbert by the Norsemen in 872, control of the city seems to have been exercised by the Anglo-Saxon Archbishop Wulfhere for a few years. The fragile authority of the Vikings in Northumbria is further emphasised by the fleeting career of Halfdan, who 'settled' the land with his men in 876 and was almost at once expelled north of the Tyne. The 'kingship' of York was anything but settled, and the next known Viking ruler of the city was Guthfrith, who held power from around 880 to 895 and was buried at York Minster, indicating that at least some of the Viking elite had converted to Christianity. From around 910, the York mint hedged its bets by producing coins that did not carry the royal name – a wise move in an era when battles and blood-feuds led to changes of ruler with monotonous regularity – but instead bore the legend 'St Peter's Money' on one side (honouring the city's patron saint) and the pagan motif of Thor's hammer on the other.

In 899, when Alfred the Great died, it seemed that the Danelaw, and in particular the Viking kingdom of York, was set to become a permanent fixture on the English political landscape. Yet almost at once events unfolded that questioned this supposition. The children of Alfred's older brother, Aethelred, had always represented a potential danger for him; excluded as they were from the succession, they could act as focal points for malcontents or even rebels. With his uncle dead, one of them, Aethelwold, decided to make a bid for the throne in place of the appointed heir, Alfred's son, Edward the Elder. He seized the royal manor at Wimborne in Dorset, but failed to gather sufficient support before Edward came up with a force of the local *fyrd*.

Hopelessly outnumbered, Aethelwold managed to slip away under cover of darkness.

He made his way to York, where he seems to have been elected king by the Vikings, although it is possible that they were merely recognising the Anglo-Saxon princeling as a convenient 'overlord' in place of Alfred, intending in due course to install him as puppet ruler of Wessex. His 'reign' seems to overlap with other Viking rulers of York, such as Sigfroth (c.895–c.900) and Knut (c.900–c.905),[66] casting doubt on the idea that he exercised any kind of sole power there. Whatever Aethelwold's precise status, his rule was fleeting, as his cousin Edward the Elder abandoned the generally defensive stance of Wessex over the preceding twenty years and launched a campaign that step-by-step pushed the Vikings out of East Anglia, the Five Boroughs and ultimately from York itself. Edward's position was strengthened by the marriage during Alfred's reign of his sister, Aethelflaed, to Aethelred, ealdorman (the 'elderman', or most senior royal official, in an area) of the Mercians. She became the ruler of English Mercia after her husband's death in 911 and helped rally local sentiment in support of what effectively became a takeover by Wessex.

In 902, Edward crossed the frontier of the Danelaw and killed his cousin Aethelwold in a hard-fought battle at the Holme (near Biggleswade in Bedfordshire). Although the Vikings had the upper hand on the battlefield, his death caused their resistance to collapse. Edward had rid himself of a dangerous pretender to his throne, but this success led to no immediate acquisition of territory, particularly as the arrival of new Norse bands in the north-west after their expulsion from Dublin the same year provided reinforcements for the York Vikings.

Disaster for the Vikings in Ireland offered opportunities for them elsewhere. One large group seems to have established a base on the River Ribble around 905. They deposited a hoard there, which included a huge quantity of hack-silver (silver coins or other artefacts that were chopped up for their value as bullion). Much of it came from Ireland, while large numbers of Northumbrian coins imply at least contact, if not cooperation, with the Viking lords of northern England. The Cuerdale Hoard was so substantial – the largest hoard of Viking silver ever found outside Russia – that it may well represent the war-chest of an army that was intended for the reconquest of Dublin.[67] The hoard was discovered by workmen repairing an embankment on the

River Ribble in 1840. Each of the finders was allowed to keep one of the coins, but the bulk of the 8,500 items, weighing more than 100 pounds (including some 7,000 coins), found its way to the British Museum. Even if they had not originally intended to stay, many of the Vikings who came east across the Irish Sea fanned out and settled across a wide area, including Cumberland, Westmorland, Lancashire and East Yorkshire (and some even made their way to the Cotentin peninsula in Normandy). As an indication of their Irish origins, they left a number of place-names ending in '–erg' (from the Old Irish *áirge* or 'shieling'). The density of names of Scandinavian origins is particularly high in the Wirral, especially in the north of the peninsula, including Irby, which may be derived from *Írabyr* ('settlement of the Irish'). Elsewhere, Scandinavian place-names are common in West Lancashire, especially on the coast north of the Ribble (with Thingwall, close to Knotty Ash, containing the telltale element *thing* or assembly, which may mean it was the site of a local meeting place). The most immediate and enduring impact of the new Scandinavian influx, however, was to provide a more secure western flank for the kingdom of York and to render communications between Viking Northumbria and Norse Dublin (after its re-establishment in 917) much easier.

The Viking exodus from Dublin also led to an upsurge in Scandinavian attacks against Wales, where a certain Ingimund is recorded attacking *Ros Melion* on Anglesey in 902/3. After his defeat at the hands of Cadell ap Rhodri, the ruler of Deheubarth, he joined the Viking diaspora in the north-west of England and settled near Chester. Although Ingimund was soon expelled from the city and failed to recapture it in 907, Chester seems to have acquired a Scandinavian element in its population; a number of ring-headed pins of Scandinavian type and arm-rings have been found in the city, while in 921 a pair of coin dies were cut there for the minting of coinage in the name of the Dublin Viking ruler Sihtric.

In 906 Edward made a treaty at Tiddingford with the Vikings of East Anglia and Northumbria.[68] Once again the peace did not last long, but this time it was Edward who took the offensive, unleashing a combined Mercian and West Saxon army across the frontier into Northumbria in 909. The following year the Vikings took their revenge, harrying far and wide in Mercia as far as Bristol, while Edward was away in Kent. Finally, the Wessex and Mercian *fyrd* caught up with the Vikings at Tettenhall in Staffordshire. In an encounter every bit as decisive as Ashdown, the Scandinavians were crushed, with three of their leaders (Ásl, Halfdan and Ivar[69]) killed, opening the way for further West Saxon expansion into the Midlands and East Midlands.

Edward took advantage of his victory by building *burhs* in forward positions, gradually making inroads on the territory of the Vikings, who were too weak to resist him. He pushed forward the line of his control deep into East Anglia, occupying Huntingdon in 917, and conquering Colchester in November the same year, while the main Danish army in East Anglia submitted to him soon afterwards. In 919, he even managed to place a *burh* in Northumbrian territory, when he constructed a fort at Manchester.

Meanwhile, the Irish Vikings had been active in the north of England under the leadership of Rögnvald, a grandson of Ivar the Boneless. In 918, he led a large army against Constantine (900–43), King of the Scots, and the English of northern Northumbria under Ealdred of Bamburgh.[70] The two armies clashed at Corbridge, located on a strategic crossing point on the Tyne just south of old Hadrian's Wall, and the honours seem to have been evenly matched. Despite the stalemate, Rögnvald was still able to establish himself as the dominant Viking leader in England. The death of Aethelflaed in June prevented her from taking up an offer of submission from the York Vikings[71] and Rögnvald moved in to fill the political vacuum.

In this way Edward the Elder was blocked from the conquest of the last major Viking territory in England, on the very point of achieving it. Although Rögnvald notionally recognised the West Saxon king as his overlord, his successor Sihtric (another grandson of Ivar the Boneless) adopted a more belligerent tone in his dealings with Edward, whose establishment of a new *burh* at Bakewell in Derbyshire in 920 posed a considerable threat to York.[72] It was left to Edward's son, Athelstan (924–39), to re-establish more cordial relations with the York Vikings; giving one of his daughters to Sihtric in marriage was no doubt deliberately calculated to this end. Yet again, however, West Saxon hopes were dashed by Sihtric's early death the following year and his replacement by Guthfrith, another grandson of Ivar, who crossed the Irish Sea to ensure that the family patrimony did not slip into the hands of Athelstan.

His patience with the dizzying succession of York Viking rulers exhausted, the King of Wessex crossed into Northumbria with a large force in 927. He soon drove Guthfrith out of York and then reinforced his position at a meeting at Eamont in Cumberland, where King Hywel of West Wales, King Constantine of Scotland, and Ealdred (son of Eadwulf, the lord of Bamburgh) all acknowledged his supremacy. To avoid any re-establishment of Viking control over York, Athelstan had the fortifications that the Danes had built there destroyed. He further stamped his authority on the city by abolishing the Anglo-Scandinavian coinage which had circulated and ordering his own issues minted there.

For seven years Athelstan's supremacy in the north of England went unchallenged, and it seemed as though Viking rule in York was ended for good, but then in 934 a new attack was launched on Scotland. The King of Wessex seems to have been afraid of a gathering coalition of enemies, both old and new; in Dublin, Guthfrith's son Olaf had come to power in 934, and Athelstan's assault that year, in which he is said to have laid waste to large areas of Scotland, may have been an attempt to pre-empt adventures by the Irish Vikings. If so, then the warning was not heeded, and in 937 Olaf Guthfrithsson set out with a large fleet to link up with the Strathclyde Britons and Constantine's Scottish army.

The combined force pushed south into England, before it was intercepted by Athelstan and his brother Edmund at Brunanburh. The location of the spot where the two armies clashed is uncertain; there is a wide variety of candidates, but the leading contender is probably Bromborough in Cheshire.[73] Although English losses were heavy, the Vikings suffered a catastrophic defeat, with five kings and seven *jarls* from Ireland counted among the dead, as well as one of Constantine's sons. Olaf limped back to Dublin, his force a mere shadow of the one that had accompanied him from Dublin just months before, the grand alliance with the Scots and Britons seemingly shattered for ever.

A poem preserved in the *Anglo-Saxon Chronicle* shows the exultation of the men of Wessex at their victory:

In this year King Athelstan, lord of nobles, dispenser of treasure to men, and his brother also, Edmund atheling, won by the sword's edge undying glory in battle around Brunanburh. Edward's sons clove the shield-wall, hewed the linden-wood shields with hammered swords . . . Their enemies perished: the people of the Scots and the pirates fell doomed. The field grew dark with the blood of men . . . There lay many a man destroyed by the spears, many a northern warrior shot over his shield; and likewise many a Scot lay weary, sated with battle.

The whole day long the West Saxons with mounted companies kept in pursuit of the hostile peoples, grievously they cut down the fugitives from behind with their whetted swords . . . Five young kings lay on that field of battle, slain by the swords, and also seven of Olaf's earls, and countless host of seamen and Scots. There the prince of the Norsemen was put to flight, driven perforce to the prow of his ship with a small company; the vessel pressed on the water, the king set out over the fallow flood and saved his life.

Then the Norsemen survivors from the spears put out in their studded ships on to Ding's mere to make for Dublin across the deep water, back to Ireland, humbled at heart. Also the two brothers, king and atheling, returned together to their own country, the land of the West Saxons, exulting in the battle. They left behind them the dusky coated-one, the black raven with its horned beak, to share the corpses, and the dun-coated, white-tailed eagle, the greedy war-hawk, to enjoy the carrion, and that grey beast, the wolf of the forest.

Never yet in this island before this, by what books tell us and our ancient sages, was a greater slaughter of a host made by the edge of the sword, since the Angles and Saxons came hither from the east.[74]

Yet for all its fame, the West Saxon victory at Brunanburh staved off the Vikings for a paltry two years. In 939 Olaf set sail again, perhaps encouraged by news of the death of Athelstan (and the succession of the eighteen-year-old Edmund). Amidst the confusion that almost always accompanied the start of a new reign, Olaf had little trouble in being accepted as King of York. By the following year his army had overrun most of the Five Boroughs, a fact that Edmund was forced to accept in a humiliating treaty following a stinging defeat near Leicester.[75] In 940 Olaf pushed northwards, deep into the old Anglian territories of southern Scotland, reaching as far as Dunbar. His death in 941 and the succession of his cousin, Olaf Sihtricsson (nicknamed *Cuarán* or 'sandal'), then allowed Edmund to recoup some lost ground, mainly in the Five Boroughs. Finally, in 943, the two kings came to an agreement very similar to that between Alfred and Guthrum sixty years earlier, setting the boundary between their realms along the line of Watling Street. As had become almost a tradition in Viking–Wessex peace treaties, Olaf accepted baptism, while Edmund stood as his sponsor.

The situation in York was complicated by the appearance of a rival Viking king, Rögnvald Guthfrithsson, who lasted only a year (943–4) and for whom, confusingly, Edmund also stood as baptismal sponsor. The following year Edmund expelled them both from York and, for the second time in six years, West Saxon armies occupied the Viking capital of the north. Edmund was killed in 946 (in a fracas when he tried to defend his steward from a man who was assaulting him) and in the turmoil following his death and replacement by his brother Eadred, there seems to have been a short-lived uprising in York, which brought the last, and most famous, of the Viking rulers of York to the throne.

Eirik, the man whom the York Vikings chose as their new king, has traditionally been identified with Eirik Bloodaxe, the former King of Norway, whose unpopular rule (during which he murdered both his brothers) resulted in his forced abdication in 936. The association between the two Eiriks seems to have arisen in the twelfth century, and there is no definite evidence in the sources that they are the same man (with one theory that the Viking ruler of York was instead another descendant of Ivar the Boneless[76]). If he was the King of Norway, then Eirik seems to have spent some time raiding in the northern isles of Scotland before receiving the summons to become ruler of York. His first reign (if indeed it existed[77]) was short, and by 947 Eadred of Wessex had already managed to impose his authority in Northumbria. The next year Eirik definitely succeeded in establishing himself at York, but the chronic division among the Scandinavians between Northumbrian-based Norsemen, their Irish counterparts and incoming Vikings from Denmark or Norway (such as Eirik himself) once again undermined attempts at a stable settlement.

Despite the support of Archbishop Wulfstan (which implies that his reign cannot have been as blood-stained as his nickname would imply), an invasion of Northumbria by Eadred in 949 led to Eirik's expulsion. Even now, the people of York clung doggedly to their independence from Wessex, and received back Olaf Cuarán (who had in the meantime also become King of Dublin[78]) as king. His second reign proved no more successful than the first and in 952 the men of York threw him out in favour of none other than Eirik Bloodaxe.

The events of Eirik's second (or possibly third) spell on the York throne are obscure. In 954, during the course of yet another invasion by Eadred, Eirik fled north towards Scotland. Somewhere along the way, at a place called 'Stainmoor', he was betrayed by Earl Oswulf (the ruler of Bamburgh) and killed by a certain Earl Maccus, son of Olaf.[79] Although it could not have been clear at the time, Eirik was the final Viking King of York, and the last Scandinavian to establish a significant powerbase in the Danelaw.[80] There was a brief upsurge in Viking activity in Wales from the 950s as those displaced from York continued to make mischief, but now the ambitions of the Viking rulers of Dublin to establish an Anglo-Irish realm including York had been shattered, so the Viking settlements on the Isle of Man became much more important as an alternative means of dominating the sea-lanes of the Irish Sea.

With its strategic location close to the coastlines of north-western England, south-west Scotland and the north of Ireland, the Isle of Man was a logical base for a seafaring power such as the Dublin Norsemen. It was from there that Viking raiders may have established a base at Llanbedrgoch on Anglesey in the 970s and 980s.[81] Yet there is no definite record of a Viking ruler there until a reference in Florence of Worcester's *History of the Kings of England* to a Maccus, described as 'king of many islands', who may have been King of Man and who was one of a number of rulers who pledged allegiance to Edgar of Wessex at Chester in 973. A Viking presence on the island must clearly pre-date that time, however, since at least one Viking coin hoard has been found from the period 955–60.[82] There are very few literary accounts of the kingdom of Man – there is a reference to a battle off Man in 987, and Manx Norsemen fought on the side of Sihtric of Dublin at the Battle of Clontarf in 1014.[83] The next secure mention is of the death of a Godred, son of Sytric, in 1070, and the accession as King of Man of his son Fingal, but nothing else is known of these two kings. In 1079 Godred Crovan seized the island. He is said to have been a survivor of the Battle of Stamford Bridge in 1066[84] and used Man as the base for building a mini-empire stretching as far as Ireland, taking Dublin and Leinster before his death in 1095. By the time Magnus Barelegs, King of Norway, arrived on Man in 1098, he found the island ravaged by a war of succession, and thereafter the island remained closely tied to the Norwegian crown (although with its own kings) until it was ceded to the Scottish crown in 1266.

Although there is little record of tenth-century Viking Man in the historical record, a number of Viking-Age burial mounds have been found. One of them, at Balladoole, contained the remains of a boat burial. Another mound at Ballateare contained evidence of possibly the only human sacrifice known from the Viking British Isles,[85] a female skeleton with a clean-cut hole sliced into her skull. In burials at Balladoole and Knock y Doonee, the remains of a boar were found in the grave, a rite that is rare in Viking graves in the British Isles, but far more common in Scandinavia, perhaps suggesting recent immigrants rather than an established Norse population.[86] Christianity seems to have been present already in the tenth century among the Vikings on Man, attested by a series of beautiful carved crosses, many ornamented in a Scandinavian style (and some of them with Norse runic inscriptions). Possibly the earliest of these, at Kirk Michael, contains the typically Viking boast by the rune-carver Gautr that he had 'made this and all Man' – in other words, he had carved all the crosses on the island. The iconography on the crosses is suggestive of a mixed population, with one cross[87] showing a carving of Odin, his foot jammed into the jaws of the wolf Fenrir on one side[88] and an image of Christ on the other face.

The most tangible relic of the Viking Age on Man is the island's assembly, the Tynwald, which lays claim to being the world's oldest parliament with an unbroken history.[89] The site is first mentioned in 1237 as *tingualla* (a word close to the Icelandic *Thingvellir*, the site of the medieval Icelandic assembly), and now consists of a tiered mound some 80 feet in circumference at the base, rising to more than 12 feet. Still to this day the Lieutenant-Governor (the queen's representative) sits on the topmost level, surrounded by the bishop, clergy and members of the legislature on the lower tiers, an echo of a time when a genuine Norse assembly met there.

Of far more lasting importance than the settlement in Man were the Viking settlements in Scotland, principal amongst them on Orkney.

Just as the tempo of Viking raids in England had grown more insistent after the arrival of the *micel here* in 865, so the Vikings in Scotland rapidly graduated from raiding to the seizing of bases. Although Orkney is said to have come under Norwegian control after an expedition by Harald Finehair of Norway in 874, it is clear that Norsemen had begun to settle there some time before this date, not least because Harald's motive was said to have been to put an end to the raiding by Vikings already established in the islands, which had begun to threaten the security even of Norway. The reconstruction of the Viking-Age history of the Orkneys is rendered simpler because we possess a detailed source – the *Orkneyinga Saga* – in contrast to the relative paucity of material from the Shetlands, Hebrides and elsewhere in Viking Scotland. Yet the saga's narrative is deceptively smooth and, without corroborating evidence from elsewhere, it is sometimes hard to be certain that the stories we possess were not carefully crafted (or modified) to suit some political agenda long after the events themselves took place.

When the Vikings arrived in northern Scotland and the islands in the ninth century, they did not enter an empty landscape. The pre-existing population was Pictish, belonging to a people first mentioned in Roman sources in AD 297,[90] and who took their name from the Latin *Picti* ('the painted ones', a possible reference to their custom of tattooing). By the sixth century, when written historical records begin to appear, the Picts had become Christianised and had begun to develop a centralised kingship. In the ninth century, however, pressure from the emerging kingdom of the Scots and from the newly arrived Vikings gradually squeezed them out. A few place-names, such as Pitlochry and the Pentland Firth[91] (the 'Firth of the Picts'), were left as testament to their presence, alongside a large number of carved symbol-stones, many of the earliest ones decorated with patterns of animals and geometric designs. The later ones (denoted Class II and Class III[92]), which post-date the conversion of Pictland to Christianity, are generally rectangular slabs with a cross on one side and a number of mysterious symbols – possibly pictograms – on the other.

The significance of these symbols – indeed, even whether they have any linguistic meaning at all – is unclear, and so they are of little help in identifying (let alone translating) the Pictish language, although it is now generally considered to be a P-Celtic language (like Welsh),[93] as distinct to the Q-Celtic or Goidelic form, which evolved into modern Gaelic and would supplant the Pictish language after Pictland collapsed following a catastrophic defeat at the hands of the Vikings in 839.

The air of mystery surrounding the Picts extends to medieval chroniclers. The author of the *Historia Norwegiae*, writing at the beginning of the thirteenth century, describes the original inhabitants of the Orkneys as 'Picts and Papae'.[94] One of these groups, the Picts, only a little taller than pygmies, he describes as having accomplished miraculous achievements by building towns, morning and evening; but at midday every ounce of strength deserted them and they hid out of fear in underground chambers. The author – or his sources – may have been led astray by the existence of 'souterrains', a kind of underground chamber which are characteristic of the Pictish area. That he also describes the Papae as Africans adhering to Judaism shows that his knowledge of the real situation was at best patchy.

The process by which the Vikings came to dominate, push out or even eliminate the local Pictish population of the Orkneys is obscure. The *Orkneyinga Saga* tradition suggests that by the time Harald Finehair reached the Orkneys in the 870s there was already an established Viking population there, capable of causing enough nuisance by freelance raiding of its own as to warrant royal Norwegian attention. The effect of Harald's expedition is probably somewhat exaggerated, since, as well as the Orkneys, he is said to have subjugated the Shetlands, the Hebrides, the Isle of Man and lands 'further west', while the settlers of the Faroes and Iceland ascribed their ancestors' migration there to resentment at the growing tyranny of Harald's rule in Norway, an improbably wide-ranging impact for a short-lived campaign. The archaeological evidence cannot, however, be used to corroborate the idea of a settlement before the 870s, as none of the pagan Norse burials so far found in Orkney date to earlier than the mid-ninth century (with the latest of them, a male grave found at Buckquoy, a little after 950).[95]

The story in the *Orkneyinga Saga* probably significantly overstates the role of Harald Finehair and oversimplifies the process by which Orkney became Viking. The insistence in Norwegian (and Icelandic) sagas and histories on Harald's role in conquering Orkney could instead have been a way of asserting the claims of the Norwegian crown on the islands.[96] According to the traditional account of the course of Harald's extended raid, Ivar (one of the sons of the Norwegian Earl Rögnvald of Møre) was killed during the expedition and, to compensate him for this loss, the king gave Orkney and Shetland to Rögnvald, who in turn passed them to his brother Sigurd. Nicknamed 'the Mighty' (*hinn ríki*), Sigurd thus became the first of the Orkney earls, a Viking line that would rule the islands for more than four centuries.

Whatever the truth about Harald Finehair's expedition, Orkney was the first convenient landfall after crossing the North Sea from Norway, and so would have been an obvious point to use as a base from which to launch raids elsewhere. The next definite report we have from the islands is of an attack on the north of Scotland around 890 by Sigurd the Mighty, allied with Thorstein the Red, the grandson of Ketil Flatnose, whom some sources describe as the ruler of the Sudreys ('the south islands' – the Norse term for the Hebrides). The local Pictish leader was a ferocious warrior named Maelbrigte Tusk (from the large tooth that protruded from his mouth). The Norse and Picts had agreed to fight with only forty men aside, but on the appointed day Maelbrigte saw that Sigurd had brought double the agreed number.[97] Badly outnumbered, the Pict had little hope of winning, and Sigurd duly killed him and cut his head off. On his return home, Maelbrigte's skull was dangling from Sigurd's saddle-bag, and the Orkney earl grazed his leg against the 'tusk'. The scratch became infected and Sigurd died, a posthumous victim of his own treachery.

The dead earl was buried in a mound by the River Oykel in Sutherland, and his ally Thorstein perished soon after in a battle in Caithness, a testament to the early involvement of the Vikings in the far north of Scotland, and the beginning of a presence there that would continue until the thirteenth century. Sigurd's son and successor, Guthorm, ruled Orkney for only a year before dying childless, whereupon Rögnvald of Møre despatched another of his sons, Hallad, to govern Orkney with the title of earl. The new ruler found a chaotic situation in which Danish Vikings were plundering unhindered as far as the coast of Caithness and, unable to bring the situation under control, he soon slunk back to Norway. Orkney was now left in the hands of two of the freebooters, Kalf *Scurfa* ('Scurvy') and Thórir *Tréskegg* ('Tree-beard'). Displeased at Hallad's cowardice, Rögnvald is said to have gathered together all his remaining sons, whose future careers he then predicted; Thórir was to succeed him as Earl of Møre, Hrollaug would go to Iceland, while Hrolf's destiny was to conquer Normandy. Only the youngest, Torf-Einar, born of a slave, had no glorious future in store for him. Instead, this least-favoured child was packed off with a single ship to Orkney and the hardly paternal counsel that, as all of his mother's family were thralls, the further away he went and the longer he stayed there, the more satisfied Rögnvald would be.[98]

Lying 60 miles to the north of the Orkneys at their most southerly point, the Shetlands never played a central role in the history of Viking Scotland, the lack of land suitable for the type of farming the Norsemen had carried out back home in Scandinavia being a principal obstacle. The islands were, however, rich in steatite, an easily quarried form of soapstone, which the Vikings valued highly for the creation of cooking and storage vessels. Little is known in detail of the early Viking period in Shetland, with the only Viking farmstead that has been excavated, at Underhoul on Unst, probably coming from a later period.

The earliest trace of Viking settlement on Shetland is probably the hoard of Pictish silver found on St Ninian's Isle in 1958. Discovered by a rather lucky sixteen-year-old schoolboy who was assisting on an archaeological dig, the hoard of some twenty-eight pieces of silver plate (and, eccentrically, the jawbone of a porpoise) may well represent the wealth of a Pictish chieftain, which was plundered by the Vikings and then buried under the floor of St Ninian's chapel, a seventh-century church which is the oldest in the Shetlands.

The most famous remains of the Viking era, however, are at the settlement at Sumburgh on the southern tip of Shetland. Known as Jarlshof, the name that Sir Walter Scott gave to the ruins in his 'Viking' novel *The Pirate,* the site was built over in the Middle Ages with a baronial dwelling (which is what Scott would have known). Beneath this later building, excavations in the 1950s uncovered a large Viking farmhouse, which occupied nearly the same area as a group of Pictish 'wheel-houses'[99] (which, in turn, had been built on top of earlier Bronze and Iron Age layers). Each of these successive phases appears to have been abandoned because of the effects of sand drifting from the nearby dunes, rather than through any act of violence. The presence of only a handful of weapons discovered in the Viking layer, together with the reuse of nearly the same site as the Pictish houses, indicates a more gradual takeover rather than the violent expulsion of the pre-existing inhabitants.[100]

Pictish place-names almost completely disappeared in the Northern Isles, the most notable exception being Orkney itself, which may derive from a Pictish word meaning 'pig' and could refer to the islands being the domain of the 'pig people'.[101] This has led to suggestions that the Vikings totally displaced the pre-existing population, either by expulsion or by killing them. The evidence from Jarlshof, however, seems to point towards assimilation (at least in Shetland). Instead the islands were probably settled by a combination of gradual Scandinavian influxes followed by a more formal acquisition around the time of Harald Finehair.[102]

Although the recollection of Viking settlement is strong in Orkney, the most spectacular remembrance of the Scandinavian period in the Northern Isles comes from Shetland. There, on the last Tuesday of each January, in the depths of the dark, bitter northern Scottish winter, the people celebrate the beginning of lighter days with a spectacular festival of fire. The name of the festival, Up-Helly-Aa, is possibly a corruption of 'Uphalliday', marking the end of the winter celebrations, and it once featured the dragging of burning tar barrels through the streets of Lerwick until, fearing a fatal conflagration, the town council banned the practice in 1874.[103] Up-Helly-Aa is still hugely impressive, with squads of costumed islanders (and one of them, that of the Guizer Jarl, dressed as a Viking) carrying blazing torches with which they set light to a reconstructed model of a Viking longship, in a re-creation of the funeral pyres of the warriors of old. The Norse longship in fact only first appeared in the ceremony in 1889, but the whole festival celebrates a pride in the Shetlands' Viking heritage, which stretches back more than a millennium.

Viking influence was less strong in the Hebrides, the third major area of Viking activity in the Scottish isles. It was, however, the area of the first-recorded Viking raids in Scotland, with a violent attack on Skye and Iona in the 790s. That the Gaelic for the Hebrides came to be Innse Gall ('Isles of the Foreigners') is an indication of the extent of early Scandinavian control there, while the entry in the Frankish Annals of St Bertin for 847 shows that already by the ninth century it was clear that the Vikings had established bases in the Hebrides: 'The

Northmen also took control of the islands all around Ireland, and stayed there without encountering resistance from anyone.'[104]

Signs of a violent occupation may come from the site at Coil-eagan an Udail on North Uist, where a small Viking fort appeared around the middle of the ninth century, followed by a development of six closely packed buildings, coupled with the complete near-simultaneous abandonment of a site that had been occupied since the Iron Age. It is likely that the first, small toehold (its defensive perimeter was only 20 feet wide) enabled the Vikings to dominate and then to expel the existing inhabitants in a process far less peaceful than the coexistence indicated at Jarlshof.

Place-name evidence, however, suggests a density of Viking population in the Hebrides far less than that in the Orkneys or Shetlands, and diminishing in the south of the islands. On Lewis, nearly 80 per cent of the village names are Norse, reducing to two-thirds in the east of Skye and far lower figures to the south. On the west coast of Scotland they fall away completely, with Ullapool (in Wester Ross) being one of the few names of Norse origin. Lewis, too, has yielded the greatest concentration of Norse archaeological sites, including the burial site at Cnip where the body of a wealthy woman wearing oval brooches and a necklace with forty-four beads was found, though no Viking settlements (such as at Jarlshof in Shetland or Birsay in Orkney) have yet been identified.

On the other side of the Irish Sea, isolated attacks from the 830s on the coast of Ireland, and the easy pickings to be had from rich ecclesiastical foundations were succeeded, just as they had been in England, by more substantial Viking expeditions. In 837, a fleet of sixty Norse ships was reported on the Boyne and the Liffey, which inflicted a serious defeat on the Uí Néill kings. The Vikings then began to infest the inland waterways of Ireland (such as Lough Neath, the Shannon, the Bann and the Boyne), striking deeper inland than ever before. In 838, the death of a Viking chieftain named Saxolb (or *Saxulf*) marks both an infrequent success by the Irish defenders and the first leader of the raids on Ireland who is known to us by name.

The first certain Viking overwintering base was on Lough Neagh in 840–41 (the entry in the *Annals of Ulster* for 842 records 'heathens still at Dublin', as though their failure to return home for the winter was considered a remarkable event). The Vikings now began to establish *longphorts,* fortified ship enclosures, beginning with one at Annagassan (or *Linn Dúachaill*) in County Louth and, more importantly, in 841–2 at Dublin. They then proceeded to found a string of similar ports along the coast, at Waterford, Woodstow, Wexford (*Veighsfjörður*), Wicklow (*Vikingaló*) and Limerick *(Hlymrekur).*

Dominating the important crossing over the River Liffey, Dublin (in Irish *Dubh-linn,* 'the black pool') soon became the Vikings' principal base in Ireland, a position it retained until the final dwindling of their power on the island in the eleventh century. Traces of the Viking settlement have been found throughout Dublin, from the Viking cemetery on its western outskirts at Islandbridge, where the skeletons of scores of warriors were discovered buried with their swords (of Norwegian manufacture), to the remains of the earliest Viking settlement around the modern Christ Church Cathedral. The exact location of the first *longphort,* which had long been believed to lie north of the Poddle River, and possibly on the site of the later Dublin Castle, has now been found in a series of burials and remains of habitation sites of the mid- to late-ninth century that lie on the other side of Dublin's 'Black Pool'.[105]

By the eleventh century an artisan quarter was thriving in Viking Dublin, containing houses and workshops of wattle bound together with hazel and ash rods, whose inhabitants have left a treasure trove of discarded and broken scraps, including soapstone moulds for casting the hammer-shaped amulets dedicated to Thor. The settlement, which was abandoned – at least by the Viking elite – in 902, and then refounded after 917, was defended by an earthen bank in the tenth century, around which another circle of banks was constructed in the eleventh century (replaced in turn by a stone wall around 1100).[106] The Vikings clearly imported elements of their political organisation in Scandinavia; a Scandinavian *thing* (or assembly) appears to have been held on a mound on College Green (in origin a prehistoric burial mound); while an official called the 'law speaker of Dublin' (*airlabraid Átha Cliath*), echoing similar titles in Iceland, is recorded as having died at the Battle of Tara in 980.[107]

The Vikings were by now firmly ensconced in Ireland, and even a series of Irish victories in 848 could not drive them out. The chronic division of the Irish – who had around 150 different sub-kingdoms grouped under the general overlordship of the kings of Connaught, Leinster, Munster, Ulster and the northern and southern Uí Néill, with one ruler or another asserting himself as 'high-king' over the rest – meant that the Vikings were able to exploit the divisions amongst their adversaries to make inroads on the coast. Yet the Balkanisation of Ireland (where conquering one sub-kingdom left scores of others still in the field) also gave it a kind of resilience in depth, which the Anglo-Saxons of England lacked.

The setbacks of 848 caused a crisis for Viking Ireland. A state of near civil war seems to have broken out among the surviving Norsemen, with a group called the *Dubh-Gaill* ('Dark Foreigners') arriving in Dublin in 851 and slaughtering large quantities of the *Fin-Gaill* ('Fair Foreigners') who were already established there.[108] The *Dubh-Gaill* then defeated the *Finn-Gaill* in a battle on Carlingford Lough in 852, and the next year a new Viking chieftain arrived, Olaf (or Amlaib, as the Irish annals refer to him), who is described as 'the son of the king of Laithlind'[109] and who, together with his brother Ivar, and a third sibling Ásl, put an end to the fighting and came to dominate Viking Ireland in the 850s and 860s.

Ireland gained a brief respite when Olaf left for the Isle of Man and Hebrides in 854–5, the first sign of the Dublin Viking rulers' penchant for involvement across the Irish Sea, which would, over time, fatally weaken their home base. The death of the high king Maél Sechlainn in 862, after a reign in which he had brought the overkings of Munster and Leinster into his obedience, allowed the Vikings to expand outwards from Dublin into the lands of the southern Uí Néill. In 864, Olaf defeated and killed Conchobar, one of the joint rulers of Meath, drowning him at the church of Clonard, but that year Ivar left Ireland for England. Two years later Olaf and Ásl took an army to Pictland, and these departures allowed an Irish fightback, which saw the destruction of many of the Viking bases in north-eastern Ireland and defeats of Viking forces at Leinster and Clondalkin, close to Dublin (where the heads of 100 Viking chieftains were collected as war-trophies by the victorious Irish).

These disasters brought Olaf hurrying back to Ireland. He struck out in all directions, raiding the church at Armagh, and by 870 felt confident enough to leave for Britain again. There he joined forces with Ivar to besiege and capture the British stronghold of *Alt Clud* (or Dumbarton

Rock), the capital of the kingdom of Strathclyde. After a four-month siege, the fortress fell – inflicting a blow from which Strathclyde never truly recovered – and both of them returned to Dublin with 200 ships laden with the spoils.[110] Although Olaf died in a further attack on Pictland in about 874, Ivar took up the kingship of Dublin, and his position was sufficiently secure that at the time of his death in 873 the *Irish Annals* refer to him as 'king of the northmen of all Ireland and Britain'.

Ivar's family continued to rule Dublin, with three of his sons obtaining the throne in succession, ending with the accession of Sihtric in 888. His rule was challenged in turn in 893 by Sigfrith, an unrelated Viking *jarl*,[111] before the two rivals temporarily patched up their differences to allow them both to go raiding together in Britain. The infighting did not cease on Sihtric's return in 894, and two years later he was murdered by a rival Viking group. The internecine feuding led to a slackening – but not the total cessation – of raiding that is referred to in Irish sources as the 'Forty Years' Rest'. In 902, the Irish took advantage of the chronic divisions among the Norsemen and came together in a coalition led by Máel Finnia of Brega and Cerball of Leinster, which overwhelmed the Scandinavian defenders of Dublin. The 'heathens' are said to have fled 'half dead after they had been wounded and broken'.[112]

A diaspora of Irish Vikings retreated to Britain, where Ingimund raided Anglesey in 902/3, while others turned their attentions to Scotland. There were a few sporadic raids on north-eastern Ireland, but the Vikings did not return in force until 913, when 'a great new fleet of heathens' attacked Waterford Harbour, led by Óttar, whom the *Anglo-Saxon Chronicle* records as having sailed from Brittany. Then, in 917, a new Viking fleet arrived under the command of Rögnvald and Sihtric, two grandsons of Ivar, and pushed aside Óttar's group. While Rögnvald took over Waterford, his brother sailed on to Leinster, defeated an Irish army at Confey and then re-entered Dublin.[113]

An Irish attempt to expel the interlopers failed in September 919 when the overking of Ulster and four other kings died in a devastating defeat at the hands of the Vikings. The renewed Norse occupation seems to have been followed by a period of some prosperity for Dublin, with a rapid expansion along the waterfront of the Liffey and a more organised network of plot-divisions appearing in the town. At Waterford, too, the focus of the Viking settlement seems to have shifted, from the probable site of the first *longphort* at Woodstown to a point further south along the River Suir.

The chimera of a joint Viking realm that transcended the Irish Sea and bound together York and Dublin continued to preoccupy the latter's Irish Viking rulers, to the point where it weakened their hold on both towns. It led Sihtric to transfer to Britain in 919 (where he became King of York in 921), leaving Guthfrith, another grandson of Ivar, as King of Dublin. His rule was marked by a complex struggle in the 920s with rival Viking centres at Limerick and Waterford that led to the foundation of new camps throughout Ireland, including at Lough Gur south of Limerick and at Linns in Dundalk Bay in 926.

A temporary check to this enlargement of the Viking sphere occurred in 926, when Muirchertach mac Néill, king of the southern Uí Néill, defeated the Vikings at Carlingford, killing 200 Norsemen. Later the same year he overcame another Viking force at Strangford Lough, an engagement in which Guthfrith's son Halfdan perished. Despite these setbacks, when Sihtric died at York in 927, Guthfrith seems not to have hesitated to take the well-worn path from Ireland to Northumbria in an effort to replace him. The rapid failure of this enterprise, and his expulsion by Athelstan of Wessex the same year, led to his premature return to Ireland.

Guthfrith died in 934, his renewed feud with Limerick having preoccupied him for most of the final seven years of his rule. With the conflict still unresolved, it was left to his son Olaf to claim victory in 937, when he smashed the Limerick fleet on Lough Ree and captured his rival king, who was also named Olaf and who rejoiced in the unflattering nickname 'Scabbyhead'. Feeling secure in his position in Ireland, Olaf now turned to the worrying phenomenon of the growing power of Wessex in northern England, which was threatening to snuff out the Viking kingdom of York for good. He joined forces with Constantine of Scotland and other northern magnates in an alliance that ended in disaster with defeat by Athelstan at Brunanburh.[114]

Despite a siege of Dublin by the Uí Néill in 938, Olaf hesitated little on hearing of his arch-enemy Athelstan's death in 939, before hurrying back over to England to claim the throne of York. Control of Dublin now passed to his cousin Olaf Sihtricsson, whose Gaelic nickname *Cuarán* ('sandal') is perhaps an indication of the degree of assimilation that was beginning to occur. But Olaf Cuarán, too, felt the pull of

York and, after barely a year on the throne of Dublin, abandoned it to another cousin, Blákári Guthfrithsson. During this period conflict with the native Irish intensified, and in 944 Congalach, overking of Brega, was able to capture and sack Dublin, killing up to 400 Vikings. As the merry-go-round of Norse kings alternated between the two cities, Olaf was pushed out of York and in 945 returned to Dublin to reclaim it by force from an unwilling Blákári. Then, when the latter regained control of the city in 948, Olaf returned to York for a final three-year stint on the throne.

All of this turmoil weakened the Viking settlement's ability to fend off Irish attacks, and Blákári lasted only a few months before being killed at a battle with the southern Uí Néill. Stability of a sort was only restored in 951, when a chastened Olaf Cuarán returned from York, having been expelled once more in favour of Eirik Bloodaxe.[115] Olaf would rule over Dublin for the next thirty years, a period in which the Viking kingdom reached the peak of its influence in Ireland, yet at the same time saw the seeds of its final downfall being sown.

There was one further area of Viking activity in western Europe, although it was probably the one in which they enjoyed the least success. During their extensive raiding against Aquitaine in Francia, the Vikings must have become aware of the rich lands to the south-west. The Iberian peninsula was divided in the early ninth century between the Islamic emirate of al-Andalus, centred on Córdoba, and a collection of small Christian states in the north, principally León and Castile, with a 'Spanish March' under Frankish control in the north-east around Barcelona. Between the two lay a debatable frontier zone, which occupied an area to the north of the River Ebro.

One of the attractions of Spain to the Vikings – other than opportunistic plundering – was slaves: both the opportunity to trade those (Franks and Anglo-Saxons) whom they had already acquired in the north and to capture new ones.[116] The inhabitants of Islamic Spain became familiar enough with the Vikings to give them a special name, the *majus* or 'fire worshippers', although whether this is a reference to any specific Scandinavian cult practice is unknown.[117] We also have a record of an embassy sent by 'Abd ar-Rahman II (who was the ruler of the Arab Umayyad emirate of Córdoba from 822 to 852) to an unknown northern king, who has been variously identified as Turgeis,

the Viking King of Dublin, or Horik of Denmark.[118] The envoy, the
poet Yahya ibn Hakam al-Jayyani – who was nicknamed al-Ghazal
('the gazelle') because of his good looks – had previously completed
a successful diplomatic mission to the Byzantine emperor Theophilus.
This second embassy was considerably less fruitful, in part because
the foreign ruler tried to humiliate al-Ghazal by making him bow
down before him, which the Arab envoy refused to do. Finally, the
king had the entrance to the audience chamber lowered so that
al-Ghazal would have to abase himself, but he is said to have entered
backwards, exposing his 'shameful parts' to the king. It also cannot
have helped that the northern queen became infatuated with the
attractive Moorish ambassador and insisted on summoning him to
her chambers almost every day in order, she claimed, to hear his
stories about life in al-Andalus.

Contacts between the various Spanish kingdoms and the Vikings
seem to have been less intense than in Francia, Ireland or Britain. Very
few Viking artefacts have been found[119] and there is only a handful of
place-names, such as Lordemanos in León and Lodimanos in Galicia
(which both mean 'north-men'), that indicate the regular presence of
Norsemen. Although there are hints that there may have been Viking
raids on northern Spain in the early ninth century,[120] the first major
recorded raid in the Iberian peninsula occurred in 844. Its wide-ranging
voyage took the Viking fleet of fifty-four ships far further than they
had probably planned. Beginning in Brittany, they first plundered in
south-western France, before carrying on to attack Christian northern
Spain (including the port of La Coruña). The Norsemen then sailed
on southwards to the Muslim-controlled lands, where in a few short
weeks they did more damage than the Christian kingdoms had inflicted
on the Umayyad emirate in more than a century, burning Cádiz and
Algeciras. The Vikings then sailed up the Guadalquivir, taking advantage of the same ability to navigate shallow waters that had allowed
them to penetrate the Seine and Loire in France, and pitched camp
on the Isla Menor near Seville. The city at the time lacked walls and
so they found it relatively easy to plunder, but, since the Guadalquivir
is unnavigable beyond Seville, they were then forced to take to the
land, where a Moorish army hastily mustered by 'Abd ar-Rahman
experienced little difficulty in crushing them.

Many of the surviving Vikings fled back to the ships, and in the ensuing slaughter some 1,000 of them were killed and thirty of their ships set ablaze by a weapon that the Vikings may not have encountered before, Greek Fire – an incendiary hurled from catapults, which had the peculiar property of remaining ablaze even on water.[121] Some 400 Vikings were taken captive and most were hanged, although a few survivors converted to Islam and remained near Seville, where it is said in later years they made a living selling cheese.[122] Those who escaped in the remaining ships made a desultory raid on the Algarve on their way northwards and then limped back to Francia.

Perhaps deterred by the adverse reports of the 844 raid, there was no further Viking raid recorded in Iberia until 859. The leaders of an expedition that year, Hasteinn and Björn Ironside, sailed into the Mediterranean (an achievement in itself) and so far to the east that they won themselves enduring fame. The fleet was large (somewhere between sixty and a hundred ships) and it seems to have set out with the extraordinary objective of sacking the city of Rome itself.[123] The expedition did not enjoy an auspicious start, though, as a raid on the hugely wealthy pilgrimage centre of Santiago de Compostela was beaten back. Hasteinn and Björn then suffered a further setback outside Seville, where they were defeated by the new Umayyad ruler, Muhammad I.

The Vikings pressed on, sailing through the Straits of Gibraltar, where they met practically no opposition – pausing only briefly for plundering sorties against Cádiz and Algeciras – and so became the first Norse fleet to enter the western Mediterranean. The two Viking chieftains then achieved another first by attacking the coast of North Africa, descending on the Moroccan emirate of Nekor, which they sacked and then held for a week. They also seized two women from the royal harem, who were only released after the payment of a hefty ransom by Muhammad of Córdoba.

The Vikings proceeded north and eastwards up the coast of Spain, attacking Valencia and the Balearics before arriving in due course on the south coast of Francia. There they raided a number of monastic houses and burned the town of Narbonne. Finally, with winter approaching, they set up camp in the Camargue, a refuge protected by its marshes from unwelcome Frankish attention. The following spring, Hasteinn and Björn sailed up the Rhône and sacked Nîmes and Arles. It seemed as if the Viking experience on the Loire and

Seine might be repeated, with this new group establishing a base in southern Francia and the Rhône, from which to raid over a prolonged period. But at Valence they were repulsed by a force under Count Gerard of Provence[124] and they decided to press on instead to Italy.

There – at least in the story as related by the Norman chronicler Dudo of Saint-Quentin – the Vikings finally reached a magnificent city, its walls and towers all made of bright white marble. Not being strong enough to assault it directly, they took it by a ruse which, even if the tale is not true, at least shows the level of cunning that their antagonists tended to ascribe to the Vikings. On arriving at the town, Hasteinn let it be known that he wished to convert to Christianity. The next day his men bore him to the city gates in a coffin, claiming that their leader had, most tragically, passed away during the night. The town's citizens permitted the funeral cortège to enter the gate, but once they were safely inside, the Vikings drew their swords and Hasteinn leapt dramatically from his coffin. The Norsemen then engaged in an enthusiastic sack of the city, which turned out not to have been Rome at all, but the much more modest town of Luni.[125]

Disappointed in their hoped-for prize, the Vikings continued their plunderers' progress through the Mediterranean. They may even have entered the eastern Mediterranean and operated in the sphere of the Byzantine empire, but their exact route cannot be traced until they tried to return through the Straits of Gibraltar in 861. This time they had to force their passage, for their way was barred by a large Muslim fleet. Although Hasteinn and Björn managed to fight their way through, it was at the cost of a large number of their remaining ships. On their retreat northwards, they did manage to capture King García of Pamplona and extract a 70,000-gold-piece ransom for his release and so, with at least these consolation prizes and some African slaves they had taken in Nekor (whom the Norsemen referred to as *blámenn*, or 'blue men'), they returned to the Loire in the spring of 862.[126]

The Umayyad response to these Viking raids was to construct a chain of forts and strengthen their navy (with 'Abd ar-Rahman II establishing a new naval base at Almería). As a result, Viking raids in Spain in the tenth century were largely directed against the Christian kingdoms of the north. Raids are recorded against Galicia in 951, 965 and 966 and a major attack occurred in 968 when a Viking force led by Gunnauð killed Sisnando, Bishop of Santiago. Emboldened by this, the same group continued to raid for three years from a base on the Ulla River, causing enormous devastation. In 972, they struck the Algarve in the Muslim-controlled area, but the Umayyads in general were easily able to fend off the few attempts the Vikings made against them.

Occasional raids did continue into the eleventh century, with a large-scale attack in 1014 against Tui on the Miño River, another on Galicia in 1029 and a major series of assaults in 1047–66 in the region of Santiago. Yet the Vikings were never able to establish themselves in Spain in the way they did in Francia. Distance and more determined resistance to their attacks meant that in Iberia the raids never reached anywhere near the level of menace that they posed in north-western Europe. As a result, of the Viking presence in Spain there is scant trace, save a few place-names, a cylindrical bone box in the treasury of León Cathedral carved in the Mammen style, the annual Romaria Vikinga festival at Catoira in Galicia, and of course the immortal memory of the voyage of Hasteinn and Björn Ironside.

Map 5 Scandinavia in the Early Viking Age

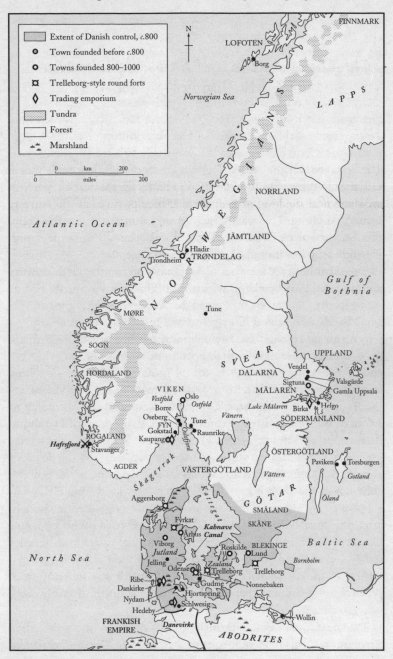

Extent of Danish control, *c*.800
Town founded before *c*.800
Towns founded 800–1000
Trelleborg-style round forts
Trading emporium
Tundra
Forest
Marshland

km   200
miles   200

FINNMARK
LOFOTEN
Borg
LAPPS
Norwegian Sea
NORRLAND
Atlantic Ocean
JÄMTLAND
Hladir
TRØNDELAG
Trondheim
Gulf of Bothnia
MØRE
Tune
SOGN
SVEAR
UPPLAND
HORDALAND
DALARNA
Vendel
Valsgärde
Sigtuna
Gamla Uppsala
MÄLAREN
VIKEN
Oslo
Vestfold   *Ostfold*
Borre
Luke Mälaren
Birka
Helgo
Oseberg
Tune
Vänern
SÖDERMANLAND
FYN
Gokstad
Raunrike
Kaupang
Oslofjord
ROGALAND
ÖSTERGÖTLAND
Hafrsfjord
Paviken
Torsburgen
Stavanger
Gotland
AGDER
VÄSTERGÖTLAND
Vättern
Öland
Skagerrak
GÖTAR
Aggersborg
SMÅLAND
Kattegat
SKÅNE
Fyrkat
Kabnave
BLEKINGE
Canal
Baltic Sea
Århus
Viborg
Roskilde
Lund
Jutland
Bornholm
Jelling
Zealand
Trelleborg
Odense
Trelleborg
North Sea
Gudme
Ribe
Nonnebaken
Dankirke
Hjortspring
Nydam
Schlwesig
Hedeby
Wollin
FRANKISH EMPIRE
Danevirke
ABODRITES

Chieftains, Myths and Ships: Scandinavia in the Early Viking Age, 800–950

The Scandinavia from which the Vikings set out on their raids was in 800 already beginning to experience a series of political changes, as the states that would ultimately form Denmark, Sweden and Norway began to coalesce. This was, though, a very slow process, with a series of false starts and premature claims of unification from writers with a nationalistic (or, more properly, dynastic) agenda.

The identities of the rulers of Denmark later in the ninth century are obscure. Two brothers, Sigfred and Halfdan, are mentioned as ruling jointly there in 873, but, given that leaders of even comparatively small bands who raided in England and Ireland are termed 'king', it is by no means certain that they held sway over the whole of Denmark (or even over more than a small portion of it). It is not until the very end of the century that the historical mists begin to part. A Viking army was defeated at the River Dyle (in modern Belgium) in 891 by the East Frankish king, Arnulf. This was accompanied, according to Adam of Bremen – whose chronicle of the Archbishops of Hamburg-Bremen includes much incidental detail about Scandinavia (which lay under the notional supervision of the German see) – by the death of two Danish kings (Sigfred and Godfred) and a decline in the political cohesion of the Danish kingdom. A very short-lived King Helgi was supplanted by a dynasty headed by Olaf that originated in Sweden (and was possibly from Skåne). Olaf was succeeded by his two sons Gnupa and Gurd, who were then followed by two rulers from another family, Sigerich and Hardegon Sveinsson. All these rulers are virtual ciphers to us, but what is clear is that Denmark was suffering from political instability and that influence from the north, from Sweden, was growing stronger.

The next mention of Danish kings comes in the 930s when Archbishop Unni of Hamburg sent a mission to Gorm (nicknamed 'the Old') in 935, but found him an obdurate pagan. Adam of Bremen's chronology is probably a little confused, as in 934 the German emperor Henry the Fowler is said to have defeated the Danish king, Gnupa, and annexed land as far north as Hedeby (leaving little time for Sigerich and Hardegon to rule before Gorm's accession the next year). About Gorm very little is known, save that he established a dynasty, the Jellings, who would rule over Denmark for the rest of the Viking Age.

What we do know comes from a series of memorials established by Gorm and his son Harald (who, for reasons that are somewhat obscure, acquired the nickname 'Bluetooth'[1]). These lie around the churchyard at Jelling, near Velje in south-eastern Jutland, now a quiet settlement, although in the tenth century it formed the heart of the Danish kingdom. As well as two runestones – one set up by Gorm in memory of his wife Thyri and another by Harald in memory of his parents – the site consists of two large burial mounds, the church itself and a number of uninscribed standing stones. At first sight hard to decipher, the complex illuminates the development of the Danish kingdom in the mid-ninth century, and in particular its Christianisation.

The first to be set in place was Gorm's runestone, a weathered rectangular slab that bears the runic inscription[2] 'King Gorm made this memorial to his wife Thyri, the adornment of Denmark.' This represents no more than a conventional tribute to the dead queen, but Gorm also raised an enormous burial mound (some 35 feet high and 230 feet in diameter) to the north of the present church, into which was set a wooden burial chamber intended for Thyri's and (ultimately) his own mortal remains. He also erected a triangular series of stones at one end of the mound, which may well be a stylised representation of a ship (from which such monuments are given the generic name 'ship-settings'). It is even possible that originally Thyri's runestone was set at the 'prow' of the ship, although it was subsequently moved and forgotten about, being eventually discovered buried in the churchyard in 1590.

For the last fifteen years of Gorm's life, Harald acted as co-ruler with his father, and by the time the old king died in 958, fresh attempts were already being made to bring Christianity to the Danes. In 948, three bishops were appointed to sees in Århus, Ribe and Hedeby.[3] Although Harald did not become a Christian before his father's death, it is clear that a favourable climate for acceptance of the new religion was emerging among his advisers some time before. It was just two years after Harald's accession to the throne that Poppo, a new missionary bishop, finally converted the Danish king (although, according to Adam of Bremen, it was the Danes' failure in a war against the German emperor rather than any religious conviction that played the central role in Harald's willingness to accept baptism).

It all came about as the result of a heated debate around the royal feasting table, fuelled no doubt by copious quantities of beer and mead. The talk turned to which of the gods was most powerful: the Danes were prepared to accept that Christ was divine, but counted him as simply one of many, and distinctly less powerful than their own deities, such as Odin and Thor.[4] Poppo could not accept this affront to the Christian religion and declared that there was only one true God, while those whom the Vikings worshipped were simply demons. To avoid the angry reaction to this offence turning violent, Harald challenged Poppo to demonstrate the truth of his argument by submitting to an ordeal.

Ordeals varied in kind, from forcing a party to a dispute to plunge his unprotected arm into a cauldron of boiling water to retrieve a ring, to binding up and throwing the accused into a pond. The latter was a technique much used in the later Middle Ages to test witches; the accused was found guilty if she floated (and survived) and innocent if she sank (and drowned). Although seeming to modern sentiments a barbaric legal instrument, ordeals were in fact reasonably common when the normal practice of taking oaths from supporters of either side to determine the truth of a case had failed, and where there seemed no prospect of satisfactory recourse to any other form of mediation.

In Poppo's case resorting to an ordeal came first, before any real attempt to mediate the dispute. The king commanded Poppo to carry a lump of red-hot iron a number of paces before dropping it. According to the rules of the ritual, his hand was then bound for several days and the wound inspected afterwards – if it was found to be infected, then the ordeal would be judged to have gone against him. The event is commemorated in a series of bronzes fixed to the pulpit in the church at Tamdrup, south-west of Århus.[5] One image shows the lump of iron being heated above a fire, and in the next Poppo removes the binding from his hand to show that the wound is clean. Harald is then depicted, duly won over, being baptised while standing naked in a barrel of water.

Harald Bluetooth may have brought Christianity to Denmark – at least to his own satisfaction – but there had certainly been Christian missionaries before his time. The first recorded was the Northumbrian St Willibrord in 714, who took time, during his forty-year-long mission to the Frisians in the early eighth century, to visit King Ongendus, who was described as 'fiercer than any wild beast, and harder than stone'.[6] The mission achieved little, not least because of Willibrord's haughtily discourteous behaviour before the Danish king.

The next attempt at proselytising the Danes came in 823, when the Frankish ruler Louis the Pious despatched Ebbo, Archbishop of Rheims, on a new mission. Although he seems to have baptised a few converts, a richer crop came in 826, when Harald Klak and 400 of his followers accepted Christianity at Mainz (although, in the way of the times, he did so largely through his need to procure imperial assistance to gain the Danish throne rather than out of any sense of religious conviction). When Harald was finally able to return to Denmark, he fulfilled his part of the bargain by bringing with him a young Christian cleric named Anskar. The success of the mission was firmly tied to Harald's political star, and when Harald was expelled from the country after just a few months, Anskar and his companion Audubert had to leave too; they had barely had time to establish a school to instruct a small number of youths in Christianity (probably at Hedeby). Anskar's next journey to Scandinavia would see him travelling not to Denmark, but to Sweden.[7]

More than a century later, Harald Bluetooth marked his conversion to Christianity by adding dramatic new elements to the family burial ground. He is said to have chanced one day on an enormous granite stone lying on a beach in Jutland, and ordered the 10-ton block to be man-hauled all the way back to Jelling. He had perhaps already ordered the erection of another mound, slightly smaller than that for his mother and placed to the south of it. This new mound almost entirely obliterated the pre-existing ship-setting, many of whose stones were buried beneath it. Oddly, when archaeologists began investigating it in 1941, they found no burial chamber inside this new memorial, and so it can never have been intended to receive Harald's own corpse (both ship-settings and burials in mounds clearly being pagan vestiges that were not encouraged in the newly Christian Denmark).

The runestone, which has been described as Denmark's 'baptismal certificate', is a triangular piece of red-black granite carved on three sides, with a lengthy runic inscription on one side accompanied by images asserting Harald's Christian credentials. It reads: 'King Harald had this monument made in memory of Gorm, his father, and in memory of Thyri, his mother, that Harald who won for himself all of Denmark and Norway and made the Danes Christian.' On the second side, a lion and a serpent (with its tail curled round into its mouth) engage in a sinuous struggle for supremacy that might symbolically represent that between the old religion and the new. The third face of the stone contains the earliest surviving depiction of Jesus Christ in native art from Scandinavia. In common with many runestones, the Jelling Stone would originally have been painted in bright colours, the merest traces of which have survived, and so the appearance of Christ – surrounded by interlocking knot patterns, his arms outstretched and his legs together as though on the cross, eyes wide open and with an expression of serene triumph – must have been striking indeed (some idea, though divorced from its setting, can be gained from the coloured replica of the stone that has been erected inside the nearby museum).

Almost as if an afterthought, a church – the current incarnation being a plain white Romanesque structure dating from about 1100 – nestles between the two mounds, stamping a definitive Christian note on a scene many of whose components flirt dangerously with paganism. Excavations in the north mound in 1820[8] found the oak-lined burial chamber, together with a scattering of artefacts including a silver cup (the decoration on which gives the Jellinge artistic style its name),[9] but there were no human remains. Although it is possible that the grave had been broken into at some time and its contents stolen (a practice vividly described in the *Saga of Grettir the Strong*,[10] where the hero enters a burial mound, does battle with the shade of Kar the Old, who is buried there, and then makes off with a treasure trove of grave-goods), the absence of human bones in the south mound suggested that something more than mere grave robbery was to blame.

The mystery was partially solved in 1976 when the church decided to install a new central-heating system. As well as the remains of two previous oak-built churches, both of which had been destroyed by fire, archaeologists discovered a grave placed just below the level of the earliest building. Interred in it were the remains of a middle-aged man, just over 5 feet 6 inches in height. The bones were not placed in an orderly fashion, suggesting that they had been disarticulated during their removal from a previous resting place. The grave also contained a large quantity of gold thread and a pair of strap decorations, which may have come from a perished garment. The balance of probability is that this burial beneath Jelling church is that of Gorm the Old, and that his remains were transferred there by Harald in a symbolic claiming of them for Christianity. They may well have been buried previously in the north mound, but what happened to the body of Harald's mother, Thyri, is unknown. Gorm's bones were buried, possibly for the third time, in 2000, again beneath Jelling church, with Queen Margrethe II of Denmark (his direct descendant) in attendance.

The complex at Jelling is not the only evidence of monumental building during Harald's reign. In the 950s additional works were carried out along the Danevirke in the south of Denmark, and ten years later a wall was constructed connecting the main fortification line to the ramparts of Hedeby. Additional improvements to the defences of Hedeby, Ribe and Århus are also attributed to Harald, but the most spectacular evidence of his building campaign is a series of monumental circular fortresses scattered throughout Denmark (and in one case in Skåne in southern Sweden, which then formed part of the Danish realm) and previously believed to be mustering points for Svein Forkbeard's invasion of England in 1013. The timbers used on them have now been dated by dendrochronology to 980–1, setting them firmly in Harald's time.

These huge fortresses, at Trelleborg in the west of Zealand (from which the type of fortification takes its name), Fyrkat in the east of Jutland, Aggersborg in north Jutland, Nonnebakken, near Odense on Fyn and another, also called Trelleborg, in Skåne, are all built to a similar plan. They have gates situated at the cardinal points of the compass, and are equipped with timber-reinforced ramparts. They vary in size from Fyrkat and Nonnebakken, which are 390 feet in diameter, to Trelleborg at 445 feet and the comparative giant, Aggersborg, whose diameter (some 790 feet) is twice that of the others. The footings of sixteen large buildings have been found inside the smaller three forts, all around 100 feet long with curved walls, while Aggersborg's larger dimensions were sufficient to house forty-eight such structures. The interior of the forts is divided into quadrants by intersecting roads, which run east–west and north–south to each of the four gates.

The precise purpose of such large fortifications is unclear, particularly as there are no signs that the interior buildings were ever repaired, indicating that they were probably occupied for as little as twenty years. They were all situated along the line of (or close to) major roads, and so may have been a means for Harald to consolidate royal power just after his 'unification' of the kingdom, but became redundant once he was secure in power.[11] This idea is reinforced by a series of improvements that he ordered on the road network throughout Denmark. The bridge at Ravning Enge in the Velje Valley is one of the largest in Scandinavia, around 2,460 feet long and 18 feet wide,[12] and has been dated by dendrochronology to 978. Throughout all this length the line of the bridge never deviates more than two inches from a straight line, and its construction required 1,100 piles, which were sunk into the swampy ground to bear its weight. It is an astonishing achievement of early medieval technology and must have involved a prodigious effort of the sort only available to a strong centralised power. Like the Trelleborg forts, the Ravning Enge bridge shows no traces of repair works, and so its operational life must have been short indeed – another sign that it, too, was built more as a statement of royal power than as a practical long-term measure.

Although Harald seems to have succeeded in unifying much of the Danish kingdom under his rule, he did not do so without external opposition. The threat from the German emperor Otto I prompted the Danes to strengthen the fortifications of the Danevirke, but an abortive attack southwards in 973 was followed by a counter-offensive which led to a German occupation of southern Jutland, including the line of the Danevirke itself. It took ten years for Harald to recover the lost ground, and it is perhaps to this time of crisis, and the need to emphasise national unity and his own power, that the building of both the Trelleborgs and the Ravning Enge bridge should be dated.

To the north Harald faced opposition from Håkon the Good of Norway, who in 954 ravaged the coastlines of Jutland and Zealand, as well as Danish-controlled Skåne. Håkon's father, Harald Finehair, had begun the consolidation of the Norwegian kingdom, and his son was equally ambitious. The Danish king tried to install his own man on the throne of Norway by giving aid to Harald Greycloak, one of the sons of Eirik Bloodaxe, whom the Norwegians had expelled around 934. Several attacks by the Eirikssons were repelled, but finally Håkon was fatally wounded in a battle at Fitjar in around 960. His court poet, Eyvind, who rejoiced in the unfortunate nickname 'the plagiarist' (Skáldaspillir), composed a sorrowful epitaph for his monarch:

> Wealth dies, kinsmen die,
> The land is laid waste,
> Since Håkon fared to the heathen gods,
> Many are thralls and slaves.[13]

Norway was then divided up between Eirik's five sons, but despite this weakening of a potential rival to Denmark, Harald Bluetooth still chafed at Greycloak's growing independent-mindedness. When the men of Trøndelag rose up against the Eirikssons, the Danish king was happy to lend the rebellion his support. Harald Greycloak fell in battle at Limfjord around 970 and Norway was then partitioned between Harald Bluetooth's new ally, Jarl Håkon Sigurdsson of Lade, and a Danish-controlled area in the south and east.

For all Harald's successful neutering of the threat to the north, his distinguished reign ended in ignominy. Shortly after the successful campaign against the Germans in 983, his son Svein Forkbeard rose up in revolt with the help of a coalition of discontented magnates. Harald was wounded in battle and fled eastwards to Wendland, ending up at the fortress of Jumne or Jomsborg (probably present-day Wolin in Poland), where, according to Adam of Bremen, he died a few years later. Harald had probably intended to use this as a springboard for a return to Denmark, as his second wife, whom he married in 965, was a Wendish princess named Tovi.[14] He is said to have founded the fortress as a centre for an independent Viking band (known as the Jomsvikings), and may have thought to have found support from them.[15]

The legends that became associated with the Jomsvikings are both heroic and colourful. The fort was said to have had a harbour large enough for 350 ships and to have housed only the strongest warriors; no woman was ever allowed to enter its gates. The *Saga of the Jomsvikings* also gives an alternative account of Harald's end, relating that the Danish king tricked the Jomsvikings (when they were suitably drunk) into agreeing to attack his arch-rival, Jarl Håkon of Lade. When they sobered up the warriors felt obliged to stick to their word and set sail en masse for Norway, where, despite their ferocious reputation, they were soundly beaten at the Battle of Hjørungavåg. The seventy survivors of the carnage were then brought before Jarl Håkon for judgement.

The Norwegian *jarl* had the Jomsvikings executed one by one, observing them closely to see if they lived up to their reputation for bravery, even in the face of certain death. One of the captives asked his comrades to watch him, saying that if there really was life after death, he would raise the axe he was holding as a sign. Yet when his head was severed, his lifeless fingers loosed their grasp and the weapon fell clattering to the ground. After nine of his comrades had been executed, an eighteen-year-old youth was dragged forward to be the tenth victim. Boldly he asked that his long golden hair be held away from his face when the blow was struck, to avoid his locks being spattered with blood. The request was granted and one of the *jarl*'s men twisted the boy's hair roughly around his hand. As the axe came down, the young Jomsviking arched backwards so that the blade instead sliced through the hand of the Norwegian executioner. Impressed at his courage and resourcefulness, Håkon then spared the youth. This did not put an end to the killing, however, and an eleventh Jomsviking, Vagn, son of Áki, was selected to meet his doom. Vagn, however, managed to pull free of his captors, seized a weapon and dealt a death-blow to Thorkel, Håkon's chief henchman, who had been overseeing the executions. After this impressive display of bravery, Vagn was invited to join the Norwegian *jarl*'s company, but he refused unless all his remaining comrades were similarly spared, a request that was granted. The story is almost certainly made up, but the saga itself may well preserve some memory of a Danish outpost on the Baltic in Wendland, which harboured a force strong enough for Harald to have hopes that it might be able to restore him to the throne.

The political consolidation of Norway proceeded much more slowly than in Denmark; the geography of the country was far more difficult than that of its southern neighbour, where most areas could be reached by a short journey overland (or by boat). There are few mentions of any central authority before the mid-ninth century, but the political centre of gravity of the petty kingdoms into which Norway was divided lay in the regions alongside the Oslofjord, notably in Vestfold, Raumarike, Hedmark and Østfold, which contained much of the best farming land in Norway. A second important region, the Trøndelag, lay far to the north near modern Trondheim, while a third nucleus of early political consolidation developed in western coastal Norway, around Sogn, Rogaland and Hordaland. It was the tensions between these three areas that defined much of Norwegian political history until the eleventh century and beyond.

Harald Finehair, who began the process of the unification of Norway, was the son of a petty king of the Vestfold named Halfdan the Black, and the grandson of Queen Åsa.[16] His mother is said to have had a dream that her son would grow to be like a tree with red roots, a green trunk and white branches, which would spread out to cover the whole of Norway (a prediction of his future greatness). Yet on Harald's accession to Halfdan's tiny realm around 870, the prospects for lasting fame (or even survival) seemed remote, as almost instantly his father's vassals took the opportunity to break away. It required years of bitter fighting to reintegrate them into the kingdom of Vestfold (which probably also included Ringerike and adjoining areas). In the meantime Håkon Grjogardsson was engaging in a similar act of consolidation around the Trøndelag, giving rise to the very real prospect of an eventual collision between their two spheres – a disaster that was only averted by Håkon's acceptance of Harald as his notional overlord.

This arrangement left Harald free to attack the west around Hordaland and Rogaland, the very area from which the first Viking raiders to cross the North Sea to Britain and Ireland had set out. After a hard-fought campaign, Harald's fleet caught up with the local *jarls* at Hafrsfjord, just west of Stavanger. Even the year is uncertain, with dates ranging from 885 to 900 being those normally accepted.[17] The dating of the battle is of some importance for the chronology of the Viking expansion in the North Atlantic, since saga tradition relating to both the Orkneys and Iceland maintains that the initial settlers were men who had fled Norway to escape Harald's increasingly tyrannical rule.[18] Unfortunately the chronology does not quite fit, as Harald only came to the throne in 870, at about the time of the first Viking settlement in Iceland, and it was at least some decades before his grip on the country became strong enough to be any threat to the independent-minded men of the west.

While Harald still had enemies, and the coexistence with Håkon in the Trøndelag was somewhat uneasy, as King of Vestfold he had emerged as the clear victor in the struggle for Norway. Harald had long before sworn an oath that he would not cut his hair or allow it to be combed until he was ruler of all Norway, a vow that gave rise to his early nickname of 'tangle-hair'. For the moment, though, he did not consider his pledge fulfilled and set out on an expedition against men who were said to have fled his rule for the Northern Isles of Scotland and were raiding the sea-lanes. Reports that his campaign extended as far south as the Isle of Man are probably an exaggeration, and there are serious doubts over the claim that Harald took control of the Orkneys and Hebrides for Norway, but some kind of expedition at least may have taken place.

Now satisfied, Harald had his most trusted follower, Rögnvald of Møre, cut his hair – a job that the earl performed with such efficacy that the king as a result acquired his better-known nickname *hafagre* or 'Finehair'. He is said to have turned now to domestic affairs, carrying out a number of administrative reforms such as the appointment of *jarls* to oversee justice in each district, including the collection of fines, one-third of which went to the royal treasury; and the establishment of a formal system by which the *jarls* would provide manpower for the army. However, many of these measures are probably reading backwards from later developments.

We possess an invaluable insight into Norwegian life at about this time from a manuscript that narrates the voyages of a Norwegian trader named Ohthere (Ottár in Old Norse). His tale has been preserved because he visited the court of Alfred the Great in Wessex in the late ninth century, and the account he gave of his travels was then appended as an additional section in the *Historiarum adversum paganos libri septem* ('Seven Books of History against the Pagans'), a Christian polemical history of the world by the fifth-century Spanish churchman Orosius.

Ohthere lived in the north of Norway, around Tromsø – or, as he described it to King Alfred, 'the farthest north of all Norwegians'. He was said to have been considered extremely rich among the Halogolanders, the men of this far-flung land, since he possessed 600 reindeer, twenty cattle, twenty sheep and twenty pigs, as well as a little land that he 'ploughed with horses'. The largest part of his wealth, however, came from the produce that he collected as tribute from the local Saami tribes. As well as furs, this included bird down, whalebone, and walrus and seal hide.

One year, Ohthere decided to find out quite how far north the coastline extended and whether anyone lived beyond the area that the Norwegians had so far explored. Setting out from the furthest point any of the whale hunters had yet reached, he sailed past uninhabited shores for three days, at which point the land veered sharply to the east. Ohthere proceeded along it for a further four days, and then the coastline turned south. After five more days' travel, he and the crew made their way up a great river, finding evidence of habitation on each bank of the waterway. The peoples he subsequently encountered included the Finns of the Kola peninsula (whom the Old English of the Orosius translation renders as *Beormas*) and another Finnic group known as the *Cwenas* (or Kvenir in Old Norse), a constellation of groups that continued to dominate the Arctic territories in the face of Norse attempts to exploit it.

Ohthere travelled such a great distance in search of walrus ivory, a precious trading commodity. He had probably reached the area of the White Sea (off the north-west of modern Russia), and although the expedition did not lead to any long-lasting connection between the two areas, it shows the extent to which commercial motives combined with sheer curiosity may have motivated some of the furthest-flung Viking voyages.

Sailing in the other direction, on his way to England, Ohthere hugged the coast of Norway (whose very name is derived from the 'North Way', the maritime route along its coastline) until, after around a month's travel,[19] he reached a place called *Sciringesheal*, which was probably Kaupang on the western shore of Oslofjord. He then travelled for five days southwards to Hedeby, where he described the islands around it as 'belonging to Denmark' – a very early occurrence of the term. Finally, Ohthere made his way to England, where Alfred the Great was described as his *hlaford* or lord – not, most probably, because the Norwegian merchant had sworn fealty to the Wessex king, but because, as was customary, foreigners paid a toll to the local ruler and in exchange came under his protection for the duration of their stay.

Ohthere was not the only traveller whose voyages were interpolated in the Old English translation of Orosius's work. Another merchant named Wulfstan, who may either have been Norwegian or English,[20] also gave an account to Alfred of his travels to Hedeby and the Baltic. From Denmark, he sailed east to Truso on the mouth of the Vistula, a voyage that took him seven days, passing by Skåne, Faster, Lolland, Langeland and Wendland, before reaching Witland, which belonged to the *Este*, a tribe that subsisted on honey and fish, where the richest drank mare's milk, leaving mead for the poor. One of their curious habits, Wulfstan reported, was to leave a man's corpse inside his house for several days; because of the extreme cold, the body did not decompose.[21]

When he died, around 933, Harald Finehair left a large number of sons, by some counts as many as sixteen, but more likely to be the nine mentioned by Eyvind the Plagiarist, the court poet of his eventual heir, Håkon the Good. It was, though, Eirik, Harald's son by Ragnhild (the daughter of a local Jutland king), who won out to become his immediate successor as King of Norway. Eirik's marriage to Gunnhild – the daughter of Gorm the Old, King of Denmark – made him a very plausible choice as Norwegian ruler, as such a dynastic link between the two realms held out the possibility of their eventually uniting, and at the very least enhanced the prospect for peace between them.

Harald's youngest son, Håkon, had been in England, where he had been fostered at the court of King Athelstan of Wessex (giving rise to his other nickname of *Adalsteins fostri*) and, on hearing of his father's death, he swiftly returned to Norway to join up with Jarl Sigurd of Hladir, who bitterly opposed Eirik's candidacy. In the face of this potent combination, Eirik put up no fight and simply sailed west to England, where he became established as King of York in 948, causing no end of trouble for his little brother's foster-father. Eirik's on–off kingship of York ended with his death in 954,[22] and his sons then chose to focus their ambitions on the crown of Norway rather than on regaining their patrimony in northern England.

Håkon the Good's rule over Norway was seriously destabilised by the alliance of the eldest brother, Harald Greycloak, with Harald

Bluetooth of Denmark, but he also faced opposition to his policy of trying to enforce Christianity, the religion of his upbringing at Athelstan's court. The coming of the new faith to Norway is remembered in the Kuli runestone found on Kuløy island off the north-west coast in 1913, which reads: 'Thórir and Hallverð raised this stone in memory of Ulfljot, Christendom had been 12 winters in the realm.' Representing the first use of the word 'Christendom' in Norwegian sources, this runestone is dated in one interpretation to the 940s, during Håkon's reign.[23]

The new king tried to encourage the observance of Sunday and also sought to Christianise the celebration of *Jól*, the old pagan midwinter festival (which had involved the drinking of large quantities of ale and the ritual sacrifice and collection of the blood of cattle). There was uproar when Håkon announced that these practices would be abolished, particularly as the king's role involved an ancient sacral element and so his participation was essential for the efficacy of the pagan rites. When Jarl Sigurd of Hladir and the other conservative notables threatened revolt, Håkon agreed to drink from a horn that had been hallowed with the name of Odin. When he tried to retain his Christian integrity by making the sign of the cross over the vessel, and those present protested and asked what he was doing, Sigurd reassured them that the king was merely making a sign in honour of Thor.

The Jarl of Hladir was not yet done with Håkon, however, and offered him the meat of a horse sacrificed to the pagan gods. This was a step too far for the king and he refused, also turning down the broth in which the meat had stewed. But in the end Håkon could see that his stubbornness was liable to cost him his throne and so he compromised by inhaling the smoke from the boiling horse meat.[24] It was neither an edifying spectacle for the Christians, nor did it really satisfy pagan sensibilities and, as tensions rose again, Håkon finally ate a piece of the sacrificial horse's liver and drank a hearty portion of the sacred broth. As a result, Håkon's memory was ever afterwards associated with his ambiguous relationship to both Christianity and paganism. His wife was reputed to be a believer in the old ways and, after Eirik's sons finally defeated and killed Håkon at Fitjar sometime between 960 and 965, his body was interred not in a churchyard (as his followers had offered the dying king), but in a pagan burial mound.

The victorious Eirikssons returned with their mother Gunhild to a Norway that was now bitterly split, with part of the east still held by Håkon's nephew, Tryggvi, while the Vestfold (under Gudrod Bjarnason) and Trondheim (ruled by Jarl Sigurd) also asserted their independence. In effect, Harald Greycloak's writ only ran in the centre and south-west of the country. By 970 Greycloak had defeated Tryggvi and brought the Vestfold under his rule, while Jarl Sigurd of Hladir was also killed and replaced by his son Håkon. The growing power of the Eirikssons worried Harald Bluetooth of Denmark sufficiently to forge an alliance with Håkon Sigurdsson, and in 974 this coalition defeated and killed Greycloak at Hals, near the Limfjord. For a time Norway was divided again, with Håkon Sigurdsson of Hladir holding the western provinces, while Harald Bluetooth took the east and south. The Jarl of Hladir, for all that he had notionally accepted Danish overlordship (with the promise of the payment of twenty falcons a year and the obligation to provide military service should it be demanded), fought stubbornly to preserve his independence, swiftly abjuring the conversion to Christianity that he had been forced to accept as part of the agreement on partitioning Norway.

In the end, Harald grew tired of his truculent vassal, and in 986 sent a fleet up the western coast of Norway to bring Håkon to heel. It was allegedly during this campaign that Harald was joined by a contingent of Jomsvikings,[25] but their defeat at the Battle of Hjørungavåg ensured the security of Håkon's rule for a decade more, until the arrival of another Norwegian princeling, Olaf, the son of Tryggvi of Vik, in 995.[26]

Sweden was the last of the three Scandinavian countries to emerge as a consolidated kingdom. Two separate realms emerged: *Svealand* ('the country of the Svear'), broadly the west of modern Sweden; and *Götaland* ('the country of the Götar'), in the east, including modern Gotland. Although there was once a belief that the coalescence of the two took place as early as the sixth century under the early Yngling kings,[27] it is more likely that this occurred towards the end of the first millennium. Sources for Sweden are sparser than those dealing with Denmark and Norway, so much of the type of information that we possess for developments in those countries during the ninth and tenth centuries is lacking for their eastern neighbour. The earliest notice that we do have concerns the missionary activity of Anskar, sent by the Archbishop of Hamburg-Bremen to convert the Scandinavian pagans.

Anskar's second mission (after his first, abortive one to Denmark) was in 829 or 830, and this time his destination was Sweden. On his way there, Anskar and his small party were attacked by Vikings, an interesting reflection on the dangers that awaited the unprotected or unwary traveller. Although they escaped with their lives, the missionaries lost all the holy books they had been carrying with them (some of which may have had bindings incorporating precious metals and jewels, making them an attractive and portable item for bandits). Finally, Anskar's party arrived at the town of Birka on Lake Mälaren, Sweden's only urban (or rather proto-urban) centre at the time.[28] They found there a local king, Bjorn, who received them well. It may well be that he was a king of the Svear, and it is certain that his rule did not extend over the whole of Sweden.

Anskar managed to convert Hergeir, who is described as the *praefectus* (prefect) of Birka, and with his assistance established a small church in the town. The number of converts, however, seems to have been quite small and Anskar soon returned to Hamburg, where he became archbishop. He made a second missionary foray around 850 on hearing of the expulsion of Gauzbert, the bishop whom he had left behind, and of the martyrdom of Nithard, one of the converts (who thus became Sweden's first documented Christian martyr). When Anskar arrived back in Birka, the king (by now a certain Olaf) explained that he would speak in support of his mission, but would have to do so in front of the local assembly or *thing* and that, if this gave its approval, Anskar would be able to preach, for 'It is the custom among them that the control of business of every kind should rest with the whole people and not with the king.'[29] As well as providing an insight into the organisation of Sweden's earliest urban centres, the incident suggests that the authority of the Swedish ninth-century rulers was somewhat circumscribed.

Because of Birka's importance as a trading centre, Christians may have continued to visit and even reside there, but for all that Anskar is known as the 'apostle of Scandinavia', the long-term effects of his missionary activities appear to have been slight. It was only when centralised royal authority developed in Sweden that Christianity began to make much headway, its spread supported by monarchs who appreciated the increase in their own authority that becoming a Christian might bring. Before then all we have are some scant records of Erik *Segersäll* ('the victorious') towards the end of the tenth century, who is portrayed as an enthusiastic Viking, engaging in pillaging raids against areas bordering on Uppland, the nucleus of his kingdom. More constructively, it may have been he who founded Sigtuna around 975, which became the Swedish royal capital (and the second urban centre in the country, after Birka). He is also said to have been baptised (in Denmark), had a Christian wife (the daughter of Prince Mieszko of Poland) and allowed a new round of missionary activity, although his conversion, as was so often the case with Viking chieftains, was skin-deep and he renounced the new religion as soon as he got home.[30]

Under Erik's son, Olof (*c.*980–1022), known as *Skötkonung* or 'half-king',[31] Sweden experienced a consolidation both in Christianity and in royal authority. He was probably Sweden's first genuinely Christian king (being baptised at Husaby around 1008) and helped with the establishment of a new bishopric for the Swedes at Skara in Västergötland. One sign of the increasing power of the monarchy was Olof's establishment of a mint at Sigtuna, which issued large quantities of coins stamped with the legend *Olaf Rex* ('Olaf the king'), while the reverse often carried the inscription *SiDei*, which may be interpreted as *Sigtuna Dei* ('God's Sigtuna'), an indication of his public commitment to Christianity. In foreign-policy terms, Olof's major achievement was the alliance with King Svein Forkbeard of Denmark against Olaf Tryggvason of Norway, which led to the Norwegian king's defeat at the Battle of Svold in 1000 and the Swedish acquisition of part of the Trøndelag.[32] Quite how far Olof's power extended within Sweden is uncertain, however, and his coins refer to him as *rex sveorum*, suggesting that the core of his kingdom remained that of the Svear and that his authority over the Götar, if it existed, was incomplete.[33]

That Olof's Christianisation of Sweden was at best partial is indicated by the tradition that he was martyred around 1021–2 for his refusal to revert to paganism. The piecemeal progress of the new religion is further suggested by a runestone found on the island of Frösö in the northern province of Jämtland. Dating from sometime in the early to mid-eleventh century, it reads: 'Austmað, Guðfast's son, had this stone raised and this bridge made, and he made Jämtland Christian. Ásbjörn built the bridge, Trjónn and Steinn carved these runes.' The revealing inscription may indicate that Christianity's advent in the far north was the work of a local chieftain and had little to do with any action by the kings at Sigtuna. Jämtland, in the border area between Norway and Sweden, seems in general to have exercised a degree of independence from both, until the defeat of the Jämtlanders by Sverre Sigurdsson of Norway in 1178 and its consequent incorporation into the Norwegian kingdom.

The comparatively weak state of Christianity in the core area of Sweden is further supported by Adam of Bremen's description of it in the later eleventh century. An anti-Christian reaction erupted in 1066 during the reign of Stenkil (nicknamed 'the Heathen'), while pagan resistance became focused on the great sanctuary at Uppsala dedicated to the worship of Odin, Frey and Thor. Although Adam had never actually been to Uppsala (where, as a Christian cleric, his welcome would doubtless have been distinctly cool), he relays with a palpable sense of horror the details that his informant gave him about the pagan rites carried out there. He tells of a huge series of sacrifices that were carried out every nine years, with nine male representatives of each living creature being slaughtered, and the corpses of the victims then suspended in the trees of the sacred grove for all to see. Even Christians were forced to take part in the bloody ritual, unless they paid a hefty fine to gain exemption.[34]

As late as 1084, when King Inge refused to participate in pagan rituals, he was denounced by his brother-in-law, Sven, who was duly installed on the throne in his place. Sven, who acquired the nickname blott ('sacrifice'), then led the notables in a ritual repudiation of Christianity, forcing each in turn to consume a portion of sacrificial horse-meat. Inge, however, did not rest idle, and from his retreat in the western part of Götaland steadily plotted his revenge. After three years he returned, trapped Sven in a house and burnt it down, with his rebellious brother-in-law still inside. Restored to the throne, and with pagan resistance cowed, Inge finally returned to the unfinished business of the Uppsala sanctuary. In around 1090, he ordered the temple's destruction and the uprooting of the sacred grove. This time there was little resistance and so, more than 250 years after Anskar's pioneering mission among the Danes, the prospect of paganism reasserting itself in Sweden vanished and the victory of Christianity in Scandinavia was complete.

Scandinavia had changed in many other ways, too, since the dawn of the Viking Age in the late eighth century. Although trading *emporia* had flourished during the seventh and early eighth centuries in north-western Europe, and had formed one of the principal targets of the early Viking attacks, urbanisation was a phenomenon that was slow to take hold in Scandinavia. It was particularly impeded in Norway and Sweden by the poor state of communications over land, and by the sheer size of those areas, which hampered the appearance of the kind of central authority that was needed to guarantee the security of large settlements.

Most people in Viking Scandinavia continued to live in isolated farmsteads, and by the early ninth century urbanisation had made such little progress that there were only four towns: two in Denmark (Ribe and Hedeby); one in Sweden (Birka); and one in Norway (Kaupang or Skiringssal). There was a curious discontinuity with later towns, and none of these places were functioning as major trading centres after 1050 (Kaupang and Birka had disappeared altogether, while Ribe and Hedeby may have been refounded later). A second wave of town foundations from the late tenth and eleventh centuries, which included Sigtuna in Sweden, Århus, Roskilde and Lund in Denmark and Oslo and Trondheim in Norway, is more closely associated with the growth of royal power in those countries and the need both for permanent royal centres and regional towns from which to dominate outlying parts of the kingdom.

The comparatively higher density of population in Viking Denmark, and its proximity to the developed markets of Frisia, France and Germany, facilitated a development of towns that was more precocious than elsewhere in Scandinavia. There were early centres at Dankirke, where fragments of glass vessels from the fifth to sixth century have been found, and at Gudme on the island of Funen, but these were at best large farms or small clusters of buildings around a harbour and do not represent genuine urban centres. The first real town was at Ribe in south-western Jutland, where finds date from as early as 710[35] (although at this stage occupation of the site seems to have been seasonal, and once the annual market was over it was temporarily abandoned).

The remains of workshops at Ribe, in which combs, glass beads and jewellery were made, are a sign of the manufacturing and trading enterprises that are a feature of all the early Scandinavian towns. It is first mentioned in the written sources in the 850s, when King Horik gave Anskar permission to preach there. Already by then an area along the Ribe River was densely settled, with around forty to fifty workshops organised into plots around 20–25 feet wide and 65–100 feet long, which clustered around the north and east banks of the river. Only around 770–780, however, did the initially seasonal occupation of the plots give way to permanent settlement. The digging of a ditch around the town in the early ninth century was probably more an indication of where Ribe's town law applied than of any attempt to bolster its defences as the era of Viking raiding got under way, for it was too shallow to fulfil any real defensive purpose. Around the middle of the century archaeological finds stop, after which there is no definite evidence of the existence of Ribe until the twelfth century (although this does not necessarily mean the settlement was abandoned or destroyed).[36]

Denmark's second town was at Hedeby in the south-east (now in Germany), which was closely linked to the Danevirke fortification across the southern neck of the Jutland peninsula. Evidence has been found of settlement there as early as 750;[37] and the city first appears in written sources around 800, when King Godfred of Denmark ordered the destruction of the Obodrite *emporium* at Reric and the removal of all its merchants to *Sliethorp*, a place under his control, which probably refers to the earliest stage of settlement at Hedeby. By the tenth century it had developed into a flourishing trading centre enclosed by a large rampart. It was certainly still in Danish hands in 1049, when it was sacked by Harald Hardrada of Norway,[38] but by the twelfth century it had been replaced as the regional centre by Schleswig.

The third permanent town to appear in Scandinavia was in Sweden, at Birka, situated on the small island of Björkö (which means 'place of the birch trees') in Lake Mälaren, a waterway that acted as a transport hub for the region and was at the centre of one of the most heavily populated areas in the kingdom. The water level was up to 15 feet higher in the ninth century, so the island was only half the size that it is today. It was preceded by a centre at Helgö on the nearby

island of Lillön, where a series of longhouses were used in the fifth
and sixth centuries as workshops, and where later finds include a figure
of Buddha, an Irish crozier head and a Coptic ladle – indications of
the international connections of the site. Finds from the cemetery
on the island show that it probably supported no more than twenty
people at a time, and so it cannot really qualify as a town.

By around 800 production at Helgö had transferred to Birka, and
the settlement there grew correspondingly. The main areas of the
Viking-Age settlement lies in the *Svarta Jorden* (the 'Black Earth')
on the west of the island, an area of around 17 acres, which may originally
have been surrounded by a wooden palisade. On its borders the land
is dotted with a large number of cemeteries, which contain as many
as 2,000 graves. Around half of these have been excavated, yielding a
rich array of finds of grave-goods, including sets of scales and weights,
part of the characteristic equipment of the merchant class that must
have formed an important sector of Birka's population. This section
of the island is still pockmarked today with the mounds and fallen
stones of ship-settings, which mark the last resting place of its
Viking-Age inhabitants.

The trading connections of this now-tranquil spot extended as far
as England in the west, Lake Ladoga in Viking Russia to the east,
Uppsala in the north, and Hedeby and the German markets to the
south. The town was wealthy and important enough to be an obvious
destination for Anskar during his Swedish mission, especially given
that its role as a trading centre meant that Christians might already
be settled there or pass through it. The level of organisation that
Anskar found there, with a royal prefect and a local *thing*, which
exercised a clear degree of independence from the local ruler, are all
indications of the town's importance. It may also be that the
Bjarkeyjarréttur ('The laws of Björkö'), which formed the basis of later
Swedish laws dealing with towns and trade, were first formulated at
Birka.[39]

The earliest objects found on the island are combs dating to the
760s, which are similar in type to examples excavated at Staraya Ladoga
in Russia. A large hoard with around 450 Islamic coins, whose final
date is around 962, is among the very latest, and it seems that by then
Birka had begun to lose its importance as a trading centre. Sometime
in the late tenth century the island's fort was burnt, though whether

deliberately or accidentally is unclear, and after this Birka was abandoned. It still retained its place in the ecclesiastical hierarchy, however, and the Archbishops of Hamburg-Bremen continued to appoint bishops to the see as late as 1060. It was also the site of the death of Archbishop Unni of Bremen, while on a visit in the 930s. Most of the unfortunate prelate was buried at Birka, with only his head being sent back to Bremen.[40] On the nearby island of Adelso lie the remains of a medieval manor house, which continued in use as a Swedish royal centre until the thirteenth century, but by then the main Swedish urban centre had transferred to Sigtuna.

Now a pretty town of low picture-postcard cottages, Sigtuna's origins probably lie in the tenth century, when a small strip between the shoreline and a rocky ridge was built up (just as at Birka, the water level was 12–15 feet higher than today). By the eleventh century Sigtuna was the only town in the Mälaren Valley, and its foundation under royal patronage and status as a royal residence ensured its success. The town also acted as a royal mint, with a large number of 'Sigtuna coins' being minted there by Olof Skötkonung in the early eleventh century.[41] On the site of the original mint site, now occupied by a somewhat overgrown lot, were found fragments of lead with the impression of a die used to strike the coins.

The range of Sigtuna's connections is indicated by the discovery of resurrection eggs and glass finger-rings from Russia, as well as a number of pottery items from the west of the Slavic world. In common with its predecessor, many of the plots excavated in the town show evidence of craft production such as amber-working and comb-making. By the 1070s Sigtuna also had its own bishop, although the see was briefly abandoned during the pagan revival of Stenkil's reign, and finally in the 1130s it was definitively moved to Old Uppsala 25 miles away.

The earliest town in what is now Norway lay at Kaupang, which is probably the same place as the *Sciringesheal* visited by the Norwegian trader Ohthere in the late ninth century.[42] Situated in southern Norway, near the modern town of Larvik, its present water level is 10 feet below that in the Viking Age, exposing much land that was under water at that time. The first comprehensive excavation of the site between 1956 and 1967[43] uncovered five houses, although none of them had hearths, indicating that the settlement may have been a seasonal one rather than having a permanent population. The site is surrounded by cemeteries, including both a large inhumation cemetery (where bodies were buried) at Bijkholberget and an extensive cremation cemetery at North Kaupang, while both of the first major finds of Viking ship-burials in Norway (at Oseberg and Gokstad) were unearthed from mounds just a few miles away.[44]

Kaupang seems to have come into use a little before 803, when plots were first laid out, with fixed buildings being erected a short time later. The number of artefacts found drops sharply after the second quarter of the tenth century, probably indicating the settlement's decline. Even after the site had been abandoned, the area continued to be of some importance, with a royal estate at Huseby less than a mile away. The slow spread of urbanism in Norway is highlighted, however, by the fact that nearly a century passed between the desertion of Kaupang and the foundation of Oslo as a royal capital by Harald III in 1048.

The story of early urbanism in Scandinavia underlines how dependent we are on archaeological sources. One of the perennial problems of deciphering events within Scandinavia (and of finding native sources about the Vikings which are not antagonistic to them) is the fact that for a long time Norse culture was pre-literate. When writing did emerge in Scandinavia around the fifth century AD, it employed not the Roman script, but a native form of writing known as runic – an alphabet of sharp angles and straight lines most suited to carving on stone or incising into wood.

The Old Norse word *rún* carries the sense of mysterious or secret knowledge, and may indicate that in their earliest form the signs were used to impart sacred knowledge or as part of rituals. In one of the most compelling stories in Norse mythology, Odin's thirst for such forbidden knowledge, which he hoped would help him avoid his ordained fate at Ragnarök (the battle at the end of the world, where most of the Norse gods will perish[45]), led him to perform a literal act of self-sacrifice in which he hung upside down for nine days from Yggdrasil, the world-tree: 'I know that I hung on a wind-rocked tree nine whole nights with a spear wounded, and to Odin offered myself to myself; on that tree, of which no one knows from what root it springs. Bread no man gave me nor a horn of drink, downward I peered, to runes applied myself, wailing learnt them, then fell down thence.'[46] The mystical sacrifice was effective, and Odin received knowledge of the runes.

The origins of the runes are not known precisely, but the resemblance of some of the signs to those in the Latin alphabet suggests that there must have been a model that came from within the Roman empire, while similarities with signs used in scripts in southern Switzerland indicates another possible source of influence.[47] The earliest example of runic writing comes from second-century Denmark, in inscriptions on fibulas from Himlingye in Zealand and Nøvling in Jutland, the first of which has been transliterated as *widuhudaR,* which may represent the name of the owner of the brooch.[48] It is clearly in an early version of the *futhark,* the runic alphabet (which is named for the first three letters of the script, just as the word 'alphabet' comes from *alpha* and *beta,* the first two letters of the Greek alphabet).

The first form of the *futhark* (known as the Elder Futhark) contained a sign for most sounds in the Proto-Scandinavian language, making a script with twenty-four letters (although only five of them represented vowel sounds). Comparatively few inscriptions using this alphabet survive, and of the 200 examples that we do have, around a quarter are from Norway, a large proportion of those from the west and south-west coast. The longest of them, the Tune inscription (found in the church of the same name in Østland), was erected in memory of a certain Woduridar, 'master of the household', by his heirs.

Around AD 500, a series of linguistic shifts affected Proto-Scandinavian,[49] leading to its evolution into the Old Norse tongue, which was spoken throughout Scandinavia during most of the Viking Age. At about the same time the *futhark* also underwent modifications. These changes are in fact rather counter-intuitive, for while there are more sounds in Old Norse than in Proto-Scandinavian – including twelve vowels – the number of runes in the new version of the alphabet (known as the Younger Futhark) actually decreased to sixteen, leading to a great deal of ambiguity on occasion as to the best way to transliterate an inscription. The script lacks a sign for the sound 'g', and so the name of the Danish king Gorm the Old had to be spelled with an initial 'k'. This problem is aggravated by the frequent lack of spaces between words (though dividers such as points or crosses are sometimes used) and the habit of omitting a double rune where one word began with the same letter as the final rune of the word preceding it.

The decipherment of runestones is, however, rendered somewhat simpler by the fact that they tend to be rather formulaic in nature. The great majority of surviving runes are found on memorial stones raised in honour of a deceased person and contain the formula 'A raised this stone in memory of B, his [wife, son, brother, sister, etc.]'. Around 3,000 runic inscriptions are known from the Viking world, including a scattering in Ireland, Britain, other Scandinavian colonies such as Iceland and the odd outlier, such as the two runic inscriptions in the Aya Sofya (Hagia Sophia) mosque in Istanbul.[50] The bulk of inscriptions (just under 2,300) are in Sweden, while Denmark has 400 inscriptions and Norway a comparatively sparse 138. Many of the inscriptions are in fact rather late, with around one-third dating from after 1050 (with many containing Christian formulae).[51] Most of them are short, some just a few words in length, but the longest – found built into the wall of the church at Rök in Östergötland in nineteenth-century Sweden – is more than 750 characters long. Probably carved in the early ninth century, it is a memorial stone set up by Varinn in memory of his son, Vemoðr, and makes reference to traditions concerning the sixth-century Ostrogothic ruler Theoderic and a series of otherwise unknown mythological beings.

There are some differences in type between the runestones found in the various Scandinavian areas, with those in northern Sweden more likely to contain elaborate artistic elements (such as intertwined serpents, although these do appear on the Jelling Stone in Denmark). Those in Norway and Denmark are more often set out in simple rows and bands, and if they contain any device other than the runes themselves, it is often a simple cross.[52] Very few runestones can be correlated with known historic events or dated precisely in any other way. The notable exceptions include the Jelling Stone mentioned above, and a few stones that commemorate men who 'took Cnut's geld' in England (which locates them to around 1018), or those that were set up in memory of the men who perished during the expedition of Yngvar the Widefarer to the east of Russia around 1040.[53] Even those inscriptions that seem to mention definite events are sometimes vexingly difficult to date, such as that found on Kuløya in the Trøndelag, which refers to the raising of the stone by Thórir and Hallvarð, 'when

Christianity had been in Norway 12 winters'. This has alternately been interpreted as referring to 1042 (twelve years after the Battle of Stiklestad), 1007 (twelve years after the death of Olaf Tryggvason) or around 1036 (a similar interval after a *thing* at Moster where Olaf Haraldsson declared Christianity to be the religion of Norway).[54]

Most runic inscriptions, however, are memorial in nature, raised to commemorate men (although they are often erected by women in memory of their dead husbands). It is possible that a primary purpose of these stones was to lay very public claim to the inheritance of property, in an age when the legal niceties of death certificates (or any kind of central record-keeping) were non-existent. This was particularly important in the case of men who had died overseas, often on Viking expeditions; the twenty-five runestones honouring those who did not return from Yngvar's expedition are a particularly notable cluster.

One of the most extraordinary surviving collections of runic inscriptions is located in the interior of Maeshowe, an Iron Age burial cairn in the Orkneys that was broken into during the Viking Age by a party that seems to have spent some time there (judging by the extent of the carvings they left). This is quite probably the group that is mentioned in the *Orkneyinga Saga*, when Earl Harald Maddaðarson of Orkney and his companions were caught by a storm just after New Year 1153–4 and took shelter in a mound known as *Orkahaugr*.[55] The mound itself has the curious quality that the rays from sunrise on the morning of the winter solstice travel along a low entry tunnel to illuminate the otherwise pitch-black interior (the awkward gait necessary to enter the mound giving rise to the earthy Viking joke in one of the inscriptions: 'Many a woman has gone stooping in here'). The Vikings (who may also have been associated with Earl Rögnvald-Kali who accompanied the Norwegian Jarl Erling on crusade to the Holy Land in 1153–5) broke in from the top of the mound and left more than thirty inscriptions in Maeshowe, including a few that cannot have been made without the assistance of a ladder, a rope or by balancing precariously on the rubble that had fallen inside when the Vikings entered.

A good indication that they were indeed returned crusaders is the carving that reads: *'Jorsalamenn* ['Jerusalem men' – that is, crusaders] broke into this mound'. Some of the inscriptions are quite laconic

('Thorfinn wrote these runes'), while others, in the manner of graffiti through the ages, sing the praises of particular women ('Ingigerd is the most beautiful of women'). Another set of carvings describes the discovery of a great hoard of treasure beginning with: 'To the north-west is a great treasure hidden. It was long ago that a great treasure was hidden here. Happy is he that might find that great treasure. Hókon alone bore treasure from this mound' and, 'It is surely true what I say that treasure was taken away. Treasure was carried off three nights before.' Whether such a treasure ever existed at all is quite doubtful, however, given that the contents of most Neolithic burials would have been of little interest to Viking-Age plunderers, and the inscriptions are probably more playful than boastful.

Many of the runic carvings are made using a special form called 'twig runes', a type of inscription that is especially widespread in Orkney, in which the sound associated with the rune is modified with reference to a numeric code. It seems a pointless exercise in such a remote spot, where the chances of anyone else happening upon the runes was slight, and where in any case the message contained in the inscriptions does not seem to merit such secrecy. The use of this esoteric runic form is instead probably more a demonstration of the skill and erudition of the rune-carver. One of the finest carvings includes the immodest declaration that 'these runes were carved by the man most skilled in runes on the Western Ocean with the axe that killed Gaukr Trandil's son in the South of Iceland'. As well as an insight into Viking boastfulness, it gives a tantalising glimpse into the background behind the saga stories, as the carver could well have been Thorhall Asgrimsson, an Icelander who accompanied Earl Rögnvald on crusade. His ancestor five generations back, Asgrim Elliða-Grimsson, slew his foster-brother Gaukr Trandilsson in a quarrel and took his axe, and the presumption is that Thorhall inherited this family heirloom and took it with him to Orkney, although whether he would have blunted the blade of such a precious item by using it to carve runes into the stone interior of Maeshowe is a different question.[56]

Runes continued in use long past the Viking Age; a particularly fine collection was found in Norway in 1955 after a fire in a medieval area of Bergen called the Bryggen. The runic inscriptions, carved on pine and bone, survived when the roof of the storage area containing them collapsed, and date mostly from the period 1250–1330. They include religious and secular texts, commercial letters, obscene graffiti and practise exercises in the *futhark* alphabet, a range that indicates that even at this late stage runic writing was anything but a half-forgotten archaism.[57] Runes, however, were not well suited for long texts, and as the written word spread into Scandinavia in the wake of Christianisation, the need for liturgical texts and later, secular books, led to the widespread adoption of the Latin alphabet, which soon became dominant. Yet as late as the nineteenth century the tradition of runic writing was still remembered and cherished, and Scandinavian farmers continued to make short runic inscriptions for items such as farm-names. That knowledge of them spread outside Scandinavia even in the late nineteenth century is indicated by the real possibility that the 'discoverer' of the Kensington Rune Stone (an alleged Viking-Age inscription found in Minnesota in 1898, which is most likely a forgery)[58] had books in his farmhouse that contained information about runes, and may well have been taught about them at school in his native Sweden.[59]

Before the conversion of the Scandinavian countries to Christianity in the tenth and eleventh centuries (and to a limited extent afterwards), the Vikings belonged to the world of pagan belief that had once encompassed much of the Germanic world of northern Europe. A great deal of what we know about the Viking religion in its heyday is derived from later (often Christian) sources, such as the account of the conversion of Iceland in 1000 by the priest-historian Ari Thorgilsson (who wrote in the twelfth century); from references in various sagas (such as the account in *Hrafnkels Saga Freysgoda* of Hrafnkell's devotion to the god Frey); from the distinctly ambivalent account of Adam of Bremen of cult practices at Uppsala in Sweden; and from references to pagan mythology in the *Gesta Danorum* of Saxo Grammaticus (writing in the early thirteenth century). A probably more authentic corpus of material survives in the form of older skaldic verses embedded in the sagas and in the series of poems referred to as the 'Poetic Edda'[60] (or 'Elder Edda' to differentiate them from the 'Prose Edda' of the Icelandic historian Snorri Sturluson, which also contains much mythological information, primarily as a side-effect of Snorri's desire to write a manual for poets that incidentally preserved elements of traditional stories).

The Edda begins with a series of poems setting out the Norse creation myths and giving an account of the various supernatural creatures
that inhabited them, followed by a series of heroic poems, many of
which deal with a legendary dynasty known as the Volsungs. The first
poem in the series, the *Voluspá* ('Prophecy of the Seeress'), outlines
the whole history of the Norse universe from its creation to its fore-
seen destruction at the end of time.

Its narrative reflects the bitterly cold Nordic winter and a corres-
ponding preoccupation with heat and fire, telling that before the
beginning of time there was only a great void called Ginnungagap,
whose northern edge was a frost-bound region called Niflheim,
bordered in turn to the south by a realm of intense heat called
Muspelheim. Where these two contrasting sections met, the frost
began to melt and the drops of water formed into a great giant named
Ymir, the first of the frost giants. The thaw also created a cow named
Audhumbla, which licked at the remaining ice and shaped a human-
like creature called Bur. His grandchildren were Odin, Vili and Vé,
the first of the Norse gods, who slew Ymir. As he died, his blood
gushed out, drowning all his progeny save Bergelmir, who survived
to become the ancestor of all the giants. The three elder gods, meanwhile, hurled Ymir's corpse into Ginnungagap and formed the land
from his flesh, the mountains from his bones and the sea from his
blood.

The gods then turned to the creation of the dwarves: dark
subterranean creatures who would, together with the giants, be their
principal antagonists in many of the Norse myths. They did not,
however, create humankind directly, merely chancing upon the almost
lifeless forms of the first man, Ask, and woman, Embla, who lacked
all 'spirit, sense and will' – qualities that Odin and his companion
gods, Hoenir and Loður, are said to have breathed into them.[61]

The Norse gods were divided into two main groups: the Aesir,
among whom were numbered Odin, Thor and most of the chief
deities; and the Vanir, who included principally Frey and his sister
Freyja (the goddess both of fertility and of war). It was a division that
probably reflects the merging of the pantheons of two separate groups
at some very early stage in Scandinavian history. The supernatural
space of the Norse world was also populated by a series of other
beings, the giants (or *jötnar*) and dwarves (*dvergar*), as well as by a

lesser category of gods called *álfar*, who were mainly connected to the Vanar. The gods were thoroughly anthropomorphised in Norse mythology, motivated by human emotions such as jealousy, anger and love and mostly conceived of in human form.

Each of these beings had its own place in a system whose complexity and, at times, precise topography set it apart from the rather less-exact notions of the Greeks and Romans. The universe was seen as a flattened disc, divided into three sections. The inner segment held Asgard, the home of the gods, in which each of the principal deities had his own halls: Valhalla for Odin, Trudheim for Thor, Folkvang for Freyja. The middle part of the world was named Midgard, the place where humans dwelt. Finally, the outermost section of the world was called Utgard ('the outer place') and was home to the giants and a host of other malevolent beings.[62] Around all of these regions was a great sea in which a huge malevolent snake, the Midgard serpent, lived, forming a great bounding circle by biting its tail and thus keeping the world in its place.

Towering through the centre of all three regions was a gigantic ash tree named Yggdrasil, at whose base lay Urd's well, where three mystical women, known as the Norns, determined the destinies of every being in the universe.[63] The tree played host to a variety of exotic creatures, including an eagle that sat in the topmost branches; a dragon named Nithogg, which gnawed steadily away at Yggdrasil's roots in an effort to topple the great ash; and a squirrel named Ratatosk, which ran up and down the length of the tree carrying scurrilous messages between the eagle and the dragon; as well as four deer, which also did their level best to kill the tree by stripping it of all its leaves.

The greatest of all the Aesir was Odin, the all-father, seen as the god of wisdom. He was not, however, omnipotent, and his thirst for knowledge and power led him to make unusual sacrifices. As well as his ordeal hanging upside down for nine days from Yggdrasil in exchange for knowledge of the runes,[64] Odin also sought to drink from a well guarded by a giant called Mimir, believing that its water would bestow great wisdom on him. The price of a draught of this magical liquid was one of Odin's eyes, which the god willingly gave, and in return he received the gift he desired. On another occasion Odin transformed himself into a snake in order to enter a cave where

Gunlod, the daughter of the giant Suttung, watched over three great cauldrons containing the mead of poetry. Odin turned himself back into human form and seduced Gunlod, sleeping with her for three nights, after each of which the giant's daughter gave him some mead. Finally, after being detected by her irate father, Odin made good his escape in the form of a giant eagle, but as he approached Asgard, he found that the giant was about to catch him. The Odin-eagle then spurted some of the mead backwards to distract Suttung and, with the aid of this decoy, just made it safely back to the company of the gods, quickly spewing out the precious liquid into buckets. He shared it with the other Aesir and handed small portions out to favoured poets, providing them with their inspiration (the story gives rise to the skaldic name for poetry itself, 'Odin's plunder'). The small portion of the mead that fell to Earth after it had served its purpose in distracting Suttung provided the share for lesser poets who still managed to produce 'jingles' without divine assistance.

Armed with the knowledge and power he had acquired, Odin reigned supreme over the other gods and beings. He was aided by two enormous ravens, Huginn and Muginn, which perched on his shoulders and were sent out each day to survey the world and report back on any matters of interest. Among his other assistants were the Valkyries, female spirits who scoured the battlefields for the souls of warriors who had died valiantly. They carried the warriors back to Odin's hall at Valhalla, where each day they engaged in single combat as training for Ragnarök (the final battle between gods and giants), while every evening their wounds healed, and they feasted on mead and the meat of the boar Saehrimnir, whose flesh was magically restored to its bones every morning.

Although Odin was in theory the most powerful of the gods, his worship was not the most widespread in Scandinavia. That honour fell to Thor, the warrior god and god of thunder, whose hammer – Mjölnir – destroyed all that it struck. Thor was described as riding through the sky in a carriage drawn by goats, and his hurling of Mjölnir caused the lightning and the falling of rain. With a magical belt that doubled his strength, Thor was the very image of a Viking warrior writ large, and, being far more approachable than Odin, was the object of veneration throughout the Norse world. His cult became more popular during the Viking Age, that of Odin having been predominant in the preceding Vendel period (in the sixth and seventh centuries) and remaining so even after that amongst the ruling aristocracy.[65] One measure of his widespread appeal is the large number of Thor's hammer amulets (with an upside-down T that mirrored the shape of his hammer) that have been found in many Viking-Age sites.

Place-names, too, may give an indication of the relative popularity of the deities in different regions: sites associated with a particular god often include his name as one element. Tyr, the god of war and martial courage, is remembered in this way almost exclusively in Denmark, while the name of one god, Ullinn (who is never mentioned in the sagas at all), is featured extensively in sites in the south-central and western regions of Norway. The name of Odin appears far more frequently in Denmark than in Norway (most notably at Odense, *Oðaens-vé*, 'the cult site of Odin'), but also has a relatively high concentration in Sweden, where he seems to have vied with Frey for popularity. The cult of Thor, to judge by the place-name evidence, seems to have been most widespread in Norway and in eastern Sweden, particularly in coastal regions.[66]

The oral preservation of the Norse myths, transmitted as poetic fossils in the works of people for whom the living pagan religion was at best a distant memory, means that it is sometimes hard to determine if stories have been reshaped to harmonise with similar Christian tales. Often the sense we have of a particular deity is incomplete, and we cannot really recover their real role in the pantheon. These tendencies combine in one of the most famous of all Scandinavian myths, that of the killing of Baldr. Loki, the agent of Baldr's destruction, is a highly ambivalent character, who is the product of the union of a goddess and a giant. A mischievous trickster, he seems constantly at odds with the Aesir, and his actions often seem to align him more with the gods' adversaries – the dwarves, giants and various monsters of the lower worlds – than on the side of Odin, Thor or Freyja.

In the story, Baldr's mother, Frigg, makes all living things swear not to harm her son, but forgets to impose the oath on the seemingly harmless mistletoe. In typical Viking fashion, the gods then entertain themselves by shooting at Baldr, secure in the knowledge that they can do him no harm. Loki, meanwhile, is aware of Frigg's careless omission, and crafts an arrow out of the forgotten mistletoe. He approaches Hodr, Baldr's blind brother (who, since he cannot see, is unable to join in the sport), offering to help him take part by aiming his shot. With the trickster god's assistance, the arrow speeds to its target and Baldr drops dead. Following a magnificent funeral, the grief-stricken gods despatch Hermód, one of the lesser war deities, to go to Hel to ransom Baldr and bring him back to Asgard. After a ride of nine days and nights astride Sleipnir, Odin's magical eight-legged steed, Hermód crosses the golden Gjöll bridge that marks the boundary with the underworld and begs its queen, Hel, to allow Baldr's release.

The underworld goddess agrees to the request only on the condition that all living things show their sorrow for Baldr's death by weeping. On hearing this, all the birds, beasts and even the rocks cry for the lost god. Finally the gods come across an old giantess, Thökk, who is hidden in a cave and has not yet shed a tear. The old crone is in fact none other than Loki in disguise. Unsurprisingly, she refuses to weep for Baldr, who as a result is doomed to spend the rest of time in the underworld. On discovering that it was really Loki who was responsible for his doom, the furious gods and goddesses seize the trickster, bind him to three sharp rocks and place him beneath a poisonous serpent. His faithful wife Sigyn collects the venom as it drips down, and so Loki remains unharmed, save when the bowl brims over and she is forced to go and empty it. Then, as the poison sears and burns into his flesh, Loki's violent writhing makes the whole Earth tremble and is believed to be the cause of earthquakes.

It is possible that the tale of the sacrificed god Baldr has been modified by Norse contact with Christianity and the story of the crucifixion of Jesus. The parallels between the stories of Ragnarök ('the fate of the gods') and Christian notions of the Apocalypse are even more striking. After three winters in which the sun does not shine (the *Fimbulvetr*), the great wolf Fenrir, which has been bound for aeons, breaks free and swallows the sun. Meanwhile Jörmungand, the Midgard-serpent, moves from his position encircling the world and attacks Midgard, the central portion of the Earth. They are joined by an array of malevolent creatures, including Surt at the head of the fire-giants and Loki, who finally shakes off his ambivalent position and definitively joins in on the side of evil. Roused by the messenger god Heimdall's horn, the gods muster, together with an army of heroic warriors from Valhalla.

Frey takes on Surt, but is killed by the giant, while Tyr, another war god, falls to the hell-hound Garm. Thor has more luck; wielding Mjölnir, he strikes a fatal blow at the earth-serpent, but the dying Jörmungand spews out venom all over the thunder god. Thor takes a few steps and falls, lifeless. Odin, meanwhile, is engaged in a bitter fight with Fenrir (said to have been the monstrous child of Loki and a giantess). Finally the wolf swallows the father of the gods whole, while Loki and Heimdall, who have been evenly matched, kill each other. With most of the gods and their opponents fallen, Surt takes his flaming sword and sets light to the world. In the ensuing conflagration, the old earth is consumed by fire.

In a possible echo of Christian notions of the resurrection of the dead on the Day of Judgement, when the flames subside a few of the younger generation of gods have survived, including Vidar and Vili, the sons of Odin, and Módi and Magni, Thor's sons, who have inherited Mjölnir from their dead father. Hodr, too, is unscathed and is joined by Baldr, who has finally been released from his bondage in Hel. Two humans (Lif and Lifthrasir) have also somehow escaped the holocaust and, under the light of the old sun's daughter, a version of the previous world is re-created, minus all of the creatures of darkness that had preyed on the old one.

To what extent the ordered but complex neatness of the Viking myths represented the reality of Norse worship is hard to determine. In the absence of official hierarchies and a fixed sacred book such as the Christian Church possessed, there must have been a great diversity of belief and a large number of local cults far in excess of those that are mentioned in the scanty records which survive. There were probably a large number of cult sites, although excavations at sites with place-name components which are believed to designate temple sites (such as '–hof' and '–vé') yielded little that could unambiguously be designated as a temple building – one at Hofstaðir in northern Iceland is most likely a longhall. However, more recently a 'cult-house' excavated at Borg in Sweden was found to have a number of Thor's hammer amulets and large numbers of animal bones (particularly of dog, pigs and horses) buried outside it; and a series of bronze and gold figurines discovered in 2002 outside an Iron Age hall in Lunda, in Södermanland, Sweden, may possibly represent victims of ritual hanging. In 1984 a dig at the church at Frösö in Jämtland yielded a large number of animal bones, which have been interpreted as sacrifices made in a sacred grove (as the remains seem to have been deposited around an ancient beech tree),[67] while a further pagan cult-site was identified at Ranheim, a little north of Trondheim, in 2012.

Viking paganism appears to have had no professional priestly class and hierarchy as Christianity possessed (with the exception of Iceland, where there does seem to have been such a group).[68] Chieftains (and kings) were required to play a role in public rituals, which made the eventual conversion to Christianity of rulers and aristocracy even more damaging for paganism. An account in the *Eyrbyggja Saga*[69] tells of a temple belonging to a chieftain, while the Icelandic *Landnámabók* refers to the obligation of chieftains at assemblies to wear an arm ring that had been hallowed by placing it on a temple altar. The rather lurid accounts in Adam of Bremen of the nine-yearly festival at Uppsala in Sweden, which culminated in a mass slaughter of nine males of every animal species, are possibly exaggerated, but they certainly preserve the sense of a major pagan sanctuary that continued to function into the second half of the twelfth century.

There are hints of local and folk beliefs in the sagas. On one occasion, King Olaf Tryggvason of Norway found himself sheltering in the house of some peasants who venerated the penis of a cart horse as a cult object. Needless to say, the disgusted king (the Christianiser of Norway) threw the strange pagan idol onto the floor, where the farmer's dog ate it. There was also a persistently strong belief in sorcery and witchcraft, rooted in the Norse belief in the potency of *seiðr*, a particular sort of magic associated with female prophecy, possibly derived from the shamanic tradition of the Saami (or Lapps), with whom the Norse came into contact in the north of Scandinavia. The Gulathing Law, a law-code that was probably first codified in the twelfth century and applied to an area in the western fjords of Norway, states that people must not believe in either 'soothsaying, witchcraft or maleficence',[70] a clear indication that the compilers of the code believed that such magical practices were still prevalent. More explicitly, the slightly later Borgarthing Laws declared that the finding of men's hair or nails or frog's feet indicated witchcraft and a charge should then be made, and also refers to the summoning of trolls.[71] The activities of Jón Ögmundarson (the Good), Bishop of Hólar in Iceland from 1106 to 1121, who is associated with a number of sacred wells and springs, suggest that the ecclesiastical authorities sought to co-opt local beliefs in the ritual efficacy of places in the landscape and to mould them to a more appropriately Christian use.

Norse pagan beliefs about life after death were complex – those who died in battle were seen as being transported to Valhalla to live a glorious afterlife, while those who suffered the ignominy of death in bed were to spend eternity in the gloomy halls of Hel. Yet there was also a strong feeling that the spirits of the dead sometimes remained close to those they had known in life. These *draugr*, or 'walking dead', might on occasion return because the proper rites had not been carried out during their burial (so that special mooring rocks were often added to ship-burials to avoid the ship and its occupants 'wandering'). There are also many references in the sagas to *haugbui* ('mound-dwellers'), the spirits of the deceased, who continued to dwell in the mound (*haugr*) that had been heaped up over their mortal remains. In *Grettir's Saga* the hero enters the mound of a man called Kar the Old, who is still present in his tomb in the form of a *haugbui*. Having helped himself to the trove of gold and silver hidden in the mound, Grettir finds himself seized by a ghostly hand as he makes his escape. Hero and *haugbui* 'engaged in a merciless struggle. Everything about them was smashed.' To and fro in the cold dark mound they fight, until finally Grettir draws his sword, Jokulsnaut, and hacks off the head of the mound-dweller. He is doubly unfortunate in having also to face a *draugr*, in the shape of Glam, a murdered shepherd, whom he also bests, but who lays a curse on Grettir that renders him increasingly fearful of the dark, an affliction that gradually causes him to go insane.[72]

Particularly important chieftains or warriors might be interred in a ship (which was then placed in a mound, either cremated or unburnt). The most spectacular account of this comes from Russia, at the eastern end of the Viking world, with the description by the Arab traveller Ibn Fadlan of a cremation ceremony. To what extent it represents a typical Viking burial – or even a Scandinavian one at all – is unknown, but the ritual was certainly a lavish one.

Ibn Fadlan was acting as secretary to the ambassador despatched by the caliph al-Moqtadir in 921 to the khan of the Volgar Bulgars, and his account of his travels includes a detailed description of a group called *Rusiyyah* (or Rus) whom he met on the way. While in general impressed by their physical stature, Ibn Fadlan was scandalised by their lack of physical hygiene and mystified by their habit of combing their hair each day. The funeral he witnessed was for a rich man, since 'If the [dead man] is poor, they make a boat, and place him in it and burn the boat.' The ceremony for the wealthy was far more elaborate, as the Vikings would 'gather his possessions together and divide them in three parts. One third remains for his family; with the second third they cut out garments for him, and with the third part they brew mead for themselves, which they drink on the day when the slave girl kills herself and is cremated with her master. They drink the mead to insensibility day and night.'[73]

A slave (usually, it seems, a female one) volunteered from among the dead man's household to accompany him into the grave. On the day appointed for the final ceremony, Ibn Fadlan went to the river to inspect the ship that was to be used in the ceremony:

around the boat had been built a large structure like a large scaffold of wood . . . Then they hauled the ship further up, until it was placed inside this structure . . . Then they brought a couch, placed it on the ship, and covered it with draperies of Byzantine brocade, and also with pillows of Byzantine brocade. Thereupon an old woman came, whom they call the angel of death, and spread the draperies mentioned over the couch. She had held the oversight over the sewing of the garment of the deceased and of their completion. This old woman kills the girl . . . When they came to his grave, they removed the earth from the timbers and raised the timbers, drew him forth in the same garment in which he had died . . . They then dressed him in stockings, trousers, boots, and a tunic and cape of brocade with gold buttons. They put a cap of brocade and sable pelts upon him and carried him into the tent that had been erected on the boat. Here they placed him upon the quilts, propped up with cushions, brought mead, fruits, and flowers, and laid these beside him.

Then they brought a dog, cleft it in two halves and laid it in the boat. Thereupon they brought all his weapons and laid them by his side. Then they took two horses, drove them until they perspired, then cleft both of them in twain with a sword and laid their flesh in the boat. Then they brought two cows, cut them in two likewise and laid them in the boat. Then they brought a cock and a hen, killed them and threw them both in to the ship. The maiden who wished to be put to death went here and there, and entered each of the tents where the head of each tent had intercourse with her saying 'Say to thy lord, I have done this out of love of thee.'

There followed the climax of the ceremony:

On Friday in the afternoon, they brought the maiden to a structure which they had erected like a doorframe. She put both her feet on the palms of the men, and was lifted up onto this doorframe, and said her piece. Then they let her down again. Thereupon they put her up a second time. She repeated what she had done the first time, and then they let her down, and let her go up again. Again she did as she had done on the first two occasions. Then they gave her a hen. She cut off its head and cast it away. Thereupon I asked the interpreter what her actions meant. He said, 'When they raised her up the first time, she said "Behold, I see my father and mother"; the second time she said: "There I see all my deceased relatives sitting"; the third time she said: "There I behold my lord sitting in paradise, and paradise is fair and green, and around him are men and servants. He calls me; bring me to him."' Then they led her to the boat. She took off the two armlets that she wore and gave them to the old woman whom they call the angel of death, who was to kill her. Then the slave girl took off two anklets that she had and gave them to the two maidens who had waited on her, and who were the daughters of the old woman known as the angel of death.

Then the people lifted her onto the boat, but did not yet let her go into the tent. There came men with shields and staves and gave her a bowl of mead, whereupon she sang and drank it. The interpreter said to me: 'With this she is bidding goodbye to her friends.' Then she was given another beaker. She took it and sang for a long time, while the old woman was urging her to finish the goblet, and to go into the tent where her lord lay. I saw then how disturbed she was. She wished to go into the tent, but put her head between the tent and the side of the boat. Then the old woman took her by the head, made her go into the tent and also entered with her. Whereupon the men began to beat their shields with the staves so that her shrieks would not be heard, and the other maidens become terrified. Then six men went into the tent, and all had intercourse with the girl. Then they placed her beside her dead lord; two men seized her by the feet and two by her hands. Then the old woman placed a rope into which a bight had been made, and gave it to two of the men to pull at two ends. Then the old woman came to her with a broad-bladed dagger and began to jab it into her ribs and pull it out again, and the two men strangled her until she was dead.

The relatives of the dead man then took torches and set fire to the ship. As Ibn Fadlan watched this spectacle, he heard a man nearby speaking and asked his interpreter what had been said. The response was curt: 'He said "They, the Arab communities are stupid." So I asked "Why?" He said "You go and cast into the earth the people whom you both love and honour most amongst men. Then the earth, creeping things, and worms devour them. We, however, let them burn for an instant, and accordingly he enters into paradise at once in that very hour."'[74] At the end of all this, the dead man's name (together with that of the king of the Rus) was written on a large birch post, and then the funeral party departed.

Although the details of the ritual described by Ibn Fadlan might have been peculiar to the particular band of Vikings he met (and possibly influenced by Slavic rituals), the late-nineteenth century saw the discovery of a number of burials in Scandinavia that confirmed the rite of interment in ships. The two most spectacular, the Gokstad and Oseberg ships, were found within a quarter of a century of each other (in 1880 and 1904 respectively), both in Norway. The Gokstad vessel (which dates from around 850) was buried near the Sandefjord, where the blue clay of the mound had acted to conserve organic material (most notably the wooden timbers of the ship) in excellent condition. As a result, the excavators were able to remove it from its burial site more or less intact. The ship is 75 feet 5 inches long, 17 feet wide and when fully laden would have had a displacement of 20 tons. It was equipped with sixteen pairs of oars, and had no fixed rowing benches (so that the crew would probably have had to sit on sea chests containing their possessions). Its mast was set on a large oak block (called the *kjerringa* or old woman) and a socket in this permitted the mast to be raised or lowered according to sea conditions, without the need to dismount it.[75]

Among the grave-goods recovered from the burial chamber were part of a bed, a game board (with antler gaming pieces), a leather purse, the closing clasp of a casket, iron fishing hooks and several metal harness mounts. A far richer haul was recovered in the front part of the ship, including three smaller boats (although what ritual purpose the inclusion of these may have had is unclear), a sleigh, a metal cauldron and six wooden beds, one of them with carved animal-head posts.[76]

The man buried in the Gokstad ship was, for the time, a comparative giant, at almost 6 feet tall. An analysis carried out of the bones in 2007 showed that he suffered from acromegaly, a sort of gigantism that enlarges the bones, which would have rendered his facial features very coarse, making his appearance striking indeed. It seems that he suffered an extremely violent death, first being struck a blow to the left leg, which made him fall, and then a substantial cut to his right leg, which probably caused him to bleed to death. In what desperate struggle this titan perished, however, will probably never be known.

The second, and possibly the finest, of the Viking ship burials was discovered in 1904 at Oseberg in Vestfold, western Norway. The initial discovery was made by a local farmer, Oskar Rom, who was engaged in some speculative digging at a large mound on his property (encouraged by the excitement generated by the discovery of the ship-burial at Gokstad twenty-four years previously). Rom unearthed some wood and brought a sample to Gabriel Gustafson, curator of the Museum of Antiquities at Christiania (as Oslo was then known). Initially sceptical, Gustafson undertook a test dig in 1903, and the following year began to excavate the 145-foot-diameter mound in earnest. Fortunately the summer was dry, making the digging easier, and the blue clay of which the mound was composed had helped – just as had been the case at Gokstad – to preserve the organic material (particularly wood), while the tightly packed layers of turf that had been heaped up to form it also created a seal, which had for centuries prevented water leaking inside.

The stern-post of the ship emerged first, but it soon became apparent that the ship had been broken into and ransacked at some point after the burial had taken place, and much of what the grave-robbers had left behind lay strewn across the entrance to the burial chamber. The weight of the mound and the stones that had been piled up inside it before the grave was sealed meant that the ship's keel had split in two, and part had been forced upwards.

The ship was broken up into 2,000 pieces, which were transferred to Oslo, together with the small finds of grave-goods, many of which were in an extremely delicate state. The pieces of this giant jigsaw puzzle were then boiled in a solution of alum, which crystallised inside the wood and made it stable, albeit fragile, and these were then coated with a solution of creosote and linseed oil. Around 90 per cent of the original wood was in sufficiently good condition to be reused, and ultimately the archaeologists were able to reconstruct almost the whole keel of the ship. The sections were reassembled and moved to a purpose-built museum at Bygdøy close to Oslo in 1926. It took almost all day to move the massive bulk of the ship from the restoration workshops along specially modified railway tracks whose 100-yard length had to be removed and relaid in front of the ship each time it came to the end of the rails – a laborious procedure carried out in front of enormous crowds of curious onlookers. Here it now sits in a massive cross-shaped hall (which it shares with the Gokstad ship). Even out of the water, the immense keel of the ship looks surprisingly sleek, although the huge and perfect bulging bulk of the Gokstad ship's sides, reminiscent of the flanks of some enormous horse, make it perhaps the most awe-inspiring of all surviving Viking vessels.

The Oseberg ship's mast and rudder both show little or no sign of use, and other features, such as the lack of means to close the oar holes in stormy seas and the dimensions of the boat itself, would have rendered it a less-than-practical vessel for active service on raids. The probability, therefore, is that it was purely ceremonial, and may, indeed, have been purpose-built for its interment in the burial mound. The identity of the occupants of the burial chamber – two women, one in later middle age, the other younger – have given rise to much speculation. Analysis of the timbers shows that the trees used to build the ship were cut down in 820 and that the ship's active life probably ended around 834, giving some possible indication of period in which the deceased had lived.

Despite the importance of at least one of those buried with the Oseberg ship, the bones were placed in the burial chamber in a rather haphazard way, perhaps lending some truth to Ibn Fadlan's account of a Viking funeral ceremony that seems in large part to have been fuelled by heavy drinking.[77] Initial analysis of the skeletons resulted in the conclusion that one of the dead women was in her twenties and the other much older, again providing an echo of Ibn Fadlan's narrative, and suggesting that the younger woman had perhaps been killed in order to be buried with her mistress. In 2006, however, both the Oseberg and Gokstad mounds were reopened (having both been sealed up in 1948, with the human remains placed back in their original resting places). Apart from the alarming discovery that the metal boxes in which the bodies had been placed were by then half-full of water and that the bones were in serious danger of dissolving, fresh scientific study of the skeletons' tooth roots found that, far from being in her twenties, the 'young woman' was actually in her fifties when she died. The older woman had abnormalities to the development of her leg bones that suggested extended periods bedridden as a young child, and again at fourteen to fifteen years of age, while she suffered compression damage to her left knee at some stage that probably left her with a limp. Her cause of death may have been identified as abdominal or breast cancer that had metastasised and spread to her bones, probably leaving her in considerable pain at the end of her life (and also giving her the somewhat dubious honour of being Norway's oldest recognised cancer patient).

Although far more is now known about the physiology of the occupants of the Oseberg burial than was the case in 1904, little of this helps in pinning down their identity. The best guess is that the older woman must have been of very high social status, and quite possibly from the royal family, and that she may have been Queen Åsa, the grandmother of Harald Finehair.[78]

Although no jewellery was found in the Oseberg ship (presumably it was looted by the grave-robbers), the remaining grave-goods are nonetheless spectacular, including most notably a large wooden cart, complete with its wheels, along which writhing beasts spiral menacingly. Set on the sides of this are four wooden heads, one of which – that of a fierce, grimacing man – is one of the most famous images from the entire Viking world. The other items included a variety of goods that the women were thought to need in the afterlife, including axes, knives, the remains of an entire ox, beds, quilts, weaving equipment and (perhaps intended for their transportation to the next world) the wagon and sledges. Among the items interred with them were the remains of a tapestry, which had almost completely disintegrated or been compressed together into cake-like lumps that were almost impossible to disentangle. Nonetheless, part of this has been reconstructed and probably represents the remains of a wall hanging that contains images of processions of human figures walking and riding, with large numbers of smaller figures, such as swastikas, knot-shapes and birds, filling almost every otherwise blank space.

Among the finds at Oseberg was the so-called 'Buddha bucket', a generally plain wooden bucket made of yew, whose handle is attached to two squatting Buddha-like figures with closed eyes, each adorned with a pair of yellow-enamelled swastikas. Although at first sight seeming to be evidence of trade with the eastern world, the bucket is most likely the product of an Irish workshop, probably representing the fruits of plunder from a monastery in Ireland.[79] Perhaps even more striking are the corner posts of one of the beds found at Oseberg. Each in the form of a dragon, they are individually carved, one of them unremittingly fierce and bearing more than a hint of menace, another alien and repellent, while a third has its eyes wide in an almost quizzical expression.

In their fullest development Viking vessels such as the Oseberg and Gokstad ships were large, open vessels adapted for both sailing and rowing, and whose particular method of construction made them well suited for long-distance raiding. They had very shallow keels, allowing them to navigate up riverways that could not be penetrated by most other vessels, heightening the feeling for their victims that the Vikings could appear almost anywhere there was shoreline or river bank.

The keel of the Oseberg vessel, some 65 feet long, curves gently, making the draught of the vessel greatest at the point where the hull was widest, and so increasing the capacity of the ship. The skeleton of the vessel was provided by a series of strakes (overlapping planks), which were riveted together using iron nails driven in and then secured by a small metal plate. The use of overlapping in this way produced a characteristic type of vessel known as clinker-built. The planking was then secured to timber ribs by lashing through holes bored in the underside.

The Gokstad ship is a little larger than the Oseberg, at some 75 feet long. Its stronger overall construction, with a keel cut in a single piece, would have rendered it more seaworthy. The hull is also rounder and the oar holes have shutters, which could be closed when under way to prevent water getting in and swamping the ship (whose sides are in any case somewhat higher than its predecessor, another modification that guaranteed a rather drier passage for its occupants). The dating of the Gokstad ship to around 850, up to half a century later than the Oseberg vessel, shows that significant improvements in ship-building techniques were being made as the era of the Viking raids opened.

The Oseberg and Gokstad ships (and a slightly earlier vessel found at Tune in 1867) are both examples of the longship, the classic Viking warship, although there are records of even bigger ships, which carried up to seventy oarsmen (such as the *Ormen Lange*, the 'Long Serpent' of Olaf Tryggvason, which had thirty-four pairs of oars). The Oseberg ship had a shield rack on the inside rail to which sixty-four shields could be fixed (the remains of which – round, painted black and yellow and each 3 feet in diameter – were found by archaeologists). When sailing into port, the shields would be left suspended to the side to strike fear into potential adversaries or those disinclined to accede to the Vikings' demand for booty. Both ships had masts intact when found (although that of the Gokstad ship was incomplete). In each case the mast could be raised or lowered when necessary by use of a mast fish (a special piece of timber attached to the mast, which made it easier to move). Steering was by means of a large side-oar attached to the starboard of the vessel (the very word starboard derives from the Old Norse *styrbord* or 'steering side'). This could be stowed when on land by swivelling it up inside the ship and unfastening the leather strap that bound it.

The sheer visual impact of such vessels should not be underestimated. The writer of the *Encomium Emmaa Reginae* in the mid-eleventh century has left an account of the departure of Cnut's fleet from Denmark in 1015, describing how 'the flashing of arms shone in one place, in another the flame of suspended shields. Gold shone on the prows, silver also flashed on the variously shaped ships . . . For who could look upon the lions of the foe, terrible with the brightness of gold, who upon the man of metal, menacing with golden façade, who upon the dragons burning with pure gold . . . without feeling any fear for the king of such a force?'[80]

We know far less about the rigging and sails of Viking ships, as very little material in the surviving vessels indicates the precise arrangements that were used, nor do the sagas tell us much. We are forced instead to rely on pictorial representations, notably the series of picture stones that have been preserved on the island of Gotland in the Baltic around 55 miles to the east of the Swedish mainland.

The island's importance during the Viking Age is indicated by the large number of Viking-Age hoards that have been found there and by the existence of numerous small harbours such as Paviken, which took advantage of Gotland's strategic position in the Baltic. Even more striking than these are the picture stones, often used as grave-markers, whose carving began in the Iron Age around AD 400, and which are almost unique to the island. Beginning with spirals, rosettes and a range of fantastic beasts, they developed to show mythological scenes, which sometimes included the portrayal of the disc of the sun and ships, a combination that may have some religious significance in denoting the means of transport needed to carry the deceased from the land of the living to that of the dead.[81] The very earliest boats shown (up until the sixth or seventh century) are, however, propelled by oars, rather than by sail.

Only in the ninth and tenth centuries did the Gotland stones become more like conventional Swedish runestones, including inscriptions in honour of a deceased person, but the pictorial element remained amongst the most inventive and varied in the Scandinavian world. Amid Valkyries plucking dead Vikings from the battlefields, and the unmistakable silhouette of Odin's eight-legged horse Sleipnir, there are a number of representations of ships with their sails unfurled, most of them showing a single rectangular sail, but others with more complicated rigging. They are almost certainly warships, as most of the carvings show warriors crowding on the deck, as if eager for battle.

(*Right*) The Lindisfarne Stone.

(*Above*) View from the beach towards the twelfth-century abbey church at Lindisfarne.

(*Left*) The tenth-centu
Gjermundbu Helmet,
the only intact Viking
Age helmet found
in Scandinavia.

(*Above*) The silver Gundestrup Cauldron, found in a bog in Denmark, is one of the most
spectacular finds from Bronze Age Scandinavia.

(*Right*) A stone ship setting at Lindholm Høje, Denmark.

(*Above*) The burial mounds at Gammla Uppsala, Sweden.

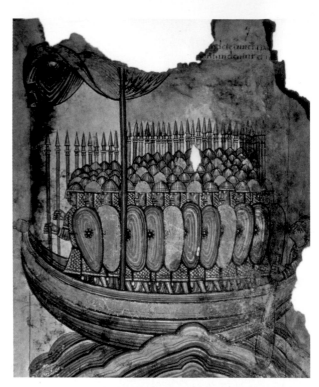

(*Left*) A Viking invasion
fleet in Francia,
from a twelfth-century
Life of St Aubin.

(*Below left*) The Danish
invasion under Ingvar
and Huba, from the
twelfth-century
*Life, Miracles and
Passion of St Edmund.*

(*Right*) The Cuerdale Hoard.

(*Below*) An aerial view of Jarlshof,
Shetland's mainland.

(*Above*) The Jelling Stone.

(*Below*) A reconstructed Viking longhouse at Trelleborg.

(*Right*) Poppo carries a red-hot lump of iron to prove the truth of the Christian religion to Harald Bluetooth (from a plaque at Tamdrup Church, Denmark).

(*Left*) A Thor's hammer amulet from East Gotland, Sweden.

(*Above*) A Gotland picture stone showing Viking Age sails and rigging.

(*Right*) The Gokstad Ship.

(*Below*) The Oseberg Ship.

The other surviving (or partially surviving) ships provide us with further information about the types of Viking vessel. One found at Ladby on Fynen in Denmark (of which only the impression left in the soil and rows of metal fastening-rivets survived) dated from around 900, and was longer and sleeker than the Oseberg and Gokstad ships. Its design made it less suitable for going under sail, and so it may have been confined to coastal Baltic waters. And the discovery in 1953 of a ship sunk in an attack on Hedeby around 985 provided an example of the very large warships that were characteristic of the later Viking Age. Its length has been estimated at nearly 102 feet, and it could carry sixty oarsmen, making its crew a formidable raiding party.

The largest Viking warship of which we have any record (albeit only in a saga) is Olaf Tryggvason's *Long Serpent*, which may have been more than 100 feet long. The building of the ship, probably around 998, was not without incident. The craftsman appointed to oversee the giant vessel was a certain Torberg *Skafhogg* ('smooth-scraper'). One evening, Torberg had to leave the work unattended. He returned later with the king to find that 'the wrights had already come, but they all stood there not at work. The king asked why they bore themselves in this manner. They answered that the ship was shamefully cut about and that some man must have gone from stem to stern and have cut one deep notch after another down the planking.'[82] Olaf was furious and offered a reward for anyone who would inform on the perpetrator of this vandalism, where upon Torberg confessed to being the guilty party. Olaf retorted that his master craftsman had to restore the ship to the same condition as before, or forfeit his life. 'Then Torberg went and chipped the planks, so that all the notches were smoothed and made even with the rest. Then said the king – and all the others too – that the ship was much finer looking after Torberg had made this alteration. The king then bade him do so on the other side and offered him great thanks.'

All Torberg's improvements were to no avail, for Olaf's fleet was overwhelmed at the Battle of Svold in 999 or 1000.[83] The king was last seen at the prow of the *Long Serpent* before leaping into the waters, fully armoured, to avoid the humiliation of capture. Although there were some who believed he had survived, or hoped that he might return once more to liberate Norway, it is far more likely that he perished after his dramatic leap from the longest Viking longship of them all.

Another treasure trove of Viking ships was discovered at Skuldelev in Denmark in 1962, when a series of wrecks was raised from the bottom of the Roskildefjord. They had been sunk to block the access channel to Roskilde in Zealand during a raid on the town, probably in the 1070s. There were three channels into the port and the scuttled vessels permanently blocked one of them, leaving a second channel that could be defended by the local fleet, and a third, more circuitous route that needed the knowledge of local pilots to navigate safely. Now housed in a square glass-topped museum set by the side of the fjord, the Skuldelev vessels are somewhat less complete than their Gokstad and Oseberg counterparts in Norway, the metal frames that stand in for those parts which are wholly missing giving them a strikingly futuristic feel. One of them (Skuldelev 2, at around 98 feet long, and possibly holding up to seventy-five crewmen) represents the most advanced development of the longship. Analysis of its timbers suggests that it was built in Ireland, in the area around Dublin, in about 1040. This was the type of vessel known as a *snekke* ('serpent'), the leviathans that carried many of the raiders in the great expeditions of the tenth and early eleventh centuries. A smaller warship, Skuldelev 5, was a comparative minnow at 60 feet long and with thirteen pairs of oars, putting it at the lower end of the longship range.

An entirely different type of vessel is represented by Skuldelev 1.[84] Stubbier and sturdier than the sleek lines of the longship, this is a *knorr*, one of the larger trading vessels that formed the backbone of the non-military fleets of the Viking Age. These specialised boats needed only a small crew (meaning there was more room for the cargo) and had comparatively few oars, making them much more dependent on sail for their propulsion. The earliest yet discovered, from Klåstad in Norway, dates to around 990 and was found with part of its original cargo of whetstones still heaped around the carcass of the ship. Skuldelev 1 was built in Norway around 1030 and is about 52 feet long, with a cargo capacity of around 24 tons. It was vessels such as this that carried the bulk of trade around the Baltic and ensured connections with the further-flung parts of the Viking world, such as Iceland and Greenland (which was especially dependent on the

Norwegian royal *knorr*, which was supposed to put into the isolated colony each year[85]).

The museum at Roskilde is one of the main centres for the reconstruction of Viking vessels, continuing a tradition that began in 1892 with the building of a replica of the Gokstad ship, which managed the crossing all the way from Norway to Chicago. Experiencing relatively little difficulty on the way, it successfully managed to upstage the 400th anniversary celebrations of Christopher Columbus's landing in the New World that was being commemorated at the World Fair that year. A reconstruction has now been built of each of the Skuldelev ships, including most recently the Skuldelev 2, which was reborn as the *Sea Stallion of Glendalough* and made the voyage from Denmark to Iceland in 2008. The journey was without serious incident, despite encountering very stormy conditions, although it was found that the vessel shipped enormous quantities of water, casting a damp light on the conditions that the crew of its eleventh-century predecessor must have endured.

The Vikings employed a variety of techniques to navigate this assortment of vessels on voyages that ranged from the strictly local, coastal variety to great strikes across the North Atlantic. The simplest, most useful method for voyages in which land was always in sight was by reference to coastal features and the approximate time taken to travel between them. Many place-names along the Scandinavian shoreline (or elsewhere in the Viking world) retain a memory of this, with toponyms such as *Kullen* ('hill'), a headland on the coast of Skåne, and the prevalence of names ending in '*-ey*' ('island'), such as Anglesey and Ramsey in Wales (an area that was only ever briefly and lightly under Scandinavian domination).[86] For longer voyages, the navigator might remember a list of such landmarks and mentally cross-reference them with the terrain he was seeing on land. One such 'chart' is preserved in the *Landnámabók*, which gives instructions for the voyage from Norway to Greenland: 'From Hernar in Norway one should keep sailing west to reach Hvarf in Greenland and then you are sailing north out of Shetland, so that it can only be seen if visibility is very good; but south of the Faeroes, so that the sea appears halfway up their mountain-slopes; but so far south of Iceland that one only becomes aware of the birds and whales in it.' Even when out of sight of land, the Vikings could use observations of the sun, stars and seabirds, including on at least one occasion of ravens, whose instinct to fly towards land helped in the discovery of Iceland.[87] Observing the prevailing winds and currents also gave experienced sailors some idea of their rough location, if other means failed, and enabled them to predict weather patterns and tailor their routes to fit them.

Less certain is the suggestion that the Vikings employed a means of 'dead-reckoning', which allowed them to estimate the longitude that they were at, using wooden boards with a pin in the centre (like the gnomon of a sundial). The shadow that the sun cast on this at a fixed time of day correlated with markings on the board, if the ship was on course. If the sun-shadow fell above it, then the vessel was north of the desired latitude and, if below it, the ship's course was too far to the south. A wooden disc found in 1948 at Uunartoq close to the Eastern Settlement in Greenland, which has been dated to around 1000, has sixteen small incisions and curved markings and has been identified as a possible example of such a sun-shadow bearing-dial.[88] Another more complete disc was discovered in 2002 at Wolin in Poland, but there is no definite evidence that this is what the object was used for, and there is no clear support (either archaeologically or in the sagas) for the use of such a device in navigation.

Even more unclear is whether the Vikings used a *sólarsteinn*, or sun-stone – a rock that had polarising qualities when held towards the sun. Although there is a mention in *Raudulfs tháttr* of a stone possessed by a farmer's son whom King Olaf Haraldsson visited, which allowed him to tell where the sun was, even if hidden by cloud, there is no evidence of such an object being used as a practical tool for navigation. On more certain ground is the story of Oddi-Helgason, nick-named Star-Oddi, who lived in Iceland in the twelfth century and was known for making a series of precise astronomical observations, such as the dates of the summer and winter solstices. Again, however, it is unclear whether his compilation is a one-off that was not generally available or known to the average Viking navigator.

Despite this uncertainty, it is not necessary to suppose immensely sophisticated navigational technology to explain the Vikings' facility at travelling throughout the Baltic, along the vast length of the Norwegian coastline, across the North Sea and then into the open Atlantic. For those who imagine such devices being routinely available to Viking sailors, there is a warning note in the number of saga accounts of voyagers driven off-course by storms, who simply did not know where they were. One notable example is Bjarni Herjólfsson, whose navigational mishaps during his search for his father, who had migrated unexpectedly from Iceland to Greenland while his son was away on an expedition, led to his initially mistaking the coastline of North America (which he was the first European to sight) for that of Greenland.[89]

From the dragon-head prows of their ships to the complex decorations on their jewellery and the patterns that snake around their runestones, almost every Viking artefact shows a love of adornment. Early Scandinavian art belonged to a tradition that embraced much of northern Europe during the Age of Migrations in the fourth to sixth centuries. From the seventh century, however, the Scandinavian world began to produce art that was independently creative, with a particular use of animal ornamentation, often with beasts intertwining to create sinuous patterns of astonishing complexity and power.

Artistic styles are notoriously difficult to date, particularly those that remained in fashion over a long period of time, as styles that are supposed to succeed each other in a neat typological sequence often overlap. Some areas are more conservative in taking up the new styles, while the presence of a particular 'dated' style in an otherwise undated archaeological context may represent an item that has been preserved in a family for decades (or even for generations).

The first Scandinavian style of the Viking Age, classified by art historians as Style E,[90] is represented by a set of twenty-two bridle-bits in gilt-bronze found at Broa on Gotland. There is a complex series of animal motifs used on them, including a stylised one with a beaked head and fork-like feet, and a 'gripping beast' – a type that would remain in use for several centuries, in which the claw-like feet of the animals often grip their own bodies. The most famous example of this style are the finds from the Oseberg ship; the decorations on the tent, the bedposts, the sledges and cart in particular adapt the animal motifs of Style E magnificently to the wooden medium on which they were carved.

The next major Viking artistic style to emerge is known as the Borre style, named for a collection of gilt-bronze harness mounts that were found in a ship-burial at Borre in Norway's Vestfold.[91] The characteristic ribbon plait, a pattern of interlaced circles, lozenges and other geometric figures, is further adorned by a gripping beast with a long snout (and sometimes what looks like a pigtail). There are also other more naturalistic animal types with heads bent backwards. The Borre style spread from Scandinavia to the Viking-occupied parts of the British Isles, where it appears in the hybrid Anglo-Norse stone sculptures and on metal items.

Roughly contemporary with the Borre style (which lasted into the second half of the tenth century) is the Jellinge style, named for a small silver cup dating from the mid-tenth century, which was found in the North Mound at Jelling.[92] Again prominently featuring a zoomorphic style, its main motif is an S-shaped beast, elongated almost into a ribbon with very narrow hips. It seems to have evolved from the Borre style (and in time metamorphosed into the succeeding Mammen style). There are objects of the Jellinge type somewhat earlier than its name-site might suggest, and a strap-end found with the Gokstad ships has been associated with it.

The Mammen style, which emerged around 950, is named for a richly adorned axe found in a male grave at Mammen in Jutland. The inlaid silver-wire decoration features a new form of beast, more like a bird, with intertwined foliage and tendrils filling much of the rest of the space. The bodies of the bird-beasts are also infilled with a pattern of dots. Despite its name, the Mammen style is that featured on the Jelling Stone itself (and the lion-like creature on the stone is a notable example of it). Other Mammen-style objects are found widely distributed throughout the Viking world, including a sculptured cross at Kirk Braddan on the Isle of Man and brooches from the Skaill hoard found in Orkney.

Around 1000 the Mammen style was supplanted by the Ringerike style, whose name is taken from an area north of Oslo where a series of carvings on sandstones in this style were found. The most obvious features are the use of vegetative decoration, with tendrils looping out of shell decorations at the base of the stones. Above the pattern of foliage is found a boldly striding animal, and snakes amongst the tendrils often complete the decorations. Amongst the best examples of the style are metal weathervanes, such as the one found at Söderala in Sweden. Additionally, many of the finest runestones in Sweden are in the Ringerike style, including such masterpieces as the Ramundsberget Stone near Eskilstuna in Södermanland, which illustrates the legend of Sigurd, the heroic slayer of the dragon Fafnir. The whole is framed by three serpents. The runic inscription is contained in the outermost, while Sigurd himself stands outside the frame with his sword plunged into the underside of the lowermost of the snakes (which stands as a representation of Fafnir).[93]

The Ringerike was roughly contemporary with the initial spread within Scandinavia of Christianity, and was the first to contain Christian iconography, although pagan symbolism was still present. It spread into the British Isles, where it appears on the Winchbombe Psalter illustrations (from the 1020s and 1030s), and the style survived in Ireland long after it had been supplanted elsewhere.

By around 1050 the Ringerike had in turn given way to a new style, the Urnes, named for a stave church at Sogn in western Norway. These characteristically Norwegian wooden churches were erected during the early period of Christianity in Norway, often bearing ornate carvings, especially on the doors. Unlike elsewhere in Scandinavia, the original wooden churches were not replaced with stone versions, and therefore many of the characteristic high roof ridges topped with a turret and spire, and projecting gables adorned with dragon-heads and other ferocious beasts, have survived to the present day.[94] As in all the other principal Scandinavian artistic styles of the Viking era, one of the main elements of the style is a stylised beast, including a snake-like creature with two legs, a standing four-legged beast, and a ribbon-like thread that terminates in an animal head. Unlike the preceding Ringerike style, there is little in the way of symmetry. As well as stave churches, the Urnes style is seen on a large number of Swedish runestones (with the inscription itself often appearing inside a snake) and on much high-quality metalwork, such as the gold Orø cross found at Issefjord in Zealand. It is also the first period in Scandinavian art when we occasionally know the identity of the artist, at least in the case of runestones, where the stone-carver sometimes included his own name. On one such stone from Södermanland, the master carver added to the inscription: 'Äsbjörn carved the stone, coloured it as a memorial, he bound it with runes' (which also, incidentally, reminds us that most runestones were originally highly coloured, and not the rather inert rocks that they can appear to be today).

The last of the main Viking styles, the Urnes, petered out in the early twelfth century; examples become much less common after 1110, although the style survived in Ireland at least until the 1130s. By then, new monarchies modelled along those in western and southern Europe had emerged in Sweden, Denmark and Norway; the last Viking raids were several generations in the past; and, perhaps appropriately, a new wave of artistic fashion had penetrated Scandinavia, with the importation of the Romanesque, which remained the dominant style for the next 200 years.

Map 6 The North Atlantic World

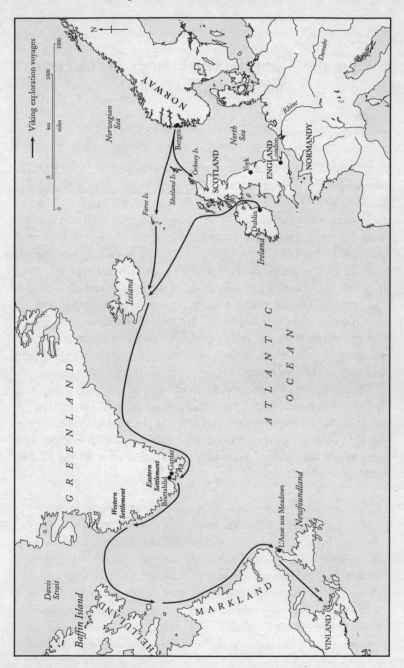

4

Across the Atlantic: The Vikings in the Faroes and Iceland, 900–1262

While some Vikings were harrying the coastlines of northern Europe, others took part in an extraordinary expansion, which would see Norse ships and colonists reaching far across the Atlantic, right to the eastern seaboard of the Americas. It all began with surprisingly modest steps. At about the same time as the first raids commenced in Britain and Ireland in the early ninth century, Viking ships started to attack (where there was an existing population) and settle (where there was not) the string of islands to the north and west of Scotland. The furthest-flung of these, and the first genuine stepping stone to the Vikings' Atlantic realm, were the Faroes, a cluster of eighteen volcanic islands that lie roughly equidistant between Norway, Scotland and Iceland, with their nearest neighbour being Shetland around 180 miles to the south-east.

When the first Vikings arrived – most likely around 825[1] – they may have found that a small settlement had preceded them. The Irish monk Dicuil, in his *De Mensura Orbis Terrae* ('On the Measurement of the World'), a handy geographical compendium composed about this time, which summarised knowledge about the lands of the known world, relates that:

> There are many other islands in the ocean to the north of Britain which can be reached from the northern islands of Britain in a direct voyage of two days and nights with sails filled and with a continuously favourable wind. A devout priest told me that in two summer days and the night in between he sailed in a two-benched boat and entered one of them. There is another set of small islands, nearly all of them separated by small stretches of water; on them for nearly a hundred years hermits sailing from our country, Ireland, have lived. But just as they were always deserted from the beginning of the world, so now

because of the Northmen pirates they are emptied of anchorites, and are filled with countless sheep and very many different diverse kinds of sea-birds.[2]

Although it is not certain that Dicuil is referring to the Faroes, it seems fairly likely that he is giving us a distant echo of a violent taking of the land (in Old Norse a *landnám*) that resulted in the expulsion of the Irish cleric's countrymen. The association is reinforced by evidence from pollen, which suggests that the natural vegetation of the Faroes – which today is largely grass, sedges and small shrubs – had already begun to be disturbed (most likely by human occupation) in the early to mid-seventh century and possibly several centuries before that.[3]

The literary evidence for the Norse settlement of the islands comes mainly from the *Saga of the Faroese*, composed a little after 1200, which focuses on the period at the end of the tenth century at the time of the islands' conversion to Christianity. The saga writer was mainly interested in the role of King Harald Finehair of Norway in Faroese history, and it is quite likely that he overstated the Norwegian role among the earliest colonists. He names the leader of the first settlers as Grim Kamban, who is said to have left Norway in the 880s to escape the Norwegian king's centralising policies. This is probably as much of an exaggeration as the similarly bold assertion in the *Orkneyinga Saga* that Harald annexed Orkney,[4] and the date of Grim Kamban's arrival is more likely to have been around 825. His nickname Kamban ('the Lame') is of Celtic origin and hints that the earliest Norse settlers on the Faroes were a mixed group (possibly from the Isle of Man, where Scandinavians did not displace the native population[5]).

Even if Harald Finehair was not directly responsible for the islands' settlement, connections with Norway were undeniably important for the Faroes, and one party of visitors from the homeland in the 890s had a huge influence on their development. It included Aud the Deep-minded, a noblewoman of high status, who stopped off on her way to Iceland and presided over the marriage of her granddaughter Olúva,[6] from whom descended the Gata, one of the leading Norse Faroese families of the Viking Age. Hiberno-Norse influence on the Faroes (and, later, Iceland) is indicated by the fact that Aud's recently killed husband, Olaf the White, had been the King of Dublin. The saga centres around the deeds of two of these descendants, the roguish

Thrand Thorbjørnsson and his brother Thorlak, who most probably lived around 970. The society it portrays is typically Scandinavian, including the description of a *thing* in operation at Tinganes on Streymoy, and violent struggles for power between Thrand and his rivals, which began with his killing of Hagrim and the brothers Brestir and Beinir. The feud continued in the next generation, as Sigmund Brestirson tried, and ultimately failed, to get his revenge.

Apart from the dramatic accounts in the *Saga of the Faroese*, most of what we know about the Viking-Age Faroes comes from archaeological discoveries. The first scientific excavations, which took place in 1941 around the village of Kvívík on Streymoy, unearthed a 65-foot longhouse with earth benches set around the outside. A further Viking-Age farm dating from about 900 was discovered at Toftanes, near Leirvik, in the 1980s. This one had a similar-sized longhouse with walls of dry stone protected by layers of turf, and a structure at one end that could have been a byre for cattle. A large number of bowls, dishes, spindle whorls and other artefacts made of steatite (or soapstone) were discovered. It is a material not found on the Faroes and must have come from Norway or Shetland, which shows that the settlers retained close links with their Scandinavian homeland. They depended on their livestock (supplemented by fishing) for a living, and sheep have always played a large role in the local economy – the name 'Faroes' itself means 'Island of Sheep' in Old Norse.

The Faroes remained part of the Scandinavian world for the rest of the Middle Ages, although little is known in detail of their history. They became part of the Norwegian kingdom in 1035, when the Faroese *thing* was downgraded to the status of a *løgting* (a law court). Thereafter, mentions are few and far between, although in 1277 and 1388 some prominent Icelanders are recorded as having stayed after being shipwrecked, and in 1364 the Faroese bishop's boat was blown off-course to Iceland, forcing him to overwinter there.[7] The islands were subsequently included in the Danish-Norwegian union in 1397, staying with Denmark after its break-up in 1814 and remaining under Danish sovereignty to this day (albeit as a self-governing territory with an extremely high degree of autonomy).

As the story of Aud the Deep-minded suggests, once they had become established in the Faroes in the mid-ninth century, the Vikings pushed further westwards, ultimately reaching Iceland around 870.

Map 7 Viking Iceland and the Faroes

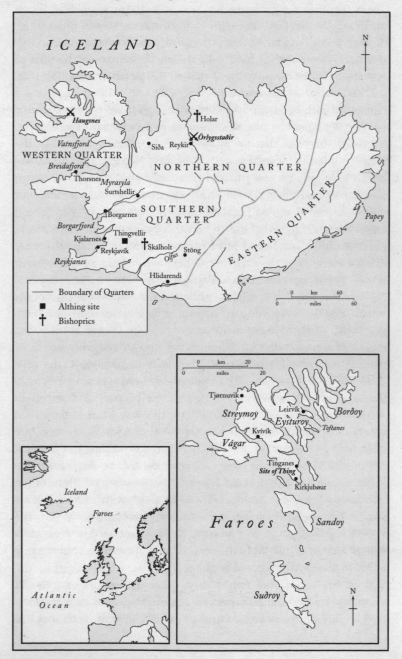

Exactly what level of knowledge the pioneering voyagers possessed before they set out on these further explorations is unclear, but if Dicuil is to be believed, the Irish had once again beaten them to it.[8] He describes a land far out in the Atlantic, six days' sail to the north of Britain, where the sun hardly dips below the horizon at the time of the summer solstice, meaning it was so light even at midnight that, as Dicuil explains – in a revealing vignette of medieval hygiene – a man could pick lice from his shirt as though it were the middle of the day.[9] We cannot be sure who these earliest visitors to 'Thule' were, or even if the place that Dicuil describes is Iceland, rather than the northern coast of Scandinavia. Yet the first Norsemen to arrive are said to have found a few *papar* (a term they used for Irish Christian hermits) in residence. These shadowy clerics soon departed, not wishing to live alongside heathens (as the ninth-century Vikings still largely were), leaving behind them 'Irish books, bells and croziers'. There are still a number of place-names in western Iceland that may reflect a memory of the elusive Irish hermits, including Papey ('Papar Island'), Papfjörður near Lón and Papafell ('Papar Hill') in Strandasysla.[10]

There are also less credible – although not impossible – accounts of Irish monks criss-crossing the Atlantic in their coracles, small animal-hide boats. Many of these form part of a genre known as *immrama*, voyage stories intended to illuminate an idea of religious search or just plain yearning for adventure. They include outlandish tales such as the *Voyage of Máel Dúin*. The eponymous hero was a warrior who built a giant coracle with room for a crew of sixty and set off in pursuit of his father's murderer. Along the way Máel Dúin visited twenty-nine islands, including one swarming with giant ants, one inhabited by talking birds and another that was scalding to the touch and inhabited by red-hot pigs. Of more immediate interest for the possible settlement of Iceland by *papar* is the story of Brendan, an Irish saint born about 844 near Tralee in south-west Ireland, who is said to have been an inveterate voyager, travelling to Wales, the Hebrides and Brittany. Intriguingly, the account of his voyages (a shorter version in Irish and a longer *Navigatio* in Latin) has him visiting an Isle of Sheep (which could be the Faroes), and encountering mountains of smoke and fire (which have been interpreted as Iceland's volcanoes) and 'crystal columns' (which might just be icebergs).

There are so many stories and so many different lands listed in these accounts that they make the Atlantic Ocean seem like a monkish super-highway. But most of the islands which the earliest Irish voyagers are said to have visited have the singular characteristic of being almost certainly non-existent, and to conclude from the story of Brendan's Voyage that he reached Iceland, Greenland, North America or even Mexico[11] is surely to stretch the sources too far.

The first Viking visitor to follow in the wake of the *papar* and visit Iceland seems to have been Naddod, who was driven off-course by a severe storm near the Faroes. Working back from later, more secure chronology, his voyage may have taken place sometime in the 830s or 840s. Storm-tossed, he finally came to an unknown shoreline, but sailed only partway around it and, struck by its chilly climate, named it 'Snowland'.[12] Intrigued by Naddod's account, a Swede named Garðar Svavarsson set out shortly afterwards and reached 'Snowland' but, with commendable egotism, decided to rename it 'Garðarsholm'. Soon afterwards (in the late 860s), a Norwegian named Floki Vilgertharson – who has an alternative claim to Grim Kamban[13] to the discovery of the Faroes – set off to find the place. Floki brought along with him some rather unusual travelling companions: three ravens, whose purpose was to discover whether any dry land lay nearby. When the journey seemed to be taking longer than he expected, Floki – Noah-like – released one of the birds, which simply flew around the ship and then came back to land on its stern. A little while later he tried again, and this time the raven flew off a short way before returning. Undeterred, Floki later released the third bird and this one, sensing land in the vicinity, flew off past the prow of the ship and failed to come back. Floki followed the course the raven had set and eventually landed at Vatnsfjörd on the north-western coast of Iceland.

Floki, ever after known as Hrafn-Floki ('Raven-Floki') for his creative navigational trick, climbed up a hill near his landing place and, from this vantage point, caught sight of a neighbouring fjord choked with drift ice. It was perilously close to winter, so Floki and his men decided to return home, but the foul weather prevented their departure, forcing them to stay until the following summer. On finally returning to Norway, Floki was so disgruntled that he rechristened the island 'Ísland' (or Iceland), a name that stuck to it ever after. Some of his companions, though, were rather more positive about the place; one of them, Thórólf, was so effusive – claiming that 'butter dripped' from the grass on the island – that from that day on he was sarcastically nicknamed Thórólf Butter.[14]

Iceland is the only land into which the Vikings expanded for which we have reasonably full accounts of the settlement. We owe this to two separate literary strands. The first derives from the very early tradition of historical writing that began with the Icelandic priest and scholar Ari Thorgilsson (1067–1148), known as 'the Learned'. The author of the *Íslendingabók* ('The Book of the Icelanders') – a brief history of Iceland, from the time of the settlement to the twelfth century – Ari was highly regarded by contemporaries for his attention to detail and his seeking out of reliable sources. Snorri Sturluson in the *Heimskringla* goes to great lengths to describe how Ari had gleaned much of his information from his foster-father, Hall Thorarinsson, in whose house he grew up, a man whose memory stretched right back to the very early days of Christianity in Iceland at the start of the eleventh century. To Ari is also attributed part-authorship of an even more precious document, the *Landnámabók* ('The Book of Settlements'), which purports to give a list of all those who took part in the original *landnám* of Iceland, together with details of the boundaries of the lands on which they settled. The original version of the *Landnámabók* does not survive. Instead we have three medieval editions.[15] The book clearly had value both as a genealogical tool – in a society where the legal system meant it was important to establish precise degrees of relationship – and as a means of settling property disputes. Even though it was first set down on paper two centuries after the settlement, much of the detail may be accurate and, as a record of the colonisation of a new land, it is unparalleled before the modern era.

The *Landnámabók*'s account of the final settlement of Iceland (following the abortive expeditions of Naddod, Garðar Svarvarsson and Hrafn-Floki) dates it to 870. Just as the *Orkneyinga Saga* explained the settlement of Orkney by reference to Harald Finehair's campaign to unify Norway, which created a large group of men eager to escape the more repressive atmosphere that was growing, so the *Landnámabók* ascribes a similar motivation to the first Norse arrivals in Iceland. A stream of settlers (mainly Norwegians) was soon said to be making their way there, among whom the pioneers were Ingólf Arnason and his foster-brother Hjorleif. Ingólf went to the new-found island twice, once on a scouting expedition and the second time to settle. On the second voyage he is said to have brought with him the pillars from the high seat at his home farm in Norway. Adhering to pagan Viking practice, Ingólf had these cast into the sea as soon as his ship came close to the Icelandic shore, swearing to build his new farm wherever they might come ashore. At first Ingólf could not find them, and so he initially settled at a site called Ingólfshöfði ('Ingólf's Head'). Then, having had time to survey the land rather better, he chose the sheltered harbour of Reykjavik ('Smoky Bay', from the abundance of hot springs in the vicinity) for his new homestead, a point where – most conveniently – he is said finally to have found the elusive high-seat pillars.

Ari's dating of the settlement to around 874 has received astonishing corroboration from the science of tephrochronology, which concerns itself with the dating of volcanic ash (or tephra) from historic eruptions. Each of these bears a very particular chemical signature, which when analysed can indicate the date of the eruption from which the ash came. Deposits from human settlement can then be dated from their position in the archaeological strata relative to the layers of tephra. Use of this technique has revealed that a short while before the first Viking settlers arrived in Iceland – or at least before they left any trace in the archaeological record – there was a volcanic eruption. This has been dated, by analysis of Greenland's glacial record, to 872 plus or minus two years.[16]

The remains of this first stage of Reykjavik can still be seen, excavated and presented in a museum at the edge of the old town. The hulk of what may be Reykjavik's oldest longhouse broods in an underground chamber (though whether it is actually Ingólf's house is uncertain). Tantalisingly, the remains of one roughly built wall have recently been unearthed, possibly the dividing line between two fields, which seems to lie *beneath* the tephra layer for the 872±2 volcano. Whether this can be confirmed and by how much it would push back the date for the Iceland *landnám* is unclear, but it certainly raises the possibility that Ingólf's settlement was not the first.[17]

The second major source for early Icelandic history is the collection of sagas collectively known as the *Íslendingasögur* (or, in English, generally as the 'Icelandic family sagas'). Set against the backdrop of the first century and a half of the Icelandic colony – and occasionally dealing with events in Scandinavia as well – they tell of the tensions between Iceland's major families, and the often tragic consequences that accompanied them. They are not intended, on the whole, to tell the story of 'high politics' or to give a coherent political narrative to Icelandic history, although a late series of sagas known as the *Sturlunga Sagas* – which are not really part of the main body of family sagas – recount the series of power struggles by which Iceland's fractious chiefdoms nearly coalesced into a coherent political whole.[18] Although the narratives can be somewhat formulaic, with a typically Viking concern to establish the exact degree of relationship between the protagonists leading to some extensive genealogies at the start of certain sagas, the best of them have a compelling power. *Njál's Saga*, one of the finest, tells how the central character Njál Thorgeirsson is drawn into the feuds caused by the murderous behaviour of his friend Gunnar Hamundarson (who is egged on by the femme fatale of the saga, his treacherous wife Hallgerð). Njál is ultimately burnt to death in his farmstead by a posse bent on revenge against his sons for their murder of Höskuld, one of Gunnar's cousins.

Some of the family sagas focus on the life of a single man, such as *Egil's Saga* (although this, unusually, dwells largely on events outside Iceland), while others (such as the *Laxdaela Saga*) are genuinely 'family sagas', recounting the history of a family over several generations. The sagas, in the form that we possess them, date largely to manuscripts of the fourteenth to sixteenth centuries, though most were evidently composed rather earlier, probably during the thirteenth century. They owed their survival not to any elite concern for the continuity of Icelandic tradition, but to the tradition of storytelling that had given rise to them, with the precious vellum manuscripts passed around for centuries on farmsteads throughout the island. It was only in the seventeenth century that their true value began to be recognised, and the Bishop of Skálholt had some of the most obviously valuable manuscripts, such as the *Flateyjarbók* and the *Codex Regius*[19] ('Royal Codex') sent back as a present to the Danish king, Frederick III, whose interest in Norse antiquities was well known. By the end of the century, collectors had begun to buy up large quantities of saga manuscripts in Iceland; the most prolific of them all was actually an Icelander by birth, Árni Magnússon, who was appointed Professor of Danish Antiquities at Copenhagen in 1701 and the next year was sent to establish a register of all the farms in Iceland.[20] During the ten years that this undertaking took him, Árni also acquired any old manuscripts that he found, eventually amassing some 6,000 documents, which filled fifty-five crates when he had them shipped back to Copenhagen in 1720. Tragically a fire in 1728 at Árni's home destroyed almost two-thirds of the precious volumes, although luckily the majority of the most valuable ones were saved.

By the nineteenth century, as nationalist consciousness rose, the Icelanders began to demand their sagas back, leading to a century of often bad-tempered negotiations with Copenhagen (where most of them had been housed in the National Library). The calls for the restitution of the manuscripts rose to a crescendo in 1945 at the time of Icelandic independence, and in 1961 the Danish parliament finally passed a bill allowing for their repatriation. Even then, a variety of legal obstacles got in the way and it was not until 1971 that the first two manuscripts were returned. In a symbolic gesture, the ones chosen to make the first return journey were the *Flateyjarbók* and the *Codex Regius*, the very ones that had been the first to be taken to Denmark. As an indication of the strength of feeling regarding the whole matter of the return, the flag at the National Library in Copenhagen was flown at half-mast when they left, while the handover ceremony in Reyjkavik was broadcast live on national television. Once begun, the handover process was extremely drawn-out, with the last of the manuscripts only being released in 1997. Even then a few of the most valuable works, such as the *Heimskringla*, were retained in Copenhagen. And those Icelandic manuscripts that had found their way to countries other than Denmark remained firmly where they were.[21]

Although the family sagas, if read too literally, give an impression of a feud-riven land where security was only won at the point of a sword, while the *Íslendingabók* is all too brief in its treatment, these sources are sufficient to construct a fair idea of the unique society that the Vikings built in Iceland. As refugees from the oppressive rule of Harald Finehair – if the picture that many of the sagas are keen to paint is to be believed – the settlers of Iceland were none too keen to exchange one form of tyranny for another, and ended up establishing a decentralised system with no king – or even any other executive authority – a system of governance that has become known as the 'Icelandic Commonwealth'. Astonishingly this entity (also known as the 'Free

State') managed to survive for three and a half centuries with just a judiciary and a legislative arm, thereby entirely discarding the executive, one of the three pillars which modern state theory holds to be indispensable.

To what extent the family sagas are to be taken as historical documents has been much debated. Whilst few would deny that the precise course of events depicted within them has at the very least been embellished – if not created – by the process of composition and transmission, scholarship on the sagas was for long dominated by the 'bookprose' school, which held that they had existed from the start in written form. The most prominent proponent of this view, the Icelandic diplomat and historian Sigurður Nordal,[22] considered that they held no historical value and that little could be learnt of the social context of Viking-Age Iceland from their study. Yet this is nowadays seen as somewhat extreme. Even if, for example, the account of the battle of 'Vinheiðr' in Egil's Saga cannot be taken as a literal description of the Battle of Brunanburh in 937 between Athelstan of Wessex and a Viking-Scottish alliance, the sagas certainly do have a lot to tell us about how Icelandic society worked, the interplay of law and power, and how a medieval society with no temporal overlord might still function successfully.

The Icelandic settlements came to be based around farms, with no towns (or even villages) appearing before the development of the urban nucleus of Reykjavik in the thirteenth century. The earliest settlers often laid claim to vast areas – with Ingólf Arnarson's original settlement in the 870s occupying the whole of the region between the Olfus River and Hvalfjord, while Skalla-Grím (the father of the hero of Egil's Saga) took extensive lands in Myrasysla. Later arrivals apparently sent grumbling messages back to Harald Finehair that this excessive land-grab left them little room in which to settle, and the king resolved the dispute – according to the Landnámabók – by decreeing that no one could claim more land than he could mark off the boundaries of with signal fires during the course of a single day.[23]

Harald's decree was either ignored or came too late, for by 930 all the land in Iceland had been settled, or at least fully claimed (more farms were built in the eleventh century, but they were established on land that already belonged to someone else). The Landnámabók records that the last area to be taken was the land between Hornafjörd and Reykjanes, because the turbulent sea conditions meant there was no good harbour and so landing ships there was fraught with peril.

The first settlers came largely from Norway, and particularly from its western regions, if the evidence of the *Landnámabók* is to be believed.[24] The unique nature of Iceland as an isolated society into which, until recently, there was relatively little new immigration after the end of the Viking Age has meant that it has become something of a laboratory for the application of new techniques in DNA analysis. Studies of mitochondrial DNA (mtDNA) – which is passed down exclusively through the female line – have revealed a high level of Celtic genetic material in the modern Icelandic make-up. This may indicate that a substantial proportion (if not the majority) of the women who took part in the initial settlement were of Celtic, most probably Irish, origin.[25] The life of Aud the Deep-minded, the matriarch of the Icelandic *landnám*, exemplifies this trend. The daughter of the Norwegian nobleman Ketil Flatnose, she married Olaf the White, the Norse ruler of Dublin. After his death she and her son Thorstein left for the Hebrides, until Thorstein's death led Aud to move to Orkney and then to the Faroes en route to a new life in Iceland, where she arrived around 895. The *Laxdaela Saga* specifically says that she took with her a number of bondsmen captured in raids around Britain, and her entourage must surely have included women who had come with her from Ireland or been taken captive during the sojourn in Scotland.

Iceland was a very conservative society, largely self-sufficient and with an abundance of sheep providing ample wool for export. The Icelandic homespun wool cloth, or *vaðmal*, was highly valued by Norwegian merchants and helped pay for the luxury goods demanded by Icelandic chieftains, which could not be produced on the island. The predominance of pastoral farming would later have serious ecological consequences, because overgrazing by sheep and cattle stripped the vegetation binding together the precious topsoil. Whereas at the time of first settlement Iceland had possessed some trees, by the tenth century almost all had been cut down for firewood or building material, meaning that severe erosion set in, quickly reducing the overall fertility of the island. It also caused the Icelanders to become dependent on driftwood carried by the ocean currents from Siberia, which was rarely of good enough quality to build ships, though adequate for limited use in housing[26] and as fuel. It became so valued that the rights to this 'driftage' became an important source of income and the subject of bitter legal disputes.

The erosion of productive land in fact seems to have lessened somewhat in the twelfth and thirteenth centuries. It then became much worse in the sixteenth century, contributing to several famines on the island and also to the near-lunar landscape of large parts of Iceland away from the coast, where the almost total absence of vegetation gives the interior the appearance of an alien desert.

At the heart of Icelandic society, and probably forming the largest group (just as in Norway), were the free farmers. Unlike in Scandinavia, this class did not owe formal allegiance to any superiors and certainly not to a monarch. There was, however, a category of 'big men' who rose above the ranks of the regular farmers. These *goðar* (singular *goði*) acted as a focus for the network of loyalties that bound Icelandic society together (and may have performed some religious function in pre-Christian times). The office or power a *goði* held was called a *goðorð*. They competed for the allegiance of the free farming community, persuading or inducing them to become the *thingmenn* (or followers) of the *goðar*. They did not, however, have a precise territory within which their writ ran (this depended on who their *thingmenn* were at any one time). Nor did they exercise the same degree of control as barons or kings elsewhere, as any one of their followers had the legal right to withdraw his allegiance and declare himself to be 'in *thing*' with another *goði*. Those chieftains who had the most *thingmenn* held the greatest sway when it came to lawsuits – since the swearing of oaths by a large number of followers was given consideration in deciding the merits of cases – or in other discussions at the Althing, the national assembly.

The system was relatively meritocratic, and a successful or ambitious farmer could become a *goði* by dint of attracting a large enough following of *thingmenn*, an avenue for social advancement that only became blocked in the thirteenth century when the Icelandic Free State began to fall apart. The *goðar* also acted as a brake against the dangerous tendency of blood-feuds to escalate out of control. A person who felt aggrieved could approach a *goði*, even a different one from the one with whom he was 'in *thing*', and ask him to act as his advocate in a case, pleading in front of the assembly (or informally persuading the other principals in a case to come to a settlement). In exchange for this intervention, the *goði* might receive the promise of a favour returned or *saemd* ('honourable recompense'), which might be the very property that was under dispute. The system could thus exert a great deal of pressure on two sides in a dispute to settle, and even provided a means to de-escalate feuds by the negotiated payment of compensation to the aggrieved party.

The sagas provide a far more profound feeling for early Icelandic society than the bare history and constitutional account can ever do. They give a vivid (and sometimes misleading) sense of real events unfolding, accentuated by the organic links between the stories and elements in the landscape that can still be experienced today. Whilst it has been said that the saga description of the landscape around Njál's farm at Bergþórshvol where he was dramatically burnt to death was clearly written by someone who had never seen the area, it is still possible to drive past Gunnarsholt, the place where, in *Njál's Saga*, Gunnar ambushed Starkað and Egil in a feud that began after a dispute over a horse-racing match.

In the saga Gunnar's opponents advance boldly, but he has been alerted to their presence and begins to pick them off even before they can reach him:

Starkað now urged his men on, and they advanced upon the three on the headland. Sigurd Hog-head was in the lead; with a thin round shield in one hand and a hunting-spear in the other. Gunnar sighted him and shot an arrow at him; Sigurd raised his shield when he saw the arrow curving high, but the arrow went right through the shield, pierced his eye, and came out at the back of his neck. That was the first killing.[27]

The slaughter continues at close quarters and, in heroic-saga style, Gunnar and his brother Hjort despatch one after another of their opponents, at little cost to themselves:

Bork and Thorkel ran forward, ahead of Thorgeir. Bork struck at Gunnar, who parried so strongly with his halberd that the sword flew from Bork's grasp. Then Gunnar noticed Thorkel on the other side within sword-reach; he pivoted on one foot and swung his sword at him. The blow fell on Thorkel's neck, and his head flew off.

In the end, however, Hjort is killed towards the end of the fight, making it a bitter victory indeed for Gunnar:

> Hjort had already killed two men. The Easterner rushed at him and struck him full in the chest, killing him instantly . . . In all fourteen of the attackers lost their lives in the battle, and Hjort was the fifteenth. Gunnar rode home carrying Hjort on his shield, and raised a burial mound over him.

Not far from the road, at a ford in the river, is a huge boulder that is said to be the point at which Gunnar made his stand. Close to this lies a burial mound in which it is said the remains of three men were found, one of whom wore an archer's finger-ring carved with a deer. It may be just coincidence, but the name of Gunnar's brother, Hjort, means 'deer' and so it is tempting to believe that this is the site of the ambush and that one of the men buried there really is the person whose death is recounted in *Njál's Saga*.

Similarly, at Hlídarendi, south-east of Reyjkavik, an old farm building sits atop a hill with commanding view of the wide plain below. From here Hallgerð, Gunnar's wife, is said to have spotted Njál's slave cutting wood on disputed common land and sent out her steward to kill him. It is hard to know, surveying the scene today, whether the story reflects a real event or whether the landscape itself suggested the story and that, in the saga-composer's mind, the two elements fused together.

Other features of the sagas reflect a less honourable side of Icelandic society. The most severe sanction available to Icelandic courts was the imposition of outlawry, which meant expulsion from the island. There were two forms of this punishment: *fjörbaugsgarðr* or 'lesser outlawry',[28] which imposed exile from Iceland for three years (as well as confiscation of property); and the more severe form, *skóggangr* or full outlawry, which involved permanent expulsion (and which could be imposed as a sentence in itself or if a man condemned to lesser outlawry failed to depart from Iceland). A full outlaw faced grave dangers: no one was allowed to offer him shelter or to help him to leave the island and he could be killed with impunity, if apprehended. In certain cases, however, the court would rule that the outlaw could be allowed to leave Iceland unhindered and could not be killed as long as he did not stray from the road, or stop for more than a certain number of nights on his way to take ship abroad.

A group of the family sagas have outlawry at the heart of their plots. In *Gisli's Saga*, perhaps the greatest of them, the main protagonist suffers a sentence of outlawry for killing Thorgrim, whom he suspects of murdering his friend Vestein. Gisli goes on the run, but is constantly plagued by bad dreams, which sap his strength ('I have two women who are with me in my dreams,' he answers; 'one is good to me, but the other tells me naught but evil, and her tale is every day worse and worse').[29] Tormented by these nightmares, Gisli moves from hideout to hideout until finally he becomes terrified of the dark and, in a weakened state, is cut down by his opponent Eyjolf, but not before killing eight men in a heroic last stand.

Many outlaws did not have the resources or, like Gisli, the wish to leave Iceland. These men took to the more inaccessible regions – of which there was no shortage – where they turned to banditry for survival. Around 40 miles to the north of Borganes in western Iceland one such hideout can still be visited. Set in a barren lava plain on which little grows save lichen, undisturbed on the lava rocks, giving the landscape an unhealthy sickly-green hue, Surtshellir is named for the giant in Norse mythology who will set the world afire with his flaming sword at Ragnarök, the final battle between the gods and the forces of darkness.[30] It is an apt metaphor for a cave system created by the intense heat of volcanic action. The more than 2-mile network of tunnels includes ample refuges for would-be bandits to conceal themselves in, amongst its stalactite-adorned and boulder-strewn passages. The caves were formed by an eruption around 900 and, during the time when they formed a bandit refuge, the rocks themselves may still have been warm from the residual volcanic heat. As early as the composition of the *Landnámabók* in the twelfth century the cave system was identified as the haunt of two brothers, Thórarinn and Auðunn Smiðkelssynir, and their band, who terrorised the surrounding region until eighteen of them were killed by neighbouring farmers in an ambush.[31]

Across one side of the largest chamber within the complex lies the *Beinahellir* ('Bone Cave'), named for the large quantity of animal bones once found there, which have long since disappeared. Across the other side of the vast cave hall is a section known as the 'Fortress', accessible only by a near-vertical slope, where a determined outlaw could defend himself against a multitude of attackers. At the back of this sits a rough circular drystone wall and a fireplace. Here there was a midden, and it seems to mark the spot where the medieval bandits took their meals, carefully crushing the bones into small pieces to extract the maximum amount of nutritious marrow from them. When the Icelandic Nobel laureate Halldor Laxness visited the caves in 1969, the pile they had left hundreds of years before was more than 3 feet deep. Now only a few scattered bones remain, trodden into the cave floor, a faint reminder that Iceland's outlaws did not exist only in stories. Laxness had a radiocarbon dating done on a fragment of cow bone that he collected here, but the calibrated date this provided was not terribly informative, yielding a range between 870 and 1260, a span that covers the entire period of the Settlement and Commonwealth.[32] A subsequent analysis performed in a 2001 excavation in the caves gave a date of 690–960 for the bones in the midden and, operating on the presumption that the use of the cave must post-date the 870 settlement of Iceland, this narrows the outlaw occupation to 870–960. To judge from the bone fragments examined in 2001, the bandit's diet was quite eclectic, including sheep (which made up 64 per cent of the total), cattle (just over a quarter) and horses, pigs and goats, which accounted for the rest. Interestingly, the outlaws had no taste for (or no access) to fish, as no such bones were found.

The cave also has a more grizzly story attached to it: in the *Sturlunga Saga* Sturla Sighvatsson[33] takes Snorri Sturluson's son, Oraekja, prisoner in 1236. He then transports the captive nearly 20 miles from Reykholt to Surtshellir, where he is said to have blinded and then castrated the helpless Oraekja 'on top of the fortress', which could well be a reference to the cave within Surtshellir.

At the opposite end of the judicial scale to the Surtshellir outlaws were the thirty-nine *goðar* who, according to the *Grágás*, the earliest extant Icelandic law code, held the right to preside at the annual spring assemblies in each region (known as *várðing*). They also brought lawsuits on behalf of their *thingmenn* and were collectively responsible for enforcing court judgements, as there was no traditional executive authority. The only *things* known for certain to have existed before 930 were regional ones (at Kjalarnes and Thórsnes), but after this the Icelanders began to experiment with a more centralised institution. It is probably no coincidence that this development occurred at about the time that the island became fully settled, when legal disputes over ownership – and the bloodshed that might ensue – were becoming a serious problem.

The setting up of a pan-Icelandic assembly came about as a by-product of the desire to establish a legal system that would bind the whole of the island. A man of Norwegian origin named Úlfjotr, who had acquired a farm at Lón in eastern Iceland, was despatched back to his native land, where he is said to have spent three years compiling a new law code for Iceland – the one he came up with was largely based on the Gulathing Law of Norway, a code that was in force in the western Norwegian provinces of Hordaland, Sogn and Firðir.[34] On Úlfjotr's return to Norway, he also advised on the establishment of a central assembly, the Althing.

The foundation of the Althing in 930 gives Iceland a good claim to having the world's oldest parliamentary assembly (although in 1799, during the time of Danish sovereignty, the Althing was moved to Reykjavik, and in 1800 was abolished altogether and not re-established until 1844, meaning, some argue, that it is not the oldest *continuous* parliamentary assembly).[35] The place chosen for the assembly lay on what is now known as Thingvellir ('Thing Plain' next to the Öxará River, near the Reykjanes peninsula). The location is spectacular: a massive cleft in the ring of hills at the back of the plain has been caused by the movement of one of the Earth's tectonic plates, which cuts through Iceland (and is the cause of the country's high level of volcanic activity). To here, for two weeks each June when the days were at their longest, *goðar* and their *thingmenn* trekked from all over Iceland. The journey might take several weeks from the most remote parts of eastern Iceland and, on their arrival, the groups established themselves in booths – turf shelters, which they returned to year after year and roofed over with homespun cloths. The sagas are full of the plots and confrontations that took place around the booths, and the slight remains of some can still be seen beside the Thingvellir cleft – little raised mounds in the ground, which retain hardly a ghost of the great events they have witnessed, such as the legal battle recounted in *Njál's Saga* between the sons of Njál and Flosi, whose kinsman Höskuldur the Njalssons had murdered.[36] With the hundreds of followers who accompanied the chieftains and those who came to set up stalls to peddle food, ale or simply for the match-making possibilities opened up by such a huge gathering, the Althing must have had more the air of a massive open-air festival than the sombre legislative gatherings of modern parliaments.[37]

Although in theory the chief official of the Althing was the *allherjargoði* ('supreme chieftain'), in reality his role was confined to the formal opening of the assembly and establishing the boundaries of the assembly's ground.[38] The centrepiece of the Althing site was the *Lögberg*, or Law Rock, from which the assembly's most important member, the *lögsögumaðr* or Lawspeaker, would annually recite one-third of Icelandic laws from memory. The reason for this was that, at least until 1117–18, the laws were not written down and relied, like the sagas, on oral transmission.[39] By the end of his three-year term in office, therefore, the Lawspeaker would have publicly declaimed the entire law-code of the Commonwealth. The practice was discontinued in 1262 once Iceland became formally a part of the Norwegian crown (after which, even though Iceland had a law-code, its terms were dictated by the Norwegian king). As a result of its long disuse, it is no longer even clear where the *Lögberg* stood. Candidates include a ledge up against the rock face at the back of the cleft and a flat shelf at the top of a large mound in front of the fault line (the place where, presumably for ease of access, a large flagpole has been planted by the Icelandic authorities to mark the spot).

Another key feature of the Althing was the meeting of the *lögrétta*, or law council. This was composed of the forty-eight *goðar* who were obliged to attend the assembly, each accompanied by two advisers. They sat on three rings of benches on the grassy slope in front of the Law Rock: the advisers on the top and bottom ranges, the *goðar* themselves occupying the middle set. Here they discussed any new laws that might be needed or the amendment of old laws, calling on the Lawspeaker when needed to advise on the exact wording of the current legislation. It was a very public form of law-making, but it avoided disputes about what had been agreed or who had spoken in its favour.

The Lawspeakers, although they had no executive authority, acquired great prestige through their tenure of the office, and the names of successive occupants were remembered right from the time of Ulfjotr (who became the Althing's first Lawspeaker). By the 950s, however, the system was beginning to break down, aggravated by a crisis brought on by a serious dispute between two of the leading chieftains of the time, Thórðr Gellir of Hvammur and Tungu-Oddi from Breiðabólstaður.⁴⁰ The case had to be referred back to the Althing because the participants did not consider that they would get a fair hearing at local assemblies (as they came from outside the *thing* district). To resolve the issue, the country was then divided into four Quarters, with three assemblies in each (except in the North Quarter, which was allocated four). These each had a court that routinely tried cases, giving access to locally administered justice. Alongside these were courts for each Quarter held at the Althing, to which anyone who felt he was not (or would not be) treated justly by the local assemblies could bring his case.⁴¹

The final major change to the constitutional structure of the courts and the Althing came while Skapti Thóroddsson was Lawspeaker (a position that he held for twenty-six years from 1004 to 1030, the longest tenure of the office by anyone in Icelandic history). Early in his Lawspeakership, Skapti established a Fifth Court to act as a final court of appeal. Judgements in the four Quarter courts at the Althing had had to be practically unanimous, and so a large number of cases had become stalled, and the institution of majority voting in the new Fifth Court was designed to bypass these deadlocked situations.⁴²

The *goðar* who played such a key part in the proceedings of the Althing also had a central role in the pre-Christian religion of Iceland. The office of the *goði* may originally have been connected with the obliga- tion to keep up a temple, while the *Landnámabók* mentions several people whom it refers to as 'priests', one of whom, Jörund, is said to have carried fire around the boundary of a piece of land he was claiming, which he then dedicated to the temple. Similarly, it mentions the payment of tolls by people to temples, which it likens to the Christian practice of paying tithes to churches. The *Vápnfirðinga Saga* also gives the name of a priestess, Steinvör, who presided over a major temple that received large quantities of such temple-tolls each year.

Although there were Christians among the early settlers of Iceland, including a few prominent ones such as Aud the Deep-minded, their numbers and influence seem to have been limited. Their adherence to Christianity may also have been somewhat conditional, as exemplified by Helgi the Lean, who settled in Eyhafjördur and who is said to have 'believed in Christ but invoked Thor when it came to making voyages and facing difficult times'.[43] During the late tenth century Christianity gained increasing acceptance throughout the Viking world, a development promoted by the conversion of King Harald Bluetooth in Denmark around 970 and by Olaf Tryggvason (995–1000) and Olaf Haraldsson (1015–28) in Norway.[44] This was a development that touched Iceland, too. Around the 980s, a series of Christian missionaries made their way to Iceland, beginning with Thorvald Kodransson (nicknamed 'The Far Traveller'), who journeyed there in the company of a Bishop Frederick for whom he acted as interpreter (as the bishop, who was probably German and had been despatched by Archbishop Adaldag of Bremen, spoke no Norse). The pair met great resistance to their proselytising and were viciously lampooned, including one scurrilous verse which suggested that Thorvald had fathered nine children on Frederick. Such libels were a serious matter and the Icelandic law-code prescribed banishment for the author.[45] The enraged Thorvald did not wait for justice to take its course and killed the two people responsible for the poem, and for this hardly Christian act he and the bishop were driven out of Iceland.

The next missionary attempt in Iceland was sponsored by Olaf Tryggvason soon after he came to the Norwegian throne in 995. Having compelled his own subjects to accept Christianity, he then proceeded to try and force it on all the regions of the Norwegian diaspora. He despatched Stefnir Thorgilsson to do his will in Iceland, but this new missionary implemented his brief in a very harsh way, breaking into pagan temples and smashing large numbers of idols. It may have been no more than his seventh- or eighth-century predecessors had done in Anglo-Saxon England or Frisia, but the reaction in Iceland was to expel him and to pass a law at the Althing, which called upon the community to take legal action against any Christians within their own families who might blaspheme against the old gods.[46]

Undeterred, in 998–9 Olaf sent a third missionary, called Thangbrand. He was rather more successful, baptising several prominent men, including Hall Thorsteinsson of Siða and Gizur the White. Some of Thangbrand's missionary techniques, however, were every bit as unorthodox as those of his predecessors. In response to a libellous verse about him composed by a certain Vetriliði, Thangbrand simply slew the poet. Predictably, Thangbrand was forced to return to Norway, where he delivered a scathing account of the Icelanders' recalcitrance in refusing to abandon paganism. Evangelisation having failed, Olaf Tryggvason turned to more forceful measures and banned Icelanders from trading in Norwegian ports, dealing a severe economic blow to the island. He also took hostage any Icelanders of good family who happened to be in Norway and threatened to kill them if their families did not convert to Christianity.

The Christian faction in Iceland was emboldened by such forceful sponsorship and, at the 999 Althing, their chieftains effectively seceded rather than engage in the heathen oaths and sacrifices that would normally have been required of them. At the start of the next summer, one of the most prominent of their number, Gizur the White, went to Norway with his son-in-law Hjalti (who had been sentenced to exile for composing a blasphemous verse against the goddess Freyja). The pair succeeded in persuading Olaf to release the Icelandic hostages in return for a promise to exercise their influence to induce their countrymen to accept Christianity.[47]

There then unfolded one of the most dramatic episodes in Iceland's history. Gizur and Hjalti arrived back in Iceland towards the end of summer 1000, just when people were setting out for that year's Althing. It was imperative that they reach it before proceedings began (to avoid a judgement against them being made in their absence), but the folk of some of the districts they travelled through refused to lend them horses. Gizur sent word ahead to his supporters that they were to gather together and meet him, since he had received word that the leading pagans were planning to keep his party from the Thingvellir by force. With these reinforcements, Gizur and his allies rode fully armed onto the Assembly Plain, there to face off against an equally threatening force of the supporters of paganism.

It looked as if there would be an appallingly bloody confrontation at the assembly. With a typically Icelandic urge towards compromise, however, immediate hostilities were averted and the two sides retired, returning the next day to hear their respective leaders give speeches before the Assembly. After Gizur and Hjalti had put their case from the Law Rock, and the advocates of paganism had done the same, the assembly rejected the Christian case and each side declared itself 'out of law' with the other, raising the spectre that the Althing might end in violence and that Iceland would break apart into heathen and Christian Commonwealths.

Fortunately, calmer counsel prevailed and the Christian leader, Hall of Síða, persuaded the Lawspeaker, Thorgeir Thorkelsson, to arbitrate on the case. It was a shrewd move as Thorgeir was a pagan and presumably his judgement in the matter would be more likely to be accepted by the non-Christian side. There have been suggestions that Hall bribed Thorgeir with money that he had received from Olaf Tryggvason, but the sources on whatever negotiations (or bribery) went on behind the scenes are not decisive.[48] Thorgeir is said to have retired to consider matters to his booth, where he spent the rest of the day and entire night sheltering 'under his cloak'. Exactly why he adopted this apparently extraordinary posture is not clear, but it is possible that it is a reference to some kind of shamanic trance[49] in which he would receive the answer to the terrible dilemma he faced.

The next morning Thorgeir summoned everyone to the Lögberg. He began his speech by emphasising the perils of Icelanders having more than one law or, as he put it, 'if we divide the law, so we will also divide the peace'. He continued that both sides had agreed to adhere to whichever law (be it pagan or Christian) that he decided should prevail. If the pagans in the excited throng gathered before the Law Rock were expecting that Thorgeir (one of their own, after all) would decide in their favour, they were to be disappointed. Instead, he pronounced that henceforth all Icelanders would be Christian and those who had not received baptism must accept it as soon as possible. He added a series of minor concessions, possibly intended as a sop to the more extremist pagans. The exposure of unwanted babies – allowed under the heathen laws – was still to be permitted; the eating of horse-flesh should continue to be sanctioned; and sacrifices to the heathen gods were still to be permitted, as long as it was done in private. The last was probably the most important concession, but, deprived of its public face, paganism was bound to wither away to a set of folk beliefs – just as it had ultimately done after Constantine the Great enacted the toleration of Christianity in the Roman empire in 313.[50]

There was a certain amount of grumbling, and many people refused to be baptised at the Althing, claiming that the waters of the Oxara River were far too cold. Instead they insisted that their conversion take place at the hot springs at Reykir in Lundar-Reykjadalur.[51] Ironically, Olaf Tryggvason died soon afterwards at the battle of Svold[52] and Norway temporarily reverted to paganism. Yet despite the loss of its most forceful champion, Christianity had come to Iceland to stay. Initially, the island had to make do with itinerant bishops, such as Bishop Bernhard Vilrádsson, whom Olaf Haraldsson of Norway sent over around 1020. Leadership of the Church in this period instead effectively devolved to the *goðar* and other chieftains, many of whom built small churches on their lands.

A number of other 'missionary bishops' spent time in Iceland in the eleventh century, the most enduring of whom were the Englishman Bishop Rudolf, who spent nineteen years there from 1030 to 1049, and Bishop Bernhard (a Saxon), who served an equally long stint from 1048. The Icelanders were not particularly happy with this succession of itinerant bishops, most of whom did not even speak Icelandic and whose behaviour was sometimes unexpected. Bishop Heinrik, who lasted for just two years in the 1060s, eventually became Bishop of Lund, where he died after a drunken binge. Finally the *goðar* resolved that Iceland must have its own permanent bishop and selected one of their own to fulfil that role. Ísleif was the son of Gizur the White, one of the most prominent Christian chieftains at the time of the conversion, and had been educated at a monastic school in Germany. As an ordained priest and the son of one of Iceland's most important families, he neatly combined an appropriate level of clerical learning with membership of the Icelandic ruling class. Ísleif was elected unanimously at the Althing meeting in 1055 and then travelled to Europe to seek recognition of his office. The handily impressive gift of a live polar bear from Greenland smoothed his way with the German emperor Henry III, who allowed him to travel on to Italy, from where, after an audience with Pope Victor II, he was sent to Bremen to be consecrated (which caused some diplomatic difficulties as King Harald Hardrada of Norway did not recognise the authority of the Bremen see).

On his return, Ísleif chose his father's property at Skálholt in southern Iceland to be his episcopal seat, and from there made steady progress in establishing the Church, despite difficulties such as the failure to establish a system of tithes and the unspecified 'abominable acts' which, according to the *Bishops' Saga*, were committed by some of his flock.[53]

When Ísleif died in 1080 he was replaced as bishop by his own son, Gizur.[54] His was one of the most successful episcopacies in Iceland's ecclesiastical history and in 1097 he managed to push through the payment of tithes, which established the Church on a firm financial basis. The survey in 1095 of the country's farms, which was needed to set a value on the tithes each must pay, also acted as Iceland's first census, and established that the number of free farmers in the country was 4,560.

Skálholt remained the site of Iceland's main bishopric until 1785, when the see was transferred to Reykjavik. In the meantime, the chieftains of the Northern Quarter had begun to complain that Skálholt was too far for them to travel, and finally Bishop Gizur conceded that they could have a bishop of their own, who was based at Hólar, more than 190 miles from Reykjavik, on Iceland's north-west coast. The first incumbent was Jón Ögmundarson (who had studied at Skálholt). After a small hitch caused by the refusal of the Archbishop of Lund[55] to consecrate him – on the grounds that he had been married not once, but twice – Jón obtained a papal dispensation excusing him his marital faults and in 1106 officially took up his office. The new bishop found his diocese steeped in pagan ignorance, and he decreed that everyone must attend Mass each Sunday. During his fifteen-year episcopacy he also abolished the traditional names for the days of the week (which were based on the names of pagan gods)[56] and – doubt-less a far more unpopular measure – tried to outlaw dancing and the singing of ballads.

As the Church grew in strength in Iceland over the twelfth century, so bishops began to interfere more in the country's social system and seek to exert a greater degree of independence for themselves from the chieftains. At the forefront of this development was Bishop Thorlák Thórhallsson, a former Augustinian friar, who became Bishop of Skálholt in 1174 and tried to abolish the practice of concubinage – very prevalent amongst the noble families as a means of cementing alli-ances, short of marriage – and to outlaw divorce. His case was hardly helped by a letter from his superior, Archbishop Eysteinn of Lund, in which he accused the Icelandic chieftains of acting 'like the beasts in a farmyard' in their marital affairs.[57] This clerical activism was taken a stage further by Bishop Guðmund Arason, who became Bishop of Hólar in 1203 and succeeded – in the face of bitter resistance from the chieftains – in establishing the bishop's exclusive right of jurisdiction over his own clergy, independent of meddling by the secular aristocracy. He also travelled extremely widely throughout his diocese, blessing springs wherever he went, and engaging with acts of generosity that led to his being very popular among the common people (from which he acquired his nickname *hinn góði*, 'the good'), but which left him facing frequent financial difficulties.

Relations between the *goðar* and the Church grew so bad that Guðmund was expelled from his see several times, and in September 1208 an armed clash erupted outside the episcopal residence at Hólar involving around 700 of the bishop's followers and adversaries. Guðmund's ragtag army included two monks, forty priests as well as a leavening of beggars and other vagrants, but it was surprisingly effective and the leader of the anti-clerical party, Kolbeinn Tumason, was killed, along with several others. Another, more formidable group of chieftains then gathered in spring 1209, forcing the bishop out of his see once more. He spent two four-year periods of exile in Norway, punctuated by further violent clashes in 1222 in which Tumi Sighvatson, another anti-clerical chieftain, was killed. Matters only really calmed down in the final four years of Guðmund's episcopacy after 1233, when old age reduced his activism and calmed the resentment against him.

Among those who had taken part in the 1209 attack on Guðmund, but who in reality was rather sympathetic to the bishop and accompanied him when he was expelled from Hólar, was a young man named Snorri from the powerful Sturluson family. Born in 1179, he was to become Iceland's best-known literary figure and historian, and one of the main protagonists of the events that saw the collapse of the Icelandic Commonwealth in the mid-thirteenth century.

Snorri was fostered at an early age at the house of Jón Loptsson at Oddi in the south of Iceland. Jón was the grandson of the priest Saemund the Learned, the author of the *Historia Norwegiae*, a history of the Norwegian kings, and so it was a household in which (presumably) manuscripts concerning Iceland's early history and culture were freely available. In 1199 Snorri made a fortunate marriage alliance to Herdis, whose father Bersi Vermundarson was – with good reason – nicknamed 'the wealthy'. In 1202, when his father-in-law died, he inherited the family property at Borg (which had also been the home of Egil Skallagrimsson). Snorri made use of the leisure this gave him both to indulge in the politicking that would result in his acquisition of properties throughout Iceland and his serving of two terms as Lawspeaker of the Althing, and to engage in the literary endeavours that brought him more lasting fame.

At a time when memories of Iceland's pagan past were beginning to fade, and with it the poetic language which had drawn its roots so strongly from that heritage, Snorri was concerned that before long this skaldic lore would be lost entirely. To guard against this, he compiled the 'Prose Edda', a multifaceted work that included the *Skáldskaparmál* ('The Language of Poetry') – essentially a guide for would-be poets that included samples of the work of numerous earlier writers, the *Háttatal*, which contained examples of dozens of traditional Icelandic verse forms and metres, as well as a section with many stories from traditional mythology. Snorri also wrote the *Heimskringla*, a history of Norway from the very earliest times down to about 1175, although whether he is the author of *Egil's Saga*, as some suggest, is less certain.

By Snorri's time the balance of power between the traditional *goðar* had begun to break down. Before the twelfth century, chieftains had only held one *goðorð* at a time (or even a share of one), but from the 1100s power became increasingly concentrated in fewer hands. There arose a class of *stórgoðar* ('big *goðar*') who occupied several chieftain-ships simultaneously, beginning the establishment of geographical domains that were the nucleus of mini-states. Within these domains the *stórgoðar* often abolished the traditional local assemblies, concen-trating judicial authority in their own hands. Snorri himself acquired several *goðarð* whilst he was at Borg, and when he moved further inland to Reykholt, around 1206, he became *goði* there as well.

From around 1220 the number of domains reduced to around ten, with two loose alliances coalescing around the Sturlungas, who had close ties with the royal house of Norway, and their rivals, the Oddi family. The next forty years saw a series of vicious conflicts between the two sides, which amounted to a state of near civil war in Iceland. Pitched battles took place between large forces on a scale that had never been seen before on the island, and which ended not with a unitary Icelandic kingdom, but with the loss of its independence to Norway. The conflicts between the *stórgoðar* are chronicled in a series of sagas, which together are known as the *Sturlunga Saga*, part of

which was composed by Snorri Sturluson's own nephew, Sturla
Sighvatsson. At the same time the richer farmers developed into a
class of *stórbaendr* ('big freemen') who, tired of the bloody squabbles
between the *stórgoðar*, tended to look more and more to the Norwegian
kings as a guarantor of some kind of security.

The factions became tied up with a civil war in Norway, which
pitched King Håkon against Earl Skuli Barðarson. Snorri Sturluson, a
supporter of Skuli, found himself on the opposite side to his nephew
Sturla. Open warfare broke out in 1236 between the partisans of the
two groupings and a pitched battle at Baer in the Borgarfjörd in April
1237 resulted in a serious defeat for Snorri's ally, Thorleif of Garðar.
Snorri was forced into temporary exile in Norway, where he became
caught up in a conspiracy with Earl Skuli, who seems to have promised
him the position of 'Earl' in Iceland should he win the throne of
Norway.[58] In the meantime the Sturlungas had suffered a catastrophic
defeat in August 1238 at Örlygsstaðir, in the north of Iceland, in the
aftermath of which Sturla and his father Sighvat were killed. The battle's
victor, Gizur Thorvaldsson, was now the dominant force in most of
Iceland, and also very much King Håkon's man.

Snorri had by this time returned to Iceland, but his treacherous
dealings with Earl Skuli had become known. Skuli himself had died
in 1240 following an open rebellion against Håkon, and the Norwegian
king was determined to wreak vengeance on anyone who had
supported him, and that included Snorri. Håkon therefore sent instructions to Gizur that Snorri was to be forced to return to Norway or,
if he refused, to be killed.

Gizur gathered together a party to enforce the king's will and on
the night of 23 September 1241 rode out to Snorri's farm at Reykholt,
catching him unawares and undefended. The great poet and historian
took refuge in his cellar, but Gizur's men hunted him down and,
without even offering him the option of falling on King Håkon's mercy
in Norway, butchered him on the spot.

The other Sturlungas, however, escaped Gizur's justice and the civil
war ground on, with Iceland's largest ever battle taking place in April
1246 at Haugsnes. Increasingly, the blood-letting was weakening the
Icelandic chieftains more than solidifying their political control; in the
aftermath of Haugsnes, Gizur and his main opponent, Thórð Kakali,
turned to King Håkon for arbitration, a clear sign of the increasing

strength of Norway's hand in Iceland. By the early 1250s the Norwegian king was beginning to acquire chieftaincies in his own name, including the extensive domain of Thórð, who had been summoned to Norway and then prevented from returning home.[59] The 1250s, though, saw no let-up in the fighting, with violent incidents such as the attack on the wedding feast of Gizur Thorvaldsson's son, Hall, in 1253, in which Gizur's wife and all of his sons were burnt to death.

Chieftain after chieftain rose to prominence and then just as quickly fell. For a while it looked as if Thorgils Skarði – one of the principal *stórgoðar* who had been held hostage in Norway from 1247 to 1250, but then returned as Håkon's man – would reach a position of dominance, but in 1258 he was captured by his rival, Thorvarð, while staying in Eyjafjörður in the north-west of the island, and executed. The Norwegian king then turned to Gizur, whom he was also detaining in Norway at the time, bestowed on him the title of Earl and sent him back to Iceland in return for a promise to 'restore peace' (which in effect meant securing Icelandic loyalty to Norway). Although Gizur went vigorously about reinforcing his power-base in Iceland, he did little in practice to promote that of the king, and in 1260 Håkon despatched two envoys, Ívar Arnljótarson and Páll Linsauma, to the Althing, where they read out in public letters demanding to know why Iceland was not paying tribute to the Norwegian crown. It was clear that Gizur could not continue his ambiguous position indefinitely, and the support of the *stórbaendr* class for Norwegian intervention made his position unsustainable. So, at the 1262 meeting of the Althing, those present swore 'Land, people and tribute in perpetuity to King Håkon', with a written covenant (which became known as Gizur's Covenant) setting out more detailed conditions.

Even though it took until 1264 to secure the agreement of the leading men of the Eastern Quarter, the Icelandic Commonwealth was now in effect at an end. The terms of Gizur's covenant stipulated that each tax-payer should pay a quantity of home-spun cloth annually to the king, and that six ships were to sail from Norway to Iceland each year. The latter condition was not kept to for long, and another clause promising that the Icelanders would be allowed to enjoy 'Icelandic laws' was similarly soon breached. After 1262, the laws of Iceland were no longer determined at the Althing; the law-scrolls of the Commonwealth – which are collectively known as the *Grágás*

('The Grey Goose Laws') – became at a stroke redundant and were replaced in 1271 by a new code known as *Járnsiða* ('the Ironside Laws'). This was extremely unpopular in Iceland, as it was little more than a lightly adapted version of the Norwegian code. Fearing a revolt that might lead to the loss of his recently acquired new domain, King Magnus conceded a new code to the Icelanders, which became known as the *Jónsbók*, and which was more closely modelled on the traditional *Grágas*. Mollified, the Althing accepted the new laws in 1281 and Magnus earnt himself the title *lagabaetir* ('Law Mender'), although he did not live to enjoy the new harmonious relations with Iceland, having passed away the previous year.

By then, however, the Viking Age in Iceland was well and truly at an end. Although the compilation of the family sagas kept knowledge of the heroic traditions alive in Iceland (and in a form more complete than we have from any other part of the Scandinavian world), the island itself became something of a backwater, economically relatively weak and exercising little influence on its Norwegian overlords. Those whose ancestors had fled Norway to escape the oppression of Harald Finehair ended, four centuries later, firmly under the thumb of his royal descendants.[60]

Map 8 Viking Greenland

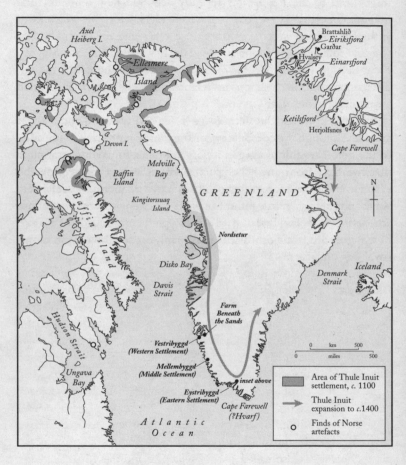

Axel
Heiberg I.

Ellesmere
Island

Devon I.

Baffin
Island

Melville
Bay

Kingitorssuaq
Island

Baffin Island

Nordsetur

Disko Bay

Davis
Strait

Farm
Beneath
the Sands

Vestribyggd
(Western Settlement)

Mellembyggd
(Middle Settlement)

Eystribyggd
(Eastern Settlement)

Hudson Strait

Ungava
Bay

Atlantic
Ocean

GREENLAND

Denmark
Strait

Iceland

N

inset above

Cape Farewell
(?Hvarf)

Inset (top right):

Brattahlið
Eiriksfjord
Garðar
Hvalsey
Einarsfjord

Ketilsfjord
Herjolfsnes

Cape Farewell

Scale / Legend:

0 — km — 500
0 — miles — 500

Area of Thule Inuit
settlement, *c.* 1100

Thule Inuit
expansion to *c.*1400

Finds of Norse
artefacts

5

The Colony that Vanished: Greenland, 1000–1450

The enormous bulk of Greenland, the world's largest island,[1] lies just 318 miles from Iceland at its nearest point. In Norse times, the voyage from Snaefellsnes in western Iceland to Hvitserk on the eastern seaboard of Greenland took only four days (assuming favourable conditions).[2] Yet this closest landfall is far from promising, for much of Greenland's 835,000-square-mile landmass is permanently covered in ice, and the east coast is particularly bleak, a white rocky wilderness almost devoid of areas suitable for the type of pastoral farming that the Norse had transplanted to Iceland.

It is possible that ships bound for Iceland were occasionally driven off-course to Greenland, but the first definite rumour of land to the west came sometime between 900 and 930, when the Norwegian Gunnbjorn Ulf-Krakason found himself swept past his intended destination and he sighted what he thought to be a series of small islands.[3] For at least fifty years no one appears to have chanced on the *Gunnbjarner sker* (Gunnbjorn's skerries) again, and their location has never been satisfactorily confirmed. Indeed, they may very well never have existed at all, being simply an optical illusion,[4] a mirage projected from the real coast of Greenland. References in the *Landnámabók* ('Book of Settlements') to Hvitramannaland (the 'Land of White Men') are even more tantalising. The Icelander Ari Marsson was said to have been blown there (possibly in the early 970s) and to have found the place (which was also called *Irland Mikla*, 'Ireland the Great') already inhabited. He spent some time there and was even baptised, suggesting to some a Norse or Celtic colony already existing in Greenland.[5] In the absence of any independent source or archaeological evidence of Ari's landfall, however, his achievement must remain in doubt, and the details of a functioning Scandinavian society suggest that his sojourn was probably closer to Scandinavia than to Greenland.

It was certainly not in search of a mirage that a hot-tempered young adventurer set sail in the summer of 982. Eirik *Rauði* ('the Red'), whose nickname may refer either to his red hair or his fiery temper, was an exile twice over. Around 970 he left Norway in the company of his father, Thorvald Asvaldsson, who had been sentenced to outlawry for manslaughter following a feud. From the family farm at Jaeren (the region around Stavanger), Eirik and Thorvald made their way to Iceland, but when they arrived, the pair found that the best land had long ago been settled and they were forced to establish a new farm-stead in the harsh terrain of Drangar in the west of Iceland. After his father's death, Eirik moved closer to the territory of his Icelandic wife's family in Haukadal, in one of the coves of the Breidifjord. The ruins of a late tenth- or early eleventh-century longhouse still lie there, sited partway up the slope of a fertile valley, but it is uncertain whether the remains are genuinely those of Eirik's farmstead (though the nearby reconstruction, its timbers built with recovered driftwood, offers a welcome respite from the wind).

It was better land, but the hot-tempered Eirik was soon drawn into another feud, after his slaves accidentally set off a landslide which destroyed the house of one of his neighbours. In the resulting fracas two of Eirik's servants were killed, and in retaliation for this he in turn slew a pair of the neighbour's men.[6] Inevitably Eirik was forced to leave Haukadal, finding refuge at Tradir on Suðurey Island off the far north-west coast of Iceland. But his penchant for attracting trouble soon meant that there, too, he was drawn into a fresh feud.

It may have been Eirik's expectation that he would not have to stay too long at Tradir that led him to lend the pillars of his high seat to Thorgest Gamli, a farmer on the mainland; but when he asked for them back, Thorgest refused. Once again, raised voices turned to violence and two of Thorgest's men were slain. Various neighbours took the part of one side or the other, and in an effort to avert further blood-letting, the local *thing* at Thorsnes outlawed Eirik, condemning him to *fjörbaugsgarðr* (three years' banishment from Iceland).[7]

With both Iceland and Norway now closed to him, Eirik decided to stake his luck on finding Gunnbjorn's skerries to the west. Exactly what point he first reached along Greenland's eastern coast is uncer-tain, but it will not have been an inviting landscape that greeted him, with its forbidding snow-clad mountains and the white desolation of the interior icecap hardly speaking of a habitable land, and he might well have been forgiven for turning right back to Iceland.

Undeterred, however, Eirik and his companions made their way southwards, finally rounding Cape Farewell and turning north near a place he called Hvarf (possibly a cape off Semersoq Island).[8] He spent some time investigating the area, later to become the nucleus of the Norse settlement in Greenland. He found the fjords with their abundant shelter for shipping and the lush expanses of dwarf willow and juniper on their inner reaches a tempting prospect for settlement, in contrast to the often barren terrain of Iceland. With an aptitude for self-promotion that was pretty much essential for a successful Viking colonist, Eirik named the place where he settled the first winter 'Eirik's Island'. The following spring, the Norsemen sailed back down the fjord (which, with similar deference to their leader, they named 'Eirik's Fjord'). Having spent a season exploring the neighbouring fjord, and finding some evidence of previous habitation in the shape of house ruins and the remains of boats – possibly evidence of the earlier Dorset Eskimo inhabitants of the region[9] – Eirik made his winter quarters at a place he named 'Eirik's Holm', further stamping his own name on the infant toponymy of the region. Once the sailing season got under way in 984, Eirik ordered his men northwards, passing by Hrafnsfjord (modern Unartoq) until further progress was hindered by ice floes, and he turned back south to spend his third Greenland winter at Eirik's Island.[10]

His three-year term of exile over, Eirik returned to Iceland in the spring of 985. With him he probably carried a precious cargo of goods guaranteed to attract interest at home: bear skins, seal and walrus hides and walrus ivory. The obvious natural riches of the new land, enhanced in the telling by Eirik's canny naming of it as Groenland (or Greenland),[11] meant that he had little trouble in attracting recruits for the establishment of a new colony. Moreover, as Eirik himself had discovered just fifteen years before, the best land in Iceland was all taken and the opportunity of being in at the beginning of an entirely new landnám (a 'taking of the land') was too good for the ambitious but ill endowed to spurn.

It was a veritable armada of twenty-five ships that set sail for Greenland in the spring of 986, mostly crewed by men from western Iceland, their vessels heavily laden with family, slaves and cattle; everything, in short, that they needed to replicate the Icelandic way of life in Eirik's new land. Unfortunately, not all of them made it; only fourteen ships reached the coast of Greenland. The rest were either driven back or sunk, possibly by a natural phenomenon known to the Norse as *hafgerðing* ('sea-hedge'), which was periodically reported in the waters between Iceland and Greenland, in which a huge wave hundreds of yards long (possibly caused by an undersea earthquake) simply swamped any vessels in its path.

A description of the terrifying spectacle was given by one of the few Christians known to have accompanied Eirik's fleet, a Hebridean Viking aboard the ship captained by Herjolf Bárðarson (later to become one of the new colony's leading men). The *Hafgerðingadrápa*, the poem he wrote about his experience, asks God to protect his path in the face of the 'Sea Breakers'.[12] A more explicit evocation from the *Speculum Regale*, a thirteenth-century instruction manual for princes,[13] describes the phenomenon 'as if all the gales and waves found in the sea have been collected into three heaps, out of which three billows are formed; these hedge in the entire sea, so that no opening can be seen anywhere; they are higher than lofty mountains and resemble deep overhanging cliffs.' The trustworthiness of the account of this sea-hedge is, however, slightly undermined by the preceding section, which discusses the mermaids to be found in Greenlandic waters; if one catches a fish and throws this at a ship, the sailors are doomed, whereas if the mermaid eats the fish, then the sailors' lives may be spared. Just like Gunnbjorn's skerries, the *hafgerðing* may have been a mirage, an optical effect caused by a temperature inversion that preceded an approaching storm front.[14] Prosaically, perhaps, it was probably this storm rather than any freak of nature that caused the loss of almost half of Eirik's fleet.

Travel to Greenland would never be risk-free, and to be shipwrecked on the eastern coast meant almost certain doom from starvation or exposure. Sometime before 1169, Einar Thorgeirson trekked across the ice-cap and perished just a day's journey from the Western Settlement, along with the two companions who had set out with him. Einar's family was clearly an ill-fated one, for his brother Ingimund, a priest, was wrecked off East Greenland in 1188, and his body was discovered in a cave some fourteen years later (where it was allegedly undecayed and found alongside a set of wax tablets, which explained the fate of the ship's crew). One man, Corpse-Lodin, even made a macabre living out of scouring the beaches, coves and caves of the East Greenland coast in search of the corpses of shipwrecked sailors, which he then boiled down to the bare bones so that these could be transported back to the settled areas for proper burial.

The most notorious wreck of all took place in 1125 when Arnbjörn Austman's two ships ran aground off the unsettled coast.[15] When a hunting party led by Sigurd Njalsson stumbled upon the scene some four years later, they found that the survivors of the shipwreck had built a large hut. Inside there was just a single man, but he had already succumbed to insanity and, panic-stricken at the sight of his would-be saviours, fled and fell to his death in a ravine. Sigurd's group collected the corpses of the others, boiled the flesh from their bones and took these and whatever cargo they could salvage (including the precious iron nails from one of the ships) to the episcopal seat at Garðar. The skeletons they handed over to the bishop for decent burial, but they kept the cargo, which they regarded as their due according to the laws of Greenland.

Unfortunately, Arnbjörn's family in Norway came to hear of the affair, and his nephew Össur set sail for Greenland the next year, together with a number of other relatives of men who had died in the wreck, intent on recovering this cargo. They pleaded their case before Bishop Arnald at Garðar, but were summarily dismissed and had to overwinter in Greenland, before the matter was heard the following spring at the Garðar *thing*,[16] the island's main assembly. They were opposed by Einar Sokkason, Arnald's strongest supporter, who attended with a large contingent of *thingmenn*. Einar vigorously opposed attempts to apply Norwegian law in the case (which, if successful, might have resulted in the cargo being returned to the Norwegians) and the *thing* once again dismissed Össur's case. In the ensuing fracas, Einar struck Össur dead, and a subsequent attempt to broker an agreement between the Norwegian traders and the Greenlanders ended in a battle at Garðar on a spit of land between Einarsfjord and Eiriksfjord, in which a large number of men (including Einar) were killed. Yet another argument then blew up over the appropriate amount of blood-money each side would pay, and the Norwegians escaped, empty-handed, back to Norway. In all, eleven men had died in the disputes over the shipwrecked cargo (which was clearly regarded as valuable enough to fight over) – vivid testimony that, whatever the theoretical mechanisms for solving disputes, bloodshed and violence were an almost inescapable part of the legal process in Viking times.

Those aboard the fourteen settlers' ships that made it intact to Greenland in 986 took full advantage of the three years of scouting which their leader had undertaken. Eirik himself established his farmstead at Brattahlid (the name means 'Steep Slope') on the upper slopes of Eiriksfjord, in the modern district of Qassiarsuk, an area that enjoyed the best grazing land along the whole coast. The leading men in the flotilla took possession of other prime tracts of land, with Herjolf Bardarson settling Herjolfsfjord and Ketil Fiflski acquiring Hrafnsfjord; the farms they established became the nucleus of the *Eystribyggd* ('Eastern Settlement' – around modern Qaqortoq). A smaller group pressed some 375 miles further west along the coast, where they founded the smaller *Vestribyggd* or 'Western Settlement' (closer to today's Nuuk). As more and more Norsemen came to join the new colony, both of these settlements expanded, with the arrival of men such as Thorbjörn Vifilsson, who had supported Eirik the Red during his legal troubles back in Iceland in 982, and who was rewarded with a tract of land at Stokkanes, which had originally formed part of Eirik's portion.[17] Contemporary sources indicate that eventually there were 190 farms in the Eastern Settlement and ninety in the Western Settlement, with a small group of twenty farms between the two, which was sometimes referred to as the Middle Settlement (although it was really an outlier of the *Vestribyggd*).

Modern archaeology, however, has revealed that there were in fact around 500 Norse settlement sites in the Eastern Settlement, and about 100 in the Western Settlement (although not all of these were occupied at the same time). A great deal of speculation has surrounded the eventual size of the Greenland Norse community at its maximum. One estimate in the 1960s gave a number as high as 37,333,[18] but the modern consensus is around 4,000–5,000, with the lowest estimate coming in at 2,000.[19] This represents only a tiny fraction of the size of the Icelandic population, which may have reached 80,000, and so, although the Greenland colony was quite capable of sustaining itself under normal circumstances, it was small enough to be very vulnerable to any kind of demographic shock.

As they had done in Iceland, the Viking settlers sought to transplant the Norse pastoral lifestyle wholesale to Greenland. They were fortunate in that sea temperatures there may have been several degrees warmer on average than today, during a period known to climatologists as the 'Medieval Warm Period'. The sea-ice did not extend as far south as it now does, leaving greater areas open for navigation and for fishing (not to mention creating slightly more clement winters, though even in Norse times the average daytime temperature would rarely have crept above 10°C in summer). The milder conditions encouraged species such as macrophyllous birch (whereas in colder climates its relative, dwarf birch, is more prevalent), while right whales were recorded in Greenlandic waters at a latitude greatly to the north of their current range. There were significant climate oscillations even within the Medieval Warm Period and the 'Little Ice Age' that succeeded it, and so the Vikings would have been subjected to cold spells even within this phase of higher temperatures. The survival of the Norse colony for more than four centuries shows that their society was resilient enough to survive these.[20]

Farms such as Eirik's at Brattahlid were generally sited on grassy slopes on the inner reaches of the fjords. The earliest farmsteads were built in the traditional longhouse style, largely from turf, for good timber was as scarce in Greenland as it had been in Iceland. The remains of what was probably Eirik's original residence were excavated in 1932, embellished with thick stone walls covered with turf strips and enclosing an area some 47 feet by 15 feet. As befitted the home farm of the colony's leader, it seems to have been a prosperous place and was provided with four barns and two byres for the cows. In general, the Norse farms on Greenland mixed the herding of cows with sheep and goats, which could be kept outside in the colder months and so required less winter feed.[21] There are indications that it was sometimes possible to grow a limited amount of corn, but Greenland-cultivated cereals never played any significant part in the diet, and instead the Norsemen supplemented it by hunting, mostly for seal and caribou. Oddly, considering the comparative proximity of the exceptionally rich fishing grounds of Newfoundland, few fish bones have been found at Greenland Viking sites. This suggests an abundant source of nutrition that the Norsemen simply ignored (although fish bones are small and dissolve easily, so their absence from archaeological layers is not an absolute guarantee that the Norse did not eat them). In a few isolated farms where the pasture was poor or non-existent, meat acquired by hunting must have formed the bulk of the diet.

As the Greenland colony developed, the longhouse form was found to be less practical for the cold winters and a new form of 'passage house' developed, with rooms set to the side of an interior corridor, an arrangement that required less heating fuel than the single large room of the traditional Nordic dwellings. The remains of an even more complex structure were found in 1990, when two Inuit caribou-hunters from Nuuk chanced upon sticks of wood poking up from the base of a river bluff. This turned out to be the remains of a Norse-era building, which archaeologists have dubbed 'The Farm Beneath the Sand'[22] because of the five-foot layer of sand which had been deposited over the site by the action of the river over the centuries.[23] They found that a very early (mid-eleventh-century) longhouse (around 39 feet by 16 feet) had been later replaced by a modest passage-house-type building with eight or ten rooms, although the Farm Beneath the Sand then became more and more elaborate during its period of occupation (which stretched to the early fourteenth century), growing eventually into a labyrinthine collection of some thirty chambers.

Excavation revealed that the inhabitants kept mostly sheep or goats, which they seem to have raised largely for milk and wool (as few bones of these domesticated animals were found in middens), while the meat component of their diet came from hunting game, principally caribou, seal and hare. The Western Settlement, in which the Farm Beneath the Sand lay, was ideally located for access to the rich hunting grounds of the *Norðsetur*, the area of the north-western coast of Greenland that began around Disko Bay. There, the Norsemen could hunt walrus, both for ivory and for the hide, which made extremely tough and flexible ropes; and narwhal, whose horns were sold to unsuspecting buyers back in Europe and the Middle East as 'unicorn' horns. Such products made up a particularly valuable portion of Greenland's trade to Scandinavia, as many of its other products, such as fish, were either little in demand there or could be obtained from far more conveniently accessible sources.

The Norsemen probably made a single hunting trip to the *Norðsetur* each year, returning to the Western Settlement before the winter closed in. In 1823 a local Inuit found a small runestone embedded inside a cairn on Kingitorssuaq Island, more than 500 miles north of the Western Settlement. The inscription stated that three Norse hunters – Erling Sigvatsson, Bjarni Thordarsson and Eindridi Oddsson – had built the cairn 'on the Saturday before Rogation Day'. The runes are generally taken to date from between 1250 and 1300[24] and, because it would have been very hard to be at Kingitorssuaq on Rogation Day (25 April) and reach the Western Settlement before winter set in (or next to impossible, if the Little Rogation Days, which generally fall in May, are meant[25]), the hunters were almost certainly forced to overwinter on the island.

A fourteenth-century account of an expedition to the Norðsetur in 1266[26] tells how the Norsemen ventured far to the north of their usual hunting grounds, but found no sign of human habitation. The church authorities then despatched another boat, which pushed even further northwards, sailing from Kroksfjordshede (at the northern edge of Disko Bay) and reaching a region in which the crew spotted many glaciers and polar bears. Although the expedition could not land, they saw some signs of a people they called skraeling, and on their return journey found further evidence of these people near Snejfeld ('snow mountain'). The term is the same one used by the Saga of the Greenlanders and the Saga of Eirik the Red for the indigenous peoples of North America.[27] Although its etymology is not entirely clear, it is most probably related to an Old Norse term meaning 'wretch'.

Who exactly were the skraelings? The Viking settlement of the Faroes and Iceland had been greatly facilitated by the absence of an indigenous population. Greenland, in contrast, had been settled previously, but the Norsemen were fortunate enough to arrive during a kind of cultural hiatus between the disappearance of a palaeo-Eskimo culture known as the Dorset and the arrival of the Inuit Thule culture from further west around 1300. The Dorset culture had spread into Greenland from North America around 100 BC and within two centuries had reached far up the eastern coast. Walrus- and seal-hunters, the Dorset people did not use the bow and arrow, but armed themselves instead with heavy hunting spears (often barbed for fishing) and closed-socket harpoons. Following the onset of a cooler climatic phase around AD 500, the Dorset retreated, until by around AD 700–900 they occupied only a restricted area around Disko Bay and in the far north of Greenland. If the Vikings encountered any of the Dorset folk, they would have been the very last of their kind.[28]

The successor culture to the Dorset in Greenland (and North America) was the Thule, which appeared at the turn of the first millennium in the north of Alaska.[29] The Thule made a number of technical advances, which allowed them to thrive in Arctic conditions. They used longer harpoon points – more suitable for hunting large sea mammals than the shorter barbs of the Dorset – and the kayak, the sea-canoe that became an indispensable aid both to hunting and transportation at sea. The Thule also used dogs and sledges and developed an underground house style with sunken passages and thick peat walls, strengthened with whalebone ribs that prevented precious heat from escaping their dwellings. They migrated in time towards Hudson Bay and then to north-western Greenland, possibly traversing Melville Bay to reach the vicinity of Upernavik and Umánaq. By the thirteenth century the Thule may have reached far enough south in the region of the Norðsetur for the expedition of 1266 to find evidence of them.

There are few further direct mentions in the sources of the skraelings until Ivar Bardarson's Description of Greenland (composed in around 1368), in which he writes that 'the skraeling have the whole of the Western Settlement, there are . . . no inhabitants, neither Christian nor Heathen'. The Icelandic Annals for 1379 mention an attack on the settlements. Whatever the ambiguity about how far the Thule Inuit had migrated in the 1260s, a century later they had clearly reached the Viking settlements, and in force.

Archaeologists have discovered a number of Norse artefacts in Inuit contexts both in Greenland and in North America that indicate a greater degree of interaction between the two communities than the bare written record suggests. Around the Disko Bay area, some twenty-three items have been found, including knives, wool shears and even a chess piece, with a further thirty-two artefacts coming from areas further north, including Melville Bay and the district of Thule. The Inuit may have acquired these through direct contact or indirectly, through trading networks, although some fifty-seven finds in Thule houses in the Western Settlement itself are believed to have been scavenged after the abandonment of the area by the Vikings in the fifteenth century.[30] The majority of Norse items found in Inuit houses were made of worked metal, a precious commodity given that the Inuit did not know how to forge iron and were otherwise dependent on iron from meteors for the creation of metal tools. Curiously, these scavenged iron pieces included a large number of broken bell fragments – unlikely items for trade – and it is not clear whether the Inuit obtained these as they occupied abandoned Norse settlements or, indeed, why they should have bothered to keep them at all.

A further range of Norse or Norse-inspired items were found on the Arctic islands of Canada and the North American mainland, which are taken either to represent items passed down along trade routes from Greenland or to be evidence of intermittent Norse contact with North America. More than fifty artefacts of Norse origin have been found on eastern Ellesmere Island in Canada, including a carpenter's plane, lumps of chain mail and ship rivets, and part of a trader's balance which was discovered on the north-west of the island. A number of statuettes and other carvings are probably Inuit representations of the Norse, identified by hair-styles such as the topknots, facial features or by clothing that is not characteristic of the Inuit, such as hooded capes. There is a certain irony in the fact that the few images we have of Viking Greenlanders come from the very people who were to supplant them.

A distant echo of Norse Greenland has also survived through a series of Inuit folk-tales collected by the Danish geologist Hans Rink in the late nineteenth century.[31] A number of these concern the Kavdunlait, which may be an old Inuit term for the Norse. In one of them, these Kavdunlait are said to have established camps at Kakortok, which were then approached by an Inuit kayaker. He was challenged by one of the Kavdunlait to strike him with his lance, but the Inuit refused to do so. Then the Kavdunlait chieftain, Ungortok,[32] intervened and ordered the Inuit to strike the Norseman, who fell down dead. Ungortok let the Inuit go, saying that he had only done as the Kavdunlait asked, but the incident led to a feud erupting between the groups when the original kayaker returned two years later and killed another Kavdunlait, this time unprovoked. In retaliation, the Norsemen slew a group of Inuit and pursued two brothers who had survived. A chase ensued, during which Ungortok cut off the arm of the younger one as he stumbled on the ice.

In another tale, the Inuit encountered the Kavdunlait for the first time and competed with them in a series of games of skill. One of the Kavdunlait challenged an Inuit to a contest in which a piece of skin was stretched over a target, which was then set on a little island offshore. The two competitors had to hit the target with an arrow, and the one whose shot struck furthest from the centre would be hurled from a cliff. The Kavdunlait took the first turn and his arrow landed close to the middle, but the Inuit's shot was truer still and landed plum in the centre. The other Kavdunlait then insisted that their compatriot stick to the rules by throwing himself over the cliff edge, and they assured the Inuit they would not seek vengeance, saying it was as much as he deserved for wagering his life in such a foolish manner. Although these tales cannot be tied to any specific date or historically verifiable event, they do indicate a memory that relations between Norse and Inuit were at best those of uneasy rivals, and that at times they descended into outright violence.

Although most of the original 400 or so Norse settlers in Greenland were probably pagans, little trace of their beliefs has survived. The sole concrete evidence comprises a few pieces of soapstone from Brattahlid and Herjolfsnes inscribed with Thor's hammers. Some memory of pagan belief is indicated by an account of how Thorkel Farserk, one of the first wave of colonists, was buried in a mound near his farm at Hvalseyarfjord, and that his spirit had been there 'round about the house, ever since'.[33] That Christianity came early is indicated – quite apart from the presence of the Christian author of the *Hafgerðingadrápa* in the *landnám* fleet – by the story in the *Saga of the Greenlanders* that Eirik's son, Leif, was sent back to Norway fourteen years after the original settlement (so about 1000) and was baptised during his stay there.

Leif Eiriksson's return home to Greenland was eventful. He was said to have been blown off-course and discovered the new territory of Vinland (in North America).[34] When he did make it back to Brattahlid, he persuaded his mother Thjodhild to embrace Christianity. Leif's father was less easily convinced, however, and when Thjodhild asked for permission to build a church at Brattahlid, Eirik consented only on condition that it was built 'a small distance' from the farm, so that he would not be forced to look at it. Far more vexing to the Brattahlid patriarch, one presumes, was Thjodhild's obstinate refusal to share the marital bed after her conversion.

The tale remained just a saga story until 1961, when work began on a new school at Qassiarsuk (the modern settlement at Brattahlid) and workmen excavating the foundation trench disturbed several skulls. Archaeologists were called in and found a small church (just 6½ by 11½ feet), encircled by a cemetery (several of whose graves the builders had disturbed). The church was built mainly of turf, with its west gable of precious wood and a small core of stone. Sited around 300 yards from where the main farm had been, it seems possible that this was Thjodhild's first church and that, tantalisingly, the graves must include both her own and that of Eirik, the original first European couple of Greenland.

In total, the remains of 144 corpses were found in the Brattahlid churchyard, of whom twenty-four were children, sixty-five adult males and thirty-nine women (a further sixteen skeletons were of adults, but the sex could not be determined).[35] The small number of child burials is surprising, as high rates of child mortality in medieval times should have meant a much higher proportion of juvenile burials, but it is possible that less care was taken over the disposal of infants' bodies and these were interred around the farms rather than receiving special burial in the churchyards. The men were not noticeably smaller than their northern European counterparts in the twenty-first century, and were on average 5 foot 7½ inches tall, although the women, at 5 foot 1½ inches, were significantly shorter.

The corpses yielded some interesting data about the health of the Norse community. Most showed little or no trace of tooth decay (signifying a diet low in sugars), while a majority of the adults suffered from degenerative arthritis, which must have been painful and, in the most extreme cases, crippling. It was not possible to determine the cause of death, save in one case, that of a man around thirty, whose skeleton had a heavy iron knife protruding from the left side of his chest. Although quite possibly a murder victim, the reason why the knife was not removed from his corpse before burial is even more intriguing than the manner of his death.

Another oddity of the cemetery was the discovery of a mass grave to the south of the church, in which hundreds of bones had been piled in no particular order, save for thirteen skulls carefully set facing in an eastward direction. Again, we will never know who the deceased were, but one fascinating notion is that they represent the interment of corpses found in eastern Greenland and then brought back by Corpse-Lodin or one of his fellow bone-collectors for Christian burial.

The tiny size of the church, which almost certainly represents the Brattahlid farmstead's private chapel, is representative of the very earliest phase in Greenland Christianity, during which there would have been very little in the way of a formal church hierarchy. The majority of the other churches that have been found on Greenland are just as small and are located close to home farms, where they would have been supervised by the local landowner. Indeed, there was clearly a shortage even of priests, and so, as a temporary measure, corpses were often buried in the ground with a stick driven in the chest. When eventually a priest did come into the locality, he would remove the stick and then pour holy water into the hole, this being adjudged as adequate replacement for a full Christian burial in hallowed ground.

Just as in Scandinavia, the Church was eager to impose discipline on its new Greenlandic converts, and the establishment of a bishopric and its obedience to the archbishopric back in Europe was a vital part of this. The Greenland Norse were left largely to their own devices for the first century or so, having to make do with the occasional itinerant or missionary bishop. The earliest recorded of these was Eirik Gnuppson Upsi (a nickname meaning 'pollock' or 'coal-fish'), who is said to have been active at the beginning of the twelfth century.[36] Eirik is a rather shadowy figure, seeming to have no fixed see or source of authority, and in 1121, according to the *Icelandic Annals*, he travelled to Vinland on some form of missionary journey and thereafter disappears from the record.[37]

That Bishop Eirik probably did not return to Greenland is indicated by the account of a *thing* summoned by Sokki Thorisson at Brattahlid in 1124, at which he expressed his desire that 'the country no longer be without a bishop'. A delegation was duly despatched to Sigurd Jorsalafar, King of Norway (1103–30). It was led by Sokki's son, Einar Sokkason, and carried with it the sweetener of a live polar bear, which was only to be handed over once the king had acceded to the Greenlanders' demand for the consecration of a new bishop.

The post of first Greenlandic prelate fell to Arnald, a simple priest, who was initially very reluctant to take the position (because of the isolation from his family and friends that it entailed), but eventually relented and was consecrated at Lund in Sweden. After being forced to spend the winter in Iceland when adverse weather penned his ship in harbour there, the new bishop arrived in his Greenland see in 1126. The site Arnald chose for his cathedral was at Garðar, centrally located in the Eastern Settlement on land that had belonged to Eirik the Red's daughter Freydis (today the settlement of Igaliku). The episcopal complex, excavated in 1926 by the Danish archaeologist Paul Nørlund, was quite substantial, with a central longhouse about 100 feet long and a grand ceremonial hall, which at some 1,500 feet square provided a disproportionate amount of entertaining space for such a far-flung location.[38] The cross-shaped church, whose foundation courses of well-dressed stone still dominate the site today, was equally grand, complete with what may have been a bell-tower to the south-east (which would make it the only such campanile discovered in Greenland).

Bishop Arnald enjoyed his position for twenty-four years, before resigning and returning home to take up the bishopric of Hamar in Norway. From then until the last known resident bishop in the late fourteenth century, all the holders of the office were Norwegian, although there were often considerable gaps between episcopacies because the great distance from Greenland to Norway and the infrequency of voyages between the two meant that news (and bishops) took time to travel. Arnald's successor Jon Knut was consecrated in 1150 and died in 1187. He was certainly in Iceland in 1186, but there is no definite evidence of him in Greenland. His successor Ingimund died in a shipwreck off the Greenland coast[39] and so the next bishop actually able to take up his see was Jon Smyrill ('Sparrowhawk') Arnason, who held the post from 1189 to 1209.[40]

It may have been under Smyrill that the Garðar church was substantially enlarged to give it its final length of 89 feet, and his *may* be the skeleton of a bishop found interred in the chancel of the church during the 1926 excavations, which was of a tall man (some 5 foot 7 inches in height) who died in middle age. On one of the man's fingers was a gold ring and at his side lay the remains of a crozier, its head intricately carved in walrus ivory – clear signs that the deceased was a bishop. But equally the dead man could be one of Smyrill's successors, such as Helge (who died in 1230), Nikolas (around 1240) or Olaf (who passed away in 1280 or 1281).[41]

Bishop Nikolas had been dead four years before Olaf was consecrated Bishop of Garðar, and it took a further year for him to reach Greenland. He brought with him an alarming message from King Håkon Håkonsson of Norway: that the Greenlanders must submit to the Norwegian crown. Håkon had been throttling the political independence of the Shetlands, Orkney and Faroes and, most importantly, seeking to incorporate the Free Republic of Iceland into his realm.[42] It is therefore unsurprising that his ambitions extended to securing Greenland as well. The Greenlanders were in no position to argue, as they were dependent on trade with Norway, and without the co-operation in some form of the Norwegian crown, the Settlements would struggle to survive. So it was that in 1261, a year ahead of

Iceland, a delegation of Greenlanders travelled to Norway and pledged that they would pay tribute, thereby acknowledging their allegiance to the Norwegian king.

It was on the basis of this agreement that Greenland remained under the Norwegian crown until 1397. When Norway was joined in personal union with Denmark under the Union of Kalmar that year, it became in effect a Danish possession. After Norway separated from Denmark in 1814, Greenland remained attached to the Danish crown (and has remained under Danish sovereignty, albeit with increasing autonomy, until the present day). Although the Norwegian crown obtained a de facto monopoly on trade with Greenland through its ability to forbid unauthorised vessels from sailing there (and by the end of the thirteenth century it had tightened its hold still further by enacting that the Greenland trade was the exclusive privilege of Norwegian merchants from Bergen), this did not mean any marked increase in the frequency with which ships made the journey. Even though agreements with the Norwegian king laid down that ships were supposed to sail to Iceland each year, there were at least four years in the fifteenth century when no ship came[43] and the voyages to Greenland would have been even less frequent. In the whole of the thirteenth century only thirteen sailings there are recorded in the sources. Although only those that were remarkable in some way, such as shipwrecks, would have been noted, even a doubling or trebling of this figure hardly amounts to regular traffic. After the wreck in 1369 of the *Groenlands Knörr*, the royal vessel that carried out the trade, the maritime connection between Norway and Greenland became even more tenuous.

What notices we do possess have an almost accidental quality about them. In 1347 a Greenland ship, which had been gathering timber in Markland (on the coast of North America), was driven on to Iceland.[44] The *Icelandic Annals* for the year are laconic, simply remarking that 'A ship came from Greenland to Straumfjord, it had sailed to Markland but had then been driven off course over the sea, with a crew of 18.' If anything, the episode shows that the Greenland Norse, although increasingly cut off from European contacts, were not turning inwards, but continued to exploit the natural resources of North America's eastern seaboard.

Almost the only description we have of conditions in

mid-fourteenth-century Greenland itself is that of Ivar Bardarson, who travelled there sometime after August 1341 (when he was provided with a permit to travel by the Bishop of Bergen). From 1349 to 1368 he acted as the episcopal *officialis* (or steward) in the interregnum before the arrival of Bishop Alf, the very last known occupant of the see actually to be resident in Greenland. At some point during his tenure, Ivar made a journey northwards to the Western Settlement and his terse but alarming report has been taken to mean that the *Vestribyggd* had already been lost. 'The Skraelings have the whole Western Settlement,' he wrote, 'but there are horses, goats, cows and sheep, all of them wild. There are no people, neither Christians, nor heathens.' An addendum to Ivar's accounts states that he was sent to expel the *skraelings* from the Settlement, but finding no one alive there, the expedition slaughtered the animals and sailed back home.

Ivar's testimony implies a sudden abandonment, with the settlement's animals left to fend for themselves. An echo of this came during the excavations of the Western Settlement, when a complete goat skeleton was found buried in the rubble of the Farm Beneath the Sand, having clearly died some time after the farm was abandoned. In contrast, another nearby farm[45] contained the skeleton of a hunting dog, with incisions in its bones suggesting that it had been deliberately butchered (and presumably its meat eaten) – a clear sign of economic distress, since such dogs were valuable and would not normally have been used for food. At the chieftain's farm in Sandnes, a further nine skeletons of hunting dogs were found beneath collapsed roofs, the dogs having probably been abandoned when the community was deserted.

Fewer walrus bones are found in the middens of the Western Settlement from the early fourteenth century, evidence that regular expeditions to the *Norðsetur* may have ceased, and that trade in the northern goods that had provided the economic lifeblood for the Western Settlement was dwindling. Living conditions were probably increasingly difficult and one bad winter could have permanently damaged the viability of the settlement. It is quite possible that by the time Ivar Bardarson wrote his report, the Western Settlement had already been partially abandoned and the Inuit attack was launched against just a few surviving farmsteads.

A further sign of trouble comes from the letter that King Magnus

Eriksson of Denmark sent in 1355 appointing a certain Poul Knudsson to lead an expedition to Greenland to preserve Christianity on the island. Although the letter has been transmitted in a very late copy and there is no evidence that Knudsson actually set out on his mission, the document does at least indicate a level of concern at the royal court that, somehow, things were not going well in Greenland.

By the time Bishop Alf arrived to take up his see in 1368, it may well, therefore, have been a shrunken one, as the colony reverted to its original core in the Eastern Settlement. The vessel that carried him was the very last official trip to Greenland by the royal *knörr*. The ship returned safely to Norway, but was wrecked off Bergen in 1369 just as she was setting out on a new trip.[46] No replacement was ever built and, though an official from the royal court was present in Greenland in 1374, it is not clear how he got there.[47] By the time of Bishop Alf's death in 1378, Greenland was, to all intents and purposes, cut off from regular contact with Europe. It is telling that, though the papacy continued to appoint titular bishops of Garðar until the death of Bishop Vincenz Kampe in the 1530s, not one of them actually visited his far-flung see.

Among the many theories seeking to explain the demise of Viking Greenland is that conflict between the Inuit and the Norsemen so damaged the remaining Eastern Settlement as to make it unviable. There is one account of such fighting between the two groups, though it is hard to say if it is an isolated incident or whether it represents a wholesale breakdown in relations. In 1379 an entry in the *Icelandic Chronicle* relates that 'The Skraelings attacked the Greenlanders, killed eighteen men and carried off two boys, whom they enslaved.' The *Historia Norwegiae* also contains a passage describing the *skraeling* as a people who, if 'struck with knives and survive, their wounds grow white without bleeding, but if the blows are fatal the blood scarcely stops flowing'.[48] Although the details are fanciful, they do betray at least a degree of ignorance and distrust by the Norse of their Inuit neighbours.

In reality, the Inuit way of life meant that the inner fjords, which the Norsemen continued to farm, were of relatively little economic value to them, as they preferred the outer fjords and open coastline, where fish and seals were far more abundant. Friction and suspicion there may have been, but outright warfare was unlikely. A more positive light is cast on relations between Inuit and Norse by the tale of Björn Einarsson Jorsalafari ('the Jerusalem Farer'), who was driven onto the coast of Greenland while returning to Iceland from a pilgrimage to the Holy Land. During his two years' enforced stay, he was appointed sheriff by the Norwegian king and rescued a young Inuit boy and girl who were stranded on a rock off the east coast. The pair – described as 'trolls' – became his servants and were so devoted to him (the girl caring for Einarsson's infant son) that when he was finally able to undertake the voyage home in 1387, the distraught Inuit cast themselves into the sea and drowned.

In the late fourteenth century relations between Greenland and the rest of the Norse world still carried on. A lawsuit heard in Bergen in May 1389 concerning the illegal importation of goods from Greenland (and Iceland) into Norway[49] indicates that, even at this stage, the Norwegian crown was keen on exerting its influence there – or at least in preventing others from profiting from its rather lax overlordship. These contacts, however, did not have long to run.

On Sunday 16 September 1408, a wedding took place in Greenland in the church at Hvalsey. The marriage being celebrated was between Sigrid Björnsdóttir and Thorsteinn Olafsson, an Icelandic sea captain who had arrived in Greenland two years before, drifting off-course from Iceland as so many had done previously. It seems to have been a perfectly ordinary occasion, with banns being read on three successive Sundays, yet it is also the very last concrete mention that we have of Viking Greenland in the written sources. We only know of its existence because the couple (and Olafsson's original travelling companions) returned to Iceland and made affidavits in 1414 and 1424 to attest that the wedding had been held lawfully and to give evidence concerning a man named Kollgrim, who had been condemned to death by burning at Hvalsey in 1407 for seducing another man's wife. Thereafter, all we have is the testimony of archaeology and the certainty that at some point after 1408, and most likely in the second half of the fifteenth century, the Norse colony in Greenland disappeared.

The story of the Hvalsey wedding carries no hint of impending disaster, but when the next known European visitors came upon the Western Settlement in 1723, they found just ruined buildings, and no sign of the inhabitants. What exactly was it that led to the contraction, and then the disappearance, of Norse Greenland? The failure of the colony has been variously blamed on the southward advance of the Inuit from the Norðsetur, leading to violent clashes; on climatic change that made the Norsemen's way of life increasingly difficult to sustain; on disease; on attacks by European pirates; or on a wholesale migration of the population to an unknown destination.

The almost complete lack of written documents from the last phases of Viking Greenland means that the full story of the end of the Settlements will probably never be known in detail, but it is likely that it was a combination of factors, rather than any single calamitous event, that brought them to an end. Puzzlingly, some of the later archaeological evidence is indicative more of prosperity than of prolonged decline. In three of the major centres of the Eastern Settlement (Hvalsey, Herjolfsnes and Garðar), great feasting halls were built in the early fifteenth century – hardly the actions of a community on the edge of starvation, or fearful of imminent invasion by hostile Inuit.

Environmental stress is a very plausible possible explanation for the collapse of the Viking colony. The period from 1250 saw a general decline in temperatures in the North Atlantic in the order of 2°C and an increase in temperature instability, which persisted until the fifteenth century.[50] The cooler climate and harsher winters that resulted may have rendered formerly marginal land unusable and pushed a community previously on the edge of starvation into abandoning its lands, although there is no evidence that the Norse Greenlanders were anything but reasonably prosperous before 1250, and Iceland, which experienced a similar climate change, suffered no such demographic catastrophe.

If climate change was not to blame, then caterpillars may have been. The larvae of one species, Agrotis occulta, have been found in fourteenth-century levels at various sites in the Western Settlement. These larvae, which tend to proliferate in the spring – just when the cattle, weak and lean from their enforced winter period indoors, emerge to find fresh fodder – can strip entire fields bare of foliage.[51] Yet while such an event may have made life on individual farms difficult, it is unlikely that, alone, it can have had much more than a slight effect on the viability of the Settlements as a whole. Far more probable is that the settlers' very way of life contributed to its own destruction. When the Vikings arrived in Greenland they found a virgin land which, though harsh, seemed more fertile than the farms they had left behind. Yet just as overgrazing contributed to loss of topsoil and erosion in Iceland, so analysis of pollen from ice-cores in Greenland[52] indicates that the vegetation that had covered the landscape at the time of Eirik the Red's arrival in 986 was gradually replaced by grass-sedge. This resulted in less available pasture for the pigs, cattle and sheep that formed an important – if far from exclusive – part of the Greenlandic Viking diet.

Although there is little historical documentation of conflict between the Inuit and Vikings, the archaeological record does show the Inuit gradually expanding southwards from their initial toeholds in the north of Greenland. The two cultures' spheres of influence probably first overlapped around 1150 in the Norðsetur, and by 1300 the Inuit had begun to settle on the margins of the Western Settlement.[53] Although the Norse artefacts found in the Inuit settlements in northern Greenland show some kind of contact between the two groups, the Vikings failed to learn critical survival techniques from the incoming group. They never adopted the Inuit *kayak* or the larger *umiak*, skin boats that got around Greenland's lack of timber and allowed fishing in coastal waters. They also did not learn the use of the harpoon, which meant they could only hunt seals such as harp seals that either came close to harbour (generally by use of lines of nets) or could be clubbed to death on the ice itself. Ring-seals, which have to be hunted at breathing holes in the ice using harpoons, are rarely found in Norse middens, indicating that the Vikings were denying themselves a precious additional source of meat, which might have made a crucial difference during especially harsh winters.[54]

The churchyard at Herjolfsnes lies at the southernmost tip of Greenland, a position exposed to the full fury of wind and water. The Viking-era cemetery there was already being washed away into the sea by the time it came to the attention of Danish archaeologists in the 1920s, and only a timely rescue excavation by Paul Nørlund in 1921 unearthed some of the most important testimony that we possess of the last stages of the Eastern Settlement. The site had already been identified as promising in 1840 by the owner of a local trading post, O. Kielsen, who come across pieces of ancient cloth from a man's

smock at the water's edge and directed a dig in the churchyard –
without, however, finding anything of further interest.

Nørlund's excavation was far more fruitful and he discovered the
remains of dozens of fourteenth and fifteenth-century Greenlanders
whose funeral garments had been preserved by the frozen soil in
which their corpses had been interred. These included no fewer than
thirty dresses, woven from a four-threaded twill, most of them with
narrow waists, long sleeves and low necklines, which were very similar
to fourteenth-century clothing styles found in Scandinavia. Some of
the dead had been buried with their best hats, most remarkably a type
of hood known as 'liripipe' from the long cloth ribbon that hung
down the back, making the wearer look like a rather self-conscious
jester. These could also be wrapped around the wearer's face to give
extra protection against the cold, giving a positively outlandish appearance. Liripipes were the height of fashion in fourteenth-century
northern Europe, where they had become associated with dandyish
tendencies. Their appearance in Greenland shows that, even in their
furthest North Atlantic outpost, the Norsemen were well aware of
the latest styles back in Scandinavia and were keen to ape them. So
much so that in 1357 the Skálholt priest was forced to issue an edict
forbidding the wearing of liripipes more than a cubit long.[55]

A few of the items of clothing are definitely of fifteenth-century
date. A man's overgarment with button-holes at the front must be
later than 1400, since buttons did not come into general use until then.
A Burgundian-style cap, tall and shaped like a stove-pipe, was initially
dated to the late fifteenth century, causing huge excitement amongst
scholars, as this would have pushed back the probable date for the
end of the Eastern Settlement by several decades, but it is now generally considered to be from around 1450, the consensus date for the
disappearance of the Norse colony.[56]

The remains found at Herjolfsnes were also initially believed to
indicate a population in crisis. Although the skeletal material was in
very poor condition, measurements of the cranial size were taken to
show that the skulls of these late Norse Greenlanders were smaller
relative to those of their *landnám* ancestors and that they were thus
mentally degenerate (perhaps caused by inbreeding or deficiencies in
their diet). The skeletons were also considered to be much shorter
than their fifteenth-century cousins back in Scandinavia, a regression

explained by the worsening climate in Greenland, which led to an impoverished diet. Subsequent analysis, however, has shown that, while the Herjolsfnes skeletons were somewhat shorter on average than contemporaneous finds in Denmark, Norway or Iceland, it was not by much.[57]

On balance, the evidence from Herjolfsnes shows a community functioning pretty much normally, interring its dead with full Christian burial, able to acquire the latest fashions from Europe, and showing no evidence of nutritional crisis or any other signs of a population blighted by disease, other than the normal pattern of ground-down teeth and endemic arthritis from which their ancestors at Garðar had suffered several centuries before.

If it was not famine brought on by caterpillars or global cooling, attacks by Inuit or the mental degeneration of the population that caused the collapse of Viking Greenland, what was it that brought about its downfall? There is some evidence that as trade links between Norway and its Greenland colony faded away, so other European powers (or at least their merchants) stepped in to take the Norwegians' place. As early as 1415, Erik VII of Denmark-Norway complained to Henry V of England that English ships were sailing without permission to lands under his overlordship, a problem that was clearly not solved at the time, as it became the subject of a treaty in 1432 between the two countries, by which the English king resolved to forbid the trade.[58] The 'trading' undertaken by English seamen was in practice little different from piracy, and, although there are no records of attacks on Greenland (as, indeed, there are no records at all from this period), several raids are recorded by English freebooters on Iceland in the 1420s, and even one on Finnmark in northern Norway in 1423. The effects of even one such attack on the thinly populated Greenland coast (where, after the disappearance of the Western Settlement, the remaining Norsemen probably numbered no more than 3,000 and possibly as few as 2,000) could have been devastating. With little prospect of their victims being able to call on any kind of assistance, the pirates would have been greatly tempted to return to prey on such a soft target.

A distant echo of such an event may be found in a letter dated 1448 from Pope Nicholas V to the Bishop of Skálholt in Iceland, instructing him to send a priest to minister to the population of Greenland, which had 'been without a bishop for 30 years following the attack by the heathens, when most of the churches were destroyed and the inhabitants were imprisoned'. Although the 'heathens' blamed for the atrocity could be interpreted as Inuit, the letter could equally contain a veiled reference to English (or other European) pirates. An Inuit story collected by Niels Egede, the son of the Danish missionary Hans Egede who settled in Greenland in 1721, may corroborate this. It tells of three boatloads of foreigners who arrived from the south-west and attacked and plundered the Norse settlements, killing some of the inhabitants. Although the Norsemen captured one of the boats, the other two got away. The following year a much larger flotilla arrived, massacred large numbers of Norsemen, took some captive for resale as slaves and made off with all the settlement's cattle. Most of the surviving Norse are said to have departed by boat, leaving only a small number behind. The pirates returned again the following year, and the local Inuit, together with the few remaining Norsemen who had taken refuge with them, then fled inland. When they returned, they found the Norse farms utterly pillaged and destroyed, and thereafter they went back to the Inuit and intermarried with them.[59]

If this is true, it may be that a series of attacks by pirate-traders damaged the Eastern Settlement to the point where the survivors simply gave up and emigrated. If so, there is, unfortunately, not a shred of evidence as to where they might have gone. Obvious candidates include the North American mainland, though the reduced numbers of Norsemen would have made it little more inviting to them as a prospect for permanent settlement than it had been during the abortive attempts to colonise it in Leif Eiriksson's time,[60] and Iceland or Scandinavia itself. The idea of a more or less orderly departure is supported by the almost complete absence of precious items in the archaeological record, particularly of ecclesiastical vessels in the churches. Some more sudden catastrophe, such as plague or Inuit attack, would have left the community with no time to hide or remove their valuables.

Another possibility is of 'internal migration' to a more inaccessible spot, or of the survivors blending in with the Inuit population and in time becoming indistinguishable from them. The chimera of a hidden Norse colony located in an inaccessible part of Greenland or Arctic Canada became the driving force behind a number of expeditions from the sixteenth century onwards to locate the imagined survivors of the Viking settlements. Equally attractive to many was the hypothesis that the Norse and Inuit had simply intermarried. The Norwegian explorer Fridtjof Nansen – who in 1888 led the first expedition to cross the frozen interior of Greenland – was among the distinguished champions of this 'blond Eskimo' theory.[61] Scientific examination of the claim only became possible with the advent of DNA testing in the late twentieth century, and in 2002 two Icelandic anthropologists, Gísli Pálsson and Agnar Helgason, took samples from 395 Inuit in Greenland and northern Canada. They found no evidence of any DNA markers that would indicate Scandinavian ancestry, a stark contrast with similar studies in northern England, Scotland and Ireland.[62]

As to the date of the colony's disappearance, the testimony of the Hvalsey wedding suggests that Viking Greenland was still a fully functioning community in 1408, while the archaeological evidence from Herjolsfnes indicates that it continued in this way at least to some point between 1425 and 1450. Anecdotal reports hints at some kind of attack in 1418, with further assaults in the period after 1420, but thereafter it is hard to be conclusive. An isolated document from Bergen around 1484 mentions a brawl in which a party of Germans killed some other foreign sailors who had enraged them by boasting about the precious goods they obtained in Greenland.[63] If this is to be believed, then as late as the 1480s there was still somebody left in Greenland with whom trade could be conducted.

It is reasonably safe to presume that there still was an Eastern Settlement in the 1420s, but that by 1450 or shortly thereafter it had been abandoned. The Norwegian crown and the papacy, though, continued to act as if nothing was amiss with the Greenland colony, periodically restating their rights or appointing bishops to the phantom see at Garðar. In 1492, Pope Alexander VI nominated Martin Knudsson, a Benedictine monk, as titular bishop, including in his letter of appointment a suspiciously detailed account of the state of affairs in Greenland, stating – almost certainly correctly – that no ship had sailed there for the past eighty years, but adding that many of the inhabitants of the colony, who had been without a priest for a similar period of time, had lapsed into heathenism and that those who remained faithful had no sacred vessels or other relics of Christianity save a corporal (the cloth onto which the chalice is set during the Mass).[64]

Knudsson never sailed for Greenland, but it looked for a time as though his successor, Vincenz Kampe (appointed in 1519), might do so. Christopher Columbus's discoveries in the 1490s had become well known in European courts, and Christian IV of Denmark seems to have had designs on the former – or possibly even still extant – Norse colonies in Greenland as a springboard for Danish expansion in North America. An expedition was ordered under Søren Norby in 1520, but the luckless admiral was prevented from sailing by an uprising against Christian, who was forced to flee to Gotland.

A series of mid-sixteenth-century accounts of travels to Greenland are probably fictitious, although one of them, by 'Jon Grønlaender', who was said to have been blown off-course towards the Greenland coast around 1540, contains some fascinating details. Grønlaender is said to have seen stone-built houses and sheds for drying fish, and in one of the dwellings he came across a body, lying face down. The dead man wore clothes partly made of sealskin, and by his side lay a very worn knife. As the body was not decomposed, the man must have died not long beforehand. It is tempting to believe this is an account of the very last Greenland Viking, who lived a solitary existence, husbanding his last precious metal blade and finally dying shortly before rescue (in the shape of Jon Grønlaender) arrived.

Unfortunately, Grønlaender is probably just as much of a mirage as Gunnbjorn's skerries or the *hafgerðing*. Danish kings continued to plot expeditions to Greenland that never came to fruition, and in 1568 Frederick II even issued a letter to his imagined Greenland subjects in which he promised that royal ships would henceforth call there twice a year (and appointed Kristian Olborg as captain of the first). Yet the first concrete testimony of Greenland for 170 years comes from two English explorers, Martin Frobisher in 1578 and John Davis in 1586, both of whom seem to have landed on islands off the coast of Greenland. Frobisher even kidnapped an Inuit whom he encountered paddling a kayak, together with his wife and child.[65]

The Danish kings still entertained hopes of finding their long-lost subjects in Greenland, and Christian IV despatched three expeditions to find them (in 1605, 1606 and 1607). Although ships from the second landed on the west coast of Greenland (where they collected a quantity of what they thought was silver ore and took six more unfortunate Inuit captive), they did not find the Norse settlements. The final voyage was hampered by the persistent conviction that Eirik the Red had settled on Greenland's eastern coast and so, predictably, it found nothing.

Danish interest in Greenland waned rather thereafter, and only in the early eighteenth century did a renewed burst of activity definitively secure Danish sovereignty in the area and finally locate the ruins of the Viking settlements. In 1721 the missionary Hans Egede landed at Igdluerunerit in Godthaabsfjord as part of an effort to establish a mission station there. Egede's explorations in the interior finally brought him to the ruins of the Western Settlement in 1723, and later, as he surveyed possible alternative sites for the mission, to the broken-down remains of the Eastern Settlement. He was particularly fascinated by the shell of the church at Hvalsey, but continued to believe, despite his failure to find any descendants of the medieval Norse, that somewhere, hidden in an inaccessible spot, such a community must survive.[66] Further expeditions set out in search of the elusive Vikings led by Captain Løvenørn in 1786, the Englishman William Scoresby in 1822 and under the auspices of the Danish navy in 1828. Only a final attempt in 1883–5, which surveyed the east coast inside the ice-belt, finally laid for good the ghost of a hidden Norse colony.[67]

The search for the Greenland Vikings had gone on for four centuries, almost as long as the life of the colony itself. The debate as to what exactly caused their disappearance began almost as soon as it became clear that Eirik's descendants were not lurking in some inaccessible part of Ellesmere Island or even submerged into the Inuit gene pool. Whatever the reason for the colony's collapse, the tiny size of the community – between 2,000 and 4,000 – means that over the course of a century it would only have required a net attrition rate of ten or twenty people each year (whether by excess of deaths over births, from migration, or through attacks by slavers) to reduce the total size of the population by half.

For something like four and a half centuries the Vikings in Greenland succeeded in maintaining a fair replica of the society that they had left behind in Iceland, a free republic whose detailed history will probably for ever remain obscure. Yet for all its isolation and the mystery surrounding its demise, Viking Greenland was not the most remote of the North Atlantic colonies. That honour goes to North America or, as the Vikings named it, Vinland.

Map 9 The Viking Exploration of North America

⊙	Norse settlements
○	Finds of Norse Artefacts
→	Vinland voyages *c.*1000–1015
→	Later hunting and timber-gathering voyages, to 1347

Arctic Ocean

Axel Heiberg I.

Ellesmere Island

Devon I.

Melville Bay

GREENLAND

Baffin Bay

Iceland

Denmark Strait

Baffin Island

Disko Bay

Davis Strait

Hudson Strait

HELLULAND

Western Settlement

○ Tanfield Valley
possible Norse settlement site

Eastern Settlement

Cape Farewell

Ungava Bay

Hudson Bay

MARKLAND

Labrador

Strait of Belle Isle

○ L'Anse aux Meadows

Atlantic Ocean

Newfoundland

St Lawrence

VINLAND

Find of Maine Penny ○

Nova Scotia

Godard Point

Cape Cod

N

0	km	500
0	miles	500

6

The Search for Vinland the Good: The Vikings in North America, 1000–c.1350

Up until 1962, no area of Viking studies excited so much interest and produced so much material on the basis of so little evidence as the story of the Viking discovery of North America. The root of the problem was that the two relevant sagas, the *Saga of Eirik the Red* and the *Saga of the Greenlanders*,[1] gave clear descriptions – albeit often contradictory – of a series of Viking voyages to North America and of an attempted colonisation of the continent, and yet, despite all their stirring tales of discovery, there was no undisputed archaeological evidence that the Vikings had ever been there at all.

The accounts of the two sagas – collectively known as *The Vinland Sagas* – differ significantly, but both indicate that sometime around the year 1000 (and probably in 1001 or 1002), Vikings from Greenland sailed west and came across a new coastline, which they explored and, in subsequent years, attempted to settle. *Eirik's Saga* mentions only two voyages, while the *Saga of the Greenlanders* – believed to be the older of the two (and dating from before 1263)[2] – gives a more complex account of six exploratory sailings. According to the latter version, the North American mainland was first sighted shortly after 986[3] by Bjarni Herjólfsson who, like so many sea-captains in the sagas, was driven off-course while sailing from Iceland to Greenland, where his father had gone to join Eirik the Red's new colony.[4] Bjarni had been on a trading trip to Norway and was totally unaware that his father had emigrated. He decided to follow him, but, understandably a little hazy about the precise sailing route from Iceland to Greenland, he got lost in an extensive bank of fog and, when the mist cleared, found himself sailing along an unknown coastline, forested and punctuated by low hills.

Opting for caution, Bjarni decided against landing and pressed on northwards for two days until the landscape changed, turning flatter, but still tree-lined. His crew urged Bjarni to go ashore and take on fresh provisions of food and timber, but he refused and pushed on for three more days until the ship came to a much more forbidding land of soaring peaks and glaciers. Here, too, Bjarni would not make landfall, saying that the place was good for nothing and not even worth exploring. After a further four days' sail, their progress assisted by stronger winds, the Icelanders came to a fourth land, which looked a lot more like the descriptions of Greenland that Bjarni had heard in Iceland. By an extraordinary coincidence, he had arrived at Herjolfsnes in Greenland, the site of his father's farm, where he is said to have spent the rest of his days.

The *Saga of the Greenlanders* goes on to tell that a number of years later, Eirik the Red's son Leif went to visit Bjarni and recruited thirty-five crewmen for a voyage in search of the land that Herjólfsson had seen fifteen or so years before. Originally, Leif Eiriksson had intended that his father should lead the expedition, but Eirik had a riding accident just before reaching the ship and returned home to his farm at Brattahlid, possibly a diplomatic manoeuvre to give his blessing to the venture, while allowing his son to act as its leader.

Having taken good note of Bjarni's account, Leif decided to retrace his steps and so arrived first at the land which his predecessor had visited last. Just as Bjarni had described it, he encountered a landscape of glaciers, mountains and great flat slabs of rock, which he named Helluland ('slab-land'). Leif then directed his ship southwards and soon came to the flat, forested land that Bjarni had visited second, and here he put a boat ashore, making the earliest known landing by Europeans in the Americas. After a very brief stay, Leif ordered his men back to the ship, and sailed on southwards from what he dubbed Markland ('wood-land'). The vessel remained out of sight of land for two days and, when the Norsemen did catch a glimpse of a fresh shoreline, it was a far more inviting prospect, with just the right kind of fertile pasture-land to gladden the heart of any Viking intent on a new *landnám*. The rivers here were also full of salmon, and they decided to stay and build what the saga describes as *buðir* or 'booths', a term associated with the structures built to house chieftains' followers during the annual *things* in Iceland (and which implies a temporary shelter).[5]

During the months Leif and his crew spent in the *buðir* they were amazed to find that the winter was frost-free and that, on the shortest day, the sun could still be seen from breakfast time to the middle of the afternoon.[6] A scouting party was sent out to explore the surrounding countryside, and one of its members, a rather trouble-some German named Tyrkir, went missing. When he eventually turned up, he was beside himself with excitement, prattling away in his native tongue, much to the bemusement of his Norse companions. When finally he became more coherent, he reverted to Norse and explained that he had found vines and grapes. From this discovery, Leif is said to have named the area Vinland (or 'wine-land').[7] For reasons that are not immediately obvious, Leif then had his crew spend some considerable time gathering a cargo of grapes – or possibly raisins – for transportation back to Greenland.

Already at this point the narrative in *Eirik's Saga* has departed from the timeline of the *Saga of the Greenlanders*, although many of the details are similar. Critically, several characters in the latter are left out entirely, so that there is no mention of Bjarni Herjólfsson's prior sighting of the new land; Leif is said instead to have drifted acciden-tally onto the coast of Vinland on his return to Greenland from Norway, where he met Olaf Tryggvason and was commanded by the king to convert the Greenlanders to Christianity. Having discovered the three lands – but not, in this version, having named them – Leif returned to Greenland, saving the crew of a shipwrecked vessel on the way (for which he received his later nickname of Leif 'the Lucky'), and then proceeded to deliver on his promise of Christianising his homeland.[8]

Eirik's Saga also entirely misses out the second voyage to Vinland, this time by Thorvald Eiriksson, who borrowed his brother Leif's ship and set out for Vinland with a crew of thirty. They are said to have stayed the winter in the booths that Leif and his men had built the previous year (which by now had become known as Leifsbuðir, 'Leif's booths'). In the spring, Thorvald sent a party out to the west to explore. This group came across signs of human habitation for the first time – a container that the Vikings believed was for drying corn. The following summer the Norsemen discovered a wooded fjord, which Thorvald, still keen to settle the land, decided was the ideal spot on which to build his farm. Unfortunately, it was also the place where the Vikings encountered their first Native Americans, whom they took by surprise while they were resting under their skin-boats. They killed all but one man, who escaped and later returned with reinforcements while the Norsemen, in turn, were asleep. In the ensuing skirmish Thorvald was fatally wounded by an arrow, despite a protective breastwork of branches, which he had ordered erected along the side of the ship. *Erik's Saga* reports that the one responsible for Thorvald's death was not a *skraeling* (as the Norsemen came to call the local inhabitants), but a 'monopod' – a man with a single foot – a character seemingly straight out of Herodotus's *Histories* or some fantastic medieval traveller's tale.[9] Having buried their leader at a place that became known as Krossanes ('Cross Head'), Thorvald's disheartened followers returned home.

A new sortie to Vinland was planned by Thorstein, another of Erik's sons, but he fell victim to an epidemic in Iceland and died before he could set out. In a particularly baroque touch, the saga writer has his shade rise from the dead to predict the future of his widow Guðrið, who soon thereafter remarried, this time to a wealthy Icelander named Thorfinn Karlsefni. It is his voyage to Vinland that forms the centrepiece of *Erik's Saga* (and to an extent of the *Saga of the Greenlanders*) and the divergences between the two accounts have caused much subsequent puzzlement to historians trying to analyse the texts.

Guðrið and her new husband set off – the year was probably sometime around 1010[10] – and settled down at Leifsbuðir (which they had offered to buy, but which Leif, ever with an eye to commercial opportunities, refused to sell to them).[11] They were accompanied by sixty men, five women and a quantity of livestock, clearly more of a colonising than a scouting expedition. All went well for a while, as the Norsemen were able to exploit the abundant local stocks of fish and hunting game and, when this proved insufficient, survived off the meat from the carcass of a rorqual (a type of baleen whale) that was fortuitously washed onto the beach. Even the first encounter with the *skraelings* went well – despite an early scare when they were terrified by the sound of the Vikings' bull roaring – and the Norsemen received a pile of valuable furs in exchange for a supply of butter, which the *skraelings* greedily gobbled up.[12]

Shortly afterwards, Guðrið gave birth to a baby boy, whom she and Karlsefni named Snorri, and who has the honour of being the first recorded child of European descent born in the Americas.[13] It was not long, however, before the *skraelings* became bolder and one of them was killed while trying to steal weapons, which the Vikings had steadfastly refused to trade with them. A revenge attack was inevitable and Karlsefni prepared for it, forcing the issue at a spot where a lake and a forest meant that the Norsemen could not easily be outflanked. Although the *skraelings* were beaten off and their chieftain killed, Karlsefni realised that, few as they were, the Vikings could not resist such attacks indefinitely. After staying a further winter – which the impossibility of sailing back home through the winter ice constrained them to do – he ordered the colony abandoned and a return to Greenland.

This was not quite the end for Viking Vinland (at least not according to the *Saga of the Greenlanders*) for there was a final, very ill-fated expedition led by yet another of Eirik the Red's children, this time his daughter Freydís.[14] The joint venture with Finnbogi and Helgi, both Icelanders, ended in disaster when Freydis – in the grand saga tradition of strong-minded women – provoked a quarrel and then engineered their murder. Under such circumstances it is hardly surprising that the survivors returned to Greenland the next spring, carrying another cargo of furs and bearing a secret they all swore never to tell (but, as it appears in the saga account, one of them at least clearly did).

Eirik's Saga misses out Freydis's voyage entirely (and has her instead playing a heroic role during Karlsefni's expedition, when she is said to have carried a sword into battle and bared her breast, terrifying the *skraelings* so much that they fled). Instead, it assigns as much as possible of the Vinland glory to Karlsefni, attributing to him the naming of Helluland, Markland and Vinland. Its description of his initial explorations also adds a number of place-names to the mix for historians and archaeologists on the hunt for the location of Norse Vinland; having passed Markland – which conforms to the description of it in the *Saga of the Greenlanders* – they came to a shoreline with long beaches, which they called Furðustrandir ('Marvel Beaches', so-called for their extraordinary length). Two scouts, fleet-footed Scots named Haki and Hekja, were sent out to explore, and it is they who are said to have discovered the grapes and what the saga describes as 'self-sown corn'.

In this version, Karlsefni initially settled down on the interior of a fjord he named Straumfjord, where the party suffered badly from lack of food during the winter. The following spring the Vikings – minus one ship under Thorhall the Hunter – sailed southwards in search of a more promising spot for the colony. After some days' sail they found a place they named Hóp, where a river ran down to the sea from an inland lake, with fields of the same self-sown wheat that the Scots had found, grapes and a general abundance of fish and game. It all sounds so impossibly idyllic, and the similarities to the fabled *Insulae Fortunatorum* ('the Blessed Isles') described by the seventh-century Spanish encyclopaedist Isidore in his *Etymologiae* may indicate that the saga writer borrowed a convenient piece of literary topography for his own account.[15]

On their way to Hóp, the Vikings had encountered a group of *skraelings* sailing in nine skin-boats, armed with peculiar staves that made a rattling sound when waved. There was little contact between the two groups, but the *skraelings* returned the following spring in far greater numbers, again swinging their staves – the saga said they did so 'sunwise', a peculiarly precise touch – and they traded with the Vikings, eager to swap their furs for lengths of red cloth (as opposed to the butter of the *Saga of the Greenlanders*). Terrified by the roaring of Karlsefni's bull, the *skraelings* fled and returned three weeks later, this time swinging their staves 'anti-sunwise', presumably a sign of displeasure or hostile intent. Despite hard fighting, in which the Vikings lost two men but slew a large number of *skraelings* – and during which Guðríð performed her bare-breasted rallying act – Karlsefni's side eventually prevailed. The Vikings then retreated north from Hóp to Straumfjord, where they had left around 100 men.[16] This would mean that Karlsefni had engaged in his southward exploration to Hóp with just forty men (nine having earlier departed with Thorhall the Hunter). Also, given the small size of the Greenland colony at the time, it shows what a large risk, in demographic terms, the Vikings were taking by their voyage to Vinland. Just as in the *Saga of the Greenlanders* account, Karlsefni realised that the numbers and hostility of the *skraelings* made it impossible to settle down in Vinland and he decided to return to Greenland. The departure, though, was delayed until the following spring and was not without incident, as one of the ships, captained by Bjarni Grimólfsson, became worm-eaten and sank soon after setting off. On the way back Karlsefni's vessel picked up two *skraeling* boys in Markland, whom the Vikings took back to Greenland and had baptised.[17]

Yet for all the rich saga tradition of Viking settlement of North America, there was no concrete evidence on the ground. In the absence of an actual Viking site, interest in finding artefacts from Vinland began surprisingly early, fuelled by the publication by the Danish antiquary Carl Christian Rafn, the first secretary of the Royal Society of Northern Antiquaries, of the *Antiquitates Americanæ*, a compendious collection of all known archaeological and written sources relevant to Vinland.[18] Rafn supposed the location of the Vinland of the sagas to lie on the coastline between Massachusetts and Rhode Island. A year before the issuing of his final volume, an exhibition at Christiansborg Palace in Copenhagen presented a range of finds from Greenland and Vinland to the Danish public, including the Kingitorssuaq Runestone, which had been discovered thirteen years previously.[19]

The thirst for Viking artefacts in the United States was insatiable, to the point where almost any ancient find that could not obviously be attributed to Native Americans was marked down instead as evidence of Norse activity. This included the Dighton Rock, a 40-ton sandstone boulder at Berkley on the Taunton River in Massachusetts, part of whose surface is covered in petroglyphs, which were seized on as evidence of either Phoenician or (according to C. C. Rafn) of Viking exploration. In the end, however, they proved after all to be of Native American provenance.

One curious contribution to the genre came from the poet Henry Wadsworth Longfellow, who embarked on a grand study tour of Europe in 1835–6,[20] which took him to London, Stockholm and finally, in September 1835, to Copenhagen. With him he carried letters to various Danish academic luminaries, including Rafn, whom he met. Longfellow described him as 'an Historian and publisher of Old Icelandic books, which he transcribes from the MSS of which the libraries are full . . . his eyes are always staring wide, so that he looks like the picture of a man who sees a ghost. He is, however, a very friendly, pleasant man, and gives me lessons in Icelandic.'[21]

Longfellow made good use of his tutorial in the Icelandic sagas and language, later penning several poems on Norse themes. The most famous of them at the time was 'The Skeleton in Armor', inspired by the discovery in 1832 of a corpse near Fall River, Massachusetts, which had been interred wearing a suit of crude chain-mail armour and a brass breastplate. Speculation raged as to the identity of the body, with some claiming it might be an ancient Egyptian or Phoenician traveller. Longfellow, however, was in no doubt that what had been unearthed was the burial place of a real Viking warrior, or, as he more poetically put it:

> I was a Viking old!
> My deeds, though manifold,
> No Skald in song has told,
> No Saga taught thee!

The skeleton and most of the artefacts associated with it perished in a fire at the Fall River Museum in 1843, although subsequent analysis of the metal tubes found with the body (which had survived the blaze) revealed them to be brass and of a type also found in other burials in Massachusetts that are definitely Native American.[22]

More durable than the Fall River skeleton – both physically and in the imaginations of those hungry for genuine American Viking arte-facts – was another of the inspirations for 'The Skeleton in Armor', a round tower at Newport, Rhode Island. No lesser scholar than Rafn had written about it: 'I am persuaded that all who are familiar with Old-Northern architecture will concur, that this building was erected at a period decidedly not later than the 12th century.'[23]

The tower, which has experienced later adaptations that make its close dating even more difficult, is first mentioned in documents in 1665, and so is clearly of seventeenth-century date or earlier. Some 28 feet high, constructed of dry stone, and held up by eight squat pillars at its base, it originally had two internal rooms, although the roof of the upper one has long since collapsed. Benedict Arnold, an early colonial governor of Rhode Island (who died in 1678), refers to the building in his will as his 'stone-built wind mill', and opponents of a Norse origin for the structure have taken this to mean that he had it built himself.[24] Parallels have been drawn with a mill of not dissimilar design at Chesterton in Warwickshire, which Arnold is said to have used as a model. It is unclear, though, whether that building was actually in use as a mill (rather than an observatory) pre-1700, and so it is not a definitive proof of the Chesterton theory.[25]

There are elements about the Newport Tower's design that do not entirely chime with the thesis that it was an early colonial mill. The walls are some 3 feet thick, and it has been estimated that it would have taken 450 tons of granite, the timber from four 60-foot-high trees and the labour of sixteen men working for a year to build it.[26] Of course it similarly begs a number of questions to presume that a small Norse colony, which (given the size of Greenland's population) can never have been more than a few hundred strong, could have devoted such a huge amount of effort to building a mill (or even a tower), when they have left no other stone structures in the Americas and nothing remotely similar in Greenland.[27]

Other seventeenth-century buildings have been excavated in the area surrounding the tower, and radiocarbon dates on the mortar of the tower are clustered around the period 1635–98,[28] which would support the Benedict Arnold thesis. Attempts have been made to cite maps produced by the Italian explorer Giovanni da Verrazano as evidence for the existence of a stone structure at Newport at the time of his voyage in 1524. The 'Norman villa' on his map is, however, placed far to the north of Rhode Island, in the vicinity of Long Island, and, although it probably indicates some kind of settlement, it is not clear what. Furthermore, if da Verrazano really had found an imposing stone building such as the Tower, it seems strange that he mentioned it only in a cryptic reference on his map and, moreover, displaced it from its true position by 100 miles or more.

The Newport Tower theories, though, refuse to die. In addition to its attribution to the Vikings, it has been supposed variously to have been constructed by early medieval Irish monks, by a pair of four-teenth-century Venetian brothers,[29] by sixteenth-century sailors as a lighthouse, by Earl Henry Sinclair of Orkney (imagined by eighteenth-century antiquaries to have ruled over an island kingdom in the Atlantic), or even by a fleet of Chinese explorers in 1421 led by the 'three-jewelled eunuch' Admiral Zheng He.[30]

Enthusiasm for Viking discoveries in America was at first rather tempered by the lack of availability of the sagas in English. The first recorded translation was of a fragment of *Håkon's Saga* by the Scot James Johnstone in 1782. *The Vinland Sagas* themselves were not generally accessible (even in Old Norse) until their publication by Rafn in the *Antiquitates Americanæ*. They then came to the attention of the English-reading world with the publication in 1841 by North Ludlow Beamish of *The Discovery of America by the Northmen*, which drew heavily on Rafn's work. As the nineteenth century went on, increasing numbers of Scandinavians migrated to the United States and Canada[31] and as their numbers rose, so too did a feeling that Christopher Columbus had received rather too much credit for the European discovery of America. In 1874, Professor Rasmus Anderson of Wisconsin University encapsulated this feeling in his exploration of the Norse antecedents of the United States entitled *America Not Discovered by Columbus*.

Resentment at the general acceptance of Columbus as prime discoverer was heightened by the celebrations planned in 1892 to commemorate the 400th anniversary of his landing in the New World. Funds were raised by public subscription in Norway to build an exact replica of the Gokstad ship, in an attempt to upstage the event at Chicago's Columbian Fair.[32] The *Viking* set sail from Bergen on 29 April 1893 with a crew of eleven, and arrived in Chicago twenty-seven days later, having made its way via New York and the Erie Canal and Great Lakes. As an affirmation of the sea-worthiness of Viking vessels it was astonishing, and it did rather divert attention from the 'Columbus' themes of the expo, much as those behind the project had desired.[33]

With interest in things Norse reaching an unprecedented level, it is no coincidence that the next decade saw a rash of 'discoveries' in the United States. The one that has proved most stubbornly persistent is a runestone unearthed by Olaf Ohman, a migrant Swede, on his farm outside Kensington, Minnesota. According to Ohman's story, which he somewhat modified as time went on, the stone – around 30 inches by 16 inches – was found underneath the root of an aspen tree. Sometime after the stone slab was dug up in 1898, Ohman's young son noticed strange carvings on it, which the farmer then recognised as runic writing. And so began a century of claim and counter-claim. After a brief period of display in the window of a local bank, a copy of the inscription was sent to Professor O.J. Breda, a philologist at the University of Minnesota, and then in 1899 to another philologist, Professor George Curme at Northwestern University, both of whom dismissed it as a fake. Other eminent scholars, including Professors

Gustav Storm and Sophus Bugge[34] of Christiania (Oslo) University, also pronounced the runestone to be a fraud.

The stone, though, found its champions, including its most vociferous proponent, the Norwegian-American author Hjalmar Holand, who published the first translation of the runes in 1912. They were said to declare that 'We are eight Swedes[35] and 22 Norwegians on a journey of exploration from Vinland westward. We set traps by two shelters a day's march north of this stone. One day some of us went fishing. On our return to camp we found 10 men dead, red with blood. May the Blessed Virgin Mary save us from evil. We left 10 men by the sea looking after the ships 14 days' journey from this island. In the year 1362.'[36]

Holand sought to link the stone with the expedition of Poul Knudsson, which King Magnus of Denmark authorised in 1355, arguing that the Kensington Runestone was the record of an extension of this effort. Yet, quite apart from the fact that there is no independent evidence that Knudsson actually set out on his journey,[37] there are a number of other significant obstacles to accepting the Runestone's authenticity. The first is the location of the find – several weeks' journey from the only currently accepted Viking site at L'Anse aux Meadows. It would have taken at least a fortnight to sail down the Red River to enter Lake Winnipeg, followed by a substantial overland trek to reach Kensington, all the while traversing territory occupied by large numbers of Native American tribes, for little discernible gain. Nor have there been any other archaeological traces of Norse activity so far to the south and inland – although absence of evidence does not mean that it might not be found in the future.

More telling is the linguistic data. The Runestone bears one of the longest runic inscriptions found to date *anywhere* in the Viking world. To have carved such a stone would have taken considerable time, and is not the sort of activity that a small party exploring in hostile territory many days' journey from a safe haven might have been expected to indulge in. The contrast is instructive with the brevity of the inscriptions scratched on the interior of Maeshowe in Orkney by eleventh-century Vikings who were threatened by nothing more violent than the storm that caused them to take shelter there.[38]

The language and form of the Kensington Stone runes also indicate that it is either a fake or linguistically unique. The inscription includes an umlauted form of 'o', which did not begin to appear in Swedish until the sixteenth century, and runes for 'j' and a version of 'n', which had fallen into disuse several centuries before 1362.[39] The text itself contains various anachronistic usages, such as *dags rise* for a 'day's journey' instead of the expected form in Old Norse of *daghs faerdh*. Even more revealing is that several of the aberrant rune types have been linked to forms used in the central Swedish province of Dalarna in the nineteenth century – precisely the area where several of Ohman's associates around Kensington had originally come from. Ohman himself admitted to having studied runes at school and he had in his possession a copy of a history of Sweden that discussed runic alphabets.[40] Several others in Ohman's circle may also have possessed the requisite knowledge to attempt such a forgery.

The Runestone, therefore, is almost certainly a fake, albeit a sophisticated one, which answered the need for Viking artefacts[41] at a time of rising consciousness among Scandinavian-Americans of their position as the heirs of Leif Eiriksson. Even so, it continues to have its steadfast defenders; from February 1948 to February 1949 the Kensington Runestone even formed the centrepiece of an exhibition at the Smithsonian Institution in Washington. Today, it is the prize exhibit at the Runestone Museum in Alexandria, Minnesota, while a giant replica of the stone has been placed in the 'Kensington Runestone Park' that is centred on Ohman's original farmstead.

New evidence appears from time to time on one side or other of the Kensington Runestone debate – such as the assertion in 2005 that other rune forms on the stone (such as a dotted 'r') are characteristic of Gotlandic script of the 1300s.[42] However, the polemic surrounding the stone is as nothing compared to the fierce debate that has raged around the most famous Viking 'artefact' of them all, the Vinland Map. The map first came to light in 1957, when an antiquarian bookseller in New Haven, Connecticut, showed a fifteenth-century manuscript to Thomas Marston, the curator of Medieval and Renaissance Literature at Yale University Library, and his colleague Alexander Victor, the library's maps curator. Bound up with the *Tartar Relation* (a hitherto unknown account of an embassy by the Franciscan friar Giovanni de Piano Carpini to the court of the Mongol ruler Ögodei Khan in 1245–47) was an apparently contemporary world map, which included a depiction of

Greenland and the eastern seaboard of North America, including the place-name 'Vinland'.

If genuine, this would be an astonishing find. The earliest known cartographic representation of North America had previously been the Canerio map, drawn by a Genoese map-maker around 1503. The first maps actually naming 'Vinland' (or Vinlandia) began to appear only in the late sixteenth century, starting with the rather crude Stefansson map of 1570, which includes labels for 'Promontorium Vinlandia' and 'Skralinge Land'. There had been a number of fifteenth-century maps of the Atlantic that showed a variety of mythical islands bearing names such as Antilia, or the 'Isle of Brazil'[43] (the former appears on a Venetian nautical chart from 1424). There, is, however, no evidence that any of these referred to North America (although they may well display knowledge of Greenland, which appears as 'Ilha Verda' – literally meaning 'green land' – on a Catalan chart from around 1480).

Although the map that the Yale curators saw covers the entire world (or at least those parts of it supposed to have been known to its purported fifteenth-century creator), its principal interest lay in its depiction of an island in the middle of the Atlantic, which bears the label *Vinland Insula*. From this the map soon gained the nickname 'The Vinland Map', by which it has been known ever since. It also bears a series of inscriptions, which seem to support the idea that it contained information genuinely derived from the voyages to the Americas detailed in *The Vinland Sagas*. Part of one of them read:

> By God's will, after a long voyage from the island of Greenland to the south toward the most distant part of the western sea, sailing southwards amidst the ice, the companions Bjarni and Leif Eiriksson discovered a new land, extremely fertile, and even having vines, the which island they named Vinland. Eric, legate of the Apostolic See and Bishop of Greenland and the neighbouring regions, came to this vast and very rich land in the name of God the Almighty in the last year of our most blessed father Pascal, remained a long time through both summer and winter, and later returned north-eastward to Greenland.[44]

Apart from the obvious reference to the saga account of the discoverers of Vinland, the map's annotation mentions Bishop Eirik Gnuppson

Upsi, who is known from the *Icelandic Annals* to have gone to Vinland in 1121.[45] The discrepancy between the year implied in the Vinland map inscription (which would be 1117, the last year of the reign of Pope Pascal) and the date given in the Icelandic records is a minor one compared to the concerns that soon began to be raised about the map's authenticity. Its provenance was shrouded in uncertainty from the outset – it had been bought by the antiquarian bookseller Laurence Witten in Barcelona from the art dealer Enzo Ferrajoli de Ry, who maintained that it had come from a 'private collection', which he was not prepared to identify.[46] There were also a number of holes in the manuscript caused by the action of bookworms, which did not match up between the Vinland Map and the *Tartar Relation*. This particular puzzle seemed to be solved by the serendipitous appearance in April 1958 of another medieval manuscript containing a section of the *Speculum Historiale* ('The Mirror of History') of Vincent of Beauvais. This new find also contained wormholes, which would match those on the Vinland Map and the *Tartar Relation*, if it were supposed that it had once been bound between them.

Victor bought the map but, although an initial examination at Yale declared it authentic and a book detailing those findings and introducing the map to the public was published in 1965,[47] doubts lingered. An examination of the map at the British Museum in 1967 found anomalies in the script, which Marston had confidently declared to be identical to that in the *Speculum* and *Tartar Relation* manuscripts and to be a type of 'bastard book cursive' typical of Germany, France and the Low Countries around 1415–60.[48] More seriously, analysis of the ink on the Vinland Map revealed it to be different in composition from that on the other two documents and, indeed, from most other medieval European manuscripts, having no trace of iron in it.

In 1974 the map was sent for more detailed examination to the McCrone Research Institute in Chicago. This found that the ink used on the manuscript contained traces of a milled-form anatase (a form of titanium dioxide) that indicated it to be of twentieth-century origin. Walter McCrone considered that the anatase was probably of a type patented in 1916 for use in the paint industry, leading him to conclude that the map had been drawn around 1920. Further analysis at University College London by researchers using advanced spectroscopic techniques confirmed the presence of anatase in the map's ink, in contrast to its absence from the other two manuscripts.[49]

The map's cartography also indicates that it is very probably a forgery. It depicts Greenland as an island, a fact that was not known for sure until the twentieth century. Even in 1965, when the map was published, no one had actually circumnavigated it.[50] Furthermore, there are indications, such as the identical position of Greenland on the Vinland and Canerio maps, that the composer of the Vinland Map drew on sixteenth-century Portuguese models for his cartography.[51]

As to the identity of the forger, the pool of people with the necessary knowledge and skill to produce it must have been very small. One prime candidate is the Austrian Jesuit priest Josef Fischer, who wrote an introduction to a book on Norse discoveries in 1902. While researching this in the archive of Wolfegg Castle in Swabia, he had unearthed the Waldseemüller map, which dates to 1507 and bears the first published appearance of the name 'America'. What the forger's motive was in producing such a sophisticated fake is unclear, but the production of the Vinland Map might simply have been another attempt – more credible than the Kensington Runestone – to give *The Vinland Sagas* a grounding in fact.

Not all 'Viking artefacts' uncovered in the Americas before the discovery of L'Anse aùx Meadows were fake. A genuine find was turned up in 1957 by two archaeologists digging at the Goddard Farm in Naskeag Point, central Maine. Although the Goddard site is a Native American one – and a rich one in material terms – it was a single silver coin embedded in the midden there that proved to be the most significant discovery. At first its importance was not recognised and it was misidentified as a twelfth-century English coin 1100–1135. It was not until 1978 that a British numismatic expert realised that the coin was not English at all, and a re-examination by the National Museum of Norway's coin curator, Kolbjørn Skaare, found that it was a Norse penny, probably minted between 1065 and 1080. Analysis of the settlement pattern at the site indicated that it was occupied by Native Americans in the period 900–1500 and then abandoned and so, crucially, the coin must have been deposited before the next set of Europeans visited the area in the sixteenth century. The Goddard site was a hub in a series of trading networks that stretched as far north as Labrador, and clearly goods arrived there from some considerable distance. A particular set of thirty stone tools and hundreds of stone flake fragments from Goddard were made of Ramah chert, which is only found in northern Labrador, and these, together with a polished jade knife and a scraper from the Dorset culture, indicate that the settlement traded (though perhaps not directly) with Labrador. Although it is impossible to know exactly how the coin got to Maine, or how long it took to get there, it does show with some certainty that there were still Norsemen in the Americas some time after 1065, half a century after the most likely date of the voyages recounted in the sagas, and that one of them traded or lost the penny.

Almost every piece of information related in the sagas has been picked over numerous times in an attempt to establish the location of the elusive Vinland and, by analogy, Markland and Helluland, an activity that resulted in much feverish (and fruitless) speculation, before a genuine Viking-Age site was discovered in 1961. Most attempts to identify the area in which Vinland lay used incidental references in *The Vinland Sagas* to try and narrow down the location of the various places mentioned. The description in the *Saga of the Greenlanders* of the sun being visible between breakfast and the afternoon meal (*dagmál*) on the shortest day has been interpreted to mean that the sun was up by 9 a.m. and did not set until after 3 p.m., which would imply a latitude of somewhere between 40°N and 50°N, and a location for Vinland anywhere between New Jersey and the Gulf of St Lawrence.[52] The references to grapes and self-sown wheat in the sagas have also provided fertile ground for scholarly speculation, with wild grapes no longer occurring to the north of southern Novia Scotia, while the reference to self-sown wheat, if it refers to a form of wild rye,[53] would indicate roughly the same area. Conversely, the saga report that Leif's expedition found salmon in Vinland suggests an area no further to the south than Maine.

The use of the term '*skraeling*' in the sagas has also been much discussed as a means of narrowing down where the Vikings may have landed and the type of peoples they encountered there. It first appears in the *Book of the Icelanders*, composed by Ari the Learned, who died in 1158. His discussion of the colonisation of Greenland contains a reference to 'the same kind of people had lived there as those who inhabit Vinland, and whom the Greenlanders called skraelings'. Some decades later, around 1170–5, the author of the *Historia Norwegiae* refers to 'dwarves called skraelings' who are said to live 'beyonde the Greenlanders' and who are said not to bleed when they are wounded.[54]

At first sight it might seem logical that the natives whom the Norse encountered in North America were Dorset Eskimo or Thule Inuit people. Although the Thule do not seem to have migrated as far south as Greenland's Western Settlement in the mid-twelfth century, the Norse may have come across them in the *Norðsetur*, Greenland's northern hunting grounds, or perhaps some remnants of the Dorset culture that preceded them.[55]

The Dorset lived in northern Labrador (one possible candidate for Helluland) at least until 1300 and so might have been encountered by the Norsemen there. Further south, too, there may have been Dorset Eskimos in Newfoundland at the time of Leif Eiriksson's voyage, where they travelled in search of harp seal.[56] Yet there are elements in the saga description of the *skraelings* that do not match what we know of Inuit or Dorset culture. The structure for drying corn, which Thorfinn Karlsefni and his men spotted, is more characteristic of those used by ancestors of Native American groups such as the Beothuk or Micmac than of the Inuit, while another saga reference to the nine men that Karlsefni's expedition found sleeping under three boats does not sound as if it is referring to an Inuit kayak, as these were far too small to provide such shelter.[57]

The confirmation that the manufacturers of the Vinland Map, the Kensington Runestone and a host of other false Viking artefacts sought came when the Norwegian author Helge Ingstad announced that he had found a Viking settlement at L'Anse aux Meadows in Newfoundland. Initially Ingstad was greeted with a chorus of scepticism, in part because many scholars had placed Vinland elsewhere, mostly further to the south (with Christian Rafn plumping for Cape Cod, and Gustav Storm opting in 1887 for Nova Scotia).

L'Anse aux Meadows, the site of Ingstad's discovery, lies in the far north of Newfoundland alongside the Strait of Belle Isle and facing Labrador. A series of test excavations in 1956 by the Danish archaeologist Jørgen Meldgaard at nearby Pistolet Bay had discovered nothing, but when Helge Ingstad arrived in Newfoundland in 1960 to prospect possible sites for Leif's booths, a local man named George Decker took him to Épaves Bay, where a plain covered in dwarf willow and grass was cut through by the sparkling water of Black Duck Brook. Decker showed him a grassy terrace near the head of the bay from which some small heather-covered mounds protruded.

Ingstad was convinced this might represent the remains of the long-sought-after Norse settlement of Vinland, and in 1961 he and his wife, Anne Stine Ingstad, began excavating. The seven summers that the Ingstads spent digging at L'Anse aux Meadows yielded spectacular results, in sharp contrast to the century of disappointment and forgeries that had preceded it. Their initial digs, and subsequent excavations under the auspices of Parks Canada from 1972, uncovered eight or nine Norse-era buildings constructed of turf. The site was revealed to have been previously occupied by Dorset Eskimo, and in later centuries by Native American groups.[58] However, it seems there were no native peoples living in the close vicinity at the time. This (given the bloody clashes between Vikings and *skraelings* which the sagas recount) would have greatly recommended it as a location for settlement. The two biggest structures – 'House A' (around 79 feet long and 15 wide), which lies closest to the brook, and 'House F' (around 65 feet long and 49 feet wide with six rooms), which was sited furthest east along the terrace – were both sufficiently large to indicate something rather more than temporary accommodation for a few passing Norsemen.

The most conclusive evidence that L'Anse aux Meadows was indeed a Viking site came from the 125 or so artefacts that the Ingstads found; around 100 of these were iron nails or nail fragments – not a material that was available to the native population, except in the form of meteorite iron from Greenland, which could not have been worked into nails. Another 650 items found by the Parks Canada excavations – many in the boggy ground that surrounded the houses – were made up largely of wooden debris left over from carpentry undertaken by the inhabitants of the site. More compelling yet was the remains of 'House J', a single-roomed structure in which the remnants of slag and bog-iron indicated that iron had been smelted there, with the remains of a charcoal kiln found next to it acting as further proof of the house's role as a smithy. Other, smaller houses on the site appear to have been residential, with finds including iron rivets, parts of wooden vessels, a stone lamp, a ring-headed bronze pin of Viking-Age type and a spindle whorl made of soapstone.

What kind of settlement does the site at L'Anse aux Meadows represent? It is certainly tempting to equate it to Leifsbuðir, which would neatly resolve the question of where Viking Vinland is. Yet this would not answer the complicating question of where the Hóp and Straumfjord of the *Saga of the Greenlanders* should be supposed to lie. The two largest buildings, each with a private chamber at one end, are suggestive of someone with elite status and may have housed an entire ship's crew together with its captain. The discovery of the spindle, indicating that weaving – an activity exclusively the domain of women – took place on the site, implies that whoever lived at L'Anse aux Meadows, they probably brought their families with them.

Although this suggests a colonising venture, other aspects of the site indicate a more temporary occupation. None of the houses show any signs of repair – although some of them were eventually destroyed by fire. The roofs of turf buildings generally need maintenance at least once every twenty years, and that the houses at L'Anse aux Meadows did not undergo any such remedial work indicates that their maximum period of occupation must have been around two decades. Further evidence of the short duration of the L'Anse aux Meadows settlement is the lack of a cemetery, which would surely have been needed after any prolonged period of habitation, and the small size of the site's rubbish middens.

The amount of iron slag and bog-iron that has been found at the site amounts to a total of just 6 or 7 pounds, which is hardly indicative of constant large-scale production over a number of seasons, but is closer to the amount of smelting needed to effect spot repairs on a single vessel. The excavation of a large number of nails and iron rivets, which almost certainly came originally from a ship, is also supportive of this theory. Some of the nails have even been found to have split marks, indicating that they were removed with a chisel from the place where they were originally embedded (presumably in the ship's timbers).[59] In addition, even though some women at least were clearly present at L'Anse aux Meadows, no byres or barns have been found at the site. If the Norsemen came to Newfoundland with their families, then they did not, it seems, come to L'Anse aux Meadows with their livestock.

Tantalisingly, the remains of three butternuts (*Juglans cinerea*) were also found at the site, a fruit whose range extends only as far north as the St Lawrence Valley around New Brunswick (having more or less the same range as wild grapes), suggesting that the Vikings who occupied L'Anse aux Meadows must have journeyed at least that far south. Initial radiocarbon dates for wood taken from the site cluster around the tenth century, which, given that some of the material must have been driftwood or timber from trees cut down some decades before being deposited in Newfoundland, is not inconsistent with the dates derived from the sagas of 1000–20 for the Vinland voyages. Subsequent radiocarbon analysis has refined this to the period 980–1020,[60] a more or less precise match with the saga material.

Instead of being a colonising venture, it seems more likely that L'Anse aux Meadows was a kind of staging-post or gateway to the rest of Vinland. Ice conditions in the seas around Greenland meant that it was not generally possible to sail from there until midsummer and so, in order to avoid being stranded, the return voyage from Vinland had to be completed by October. Considering that reaching landfall at L'Anse aux Meadows would have taken around two weeks from Greenland, then the wisdom of having a secure base to act as a platform from which to explore the rest of 'Vinland' is clear. Yet does this mean there might be other, possibly larger Norse sites yet to be discovered along the eastern seaboard of North America? The population that could be housed in the buildings at L'Anse aux Meadows has been estimated at about seventy[61] and given that the entire population of the Greenland colony at the time may have been only 400–500,[62] then a second such substantial settlement would have meant sparing one-third of the Greenlandic population for this colonising venture, which seems extremely unlikely. One possible candidate for a smaller waystation has, however, emerged. In October 2012, the Canadian archaeologist Patricia Sutherland announced that excavations at Tanfield Valley on the south-eastern coast of Baffin Island had yielded a whetstone with fragments of bronze and smelted iron embedded in it, both metals whose manufacture was unknown to local native peoples, but which could be produced by the Greenland Norse. Taken together with fragments of yarn found at Tanfield, which resembled that woven in Greenland at the time, this has suggested that the buildings found at Baffin may be the remains of a permanent Viking trading post. If this is the case, then Tanfield Valley might represent the second Viking site to be identified in North

America, but quite how many Vikings lived there, over what period and whether they did so permanently, or as part of a seasonal trading pattern, is uncertain.

There are signs that at least some of the inhabitants of L'Anse aux Meadows may have come from Iceland. Five fire-starters (flint-like tools used to create sparks for starting fires) made from jasper originating in western Iceland were found by archaeologists, while four similar tools were made of Greenlandic jasper and one from stone taken from central Newfoundland, around 150 miles to the south-east (itself suggesting a range of inland exploration that would otherwise be unknown to us). But even if one or two ships' crews came from Iceland, it still does not alter the fact that Vinland's position made it dependent on Greenland, which in the early eleventh century could not possibly provide enough manpower to sustain it.

The occurrence of three different named sites in the sagas (Leifbuðir, Straumfjord and Hóp) does present complications, and should alert us that Vinland is in truth a region and not any particular place. Whether the Straumfjord of the *Saga of the Greenlanders* is the same as the Leifbuðir of *Eirik's Saga* is unclear – a problem which, together with the search for the location of Hóp, has given rise to a substantial literature. Candidates for Straumfjord have included L'Anse aux Meadows itself and the Avalon peninsula of southern Newfoundland, while writers have sought Hóp in places as far afield as St Paul's Bay on the Gros Morne peninsula, some 120 miles south of L'Anse aux Meadows, and the Hudson River.[63]

As to how and when the Viking colony in America died out, the picture is rather clearer. The evidence both from the sagas and from L'Anse aux Meadows suggests that the period from Leif's first landing in Vinland to the final exploratory voyage was around twenty years, and that these were not followed up by further large-scale expeditions. This does not mean that after 1020 the Vikings never visited Vinland (or Helluland or Markland) again; there is evidence, both literary and archaeological, that they did so. An analysis of parts from ships unearthed at Norse ruins in Greenland showed that six out of ten samples were made from larch, which is not found in Greenland, but is native to North America.[64] Furthermore, at the Farm Beneath the Sand in Greenland's Western Settlement,[65] fragments of bison hair and fibres from the fur of brown and black bears were found, which can only have come from North America. The Maine penny is also an indication of contacts between Vikings and native traders at least until the mid-eleventh century, although it is conceivable that it was traded all the way from Ellesmere in the sub-Arctic rather than through direct contacts in Vinland.

As far as documented contacts go, we have only the cryptic reference to Bishop Eirik Gnuppson's journey to Vinland in 1121 and then the Greenlandic ship that arrived in the outer Straumfjord in Iceland in 1347. It was not large – the author of the *Icelandic Annals* stresses that even the smaller boats in Iceland were bigger – but it is recorded that the vessel was on a trip to Markland when it was blown off-course. The purpose of the expedition is not noted, but it is a fair guess that it was in search of timber. According to *The Vinland Sagas*, Markland had an abundance of timber, but without it the Greenland Norse otherwise had to rely on driftwood. There were doubtless other, unrecorded voyages from Greenland to North America – the 1347 expedition would have gone unremarked, had the ship not been driven to Iceland – and some of them may have occurred even later. But it is an intriguing thought that 350 years after the first Viking landings in North America and just 150 years before Columbus 'discovered' the Americas, it would still have been possible to encounter a Viking landing party engaged in the humdrum activity of chopping down trees for building wood.

Map 10 The Vikings in Russia

Area controlled by the Rus, *c.* 912

N

*Norwegian
Sea*

NORWAY

SWEDEN

*Gulf of
Bothnia*

FINNS

Kaupang

Birka

Lake Ladoga

Lake Onega

DENMARK

*Baltic
Sea*

Grobina

Neva

Staraja Ladoga

Beloozero

Novgorod

Volkhov

Lake Ilmen

Jaroslavl

Hedeby

Jumne

Truso

Suzdal

Vladimir

Wollin

Volga

Elbe

SLAVS

Gnezdovo

Bolghar

Danube

Dnieper

Chernigov

Kiev

Don

PECHENEGS

Volga

HUNGARY

Berezany

Danube

*Sea of
Azov*

KHAZAR
KHANATE

Itil

Naples

BULGARIA

Black Sea

Constantinople
(Miklegard)

BYZANTINE

EMPIRE

*Caspian
Sea*

*Mediterranean
Sea*

Bardha'a

Baku

Kura

ABBASID
CALIIPHATE

7

Furthest East: The Vikings in Russia, 800–1040

Swedish Vikings and traders, denied the easy access to the western seas enjoyed by their Danish and Norwegian counterparts, turned east instead. Here, from as early as the mid-seventh century, they began to colonise the shores of the Baltic Sea (founding a colony at Grobina in Latvia around 650[1]). By the mid-eighth century they had pushed deeper into the Russian interior, gradually taking control of trade routes down the Dnieper and establishing a series of settlements (or colonising existing ones) that would form the nucleus of what eventually evolved into the Russian state.

Memories of Scandinavian involvement along the eastern Baltic coastlines ran very deep; the Swedish king Yngvar (probably dating to the seventh century) is said to have harried the lands of the Estonians (and died during one such campaign), while the last of the Swedish Yngling dynasty, Ivar *Vidfadmi* ('the Far-Traveller'), is described as having a realm that encompassed Sweden, Denmark, Saxony and much of the Baltic.[2] It is not until the mid-ninth century, however, that such involvement emerges from the mists of semi-legend into a more historical framework. Even then, attempts to understand the process by which the Vikings came to establish a number of principalities based around Kiev, Novgorod and a series of other trading towns are bedevilled by controversy. This focuses mainly on the extent to which the incoming Vikings adapted themselves to existing Slavic institutions and were absorbed by pre-existing Slav (and Finnic) populations, or whether, in contrast, the states they founded were fundamentally Scandinavian affairs. The proponents of the theory that the settlements were basically Slavic are known as 'anti-Normanists', in contrast to the 'Normanist' protagonists of a purely Viking ancestry for the proto-Russian states.[3] Unsurprisingly, the anti-Normanist theory has long held sway in Russian historiography, and particularly in Soviet times, when it was an almost obligatory orthodoxy. Scandinavian historians, in contrast, have tended to emphasise the Viking role in the foundation and development of states in the area. The truth, as ever, almost certainly lies in the middle – the Vikings did not arrive in a deserted landscape or develop totally virgin sites, and thus there must have been a significant Slavic component even at the early stages of the Viking settlement of Russia.

Exactly when the Vikings moved southwards into Russia from bases they established in the eastern Baltic such as Grobin, Apuola and Elbing (on the Bay of Gdansk) is unclear.[4] There is documentary evidence, however, that by the 830s they had certainly managed to penetrate down the Dnieper as far as Constantinople. The Frankish *Annals of St Bertin* relate the story of a diplomatic mission from the Byzantine emperor Theophilus, which arrived at the distant court of the Frankish ruler, Louis the Pious, at Ingelheim in 839. The Greek ambassadors are said to have brought with them a group of men 'called Rhos' who had themselves come as envoys to the Byzantine emperor, but who had been unable to return by the way they had come, as this was now blocked by hostile tribes, and so instead they had taken the far longer route westwards into Francia. Louis had the men interrogated and found that they belonged to the Swedish nation (*Suenones*), whose ruler was known as the *khagan*. He suspected the men of being spies, and kept them at court until he could be satisfied of their good intentions. The *Annals* do not relate what happened next, but presumably in the end the Frankish king allowed them to go on their way.[5]

The episode features the first appearance of the name *Rhos* or *Rus*, the term by which the Scandinavian settlers of Russia became known, and from which ultimately the country took its name. The term's origin is unknown, although it could be derived from *Ruotsi*, the Finnish term for Swedes,[6] or alternatively from the Old Norse *roÞer*, meaning 'rowers'. More fanciful interpretations include that put forward by the Italian historian Liutprand of Cremona, who believed that it derived from the Greek word for 'red' and referred to the ruddy complexions of the Norsemen; and the theory that the name comes from a tribe of Alans called the Rukhs-As who lived in the Caucasus.[7] The term Varangians, by which the Norsemen were alternatively known, and which came to refer to mercenaries from Scandinavia – and specifically those in the service of the Byzantine emperor[8] – could derive from the Old Norse *vár* ('pledge'), which may denote a group of men sworn to mutual support, either warriors or merchants.[9]

The written account of the Viking advent in Russia is very problematic, as it relies on interpretation of the *Povest' Vremennykh Let* ('The Chronicle of Bygone Years' or *Russian Primary Chronicle*), which was composed around 1116.[10] The Rus are first mentioned in it in 852, when the 'Russes attacked Tsargrad [Constantinople]'. Then in 859 comes the entry: 'The Varangians from beyond the sea imposed tribute on the Chuds, the Slavs, the Merians, the Ves', and the Krivichians.' In 860–2, the *Chronicle* further records:

> The tributaries of the Varangians drove them beyond the sea and, refusing them further tribute, set out to govern themselves. There was no law among them, but tribe rose against tribe . . . They said to themselves, 'Let us seek a prince who may rule over us and judge us according to the Law.' They accordingly went overseas to the Varangian Rus . . . The Chuds, the Slavs, the Krivichians, and the Ves' then said to the people of Rus', 'Our land is great and rich, but there is no order in it. Come to rule us and reign over us.' They thus selected three brothers, with their kinsfolk, who took with them all the Rus' and migrated. The oldest, Rurik, located himself in Novgorod; the second, Sineus, at Beloozero, and the third, Truvor, in Izborsk. On account of these Varangians, the district of Novgorod became known as the land of the Rus'.[11]

Although the precise details of the story cannot be relied upon too much, the account probably represents a memory of the takeover of a pre-existing centre established by Slavs at Kiev for the collection of tribute among the surrounding tribes. The political make-up of this arena into which the Vikings were now entering was not a simple matter of a patchwork of Slavic tribes. More organised states held sway in the region, too. The Khazars – a people of Turkic origin, whose lands lay between the Volga, the northern Caucasus and the Sea of Azov – had steadily extended their control westwards during the seventh century. Their empire, the world's only Jewish state between the Roman conquest of Palestine and the foundation of the State of Israel in 1948, had, after a bitter war against the Arabs in 722–37, reached a modus vivendi with the Abbasid caliphate (based at

Baghdad), which allowed it to expand north and west from its base around the Caspian Sea into the forest zone of Russia. In doing so, the Khazars absorbed or subjugated a series of Finnish and Slavic tribes from whom they collected tribute, mainly in furs, beeswax and other forest products. They also came to exercise hegemony over the Volga Bulgars, another Turkic group, who had settled on the Volga around 675 and whose capital Bolghar (near modern Kazan in Russia) was an important trading entrepôt. It was probably some disturbance in this system caused by Scandinavian incomers from the north that is remembered in the *Primary Chronicle* account.

More tangible evidence of the earliest Scandinavian settlers in Russia comes from a series of settlements in the north of Russia, beginning with Staraya Ladoga ('Old Ladoga'), a small trading settlement set up by local Slavs around 750 on the left bank of the Volkhov, north-east of St Petersburg. Into this conduit for trade further to the east, and for the proceeds of tribute collection amongst the Slavs and Finnish tribes to the west, there flowed large quantities of Islamic silver coins (often known as dirhams), the first hoards of which appear as early as 780.[12] The prosperity this brought to Staraya Ladoga allowed the settlement to grow considerably in the 830s, with new houses being built to the north and the expansion of local manufacturing, such as the working of metal, antler and amber. Unlike their counterparts in western Europe, the Vikings did not come to Ladoga to prey on local monasteries and pillage prosperous nearby towns; there simply were no such appetising targets. The purpose of their colony must have been primarily to tap into local trading networks, including the gathering of furs as tributes, which they could then carry to Bolghar or further south to the Khazar capital at Itil.

At first the northern traders – probably mainly from Sweden – simply visited, but at length they came to stay and Staraya Ladoga became a more predominantly Norse settlement (which they called Aldeigjuborg), with an extensive Scandinavian-style cemetery on its outskirts. Hundreds of burial mounds dot the landscape, eloquent testimony to the travels of merchants who passed up the River Neva to Lake Ladoga and then to the confluence of the Volkhov. Still later archaeological levels include Slav-style single-roomed cottages, and so it is supposed that by the tenth century the Vikings at Staraya Ladoga had become assimilated, or at least had absorbed many of the practices of the local Slavic population.

Eventually the Viking Rus felt the need to control the trade further down the river and established a new settlement at Riurikovo Gorodishche on Lake Ilmen. With a more fertile hinterland than Ladoga, Gorodishche was able to support a larger population and became in turn the launching point for still further Scandinavian expansion, as the Norsemen moved east, founding new settlements such as that at Beloozero, on the lake of the same name. From all of these bases the Vikings used a mixture of force and economic induce-ment to dominate the local tribes, forging alliances with local chieftains to gain access to furs and other trade goods. Eventually they began to push southwards towards the Dnieper, reaching Kiev, and shortly after 900 they set up a base at Gnezdovo (around 8 miles west of Smolensk), from where they could dominate the routes between the Khazar empire to the south-east and the southern shores of the Baltic.[13] The importance of this settlement is indicated by the size of its cemetery, which has more than 3,000 burial mounds. Although only around a small proportion can be identified as exclusively Norse, the presence of a large number of Scandinavian artefacts suggests that the site was a significant centre of Rus power on the Middle Dnieper.[14]

We are fortunate in possessing a number of Arabic descriptions of the Rus, notably that by the Persian geographer Ibn Rusteh in the early tenth century.[15] He recounts:

The Rus live on a peninsula surrounded by a marsh. The peninsula on which they live is three days' journey in extent and is covered in wood and thick scrub. It is extremely unhealthy and the ground is so sodden that it moves underfoot. Their leader bears the title Khagan-Rus. They make war against the Slavs; they take them prisoner and sell them to the Khazars and the Bulgars. They do not cultivate the land and live off what they pillage in the lands of the Slavs. At the birth of an infant, the father places a naked sword in front of the baby and says 'I leave you no fortune, no inheritance, save what you can take at the point of this blade'. They have no villages, no estates or fields. Their only occupation is trading in sable and squirrel and other kinds of skins . . . Their garments are always clean, and the men adorn themselves with golden arm-rings. They treat their slaves well and wear showy clothes, since they engage in trade . . .[16]

Another account of the Rus comes from Ibn Fadlan, who partici-
pated in an embassy from the Abbasid caliph al-Muqtadir to the king
of the Volga Bulgars in 921–2.[17] Ibn Fadlan came along as the expedition's secretary and provided a vivid description of the Rus whom he
met encamped by the River Itil (the Volga). He was admiring of their
physique, noting that they are 'as tall as date palms, blond and ruddy',
while each of them 'has an axe, a sword and a knife with him and
. . . never let themselves be separated from their weapons. The swords
are broad bladed, provided with rills, and of the Frankish type.'[18] Ibn
Fadlan describes how the Rus prayed to wooden idols placed into the
ground near their ships, and built wooden houses close to their moor-
ings; their slave girls and concubines wore neck-rings of gold and
necklaces of coloured glass beads. But he is repelled by what he regards
as the Vikings' filthy habits, as they all wash their faces and hair from
the same bowl. Their lack of cleanliness, he concludes, makes them
like 'wild asses'.

Ibn Fadlan encountered the Rus far to the east of their core territory and, by the time he met them in the 920s, they seem to have
been already well established in western Russia. The *Russian Primary
Chronicle* gives an account of these developments, which, if oversim-
plified, may contain a core of truth. Within two years of the
Varangians' arrival in Russia, two of their leaders, Sineus and Truvor,
both died, and the third brother Rurik took over their territory, after
which he based himself at Novgorod.[19] A short time later a party of
Vikings, dissatisfied with the prospects for enrichment there, sailed
further down the Dnieper, finally spying 'a small city on a hill', which
they promptly seized. Their prize was Kiev, which was most probably
a pre-existing Slav settlement, but its capture did not slake the Vikings'
thirst for plunder, and a group led by Askold and Dir carried on
southwards towards Constantinople.[20]

The Rus reached the Byzantine capital, which they would come to
know as Miklegard, 'The Great City', on 18 June 860, and the unexpected appearance of these new barbarians prompted panic among
the Greeks. 'Why,' wailed Patriarch Photius, who was entrusted with
the defence of the city in the absence of Emperor Michael III on
campaign against the Arabs, 'has this dreadful thunderbolt fallen on
us out of the furthest north?'[21] The Rus are described as sailing on a
calm sea towards Constantinople, their swords raised aloft 'as if

threatening death'. In two sermons composed to steady the nerves of the citizenry (although their content is quite likely to have had the opposite effect), Photius links the advent of the Rus to biblical prophecies such as that in Jeremiah when the Israelites are warned: 'Behold a people cometh forth from the north country . . . they are cruel and have no mercy; their voice roareth like the sea.' The Rus are said to be 'an obscure nation, a nation of no account, a nation ranked among slaves', which made the shock of their appearance at the city walls all the more profound.

In the end the attack did not amount to much, despite the patriarch's graphic description that 'everything was full of dead bodies; the flow of rivers was turned into blood; some of the fountains and reservoirs it was no longer possible to distinguish, as their cavities were made level with corpses'.[22] Photius ascribed the city's escape to divine intervention brought down on the Vikings by processions around the city wall: the mystic power of the *Himation*, the sacred robe of the Virgin Mary, which the citizenry held aloft, is said to have caused a tempest to blow up, scattering the invaders' fleet. Whether Askold and Dir's expedition really did encounter a storm, or whether they were otherwise deterred from continuing their raid, the pair did not last long afterwards. They were killed, according to the *Primary Chronicle*, by a relative of Rurik called Oleg, who then established himself in Kiev.

The Vikings' eastern trade (as measured by the inflow of Islamic dirhams) increased significantly in the 860s–880s, the period immediately after the attack on Constantinople, and the prospect of increasing riches may have encouraged the Rus to consolidate their hold on the trade routes. After a brief dip in the late ninth century, mercantile traffic once again surged, as the Samanids of central Asia, in the throes of constructing a new empire, began to produce silver dirhams in large quantities.[23] The routes by which trade reached the Rus-controlled areas shifted northwards and no longer went via Itil on the Volga, but instead through Transoxiana (in Samanid-controlled territory) and then across the steppe to Volga Bulgar. This influx of silver brought great prosperity to the Viking settlements in Russia, although much of it ultimately made its way to Scandinavia, where it formed a great part of the large number of hoards found on Gotland.

To what extent the followers of Oleg were independent actors, free of Khazar (or Bulgar) overlordship, or indeed whether the political situation was more complex still, with larger numbers of independent Scandinavian groups than the sources suggest, it is difficult to know, given the great bias of the *Russian Primary Chronicle* towards relating the dynastic history of the house of Rurik. The *Chronicle* gives an account of a series of campaigns by Oleg against the Slav tribes in the area around Kiev; in 883 he is recorded as having attacked the Derevlane (and taken a large tribute of black marten fur from them), while in the succeeding two years his armies struck the Severiane and Radimichi in turn (the latter are recorded as having previously paid tribute to the Khazars).

Now well established on the Middle Dnieper, the Vikings then struck south. In 907 Oleg is said to have led a second attack on Constantinople (although there is some doubt as to the historicity of the raid).[24] He embarked in a fleet of 200 ships, taking the same route as Askold and Dir before him. Yet when Oleg arrived at Miklegard, he found the Golden Horn, the city's natural harbour, had been blocked off by a chain.[25] The Rus prince was not to be turned aside, and simply mounted his ships on wheels and had them bypass the obstacle by rolling over the land into the Horn (a stratagem also used by the Ottoman Turks in 1453). Seeing the danger, the Greeks promised to pay Oleg tribute in return for his departure in peace, though not without first having attempted to assassinate him with poisoned food and wine. Pagans still, the Norsemen swore oaths by their god Perun not to continue with their attack, and departed, laden with gold and new silk sails for the ships.

There are some reasons to believe that, even if Oleg's 907 attack is apocryphal, Viking attacks were something the Byzantines felt they needed to guard against. The *Taktika* of Leo VI, a military manual from the 890s detailing tactics to be used by the imperial navy against a variety of foes, makes reference to the 'northern Scythians' who employed small, rapid vessels in their assaults, which seems very likely to be a reference to the Rus.[26] In any case, the agreement of 907, which stipulated that the Rus would not be allowed to stay within the city itself, was supplemented by a further treaty in 911, which set down in much greater detail the terms under which the Norsemen were permitted to trade there. Interestingly, the Rus envoys in 911 are listed as Karl, Ingjald, Farulf, Bermund, Hrollaf, Gunnar, Harold, Karni,

Frithleif, Horarr, Angantyr, Throand, Leithulf, Fast and Steinvith. Although transcribed in the actual treaty into Greek, these are exclusively Scandinavian names and indicate that at this point in the early tenth century Slavic influence on the Viking elite at Kiev was still comparatively slight.

The clauses of the 911 treaty deal with the ransom of Christian prisoners held in Rus territory and the obligation to return slaves who had escaped, as well as the procedure for dealing with criminal acts committed by the Rus while in Byzantine territory. The treaty states that such crimes were to be settled amongst themselves if they concerned only Norsemen, but were to be dealt with according to imperial law if they concerned others. The Rus were to be permitted to reside in the city for six months (a privilege otherwise accorded only to Syrians) and were exempted from all the normal customs dues.

Oleg died in 914. There had been a prophecy that his favourite stallion would be the cause of his death, and so Oleg had the animal sent away (although he ordered that it should still be cared for). Finally, after four years, Oleg found that he was missing the horse and went to visit the stables where it was kept. On being told the beast had died, he ordered its skull brought to him and stamped on it, but as he did so a venomous snake slithered out from beneath the shattered bones and bit him. It was thus the very act of showing his contempt for the oracle that brought about Oleg's doom. However he really died,[27] Oleg was succeeded by his son Igor, although the gap of several decades between these two events casts some doubt on the chronology of the *Russian Primary Chronicle*.

In 941, Igor renewed the attack against the Byzantine empire, gathering a large fleet – though probably not the 10,000 vessels the *Primary Chronicle*, in a fit of hyperbole, claims he mustered[28] – which he launched on a series of raids around the Black Sea. This time, the Byzantines countered with Greek Fire, a secret weapon developed in the late seventh century to counter invading Arab fleets, whose precise ingredients have not been established.[29] It probably contained some kind of petroleum and saltpetre and may have been in the form of a gel – something like napalm – which was initially delivered by hurling it in earthenware pots (like hand grenades) or by tossing from a trebuchet. Eventually the Byzantines seem to have learnt to pump it out of tubes, like a flame-thrower. Whatever it contained, Greek Fire's devastating impact on enemy ships – continuing to burn even in contact with water – is clear: the terrified Rus are said to have hurled themselves from their ships, preferring drowning to being burnt alive in the flames. Some of them are said to have caught alight, even in the water, while many of the rest, wearing heavy cuirasses and helmets, simply sank to the bottom. A chastened Igor retreated with the remains of his fleet, which according to one source amounted to just ten vessels from the whole grand flotilla.[30] Nonetheless, Igor returned with another fleet in 944, this time reinforced by an army including Slavs and Pechenegs (a nomadic group that had emerged into the historical record with an attack against the Rus in 941, but who were now temporarily allied with them). Forewarned of the approaching armada, the Byzantine emperor Constantine VII Porphyrogenitus bought Igor off with a handsome gift of gold and silks, although the Pechenegs still inflicted terrible damage, as they were left behind in the Balkans to plunder their way home to Kiev.

The agreement to leave the Byzantines alone was confirmed by a new treaty in 944, the terms of which were rather less favourable to the Rus than that of 911; they would now need to produce certificates stating how many ships they had brought with them before being allowed to trade, and were henceforth restricted to the purchase of fifty bezants worth of silk.[31] The Rus were also no longer allowed to remain for the winter at the mouth of the Dnieper, thus preventing them from basing a fleet of larger warships there – a wise precaution in view of the Vikings' progression from overwintering to conquest and settlement elsewhere in Europe. Another telling change from the 911 treaty is that the names of those who witnessed it on the Rus side are less overwhelmingly Scandinavian – the creep of Slavicisation had clearly reached the Kievan elite.

The final stipulation about not overwintering means that the account written by none other than Emperor Constantine Porphyrogenitus of a Rus trading convoy (in his *De Administrando Imperio*, 'On the Administration of the Empire', a kind of guidance manual for future emperors) must date from a little before the 944 treaty. The Rus fleet, Constantine explains, gathered each winter before the spring thaw at Kiev, spending the time until the river became completely navigable in June in building new boats (which the emperor describes as being hollowed out of a single tree trunk). On the appointed day the fleet mustered at Vitichev[32] and then descended down the Dnieper together. The principal hazards were twofold. The first was a 45-mile section of rapids (between modern Dnipropetrovsk and Zaporizhia in the Ukraine), where the river was only navigable at the highest June water, and even then the cargoes had to be unloaded and carried by slaves while the Rus carefully navigated their vessels through the treacherous rocks using poles. At some points even this was not enough, and the ships had to be portaged – carried overland until a more tranquil section of water was reached. The emperor records the evocative names that the Scandinavians gave these rapids, including *Essupi* ('the drinker'), *Gelandri* ('the yeller'), *Aifor* ('the ever-fierce' or 'impassable') and *Leanti* ('the laugher').

If the hazards of the river were not enough, there was the equally dangerous threat that the nomadic tribes whose territory bordered the river might attack the Rus as they were at their most vulnerable, during the portage of the boats. In 972, the Pechenegs did just that, killing Igor's successor, Svyatoslav. Finally, if they had navigated safely between rapids and nomads, the convoys arrived at St Gregory's Island.[33] Here, in the shadow of a great oak tree, the Vikings made sacrificial offerings in gratitude at their safe deliverance, before proceeding on to the island of Aitherios (Berezany, on the Black Sea near Odessa), where they rested for several days before the much more straightforward journey along the Black Sea coast to Constantinople itself.

His ambitions towards Constantinople temporarily thwarted, Igor turned his attention eastwards towards the areas dominated by the Khazars, the Bulgars and, further to the south and east, by the Arabs. Securing the trade routes here under permanent Rus control might prove every bit as lucrative as the violent extraction of more favourable trading terms from the Byzantine emperors. Already in 912,[34] a Viking expedition had raided the Caspian (helped by an agreement with the Khazars, who prudently offered the Rus free passage in exchange for a share of the plunder). The Viking raiding fleet, described by the Arab writer al-Masudi as having numbered around 500 ships (each carrying 100 men, to yield an improbably large force of 50,000 warriors), proceeded up the River Don to the Volga and thence to the Caspian Sea. The Rus had the advantage of surprise, as apparently no warships had ever been seen in these waters before, and they were able to raid freely, attacking as far as Baku (in modern Azerbaijan) and even reaching Ardabil, in north-western Iran, some three days' journey from the sea.

After several months, laden down with booty, the Vikings passed back through the Khazar lands and duly handed over the agreed share of plunder. Although the *khagan*, the Khazar ruler, himself had no interest in betraying them, many of his Muslim subjects were inflamed by the attacks against their co-religionists, and they formed a huge force of 150,000 men and fell on the Norsemen. The battle lasted three days and around 30,000 Vikings fell in the disaster, with only around 5,000 escaping in their ships down the Don to relative safety among the Bulgars.[35]

In 943–4, a Viking force returned to the Caspian, this time despatched by Igor. This made its way up the Kura River in the Caucasus, and defeated a force of levies under the governor of Bardha'a. The Rus then captured the town, amid wholesale slaughter of its citizens, but a large number of the raiders died soon afterwards in an epidemic. This made it easier for Marzuban ibn Muhammad, the ruler of Azerbaijan, to besiege the Vikings and then draw the invaders out of the town, surround them and cut them to pieces. The survivors barricaded themselves into the citadel of Bardha'a and then slipped away at night, making off with only a fraction of the plunder they had gathered.

Igor was almost certainly not present on this catastrophic raid but he perished soon afterwards in 945, during a tribute-collecting expedition among the Drevljane, who had refused an increased demand for payment and then attacked Igor's party when he came to enforce the levy in person. He was succeeded as Grand Duke of Kiev by his son, Svyatoslav, the first of the royal line to bear a Slav name. Although by now the Rus principalities were also increasingly Slavic in nature, the career of Svyatoslav, who ranged widely along the Volga, the Danube and fought against Byzantium, has much of the heroic Viking Age about it. His appearance, as portrayed by Leo the Deacon (in his description of Svyatoslav's meeting with the Byzantine emperor John Tzimiskes on the Danube in 971), could equally well apply to a host of Viking chieftains of the previous century:

He was of moderate height – neither taller than average, or particularly short; his eyebrows were thick; he had grey eyes and a snub nose; his beard was clean shaven, but he let the hair grow abundantly on his upper lip where it was bushy and long; and he shaved his head completely, except for a lock of hair that hung down on one side as a mark of the nobility of his ancestry; he was solid in the neck, broad in the chest and very well articulated in the rest of his body; he had a rather angry and savage appearance; on one ear was fastened a gold earring, adorned with two pearls and a red gemstone between them; his clothing was white, no different from that of his companions, except in cleanliness.[36]

The first target of Svyatoslav's armies was the Khazar empire. The attack probably took place sometime in the 960s[37] and the Rus army soon took a town called Biela Viezha ('White Tower'), which may have been Itil, the Khazar capital. A contemporary account (from around 965) tells of the devastation of the town's orchards, as the invaders left nothing but ruins behind them. The Khazar state collapsed and never recovered, removing a useful buffer state in the Caucasus and opening the way for later nomadic invasions, which the Rus would have cause to regret. As late as the eleventh century the site of Itil was still a field of ruins.

Still ambitious to expand the territory under his control, Svyatoslav then embarked on a campaign against the Bulgars on the Danube. He was encouraged by the Byzantine emperor Nicephorus Phocas (963–9), who hoped that whichever one of them emerged victorious, two potential foes of Byzantium would have been weakened in the fighting. Armed with a bribe of 1,500 pounds of gold from Nicephorus, Svyatoslav made rapid progress, his cause boosted by the death of the great Bulgarian tsar Symeon and his replacement by a rather less warlike successor, Peter. The Rus army rampaged through Bulgaria, confining the Bulgars to the town of Dristra, and sacked several major settlements, before halting somewhere near the bend of the Danube (possibly in the old late-Roman fort at Dinogetia).

There Svyatoslav heard the unfortunate news that his mother, Olga, had fallen ill. The Kievan prince hurried homewards, leaving the bulk of his fleet behind and, though suffering an attack by the Pechenegs on his way back, reached Kiev just before she died in 969. On his return to Bulgaria later the same year he found that most of the Rus gains had been lost to a new Bulgarian tsar, Boris, whose generally pro-Byzantine stance made Svyatoslav a rather less convenient ally for the Greeks. The Rus faced far more stubborn Bulgar resistance than before, but when the new Byzantine emperor John Tzimiskes – who had had Nicephorus murdered in his bedroom – offered to continue the payment of tribute to the Scandinavians if they left Bulgaria, he found Svyatoslav surprisingly unreceptive. There was an exchange of blustering messages between the two rulers, in which the Kievan ruler demanded that his Byzantine counterpart should head for Asia, since the only price the Rus would accept to return to Kiev was all the imperial territories in Europe, while Tzimiskes retorted acidly that Svyatoslav should have a care, lest he suffer the same fate that had befallen his father's fleet when it attacked the empire in 941.[38]

A Byzantine offensive against the Rus faltered when Bardas Phocas, the general leading it, rebelled against John Tzimiskes and left for Cappadocia in Asia Minor to muster support there. The emperor was forced to conduct the campaign in person, and nearly destroyed the Rus army holed up in Pereyaslavets, from which only a small party managed to break out. Further setbacks for the Vikings followed, with many of their leading warriors killed. A final battle in July 971 was hard fought, with the Byzantines benefiting (as they often seem to have believed) from supernatural aid, this time in the shape of a mysterious man riding a white horse, who led a decisive charge at the critical moment in the fighting. Admitting defeat, Svyatoslav negotiated terms with the Byzantine emperor on an island in the Danube.[39]

Whether Svyatoslav's position back at home in Kiev was weakened by his lack of success against the Greeks will never be known. At some point, as he made his way back up the Danube with the remnants of his army – presumably while he was trying to traverse one of the many rapids – Svyatoslav's party was ambushed by a big force of Pechenegs who had been lying in wait. Large numbers of Vikings were slaughtered, including the Prince of Kiev. Svyatoslav's skull was hollowed out and inlaid with gold, to be used as a drinking cup by the victorious Pecheneg chief – a charming habit of the steppe nomads, which had been previously visited on the Byzantine emperor Nicephorus I after his defeat by the Bulgarian Khan Krum in 811, although on that occasion it was silver rather than gold that was used as the lining for the macabre drinking vessel.

Svyatoslav's death was followed by a vicious civil war amongst his sons, Yaropolk, Oleg and Vladimir. Yaropolk killed Oleg, but in 978 he in turn was treacherously murdered by his remaining brother while attending a meeting to discuss peace between them. Vladimir then seized the throne with the aid of a large band of mercenaries whom he had recruited from Sweden and with the assistance of Blud, a Slav general who had defected from Yaropolk's camp.[40] Once secure on the throne, Vladimir attacked several neighbouring tribes, including the Radomichi, in an effort to increase the core territory of Kiev. He built a series of strongholds in the south of the realm, intended to act as bastions against the Pechenegs, and also sent a fleet against the Volga Bulgars.

Vladimir was still a pagan (although his mother Olga was a Christian, few other leading Rus had followed her lead), and is said to have flirted briefly with conversion to Islam. The *Primary Chronicle* tells how Vladimir called for representatives of the main religions to report on the mode of worship in their home countries. There came in succession ambassadors from the Volga Bulgars (who were Muslim), from the Khazars (who were Jewish), from Germany (which was Catholic) and from Constantinople (which was Orthodox). Having heard them out, Vladimir despatched his own envoys to confirm his impressions. On their return, these nobles reported:

> When we journeyed among the Bulgars, we beheld how they worship in their temple, called a mosque, while they stand ungirt. The Bulgar bows, sits down, looks hither and thither like one possessed, and there is no happiness among them but instead only sorrow and a dreadful stench. Then we went among the Germans, and saw them performing many ceremonies in their temples; but we beheld no glory there. Then we went to Greece, and the Greeks led us to the edifices where they worship their God, and we knew not whether we were in heaven or on earth. For on earth there is no such splendour or such beauty, and we are at a loss how to describe it. We only know that God dwells there among men, and their service is fairer than the ceremonies of other nations. For we cannot forget that beauty.[41]

Vladimir had already given some indication of his final decision, for he had found the insistence of the Muslims on abstinence from pork and wine a most disagreeable prospect; '"Drinking", he said, "is the joy of the Russes. We cannot exist without that pleasure."' As for the German Catholics, Vladimir was horrified by their promotion of fasting, while the Khazars he rejected on the grounds that the Jews had been driven out of their Holy Land, and so God must be angry with them. That left the Orthodox creed. Whether Vladimir was enticed by the aesthetic grandeur and mystique of Byzantine ceremonial or, more likely, by the very real diplomatic advantages to be gained by becoming a fully fledged Christian ruler within the Greek imperial sphere, in 988 he agreed to accept Christianity from Constantinople. In exchange he was to receive the not insubstantial inducement of Emperor Basil II's sister, Anna, in marriage. The story that Anna was none too keen on marital exile in far-off Kiev is reinforced by Vladimir's attack on Byzantine-held Cherson in the Crimea, hardly the act of a would-be brother-in-law. The Rus are said to have captured the city after a traitor inside shot an arrow, to which was attached a message informing Vladimir how to cut off the town's water supply. With Cherson in his hands, the marriage negotiations seem to have proceeded much more smoothly and both the wedding and Vladimir's own baptism took place soon afterwards in Kiev. As a symbolic gesture, Vladimir had the pagan idols of the old religion cast down, having the most important – that of Perun (which was made of wood, with a head of silver and a moustache of gold) – tied to a horse's tail and dragged down the Borichev hill to the stream at its foot. There, in a macabre re-creation of a human sacrifice, he ordered twelve men to beat the image of the fallen god with cudgels.

The change in nature of the Kievan Rus state from Viking outpost to Slav kingdom was almost complete. The Scandinavian warriors who had long been welcomed in the Rus lands (which the Vikings called Gardariki, 'the kingdom of fortresses') were now something of an inconvenience to Vladimir. Although he had employed them in his own ascent to power, he wanted no such destabilising bands of unemployed warriors causing mischief, now that he had secured both the throne and diplomatic respectability. He resolved the problem, as well as gaining favour from Basil, by sending a large number of these Varangians (as the mercenaries were known) to support the Byzantine emperor in putting down the rebellion of Bardas Phocas.[42] This force, perhaps as large as 6,000 strong, was the origin of the Varangian Guard, which would form the nucleus of the Byzantine Imperial Guard for the next two centuries.[43]

Vladimir died in 1015, and his death was followed by another bitter succession struggle. One of his sons, Svyatopolk, was driven mad by the effects of his final defeat in battle, while the victor, Yaroslav, was forced into grudging acceptance of a division of the principality between himself and his remaining brother, Mstislav, who ruled from Chernigov. Yaroslav, who based himself in Novgorod, was not particularly popular in his own lands, but was very particular about keeping up connections with his ancestral homeland, and thus obtained rather more approving mentions in the sagas. On no fewer than six occasions he is said to have called on 'Varangians' from overseas to reinforce his armies.[44] He chose as his wife Ingigerd, the daughter of Olof Skötkonung of Sweden, and gave shelter at various times to Olaf Haraldsson of Norway after he was expelled in 1028, and later to Magnus Olafsson and his brother Harald Hardrada, in the aftermath of Olaf's defeat and death at the Battle of Stiklestad in 1030. He strengthened the Scandinavian connection by giving his daughter Elizaveta in marriage to Hardrada (although there were limits to sentimentality in that regard, and other daughters were married off to Andrew I of Hungary and Henry I of France). He further underlined his status as a Christian monarch, rather than a Viking adventurer, by building St Sophia in Kiev, Russia's first cathedral, in 1037, while advances that he made against the Chud to the north and in pushing the boundaries of the Kievan principality to the west made him the most powerful yet of the Rus princes.

Yaroslav's most serious misstep was an ill-judged attack on Constantinople in 1043, which ended with the destruction of the Kievan fleet and a severe dent to his own prestige. By then, the last hurrah of Viking Russia had taken place, an expedition in the grand old style led by Yngvar the Widefarer, which set off around the year 1040. It seems to have been a large-scale raid aimed against the Muslim lands around the Caspian, and is remembered by a series of twenty-five runestones (all of them in Sweden) commemorating those who fell on the expedition. One, from Gripsholm, records: 'Tola had this stone raised for his son Harald, Yngvar's brother. They journeyed boldly, far afield after gold: in the east they gave food to eagles. They died in the south, in Serkland.' (*Serkland* is the generic Old Norse term for the Muslim-controlled lands.) Another, more laconic inscription simply records the names of the deceased and the lands to which they had travelled: 'Ormika, Ulfair, Greece, Jerusalem, Iceland, Serkland.'

Apart from the runestones, the only real source for Yngvar's expedition is the *Yngvar Saga*, which relates how the expedition's leader won early fame as a warrior, but found that Olof Skötkonung of Sweden would not grant him any land. Rebuffed, he went to the court of Yaroslav and set out to explore the lands to the east of Gardariki, pressing far down the largest river (probably the Volga). His adventures included the utterly improbable (encountering a dragon in flight and seizing a great silver cauldron from a giant); the barely credible, such as his sojourn at the court of a beautiful queen, Silkisif; and the almost plausible, such as encountering a fleet armed with Greek Fire (although the saga then once more descends into the fantastic, as Yngvar kills a giant, carries his enormous foot away and uses it as bait to lure away a dragon, whose mound the Vikings then rob). Finally, Yngvar finds a haunted hall in which the standard of the long-dead King Harald of Sweden has been hidden. When he takes the banner, a curse falls on him and he and many of his men die of disease on the way home.[45]

By this time other changes, too, had radically modified the nature of Viking Russia. The flow of dirhams being imported from the Islamic lands had slowed in the 960s and came to a virtual halt in the 1030s (so that hoards of this date are rare in Gotland, where the bulk of dirhams have been found). Arabic coins were replaced by Anglo-Saxon and German issues, many of the latter minted using silver from the Hartz Mountains, where production was just stepping up. And, more importantly, the supply of Viking mercenaries also dried up and traditional links of family and shared culture withered. The Kievan rulers became more and more part of a Slavic culture that looked southwards to Constantinople for its inspiration rather than northwards to Scandinavia. By the mid-eleventh century the Viking Age in Russia can be considered at an end.

Map 11 New Empires of the Eleventh Century

Ruled by Cnut, October 1016

Acquired by Cnut by end 1016

Acquired by Cnut, 1019

Acquired by Cnut, 1028

Norwegian Sea

Atlantic Ocean

Faroes

EARLDOM OF ORKNEY

Shetland

Brough of Birsay

Egilsay

Papa Stronsey

Skaill *Orkney*

Burray

Kirkwall

SCOTLAND

Stiklestad, 1030

Trondheim

TRØNDELAG

Hardangerfjord

HORDALAND UPPLAND

Mostere

VIKEN

ROGALAND

N O R W A Y

Nesjar, 1015

AGDER

S W E D E N

Sigtuna

Vänern

Vättern

North Sea

RAUNRIKE

D E N M A R K

Helga Å, 1026

Jutland Roskilde

Lund

Bornholm

Svold, 1000

Hedeby

WENDLAND

Bamburgh

NORTHUMBRIA

Gainsborough

E N G L A N D

Wallingford Oxford

Malmesbury London *Ashingdon, 1016*

Bath

SOMERSET Greenwich

DEVON Canterbury

Wareham *Isle of Wight*

Aachen

English Channel

Rouen

NORMANDY Paris

Elbe

Rhine

Danube

N

8

New Empires in Britain and Scandinavia, 950–1150

The expulsion of Eirik Bloodaxe from York in 954 seemed to mark the end of the Viking threat to Britain. Alfred the Great's descendants had unified England under the House of Wessex and the last independent Scandinavian settlement in England had fallen. The reign of Edgar (959–75), the main events of which were a series of reforms to the Church and the coinage, was so tranquil in comparison to those of his predecessors that he acquired the nickname 'The Peaceable'. A shadow, though, crossed the land after his death, as Edward and Aethelred, his two sons (by different queens), vied for the kingship. Edward, supported by Dunstan, the reforming Archbishop of Canterbury, was initially successful. But then, three years later, Edward was murdered in distinctly murky circumstances while he was visiting Aethelred and his mother Aelfthryth at Corfe Castle. As the *Anglo-Saxon Chronicle* puts it, 'No worse deed for the English race was done than this, since they first sought out the land of Britain.'[1]

Many believed that Aelfthryth herself was responsible,[2] driven to murder out of ambition for her son, but such lingering suspicions did not prevent Aethelred from succeeding to the throne. The new king was just eleven or twelve years old, and the taint of regicide was hardly the most auspicious way to begin his reign. Yet, under the tutelage of his mother and advisers such as Bishop Aethelwold of Winchester and Aelfhere, the Ealdorman of Mercia, there was every expectation that his reign would be as long, peaceful and prosperous as that of his father.

Long Aethelred's reign certainly was, but it was so disastrous that he earnt himself the nickname *Unraed* – which does not, as commonly supposed, mean 'Unready', but rather 'Ill-Counselled' – for his failure to prevent the catastrophe that engulfed England.[3] Within a year of Aethelred's consecration in May 979 at Kingston-on-Thames, the first Viking raids for decades saw Southampton sacked, the Isle of Thanet ravaged and bands of Norsemen spreading devastation through Cheshire. Whether the raiders were pulled by their awareness of the new king's tender age and the dubious circumstances of his accession, or were instead pushed (as the sagas imply) by the increasing strength of the Scandinavian monarchies under rulers such as Harald Bluetooth of Denmark, is difficult to determine.

These first raids were freelance affairs and, although damaging, did not seriously threaten to destabilise England. An attack on Cornwall followed in 981, and then another on Portland in Dorset the next year. The following decade was punctuated by further raids and rising tension between Aethelred's court and Duke Richard of Normandy, who was suspected of harbouring Viking fleets in his ports.[4] A peace treaty between Wessex and Normandy, brokered by the papal envoy Leo, Bishop of Trevi, was signed in 991, which contained the provision that each side promised not to shelter the other's (unspecified) enemies.

The pact may have brought hope, but it did not bring peace. Barely six months later a huge war fleet, of perhaps ninety-three ships, made its way along the east coast of England, raiding Sandwich in Kent, and then falling upon Ipswich before it came to land at Maldon in Essex. This time the attackers were led by no small-time Viking free-booter, but by Olaf Tryggvason, a man of noble blood, the son of the ruler of Viken around Oslofjord and, the sagas would later claim, the great-great-grandson of Harald Finehair himself.[5]

Maldon was the second-largest town in Essex at the time (after Colchester)[6] and although the Vikings could easily have sailed up the River Blackwater, which is still tidal at that point, they chose not to do so and instead encamped on Northey Island, which is around a mile downstream.[7] The island was accessible to the mainland only by a tidal causeway (which had existed since Roman times). As a result, passage to or from the island was only practicable at low tide, making surprise attacks on the Viking camp impossible, but equally impeding their ability to conduct a raid or manoeuvre to face an attacking force.

The Norsemen were soon confronted by a group of local levies led by Byrhtnoth of East Anglia, who was Aethelred's most experienced ealdorman (the highest-ranking local official in Anglo-Saxon England), having held the position since 956. The lack of time available to call up any but the *fyrd* of Essex meant that he probably only had 500 or 600 men, as against possibly five times that number in Olaf's army.[8] The course of the battle, which is dealt with somewhat peremptorily in the *Anglo-Saxon Chronicle* (which also mistakenly puts its date as 993 rather than 991), is better known from an Old English poem known as 'The Battle of Maldon'.[9] According to this, Byrhtnoth lined his men up along the river, instructing them to form a shield-wall as he rode up and down on horseback to inspect the formation.

Seeing the approaching Anglo-Saxon force, the Vikings sent over a messenger to demand a payment from Byrhtnoth in return for departing in peace. The ealdorman understandably dismissed this attempt to extort a bribe. With his enemy bottled up on the island, and their only hope of reaching Maldon being across the narrow causeway where they could be easily picked off, Byrhtnoth had the luxury of being able to wait until more substantial reinforcements arrived. He arrayed his men along the river bank to either side of the causeway and waited for the Vikings' next move.

Olaf's men unleashed an arrow-storm against the English, a characteristic attempt to thin an opponent's ranks before the main battle. The tide, however, was now beginning to ebb, exposing Byrhtnoth to a possible bid by the Vikings to force the causeway. At high tide, the water is around 6 feet deep, and so it was only now that such a crossing was possible. The English ealdorman ordered three champions to block the passage, which – at only about 6 feet wide, and with the water to either side still hindering any attempt to bypass them – the English warriors could have done without having to face more than a few of their opponents at any one time. The trio of Wulfstan, Maccus and Aelfhere fought valiantly 'as long as they could wield weapons',[10] and seem to have beaten off the initial Viking assault.

The Vikings and Byrhtnoth now engaged in a further round of parlaying, with the Norsemen asking for permission to cross the causeway so that the two sides could fight on equal terms. The ealdorman is said to have agreed, allowing the Vikings onto the mainland, 'on account of his pride'.[11] Exactly why he did so has been the subject of much debate, with explanations ranging from the literal – that he genuinely believed his own numerically inferior forces could beat the Vikings – to a view that he wanted to engage Olaf's force before the Scandinavians could sail off and attack an even less well-defended town.

Whatever the reason behind it, the result of Byrhtnoth's bravado was catastrophic. The Vikings must have surged across and, though 'The Battle of Maldon' poet is rather imprecise on the actual course of the combat, he refers to the Vikings as wolves, 'beasts of battle' who feasted on the corpses of the dead. The English formed up in a shield-wall, but were gradually overwhelmed. At the height of the fray, Byrhtnoth was struck in the arm. He broke off the shaft of the spear that had penetrated his armour, but fell to the ground, fatally wounded. At this point a certain Godric, son of Odda, mounted Byrhtnoth's horse and fled. Thinking that their commander was abandoning them, many of the English followed him, while those who stood firm were cut down to a man.

Byrhtnoth's body was collected by the monks of Ely Abbey and buried in the minster. The Vikings had decapitated his corpse and carried off the head, so a ball of wax was set in its place in the coffin.[12] Although the 'Maldon' poem may well be more literary artifice than accurate reflection of the battle,[13] Aethelred's forces clearly suffered a serious setback and the political effects were profound. The *Anglo-Saxon Chronicle* records that later that year, the Norsemen were paid a tribute of 10,000 pounds, the first time that such a bribe had been paid to them, 'because of the great terror that they were causing along the coast'.

Predictably, and as would be the pattern for the next two decades, the payment acted as an inducement rather than as the intended deterrent to further Viking raids. In 992, a fleet that had been assembled to head off a new Viking army was defeated, apparently betrayed by Aelfric, Ealdorman of East Anglia.[14] Then, in 994, a dangerous new protagonist joined the renewed Viking assault in Britain. Svein *Tjúguskegg* ('Forkbeard') had replaced his father, Harald Bluetooth, as King of the Danes after a rebellion in 987.[15] Initially preoccupied with asserting his authority over Denmark, in 994 he joined the Norwegian Olaf Tryggvason in an attack on London. Although they were driven off, their subsequent ravaging of the south coast forced Aethelred to allow the Vikings to overwinter in England and to pay them 16,000 pounds of silver to desist from further raiding. One positive result of this truce was that Olaf agreed to accept Christian baptism and to leave England for ever – a stipulation which, perhaps surprisingly, he adhered to, thus splitting up the potentially devastating alliance between Danes and Norwegians. His departure had the useful side-effect, from Aethelred's point of view, of causing Svein, too, to return to Scandinavia to head off any attempt by Olaf to expand into Denmark.

For the next five years Aethelred enjoyed a respite, until Svein's defeat of his rival at the Battle of Svold in 1000[16] enabled the Danish king to turn his attention to England again. There had been some Viking raids in the interim, notably those carried out by an army that arrived in 997 and which for the next two years ravaged the south coast until it retired to Normandy in 1000, but these did not pose the same threat as the incursions of the early 990s. Aethelred's displeasure at Duke Richard II of Normandy harbouring this particular Viking fleet led to negotiations that resulted in the king's marriage to the duke's sister Emma, and the expulsion of the Norsemen.[17]

It was possibly this force, pushed out of its Norman haven, that attacked Devon and Somerset in 1001 and then overwintered on the Isle of Wight. Terms were finally negotiated with the raiders, who extorted a payment of 24,000 pounds. The price of peace was rising steadily, and all the time the respite that the tributes won was growing ever shorter. Frustrated that his pay-offs to the Danes had not had the desired effect, and fearing that the invaders might soon return and even try to seize land for settlement, Aethelred resolved to take more decisive action. Sometime in the late summer of 1002 he issued an order for the killing of 'all the Danish men that were in England'. The massacre took place on St Brice's Day (13 November): John of Wallingford, writing in the thirteenth century, records that 'They spared neither age nor sex, destroying together with them those women of their own nation who had consented to intermix with the Danes . . . the children were dashed to pieces against posts and stones.'

The St Brice's Day Massacre has left one of the more macabre legacies of the Viking invasions of Britain. These are the 'Dane-skins' kept in various churches of the former Danelaw, which are said to be the flayed skins of victims of the massacre. Most of them are almost certainly animal skins to which the grizzly legend became attached, although there is some suggestion that the skin stretched over the church door at Hadstock Church (near Saffron Walden in Essex) may be the genuine article (though whether of a Dane who perished at Aethelred's orders is impossible to determine).[18] There was great excitement in 2008 when the bones of thirty-seven adult males (mainly aged between sixteen and twenty-five) dating from the Viking era were found buried in a Neolithic ditch being excavated in the grounds of St John's College, Oxford. Evidence of charring to the bones suggested that they might be victims of the St Brice's Day Massacre. It was

consistent with the account of a royal charter of 1004 that recorded
how the Danes in Oxford, who are said to have sprouted up 'like
cockle among wheat', took refuge in the Church of St Frideswide,
and the local people – unable to gain entry to cut them down – simply
burnt the building to the ground. Subsequent analysis, however, has
indicated that the victims, although of Scandinavian origin, were very
probably warriors who died some decades earlier, possibly executed
after being captured.[19] Victims of a massacre they may well have been,
but not of that ordered by Aethelred in 1002. Evidence of another
11th-century massacre was uncovered in 2009 near Weymouth in
Dorset. The fifty young men – analysis showed they were between
18 and 25 years old and came from Scandinavia and the Baltic – had
all been decapitated and their skulls placed to one side of a mass burial
pit. Whether an unfortunate Viking raiding party, or more victims of
the St Brice's Day Massacre, we simply do not know.

Just like the *gafol* (the tribute payments to the Vikings), the cold-
blooded slaughter of much of England's Danish population had
precisely the opposite effect to the one Aethelred had planned. The
very next year Exeter was stormed by a Viking army led by none
other than Svein Forkbeard, who is said to have sailed over to wreak
revenge for the death of his countrymen.[20] He travelled via Normandy,
where he made a treaty with Richard, who agreed to take in wounded
Danes in exchange for a share of the booty. The *Anglo-Saxon Chronicle*
takes a fairly dim view of the quality of opposition to Svein's invasion,
blaming lack of organisation and treachery for their losses (in 1003
Ealdorman Aelfric of East Anglia was again accused of betraying the
English cause by feigning sickness at a crucial moment, resulting in a
devastating defeat for the English levies at the hands of the Danes[21]).

By 1007 Aelfric had been supplanted as the leading English noble
by Eadric Streona, who was appointed Ealdorman of Mercia that year.
A figure who looms large in the list of those responsible for the disasters of Aethelred's reign, Eadric is described as having a dubious past,
being complicit in the murder of Ealdorman Aelfhelm of Northumbria
in 1006.[22] His appointment came just after Aethelred had authorised
the payment of the largest tribute yet to the Danes: of 36,000 pounds
to a force based on the Isle of Wight that had been laying waste to
large areas of Hampshire and Berkshire.

Aethelred managed to take advantage of a brief pause in Danish activity to reorganise the Midlands into shires and to re-form the military levy, so that every 310 hides of territory should contribute a ship to the national defence, and every eight hides a helmet and a shirt of mail.[23] He also had the fortifications of some *burhs* strengthened (possibly including Wareham, Malmesbury and Wallingford), and the general air of martial renewal was reinforced by the issue of 'Helmet' coins, which portrayed Aethelred wearing military headgear in place of the normal royal crown. He was assisted in this programme by Wulfstan, the Archbishop of York since 1002, who, as well as being a vigorous proponent of church reform, assisted the king in the drafting of all his royal law codes.[24]

In the end, none of Aethelred's reforms mattered. On 1 August 1009, a huge new Viking army arrived in England, led by the Dane Thorkell the Tall, who is said to have come in revenge for the death of his brother Hemming, leader of an earlier raid that year.[25] Aethelred's initial response was not a tribute payment, not a military strike to cut off the Scandinavians before they could become established, or even a further massacre of Danes. Instead – doubtless under the influence of Wulfstan – he ordered a national outpouring of prayer. The legislation enacted at Bath in the first part of 1009 set out a large-scale programme of fasting, prayers and penance. During the national three-day fast there were to be processions, thirty Masses said by each priest every day, and at monasteries in particular Masses were to be said 'against the heathen'.

The *Sermo Lupi ad Anglos* ('Sermon of the Wolf to the English'), of which Wulfstan was almost certainly the author, contained an evocative condemnation of the Anglo-Saxons for their moral laxity, which had led to God's judgement on them in the shape of the Scandinavian invaders. In a rhetorical flourish employed by previous Anglo-Saxon writers, such as Bede, the author of the *Sermo* pointed to the fate of the Britons five centuries before, whose similarly sinful state had caused God to allow their defeat at the very hands of Aethelred's own ancestors.[26]

God failed to smile on the Anglo-Saxons for their piety or to smite their Viking tormentors, and at Christmas 1009 Thorkell's army sacked Oxford and then overwintered in Kent. In May 1010, they encountered the English army under Ealdorman Ulfcytel. In a hard-fought battle the English were driven from the field, having lost a number of nobles. With East Anglia subdued and the way open to the East Midlands, Thorkell was now joined by Olaf Haraldsson, the future King of

Norway, and during a joint attack on London they are said to have
pulled down London Bridge, an event commemorated in the children's
nursery rhyme 'London Bridge is Falling Down'.[27]

By 1011, Thorkell had overrun East Anglia, the Midlands and much
of Wessex. As the despairing Aethelred desperately sued for peace,
offering the by-now-customary handsome tribute to buy off the
invaders, Thorkell's army besieged Canterbury. The city fell at the
end of September, and amongst the clutch of high-value prisoners
taken by the Vikings was Aelfeah, the Archbishop of Canterbury.
Finally, on Easter Day 1012, an English delegation led by Eadric Streona
came to negotiate a peace. The payment he promised was a stupen-
dous 48,000 pounds, the largest amount yet handed over to the Vikings.
But it was not enough, as Thorkell's men demanded a separate
payment against the archbishop's freedom. Aelfeah refused to let this
supplementary tribute be raised and, angered at being deprived of an
extra slice of money, a group of drunken Vikings began pelting him
with ox bones, and then one struck him on the back of the head with
an axe. This final blow proved fatal and so, amid the raucous squalor
of an over-rowdy Viking feast, England's leading churchman perished.

Aelfeah's body was carried to London and soon afterwards he began
to be venerated as a martyr. Of more immediate consequence was
the defection to Aethelred's side of Thorkell, long the scourge of the
English, together with his complement of forty-five ships. The Anglo-
Saxon king may now have felt himself secure, but in July the following
year Svein once more set sail for England, this time accompanied by
his son Cnut. The fleet was large and magnificently accoutred. The
Encomium Emmae Reginae states: 'On one side lions moulded in gold
were to be seen on the ships, on the other birds on the top of the
masts indicated by their movements the winds as they blew, or dragons
of various kinds poured fire from their nostrils. Here, there were
glittering men of solid gold or silver nearly comparable to live ones.'[28]

On making landfall, Svein made his way rapidly up the Trent to
Gainsborough in Lincolnshire. He received the surrender of Northumbria
and the Five Boroughs; in short, much of the old Danelaw. There was
so little opposition, and the surrender of northern England was so
rapid, that it is hard to believe it was not prearranged. Tension between
Aethelred and his sons by his first marriage (most notably Prince
Aethelstan[29]), who feared their dispossession by their half-brothers by

Emma (Aethelred's second wife), also weakened the English resolve. Svein's host moved southwards and before long Oxford and Winchester had submitted to him. Only at London, where Aethelred and Thorkell had based themselves, was there any sign of resistance.

Svein bypassed them and moved off to Bath, where he received the important submission of Aethelmaer, son of the Ealdorman of western Wessex. The Londoners, seeing that they were now virtually alone in clinging to Aethelred's cause, gave up hope and surrendered. In the meantime, Queen Emma and her children, Alfred and Edward, had fled to the court of her brother Richard in Normandy. Aethelred tarried a while, seeking refuge first with Thorkell's army, which was stationed at Greenwich, and then on the Isle of Wight, before slipping across the Channel to join his wife a little after Christmas 1013. By then, resistance to the Danes had totally collapsed and Svein was acclaimed King of England. To strengthen his position, he had his son Cnut marry Aelfgifu, the daughter of Ealdorman Aelfhelm of Northumbria, thus cementing a dynastic alliance between the Danish royal family and the Anglo-Saxon nobility.

It looked as if the Danes had finally achieved their centuries-old ambition of conquering England, ironically without much of a fight. All their plans were thrown into disarray, however, by the sudden and unexpected death of Svein Forkbeard on 2 February 1014.[30] With Cnut's position uncertain – he faced opposition from his brother Harald to any claim to the Danish throne – the English nobility performed a volte-face and called for Aethelred's return.

In penance for his previous misrule, Aethelred was forced to agree to govern 'more justly than he had before', and to 'improve each of those things which they all hated'.[31] His promise to declare 'every Danish king outlawed from England for ever' must have come more easily to Aethelred, but there remained the problem of the Danish fleet, which had declared Cnut as king, and which was still supported by a group of Prince Aethelstan's partisans. The alliance ranged against him was too strong, however, and Cnut retired to Denmark, pausing briefly at Sandwich to drop off some of his hostages, whose noses and ears he had hacked off.

Aethelred's second, brief reign was scarcely more tranquil than his first period on the throne. After the necessary business of dealing with those who had supported Cnut, including the murders of Sigeferth and

Morcar (the principal nobles who had remained loyal to the Danish cause to the end), Aethelred fell seriously ill in the summer of 1015. Unfortunately, the king's incapacity coincided with the return of Cnut, who had come off worst in the tussle for the Danish throne with his brother Harald and had opted instead to try for a tilt at the English crown.

The situation was further complicated by the appearance of Edmund Ironside, Aethelred's second son, with a fresh army and a new force recruited by Eadric Streona. In theory, Edmund (whose nickname derived from his reputation for great bravery) was in open revolt against his father, but Eadric, who might have rallied loyalist sentiment to Aethelred, in the end defected to Cnut, taking with him forty precious ships. Further confusion arose when Aethelred seemed to rally in the autumn, rendering Edmund's position distinctly uncomfortable. He managed to entice his father to join him in person, but some of Aethelred's advisers persuaded the ailing king that Edmund was in fact plotting to depose him and so he returned to London.

The complex three-cornered fight for England unwound in 1016, beginning with the death of Aethelred in April. Cnut's position was already reasonably secure in the Danelaw, and just before the king's death he had been preparing for an assault on London. While the *witangemot*, the royal council,[32] opted to recognise Edmund as king, the Danish fleet finally reached London in early May and laid siege to it.[33] Cnut is said to have demanded an enormous ransom of 60,000 pounds to allow safe passage for Queen Emma, who was marshalling the defences, and her two sons. Edmund, however, had slipped away to the West Country, where he raised another army and, after skirmishes with Danish forces that Cnut had sent to intercept him, managed to relieve London.

In an effort to regroup, Cnut moved northwards to Essex and Mercia and then struck south again, pushing Edmund back into Kent. At this point Eadric Streona, whose reputation for perfidy seems to have been well earned, decided to defect once again and join Edmund. The combined English forces pursued Cnut, overtaking him somewhere in Essex at 'a hill which is called *Assandun*'[34] (or Ashingdon). The battle that followed was a disaster for the English – the *Anglo-Saxon Chronicle* records that the treacherous Eadric fled from the battlefield and his withdrawal began a rout. The dead included Ealdorman Aelfric of Hampshire, Ulfcytel of East Anglia, Bishop Eadnoth of Dorchester,

Abbot Wulfsige of Ramsey and a clutch of other nobles. Edmund, however, survived, but with his chances of seizing undisputed control of the English crown dashed, he was forced into an agreement with Cnut at Alney, which left him in control of little more than Wessex, while his Danish rival was recognised as sovereign in the North, Mercia and East Anglia. This uneasy and highly unstable arrangement cannot have been destined to endure for long without renewed conflict between the unwilling co-rulers. In the event, Edmund never really recovered from wounds he had received at Ashingdon, and on 30 November 1016 he died. After three years of confusion, Cnut was now unrivalled King of England.

The complex political manoeuvrings during the crisis of 1013–16 revealed the weakness of the Anglo-Saxon position, in that decades of failure to face up to the Danish challenge had left the country divided and prone to factionalism amongst the nobility. But it equally demonstrated its underlying strength, as the Danes had only been able to overcome English opposition because of the unusually rapid attrition amongst the Anglo-Saxon royal family (with Aethelstan, Aethelred and Edmund all dying in rapid succession). Even now, Cnut's position was ambiguous, and it was only in 1017 that he was 'chosen' to be king.[35] He made few concessions to the native English nobility, setting Scandinavians as earls over East Anglia (Thorkell) and Northumbria (Erik, his brother-in-law). The mercurial Eadric Streona was left in place as Ealdorman of Mercia, but only until Cnut was reasonably sure that he would face no major rebellions. At Christmas 1017 the new king had his untrustworthy ally murdered, putting to a brutal end a career that had seen the Mercian ealdorman support at one time or another almost every one of the various claimants to the English throne.

Cnut further cemented his position by marrying Aethelred's widow Emma, which provided him with a connection to the royal house of Wessex, as well as handily creating a marriage alliance with the Duchy of Normandy (as Emma was Duke Richard's sister). It also set aside Cnut's still very much alive first wife Aelfgifu, by whom he had two sons, Svein and Harald.[36] In 1018, he also raised an enormous levy to pay off the warriors whom he had brought over with him from Denmark. The sum, around £82,000 of silver, was the largest tribute ever paid to a Viking army, exceeding, ironically, all those that had been paid out by Aethelred in an effort to stave off their depredations.[37]

Harald, who had succeeded Svein Forkbeard on the Danish throne, died in late 1018 or early 1019 and Cnut rushed to Denmark with a small force to secure his kingship there. In England he had retained the services of only forty ships, enough to provide security, but not, it turned out, to deter conspiracies, and news of a plot in 1020 brought him rushing back across the North Sea, after which he had Eadwig, another of Aethelred's sons, put to death.[38] The other possible contenders for the throne, the children of Edmund Ironside, were too young to pose a threat. After a spell in Sweden they had in any case ended up in far-off Hungary. Edward and Alfred, Aethelred's sons by Emma, were also not of an age to be seriously considered as replacements for Cnut, although their presence in Normandy was at a rather less comfortable distance for the pro-Danish faction in England.

Throughout Cnut's rule the majority of appointments to senior positions remained Scandinavian. Thorkell the Tall, who had played such a pivotal role in the progressive Danish conquest under Svein and Cnut, proved to be a worryingly over-mighty subject. On Thorkell's recall to Denmark in 1023 he almost destabilised the king's rule there, forcing a rapid reconciliation and return to England. For the most part, however, Cnut's rule in England after 1020 was tranquil, supported by a tactical alliance with Archbishop Wulfstan of York, who kept the Church and the remaining Anglo-Saxon nobility onside.

Cnut's struggle with Olaf Haraldsson of Norway left him preoccupied for much of the 1020s, particularly after Cnut's defeat at the Battle of Holy River in 1025, and it was only following Olaf's death at the Battle of Stiklestad in 1030 that he was able to return to England.[39] This final period of Cnut's direct rule in England also saw the emergence of the native Anglo-Saxons, who (together with their families) would dominate the English scene for the next thirty years, beginning with Leofric, who became Ealdorman of Mercia around 1032, and Godwine, whose career began as a local notable in Sussex in the 1030s.[40]

When Cnut died of natural causes in 1035, the Danish kingdom of England was barely twenty years old, but it had only another seven years to live. Cnut's regular absences in Denmark (as well as a pilgrimage he undertook to Rome in 1027) meant that England was never truly integrated into a larger Scandinavian empire and its institutions (and, in the case of the Church, those running them) remained overwhelmingly English. Cnut's death triggered yet another succession crisis – his three sons each found themselves in a different part of his empire: Svein, with his mother Aelfgifu, had been sent in 1030 to govern Norway; Harthacnut, his son by Emma, had been established as joint king in Denmark. This left Harold (known as Harefoot), his younger son by Aelfgifu, in England. Harold had not been appointed to an earldom or other senior position, a possible indication that Cnut intended his empire to remain intact under Harthacnut. However, just as Cnut died, Svein was expelled by the Norwegians, who then attacked Denmark, occupying Harthacnut's attention and preventing him from travelling to England to secure his throne.

Even though Harthacnut had the powerful support of Earl Godwine of Wessex, the countervailing alliance of Queen Emma and Earl Leofric of Mercia – both keen to prevent the Wessex earl from becoming too dominant – had led to a messy compromise under which Harold was recognised as king north of the Thames, while Emma would act as regent in the south, but very much under Godwine's watchful eye. It all seemed like an unhappy repetition of the short-lived division of England in 1016 (and a reminder that, whatever the subsequent history of England as a united nation, its union was by no means secure in the mid-eleventh century). Then, in 1036, Emma decided to make a bid for power over the whole kingdom by bringing over her two sons by Aethelred, who were still languishing in exile in Normandy.

Edward and Alfred's position had been significantly weakened by the death of their protector, Duke Robert of Normandy, in July 1035 while returning from a pilgrimage to the Holy Land. This left them nominally in the care of the new ruler, William, who was just seven or eight years old, and whose supporters had more than enough on their hands securing the young duke's succession. Edward and Alfred nonetheless left the sanctuary of Normandy, heartened no doubt by their backing of their mother by Cnut's old housecarls, who were stationed at Winchester. Edward sailed to Southampton, but, finding little support there, withdrew to France. Alfred, however, landed further east and was soon arrested by Earl Godwine's men as he tried to make his way to Emma's court. Many of his companions already having been killed, Alfred's eyes were put out and he died of his wounds at Ely in February 1037.

Godwine now threw his weight wholeheartedly behind Harold's kingship and Emma fled to the court of Count Baldwin V of Flanders, a far safer haven than Normandy during the turbulent minority of her great-nephew William. Harold's remaining three years on the throne were relatively uneventful.[41] A storm loomed in 1040, when Harthacnut finally made peace with the Norwegians and gathered a large fleet of some 60 ships to press his claim on the English throne. A civil war was averted only by Harold's death at Oxford on 18 March, after which the royal council hastened to send envoys to offer the crown to his brother, who had made his way to see Emma in Bruges and was gathering his invasion force there.

Harthacnut did not endear himself to his new English subjects. Virtually his first move was to levy another large Danegeld of £21,000 to pay off half his fleet, whose crews had been denied the rewards they might have received if the expected campaign had gone ahead. He also had his brother's corpse disinterred and abused, and allowed Earl Eadwulf of Bamburgh to be killed while under safe conduct; and, not coincidentally, he then granted Northumbria to Eadwulf's killer, the Dane Siward. He did, however, permit the safe return of Edward from Normandy. Harthacnut's motive in this is unclear; he may have felt his main native English rival for the kingship was best kept under close supervision, while many other English notables, including particularly Earl Godwine, were associated with Harold's rule and so could not be trusted as collaborators.

Whether Danish king and English prince might have worked harmoniously together in the longer term was never tested, as Harthacnut died suddenly in June 1042 after attending a wedding feast at Lambeth. He was just twenty-three or twenty-four years old, and is said to have been taken ill as 'he was standing at his drink, and he suddenly fell to the earth with fearful convulsions, and those who were near caught him, and he spoke no words afterwards. He died on 8 June.'[42]

Harthacnut was the last of Cnut's surviving children, both Svein and Harold having already died. The only plausible claimant for the English throne, therefore, was Edward, although at thirty-seven, unmarried and with no children, there must already have been worries about whether he would provide a suitable heir. In the absence of a Danish candidate, the nobility rallied around Edward, and he was crowned at Winchester on 3 April 1043. Very likely as part of the settlement between them, Edward married Godwine's daughter, Edith, in January 1045, thereby cementing the Wessex earl's position as, in effect, a member of the ruling family. The one remaining political uncertainty was the rights that King Magnus of Norway claimed over the English throne, on the grounds that Harthacnut – as the Norwegian king maintained – had made an agreement that whichever of the two sovereigns died first, his lands should be inherited by the survivor. At the time of the treaty Harold (and not Harthacnut) was King of England, so the agreement, even if it did exist, was of very dubious validity. In any case, Magnus chose not to send a fleet to England to press the point. His claim, however, would cast a very long shadow and was used by Harald Hardrada, his successor as King of Norway, as the legal pretext for his invasion of England in 1066.[43]

Relatively little is known of Svein Forkbeard's domestic rule in Denmark – his preoccupation for much of his reign with adventures in England and his struggle to maintain Danish influence in Norway and prevent Olaf Tryggvason securing control there saw to that (although the *Encomium Emmae Reginae* does praise him for his peaceful rule over the country). The reign of his son Cnut, who inherited the throne in 1018 on the death of his brother Harold, had more of an impact in Denmark, but once more the Danish king's constant involvement with England left him comparatively little time to attend to his Scandinavian patrimony. It was not until 1028 that he secured control of Norway (which he had temporarily lost to Olaf Haraldsson) and so re-created the empire of his father. Elsewhere his influence began to extend into Scotland, where in 1031 he received the submission of King Malcolm II and two other rulers, one of whom may have been Macbeth, the *mormaer* (steward of Moray), who was later to be immortalised by one of Shakespeare's plays. In the Irish Sea, Cnut's fleet may have taken part in 1030 in a raid against North Wales in support of a Dublin Irish outpost there.[44] Both developments suggest that, with his core possessions in Scandinavia and England relatively secure, Cnut was looking to expand his control beyond them.

Positive effects of Cnut's North Sea empire on Denmark included his introduction of a new coinage, based on Anglo-Saxon models, and his importation of churchmen from England as part of a bid to assert the independence of the Danish Church from the see of Hamburg-Bremen in Germany. This caused relations with the German archbishops to descend to such a low point that in 1022 Archbishop Unwan captured

Bishop Gerbrand of Roskilde while he was returning from England and forced him to swear an oath of obedience to Hamburg-Bremen.

In 1027 Cnut went on a pilgrimage to Rome. It was probably motivated more out of a desire to show that he was an established Christian monarch, and to be viewed as the equal of his counterparts elsewhere in Europe, than from any sense of piety. Its effects in Scandinavia were almost disastrous, as the kings of Norway and Sweden (Olaf Haraldsson and Anund Jakob) joined together to unseat him in alliance with his own brother-in-law Ulf, who was acting as regent for Cnut's son, Harthacnut, in Denmark. On his return from the pilgrimage Cnut put down Ulf's rebellion comparatively easily, to the extent that he was able to visit Rome again in 1028, but a large part of the rest of his reign was taken up in asserting his claims over Norway. His death in 1035 left Harthacnut in control of Denmark. Cnut had probably originally intended him to be King of England too, but attacks by Magnus of Norway meant that he was forced to remain in Denmark and acquiesce in his half-brother Harold Harefoot's seizure of the English throne.

Denmark experienced another period of Norwegian rule from Harthacnut's death in 1042, when the Danes chose Magnus of Norway to be their king, until 1047, when Harthacnut's cousin, Svein Estrithsson,[45] was recognised as ruler. The continued threat from Norway under Harald Hardrada stifled any Danish ambitions either for expansion or for consolidation at home, and the treaty in 1064 between the two countries that brought an end to half a century of intermittent warfare must have come as a relief to both kings.

Norway, which had lain in the shadow of the Danish kings for most of the mid- to late tenth century, finally emerged as a fully independent kingdom again under Olaf Tryggvason. His father was Tryggvi Olafsson, the ruler of the eastern part of Viken, whom Harald Bluetooth of Denmark had deposed in the 970s.[46] Harald was born around 963 after his mother Astrid escaped her husband's killing by Harald Greycloak, one of the sons of Eirik Bloodaxe. Suggestions that he was descended from Harald Finehair through an alleged liaison with a Sami girl called Snaefrith are, however, almost certainly a later gloss to lend legitimacy to a claim to the Norwegian throne that otherwise looked distinctly shaky.[47] Mother and baby hid in Sweden for three years, as Harald Greycloak's agents desperately sought to locate and dispose of a serious threat to his rule. Eventually Astrid managed to flee, first to Sweden and then towards Russia and the court of Prince Vladimir of Novgorod, with whom her brother Sigurd had taken service. However, on the way there the pair were attacked by Estonian Vikings and taken into slavery. They were separated, and although Astrid was freed by a wealthy Norwegian, Olaf remained in servitude. Then, six years later, Sigurd happened upon the boy at a Novgorod slave market and asked what family the fine-looking youth was from. The response made him realise that he had found his long-lost nephew, and Sigurd bought him from the farmer in whose service he had been and took him back to the royal court, where Olaf was brought up.

At the age of eighteen Olaf embarked on the conventional career of a Viking, joining in raiding expeditions, including one on Bornholm (to the east of Denmark), and making a short-lived marriage to Geir, the daughter of King Boleslav of Wendland (into whose lands he had been storm-driven). He then turned his attention to the British Isles, and was probably present at the Battle of Maldon in 991, before joining forces with Svein Forkbeard. The failure of their joint army's attack on London in 994 led to Olaf's acceptance of baptism under the patronage of Aethelred II of Wessex, although the payment to him of a geld of some 22,000 pounds of silver[48] was an additional incentive. As part of the treaty, Olaf agreed not to attack English interests and to leave English vessels abroad in peace if he came across them. With a seasoned army of Vikings, a handy treasure chest to provide for their pay and the newly acquired status of a Christian prince, Olaf decided on a venture that was not denied to him by the terms of his agreement with Aethelred – an attempt to gain the throne of Norway. He had probably heard that the position of Jarl Håkon of Hladir (who had ruled Norway under Danish overlordship from the 970s, and after 985 more or less independently) was weakening.[49]

It was in northern Norway, in the Trøndelag, that the newcomer received greatest initial support – it is possible that the independent-minded men of the region chafed at Håkon's rule and had contacted Olaf while he was still in England. Olaf landed at Moster, to the south of the Hardangerfjord, and made his way rapidly northwards. As it happened, he arrived back in Norway at just the time that Håkon was killed, his throat apparently cut by his own thrall, Kark.[50] The possibility that the Danes might take the opportunity of the ensuing confusion to throttle Norwegian independence must have worried the Trøndelagers, and so Olaf was proclaimed king at the *thing* in Trondheim. With this support, he then set about securing the rest of Norway.

He began by gaining the adherence of the chiefs of Vestland, who acknowledged him as their king at the Gula *thing* in 996 in exchange for a fair degree of autonomy under the local chieftain Erling Skjalgsson, although they did also agree to accept baptism.[51] The exact progress of Olaf's subjugation of Norway, and indeed of his propagation of Christianity, is bedevilled by serious disagreements in the sources. Adam of Bremen, who reviled the Norwegian king because of his attempts to establish an autonomous Norwegian Church, alleged that 'Some relate that Olaf had been a Christian, some that he had forsaken Christianity; all, however, affirm that he was skilled in divination, was an observer of the lots and had placed all his hope in the prognostication of birds . . . In fact, as they say he was also given to the practice of the magic art, and supported as his household companions all the magicians with whom that land was overrun and, deceived by their error, perished.'[52] The Icelandic sources, in contrast, have a touch of the hagiographical about them, as they laud Olaf's sanctity and his success in Christianising Norway.

Although suggestions that Olaf Tryggvason destroyed pagan temples in the Trøndelag may be transferred from his successor Olaf Haraldsson, he did base himself there, founding a small town near the mouth of the River Nid as his royal capital. He wished, no doubt, to avoid Hladir, the old base of the *jarls*. This new town became known as Nidaros and later Trondheim. His presence did not make the hearts of the men of the Trøndelag grow any fonder, while his comparative neglect of the inland areas of Norway meant that by 1000 his grip on the whole country was beginning to slacken. His enemies had also begun to make common cause, and Svein Forkbeard, Olof Skötkonung of Sweden and Eirik, the son of Håkon, the former Jarl of Hladir, all of whom had much to gain by Olaf's downfall, began to muster armies against him. Olaf's most significant ally was his brother-in-law Erling, whose network of connections stretched as far as the Trøndelag, through the marriage of his sister to Sigurd of Trondenes, from one of the most influential north Norwegian families.

In 1000, disaster struck while Olaf was on his way to Wendland. He had opened hostilities with Denmark, claiming that Svein Forkbeard owed him Zealand as the dowry for his sister Tyra.[53] Having made little headway, he was making his way to the Wendish court to forge an alliance that would create a threat to the east of Denmark and so reduce the growing pressure on Norway from Svein. On his way there, Olaf fell into an ambush at Svold off Rügen (near the modern town of Stralsund in Pomerania), where Svein and Olof Skötkonung were lying in wait for him.

The sight of Olaf Tryggvason's flagship, the enormous *Long Serpent*,[54] must have given his enemies pause for thought, although initially they were even overawed by a rather smaller vessel that belonged to Erling Skjalgsson. The battle, once joined, was hard fought, but gradually Olaf's ships were overcome and, at the very end, rather than face capture by the Danish king, he jumped in full armour into the waves. Although Snorri Sturluson recounts that many men believed he had been rescued by a passing Wendish ship, and some even swore that they had encountered him in the Holy Land, he concludes that 'King Olaf never again returned to his kingdom in Norway'.

Despite his rapid elevation to the status of a national saint, Olaf's rule over Norway had lasted barely five years. He had, however, succeeded in consolidating Norwegian independence from Denmark, and his English connections and his cultivation of ecclesiastical links with England (as opposed to Germany) had also helped boost the standing of the Norwegian Church.

After Olaf's death Norway was partitioned, with the Swedes receiving coastal territories in Gautland, Svein Forkbeard taking direct possession of the Viken, while the rest was divided between Jarl Eirik Håkonarson of Hladir – who, as Svein Forkbeard's son-in-law, was in effect subject to Danish interests – and his brother, Jarl Svein. Meanwhile in the west, Olaf Tryggvason's former faithful follower Erling still held sway until Jarl Eirik dispossessed him of much of it, though never quite pushing Erling from his control of Rogaland.

The man who rescued Norway from both Danish overlordship and its fragmented state was another Olaf, whose support for Christianity marks the real start of the religion's dominance in the country, and whose untimely death gave him the status of the first Norwegian royal saint. His date of birth is conventionally given as 995, although the coincidence with the death of Olaf Tryggvason (whose spiritual heir the second Olaf in many ways was) is probably indicative of a selective moulding of the facts to shape the desired narrative. Ari Thorgilsson paints him in the *Íslendingabók* as a great-great-great-grandson of Harald Finehair, but again this is almost certainly an attempt to lend his claim to the throne a legitimacy that he did not in truth possess.[55] Snorri Sturluson portrays him more prosaically as the son of Harald Grenske, a minor king who ruled a territory around Viken.[56] His mother Åsta remarried after Grenske's death, and to her second husband she bore another son, Harald Hardrada, a half-brother who was to be the source of much trouble for Olaf Haraldsson.

Little is known for sure of Olaf's youth, although Snorri Sturluson in his *St Olav's Saga* ascribes to him an almost conventional early career as a Viking in the Baltic, taking part in raids on the coasts of Denmark, Sweden, Gotland and Estland and returning to spend the winters in Novgorod.[57] At just fifteen years old, if the traditional date of his birth is to be believed, he took service with Thorkel the Tall in the army that ravaged the south of England in 1009–11 (and which brutally murdered Archbishop Aelfeah). When Thorkel allied with Aethelred in 1012, Olaf took his share of the £48,000 with which the King of Wessex had bought off the Viking army. He took his followers southwards, where he plundered in Spain, before travelling to Normandy in 1013. There he was well received by Duke Richard II and agreed to convert to Christianity. Olaf also met the exiled English King Aethelred II and accompanied him on his return to England in February 1014 after Svein Forkbeard's death. Although he initially retook large parts of England for Aethelred,[58] the return of Cnut the following year and the seeming eclipse of the cause of the House of Wessex made Olaf reconsider his position, particularly as a number of leading Norwegians (including Jarl Eirik Håkonarson) had accompanied the Danish king to England, leading to something of a power vacuum in Norway.[59]

Olaf set sail for Norway with two merchant ships and just over 250 men. It was a small force for the enterprise that he proposed, but he expected to gain support in his ancestral territories around the Oslofjord. Equally, though, Olaf must have feared the opposition of Erling Skjalgsson, his one remaining plausible rival still actually present in Norway. He landed at Selja in Sogn on the west coast, and defeated a small force led by Håkon Eiriksson, who had inherited his father's lands – a setback for Olaf's opponents that Snorri puts down to the young *jarl* being only fifteen at the time. Olaf moved rapidly north and captured Nidaros, but was then driven out by local forces loyal to Jarl Svein.

Olaf escaped the clutches of the men of Trøndelag, however, and in March 1016 the fleets of the two sides met at Nesjar on the Oslofjord. Svein had with him all the leading chieftains of the Trøndelag. Olaf's men may have been better equipped, and Jarl Svein's quarrels with his subordinates led to a disjointed leadership, which ended with his flight and that of most of his followers. With the prospect of the return to Norway of Jarl Eirik, Svein's brother, following Cnut's final victory in England in 1016, Olaf now hurried to subdue all his remaining Norwegian rivals, and in particular Erling Skjalgsson, whom he had the Gula *thing* deprive of most of his privileges.

Internal opposition to Olaf came to a head through the meddling of Cnut of Denmark, who resented the alliance he had made with Olof Skötkonung of Sweden in 1019, and who was also displeased that Olaf had refused to accept Danish overlordship. In spring 1022, Olaf summoned Erling Skjalgsson to Tønsberg to answer for his attempts to reassert himself in the Gula *thing*. Trouble between the two culminated in rebellion in Vestland in 1024, after which Erling's successful opposition to the execution of one of the rebels inflicted a damaging blow to Olaf's prestige.

By spring 1024 the rift between Olaf and his most powerful Norwegian vassal had become irreparable, and Erling sought the assistance of Cnut, who was more than happy to aid anyone ill disposed to Olaf's growing power. Erling's two sons, Aslak and Skjalg, visited England and appear to have secured promises of assistance from Cnut. Finally in summer 1026, provoked by an alliance between Olaf and Anund Jakob of Sweden (who had succeeded Olof Skötkonung in 1022), Cnut set sail in person for Norway with a large fleet. The Swedes and Norwegians had been separately harrying the coastal areas of Zealand and Skåne, but, faced with the superior force that Cnut had assembled, they retreated northwards to the mouth of the Helga-á (Holy River) in Skåne. The details of the battle are obscure – Jarl Ulf, who had been Cnut's regent in Denmark, is reported as fighting on both sides – but what is clear is that Cnut came out victorious; Anund Jakob headed swiftly back to Sweden, while Cnut had the (possibly) treacherous Ulf murdered in Roskilde. Olaf's supporters in Norway began to melt away. A verse by Olaf's skald Sighvat Thorðarson laments that Cnut's wealth meant that he was able to buy the support of neutrals in Norway: 'the king's enemies are walking about with open purses; men offer the heavy metal for the priceless head of the king'.[60]

Olaf was not a man to give up easily and he rallied support, evading capture until Cnut had returned to Denmark, whereupon he re-emerged to confront his arch-rival Erling. On 21 December 1028, their two fleets clashed at Sola. Apart from his flagship, which could carry 240 men, Erling had mostly just fishing vessels and other small ships under his command, and he was quickly surrounded and captured. Olaf promised him quarter, but in a hot-blooded scene one of his followers, Aslak Fitjaskalle, split the captive chieftain's skull in two with his axe. Olaf, horrified, turned to Aslak and remarked that with that blow he had struck Norway out of his hand.

His words turned out to be prophetic, for in the wake of Erling's murder, Olaf's support dissolved, as the people of Rogaland, Hordaland and Agder rallied to the dead man's sons, and many of his former supporters lapsed into, at best, guarded neutrality. Olaf soon realised that his cause was hopeless, and he fled via Sweden to the court of Yaroslav at Kiev.[61] It was not long, however, before Olaf received the good news that Jarl Håkon Eiriksson had drowned in a shipwreck off the Pentland Firth in Scotland. Meanwhile, Anund Jakob was chafing at Cnut's new position of dominance and so was quite happy to contribute 400 Swedish Vikings to a renewed attempt by Olaf on the throne.

Olaf had also raised a force of 240 warriors in Russia, and in the summer he made his way into northern Norway, where he met up with his young half-brother Harald. Olaf's return was met with near-universal opposition in the Trøndelag, and a large force of local farmers joined forces with men from Hålogoland (even further to the north). Levies were raised from Rogaland, Hordaland and Sogn to the south to produce a force, which, at more than 14,000 men, was said to be the largest Norway had ever seen. Olaf, in contrast, could muster barely a quarter of that number.

In the resulting battle at Stiklestad on 29 July (or 31 August[62]) 1030, the outcome was almost inevitable: Olaf's army was crushed and he was killed. The one notable survivor was Harald Hardrada, who escaped the battlefield and ultimately made his way to Russia. The victorious Cnut reneged on previous promises to give Norway its liberty and handed it over to the rule of his son, Svein, and his English mistress Aelfgifu.

Apart from his struggle against Erling, which sapped much of his energy, and the near-constant attempts by Cnut either to reduce him to the status of a subordinate king or to unseat him, Olaf is best known for bringing Christianity to Norway. It is likely that the new religion had already become embedded to some extent in western Norway (with the encouragement, albeit brief, of Olaf Tryggvason and Håkon the Good). The process was also promoted by the proximity of western Norway to England; many men from these regions would have come into contact with Christianity during their service in the various Scandinavian armies that attacked the country during the late tenth century, while Erling Skjalgsson had been a Christian since at least the mid-990s.

Olaf, however, took a more direct approach to the spread of Christianity, in line with his general attempt to reduce the power of local chieftains and centralise power on the royal court. Adam of Bremen describes how Olaf had women who clung to paganism burnt as witches, while at a *thing* held at Moster in 1024 he declared that Christianity would henceforth be the religion of all Norwegians. In these actions he was encouraged by an English bishop named Grimkel – a sign of the Norwegian king's desire to remain separate from the ecclesiastical jurisdiction of Germany. A section of the Gulathing Laws (dating from about 1250) stipulated that the Christian feast days and fast days were to be observed, as they had been laid down by 'St Olav and Grimkel and the Moster *Thing*', an indication that Christian Church and Christian monarchs were now working hand in hand – the one to extirpate the remnants of paganism, the other to use Christianity to provide divine sanction for the increasing power of the monarchy – and of both parties' wish to reduce the role of traditional chieftains in the secular and sacred spheres.

Olaf's posthumous reputation for sanctity grew under the guidance of Bishop Grimkel, who had his body translated from the battlefield to lie in the church of St Clement at Nidaros (which the king had had built some twenty years before). Here, a series of miracles were ascribed to the 'saintly' Olaf, no doubt much to the chagrin of Svein and his mother, whose rule was becoming increasingly unpopular. A new set of exactions, which included a ban on anyone leaving Norway without royal permission, and the ordaining of a Christmas 'gift' to the court from every householder (including a quantity of malt, a large ham and butter), fuelled the sentiment that Norway was now being ruled by foreigners. When Grimkel opened the royal grave a few years later, he found Olaf's body uncorrupted – thought in medieval times to be a sure sign of the sanctity of the deceased. By 1040, just ten years after Stiklestad, the Olaf cult seems to have been well established; a work by the former royal skald Sighvat speaks of a blind man being cured when water with which the king's body had been washed shortly after the battle splashed up against his face, while by the mid-eleventh century there were churches dedicated to St Olaf throughout the northern world, in Iceland, Scotland and England, including one at York.

Relying on the posthumous (and saintly) support of his father, and on the thoroughgoing unpopularity of Svein's regency, Olaf's son Magnus (whom he had left behind in Kiev when he set out on his ultimately fatal return to Norway in 1030) returned to claim the Norwegian crown in 1035. Cnut had recently died and, deprived of the powerful protection of his father, Svein fled to Denmark and the court of his brother, Harthacnut. The latter was not so willing to give up Danish claims on Norway, and the period after 1035 saw a tussle between Magnus and Harthacnut, with fleets mustered on both sides, until a treaty between the two made at the Göta River in 1040 brought an end to hostilities and agreed that should either die without a male heir, the survivor would inherit both kingdoms. The pact came into operation in 1042 when Harthacnut died with no son, and Magnus was duly elected King of Denmark. He neutralised opposition from Svein Estrithsson (the son of the Jarl Ulf whom Cnut had had murdered after the Battle of the Holy River) by appointing him regent of Denmark and then, when Svein proved too independent-minded, driving him out of the country altogether.

By 1045, secure in both Norway and Denmark, and with a massive victory against the Wends in 1043 under his belt, Magnus was thought likely to turn his attention to England (which ought, by the terms of his agreement with Harthacnut, to have fallen to him as well). In 1045, the English king, Edward the Confessor, stationed a fleet off the Kent coast at Sandwich, waiting for a Danish-Norwegian fleet to arrive. Yet Magnus sent no expedition, and before long would be so preoccupied with a new rivalry with his uncle, Harald Hardrada, that England gained itself a twenty-one-year-long reprieve.

The emergence of a unified kingdom in Sweden lagged far behind the consolidation of centralised monarchies in its Scandinavian neighbours. The historical division between the kingdom of the Svear (based around Lake Mälaren) and the Götar (to the east and west of Lake Vättern) was deep-rooted and the dense forests which separated them impeded the rise of political units that incorporated both regions. The earliest king of whom we have any literary mention, who ruled around Birka when St Anskar's mission arrived there in the 820s, seems to have had a fairly circumscribed domain and depended, moreover, on the support of a local assembly for the exercise of his power.

Even Olof Skötkonung (c. 980–1022), the first king to be associated with both the Svear and the Götar, while his authority was strong in a core area around Sigtuna in Svealand, probably exercised at best only partial control in Götaland. Olof's position as the first genuinely Christian king in Sweden (he was baptised at Husaby about 1008), and his foundation of Sweden's first mint at Sigtuna in 975, makes for a deceptively simple comparison with his contemporaries Harald Bluetooth of Denmark and Olaf Haraldsson of Norway, whose achievements in unifying their respective countries are far better attested.

For at least two centuries Sweden, however, remained more a federation of provinces than a unified kingdom. Olof was succeeded by his sons, Anund Jakob (1022–c.50) and Emund (c.1050–60), but the Swedish kingdom was overshadowed by its increasingly assertive neighbour to the south, and in the 1020s Cnut of Denmark actually controlled Sigtuna for a time. Around 1060 a new dynasty emerged to rule Sweden, this time more closely associated with the kingdom of the Götar. Stenkil, who married one of Emund's daughters to enhance his claim to the throne, was chosen as king by his fellow aristocrats and had his power-base in Västergötland. But neither his rule nor that of the four sons who followed him was particularly secure, with several of the brothers exercising co-regencies, while the country was riven by pagan uprisings in 1084 and 1120. In the first, King Inge was deposed when he refused to perform time-hallowed pagan rituals (although he had his revenge when he seized back his throne around 1090 and had the main cult centre at Uppsala destroyed).

By the 1120s, the Svear kingship had become fragmented and it seemed that Sweden's political destiny might lie in Balkanisation rather than unification. The next decade, however, brought resumed consolidation of royal power, following the accession of Sverker I, an aristocrat from Östergötland. He oversaw the arrival of the Cistercians in Sweden, who established a monastery at Alvastra in 1142, a sign of the growing influence of the Church, which in turn helped enhance royal authority. Even so, Sweden did not enjoy a stable monarchy, as Sverker was murdered in 1156 by Erik Jedvardsson, who led a rival aristocratic faction based in Västergötland and then seized the crown for himself.

The partisans of the two families contested the Swedish crown for the next century, until the death in 1250 of the last of Erik's descendants, Erik 'the Lisping and Limping'. Despite the often turbulent alternation of power between the Erikssons and the Sverkerssons, the administration of the kingdom became more established and the extent of royal authority gradually increased. Erik Jedvardsson is associated with the establishment of the law-code of Uppland (although this was a provincial, not a national, code and was finally codified only in the thirteenth century). He also conducted a raid into Finland in the 1150s (described by his supporters as a 'crusade' against the pagan Finns), which was a sign of the growing confidence and ability of the Swedish kings to project their power outside their traditional heartland. Erik was assassinated in Uppsala in 1160, probably on the orders of his immediate successor, Magnus Henrikson, whose one-year reign was the only break in the dynastic stranglehold of the feuding Erikssons and Sverkerssons.

Soon after his death a cult grew up around the site of Erik's murder, and he came to be regarded as Sweden's first royal saint. Although this cult was unofficial at first, it was promoted by his family and supported by the Church at Uppsala, particularly after its selection as the site of a new archbishopric in 1164. By 1256 the veneration of Erik had received papal sanction, when a Bull of Alexander IV granted indulgences to pilgrims who visited his grave.

Erik's son, Knut, who became king in 1167, enjoyed a comparatively tranquil reign after a revolt in 1170, dying naturally in 1195. He was the first ruler to be regarded outside Sweden as ruler of both the Svear and the Götar, being addressed as such by Pope Alexander III in 1171–2.[63] Knut also made Sweden's first treaty with a foreign power (Duke Heinrich of Saxony) and reintroduced a Swedish-minted coinage after a 150-year break following the time of Olof Skötkonung.[64] Sweden had experienced no dramatic wars of unification and no one ruler who could be singled out as its unifier. Even so, in 1200 – although the country had a long way to go to the establishment of a strong central administration, permanent taxation and a national law-code, all developments that took place under the Folkung dynasty (which came to power in 1250) – its political unity, at least, was reasonably assured.

Norway and Sweden were not the only Scandinavian countries to yield a royal saint in the eleventh century. Denmark had St Knud of Odense, and even little Orkney was not to be outdone: the chronic divisions between the earls from the late tenth century would ultimately lead to the islands having their very own royal patron. The death of Earl Sigurd in 891[65] had been followed by a period of rule by Einar, the illegitimate son of Earl Rognvald of Møre, who rejoiced in the unusual nickname Torf-Einar ('Turf Einar'), possibly because his mother was said to have been a slave and so associated with menial tasks such as the cutting of turf.[66] The new Orkney earl's principal difficulty was in his dealings with Harald Finehair of Norway. His father, Rögnvald, was killed by Halfdan *Háleggr* ('Long Legs'), the Norwegian king's son, who promptly fled to Orkney and expelled Einar. The deposed earl bided his time briefly in Scotland and then returned to defeat Halfdan, whereupon (according to the saga) he performed the rite of the blood-eagle on him by carving his ribs out and then pulling his lungs through his back, to create a bloody simulacrum of an eagle.[67]

Understandably furious, Harald made a second expedition to the Orkneys, but, in view of the mitigating fact that Halfdan had burnt Torf-Einar's father to death, he contented himself with imposing a fine of sixty gold marks. Einar, meanwhile, made the best of a bad situation by insisting that the *odal* rights of the leading men of the islands became his property, in exchange for paying the portion of this enormous fine, which the more modest landowners could not afford. These preciously guarded rights had allowed the holder of *odal* land to pass it on, but not to alienate it outside the land without permission. Little more is known of Torf-Einar than this single incident and that he 'ruled over Orkney for many years'. His death was followed by the first of many divisions of the earldom into three parts, which would ultimately sap its strength and undermine its claim to primacy amongst the Viking lordships of the Northern Isles. Two of the three heirs, Arnkell and Erlend, joined forces (or were forced to join) with Eirik Bloodaxe in his campaign to secure the kingship of York and were killed in the ambush at Stainmore that resulted in Bloodaxe's own death in 954. The remaining son of Torf-Einar, Thorfinn *Hausakljúfr* ('Skull-splitter'), was not initially able to assert his rule over Orkney, for Eirik's widow Gunnhild and their sons based themselves there for a while before returning to Norway.

After Thorfinn's death in 976, Orkney was torn apart in a series of dynastic killings that saw Ragnhild, the daughter of Eirik Bloodaxe and the wife of Thorfinn's son Arfinn, implicated in the assassination of three successive earls (two of them her husbands) and in fratricidal murders which included that by Earl Ljot of his brother Skuli, who was conspiring with the Scots. A semblance of stability was finally restored in 980 with the accession of Earl Sigurd whose rule lasted until 1014. His reign, together with that of his son Thorfinn (1014–65), saw the peak of Orkney's power, when its influence reached as far as the Isle of Man and Ireland. Sigurd succeeded in retaining a toehold in northern Scotland in Caithness, after a battle early in this reign where he secured the support of the Orkneymen by promising to return to them the *odal* rights that his ancestor Torf-Einar had extorted from them; it was the first battle in which Earl Sigurd unfurled his famous raven flag, a banner under which his men would fight many engagements. In 987 and 988 he invaded the Isle of Man, defeating King Godfrey and returning with a huge amount of treasure (and the rights to collect tribute), which enabled the Orkney earl to fund raiding expeditions for the rest of his reign. It is possible that the Burray Hoard, consisting of a large number of silver neck-rings, represents part of Earl Sigurd's treasure. Even this, however, does not match the Skaill Hoard, the largest ever discovered in Orkney, found in 1858 by a schoolboy named David Linklater, who was chasing a rabbit into its hole. Its components weigh 18 pounds, and it dates probably from the period 950–70, some decades before Sigurd's rule.

In 995, Sigurd met his match when he encountered Olaf Tryggvason on his way back to Norway. Having become a Christian the previous year, Olaf was in a fierily evangelical mood when he met Sigurd at Osmundwall on the island of Hoy, where they had both by chance put in. The Norwegian prince threatened Sigurd with death and the ravaging of the entire Orkneys if he did not accept the new religion. Faced with a clearly superior force, Sigurd quickly agreed to abandon the ways of his ancestors and was baptised. The *Orkneyinga Saga* implies that the whole of Orkney followed suit, but it is probable that the conversion was much more gradual, with the patronage of the earls accelerating rather than completing the process.[68]

Sigurd met his death at Clontarf in 1014, as part of the grand coalition that King Sihtric of Dublin had summoned to contain the growing power of the Irish high king Brian Boruma.[69] He had been initially sceptical about joining this and it took the promise of lands in Ireland and the hand of Sihtric's mother, Gormflaith, to persuade him to participate. The force that he brought, containing men from the Orkneys, Shetland and the Hebrides, is indicative of the reach of the Orkney earl. It availed him little, for the enchantment of his raven banner, which was supposed to guarantee victory to its bearer, failed him and huge numbers of Orkneymen fell, Sigurd among them.

Orkney was divided once more, this time between Sigurd's three grown-up sons, Sumarlidi, Einar Wry-mouth and Brusi. A younger son, Thorfinn, was left in the care of his grandfather, King Malcolm of Scotland, and it was only after the death of Sumarlidi that the young man gained possession of one-third of Orkney. A quarrel, however, broke out between Einar, Brusi and Thorfinn (and his protector Thorkell Fosterer) over Caithness, which Thorfinn held, and which he argued did not count as part of the Orkneys for the purpose of the division into thirds. After a feast held in 1020 at Thorkell's hall at *Hlaupandanes* (Skaill, Deerness), which was supposed to lead to a reconciliation, the Fosterer murdered Einar, whereupon Brusi claimed that he should inherit his murdered brother's third, while Thorfinn maintained that the surviving brothers should split the earldom equally. Both earls appealed to Olaf Haraldsson of Norway, once again binding

Orkney closer to the Norwegian sphere of influence, as Olaf's final decision was that the disputed third was forfeit to the crown of Norway, although it was then entrusted back to Brusi as regent.

Only in 1029 did Thorfinn succeed in gaining control of the contested third and anything like the power that would justify his later nickname of 'The Mighty'. Even so, it is probably not a coincidence that he was able to do so at just the time that Olaf was exiled from Norway and then soon afterwards killed at the Battle of Stiklestad. Thorfinn's royal capital was on the Brough of Birsay, a small island whose relative difficulty of access by a tidal causeway provided suitable security at a time when attacks by raiders (or even relatives) was a constant possibility. It had previously been a Pictish settlement (the remains of a well still mark the principal survival from that period), and its reuse as a Viking royal centre is one indication of continuity between the two cultures. The outlines of the foundations of the Viking buildings can be seen on the island even today, together with the ruins of the church that may have been the 'Christchurch' – the first cathedral on Orkney – possibly built during the reign of Earl Thorfinn (although its square tower and general Romanesque appearance may suggest a date a little later, in the early twelfth century). There is a degree of uncertainty regarding its identity, however, and there is an alternative view that the present church on the larger neighbouring island of Birsay may in fact represent the first church.[70]

Brusi's son, Rögnvald, had been left in Norway as a hostage against his father's good behaviour as Orkney earl. He fought on Olaf Haraldsson's side at Stiklestad (where he is said to have helped the young Harald Hardrada escape from the battlefield). He assisted in Magnus the Good's return to Norway in 1035, and the grateful new Norwegian king bestowed on him both his father Brusi's portion of the Orkney earldom as well as the royal third. Thorfinn was preoccupied with campaigning in the Hebrides and Ireland and was forced into a grudging acceptance of this diminution of his power. The unsatisfactory compromise came apart when a new force destabilised the equilibrium, with the arrival in 1046 of Kalf Arnasson, who was said to have killed Olaf Tryggvason on the battlefield of Stiklestad and whose niece, Ingebjorg, was Thorfinn's wife. Kalf came with a powerful host, which Thorfinn used to defeat Rögnvald Brusason at the Battle of Rauðabjorg and drive him out of the Orkneys into exile in Norway. Rögnvald did not stay away long, however, and, although he only had a single ship and its crew, he slipped back to Orkney, caught Thorfinn unawares and almost killed him by setting light to the house in which he was staying.

Things were never settled simply amongst the Orkney earls. Thorfinn broke out of the burning house and managed to reach Caithness in a rowing boat. Soon afterwards he repaid the favour by descending on Papa Stronsay, where Rögnvald and his men were collecting malt for the Yuletide ale. Thorfinn's men set fire to his house and, though Rögnvald initially escaped disguised as a priest, his hiding place was betrayed by the barking of his pet dog and he was butchered.

Thorfinn ruled Orkney for the next twenty years, enjoying more tranquil relations with Harald Hardrada after he ascended to the throne of Norway in 1047 than he ever had with Magnus. In 1048, the Orkney earl even emulated Cnut the Great's pilgrimage to Rome by making his own visit to the Eternal City, where he was absolved of his sins by Pope Leo IX. Just after his death in 1065, Orkney became entangled once more with Norwegian ambitions, as Harald Hardrada's fleet put in there on the way to his doomed bid to seize the English crown. The new joint earls, Paul and Erlend, were persuaded to join the expedition and were fortunate to be among the very few magnates who survived the Battle of Stamford Bridge, in which Harold of Wessex crushed the Scandinavian coalition arrayed against him.[71]

Although Paul and Erlend managed to rule the Orkneys in relative harmony for the next thirty years, the rivalry between their sons and grandson would bedevil the earldom for the next four generations. Paul's son Håkon and Erlend's son Magnus got on so badly that, in a bid to avoid bloodshed, Paul persuaded Håkon to leave Orkney and go to Norway. During his trip there in 1093, Håkon visited a seer and asked for a prediction of his future. The soothsayer, after much equivocation, reluctantly foretold that Håkon would commit a terrible crime that he could never atone for, but that he would eventually rule over the whole of Orkney.

Håkon next visited Norway, where he made the mistake of encouraging King Magnus Barelegs to raid the Northern Islands, hoping that the Norwegian king would take the Hebrides and leave the Orkneys for him to rule as sole earl. Magnus, however, was more ambitious and informed Håkon that, if he undertook such a voyage, he would take all the isles for himself.[72] He was true to his word and, during his wide-ranging expedition in 1098–9, which encompassed the Hebrides and south Wales, Magnus captured both Paul and Erlend and shipped them back to Norway, where they died the next year.

Magnus Erlendsson was also taken prisoner by King Magnus, and offended the Norwegian king's Viking sensibilities by refusing to take part in a battle on Anglesey, instead choosing to chant psalms while the din of battle echoed around him. Finally, however, he managed to escape his captor and made his way to England. By 1105, Magnus's cousin, Håkon, had succeeded to the Orkney earldom, which had been briefly ruled directly from Norway by Magnus Barelegs's son, Sigurd. The next year Magnus Erlendsson, who had been appointed Earl of Caithness by King Edgar of Scotland, returned to Orkney to claim what he regarded as his rightful share of the earldom. After Magnus received confirmation of his title from King Eystein of Norway, the two cousins settled down into the type of uneasy cohabitation that had become almost customary (and most often disastrous) amongst the Orkney earls.

Eventually, in 1114 Earl Magnus was forced out and spent twelve months in exile at the court of King Henry I of England. When he returned the next year with five shiploads of armed men he caught Earl Håkon, who was in Caithness, totally by surprise.[73] Matters were heading towards serious violence when the two rival earls met at a *thing* sometime before Palm Sunday in 1115. They were finally persuaded to suspend hostilities and to agree to meet again at Easter the following year on the small island of Egilsay.

The resulting encounter was one of the most dramatic recorded in the sagas. Each earl had agreed to bring just two ships, as a token of their peaceful intent. Magnus arrived first. As he came in to land, a huge wave swamped his ship. It was taken as a bad omen and when evening drew in, Magnus sighted Håkon's flotilla approaching the island, composed not of a pair of vessels, but of eight warships. Magnus knew at once that he had been betrayed, but there was little he could do. His men begged him to hide, but he refused and spent the night in the small church on the island, praying for strength to face whatever the next day might bring.

At daybreak, Håkon and his men came ashore. As they approached,

Magnus told his retainers not to risk their lives by defending him in the face of hopeless odds. Håkon's followers soon violated the sanctuary of the church and dragged their master's rival out to face execution. At first Magnus sought to bargain for his life, suggesting that he would leave Orkney and go on pilgrimage to the Holy Land; when this was refused, he offered to accept imprisonment in Scotland; and finally, when this too was rebuffed, he pleaded, saying that he was prepared to undergo blinding or maiming and be imprisoned for the rest of his life. Håkon was inclined to accept this final proposition, but his chief followers refused, saying that if he did not kill Magnus, they would kill Håkon instead.

Magnus ordered his standard-bearer Ofeig to do the deed, but he declined and the role of executioner fell to Lifolf, Håkon's cook. The poor man was totally unaccustomed to killing, began to tremble violently and sob. Magnus reassured him and advised him 'Stand thou before me, and hew on my head a great wound, for it is not seemly to behead chiefs like thieves. Take good heart, poor wretch, for I have prayed to God for thee, that He be merciful unto thee.'[74]

The place where Magnus's head fell to the ground, which had been rocky and barren before, was transformed, according to tradition, into a green and fertile field. A church now stands there, an abandoned shell, with a large part of its great round tower fallen. The walls of the nave are complete to the second floor, but inside all is bare, with the still emptiness containing not the merest hint of the violent murder that took place on the spot. This was not, however, the final resting place of Magnus's body, for Håkon, in a fit of penitence, permitted it to be carried back to Birsay and buried there. Almost predictably, whispers of miracles associated with the dead earl began to circulate.[75] Håkon died in 1123, having made a pilgrimage to Rome and been absolved of his crime, and his son, Paul the Silent, and Bishop William (who seems to have been appointed around 1102 by Magnus Barelegs of Norway) tried to suppress the growing cult of Earl Magnus. William's opposition collapsed when he was struck blind while praying in the Christchurch, and his sight was only restored by appealing for mercy at the tomb of Magnus. William then had Magnus's bones exhumed and put to a test by fire. When the knuckle bone failed to burn and even changed shape to appear in the form of a cross, William was finally convinced of the murdered earl's sanctity.

In the meantime Magnus had appeared in a vision to a farmer from Westray called Gunni, insisting that Earl Paul translate his relics to a new shrine in Kirkwall on the mainland. At length Gunni travelled to Birsay with an account of his dream, and the relics were duly moved to the church of St Olaf in Kirkwall. The church in which they finally came to rest, the present cathedral, was commissioned by Earl Rögnvald in 1136[76] to hold the relics of the saint (who also happened to be his uncle). Towering above Kirkwall, its stunning bright and red stone form is one of the finest pieces of northern Romanesque architecture and a strikingly large monument for such a modestly sized place. It is nonetheless indicative of the importance of Orkney in the Viking world, and particularly of the self-image of the Orkney earls, even in the twelfth century, as important players.

Although Magnus, and in particular his bones, had been the main motivation behind the building of the new Kirkwall Cathedral, and they were duly enshrined about the 'high altar', over time they were completely forgotten. In 1848, while work was being performed on one of the pillars near the original site of the altar close to the north arcade of the choir, a cache of bones was discovered in a box. Some thought these were the bones of Magnus himself, while others argued that they represented those of St Rögnvald (the founder of the cathedral having himself been canonised). Then, in 1919, during a major programme of restoration of the cathedral, the clerk of works noticed some loose stonework on the south side of the choir. On investigation he found a cavity, with a small oak box lying inside. The contents of this turned out to be another set of bones, of a man of around 5 foot 7 inches in height, about twenty-five to thirty-five years old, of light build and – most significantly – with a gash on the rear of the skull, of a type that might have been caused by an axe blow (the wound was clean-cut and not caused by crushing).[77] It is all so consistent with the *Orkneyinga Saga* story of Magnus's death that it is almost certain these are the bones of the saint himself, translated to their last hiding place at some point in the later Middle Ages.

Having been examined, the bones of St Magnus Erlendsson were replaced in a new lead-lined casket and reinterred in the niche above the southern choir, the spot being marked by a discreet red cross in the pillar below. For a man who preferred his psalms to pillaging, it is a most appropriate resting place.

Map 12 Viking Normandy

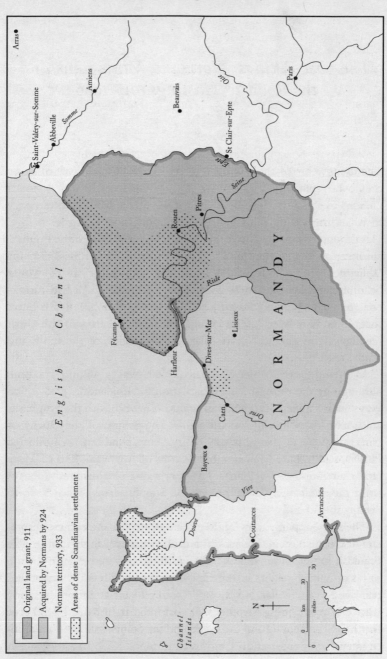

The Last Vikings: Normans, Varangians and the Road to Hastings, 911–1066

The dying years of the Viking Age are marked by the lives of three men who epitomised its values and whose intersecting destinies collided in a violent clash over the throne of England – the territory in which the Viking raids had begun almost three centuries before: Harald Sigurdsson, the Norwegian king (better known in the English-speaking world as *Hardrada* – 'hard counsel' or 'ruthless'); Duke William of Normandy (or William 'the Conqueror' as he would become); and Harold Godwinson, King of England. All had careers etched in blood and possessed a ruthless sense of ambition, attributes that would have been just as familiar in the far-off days of the Great Heathen Army or the North Atlantic colonisation of the ninth and tenth centuries.

Normandy, over which William ruled, was a Viking creation, although by the time of his embarkation for England in 1066 it was very much a mixed Scandinavian-Frankish hybrid, with the emphasis, culturally and politically, on the latter. The genesis of the Duchy of Normandy lay in the activities of a Viking band led by Rollo (or Hrolf), said to have been one of the sons of Rögnvald, Earl of Møre (and therefore a Norwegian).[1] The very name of Normandy derives from the *nordmanni* ('North-Men', or Scandinavians) who came to occupy it.

The story, as penned by Dudo of Saint-Quentin, the earliest chronicler of Normandy (in the late tenth century), is enticingly simple. The Frankish king Charles the Simple was under severe pressure from a series of Viking raiders in the first decade of the tenth century, and one band in particular, led by Rollo, came to his attention. In many ways this group must have been almost indistinguishable from those that had been penetrating the Loire and the Seine since the mid-ninth century, but in autumn 911 Charles summoned Rollo to a meeting at

Saint-Clair-sur-Epte (a small settlement in the modern Val d'Oise), where he offered him extensive lands in Normandy in exchange for becoming the king's vassal and agreeing to defend the realm against his erstwhile Viking kinsmen. The land was granted in full ownership (*in alodo et in fundo*) to Rollo and was said to cover virtually the entire future duchy of Normandy.[2] Rollo was also to accept Christian baptism and was given Charles's daughter Gisela in marriage.

Despite Dudo's assertion that Rollo received the whole of Normandy from Charles, it is more probable that, at least initially, he obtained (or occupied) only upper Normandy between the Epte and the Seine. Later land grants increased his territory into the Bessin and Hiémois (in 924), and by 933 the Normandy Vikings seem to have expanded into the Cotentin and Avranchin.[3] Other elements of Dudo's account are even more fanciful. Aping the classical tendency to trace the descent of great empires from one or more heroes of the Trojan War (a much more satisfactory pedigree to a Christian cleric than the Norse predilection for pagan gods, such as Odin or Thor, as ancestors), he described the Normans as having originated in 'Danmark' (or Dacia), and claimed that their forefather was the Trojan Antenor, who had become King of Dacia. The reason for the Viking migration from Denmark, Dudo explains, was their custom of polygamy, which led to overpopulation (the latter, if not the former, being a reason also cited by modern historians). Dudo also has Rollo dream of a mountain in which there are birds of many different colours and species, which he interprets as a calling to go to a foreign land, where he will unite people of many races under his rule.[4]

The description of the meeting at Saint-Clair-sur-Epte is scarcely less colourful. As a proud Viking war-leader, Rollo was unwilling to abase himself to kiss the Frankish king's foot, as the ceremony of fealty demanded. Instead, one of Rollo's followers was chosen to enact this humiliating part of the proceedings, but the importunate stand-in seized Charles's foot, causing the king to topple over backwards. One can imagine that, if true, this outrage would have caused the alliance between Rollo's Vikings and the Franks to be of very short duration indeed.

The first real evidence of the arrangement between the two sides comes in a charter of Charles the Simple dated 14 March 918, which mentions a portion of his lands that the Frankish monarch had 'granted to Rollo and his Companions for the safety of the Kingdom'.[5] In truth, this territory was probably not under Charles's control in the first place, but Rollo's settlement, which concentrated initially on the area around Rouen, acted as a useful block against the depredations of other Viking groups. It was a tried and tested tactic, having been used to good effect with the cession of Frisia to Harald Klak in 826, and the offer of Nantes as a fief to the Vikings by Robert of Neustria in 921.[6]

At first Rollo kept to his side of the bargain, for in 923 he is seen on campaign with the Frankish king near Beauvais. But the following year the Normandy Vikings (who soon became known as Normans) defected to Charles the Simple's rival, Ralph of Burgundy. Rollo's new ally granted him Bayeux and Maine, but this pact did not last long either and the Normans took to raiding along almost the whole length of their border, towards Amiens, Flanders and Arras. The Scandinavians' predations were halted by a serious defeat that Rollo suffered at the hands of the counts of Flanders and Vermandois at Eu, and thereafter the fledgling duchy (still technically a county until the early eleventh century)[7] settled down to become one of a constellation of over-mighty lordships that jostled for power with the feeble later Carolingian kings.

Although contemporary Frankish writers complained that the Normans reverted to pagan practice whenever it suited them, and lamented that Rollo (even though baptised) had hedged his bets on his deathbed in 942 – by ordering the sacrifice of some Christian slaves to appease Odin and Thor, the gods of his ancestors – his son and successor William Longsword was definitely a Christian. William spoke Norse and had a Danish concubine, but this did not shield him from the attempts of other Viking groups to operate in Normandy, most notably the revolt by Riulf, who accused Longsword of adopting too many Frankish ways.[8] An independent Viking chief named Harold also seems to have succeeded in taking over Bayeux for a time. In 944, the Scandinavian colony seemed set to collapse when a joint attack by Louis IV and the Duke Hugh the Great[9] resulted in the temporary loss of Caen, until the two Franks fell out and William regained control of Normandy.

By around 965 William was secure, married to a daughter of Hugh the Great and largely eschewing the Viking-style raiding of his neighbours. His administration became more sophisticated and adopted Frankish practices, such as the issuing of charters and the adoption of the Frankish titles of marquis and count. This is unsurprising, as the original Scandinavian colonists do not seem to have been a majority; place-name evidence suggests that the largest number settled in the north of the Cotentin peninsula, in the Pays de Caux, and certain other coastal regions.[10] Settlement names such as Tocqueville ('Toki's ville') and Auberville ('Osbern's ville') and those containing the suffix '–tot' ('house site'), such as Hautot, or '–bec' ('slope'), as in Bricquebec, betray the presence of these incomers, although the vast bulk of place-names remained French in form. The place-names tell us something, too, about the origins of the settlers. The many personal names of Viking type that were incorporated in names ending in '–tot' generally indicated that they came from the Danelaw, and thus had come from England rather than directly from Scandinavia (unlike Rollo, who is definitely said to have been Norwegian). This is reinforced by several Anglo-Saxon names that became part of hybrid place-names in Normandy (such as Dénestanville, or 'Dunstan's ville'). In the Cotentin, moreover, there are clusters of names that show possible Irish (or Hiberno-Norse) settlement, such as the name Dicuil in Digulleville.[11]

The Scandinavian language itself seems to have faded quickly: Dudo recounts how in the 940s William Longsword was forced to send his son Richard to Bayeux to learn the Norse language, as it was no longer a living tongue around the ducal court at Rouen. This is probably an exaggeration, since as late as 1025 one of Olaf Haraldsson of Norway's skalds was received at Rouen, where presumably there were still those who could appreciate his poetic art.

Certain other Scandinavian customs persisted, however, and there was still a slave market at Rouen in the late tenth century.[12] The dukes also had the power to exile miscreants (called *ullac*), which resembled the custom of outlawry in Scandinavia (and particularly Iceland), while other laws concerning the rights to salvage from shipwrecks and the division of land among heirs were more similar to Norse than Frankish custom.[13] Even after the death of Richard I, the Norman rulers retained close contacts with Scandinavia, and Richard II (996–1025) concluded a peace treaty with Svein Forkbeard of Denmark just before the latter invaded England in 1013. It was about this time also that Olaf

Haraldsson of Norway arrived in Normandy, bringing with him a host to assist Richard II in a campaign against the Count of Blois. In a sign of the changing times for the Viking homeland in Scandinavia, Olaf accepted baptism once the fighting was done and foreswore further raiding, withdrawing his forces from Svein's attack on England.

The close ties between the Normans and their Viking cousins had already begun to fray a little earlier. In 991, Duke Richard I and Aethelred II of England had reached an agreement not to harbour each other's enemies, a pact aimed largely at choking off Viking activity. The marriage in 1002 between Emma, Richard's sister, and Aethelred was intended to cement this alliance (though the visit by Svein to Normandy in 1003, after he had harried Yorkshire, must have come close to breaching the Anglo-Norman concord). When Svein finally succeeded in deposing Aethelred in 1013, it was to Normandy that Emma and the royal family fled, and three of her children – Edward, Alfred and Godgifu – went there again in 1016 after the death of Edmund Ironside.[14]

Normandy's period of relative stability ended in 1026 with the death of Richard II. His successor, Richard III, lasted just a year, his short reign being marred by a rebellion by his own younger brother Robert (who became duke in turn in 1027). Robert faced serious pressure along the borders from Alain III of Brittany, who attacked the Cotentin in early 1030, although this did delay Robert's planning of an invasion of England in 1033 to restore the sons of Emma to the throne. The expedition was then prevented from setting sail by unfavourable winds and, thus deprived of the chance to become 'Robert the Conqueror', the Norman duke (perhaps unwisely, given that his heir William was both of doubtful legitimacy and a minor) departed on a pilgrimage to the Holy Land.

Although Robert did reach Jerusalem, he fell ill and died in 1035 during the return journey at Nicaea, leaving the seven-year-old William to inherit the duchy. The young duke's survival was only guaranteed by a group of loyal advisers who had served his father, and his position remained extremely tenuous until 1047, when the revolt of his cousin Guy of Brionne was defeated at Val-ès-Dunes near Caen with the help of Henry I of France. Even then William was not secure, as two of his uncles, Count William of Arques and Archbishop Malger of Rouen, rebelled in 1053 – a threat made even more serious by their coalition with Henry I, Geoffrey Martel, Count of Anjou and Count Guy of Ponthieu. The Norman defeat of the main French army at Mortemer in 1054 left William for the first time in a position to project his power outside Normandy. Then the death of Henry I of France in 1060, and the succession of the eight-year-old Philip I, whose guardian just happened to be William's father-in-law Count Baldwin V of Flanders, meant that the Duke of Normandy was finally free to act without fear of attack by the French king.

It was on one of these campaigns in 1064–5, against Duke Conan of Brittany, that William was accompanied by a noble guest from abroad. The leading English earl, Harold Godwinson, was apparently on a mission from Edward the Confessor, and landed near the mouth of the Somme. He was met by William's longtime rival, Guy of Ponthieu, who, seeing the opportunity to make mischief, seized the Englishman and imprisoned him in his castle at Beaurain. William put pressure on Guy, and Harold was released into the Norman duke's custody and taken to Rouen, where, half-guest, half-hostage, he agreed to join the expedition against Conan. Having distinguished himself in actions against Dol and Dinan, Harold was knighted by William. He then took some kind of oath, which Norman sources later represented as an act of homage to the Duke of Normandy and a promise to support his claim to the English throne when the time came.

William of Poitiers, Duke William's chaplain, who wrote a history of the Norman conquest of England, claims that Edward the Confessor had 'sent to him Harold, of all his subjects the most distinguished in riches, honour and power, whose brother and nephew had previously been received as hostages for the duke's succession'.[15] One alternative explanation for Harold's visit to Normandy was to persuade Duke William to release those hostages, who had been held since the 1050s. His landfall in the territory of Guy of Ponthieu might also suggest that he was not initially bound for Normandy at all, but may have been heading for his family's traditional allies in Flanders.[16]

William most probably received the news of the death of Edward the Confessor sometime in January 1066 and immediately began mobilising his army and marshalling diplomatic allies to press his claim to the succession. He sent Gilbert, Archdeacon of Lisieux, to plead his case to Pope Alexander II, pointing out that Harold had broken his oath to support William's candidacy for the English throne, and offering as an additional incentive a wholesale reform of the English Church. The Pope concurred and sent Gilbert back with a papal standard, a battle flag under which the Norman duke could fight for England.[17]

William despatched a mission to Emperor Henry IV, seeking to invoke a treaty by which each had promised to come to the other's aid if threatened by an enemy, but no assistance was forthcoming. He sent another embassy to the Danish king Svein Estrithsson who, if he did offer any support to William, did so as a counterweight to the claims of Harald Hardrada, since a Norwegian conquest of England would have been most unwelcome to Denmark. William was also visited by Tostig, the exiled former Earl of Northumbria, who presumably offered to support his claim against his brother Harold in exchange for restoration to his earldom.[18]

Once his forces were ready, William marshalled them at the mouth of the River Dives and awaited a favourable wind. He languished there for four weeks, before moving his force to Saint-Valéry-sur-Somme for a further wait. The positive effect of this delay (at least for the Normans) was that the army of King Harold, which had been waiting along the south coast to intercept any landing by the Normans, exhausted its supplies and was demobilised on 8 September. Finally, on 27 September, when it seemed as though the season would grow too late for campaigning and the embarkation for England might never take place, a favourable wind began to blow across the Channel. Apart from a minor panic when William's ship lost touch with all the rest midway, the crossing was uneventful.[19] The invasion fleet of Duke William of Normandy landed at Pevensey on the Sussex coast in the early morning of 28 September 1066. It was, though William could not have known it at the time, just two days after Harold Godwinson's victory over Harald Hardrada at Stamford Bridge.[20] William decided to take a cautious approach, remaining sufficiently close to his landing site to beat a hasty retreat to Normandy should it become necessary. He built a new defensive wall inside the old Roman Saxon shore fort at *Anderitum* and then proceeded to ravage the neighbouring area. Unless he wished to tolerate the outrage of this foreign interloper laying waste to large sections of southern England, the Anglo-Saxon king would have to come to the Norman duke.

* * *

When Harold's predecessor, Edward the Confessor, came to the throne, he was the most convenient of the few available candidates, being the only surviving son of Aethelred II, and Harthacnut's recognition of him as co-ruler in 1041 further smoothed the way to his succession. Magnus the Good of Norway also laid claim to the English throne, through his alleged agreement with Harthacnut that whichever of them died first would inherit the lands of the other and, in the case of the Danish crown, this would include England. There was a scare in summer 1044, when Edward mobilised an army in expectation of a Norwegian invasion, but Magnus was, on the whole, too preoccupied with his struggle with Svein Estrithsson over Denmark to mount any expedition to England. Magnus's death in 1047 and the continued warfare between his successor, Harald Hardrada, and Svein then postponed the issue for nearly twenty years. There were, though, small-scale Scandinavian raids on the south coast in 1048, when Sandwich and the Isle of Wight were attacked, and the following year a contingent of Vikings from Dublin raided the Welsh coast.

On the whole, however, Edward was more preoccupied with reforming the Church and with gradually installing his own supporters in earldoms and other senior positions. Of the Danish retainers of Cnut, Siward remained in place as Earl of Northumbria, whilst among the English notables Godwine, Earl of Wessex – who owed his rise to the service he provided Cnut on an expedition to Denmark in 1019[21] – became the most prominent. Although Godwine tussled with Earl Leofric for influence in Mercia (where the latter was earl over the western portion), the marriage of his daughter Edith to Edward in 1045, which made him the king's father-in-law, rendered his power almost unassailable.

Godwine's family continued to amass positions of influence. His eldest son Svein was elevated to the earldom of Herefordshire in 1043; and his second son Harold became Earl of East Anglia two years later. The acquisition of an earldom in Oxfordshire by Edward's nephew, Ralph, in the late 1040s[22] acted as only a partial counter-balance to the House of Godwin's growing power.

By around 1050, it was becoming clear that Edward, by then in his forties, was unlikely to produce a male heir (who would have been Earl Godwine's grandson). Attention turned to an alternative successor, and Godwine widened his circle of allies through the marriage around

1051 of his third son Tostig to Judith, the half-sister of Count Baldwin V of Flanders. The murder in 1049 of Earl Beorn, the brother of Svein Estrithsson of Denmark, removed another contender for the throne, although the circumstances of his death – abducted and killed by Godwine and Svein Godwinson – very nearly provoked a Danish invasion.[23]

Throughout the 1050s the struggle for influence at Edward's court continued, with a Norman element coming increasingly to the fore. This is hardly surprising, as Edward's mother Emma was the sister of Richard II of Normandy, and he (together with his brother Alfred) had spent considerable time in exile there during the period of Cnut's initial ascendancy and until his own recall to England in 1041. The exile of Earl Godwine in 1051 (for refusing to punish the men of Dover for their part in an attack on Eustace of Boulogne, Edward's brother-in-law) probably led Edward to rely even more on his Norman connections. There are indications that Archbishop Robert of Canterbury may have visited Duke William in 1051–2 in Normandy as part of negotiations to secure an alliance against Godwine that left Wulfnoth, the earl's son, and Håkon, his grandson, as hostages at the Norman court.[24] What other messages Robert may have passed on to William are unknown, though it may well be that he made promises concerning the English succession.

In June 1052, Godwine attacked the south coast, joining up at Portland with another fleet that Harold had brought over from Ireland. Facing only ineffectual resistance from Edward's navy led by Earl Ralph, the Godwines ravaged the north Kent coast. Joined by the Londoners, the invading army then marched to meet Edward at Southwark. All the king's careful diplomacy of the previous two years was undone, and Godwine and Harold were allowed to return to England. Most of the king's French (in other words, Norman) advisers, including Archbishop Robert of Canterbury, fled from London and took passage from the Naze in Essex on a leaky boat bound for Normandy.

The last thirteen years of Edward's rule were overshadowed by the renewed supremacy of the Godwines, even after the death of the earl in 1053. Harold succeeded him as earl of Wessex, and the family's power was cemented by his brother Tostig's acquisition of the earldom of Northumbria in 1055. Harold's position was further strengthened by his victory the same year over Gruffudd ap Llywelyn, the ruler of Gwynedd, who had invaded Hereford together with an Irish-Norse band that had joined forces with Aelfgar, the exiled Earl of East Anglia.[25] The Godwines acquired a further earldom when Gyrth became Earl of East Anglia in 1058, and the deaths of Earl Leofric of Mercia and Earl Ralph in 1058 also removed senior figures who might, at the very least, have placed obstacles in the way of Harold's inexorable rise. With the hapless Earl Aelfgar, who had briefly come back into favour, exiled once more in 1058, Harold seemed in a strong position to dictate the course of the succession himself.

Although Harold may at this point have entertained ambitions of the crown for himself, what he certainly sought to avoid was a Norman acquisition of the throne. It was probably as a result of this that the last available native English candidate from among the descendants of Alfred the Great was sought out. Edward the Exile, the son of Edward the Confessor's half-brother, Edmund Ironside, had been sent to Sweden in 1017 and, after a stint in Russia, had ended up in the 1040s in Hungary, where he married Agatha, the niece of the Emperor Henry II. In 1054, Bishop Ealdred of Worcester was despatched to persuade him back, but it took a further three years for the exiled prince to return. Unfortunately for this neat piece of succession-planning, Edward the Exile died in April 1057, just months after reaching England, and before he even had a chance to meet King Edward. He left behind him a son, Edgar (later known as the Atheling), who at five years old was far too young to be considered a serious claimant to the throne.

Harold Godwinson, meanwhile, went from strength to strength. He had his ally, Stigand, appointed Archbishop of Canterbury in 1052, although the irregular nature of his translation to the see caused problems with successive popes.[26] A successful raid by Tostig into Scotland in 1058 led to King Malcolm visiting England to make peace with Edward. Then in 1063 Harold launched a naval attack against Gruffudd ap Llywelyn in Wales, destroying his main base at Rhuddlan and joining up with a land invasion by Tostig to force a complete Welsh surrender.

Harold seemed destined now to be, if not the next King of England, then at least the king-maker. But the political landscape of Anglo-Saxon England was shaken up one last time when the thegns (the

lesser aristocracy) of Yorkshire and Northumberland rose up in revolt
in 1065 against Earl Tostig, whom they accused of undue harshness.
The rebels chose Morcar, son of Aelfgar, the previous incumbent, to
be their new earl. Once they were joined at Northampton by Earl
Edwin of Mercia, the coalition was too strong for King Edward to
resist and he sent Tostig (and his wife Judith) into exile in Flanders.

Tostig was not universally vilified, and the *Life of Edward the Confessor*
describes him as 'this distinguished earl, a son and lover of divine
peace', who had governed his earldom so well that he 'had in his time
reduced the number of robbers and cleared the country of them . . .
that any man, even with any of his goods, could travel at will even
alone without fear of attack'.[27] He did not remain quiet for long in
Flanders and is said to have visited William of Normandy, perhaps
offering his own support for the duke's claim to the English throne.
Sometime in late April, Tostig landed on the Isle of Wight and
proceeded to ravage the south coast as far east as Sandwich and Kent.
He then moved north with sixty ships and landed at Lindsey in
Lincolnshire. He probably hoped to exploit residual loyalty to him in
Northumbria, but was defeated by Edwin and Morcar and, with only
one-fifth of his original fleet remaining, made his way to Scotland,
where he joined forces with Harald Hardrada.[28]

King Edward had in the meantime suffered a series of strokes, and
throughout November and December 1065 lay gravely ill at Westminster.
On Christmas Eve, the king had another heart attack, but was well
enough to attend church. The following day, however, his health took
another turn for the worse and he fell into a coma. At the very end,
Edward miraculously recovered enough strength to deliver a prophecy
warning of a dire future for England and to bequeath his kingdom
to Harold. As he offered his hand to the Wessex earl, he pronounced
with his last breath, 'I commend this woman and the whole kingdom
to your protection.'[29]

Edward the Confessor died on 5 January 1066 and was buried in
Westminster Abbey, the church that he had commissioned and which
had been consecrated just a week before. Harold was crowned the
very next day, taking advantage of his consolidated position as the
leading English noble and of the late king's apparent (and most convenient) deathbed designation of him as heir. In a very real sense his
claim to the throne was shaky, with his marriage to Edward the

Confessor's sister being as close as he could claim to membership of the House of Wessex. Yet William of Normandy's own candidacy for the English throne was every bit as tenuous, deriving as it did from the marriage of his great-aunt Emma to Aethelred the Unready. And yet, as there were no available blood-descendants of Alfred the Great to hand (Edgar Atheling being still too young), the acceptance of Harold as king by the *witangemot* or royal council must have seemed the only sensible way to secure a ruler who would defend native English interests.

The first few months were surely tense, as Harold was well aware that Tostig, Harald Sigurdsson of Norway and William of Normandy would all be happy to see him pushed from his newly won throne. The waiting was punctuated by a series of appointments, possibly including that of Waltheof as earl of a territory in the East Midlands.[30] A moment of particularly ill omen occurred on 24 April 1066 when a comet appeared, which was clearly visible in the sky for a whole week. It was the visitation once every seventy-six years of Halley's Comet, but many of those who saw it interpreted it as portending a terrible doom about to fall upon England. The waiting would soon, however, be over, and the first to strike against England was Harald of Norway.

The half-brother of King Olaf Haraldsson, Harald was the son of Sigurd Halfdansson and, according to the conveniently manufactured genealogy of the sagas, the great-great-grandson of Harald Finehair. He also had royal connections on the maternal line, as his formidable mother, Ásta Guðbrandsdóttir, had previously been the wife of Harald Gudrodsson, a great-grandson of Harald Finehair (the marriage from which Olaf Haraldsson was born). Born around 1012, Harald was about three when Olaf secured the Norwegian throne after his defeat of Jarl Svein in a naval battle at Nesjar in 1016. The *Heimskringla* relates the story that Ásta held a great feast to celebrate her son's new status, to which she also invited her three sons by Sigurd. Olaf decided to test the mettle of the Sigurdssons by pretending to fly into a terrible rage. Harald's brothers, Guthorm and Halfdan, were terrified, but little Harald simply pulled the beard of his furious stepbrother. The next day Harald's two elder brothers were seen constructing play farmhouses by the side of a pool, while Harald had built wooden boats that he floated on the pond. Observing this, Olaf remarked,

'You may have command of warships one day, my kinsman.' Finally, Olaf asked each of the brothers what he most desired: Guthorm chose cornfields, Halfdan wished for cattle, whilst Harald's choice was housecarls.[31]

It was an ambition that would be achieved one day. Harald did not encounter his illustrious kinsman again for more than fifteen years, and then it was in inauspicious circumstances. After Olaf's expulsion by a pro-Danish alliance and an abortive attempt to return,[32] the Norwegian king finally obtained succour at the court of Yaroslav of Kiev and, more importantly, fresh equipment for his band of 250 warriors. Early in 1030, Olaf set out, leaving behind his young son Magnus in Yaroslav's care. Passing through the frozen wastes of Russia in wintertime, Olaf finally crossed to Gotland and then to the court of the Swedish king Onund, who declined to join his expedition, but did send 400 warriors and allowed the Norwegian to recruit as many as would join his standard. By the time he reached Norway, Olaf had also secured the support of Dag Ringsson of Uppland, an inveterate opponent of Danish rule in Norway. Yet the local notables and peasantry instead opposed him, and it was an army largely composed of these 'bonders' (from *bønder*, the Norwegian term for free farmers) that Olaf faced late that summer when he came to Stiklestad, a farm near Vaerdal in the northern Trøndelag.

Harald Sigurdsson had joined his half-brother by this time and, still just sixteen, he begged to be allowed to take his place in the battle-line. Olaf initially refused, but Harald protested, 'if I am so weak as not to be able to wield a sword, then my hand should be tied to its hilt'. Dag Ringsson, whose force was supposed to make up the right wing, was delayed in reaching the battlefield and so Thore Hund, at the head of the bonder's army, had already launched his attack by the time Olaf's army was complete.

The Norwegians and their allies surged forward with the cry 'Forward Christ-men, forward cross-men, forward king's men', a reference to Olaf's role in bringing Christianity to Norway. Yet by the time Dag Ringsson's contingent was fully deployed, Olaf's army had already suffered badly in the 'storm of steel' that engulfed Stiklestad. In the melee Olaf was wounded in the thigh by Thorstein Knaresmed. Barely able to support himself, the king dropped his sword and was then despatched by Thore Hund and Kalv Arnesson.

The remnants of Olaf's army and Dag Ringsson's late-arriving contingent fled the battlefield. Harald had somehow escaped the carnage and, badly injured, was rescued by the Orkneyman Rögnvald Brusason.[33] Rögnvald carried Harald to the shelter of a remote farmhouse, where he stayed until he was strong enough to venture the mountain crossing into Sweden. All the while, according to Snorri Sturluson, the farmer's family was completely unaware of the identity of their ailing guest. From Sweden, Harald and Rögnvald sailed east to Russia, where they were received as honoured guests by Grand Duke Yaroslav. The Kievan prince appointed Harald joint commander of his army, a move possibly conditioned by his less-than-cordial relations with his brother Mstislav (who ruled the eastern part of the principality from Chernigov), which made reinforcements from Scandinavia all the more welcome.

The *Orkneyinga Saga* tells that Rögnvald Brusason took part in ten battles in Yaroslav's service, although it is not known whether he and Harald fought together.[34] A line of verse from Harald's skald, Thjodolf, tells of his fighting against the 'Laesir', probably a reference to the Poles and an indication that Harald's Norwegians took part in the joint invasion of Poland by Yaroslav and Mstislav in 1031. Between then and 1034 (the most probable date of his departure from Russia), Harald's movements are obscure. The campaigns east of the Baltic, to which Snorri refers, may represent the kind of armed tribute-taking winter expeditions that the Viking Rus rulers customarily undertook as a way of exacting forced contributions from neighbouring Finno-Ugric and Slav tribes.[35] Harald and Eilif are also said to have been entrusted with the defence of Gardariki (the Norse name for Russia), although this probably refers to a role in safeguarding the northern part of the realm rather than an outright takeover of the defence of the whole country.[36]

Harald would have found ample other opportunities for action in Yaroslav's service. In 1032, there was an expedition to the Iron Gates, probably against Ugrian tribes north-east of the Pechora River near the Urals, while the Rus princes faced a constant challenge from the Pechenegs who roamed the steppelands north of the Black Sea around the Dnieper.[37] Perhaps Harald would have remained indefinitely in Yaroslav's service (at least until the call of the Norwegian throne lured him back to Scandinavia), had it not been for his infatuation with his host's daughter, Elizaveta (or Ellisif, in the Norse version of her name). Harald referred to her as 'the bracelet-goddess in Gardar', and the two were eventually married, but at the most probable date of his departure the princess was still only ten years old. Yaroslav is said to have refused her hand in marriage to Harald until the Norwegian had proved himself in glory and riches. Perhaps Yaroslav did have his eye on a strategic marriage for Ellisif, but wanted to be sure that Harald was not just another ephemeral Scandinavian princeling, before letting go of one of his most precious dynastic assets.

The most obvious path to wealth and glory for an ambitious Norse warrior in Russia lay to the south, to the Byzantine imperial capital of Constantinople (or Miklegard – the 'great city', as it was known to the Vikings). Harald probably took the same well-worn route down the Dnieper that the Russian trading fleets used each year.[38] Vulnerable to steppe raiders such as the Pechenegs, the merchants with whom Harald travelled must have been grateful for the extra armed escort.

So it was around 1034 that Harald Sigurdsson arrived in Miklegard to join the Varangian Guard, the Emperor's elite corps of Scandinavian troops. He was not the first of his countrymen to come in search of employment as a mercenary, but he was certainly the most illustrious. Like so many before him, he was clearly awestruck by the imperial capital, and his reaction on reaching the Bosphorus and catching sight of the fabled city has been preserved in a skaldic verse by Bolverk Arnorsson, who later became one of Harald's court poets: 'Bleak gales lashed prows, hard along the shoreline. Iron-shielded our ships rode proud to harbour. Of Miklegard, our famous prince first saw the golden gables. Many a sea-ship fine arrayed swept toward the high-walled city.'[39]

The Byzantine military renaissance in the tenth century owed much to the military prowess of emperors such as Nicephorus Phocas, John Tzimisces and Basil II, but it also benefited a great deal from their use of foreign mercenaries, including Normans and other western Europeans (usually referred to collectively as 'Franks'), as well as Scandinavians. In 866, a treaty between the Byzantines and the Rus had included a clause that the Russians should provide troops to the emperor, and in the tenth century there are intermittent mentions of Rus in Byzantine military service, such as the 700 Norsemen who are said to have taken part in an expedition against Crete in 961.[40]

The general name for the foreign troops who guarded the imperial palaces in Constantinople itself was *Hetairia* ('friendly troops'). Membership of this elite band was clearly quite a lucrative affair, since entry into these units involved the payment of a fee, which in the case of the Grand Hetairia (the senior division of the household guard) amounted to 16 pounds of gold.[41] It was not until the reign of Basil II (976–1025) that a separate regiment of Scandinavians was established, when the emperor – under severe pressure after a defeat by the Bulgarians, and faced with twin revolts by Bardas Scleros and Bardas Phocas – appealed to Vladimir of Kiev for aid. In exchange for the promise of the hand in marriage of Princess Anna (Basil's sister) the Kievan ruler despatched 6,000 warriors to Constantinople.[42]

These soldiers were used to form a new elite unit, the Varangian Guard. The Norsemen duly helped Basil defeat Bardas Phocas, finally crushing the rebels at Abydos in April 989. The Varangians took part in many of the subsequent campaigns of Basil, who restored the borders of the empire to their greatest extent since the loss of Africa and Levant to the Islamic expansion of the seventh century. They were present during his expedition to Syria in 999 (which retook Emesa) and also in Armenia in 1000–1. In the field they were noted for their ferocity (participating in the massacre of the entire population of twelve districts of Georgia during a campaign there in 1021). They were also despatched to put down a revolt around Bari in southern Italy in 1009. Ironically, the leader of that rebellion invoked the assistance of the Normans of the region, leading to a situation in which troops of Scandinavian origin (or at least descent) were fighting on both sides.[43]

When not on active military service, the main duty of the Varangians was to act as a personal bodyguard for the emperor. At imperial coronations they were awarded the honour of walking on either side of the emperor, and whenever he attended church services, two Varangians stood guard behind him, bearing the large axes that were their most characteristic weapon.

Although the regiment was at first almost exclusively Scandinavian, its officers were generally Greeks. There were some exceptions to this, such as the Nabites who commanded the unit under Alexius, who may have been a Norseman,[44] and the Ragnvald commemorated by a runestone in Uppland in Sweden, who is described as the 'leader of the war-troop of the land of the Greeks'. The Varangians' status as outsiders meant that they were often relied upon to undertake tasks that native Byzantine troops might have baulked at performing. These included the duty of the *Manglavites*, one of the junior officers, to walk in front of the emperor during processions, beating the crowd with a jewelled whip to keep it at a safe distance from the imperial presence, and the role of the Guard in the deposition and blinding of Emperor Michael V in 1042.

The Varangian barracks seems to have been situated in the Numera, near the Hippodrome, a convenient location close to the imperial palaces. As a distinct foreign community in the vast metropolis of Constantinople, the Varangians developed their own institutions and had their own church dedicated to the Blessed Virgin Mary and the royal Scandinavian saint Olaf. Hneitir, the sword of the martyred Norwegian king, hung over the church's high altar. It is said to have been picked up in the aftermath of the Battle of Stiklestad in 1030 by a Swede, one of whose descendants subsequently took service in the guard. The Swede is said to have gone on campaign with the Varangians and each night, as he fell asleep, he kept his hand on the sword's hilt, and the blade beneath his pillow. Three nights in a row he found, on waking, that it had moved several feet away. The story of the sword's miraculous movements reached the emperor, who summoned the Varangian to him. The Swedish warrior then explained the provenance of the blade, and the emperor gave him triple its worth in gold and placed Hneitir above the altar of the Varangian church.

The Varangian Guard had, therefore, been established for around forty years by the time Harald Sigurdsson arrived in Constantinople. We are fortunate in having a number of sources for Harald's time with the Varangians, including the *Advice to an Emperor*,[45] an anonymous tract whose title is self-explanatory, which refers to Harald as 'Araltes' and says he brought with him 'five hundred valiant men' whom the emperor then sent to Sicily. Other information about Harald's activities in the Byzantine empire is contained in Scandinavian sources, including the *Heimskringla*, as well as skaldic verses embedded in various sagas. A number of stories seem to have been carried back to Iceland by Halldor Snorrason, who served with Harald in the Varangian Guard, and were later incorporated into sagas, and these have the benefit of having come from a first-hand source.

As far as any chronology can be constructed from the mixture of incidental references in Greek sources, elliptical verses and heroic exaggerations, it seems that Harald arrived at about the time that Michael IV succeeded Romanus III as emperor in 1034 and was tasked first with suppressing pirates in the Aegean (where he got 100 gold pieces for every vessel he seized). The Varangians were then sent under General Georgios Maniaces (called 'Gyrgir' in the Norse sources) on campaign in Asia Minor. Harald is said (in the *Heimskringla*) to have gone to 'Serkland', where he 'took 80 cities of the Moors'.[46] He then seems to have gone to Palestine, where *Harald's Saga* rather grandly claims that 'all cities and castles were opened for him, and surrendered without a struggle into his hand'. There was in fact no campaign in Palestine at the time, and it is likely that instead Harald accompanied the masons who were sent in accordance with a 1036 treaty between Michael IV and the caliph Mustansir-Billah to repair the Church of the Holy Sepulchre.

Harald was then sent to serve under Maniaces once more, this time in Sicily, where Michael IV's Arab ally, Akhal-Aboulaphar, was struggling against the rival emir Abu-Hafs[47] – an attempt to reinforce him, led by Constantine Ophos, the catepan (governor) of Byzantine Italy, having failed miserably. As well as the Varangians, Maniaces had a force of 300 Normans from Salerno who were led by William Iron Arm and Drogo, the sons of Tancred de Hauteville.[48] The expedition was ultimately somewhat inconclusive: the Norsemen won a naval victory off Sicily, where the blood poured 'to the planks in the bottom of the sea', but Maniaces's martinet streak alienated the Normans, who defected, ignited a rebellion in southern Italy and caused the Byzantine general to lose all the territory that the Varangians had gained, with the exception of Messina.

Relations between Harald and his Greek superior are portrayed in the sagas as poisonous, and a number of incidents reveal the tensions between them – bad blood that would ultimately prove almost fatal to the Norwegian prince. On one occasion the Varangians wanted to pitch their tents on the side of a slope rather than the marshy lower area that Maniaces had instructed them to camp in. Harald is said to have arranged the drawing of lots to determine the matter, but he cheated the Byzantines by making false marks on the tokens, and so won the right to spend the night on the ground of his choosing.

Some of the more picaresque tales that became attached to Harald's name are probably elements borrowed from other tales, to which his larger-than-life figure acted as a convenient hook. He is said to have taken one city by capturing all the birds that normally nested under the eaves of its houses and then coating the unfortunate creatures' wings with wax and sulphur, which he had his men set alight. The birds then flew back to their nests, started a massive blaze and, in the ensuing confusion, the Varangians stormed the city. Harald is also said to have smuggled his men into another fortress by pretending to be dead. The defenders allowed the Scandinavians to pass through the city gates bearing his lifeless body, but, once inside, drew their swords and the 'resurrected' Harald sprang from his coffin, leaving the astonished townspeople powerless to resist.

The story of the birds, however, appears attached to a number of other historical personages, including the Russian queen Olga on her taking of a town called Iskorot, and in the thirteenth century it was a stratagem said to have been used by Genghis Khan. An alleged Viking exponent of the trick was the Danish leader Guthrum who, during Danish attacks on England in 879, is said to have used blazing sparrows to capture Cirencester (which was for a time thereafter known as Sparrowchester).[49] The story of the fake funeral is even more widespread, appearing twice in *Saxo Grammaticus* (being told about the legendary Danish king Frodo's captures of Polotsk and London), in William of Apulia's account of Robert Guiscard's capture of an Italian monastery, and, most famously of all, about Hasteinn's attack on the Italian city of Luna[50].

The Varangians were recalled from Sicily to take part in the suppression of a revolt in Bulgaria by Peter Deleanos that posed a dangerous threat to the Byzantine hold on the Balkans. For his part in that campaign (from 1040–1) Harald received the epithet 'burner of the Bulgars' from Norse poets, as well as the more tangible reward of promotion to *spatharocandidatus*, the highest rank definitely recorded as having been achieved by a Scandinavian in the Varangian Guard, although it did not amount to an independent field command.

At about this time Harald's fortunes took a dramatic turn for the worse. Michael IV died in December 1041, and his successor Michael V was far less sympathetic to the Varangians. Even worse, he released Harald's nemesis, Georgios Maniaces, from prison. The irascible general had got himself into trouble for striking Admiral Stephanos – who also happened to be Michael V's father-in-law – who had accused him of allowing an Arab fleet to escape in Sicily. Once restored to imperial favour, Maniaces seems to have engineered Harald's arrest, together with that of two of his closest companions, Halldór Snorrason and Ulf Óspaksson, on a charge relating to the embezzling of money due to the emperor. This could either refer to a tax-collecting expedition where the required amount was not handed over or to retaining the bounty of 100 gold pieces that Harald was supposed to give to the imperial authorities for each enemy ship he captured in Sicily.

The Norsemen are said to have been held in a dungeon near the Varangian Church.[51] Once more a series of colourful stories became associated with their imprisonment, most notably that of the 'dragon' or huge serpent which was said to have shared their quarters, and which Harald managed to stab to death while Halldór and Ulf clung frantically to the monster's head and tail. Their final release came about through another shift in the almost comic-opera twists and turns of eleventh-century Byzantine imperial politics. Michael V had bungled an attempt to get rid of his adoptive mother, the popular Empress Zoe. This led to a mob storming the imperial palace and releasing a number of prisoners, including Harald and his companions. Zoe's sister Theodora, who had been living a quiet life in the convent of Petrion (to which she had been despatched in 1030 to remove a possible rival), was then installed as co-empress, much to Zoe's chagrin. After a siege of the imperial palace, in which 3,000 people are said to have died, the now-friendless Michael V took refuge in the Studion monastery. He failed to find sanctuary there, however, for Harald and the Varangians were sent to arrest the fugitive emperor and his uncle Constantine. They were dragged away from the high altar and blinded – some sources say it was Harald himself who put out the eyes of the noble pair (he is referred to in a poem by his skald Thjodolf as being 'The destroyer of the wolf's grid, had out both the eyes of the Great King').

It may be that Harald sensed his position was still vulnerable to yet another change in the political environment. The situation was indeed volatile, for Theodora was soon sidelined again when Zoe married the prominent bureaucrat Constantine Monomachus, who was thereby elevated to the imperial throne as Constantine IX. More likely, it was the news that his nephew Magnus (son of Olaf II) had been recalled to the Norwegian throne that made Harald decide to return home to Norway. His initial petition to Constantine IX to be allowed to leave was refused – Maniaces had revolted in Sicily and the emperor was understandably reluctant to risk a large number of the Varangians departing alongside their leader. Norse sources confuse the issue with an almost certainly fabricated tale of Harald's love affair with a Greek noblewoman, Maria, said to be related to Empress Zoe. This Maria is said to have aided Harald's escape by allowing him to climb through an escape hatch in the building where she was concealing him.[52]

However they managed to slip away, once safely aboard their two ships, the Varangians were confronted by an iron chain that was strung across the Golden Horn to prevent enemy vessels from entering, and which equally impeded their own escape. As they approached the obstacle, rowing furiously, Harald ordered all those who were not manning the oars to take their bedding and other possessions and go to the stern, thus making the ships ride high up onto the chain. Then he commanded his men to rush down to the bows, in turn causing the vessels to pitch forward and ride over it. The tactic was perhaps a little too ingenious, as one of the galleys broke apart when it was clearing the chain, and many of the Norsemen were drowned. Harald, though, got away, and made his way into the Black Sea and then to Kiev.

Harald is said in the *Advice to an Emperor* to have remained on friendly terms with Byzantium, and even to have allowed a Greek missionary to come to Norway.[53] There is no evidence, however, that he kept in touch with his former Varangian colleagues. The Guard continued to serve successive Byzantine emperors for at least a century more and survived in some form into the fourteenth century. The Varangians also took part in the fight against their Norman cousins in southern Italy in the 1060s (where a memory of their presence was preserved in the name of a church near Taranto, which was dedicated to Santa Maria dei Guaranghi ('Saint Mary of the Varangians').[54]

Under Romanus IV, a contingent of Varangians joined in the fateful campaign in Asia Minor that ended with the disastrous defeat by the Seljuqs at Manzikert on 19 August 1071. Doubtless many of the Norsemen perished, but enough survived to serve in the army of

Alexius I Comnenus when he faced the Norman invasion of the Balkans under Robert Guiscard in 1081. At Dyrrachium on 18 October 1081, the Varangians (and a company of pro-Byzantine Norman loyalists under a certain Humbertopoulos) acquitted themselves well, before Guiscard's wife Sigilgaita rallied the Norman right wing as it was about to be pushed into the city. The panicked Varangians fled into the nearby church of St Michael, where the roof caved in and most of them perished when the building was set on fire by the victorious Normans. A particular edge was added to this encounter by the presence of a number of Anglo-Saxon refugees from the Norman conquest of England, who joined the Varangian Guard in increasing numbers at the end of the eleventh century, and who were, one presumes, itching for the chance of a revenge match against William the Conqueror's cousins.[55]

The advent of the Crusades in the late eleventh century injected fresh Viking blood into the Varangian Guard, as several Scandinavian monarchs took the cross and made their way to the Holy Land. King Sigurd I of Norway did so in 1108 and was, after some hesitation, allowed to enter Constantinople. The normal run of tall tales attached to his visit, including one that relates how Sigurd invited Alexius I and Empress Irene to dinner, but the empress, wishing to test the foreigner, bought up all the firewood in Constantinople to make cooking impossible. The resourceful Sigurd had walnuts gathered up as fuel and was still able to present a worthy feast to the imperial couple. When he returned home, a large part of Sigurd's retinue remained behind, providing as many as 5,000 fresh recruits for the Guard.

The last influx of Scandinavians into the Varangian Guard probably came at the time of Earl Rögnvald-Kali of Orkney's pilgrimage to the Holy Land (he set out between 1151 and 1153, a little too late to join in the main action of the Second Crusade). He left Orkney in the company of Eindridi the Younger, who had taken part in the main crusade, and whose tales of the action to be had in the Holy Land were probably what persuaded Rögnvald to venture on the journey. Departing with fifteen ships, the flotilla was depleted once past the Straits of Gibraltar, as Eindridi (who had all the while been on a mission to recruit fresh Varangians) abandoned Rögnvald and took six ships to Marseilles, from where he probably made his way straight to Constantinople. Rögnvald, meanwhile, carried on to Crete and

Jerusalem. On his return journey he put in at Constantinople, where those Norsemen who were tempted to stay behind and serve in the Varangian Guard were rather dissuaded by the news that they would be under the command of Eindridi, whose earlier disappearance from the fleet had made him unpopular. Rögnvald did leave the Emperor Manuel I his ships (as he returned back to western Europe overland), which may have amounted to six full crews, or around 900 men.[56]

The Varangian Guard probably suffered terribly in the disastrous defeat at Myriocephalon in 1176 when Alp Arslan's Seljuq Turks overwhelmed the army of Manuel I in a mountain pass in central Anatolia. It was by now largely an Anglo-Saxon unit rather than a Scandinavian one (a fact underlined by the letters that Alexius III wrote on his ascent to the throne in 1195 to the three Scandinavian monarchs, Sverre of Norway, Knud Karlsson of Sweden and Knud VI of Denmark, pleading for new recruits for the Varangian Guard). The unit itself carried on, although again severely diminished after the taking of Constantinople by the Fourth Crusaders in 1204. In the thirteenth century the Varangians appear largely as ceremonial troops, and they are last referred to in a proclamation of John V in 1341, when they were said to be 500 in number – a mere shadow of the 5,000 Viking warriors who had made up the Guard's initial number three and a half centuries earlier.

Two curious reminders of the passing of the Varangians' sojourn in Constantinople survive. The first is a runic inscription on a marble lion that once stood at the harbour entrance to Piraeus, but which was removed by the Venetian general Francesco Morosini when he captured Athens in 1668 and was placed in front of the Arsenale in Venice. The runes are extremely worn and have become progressively more so over time, making them almost impossible to decipher (or even transcribe). Various optimistic attempts to do so have been made, the most notable by the Danish scholar C. C. Rafn in 1856, who interpreted part of the inscription to mean that it had been carved at the request of 'Harald the Tall', which Rafn took to mean Harald Sigurdsson himself. In contrast, the Swedish runologist Erik Brate concluded in 1919 that the runes had been carved as a memorial to 'Horsa, a good farmer', while in 1930 Erik Moltke could only identify two male names, Ulf and Smid, who performed some unidentified act 'in this port'.[57] In the absence of any scientific advance that may unlock the form (and therefore the meanings of the inscription), the marble lion will act only as a proof that there were Scandinavians in Piraeus, but not who they were or what they were doing.

Briefer still, but in some ways more eloquent, are two fragmentary runic inscriptions found in the southern gallery of the Aya Sofya mosque in Istanbul (the former church of Hagia Sophia). The first, discovered in 1964, consists simply of the single name 'Halfdan', while the second, identified nearby in 1975, reads 'Ári (or Árni) made this'. It is tempting to believe that these represent the bored doodlings of members of the Varangian Guards, hidden high up in the gallery, while their colleagues, axes poised, stood behind the emperor during a church service, poised to strike any would-be assassins.

Harald remained at Yaroslav's court in Kiev for around three years, finally marrying Princess Ellisif in early 1043.[58] The information he could have provided about the Byzantine fleet and its tactics may have influenced the Kievan ruler to launch a naval assault against Constantinople the same year. Unfortunately no amount of descriptions of Greek Fire – the Byzantine naval 'secret weapon' that burnt as well on water as it did on wood, and was probably a compound of naphtha – could prepare the Kievan Rus for the extent of the damage it could inflict and this, combined with a huge storm which dispersed their fleet, meant the whole expedition ended in disaster.[59]

In the autumn of 1045, Harald would have heard of the success of his nephew, Magnus the Good, in defeating his Danish rival Svein Estrithsson at Helganes off Jutland, causing the Danish king to flee to the court of Anund Jakob of Sweden at Sigtuna, and allowing Magnus to take possession of Denmark. Harald must have decided that once Magnus had consolidated his position as king of both Norway and Denmark, then his own chance of claiming the Norwegian throne would vanish. So, late in the year, he set sail for Scandinavia. Instead of going straight to Norway, he went first to Sweden, to Sigtuna, where he made common cause with the exiled Estrithsson. Together, the pair spent the spring of 1046 ravaging the Danish islands, Svein with the more obvious motive of regaining his throne and Harald, presumably, with the intention of making so much trouble for his nephew that Magnus would concede some share of power in Norway to him.

Magnus took the hint and offered Harald the joint kingship of

Norway, which he accepted. The scene of reconciliation between nephew and uncle is a typical piece of saga theatre. Snorri Sturluson tells that Harald brought with him treasure-chests laden with gold from the spoils of his Varangian campaigns and challenged Magnus to produce a similar hoard. The embarrassed young Norwegian king could only proffer his gold arm-ring, given to him by his father Olaf Haraldsson. Harald then retorted that by rights this belonged to him anyway, as Olaf had originally given the ring to his own father, Sigurd. Snorri recounts such a number of tales of the ill will that was growing between Harald and Magnus that it is clear full-scale civil war would have broken out, had Magnus not become gravely ill and died while the two were in Denmark to receive the submission of their subjects there (Harald's alliance with Svein Estrithsson having proved strictly an affair of convenience).

Svein took advantage of Harald's preoccupation with securing his position in Norway to return to Denmark. Unopposed, he was proclaimed king and the two erstwhile allies spent the next two decades intermittently at war. Among the attacks was a damaging raid on Hedeby in 1049, when Harald burnt the port to the ground, probably sealing its decline. There was another sometime between 1040 and 1050 on Roskilde, which led to the sinking of the five Roskilde ships to block the navigation channel into the port and impede the Danish attack.[60] The raiding certainly continued up until an attack on the island of Fyn in 1051, but there may have been a gap of some years before the next attested attack in 1061, when Harald's ships faced determined resistance off Jutland and were nearly trapped by Svein's fleet.

His royal pride bruised, Harald responded by ordering the construction of the largest longship ever built, which had thirty-five pairs of rowing benches (one more than Olaf Tryggvason's fabled *Long Serpent*). He challenged Svein to meet him in a sea battle and so, in spring 1062, Harald's 150 ships faced Svein's rather larger force of 300 vessels.[61] The naval engagement that took place at the mouth of the Nissa River was conducted in the customary fashion, in which most of the ships were lashed together in a central formation, making manoeuvring extremely difficult. Initial lengthy bombardments with arrows (a skaldic verse by Thjodolf recounts that 'All night long, Norway's lord let arrows fly from yew-bow to shining shields') were followed by boarding and a bloody clearance of the opponent's deck.

The fighting went on long into the hours of darkness, until finally Svein's flagship was captured. The king himself managed to escape in disguise after he took refuge with a local farmer's wife. In 1064, Harald and Svein met again at the Göta River, but this time to cement a permanent peace. This essentially confirmed the boundaries of each kingdom and agreed that no compensation was to be paid for any deaths or damages caused during the conflict. After fifteen years of bitter and bloody warfare, neither Svein nor Harald had anything to show for it.

Harald may already have had his mind set on further-flung conquests, but first of all he set his own house in order, heading in late summer to Uppland, where Jarl Håkon Ivarsson was assembling an army against him. They met at Vanern, where Håkon's Gautlanders, forced to advance across marshy ground to attack Harald's army positioned atop a ridge, fell in huge numbers. Harald then spent a number of months exacting his revenge on the men of Uppland, maiming leading opponents and burning the farms of the particularly recalcitrant.[62]

That winter, Harald received a visitor at his winter residence near Oslo. Tostig, smarting from his exile in Flanders, is said to have made his way to Norway since, as he told Harald, 'all men know that no greater warrior than you has come out of the northlands'.[63] Harald's continuous attacks on Denmark demonstrated that he considered himself to have inherited Magnus the Good's claim to it and, by a tortured piece of logic, to England too, given that Harthacnut (with whom Magnus had made that agreement) had also been the ruler of England.

Although Snorri describes the encounter between deposed earl and Norwegian king in some detail and has Harald agree that there was 'truth in Tostig's words', it is more likely that Tostig sent an envoy in his place. Tostig's proposal – of a joint invasion of England to which he would be able to bring (he hoped) an uprising in his favour, once the Norwegian army reached his old domain around York – fell on extremely receptive ground. Tostig fulfilled the first part of his bargain with his raids in spring 1066 along the south coast, and then up as far north as Lindsey in Lincolnshire.

When these failed to provoke the hoped-for rebellion, he made his way north to Scotland to rendezvous with Harald, who had arrived there with a fleet that Snorri puts at over 200 warships. As well as intelligence from his abortive raids, Tostig may have brought information about Duke William's plans, for the two had apparently met in

Map 13 The Stamford Bridge and Hastings Campaigns, 1066

→ Harald Hardrada and Tostig's movements

- - → William of Normandy's movements

····› Harold Godwineson's movements

Tostig

Harald Hardrada

Newcastle

Hardrada & Tostig

Scarborough

Stamford Bridge

20 Sep. Hardrada defeats Earls Edwin and Morcar

York

Ouse

Fulford

Riccall

16 Sep. Hardrada lands at Riccall

25 Sep. Harold defeats Hardrada and Tostig

1–6 October Harold's march southwards

Humber

Doncaster

North Sea

Chester

Trent

Lincoln

Shrewsbury

Nottingham

Welland

Norwich

Gt Ouse

1–6 October Harold's march southwards

Huntingdon

Warwick

Cambridge

E N G L A N D

Hereford

Severn

Gloucester

Oxford

20 Sep. Harold sets out from London

Thames

London

Rochester

Canterbury

Salisbury

Dover

Winchester

14 Oct. William defeats Harold

Pevensey

Battle

Hastings

28 Sep. William lands at Pevensey

27 Sep. William sails from Saint-Valéry

English Channel

Saint-Valéry-sur-Somme

Somme

Fécamp

Rouen

N

Bayeux

Caen

Dives-sur-Mer

N O R M A N D Y

Seine

0 km 50

0 miles 50

Normandy in April or May. Harald had made landfall first in Shetland and then in Orkney, where he recruited reinforcements including Paul and Erlend, the joint earls, and Godred Crovan, the Viking ruler of Man and the Hebrides, before sailing south towards England.

The exact size of Hardrada's army is unknown, but assuming around sixty men per fighting vessel, it may have amounted to some 12,000 warriors. The fleet made landfall near the mouth of the Tyne, sacking Cleveland and Scarborough and defeating a force of local levies near Holderness. Tostig and Hardrada then boarded their ships again and made their way up the Humber and the Ouse to Riccall, just 10 miles from York. Here, around 16 September 1066, they disembarked again, left a portion of the army behind and marched on the city. Capturing what was in effect the capital of the North, and the historic centre of the Viking kingdom of York, would represent a significant prize and should have been expected to unleash the torrent of sentimental and opportunistic support for Tostig and his Norwegian patron upon which the allies were counting.

They were met by an army raised by Earls Edwin and Morcar. Word had probably reached them of the raids on the Tyne, but it must have been a scramble to gather together sufficient levies from the nearby counties of Cheshire, Staffordshire and Shropshire to add to their own force of housecarls. The two sides clashed at Fulford, on the north bank of the Ouse, on 20 September and the encounter ended in a defeat for the English, with large numbers of them drowning in the river as they attempted to retreat.

The victorious Harald and Tostig must have thought they had the luxury of regrouping their army, pulling in reinforcements from those who would now flock to their victorious cause and then marching southwards towards London, with momentum firmly on their side. York surrendered to the allies first, and then Harald made his way to Stamford Bridge on the Derwent, probably with the intention of receiving hostages from the neighbouring regions. He reckoned, however, without the extraordinarily quick reaction of Harold Godwinson, who had probably received news of the Norwegian invasion only between 18 and 20 September.

Even though he had dismissed the bulk of his army less than two weeks before, Harold quickly issued a summons to the *fyrd* to gather again and then set out from London (around 20 September) with a force composed of his housecarls and any troops he had been able to gather up on the line of his march. This scratch army travelled the 200 miles from London to York in just five days, an astonishing rate when it is considered that highly trained Roman legionaries were only expected to advance 20 miles in a day when fully laden.[64] The next day, Harold marched through York, which neither resisted him, nor, it seems, warned Harald Hardrada and Tostig of the arrival of the English host. Harold was also probably able to gather reinforcements for his own army from amongst the survivors of the Battle of Fulford.

It is around 16 miles from York to Stamford Bridge, and the English host covered the ground rapidly. The Norwegians were taken completely by surprise as they rested in the summer heat by the river. The first they knew of Harold's approach was when it crested the ridge of a nearby hill and they could make out the great cloud of dust that the mass of Anglo-Saxon warriors kicked up in their wake. King Harald's Saga memorably describes their shock as 'the closer the army grew, the greater it grew, and their glittering weapons sparkled like a field of broken ice'.[65]

The twelfth-century accounts of the battle by Henry of Huntingdon and William of Malmesbury tell that a lone Viking warrior, axe in hand, stood his ground on the bridge and single-handedly prevented the Anglo-Saxon army from crossing to the east side of the Derwent, where Harald and Tostig's men, many of whom had left their body armour behind with the fleet at Riccall, were scrambling to react.[66] There was some disagreement between the two allies, as Tostig advised retiring to the fleet, while Harald spurned cautious counsel and ordered his men to form up into a shield wall, with its wings curved so far back that it was almost circular. At the centre, inside the circle, Harald Hardrada positioned himself next to his great banner, 'Landwaster',[67] while the archers also sheltered behind the protective barrier of the shields. Eystein Orri, Harald's marshal, was sent back to Riccall to summon reinforcements from among those who had been left guarding the fleet.

There was a brief lull as Harold Godwinson sent out twenty riders to parlay with his opponents. They were instructed to ask if Tostig was with the Norwegian army and, when the reply came in the affirmative, they passed on Harold's greetings and offered him the whole of Northumbria in exchange for peace. Tostig enquired in turn what terms would be offered to Harald Hardrada. The response from his brother was curt: the Norwegian king could expect only 'seven feet of earth, or as much more as he is taller than other men'.[68]

Harald in turn is said to have asked if anyone knew who the man was who had 'spoken so well', and, on learning that it was none other than the English king, retorted rather acidly, 'What a small man.' Shortly after this exchange, the battle was joined. The description in the sagas is rather formulaic. *King Harald's Saga* tells of an initial English cavalry charge, but for the most part there were a series of volleys of spears and arrows followed by bitter hand-to-hand fighting as Harold Godwinson's men tried to break through Hardrada's shield-wall. At a certain point – and accounts vary as to whether this was a deliberate tactic by the Norwegians, a reaction to a feigned flight by the English or simply out of frustration at being on the defensive for so long – a group of Norwegians broke out of the shield-wall and charged the English. Seeing the danger, Harald joined the fray and was consumed by a berserk fury, lashing out uncontrollably, and unconcerned for his own safety.[69]

Lacking their mail coats, many of the Norwegians were cut down. Even so, the ferocity of Harald's assault might have turned the day, as 'Neither helmets nor byrnie could stand against him. All who were nearest turned away.' But then, as it seemed the battle might still be won, Hardrada was struck in the throat by an arrow and killed.[70] As news spread that the Norwegian king had fallen, the battle died down. Harold Godwinson again offered his brother the earldom of Northumbria and free passage to the Norsemen to return home, but Tostig refused and took up position beside 'Landwaster'. Among the group of notables who stood with him next to the fallen king's flag was Harald's favourite skald, Thjodolf, who took time to compose a death-poem – a poetic knack under pressure that many Norse skalds seem to have mastered: 'needless and for nothing out of northland Harald brought us,' he lamented, 'badly bested we are now and ended in the life of he who boldly bade us battle here in England'.[71]

Thjodolf's premonition was accurate. The Norwegian shield-wall grew thinner and – although the sagas do not say exactly when or how – at some point Tostig, too, was slain. The battle was not quite done, for it was at this point, with the field littered with his dead and dying countrymen, that Eystein Orri arrived with the men he had mustered from the ships. The heat of the day was said to have been intense and many of these Norwegians, who this time had donned their armour, threw it off. A number even died of heatstroke. In any case, the reinforcements were not enough and this section of the engagement, dubbed 'Orri's Battle' in the saga, ended equally badly for the Norwegians. Most of them were slaughtered – the *Anglo-Saxon Chronicle* implies that many died by drowning as they retreated to the ships or were burnt (possibly aboard their vessels). A few, however, escaped the carnage, the most notable being Hardrada's son, Olaf Haraldsson, and the two earls of Orkney, Paul and Erlend, who had remained guarding the ships all the time.

Harold allowed the survivors to leave. Twenty-four ships were all that was needed to take them back, first to the north-east and then to Orkney, where Olaf passed the news of his father's death to his mother, Ellisif. The party spent the winter in Orkney and then, when sailing conditions permitted, returned to Norway in the summer of 1067. Behind them on the battlefield of Stamford Bridge they left thousands of corpses, so many that Ordericus Vitalis in the twelfth century could record that the bleached bones of the dead could still be seen heaped up.[72] Tostig's body was treated with greater dignity and, on Harold's orders, was carried back to York for burial, while that of Harald Hardrada was sent back to Norway sometime in late 1067 and was laid to rest in the church of St Mary at Nidaros.

Harald Hardrada's demise was a bitter end to the career of one of the most famous Vikings of all. For all the glories in between, it was bracketed by two defeats, at Stiklestad in 1030 where he witnessed the death of his brother Olaf Tryggvason, and at Stamford Bridge where he came tantalisingly close to seizing the throne of England and re-creating Cnut's North Sea empire. Whether he might in turn have garnered enough support from the Anglo-Saxon nobility to defeat William of Normandy is another matter. Although the Norse still occupied substantial parts of northern Scotland and the Isles, and Scandinavian monarchs would still launch raids against England (or dream of doing so), no Viking ever again came as close to the conquest of Britain as Harald Hardrada did in 1066.

Harold Godwinson's movements in the immediate aftermath of Stamford Bridge are uncertain. What is clear is that he cannot have had very much time to rest his army before heading back southwards. It is

The fearsome man's head
found on the wooden cart
in the Oseberg Ship.

(*Above*) Sigurd roasts the dragon's heart, while Regin stands by with a sword (*left*) and Sigurd kills Regin (*right*) from the stave church at Hylestad, Norway.

(*Right*) The twelfth-century Viking stave church of Gol, from Hallingdal, near Stavanger, was disassembled and moved to Oslo in 1884.

(*Left*) A serpent encloses the runes in this eleventh-century runestone at Jarlabanke Bro (bridge) in Sweden.

bove) The Thingvellir cleft, the site of the
elandic Althing assembly.

(*Right*) The reconstructed church of Thjodhild at Brattahlid, Greenland.

(*Left*) A Thule Inuit carved wooden doll, possibly representing a Norseman.

(*Right*) Viking turf longhouses at L'Anse aux Meadows, Newfoundland.

(*Below*) The church at Hvalsey, Greenland.

(*Above*) The Newport Tower.

(*Left*) The Baptism of Vladimir of Kiev, from the *Radziwill Chronicle*.

(*Right*) King Cnut and Queen Emma making a donation to the New Minster at Winchester.

Scenes from the Bayeux Tapestry:
Duke William of Normandy's fleet crosses the English Channel (*above*);
King Harold – possibly the figure with an arrow in his eye – is killed (*below*).

(*Above*) The Norman castle at Melfi in Italy's Basilicata region, originally built in the eleventh century.

(*Above*) A ball from the heyday of the Viking revival in nineteenth-century Stockholm (featuring horned helmets).

likely that he heard of Duke William's landing at Pevensey on 1 October, just three days after it had occurred, and he was by that time probably already on his way back from York. William, meanwhile, had also been alerted to Harold's victory at Stamford Bridge by Robert FitzWymark, a Norman who had been resident in England for some years.[73]

There are indications that Harold may have suffered desertions on his way to London, or that at least he reached the south ahead of a substantial portion of his army.[74] He probably arrived in London on 6 or 7 October and, once there, had to make the decision as to whether to attack William or wait for the Norman army to come to him. Harold's mother, Gytha, is said to have tried to dissuade him from an immediate assault, although the story that his brother Gyrth pointed out that Harold had sworn an oath to uphold William's claim to the throne and so could not lawfully fight him was probably concocted by Ordericus Vitalis and is symptomatic of the pro-Norman chroniclers' tendency to stress that William had only come to England to claim what was rightfully his.[75]

Harold brushed aside all opposition and decided to confront William head-on by marching towards Hastings. Flush from his victory at Stamford Bridge, he was probably confident that he could see off William's comparatively small force and did not want to see an invading army overwinter on English soil (which would have been an uncomfortable reminder of the activities of the Viking Great Army at the time of his illustrious predecessor, Alfred the Great). It took Harold two days to cover the ground between London and Hastings, around 50–60 miles, much of it through the wooded terrain of the Andredsweald. Late the same evening he reached Caldbec Hill, and the 'hoary apple-tree' where he had called for his troops to muster.

The sources for what happened next are fairly plentiful, providing more information about the encounter between Duke William and Harold than almost any other battle since classical times. However, the accounts of English sources such as the *Anglo-Saxon Chronicle* and the (often significantly later) French and Norman chroniclers such as William of Jumièges, William of Poitiers (the author of the *Carmen de Hastingae Proelio*), William of Malmesbury (in his *Gesta Regum Anglorum*) and Ordericus Vitalis are hard to reconcile in detail.

The most intriguing, and certainly the most visually appealing, source for the Battle of Hastings is the Bayeux Tapestry. Its 225 feet of linen, made up of nine joined strips, are embroidered with a cartoon-like narrative of the events leading up to Hastings, interspersed with occasional Latin inscriptions, which give a gloss on the events being portrayed. The tapestry became associated early on with the name of Bishop Odo of Bayeux, William's half-brother.[76] It cannot be known for sure whether Odo did in fact commission it, but the tapestry's tendency to magnify his importance in the battle makes this a plausible suggestion. The long-held belief that the work was done by Matilda, the wife of William the Conqueror, and other ladies of the court is less sustainable.[77] The Tapestry probably was embroidered somewhere in Normandy, and it has spent most of its recorded history in France, but on certain points it seems to follow a point of view more favourable to Harold than might be expected (such as its depiction of Edward designating Harold as his heir, his fingers stretched out in a gesture of bestowal). This has led to some suggestions that the work was carried out by English nuns, albeit under the general patronage of a Norman, such as Odo, or indeed Matilda. Its inclusion of a very prominent scene where Harold seems to swear fealty to William, however, suggests that the Tapestry's true purpose was, at least in part, to support William's claim to the English throne as a just and legal one.

The exact size of the armies at Hastings is unknown. William's rhetorical flourish that he would still have fought Harold even with 10,000 men, rather than the 60,000 he claimed to have brought across from Normandy, is not to be taken seriously[78] and there were probably more like 6,000–8,000 on each side. The *Anglo-Saxon Chronicle* recounts that Harold still did not have his best troops with him, presumably because they were still making their way from York, but this may well be a way of justifying his defeat after the event. The principal difference between the two armies seems to have been the larger number of cavalry and archers among the Normans. The elite warriors on both sides would have worn a chain-mail coat of metal rings sewn onto a leather backing. The helmets were generally simple conical affairs of iron, with a wide nosepiece, while spears, javelins and swords formed the main arms on the Norman side, with the addition of two-handed axes amongst the English, which were a carry-over from their popularity amongst the Danes and Vikings generally.

William had remained close to Pevensey, strengthening both the old Roman fort there and building a new one at the neighbouring

town of Hastings, and it was around 7 miles away from the latter that
he was now camped. It may have been Harold's plan to take him by
surprise there,[79] but Norman scouts alerted William just in time to
the unexpected presence of the English host, and the Norman army
spent the night in a state of high alert. William ordered his men to
set out towards Harold's position at daybreak the next morning (with
sunrise at about 6.45 a.m., this would have been around an hour
earlier). It probably took them about an hour to reach Blackhorse Hill
(then known as Hecheland) just to the south of the day's battlefield.
Here the Normans paused, some of them donning their armour. By
chance, William put on his chain-mail hauberk the wrong way round,
but aware of the sensitivity of men on the brink of battle to bad
omens, the duke made light of the mishap. As his own shield against
fate, he is said to have gone into battle wearing the very saints' relics
on which Harold Godwinson had sworn his oath to uphold William's
claim to the throne.

The English host had reached the vicinity of the ridge of what is
now Battle Abbey late on Friday 13 October 1066, and early next morning
(probably around 9 a.m.) Harold arrayed his army along the ridge,
which is around two-thirds of a mile long, with the ground falling
away all around it (save to the north). To the west lay a series of small
streams and drainage channels, while to the east was a wooded area,
long afterwards called Saxon Wood. With the advantage of high ground
secured, Harold planted his royal banner on the crest of the ridge.

Although today the hill has been terraced (to facilitate the construction of Battle Abbey, whose ruins take up much of it) – a development
that has made the slope somewhat shallower – at the time it would
have presented a formidable obstacle for men wearing chain-mail coats
and carrying swords and shields, who had to charge up it in the face
of a barrage of spears, arrows and other projectiles. The ground
around the hill, moreover, was boggy from the water courses that
traversed the battlefield, and was hardly ideal territory for William's
cavalry to operate in. Just as Harald Hardrada's men had done at
Stamford Bridge, the Anglo-Saxons formed themselves up into a shield-
wall and waited for the Norman assault.

William himself arrayed his men a short distance away from the
base of the hill, with a contingent of Bretons, Angevins and Poitevins
under the command of his son-in-law, Alan Fergant. The Normans

occupied a position in the centre, and on his right flank William placed a division of men from Picardy and Flanders, led by his seneschal William fitzOsbern. It seems likely that the main action was preceded by volleys from the Norman archers and crossbowmen, intended to thin out the English ranks. A more picturesque account[80] relates that the first action of the battle was a display by a minstrel called Taillefer, who had accompanied the Norman army. He rode out to the front of the line, juggling swords while reciting the *Chanson de Roland*, the epic poem that tells of its eponymous hero's valiant death at the hands of the Moors at Roncesvalles, and of the vengeance exacted by the Frankish king Charlemagne. One of the Anglo-Saxon standard-bearers came forward to challenge Taillefer, but was struck dead by the troubadour, who then charged into Harold's line and was overwhelmed by the mass of infuriated English warriors.

The main phase of the battle began with the sounding of trumpets to herald a series of infantry attacks by the Normans against the English positions on the hill. As the Normans cried out *'Deus Aie'* ('God help us'), the Anglo-Saxons responded with battle cries of *'Olicrosse'* ('Holy Cross') and *'Ut, ut'* ('Out, out'). The steepness of the slope, and the volleys of spears and arrows that the ridge's defenders rained down on them, meant that the Normans' attacks had lost momentum by the time they reached the crest, and as a result they failed to make any significant dent in the shield-wall. A cavalry attack similarly made no headway.

At this critical moment the morale of a section of the Bretons holding the Norman left flank cracked and they began to retreat down the slope and away from the hill. Accounts vary as to whether their flight was caused by rumours that Duke William had been killed, whether it was just the pressure of the battle or was indeed a deliberate feint to draw out a section of the shield-wall – a tactic that seems to have been used to some effect by Harold himself at Stamford Bridge. Whatever the cause of the withdrawal, it was a critical moment for the Norman duke. If the panic had taken hold of the other parts of the Norman line, and Harold had then ordered his men forward off the ridge, the battle might have ended in utter catastrophe for William.

Instead, only a section of the Anglo-Saxon shield-wall went in pursuit of the fleeing Bretons. Harold's hesitancy may be explained by the deaths of his brothers Leofwine and Gyrth, which probably

occurred about this time.[81] William removed his helmet to show those
around him that he was still alive, and shouted out, 'See, I am here:
I am still living, and by God's help, shall yet have the victory.' Odo of
Bayeux is said to have ridden out to rally groups of retreating Bretons,
while William himself – who had three horses killed beneath him
during the battle – led a cavalry charge to cut down the now-exposed
Anglo-Saxons who had left their ridgetop refuge.

The Normans rallied quickly and those Anglo-Saxons who had
charged down the hill had been quickly dealt with. Seeing the success
of the retreat (feigned or genuine) at drawing out the English, William
ordered a series of further withdrawals. Yet the English shield-wall
still remained largely intact. Once more William was faced with a
difficult choice: if he could not lure his opponent off the hill, Harold
might well receive reinforcements, and then the Normans' already
tenuous position in Sussex might become unsustainable.

William ordered his men forward again and again. It was during
one of these attacks that the decisive moment occurred. The Norman
archers, who had probably exhausted their supply of arrows, either
received fresh supplies or were able, under cover of the infantry attacks,
to retrieve those that had fallen short of the ridge. In one of the
renewed volleys that accompanied the Norman attacks against the
thinning shield-wall, Harold was struck down and died soon afterwards. Exactly how he met his end has been the subject of intense
debate. The relevant section of the Bayeux Tapestry is ambiguous.
The panel, which is labelled *Hic Harold rex interfectus est* ('Here king
Harold is killed'), portrays beneath this text a soldier who seems to
be trying to pull out an arrow that has pierced the right side of his
face. Could this be Harold? An alternative interpretation is that it is
another man – carrying an axe and shown being struck down by a
cavalryman just to the right of the arrow-scene – who is in fact Harold.
Still another possibility is that Harold was struck by an arrow, but that
he was not fatally wounded and died later in the battle.[82] The picture
is muddied still further by a drawing of the Tapestry made in 1730 by
Antoine Benoît, which seems to show that the first figure is about to
hurl a spear and is not pulling an arrow from his own skull at all.[83] A
stone slab now marks the spot where Harold is said to have fallen – it
is here that William ordered the high altar of Battle Abbey to be
placed, as a permanent reminder of the victory God had given him.

Now set amid the ruined shell of the buildings of the former Abbey (much of which was demolished in the eighteenth century), it is a little way back from the ridge. It is tempting to suppose that Harold was dragged back here after being struck by the arrow, and that the stricken king was then dealt his death-blow (or simply expired from the wound) on the spot.

It has become fashionable to discount the arrow story, but it is included in many of the early accounts of the battle by Baudri of Bourgeuil and Amatus of Montecassino. It is also relayed by both William of Malmesbury and Henry of Huntington, so the story must have arisen very early on. However Harold died – and there is even a story in the *Carmen* that Duke William burst through the English shield-wall with three knights and personally slew his adversary[84] – what is clear is that Harold fell, and that this had a devastating effect on English morale. As William of Poitiers put it: 'the English army realised that there was no hope of resisting the Normans any longer. They knew that the loss of many troops had weakened them; that the king himself and his brothers and not a few of the kingdom's nobility had all perished; that all those who remained were at the end of their strength, and there was no hope of relief for them.'[85]

Most sources concur that the battle ended at nightfall, and it seems to have done so in a rout rather than a last stand. Harold and his brothers Leofwine and Gyrth – who might have rallied the army – were all dead. As the panicked English fled, the mounted Normans were able to cut them down in large numbers: in common with many medieval pitched battles, the majority of casualties probably occurred at this stage. Yet there were still some Anglo-Saxons who fought back, and it seems that a group made a stand at a rampart and series of ditches known as the Malfosse. When Count Eustace of Boulogne came upon them, he ignored advice and charged the position. He received a wound to the head and several Norman nobles were killed. Another account[86] states that the Norman cavalry failed to spot the rampart, as it was hidden by undergrowth, and that many of them perished there. The *Battle Abbey Chronicle* also relates the story of a weed-choked ditch in which large numbers of Normans died.

No organised English resistance survived the night, and the dead were soon stripped of their valuables. The bodies of Leofwine and Gyrth had been located at the top of the hill, but at first Harold's body could not be found. Finally the royal corpse was identified by his mistress, Edith Swan-Neck, who knew it by certain marks that 'only she could recognise'. Harold's body was brought to William, at which point his mother, Gytha, offered the corpse's weight in gold if the duke would release it for burial. William refused and is said to have had his adversary interred in a grave on the Sussex coast, so that it could continue to be the guardian of the coast that Harold had so resolutely defended in life.[87] The rest of the Anglo-Saxon dead were left for the crows to pick clean. It is hard to know exactly how many died, but if the armies on either side are counted at 7,000 each, then the fallen must have numbered at least several thousand – a shocking tally at a time when the population of a large town such as York or Lincoln was only 4,000–5,000. The carnage was so appalling that in 1070 Pope Alexander II ordered William to do penance for all the blood he had caused to be shed. It was as a result of this that William ordered the building of Battle Abbey. Far from being a victory monument, it was more the new English king's way of avoiding divine (or at least papal) retribution.

William had won by the battle through a mixture of good luck and favourable circumstances. Had Harold not had to face the Norwegian invasion in the north, then his troops would have been fresher and his army more numerous. And had the English king not been killed (by an arrow strike or other means), then he would at least have been able to rally fresh forces, while William had no such possibility of easy reinforcement. Whether Harold acted correctly in marching to meet William or whether the Norman duke was prudent in remaining close to his beach-head is a moot point, but it would not have mattered if Harold had not fallen on the field of Hastings.

Nor was William's task done. Some of his fleet had landed earlier at Romney by mistake and had been defeated by an English force there, which William now marched to deal with. As he moved eastwards, he received the rapid capitulation of Dover and Canterbury. In the meantime the men of London had proclaimed the young Edgar Atheling, just fourteen at the time, as king. With the prospect of a rapid capitulation by the capital denied him, William circled warily around London to the west, receiving the submission of Winchester and then proceeding via Wallingford, where Archbishop Stigand offered his surrender. He finally reached Berkhamsted around 10

December, where Archbishop Ealdred of York, Edgar the Atheling and Earls Edwin and Morcar submitted to him. William is said to have offered Edwin authority over one-third of England (presumably the north) and it may have been this inducement that tempted the two earls to lay down their arms.[88] With their knowledge of the fault-line that had divided northern and southern England across the boundaries of the Danelaw since the ninth century, and of the capacity of York to act as a bulwark against expansion from the south, they may well have thought of ruling at least the north of England independently of William, and possibly of using it as a springboard to push him eventually out of the rest.

If so, they were badly mistaken. William did not stay long in England after his coronation (by none other than Archbishop Ealdred), returning to Normandy early in 1067, but he was forced to return at the end of the year after Eustace of Boulogne's intemperate attack on Dover Castle almost sparked an uprising. In 1068 he then had to besiege Exeter for eighteen days in order to impose his authority on the West Country.

The greatest challenge to William's rule over England was yet to come. Svein Estrithsson of Denmark launched an invasion fleet in 1069, joining forces with Edgar the Atheling, who had raised an army north of the Humber. There were also coordinated uprisings in the West Country and along the Welsh marches,[89] but Edgar attacked York too soon and failed to take the castle. William reacted swiftly and scattered the Atheling's force. Although William then built a second castle in York, both fortresses fell when Svein arrived and joined up with the remnants of Edgar's army. William's counter-strike was held up for several weeks by stiff opposition at the Aire crossing near Pontefract, but when he finally reached York he found that Edgar and the Danes had fled and the uprising had collapsed.

Determined to stamp his authority on the north of England, William then engaged in a scorched-earth policy that was so devastating that it was known ever after as the 'Harrying of the North'. Some 100,000 are said to have died from hunger as a result, and as late as 1086, when the Domesday Survey was being carried out, many villages were recorded as lying 'waste'. Svein, meanwhile, had returned to Denmark early in 1070. The last embers of resistance burnt in the fens of East Anglia, combining a rump of Danes, the remains of Earl

Morcar's forces and a local resistance leader named Hereward the Wake (or the Exile), but they were eventually overcome in 1071, when Earl Morcar surrendered. Far from his ambition of a semi-independent earldom in the north, he then languished a prisoner for the remaining sixteen years of William's reign, dying sometime in the reign of his successor William Rufus (1087–1100).

By now William's hold on England was reasonably secure. There were further conspiracies, but none of them really threatened his rule. The most serious, in 1085, involved Waltheof, the last surviving English earl, and a threatened Scandinavian invasion fleet. This combination, together with the prospect of Knut IV of Denmark allying with Count Robert of Flanders, caused considerable alarm to William. He crossed over from Normandy with a mercenary force so large that it had to be dispersed among William's leading vassals to pay for its upkeep. In the event it was not needed, as the English side of the revolt was easily put down. Waltheof was captured and beheaded, and his Norman confederate, Earl Ralph of East Anglia, fled abroad, while Earl Roger of Hereford suffered imprisonment. Cnut, meanwhile, was preoccupied with a possible invasion of southern Denmark by Emperor Henry IV and early the following year was killed at Odense by rebels and so his fleet never sailed.

The era of the Viking raids of England ended with an invasion that never happened. Over the course of nearly 300 years the threat, and the all-too-frequent reality, of Scandinavian raids, invasions and occupation of parts of England had shaped the destiny of the country, almost leading to the collapse of native rule and in the end contributing to its unification under the overlordship of Wessex. The attempt at creating a Viking kingdom based in York failed in the end, although Scandinavian customs and a fair admixture of Scandinavian genes survived in the population of northern England. Ironically, it was a man of Norwegian Viking descent who finally overthrew the House of Wessex and established an enduring non-native dynasty, succeeding where generations of raiders, chiefs and kings since the very first raid in 793 had all tried and failed.

The End of the Viking Age and
the Legacy of the Vikings

The desire for clear-cut boundaries and well-defined beginning and endings is a natural one, but the Viking Age has no such obvious finishing line. Conventionally the period has been declared at an end (at least in the Anglo-Saxon world) with the Battle of Hastings in 1066, but England was menaced by Scandinavian invasion for a couple of decades after Harald Hardrada's death at Stamford Bridge. In Ireland, the Battle of Clontarf might set a convenient end point in 1014, when the power of the Dublin Vikings to shape events on the island was broken, but there were Norsemen remaining in Ireland centuries later than that. In Russia, historians might choose a still earlier date, selecting the conversion of Vladimir in 988 as the moment when the Slavic nature of the region took centre-stage and the Viking heritage faded away into the background.

There are even later dates that have a claim to mark the terminus of the Viking world. In Iceland it might be the collapse of the Free Republic in 1262, and for Greenland the unknown year in the fifteenth century when the Western Settlement finally came to an end. In North America an appropriate point might be 1020, when the L'Anse aux Meadows settlement was abandoned, or a substantially later date if the proponents of such faux Viking artefacts as the Kensington Runestone are to be believed. In Scandinavia, the heartland of the Vikings, the task is more difficult still: Christianisation was part of a process of social transformation that gave rise to kingdoms in the later Middle Ages not substantially different from their neighbours in France or England, but Viking raids continued decades after Christianity reached Norway, and two centuries after the first missionary activity had touched Denmark and Sweden in the 820s. More confusingly still, the 'rediscovery' of the Vikings by antiquarians, nationalists and folklorists (especially in the nineteenth century) has created a shadow

Viking world, which is often rather different from that which modern historians are finally uncovering. The best that can be achieved, for those in search of the end of the Viking era, is a series of tableaux that illustrate the final acts of the Viking era, because they either represent the final embers of the old or hint at the first sparks of the new.

The last-born child (or perhaps grandchild) of the Viking Age was the conquest of southern Italy and Sicily, which sprang not directly from Scandinavia, but instead from the Viking colony in Normandy – much as the leap across the North Atlantic to the Americas had been undertaken not from Norway, but from Iceland and Greenland. The advent of the Normans in the Mediterranean was facilitated, just as it had been in Francia, by the political weakness of the nominal ruling power in the region, in this case the Byzantine empire.

The control of the Greek emperors in Constantinople over their subjects in Italy had never been strong. They had been lost to the empire in 476, when Rome fell to Germanic barbarians, and Justinian's reconquest of the province from the Ostrogoths in the 540s and 550s had left it desperately impoverished. Italy was then shattered by the irruption of the Lombards from 568, which created a patchwork of semi-independent duchies scattered throughout the south. The destruction of Byzantium's hold there was further hastened by the Muslim conquest of Sicily, which took place in successive campaigns between 827 and 878 and was largely completed in 902 with the capture of Taormina.[1] The Byzantine empire was left with toeholds in the far south-east of the Italian peninsula, most importantly at Bari, Brindisi and Otranto. These outposts engaged in a series of localised struggles against the Lombard territories of Salerno, Benevento and Capua and the duchies of Naples, Gaeta and Amalfi, which, although theoretically imperial domains, owed about as much allegiance to Constantinople as did the equally independent-minded rulers of another notionally Byzantine territory, the doges of Venice.

The Vikings (or more precisely the Normans) first became familiar with the Mediterranean through pilgrims returning from the Holy Land, who reported back on the opportunities available for trained fighting men to earn a fortune in the armies of one of the many warring local factions. Normans fought and died in battle against the Byzantines at Cannae in 1018, on the same field on which the Romans had been crushed by Hannibal more than 1,200 years before. Amongst the first Normans to become firmly established was Rainulf Drengot, who entered the service of Sergius IV, the Duke of Naples, and was settled by him in Aversa in 1034 to assist in the Neapolitans' fight against the rival Duke of Capua. Before long, more Normans followed, many of them younger sons starved of prospects back home. Notable amongst them were the children of Tancred de Hauteville, a knight from the Cotentin in Normandy, whose patrimony was far from adequate to sustain the ambitions of a dozen sons. Of this martial brood, five would later become counts or dukes in southern Italy, making the de Hautevilles the key players in the Norman conquest of Italy.

Drogo, the eldest son, and William 'Iron Arm', who arrived around 1038, took service alternately with Lombard dukes and the Byzantine emperor (also serving the latter in a failed attempt to win back Sicily from its Muslim emirs in 1038–40).[2] Gradually, the Norman mercenaries received official status and land: William Iron Arm was granted territory in Apulia by Count Gaimar IV of Salerno and, after his death in 1046, Drogo acquired the grandiloquent-sounding title of 'Count of all the Normans of all Apulia', a status bestowed on him by the Emperor Henry III.[3]

The Normans continued to harass their neighbours in southern Italy and expand their petty realms around Benevento until finally Pope Leo IX, seeing them as a threat to the papacy's own power in Italy, made common cause with the Byzantine emperor Constantine IX Monomachus (1042–55) to expel the interlopers. Drogo had been assassinated in 1051, and so the Norman forces were now under the command of Humphrey, his brother Robert, and Richard, the Norman Count of Aversa. The papal and imperial army clashed with the Normans at Civitella (or Civitate) on 18 June 1053 and, despite facing larger numbers of German and Lombards, the superior training and the shock of the Norman charge won out. Their opponents fled, desperately seeking the shelter of the walls of Civitella. In the memorable words of Edward Gibbon,[4] 'The gates of Civitella were shut against the flying pope, and he was overtaken by the pious conquerors, who kissed his feet, to implore his blessing and the absolution of their sinful victory.' As it happens, Leo had never risked the battlefield at all and was in the town throughout, but the Normans did invest him there afterwards and then kept him prisoner in Benevento for eight months.

The end result was an alliance of convenience between the papacy and the Normans, who came increasingly under the command of Robert Guiscard, whose nickname 'the Wily' was one of which any Viking war leader of the heroic age would have been proud. He was eulogised by Anna Comnena in her *Alexiad* (a biography that is mostly a paean for her father, the emperor Alexius I Comnenus (1081–1118)), who described him as:

> a Norman by descent, of insignificant origin, in temper tyrannical, in mind most cunning, brave in action, very clever in attacking the wealth and substance of magnates, most obstinate in achievement, for he did not allow any obstacle to prevent his executing his desire. His stature was so lofty that he surpassed even the tallest, his complexion was ruddy, his hair flaxen, his shoulders were broad, his eyes all but emitted sparks of fire . . .[5]

The papal-Norman alliance, which began with an agreement at Melfi in 1059, allowed the Guiscards and their followers to push deeper into southern Italy, spreading their sphere of control into the patch-work of petty jurisdictions in Apulia. This was the era that saw Guiscard's building of his own fortress at Melfi, as well as a host of other Norman castles in southern Italy, such as San Marco Argentano and Castel del Monte. Just like their Viking forebears, the Normans of Italy acquired a fearsome reputation, this time heightened by their own favourable chroniclers, such as Amatus of Montecassino, who wrote a *Historia Normanorum* chronicling the conquest from 1016 to the death of Robert of Aversa in 1078.[6] Admiringly, Amatus described the Norman conquerors as 'strong and bold as lions', who 'always stood firm' even in the face of impossible odds.

Robert Guiscard and his youngest brother Roger got on extremely badly, their vicious quarrels continuing even after they tried to divide up rulership of the south by an agreement at Squillace in 1058. Soon afterwards Roger found a fresh arena for his ambitions and embarked on the Norman conquest of Sicily. The eastern part of the island was taken quickly (by 1060), although the conquest of Palermo was more prolonged and it did not fall into Norman hands until after a five-month-long siege in 1071. Its capture was rather marred by the death of Robert's nephew Serlo, who had stayed behind in southern Italy and was set upon there by his enemies and slain, after a defence so valiant that his murderers ate his heart 'so that they might acquire his boldness, which had been great'.[7]

Even then, just as Byzantine enclaves had long held back the Muslim tide when all else around them was lost, so isolated stretches in the south-east of Sicily resisted the Normans until 1091.[8] As Roger turned south and west, so Robert directed his gaze east, captured Bari and then began planning an attack on the Byzantine empire. This culminated in 1081 in an assault on the port of Dyracchium (Durazzo in modern Albania). Robert's daughter had been engaged to Constantine, the son of Emperor Michael VII Ducas (1071–8), and when Michael's overthrow meant the chances of a marriage tie with the imperial family had dissolved, the Norman duke decided to compensate himself by seizing a huge tract of land in the Balkans. He gathered a fleet of around 150 ships (including a large number of horse transports), captured Corfu, Valona and a number of other strategic positions, and then landed at Dyracchium. He had perhaps 30,000 men with him, including more than 1,000 heavily armoured Norman knights.

Robert's fleet was destroyed by a surprise Venetian attack (the Normans having long ago lost the facility at naval warfare that their Viking ancestry would suggest), and Guiscard settled down to besiege the port. Five months passed, and the new Byzantine emperor Alexius I finally succeeded in mustering an army and reached the outskirts of the beleaguered town on 15 October. He had with him around 25,000 men, including the elite Varangian Guard, a unit that had formerly been composed largely of Scandinavians, but which by now included a large element of Anglo-Saxons who had fled England following their own defeat by the Normans in 1066. The Byzantines clashed with Guiscard's host three days after their arrival, but this Balkan reprise of Hastings went equally badly for the Normans' foes – although Guiscard's right wing was driven back by the Varangians to the sea shore, the rest of his line held firm and the overly impetuous Anglo-Saxons found themselves outflanked, surrounded, trapped in a church and then burnt to death. An invigorated Robert sent his heavy cavalry to charge the Byzantine centre, which buckled and then broke.

It took nearly four more months to capture Dyrrachium, by which time most of northern Greece was also in Robert's hands. The prospect of a Norman empire in the Balkans was only averted by a revolt that had set most of southern Italy alight and by the alliance of Alexius I with the Holy Roman Emperor Henry IV (aided by a timely and princely bribe of 360,000 gold pieces handed over by the Byzantines). Despite Bohemond – who had been left in charge by Robert – winning an engagement near Ioannina, he was then defeated in 1083 at Larissa by a new Byzantine army (which for the first time included large numbers of Turkish mercenaries). The Norman position collapsed and Robert's death from fever in July 1085, as he was setting out from the Dalmatian coast with reinforcements, meant that it became irrecoverable. The great era of Norman conquest was over.

Norman Italy and Sicily remained in being for several centuries yet, with the kingdom of Sicily producing a hybrid Arab-Norman cultural flowering during the reign of Roger II (1130–54) and the Normans playing a notable part in the Crusades, their ardour for adventures in the Holy Land increased by the relative paucity of avenues for conquest and enrichment back home. Yet by now the Normans were part of the mainstream of Christian rulers and, though their reputation for military ferocity owed much to the boldness and tenacity with which the de Hautevilles and Guiscards had carved out the Norman empire in Italy, their deeds do not form part of the Viking story.

At the other end of the Viking world in Ireland, the late tenth and early eleventh centuries saw the political eclipse of another area of Scandinavian settlement as the Dublin Vikings, deprived of the support of their brethren in York, succumbed to the renascent power of the Irish kingdoms. Olaf Cuarán, whose long reign (in his final period on the Dublin throne, 951–80) was not lacking in ambition, fought continuously with neighbouring Irish kings, killing the King of Leinster at Belan (near Athy) in 978, and the following year capturing his successor, Domnall Clóen, and sacking Kildare. Emboldened by these successes, Olaf invaded Meath in 980, but the response of its ruler, Máel Sechnaill, was decisive; he inflicted a terrible defeat on the Vikings at Tara, described as a 'red slaughter',[9] and went on to attack Dublin. After a three-day siege the humiliated Olaf Cuarán was forced to agree to release all his Irish hostages, hand over a payment of 2,000 head of cattle and remove the obligation of tribute from all the Uí Néill territories. A broken man, the defeated King of Dublin then abdicated and travelled to the monastery of Iona to live out the rest of his days as a penitent monk.[10]

The Limerick Viking fleet had already been destroyed by Mathgamain of Dál Cais in 976, and now, with Dublin captured, the Irish Vikings ceased to be significant political players, exercising at best a partial autonomy from their increasingly powerful Irish neighbours. The Norsemen found themselves caught up in domestic Irish struggles, operating as the client of one side or another in the tussle between Máel Sechnaill and the growing power of Brian Bóruma (or Boru), overking of the Dál Cais. It was a predicament made more dangerous for the Vikings by their own chronic divisions, with the rival rulers of Waterford and Dublin seeking to dominate the other, while all the time ceding ground to their Irish overlords.

The death of the Dublin Irish king, Glúniairn, in 989 led to a dispute over the succession between his half-brother Sihtric Silkenbeard and Ivar, the Viking lord of Waterford. Although Sihtric won out (and ruled Dublin until 1036), his hold on the city was uncertain, as he suffered an almost immediate attack by Máel Sechnaill, who extracted a heavy tribute from the Dubliners, while Ivar of Waterford managed briefly to expel him twice before 995. The price of Sihtric's final restoration was an alliance with Máel Mórda, overking of Leinster (who was in fact his uncle, being the brother of his mother, Gormflaith), which set him in opposition to both Brian Bóruma and Máel Sechnaill. In 995, Sihtric suffered the embarrassing loss of the royal regalia of Dublin to Máel Sechnaill, when the Irish king took his revenge for the Dublin Vikings' attack on the church at Domnach Patraic earlier in the year.[11] As the century drew to a close, the Viking position weakened still further, with a defeat at Glen Máma at the hands of Brian Bóruma in 999, followed by the sacking of Dublin in 1000. Sihtric fled, and was allowed back only after submitting to Brian.

This new alliance meant that Sihtric had to provide men for Brian's various expeditions against Máel Sechnaill until the two Irish kings were reconciled in 1002, and then for the combined expeditions against the northern Uí Néill in 1005, 1006 and 1007. All of this must have sucked badly needed manpower away at a time when reinforcements from Britain or Scandinavia were scarce, and it allowed Gilla Mochonna, overking of southern Brega, to sack Dublin in 1005.

It was thus from a position of comparative weakness that in 1014 Sihtric began his final attempt to reassert Dublin's independence, aware that, before long, its freedoms might be completely crushed by Brian Bóruma. After a naval expedition against Munster failed with the death of his son Olaf, he sent out a call to the Viking lands for warriors to come to stem the tide of Brian's growing power. Those who responded including Vikings from the Northern Isles, the Hebrides and Scandinavia – a last great coalition that echoed the Norse contingents who had fought at Brunanburh almost eighty years before.

Brian had gathered his own army at Clontarf, a little way to the north of Dublin, ready for a final assault on the city. Among his ranks were numbered his own son Murchad and his grandson Tordelbach, his long-time rival Máel Sechnaill, as well as Ospak of Man, who thus uniquely led a Norse contingent fighting on the Irish side. Sihtric's army included Earl Sigurd the Stout of Orkney, Brodir of Man[12] and Máel Mórda of Leinster. The constellation of conflicting loyalties on the respective sides is perfectly illustrated in the person of Gormflaith, Sihtric's mother. After the death of Olaf Cuarán, her first husband, she had married in succession Máel Sechnaill and then Brian Bóruma. Brian later divorced her, leading Gormflaith to nurse a bitter grudge against the Irish high king, which made her an eager participant in the attempts to destroy the power of her estranged husband. If it was not enough that Gormflaith was at the same time the mother of one leader of the Dublin side in the battle, the sister of another and the former wife of the two leading participants on the Irish side, Sihtric then compounded the confusion by promising her hand in marriage to both Sigurd of Orkney and Brodir of Man, as an inducement for them to join his coalition.

Neither Gormflaith (known in saga sources as Kormlod) nor Sihtric were actually present at the battle between the two sides on Easter Day 1014. Brian Bóruma, choosing to make his Easter prayers in place of an early (and morale-boosting) presence on the battlefield, was also missing from most of the action. Another notable absentee was Máel Sechnaill, who stood his men aside at the last minute, preferring to see the Viking coalition and Bóruma's men weaken each other sufficiently that his own, fresh force could claim the spoils, including the greatest prize, Dublin.

This left around 7,000 men on the Irish side, probably rather greater than the numbers the Vikings could muster. Initially the fighting went Sihtric's way, until the flight of Brodir of Man on the Viking left caused his contingent to follow him. Early Viking success in the centre of the line came to an end with the death of Sigurd of Orkney (who, according to the *Orkneyinga Saga*, had picked up an enchanted standard that guaranteed success for the bearer's side, at the cost of his own life). At this critical moment, with the Vikings clearly wavering, Máel Sechnaill chose to commit his men on Brian Bóruma's side. His intervention was decisive, and in the ensuing slaughter hundreds of Vikings were cut down. Losses on both sides were heavy, with only 1,000 of the Norsemen escaping back to safety within the walls of Dublin. Among the casualties were Olaf, son of the Lawman of the Hebrides, and Máel Mórda of Leinster. Brian himself perished, when Brodir of Man emerged from his hiding place to cut down the Irish high king while he was still at prayer (only for Brodir himself to be killed as he fled from the Irish camp). The main winner at Clontarf, therefore, was not Brian Bóruma, its notional (if posthumous) victor, but Máel Sechnaill, who emerged as the most powerful Irish king.

Yet the impact of the battle can be overstated. Sihtric – whose lack of valour in sheltering behind the walls of Dublin throughout the fighting turned out to be the more prudent choice – remained king there until 1036, even finding time to go on a pilgrimage to Rome in 1028, and to ally with the English in an attack on Wales in 1030. Even Máel Sechnaill did not enjoy his success for long, and it was Brian's grandson, Muirchertach, who emerged as the dominant Irish ruler in the 1060s.[13] After Sihtric's death in 1042, however, the Dublin Viking kingdom little by little slipped further into the position of a peripheral player on the Irish scene, as the prospect that the Irish Vikings would ever dominate the island as they had done in the tenth century receded ever further. In 1052, the city was captured by Diarmait mac Mail, the Irish King of Leinster, who in the mid-1050s set his own son Murchad on the throne. Dublin received an Irish king again in 1075, when Brian Bóruma's grandson Tordelbach removed Gothfrith, who was then ruling the city, and installed his son Muirchertach in his place. His son, Domnall, became in turn King of Dublin in 1115, so that by the twelfth century the lordship of Dublin was effectively in the gift of the Irish kings.

There remained a Scandinavian community in Dublin, and the

Norse language was still spoken when the English arrived to conquer Ireland in the 1170s. Although Viking political influence had long since vanished by that time, the Scandinavians left a more tangible legacy than the saga account of their victories and eventual undoing. A scattering of Norse place-names along the south and east coast, many of them deriving from the Old Norse *øy* or 'island' (such as Scattery, Dursey and Lambay), is a testament to their century-long dominance of the coastline.[14] Old Norse also bequeathed to the Irish language a clutch of nautical terms, such as *accaire* (Old Norse *akkeri*, anchor), *stiúir (styri,* rudder) and *bad (bátr,* ship), as well as a few more warlike terms such as *Iarla* (*jarl,* earl) and, intriguingly, *rannsachadh (rannasaka,* ransack or pillage). In terms of personal names, Viking influence was deepest in the tenth, eleventh and twelfth centuries with names such as Saxolf (*Saxulf*), Amlaíb (*Olaf*), Ímar (*Ivar*) and Ragnall (*Røgnvald*) being common amongst the rulers and nobility of Viking Dublin.

On a political level the Vikings represented an external force against which the Irish kings felt impelled to unite, and they brought increasing Irish involvement in power struggles on the other side of the Irish Sea (even, for a few decades, to the point at which the establishment of a lasting York-Dublin joint kingship looked likely). The *longphorts* which the Vikings founded grew in many cases into thriving towns and trading centres and, in the case of Dublin, into the most important city in Ireland – a position it has retained ever since.

As royal power grew in Scandinavia and became increasingly centralised, the space within which autonomous Viking raiders could operate gradually diminished. One of the few bases from which traditional Viking raiding continued was in the isles of Scotland, which were far removed from the effective control of the twelfth- and thirteenth-century Scottish kings. The Norwegian rulers, too, made intermittent attempts to reassert claims over their historic possessions in Orkney, the Shetlands and the Hebrides. The last of these undertaken on a truly grand scale was that of Magnus III 'Barelegs',[15] the grandson of Harald Hardrada, in 1098. Having seen off the challenge of his cousin Håkon, who had established himself as a rival king based in the Trøndelag, but who died in early 1094, Magnus resolved to re-establish the traditional Norwegian control over the Orkneys.

The Norwegian king brought with him Håkon Paulsson, an Orkney princeling who conveniently happened to be at his court, and once he reached the islands he picked up his cousin Magnus Erlendsson, too.[16] When the Norwegian fleet reached Orkney, the fathers of the two cousins (who had been joint earls of Orkney) were deported back to Norway. The Orkney earldom was then suspended and Magnus Barelegs put his own son Sigurd in place as king. Magnus Erlendsson and Håkon Paulsson remained as Barelegs' enforced guests as he continued on a wide-ranging voyage, first visiting the Hebrides to restore Norwegian authority and then putting in at the Isle of Man, another Viking domain whose independence he sought to quash. The fleet's progress next brought it to Anglesey, quite possibly as part of a plan to restore Gruffudd ap Cynan, the King of Gwynedd, who had been driven out by an Anglo-Norman force and had taken refuge with the Dublin Vikings. The exiled Welsh king had impeccable credentials as an ally, since his mother was the granddaughter of Sihtric Silkenbeard, and he had been brought up near Dublin.

In July 1098, the combined force defeated the Norman earls Hugh of Chester and Hugh of Shrewsbury and enabled Gruffudd's return the following year.[17] While Magnus Erlendsson was permitted to stay in Wales, Barelegs returned to Norway, well satisfied with his initial efforts at a restored Norwegian empire, which included an agreement with King Edgar of Scotland acknowledging his lordship over the Hebrides. In 1102, he returned to consolidate his gains, spending most of his time in Ireland, where he allied himself with Muirchetach Uí Brian and briefly secured the kingship of the Dublin Vikings. Magnus's dreams of empire were shattered, however, when he was ambushed and killed in Ulster while embarking on the journey home. His untimely death caused Sigurd Magnusson to abandon his Orkney kingship and rush back to Norway to lay claim to the throne. The Orkney earldom was restored and Norwegian control of the islands slackened once more.

By the mid-twelfth century Orkney almost had pretensions to the status of a settled European power. Its earl, Rögnvald, had begun the construction of St Magnus Cathedral, an edifice that stands comparison with the great churches of Scandinavia and even beats a few of those in the ecclesiastical heartlands of Germany and France. In 1151, Rögnvald went off on crusade to Palestine, an act that prompted an unfortunate intervention by King Eystein of Norway, who appeared off South Ronaldsay with a large fleet and captured Rögnvald's eighteen-year-old cousin Harold Madaddsson (who had been left in charge in Rögnvald's absence). The hapless prisoner had to pay a ransom of three gold marks for his freedom and his realm and, more importantly, was forced to give up the Orkneys to Eystein before then receiving it back as the Norwegian king's vassal.

If meddling from Norway was still a problem for twelfth-century Orkney earls, they faced an even sterner challenge from the man who was perhaps the last Viking of the old school still operating in the islands. Svein Asliefsson was a larger-than-life character described in the *Orkneyinga Saga* as 'the biggest man in every way in the lands of the west, both in days present and days past, among men who were not of higher rank than he'.[18] Although never himself Earl of Orkney, Svein's activities dominate the last part of the *Orkneyinga Saga*, occupying far more space than many characters of theoretically far more exalted status.

At his hall, the largest in Orkney, despite its location on the modestly sized island of Gairsay, Svein supported eighty trained warriors. In the spring his men busied themselves with sowing seed and other agricultural tasks, but then embarked on his 'spring expedition', a classic Viking plundering cruise around the Hebrides and Ireland. Around midsummer he would return home and stay until the harvest was collected, and would then set out on an 'autumn expedition', pillaging in the grand old style until the closing-in of winter forced him back to months of heroic drinking with his men at Gairsay. It was a lifestyle whose time was nearly done, dependent on the acquisition of loot to pay for a band of men who owed allegiance to no one other than their war leader.

Svein played an often brutal part in the confused civil strife that afflicted Orkney in the mid-twelfth century. Initially he took the part of Earl Paul, an ally of his father, Olaf. In 1135, the young Svein appeared at Earl Paul's drinking hall at Orphir on the mainland of Orkney at the time of the Yule feast. Paul gave him a place of honour just opposite his bodyguard Svein Breast-rope, but an argument broke out between the two men over who was being served more ale. When finally Earl Paul rose to go to Mass, one of the others present – the earl's cup-bearer Evyind – warned Svein Asliefsson that Breast-rope

had been overhead threatening to kill him. He gave Asliefsson an axe
and told him to lie in wait behind the hall's ale-store. As Svein Breast-
rope passed by in the dark, Asliefsson struck him a fatal blow in the
forehead. Breast-rope did not die at once and, in his frenzied attempts
to defend himself, ended up killing his own kinsman Jon.[19]

The faint remains of the drinking hall where the slaying took place
can still be seen, just a few courses of stones marking the outline of
the building, now largely overshadowed by the remains of Orphir
church, whose shattered round shell (the only surviving circular church
in Scotland) is believed to have been built by Earl Håkon as part of
his penance for his killing of his cousin, (St) Magnus Erlendsson.[20]
Svein Asliefsson slipped away in the confusion and took a ship bound
for the Hebrides. His appalling breach of Earl Paul's hospitality assur-
edly earnt him a role in the saga, but it had no place in the new
Orkney that was slowly emerging.

Svein, who unsurprisingly had been declared an outlaw by Paul,
did not stay in exile long. Later the same year he returned without
warning and kidnapped the earl, who was hunting otters at dawn by
the seashore on Rousay, and spirited him away to his half-sister,
Margaret at Atholl. Here, Paul was said to have abdicated the earldom
(though some said that Svein blinded him and threw him into a
dungeon).[21] Svein now tied his fortunes to Earl Rögnvald, the future
builder of St Magnus Cathedral, whose succession he had in effect
ensured by his removal of Paul.

The Viking warrior continued his old-fashioned unruly ways for
more than a decade yet. In the confused civil war over the Orkneys,
known as the War of the Three Earls (1152–54), he supported at one
time or another each of the contenders (Harald Maddadsson, Erlend
Haraldsson and Rögnvald-Kali). Erlend, the candidate Svein initially
favoured, was murdered just before Christmas 1154 (his body found
one morning dumped in a pile of seaweed with a spear sticking out
of it), while Earl Harald treated the grizzled veteran badly, so Svein
ended up in the camp of Rögnvald. The death of Rögnvald-Kali,
murdered by Thorbjorn Clerk (who in turn had a feud with Svein
over the latter's burning to death of his grandmother Frakok), left
Asliefsson exposed, and he gave up on high politics and returned to
his old habits of a biennial Viking cruise.

In 1171, Asliefsson raided in the Hebrides, the Isle of Man and

Ireland, and took two English ships as prizes, seizing a large quantity of broad-cloth, wine and mead. In celebration he invited Earl Harald, who had been sole ruler of Orkney since Rögnvald's death, to a great feast. The earl tried to persuade the veteran warrior to give up his Viking ways, but Svein insisted that he wanted to go on one last autumn expedition and then retire. Harald's reply was prophetic: 'It is hard to tell, comrade, which will come first, death or lasting fame.'[22]

True to his word, Svein duly set out on one final raid. He took seven large warships with him, but after meeting with little success in the Hebrides, made his way to Ireland, where he ransacked Dublin and took many of the leading men hostage. Undaunted, the Dubliners dug pits around the town gates and concealed them with branches, and when Svein and his band tried to enter the town the next day to receive its surrender, they fell into the traps, where the Dubliners slaughtered them all. Only those few who had remained guarding the ships escaped. It was an ignominious, if strangely fitting end, for the last great Viking.

Magnus Barelegs's expedition was the last truly threatening projection of Scandinavian power into the British Isles, but it was not the final attempt by the Norwegian kings to exert their rights in Scotland. In the 1260s, King Håkon the Old (1204–63) tried to cap the recognition of his lordship in Iceland and Greenland by crushing the independence of Orkney. Norway had in fact never given up theoretical sovereignty over Orkney (or Shetland and the Hebrides), and its increasingly obvious attempts to give practical effect to its claims gave rise to tensions with Alexander II of Scotland, who had similar designs to incorporate the islands definitively within the Scottish realm.[23] In 1242, Alexander despatched envoys to Norway to persuade Håkon to give up at least the Hebrides in exchange for a one-off payment. The Norwegian king responded abruptly that he 'did not know he was so much in want of silver that he needed to sell lands for it'. Six years later, Håkon strengthened his claim to the Hebrides by marrying his daughter Cecilia to Harald Olafsson, the Norse King of Man and the Isles. Unfortunately, the ship carrying the couple was lost somewhere south of Shetland, leaving a political vacuum that provided the Scottish kings with a golden opportunity to expand their influence into the Isles.

Alexander II died in 1249, and it was not until 1262 that his successor,

Alexander III, felt confident enough to begin raiding the Hebrides, which prompted Håkon to despatch a large fleet that went via Shetland to Orkney. Troubled by a solar eclipse that occurred while he was in harbour at South Ronaldsay (an event which dates the expedition to August 1263), Håkon nonetheless pressed on to the Hebrides, where he was joined by the exiled Hebridean king, Dougal. As detachments of this fleet raided the Scottish mainland, Alexander prevaricated, hoping that the onset of autumn would put an end to Håkon's depredations. On 2 October 1263, as Håkon and his men were forced to put ashore by bad weather, they encountered a large force of Scots at Largs (on the north Ayrshire coast). The gale meant that the Norsemen could not be reinforced by those still aboard ship, and, although the ensuing Scots victory was not absolute, it effectively ended the Norwegians' hopes of retaking the Hebrides. Håkon retreated to Orkney, fell ill and finally died, being buried in St Magnus's Cathedral in Kirkwall. In the last days of his life he had ordered that all of the great sagas be read to him, and he passed away in the middle of *Sverre's Saga*, the tale of the doings of his own grandfather.

With Håkon dead, so died all real hope of a Viking renaissance in the islands. His son, Magnus, agreed to the Treaty of Perth in 1266, by which Norway ceded its claims to the Isle of Man and the Hebrides to Scotland in exchange for a payment of 4,000 marks (1,000 payable for each of the next four years, followed by a perpetual annuity of 100 marks a year). The Scottish side recognised the Norwegian crown's sovereignty over Orkney and Shetland, but it was in the end this yearly payment – the 'Annual of Norway' – that prised those islands from the King of Norway's grasp. The payments were very intermittent, and even after the Treaty of Perth was reconfirmed in 1426, there is little evidence that the money was actually handed over. Christian I of Denmark,[24] who had financial troubles of his own, was extremely keen to collect the arrears, but the Scottish king James II was equally obdurate in refusing to hand them over (particularly as he no longer had control of the Isle of Man). Negotiations over the money owing dragged on into the 1450s, and finally in 1460 it was agreed that Christian's daughter Margaret I would marry Prince James of Scotland. The Scottish terms for the marriage were unexpectedly harsh, including the forgiveness of all outstanding debts, the ceding of Orkney and Shetland to the Scottish crown, and that Margaret must bring with her a large dowry. After prolonged negotiation (complicated by the death of James II and Danish-Norwegian attempts to secure the allegiance of Earl William of Orkney), a marriage treaty was agreed in September 1468, with the dowry set at 60,000 florins. Orkney was to be mortgaged for 50,000 florins (with the understanding that Christian I could redeem them whenever he might find the funds). The cash-strapped Danish king could only raise one-fifth of the balance of 10,000 florins still owing for the dowry, and was forced to pledge Shetland as surety for the remaining 8,000 florins. The money was never repaid, and so Orkney and Shetland remained Scottish territory. As the Viking Age in the British Isles had dawned with a raid of ferocious violence, it ended in contrast with an unredeemed pledge by a Scandinavian monarch who had learnt that one of the prices of modernity was not simply being able to embark on a raid to raise surplus cash.

As the Viking overseas territories diminished in extent or were absorbed into their host country's political networks, and as links with the original homelands in Scandinavia (or Iceland) diminished, so the Norse tongue began to wither away. In Normandy this process had already begun within a generation or two of the Viking settlement in 911,[25] whereas in Dublin the remaining Norse still kept their language into the thirteenth century. In England the Pennington inscription from Lancashire was once taken to prove that Norse was spoken there as late as 1100, although it is now believed that the inscription is in a corrupt form of the language and does not indicate the survival of Norse as a mother-tongue.[26] Norse appears to have survived longer on the Isle of Man – although here it had to compete with the local Gaelic language – but probably died out sometime between 1300 and 1500. In Scotland the fate of Norse varied dramatically in the different territories occupied by the Vikings. In the Hebrides it may have become extinct as early as the thirteenth to fourteenth century, whereas in Caithness, Shetland and Orkney it had established itself as the dominant language and survived much longer. The general view is that the form of Norse spoken in northern Scotland and the Northern Isles, known as Norn, died out sometime between 1600 and 1850, pushed inexorably out by the Scots.

Norn had, therefore, a long career in Orkney, where it was spoken for almost a millennium after the initial Viking settlement around 800. The almost complete lack of pre-Norse names in Orkney (with the conspicuous exception of 'Orkney' itself) indicates a density of Scandinavian-speaking population that completely crowded out the indigenous language as early as the tenth century.[27] As far as can be determined, many of these initial settlers may have come from north-western Norway, as place-names in Orkney resemble most closely those in Sogn, Møre and the Trøndelag.[28] Actual evidence of Norn during the Viking Age is slight – there are only around 50 runic inscriptions, of which 33 come from Maeshowe, the writers of which may have been recent arrivals or travellers from Scandinavia,[29] while of the remaining inscriptions, most are partial or incomprehensible.[30] The existence of a dozen or more documents whose place of composition is given as Orkney or Shetland between around 1299 and the late sixteenth century is also not especially helpful, as the scribes of these may well have been educated in Norway or made their language conform to more acceptable Norwegian models when they set it down on paper. By the time sources for spoken Norn become available (from the early eighteenth century), it had clearly moved some way from its original Old West Scandinavian roots. An Orkney version of the Lord's Prayer published in 1700, a Shetland version of the same prayer and a ballad collected by George Low in 1774 for his *Tour Through the Islands of Orkney and Shetlands*[31] show a number of features in common with south-west Norwegian dialects, and in particular with Faroese, such as the retention of unstressed 'a' sounds and the simplification of verb endings to lose personal inflections.[32]

Evidence of Norn could still be collected in the late nineteenth century, and certain dialect words still extant today may represent survivals of Norn (such as 'sheltie' for the Shetland pony, which possibly derives from the Norse *hjalti* or Shetlander). But the closer orientation of the Isles to Scotland after the accession of the Scots Sinclairs to the Earldom of Orkney in 1379, and more especially after the pledging of Shetland and Orkney to Scotland by the Danish crown in 1468, meant that the language was ultimately doomed. As late as 1725 there were complaints in Sandwick on the mainland of Orkney about the 'old broken Danish language' that was being used there[33] and it seems to have survived in a few places until around 1750. In Shetland, Norn was more resistant, especially in the west, and there is reason to believe that there were native speakers of the tongue as late as 1800.[34]

Just as the Norse tongues lived on in Ireland (for a time), in the Scottish islands (for centuries) and in the Faroes and Iceland (permanently), so the memory of the Vikings persisted most strongly where their languages had survived the best. The transmission of the Viking heritage through the sagas and collections such as the 'Prose Edda' is the best example of this, but by the sixteenth century antiquarians had begun to take a somewhat more scientific interest in their Norse heritage. Amongst the first fruits of this were the histories of Scandinavia by the Swedish brothers Olavus and Johannes Magnus.[35] Then, during the seventeenth century, runic inscriptions and some Icelandic sagas became available to scholars as the manuscripts were collected from Icelandic farms, where they had been preserved for centuries, and sent back to Stockholm and Copenhagen.[36]

Not long after Enlightenment touched Scandinavia (and influenced the works of historians such as Ludvig Holberg (1684–1754) in Denmark and Olov Dalin (1708–63) in Sweden), the first waves of Germanic Romanticism lapped against the Nordic countries, inspiring a new feeling that the sagas, with all their archaic glorification of violence, encapsulated within them the true spirit of the North. The 'Nordic Renaissance' that followed brought the Vikings to the fore, although more as a reimagining of the Old Norse sagas in the light of the Romantic movement than as any genuine attempt to recover what the Viking Age had actually been like. Paul-Henry Mallet (1730–1807), a Swiss-born Professor of French at Copenhagen University in the 1750s, played a key role in this, popularising the poems of the 'Edda' for a wider European audience, so that they came to influence the British poets Thomas Gray and James Macpherson[37] and the German philosopher Johann Gottfried Herder.

After the humiliations of the Napoleonic Wars, new feelings began to stir in Scandinavia. The British had bombarded Copenhagen in 1807, while Sweden had suffered the bitter loss of Finland to Russia in 1809, and the Nordic Renaissance now transformed into a revival of nationalism, glorifying Viking empires and Viking beliefs that had once made Scandinavians the pre-eminent power of northern Europe. It was this which led to a curious episode in the afterlife of the Vikings. In 1811 the *Götiska förbundet* (Gothic Association) was founded in Stockholm, composed of academics who revived a simulacrum of the old ways, by putting on recitations of Eddic poems and quaffing mead from drinking horns. On a more serious level, the association's journal *Iduna*[38] contained articles discussing Viking culture, interleaved with patriotic articles and even poems in a version of Old Norse.

One of the society's luminaries, the historian Erik Gustaf Geijer (1783–1847), wrote a *Svenska folkets historia* ('History of the Swedish People'), depicting Viking Scandinavia as an idyllic society in which king and free farmers lived in harmony, moderated by the authority of the *things*. It was a view obviously influenced by the saga accounts of the Icelandic Free State at its height, before the bitter wars of the thirteenth century, but it came to influence a more general view of Norse society. The culmination of this movement was the work of Bishop Esaias Tegnér (1782–1846), who in 1825 completed *Frithiof's Saga*, a series of epic poems in the Viking style, but of thoroughly modern composition. The work was translated into a number of languages (including English, French, German and Russian) and became the medium through which the public in those countries came to be familiar with the world of the Icelandic sagas, at a time when the originals were not available in translation. Frithiof's doings included roving in the grand Viking style:

> Far and wide, like the falcon that hunts through the sky, flew he now o'er the desolate sea. And his vikings' code, for his champions on board, wrote he well: – wilt though hear what it be? On thy ship pitch no tent; in no house shalt thou sleep; in the hall who our friends ever knew? On his shield sleeps the Vikings, his sword in his hand. And for his tent has you heaven the blue.[39]

In the end, however, Frithiof settled down to life as a farmer, making the poem a sufficiently unshocking composition for its English translation to be dedicated in 1835 to the Princess Alexandrina Victoria (who, just four years later, ascended to the throne as Queen Victoria).

As the nineteenth century progressed, the spirit of Viking restoration in Scandinavia took deeper roots, in great part inspired by the Danish priest N. F. S. Grundtvig, who spent decades trying to replace a study of Latin grammar and the classical world in schools with that of Old Norse and Scandinavian mythology, together with a healthy dose of Christian revivalism. The folk high schools that he promoted spread to other Scandinavian countries, although without the compulsory teaching of Old Norse that he had hoped for. Amidst all this nostalgia for the Viking era, Viking balls became fashionable in Stockholm, with costumes prominently featuring horned helmets, which became a de rigueur (and utterly mistaken) part of the neo-Viking paraphernalia.

By the late nineteenth century Viking mania had spread far and wide, with the translation of genuine Icelandic sagas into English by men of such eminence as the artist and radical William Morris (who translated *The Saga of Gunnlaug Worm Tongue*, *Grettir's Saga* and *The Volsung Saga*). Morris's enthusiasm for things Scandinavian led him to visit Iceland twice (in 1871 and 1873), which he called 'the terrible and tragic, but beautiful land, with its well remembered stories of brave men'.[40] Interest in the old Norse ways became particularly fervent in Norway, Iceland and the Faroes, where it was linked with those countries' national struggle for independence from Denmark (finally achieved in 1905 for Norway, in 1946 for Iceland, and in the shape of self-government under the Danish crown for the Faroes in 1948). Snorri Sturluson's *Heimskringla* – with its account of the doings of the Norwegian kings during the period of the country's greatest power – became especially popular, a sentiment further fuelled by the discovery of the Gokstad and Oseberg ships in 1880 and 1904. The sailing of a replica of the Gokstad ship to the World Fair in Chicago in 1892, and the sudden rash of 'Viking' discoveries such as the Kensington Runestone in the United States, formed part of this nostalgic rediscovery of the Norse past.

Throughout the nineteenth century the Viking Age became an appealing repository of myths and imagery to act as a counterweight to the overwhelmingly classical and biblical fare that had formed the repertoire of many artists and writers since the Renaissance. In music the German composer Richard Wagner borrowed freely from German and Scandinavian mythology to produce his epic *Ring of the Nibelung*, first performed in 1876, while British writers such as Sir Walter Scott and William Collingwood helped to popularise a literary craze for the Vikings.

This Viking-mania had a far less positive side, when it was co-opted by Germany's National Socialists in the 1930s. The Vikings were seen by the Nazis – who were also rather fond of Wagner – as a prototype of the *Herrenvolk*, the master-race with which the German racial supremacists identified themselves. On a more practical level, from 1934 the excavations at the Viking site at Hedeby (Haithabu) came under the personal supervision of Heinrich Himmler, the head of the SS (and later of the Gestapo). The *Nasjonal Samling*, the Norwegian counterpart to the Nazis, aped their ideological masters by resurrecting Viking imagery as a modern political tool, and between 1935 and 1944 they even held several rallies at the site of the Borre Viking burial mounds.

The collapse of Fascism in 1945 did not lead to a similar decline in interest in the Vikings and, free from the taint of ideological extremism, the Viking era has gone from strength to strength in terms of public enthusiasm. The wave of interest in historical re-enactment reached the Norsemen with the foundation of the Norse Film and Pageant Society (now 'The Vikings!') in 1971, and they and other groups such as Regia Anglorum put on regular events re-creating the cut-and-thrust of Viking warfare (as well as less violent elements of the culture). Many major Viking sites in Scandinavia and elsewhere have living-history re-enactors attached to them, or a re-created Viking settlement in which visitors can gain some sense of the sights and smells of the Norse world. The steadily increasing level of interest in the twenty-first century can be gauged from the hundreds of thousands of people who visit the major Viking museums, such as Britain's Jorvik Centre in York, Denmark's Roskilde Viking Ship Museum and the Viking Ship Museum in Oslo.

For all the saga deeds and conquests of the Vikings, and for all the long historical tail that they trailed in their wake, what were their true achievements and what was their legacy for later ages? Although the Vikings were undeniably violent when opposed, and used force to achieve their ends (whether the seizing of reliquaries or the acquisition of territory), they were probably no more so than their contemporaries in more organised jurisdictions. It was the Vikings' status as the 'other' – the outsider – that made them so terrifying to contemporaries, and their ability (using the latest maritime technology) to assail coastlines which had for centuries felt secure that made them the objects of such loathing. Their reputation, if it did anything, made them more effective; the payment of ever-escalating tributes by Aethelred the Unready in eleventh-century England owed as much to the fear of what the Vikings might do, if crossed, as to what they were actually able to do.

Like the most effective beasts of prey, the Vikings sought out the weak. In Francia, Scotland, Ireland and England they attacked until they found a point of weakness, and then they battered away at this mercilessly and repeatedly until resistance collapsed or richer pickings were to be had elsewhere. And, like the best predators, the end result was probably the strengthening of that which they did not destroy.

In both England and Scotland the Viking raids so severely weakened most of the native contenders for power that in both cases a single unitary kingdom emerged as the paradoxical result of their depredations. In Ireland the effect of the Viking invasions was probably slightest, although the reduction in the number of native kingdoms that wielded any real power was probably accelerated by the activities of the Viking Dubliners. In England the case is more clear-cut; the Anglo-Saxon kingdoms of Northumbria, Mercia and East Anglia were defeated one by one and absorbed by large Viking forces, until only Wessex resisted. That it survived made the ultimate unification of England under a single king that much easier to achieve, whereas welding together a competing but vigorous Mercia and Northumbria onto an ambitious Wessex might have been next to impossible. In Scotland the Vikings simplified the multi-cornered competition between Picts, Scots and the Strathclyde Britons by fatally weakening the Britons after the sack of Dumbarton Rock in 870, and thus removing one of the competing parties from the equation.

In Francia, the Vikings came closer to the wholesale destruction of the Carolingian empire, but it was the chronic instability of the state after the death of Louis the Pious and the prolonged civil wars between his sons that gave the Vikings decades in which to embed themselves. Yet even so, they only succeeded in establishing a permanent presence in Normandy, while the central core of the French monarchy was able (for a time) to recover itself before the damaging series of rivalries with England that stretched from the mid-twelfth to the mid-fifteenth century destabilised it once more. In the east the Viking contribution to what would become the future state of Russia is hotly contested, but it is clear that Viking incomers at least played a significant role in carving out a territory for themselves, which solidified into the principalities around towns such as Kiev, Novgorod and Chernigov that would form the heartland of the early medieval Russian state.

Further afield, the impact of the Vikings was much more profound, in territories that had had little or no previous settlement and so became hosts to a totally Scandinavian way of life. There simply would be no Faroese or Icelandic society as we know it without the Viking *landnám* of the eighth to ninth centuries. In Greenland and North America, in contrast, the Viking colonies died out (extremely rapidly in the latter), leaving ruins but little of lasting consequence (save for the subsequent recolonisation of Greenland by the Danish crown in the eighteenth century).

Just as previous raiders in late antiquity and early medieval Europe settled down and became a key component in the cultural and political development of the areas they had previously raided, so the Vikings became an integral part of the countries on which they preyed. From the large Viking genetic component in parts of Scotland, northern England and Ireland to the massive predominance of Viking genes in Iceland, their imprint is everywhere. In linguistic terms, they bequeathed a mass of words to English, amongst them very common ones such as 'egg' and 'bread', and a much less pronounced (but still detectable) influence on the Irish and French languages.

The Vikings have left fewer monuments than other cultures of the classical and early medieval worlds, and many of the grander remains in Scandinavia itself (such as the fabulous Romanesque cathedral at Lund) post-date the Viking Age proper. There are, however, amazing vestiges of the Viking world to be seen, from Denmark's 'baptismal certificate' on the monumental Jelling Stone, to the remnants of the furthest-flung Viking settlement of them all at L'Anse aux Meadows in Newfoundland. Some of the Viking monuments are haunting, such as the flotilla of stone ship-setting graves at Lindholm Høje in northern Jutland, while others – like the remains of their houses, their combs and even their latrines at Jorvik in northern England – are more homely. Some, such as the scratched runes in the Neolithic barrow at Maeshowe on Orkney, are astonishing survivals, which give us an almost tangible sense of a group of Vikings huddled together for protection against the storms raging outside. Others are less concrete:

the survival of a landscape or a topographical feature that has a direct link to a description in the sagas.

The Viking empire, which at its height in the eleventh century stretched from eastern Sweden across the Atlantic to Iceland and Greenland, and eastwards into Russia, did not endure, but the manner of its construction and the deeds performed in its building are the most powerful legacy of all. Using their longships and knorrs, the Vikings built the first truly maritime empire in northern Europe, a model which showed that the seaways could be sinews every bit as effective at knitting a state together as the land routes relied upon by more conventional kingdoms. From western Norway to Lindisfarne is just a day or so's sail, and the stepping stones that the Vikings took from the Faroes to Greenland only left them out of sight of land for a few days at a time. To a land-based eye, an empire that embraced the Orkneys and Shetlands, bundled them together with the Hebrides, the Isle of Man and scattered coastal enclaves in Ireland and then sought to unite them with a large chunk of northern England seems a strange hybrid, and one whose administration would create contradictions of almost irresolvable complexity. Yet to a Viking it all made perfect sense; coming from a homeland where even traversing a short distance might best be done in a boat, the dragon-prowed longships made ideal vehicles both for travelling great distances and for binding disparate communities together.

Back on Lindisfarne, where it all began, the Viking raids caused the final evacuation of the monastic community (and of the relics of St Cuthbert) in 830, and the monks (and their founder's bones) did not come back until William the Conqueror's Harrying of the North in 1069–70 prompted their hasty return to Holy Island. By 1150 a new abbey church had been constructed, whose ruined shell now dominates the site. There, free of the shadow of the Northmen's fury, the brethren lived tranquilly – save for an odd border raid or two by the Scots – until the monastery's final dissolution by Henry VIII in 1537.

The nearby church of St Mary's, built over the original wooden church established by St Aidan in 635, incorporates elements of the original seventh-century plan, including the remains of an Anglo-Saxon arch. It formed part of the original monastic complex and is perhaps the last surviving vestige of what the original Viking raiders saw (and plundered) in 793. On the wall facing the church's high altar hangs a most curious document, an apology from the Bishop of Nidaros in Norway on the occasion of the 1,200th anniversary of the Lindisfarne raid in 1993. 'We commemorate the event of 793,' writes the bishop, 'and the sacrifices of the monks of Lindisfarne with contrite hearts.'

It is not an apology the Vikings would have approved of, nor would they have wished to be remembered for their descendants' contrition. They bequeathed us material remains, linguistic traces, a fair helping of their DNA and one of the most complete vernacular literatures from the Middle Ages. It is, though, in the power of their words and deeds to stir the imagination that the Vikings have left their most potent legacy. For a people addicted to sagas, and for whom there was nothing more important than that their reputation lived on in the memory of those who had witnessed their deeds, this is perhaps the most fitting memorial of all.

Bibliography

Primary Sources

Adam of Bremen, *Gesta Hammaburgensis Ecclesiae Pontificum* (translated by Francis J. Tschan in *Adam of Bremen: History of the Archbishops of Hamburg Bremen*, New York 1959)

Ágrip, A Twelfth-Century Synoptic History of the Kings of Norway (edited by M. J. Driscoll, London 1995)

Alcuin of York, *Vita Willibrordi* (translated by the Reverend Alexander Grieve in *Willibrord, Missionary in the Netherlands, 691–739*, London 1923)

Anglo-Saxon Chronicle (translated and edited by Dorothy Whitelock, London 1965)

Anna Comnena, *The Alexiad* (translated by Elizabeth A. S. Dawes, London 1928)

Annales Bertiniani (translated and edited by Janet Nelson in *The Annals of St Bertin*, Manchester 1991)

Annales Fuldenses (edited by F. Kurze, Hanover 1891)

Annales Regni Francorum (translated by B. W. Scholz in *Carolingian Chronicles*, Ann Arbor 1970)

The Annals of Ulster to AD 1131 (edited by Seán Mac Airt & Gearóid Mac Niocaill, Dublin 1983)

Anskar, *Vita Anskarii auctore Rimberto* (translated by C. H. Robinson in *Anskar, Apostle of the North, 801–865*, London 1921)

Asser, *Life of Alfred* (translated by J. A. Giles in *Six Old English Chronicles*, London 1848)

Beowulf (translated and edited by R. D. Fulk in *The Beowulf manuscript: Complete texts*, Cambridge, Mass. 2010)

The Borgarthing Law of the Codex Tunsbergensis . . . Diplomatic edition, with an introduction on the paleography and the orthography (edited by George T. Flom, Urbana 1925)

Constantine Porphyrogenitus, *De Administrando Imperio* (translated by R. J. H. Jenkins, London 1962)

Dicuil, *Liber de Mensura Orbis Terrae* (edited by J. J. Tierney, London 1967)

Dudo of Saint-Quentin, *Gesta Normannorum* (translated by Thomas Forrester, London 1854)

Egil's Saga (translated by Gwyn Jones, Syracuse 1960)

The Elder Edda: A Selection (translated by Paul B. Taylor & W. H. Auden, London 1969)

Encomium Emmae Reginae (edited by Alistair Campbell, with a supplementary introduction by Simon Keynes, Cambridge 1998)

Ermentarius, *Vie et miracles de Saint Philibert* (in A. Giry, *Monuments de l'histoire des abbayes de Saint-Philibert,* Paris 1905)

Fagrskinna: A catalogue of the Kings of Norway (translated by Alison Finlay, Leiden 2004)

Fragmentary Annals of Ireland (edited by Joan Newlon Radner, Dublin 1978)

Grágás (edited by Peter Foote, Andrew Dennis & Richard Perkins in *Laws of Early Iceland: Grágás, the Codex Regius of Grágás with Material from Other Manuscripts,* Winnipeg 1980–2000, in two volumes)

Gregory of Tours, *History of the Franks* (translated by Lewis Thorpe, London 1974)

Grettir's Saga (translated by George Ainslie Hight, London 1914)

Henry of Huntingdon, *Historia Anglorum* (edited and translated by Diana Greenway, Oxford 1996)

Historia Norwegiae (translated by Peter Fisher, Copenhagen 2003)

Ibn Fadlan, *Risala* in *Journey to Russia: A Tenth-Century Traveler from Baghdad to the Volga River* (Richard Frye, Princeton 2005)

Ibn Rusteh, *Les Atours Précieux* (translated into French by Gaston Wiet, Cairo 1955)

Isidore of Seville, *Etymologiae* (translated by Stephen A. Barney, W. J. Lewis, J. A. Beach & Oliver Berghof in *The Etymologies of Isidore of Seville,* Cambridge 2006)

Landnámabók (translated by H. Pálsson & P. Edwards, Winnipeg 1972)

Leo the Deacon, *History* (translated by Alice-Mary Talbot & Denis F. Sullivan in *The History of Leo the Deacon: Byzantine Military Expansion in the Tenth Century,* Dumbarton Oaks 2005)

Njal's Saga (translated by Magnus Magnusson & Hermann Pálsson, London 1964)

Ordericus Vitalis, *Historia Ecclesiastica* (translated by Marjorie Chibnall, Oxford 1969)

Orkneyinga Saga (translated by Alexander Burt Taylor, London 1938)

Orosius, *Historiarium Adversum Paganos Libri septem* (*King Alfred's Anglo-Saxon Version of the Compendious History of the World by Orosius*, translated by the Reverend Joseph Bosworth, London 1859); contains the voyages of Ohthere and Wulfstan

Örvar-Odds Saga (translated by Herman Pálsson & Paul Edwards in *Seven Viking Romances*, London 1985)

Pliny, *Naturalis Historiae* (translated by H. Rackham, London 1938–63)

The Poetic Edda of Saemund the Learned (London 1866)

Regino of Prüm, *Chronicon* (translated by Simon Maclean in *History and politics in late Carolingian and Ottonian Europe: The chronicle of Regino of Prüm and Adalbert of Magdeburg*, Manchester 2009)

Russian Primary Chronicle (Laurentian Text), (translated and edited by Samuel Hazzard Cross & Olgerd P. Sherbowitze-Wetzor, Cambridge, Mass. 1953)

Saga of the Jomsvikings (translated by Lee Hollander, Austin, Texas 1955)

Saga of the Volsungs, Saga of Ragnar Lodbrok (translated by M. Schlauch, New York 1949)

Saxo Grammaticus, *Gesta Danorum* (translated by Hilda Ellis Davidson & Peter Fisher in *The History of the Danes*, Woodbridge 1980)

Speculum Regale (*The King's Mirror*, translated by Laurence Marcellus Larson, New York 1917)

Sturluson, Snorri, *Heimskringla* (translated by Erling Monsen, Cambridge 1932)

Sturluson, Snorri, *Prose Edda* (translated by Anthony Faulkes, London 1987)

Symeon of Durham, *Libellus de Exordio atque Procursu istius, hoc est Dunhelmensis, Ecclesie/Tract on the origins and progress of this the Church of Durham* (edited by David Rollason, Oxford 2000)

Three Icelandic Outlaw Sagas (translated by George Johnston & Anthony Faulkes, London 2001); contains *Gisli's Saga*, *Grettir's Saga* and *Hord's Saga*

Vegetius, *Epitoma Re Militaris* (translated by N. P. Milner in *Vegetius: Epitome of Military Science*, 2nd edition, Liverpool 1996)

The Vinland Sagas (translated by Keneva Kunz, London 1997); contains *The Saga of the Greenlanders* and *The Saga of Eirik the Red*

Vita Edwardi Regis (edited and translated by Frank Barlow in *The Life of King Edward who rests at Westminster*, Oxford 1992)

William of Poitiers, *Gesta Guillelmi* (edited and translated by R. H. C. Davis & Marjorie Chibnall, Oxford 1998)

Ynglinga Saga in Snorri Sturluson's *Heimskringla* (edited by Erling Momsen, translated by A. H. Smith, Cambridge 1932)

Yngvar's Saga (translated by Herman Pálsson & Paul Edwards in *Vikings in Russia: Yngvar's Saga and Eymund's Saga,* Edinburgh 1989)

Secondary Sources

Abels, Richard, 'From Alfred to Harold II: The Military Failure of the Anglo-Saxon State' in Abels & Bachrach (eds) *The Normans and their Adversaries at War* (Woodbridge 2001), pp. 15–30

Abels, Richard P. & Bachrach, Bernard S. (eds), *The Normans and their Adversaries at War* (Woodbridge 2001)

Abram, Christophe, *Myths of the Pagan North: The Gods of the Norsemen* (London 2011)

A Century of Population Growth: From the First Census of the United States to the Twelfth 1790–1900 (Department of Commerce and Labor, Bureau of the Census, Washington 1909)

Adalsteinsson, Jon Hnefill, *Under the Cloak: The acceptance of Christianity in Iceland with particular reference to religious attitudes prevailing at the time* (Uppsala 1978)

Adams, Jonathan & Holman, Katherine (eds), *Scandinavia and Europe 800–1350: Contact, Conflict and Co-existence* (Turnhout, Belgium 2004)

Alföldi, A., 'Cornuti, A Teutonic Contingent in the Service of Constantine the Great' in *Dumbarton Oaks Papers* 13 (1959), pp. 171–79

Almqvist, Bo & Greene, David (eds), *Proceedings of the Seventh Viking Congress, Dublin 15–21 August 1973* (Dublin 1976)

Ambrosiani, Björn, 'Birka, a planted town serving and increasing agricultural population' in *Proceedings of the Eighth Viking Congress* (edited by Bekker-Nielsen et al., Odense 1981), pp. 19–24

Ambrosiani, Björn & Clarke, Helen (eds), *Birka Studies 2: Excavations in the Black Earth 1990* (Stockholm 1995)

Anderson, R. B., *America Not Discovered by Columbus: A Historical Sketch of the Discovery of America by the Norsemen in the Tenth Century* (Chicago 1874)

Andersson, Theodore M., *The Icelandic Family Saga, An Analytic Reading* (Cambridge, Mass. 1967)

Andersson, Theodore M., *The Growth of the Medieval Icelandic Sagas (1180–1280)* (Ithaca 2006)

Antonsson, Hakí, *St Magnús of Orkney: A Scandinavian Martyr-Cult in Context* (Brill 2007)

Appelt, Martin, Berglund Joel & Gulløv, Hans Christian (eds), *Identities and Cultural Contacts in the Arctic – Proceedings from a Conference at the*

Danish National Museum, Copenhagen, November 30 to December 2 1999 (Copenhagen 2000)

Arbman, Holger (translated by Alan Binns), *The Vikings* (London 1961)

Arge Símun V., 'The landnám in the Faroes' in *Arctic Anthropology* 28 (2) (1991), pp. 101–20

Arge, Símun V., 'Vikings in the Faroe Islands' in Fitzhugh & Ward (eds), *Vikings: The North Atlantic Saga* (Washington 2000)

Arneborg, Jette, 'The Roman Church in Norse Greenland' in *Acta Archaeologica* 61 (1991), pp. 142–50

Arneborg, Jette, 'Greenland and Europe' in Fitzhugh & Ward (eds), *Vikings, The North Atlantic Saga* (Washington 2000)

Arneborg, Jette & Gulløv, Hans Christian, *Man, Culture and Environment in Ancient Greenland* (Copenhagen 1998)

Arneborg, Jette et al., 'Change of diet of the Greenland Vikings determined from stable carbon isotope analysis and 14C dating of their bones' in *Radiocarbon* 41 (2) (1999), pp. 157–68

Arnold, Martin, *The Vikings: Culture and Conquest* (London 2006)

Ashe, Geoffrey, *Land to the West: St Brendan's Voyage to America* (London 1962)

Bagge, Sverre, *Society and Politics in Snorri Sturluson's Heimskringla* (Berkeley 1991)

Bagge, Sverre, *From Viking Stronghold to Christian Kingdom: State Formation in Norway 900–1350* (Copenhagen 2010)

Bailey, R. N., *Viking Age Sculpture in Northern England* (London 1980)

Balk, Heiki, 'The Vikings and the Eastern Baltic' in Stefan Brink (ed.), *The Viking World* (London 2008)

Barford, P. M., *The Early Slavs* (London 2001)

Barlow, James William, *The Normans in Southern Europe* (London 1886)

Barnes, Michael P., *The Norn Language of Orkney and Shetland* (Lerwick 1998)

Barnes, Michael P., *The Runic Inscriptions of Maeshowe, Orkney* (Uppsala 1994)

Barnwell, P. S. & Mostert, Marco (eds), *Political Assemblies in the Earlier Middle Ages* (Turnhout, Belgium 2003)

Barrell, A. D. M., *Medieval Scotland* (Cambridge 2000)

Barrett, James H., *Contact, Continuity and Collapse: The Norse Colonisation of the North Atlantic* (Turnhout, Belgium 2003)

Bateley, Janet & Eglert, Anton (eds), *Ohthere's Voyage: A late 9th-century account of voyages along the coasts of Norway and Denmark and its cultural context* (Roskilde 2007)

Bates, David, *Normandy before 1066* (London 1982)

Batey, Colleen E., Jesch, Judith & Morris, Christopher D., *The Viking Age in Caithness, Orkney and the North Atlantic* (Edinburgh 1993)

Beamish, North Ludlow, *The Discovery of America by the Northmen: In the tenth century/with notices of the early settlement of the Irish in the western hemisphere* (London 1841)

Bekker-Nielsen, Hans, Foote, Peter & Olsen, Olaf (eds), *Proceedings of the Eighth Viking Congress, Århus 24–31 August 1977* (Odense 1981)

Benedikz, B. S., 'The Evolution of the Varangian Regiment in the Byzantine Army' in *Byzantinische Zeitschrift* 62 (1969), pp. 20–24

Berend, Nora (ed.), *Christianisation and the Rise of Christian Monarchy: Scandinavia, Central Europe and Rus' c.900–1200* (Cambridge 2007)

Berglund, Joel, 'The Decline of the Norse Settlements in Greenland' in *Arctic Anthropology*, vol. 23, no. 1/2 (1986), pp. 109–35.

Besteman, Jan, 'Two Viking Hoards from the Former Island of Wieringen (The Netherlands): Viking Relations with Frisia in an Archaeological Perspective' by Jan Besteman in *Land, Sea and Home – Proceedings of a Conference on Viking-period settlement at Cardiff, July 2001* (edited by John Hines, Alan Lane & Mark Redknap, Leeds 2004), pp. 93–108

Biddle, M. & Kjølbe-Biddle, B., 'Repton and the Vikings' in *Antiquity* 250 (1992), pp. 36–51

Biddle, M. & Kjølbe-Biddle, B., 'Repton and the "great heathen army", 873–4' in *Select Papers from the Proceeding of the 13th Viking Congress* (Oxford 2001)

Bigelow, Gerald F., *The Norse of the North Atlantic* (Copenhagen 1991)

Blöndal, Sigfús (translated, revised and rewritten by Benedikt S. Benedikz), *The Varangians of Byzantium: An Aspect of Byzantine Military History* (Cambridge 1978)

Boulhosa, Patricia Pires, *Icelanders and the Kings of Norway: Medieval Sagas and Legal Texts* (Leiden 2005)

Bradbury, Jim, *The Battle of Hastings* (Stroud 1998)

Bradley, Ian, *William Morris and his World* (New York 1978)

Brent, Peter, *The Viking Saga* (London 1975)

Bridgeford, Andrew, *1066: The Hidden History in the Bayeux Tapestry* (New York 2005)

Brink, Stefan (ed.), *The Viking World* (London 2008)

Brooks F. W., *The Battle of Stamford Bridge* (York 1956)

Brooks, N. P., 'England in the Ninth Century: The Crucible of Defeat' in *Transactions of the Royal Historical Society*, 5th series, no. 29 (1979), pp. 1–20

Brown, Callum G., *Up-helly-aa, Custom, culture and community in Shetland* (Manchester 1998)

Brown, Katherine L. Clark & Robin J. H., 'Analysis of Pigmentary Materials on the Vinland Map and Tartar Relation by Raman Microprobe Spectroscopy' in *Analytical Chemistry* (August 2002)

Brown, Nancy Marie, *The Far Traveler* (New York 2007)

Bugge, Anders, *Norwegian Stave Churches* (translated by Ragnar Christophersen, Oslo 1953)

Bullough, Donald A., *Alcuin: Achievement and Reputation* (Leiden 2004)

Byock, Jesse, *Feud in the Icelandic Saga* (Berkeley 1982)

Byock, Jesse, *Medieval Iceland: Society, Sagas and Power* (Berkeley 1988)

Cam, Helen, 'The Legend of the Incendiary Birds' in *English Historical Review*, vol. 31, no. 121 (January 1916), pp. 98–101

Carver, Martin (ed.), *The Age of Sutton Hoo: The Seventh Century in North-Western Europe* (Woodbridge 1992)

Carver, Martin (ed.), *The Cross Goes North: Processes of Conversion in Northern Europe AD 300–1300* (York 2004)

Chadwick, N. K., *The Beginnings of Russian History: An Enquiry into Sources* (Cambridge 1946)

Charles, B. G., *Old Norse Relations with Wales* (Cardiff 1934)

Chibnall, Marjorie, *The Normans* (Oxford 2000)

Clarke, Helen & Ambrosiani, Björn, *Towns in the Viking Age* (Leicester 1991)

Clarke, Howard B., *Medieval Dublin, the Making of a Metropolis* (Dublin 1995)

Clarke, Howard B. et al. (eds), *Coinage in Ninth-Century Northumbria: The Tenth Oxford Symposium on Coinage and Monetary History* (Oxford 1987)

Clarke, Howard B., Ni Mhanoaigh, Maire & O' Floinn, Raghnall, *Ireland and Scandinavia in the Early Viking Age* (Dublin 1998)

Clausen, Birthe L. (ed.), *Viking Voyages to North America* (Roskilde 1993)

Cooper, Janet (ed.), *The Battle of Maldon: Fiction and Fact* (London 1993)

Coupland, Simon, 'The Rod of God's Wrath and the People of God's Wrath: The Carolingian Theology of the Viking Invasions' in *Journal of Ecclesiastical History*, vol. 42 (1991), pp. 535–54

Coupland, Simon, 'The Vikings in Francia and Anglo-Saxon England' in *The New Cambridge Medieval History*, vol. ii (edited by Rosamond McKitterick, Cambridge 1995), pp. 190–301

Coupland, Simon, 'From poachers to gamekeepers: Scandinavian warlords and Carolingian kings' in *Early Medieval Europe*, vol. 7, no. 1 (1998), pp. 85–114

Coupland, Simon, 'Trading Places: Quentovic and Dorestad Reassessed' in *Early Medieval Europe*, vol. 11 (2003), pp. 209–32

Coupland, Simon, *Carolingian Coinage and the Vikings: Studies on Power and Trade in the 9th century* (Aldershot 2007)

Cox, Steven L., 'Palaeo-Eskimo Occupations of the North Labrador Coast' in *Arctic Anthropology*, vol. 15, no. 2 (1978)

Crawford, Barbara E. (ed.), *Scandinavian Scotland* (Leicester 1987)

Crawford, Barbara E. (ed.), *St Magnus Cathedral and Orkney's Twelfth-Century Renaissance* (Aberdeen 1988)

Crawford, Barbara, *Scandinavian Settlement in Northern Britain* (Leicester 1995)

Crouch, David, *The Normans* (London 2002)

Crumlin-Pedersen, Ole, 'Viking shipbuilding and seamanship' in *Proceedings of the Eighth Viking Congress* (edited by Bekker-Nielsen et al., Odense 1981), pp. 271–85

Crumlin-Pedersen, Ole (ed.), *Aspects of Maritime Scandinavia, AD 200–1200* (Roskilde 1991)

Cunliffe, Barry, *The Extraordinary Voyage of Pytheas the Greek* (London 2001)

Curta, Florian (ed.), *East Central & Eastern Europe in the Early Middle Ages* (Ann Arbor 2005)

Davies, W. (ed.), *From the Vikings to the Normans* (Oxford 2003)

de Boe, Guy & Verhaege, Frans (eds), *Exchange and Trade in Medieval Europe, Papers of the 'Medieval Europe Brugge 1997' Conference*, vol. 4 (Zellik 1997)

de Paor, Liam, 'The Viking Towns of Ireland' in *Proceedings of the Seventh Viking Congress* (edited by Almqvist & Greene, Dublin 1976), pp. 29–38

DeVries, Kelly, *The Norwegian Invasion of England in 1066* (Woodbridge 1999)

di Robilant, Andrea, *Venetian navigators: The voyages of the Zen brothers to the Far North* (London 2011)

Dixon, C. E. V. & Saylor Rodgers, Barbara, *In Praise of Later Roman Emperors* (Berkeley 1994)

Dolukahnov, Pavel, *The Early Slavs: Eastern Europe from the Initial Settlement to the Kievan Rus* (London 1996)

Douglas, D. C., 'Rollo of Normandy' in *The English Historical Review*, vol. 57, no. 228 (October 1942), pp. 417–36

Downham, Clare, *Viking Kings of Britain and Ireland, The Dynasty of Ivarr to AD 1014* (Edinburgh 2007)

Dubois, Thomas A., *Nordic Religions in the Viking Age* (Philadelphia 1999)

Duczko, Wladyslaw, *Viking Rus – Studies on the Presence of Scandinavians in Eastern Europe* (Brill 2004)

Duffy, S. (ed), *Medieval Dublin VI* (Dublin 2005)

Dumville, David M., *Wessex and England from Alfred to Edgar: Six essays on political, cultural and ecclesiastical revival* (Woodbridge 1992)

Dumville, David, 'Old Dubliners and New Dubliners in Ireland and Britain, a Viking-Age story' in Duffy, S. (ed.), *Medieval Dublin VI* (2005), pp. 78–93

Edwards, Nancy, *The Archaeology of Early Medieval Ireland* (London 1990)

Einarsson, Bjarni F., *The Settlement of Iceland: A Critical Approach, Granastaðir and the Ecological Heritage* (Reykjavik 1995)

Eldjárn, Kristján, *Proceedings of the Third Viking Congress, Reykjavík 1956* (Reykjavík 1958)

Ellis Davidson, H. R., 'The Later History of the Varangian Guard' in *Journal of Roman Studies*, 37 (1947), pp. 36–46

Ellis Davidson, H. R., *Pagan Scandinavia* (London 1967)

Ellis Davidson, H. R., *The Viking Road to Byzantium* (London 1976)

Enterline, James Robert, *Erikson, Eskimos & Columbus, Medieval European Knowledge of America* (Baltimore 2002)

Farrell, R. T., *Beowulf, Swedes and Geats* (Viking Society for Northern Research, London 1972)

Farrell, R. T. (ed.), *The Vikings* (Chichester 1982)

Faulkes, A. & Perkins, R. (eds), *Viking Revaluations* (Viking Society for Northern Research, London 1993)

Faulkner, Peter, *Against the Age: An Introduction to William Morris* (London 1980)

Fell, Christine, Foote, Peter, Graham-Campbell, James & Thomson, Robert (eds), *The Viking Age in the Isle of Man – Select Papers from the Ninth Viking Congress, Isle of Man, 4–14 July 1981* (London 1983)

Fellowes-Jensen, Gillian, 'The Vikings and their Victims: The Verdict of the Names' in *Dorothea Coke Memorial Lecture in Northern Studies, delivered at University College, London, 21 February 1994* (Viking Society for Northern Research, London 1995)

Ferguson, Robert, *The Hammer and the Cross, A New History of the* Vikings (London 2009)

Finley, M. I., *A History of Sicily, volume 2: Medieval Sicily 800–1713* (London 1968)

Fitzhugh, William W. & Ward, Elizabeth I., *Vikings: The North Atlantic Saga* (Washington 2000)

Fletcher, Richard, *Moorish Spain* (London 1992)

Foot, Sara, 'Violence against Christians? The Vikings and the Church in ninth-century England' in *Medieval History*, vol. I (1991), p. 12

Foote, P. G., *On the Saga of the Faroe Islanders* (London 1965)

Foote, Peter & Strömbäck, Dag (eds), *Proceedings of the Sixth Viking Congress, Uppsala 3–10 August 1969* (Uppsala 1971)

Foote, Peter & Wilson, D. M., *The Viking Achievement* (London 1980)

Forte, Angelo, Oram, Richard & Pedersen, Frederik, *Viking Empires* (Cambridge 2005)

Frank, Roberta, 'The Blood Eagle Again' in *Saga-Book of the Viking Society*, vol. XXII (1986–9), pp. 287–318

Franklin, Simon & Shepard, Jonathan, *The Emergence of Rus 750–1200* (London 1996)

Frye, R. N., 'The Samanids' in *The Cambridge History of Iran*, vol. 4 (edited by R. N. Frye, Cambridge 1975)

Gad, Finn, *The History of Greenland, volume 1: Earliest Times to 1700* (London 1970); *volume 2: 1700–1782* (London 1973)

Garipzanov, Ildar H., Geary, Patrick J. & Urbanczyk, Przemyslaw (eds), *Franks, Northmen and Slavs: Identities and State Formation in early Medieval Europe* (Turnhout 2008)

Gaskoin, C. J. B., *Alcuin, His Life and Work* (New York 1966)

Gibbon, Edward, *The Decline and Fall of the Roman Empire* (edited by J. B. Bury, London 1912)

Gibson, Margaret & Nelson, Janet L., *Charles the Bald, Court and Kingdom* (2nd edition, London 1990)

Godfrey, William S. Jr, 'The Archaeology of the Old Stone Mill in Newport, Rhode Island' in *American Antiquity*, vol. XVII (1951–2), pp. 120–9

Graham Campbell, James, *Viking Artefacts* (London 1980)

Graham-Campbell, James, 'Some archaeological reflections on the Cuerdale hard' in *Coinage in Ninth-Century Northumbria, The Tenth Oxford Symposium on Coinage and Monetary History* (edited by D. M. Metcalf, BAR British Series 180 1987)

Graham-Campbell, James & Batey, Colleen E., *Vikings in Scotland: An archaeological survey* (Edinburgh 1998)

Graham-Campbell, James, Hall, Richard, Jesch, Judith & Parsons, David N. (eds), *Vikings and the Danelaw – Select Papers from the Proceedings of the Thirteenth Viking Congress, Nottingham and York, 21–30 August 1997* (Oxford 2001)

Gravett, C., *Hastings 1066, the fall of Saxon England* (London 1992)

Greenfield, Jeanette, *The Return of Cultural Treasures* (Cambridge 1996)

Griffith, Paddy, *The Viking Art of War* (London 1995)

Gulløv, H. C., 'Natives and Norse in Greenland' in Fitzhugh and Ward (eds), *Vikings: The North Atlantic Saga* (Washington 2000)

Hadley, D. M., *The Northern Danelaw. Its Social Structure c.800–1100* (London 2000)

Haflidison, Haflidi et al., 'The tephrochronology of Iceland and the North Atlantic region during the Middle and Late Quaternary: a review' in *Journal of Quaternary Science*, 15 (1) (2000), pp. 3–22

Hallbert, Peter (translated by Paul Schach), *The Icelandic Saga* (Lincoln, Nebraska 1962)

Hardin, Stephen, *Viking Mersey: Scandinavian Wirral, West Lancashire and Chester* (Birkenhead 2002)

Harper-Bill, Christopher & van Houts, Elisabeth, *A Companion to the Anglo-Norman World* (Woodbridge 2003)

Hart, Cyril, *The Danelaw* (London 1992)

Harvey-Wood, Harriet, *The Battle of Hastings* (London 2008)

Haywood, John, *Dark Age Naval Power* (Hockwold-cum-Wilton 1999)

Haywood, John, *Encyclopaedia of the Viking Age* (London 2000)

Hedeager, Lotte (translated by John Hine), *Iron Age Societies: From Tribe to State in Northern Europe, 500 BC to AD 700* (Oxford 1992)

Helgason, A. et al., 'A Reassessment of Genetic Diversity in Icelanders: Strong Evidence from Multiple Loci for Relative Homogeneity Caused by Genetic Drift' in *Annals of Human Genetics*, vol. 67, part 4 (July 2003)

Heller, Knut (ed.), *Cambridge History of Scandinavia, volume 1: Prehistory to 1520* (Cambridge 2003)

Hertz, Johannes, 'The History and Mystery of the Old Stone Mill' in *Journal of the Newport Historical Society*, vol. 68, part 2 (1997)

Higham, N. J., *The Death of Anglo-Saxon England* (Stroud 1997)

Hilen, Andrew (ed.), *The Letters of Henry Wadsworth Longfellow* (Cambridge, Mass. 1966)

Hill, David (ed.), *Ethelred the Unready: Papers from the Millenary Conference*, BAR British Series 59 (Oxford 1978)

Hill, D. & Rumble, A. R. (eds), *The Defence of Wessex: The Burghal Hidage and Anglo-Saxon fortifications* (Manchester 1996)

Hodges, Richard A., *Dark Age Economics: The origins of town and trade, AD 600–1000* (London 1982)

Hodges, Richard A., *Goodbye to the Vikings? Re-Reading Early Medieval Archaeology* (London 2006)

Hodges, Richard & Hobley, Brian, *The Rebirth of Towns in the West, AD 700–1050*, Council for British Archaeology Research Report 68 (Oxford 1988)

Holck, Per, 'The Oseberg Ship Burial, Norway: New Thoughts On the Skeletons From the Grave Mound' in *European Journal of Archaeology*, vol. 9, nos 2–3 (August 2006), pp. 285–310

Hollander, Lee M., *The Skalds* (Princeton 1945)

Hoppin, Richard H., *Medieval Music* (New York 1978)

Horspool, David, *Why Alfred Burned the Cakes: A King and his Eleven-Hundred Year Afterlife* (London 2006)

Howard, Ian, *Swein Forkbeard's Invasions and the Danish Conquest of England 991–1017* (Woodbridge 2003)

Howarth, David, *1066, the Year of the Conquest* (London 1977)

Hudson, Benjamin, *Viking Pirates and Christian Princes: Dynasty, Religion and Empire in the North Atlantic* (Oxford 2005)

Humble, Richard, *The Saxon Kings* (London 1980)

Ingstad, Anne-Stine, *The Norse Discovery of America* (Oslo 1985)

Jackson, Anthony, *The Faroes: The Faraway Islands* (London 1991)

Jensen, Jørgen, *Prehistory of Denmark* (London 1982)

Jesch, Judith (ed.), *The Scandinavians from the Vendel Period to the Tenth Century* (Woodbridge 2002)

Jóhannesson, Jóhannes, 'Studies in the vegetational history of the Faroe and Shetland Islands' in *Annales Societatis Scientiarum Faroensis*, supplementum 11 (Tórshavn 1985)

Jóhannesson, Jón (translated by Haraldur Bessason), *A History of the Old Icelandic Commonwealth: Islendinga Saga* (Winnipeg 1974)

Jones, Charles, *Fulford, the Forgotten Battle of 1066* (Stroud 2007)

Jones, Gwyn, *A History of the Vikings* (revised edition, Oxford 1984)

Kennedy, Hugh, *Muslim Spain and Portugal* (London 1996)

Knirk, James E. (ed.), *Proceedings of the Tenth Viking Congress, Larkollen, Norway, 1985* (Oslo 1987)

Knol, Egge, 'Frisia in Carolingian Times' in *Viking Trade and Settlement in Continental Europe* (edited by Iben Skibsted Klaesøe, Copenhagen 2010), pp. 43–60

Krogh, K. J., *Viking Greenland* (Copenhagen 1967)

Lamb H. H., 'The Early Medieval Warm Epoch and its Sequel' in *Palaeogeography, Palaeoclimatology, Palaeoecology*, vol. 1 (1965), pp. 13–37

Lamm, J. P. & Nordström, H.-Å. (eds), *Vendel Period Studies – Transactions of the Boat-grave symposium in Stockholm, February 2–3 1981*, Museum of National Antiquities, Stockholm Studies 2 (Stockholm 1983)

Lamm, Jan Peder & Nylen, Erik, *Stones, Ships and Symbols: The Picture Stones of Gotland from the Viking Age and Before* (Visby 1978)

Larsen, Anne-Christine (ed.), *The Vikings in Ireland* (Roskilde 2001)

Lawson, M. K., 'The Collection of Danegeld and Heregeld in the Reigns of Aethelred II and Cnut' in *English Historical Review*, vol. 99, no. 393 (October 1984), pp. 721–38

Lawson, M.K., *Cnut: The Danes in England in the Early Eleventh Century* (London 1993)

Lawson, M.K., *The Battle of Hastings* (Stroud 2003)

Lee, Thomas E., 'The Norse Presence in Arctic Ungava' in *The American-Scandinavian Review*, vol. 61 (3) (Autumn 1973), pp. 242–57

Lehn, Waldemar H., 'Skerrylike mirages and the Discovery of Greenland' in *Applied Optics* 39, no. 21 (2000), pp. 3612–29

Leman, Edward, *The Norse Discoveries and Exploration of America* (Berkeley 1949)

Lennard, Reginald, 'The Economic Position of the Domesday Sokemen' in *The Economic Journal*, vol. 56, no. 226 (June 1947), pp. 179–95

Le Patourel, John, *The Norman Empire* (Oxford 1997)

Lewis, Michael J., *The Real World of the Bayeux Tapestry* (Stroud 2008)

Lewis-Simpson, S. (ed.), *Vinland Revisited. The Norse World at the Turn of the First Millennium. Selected Papers from the Viking Millennium International Symposium 15–24 September 2000, Newfoundland and Labrador* (St John's, Newfoundland 2003)

Lichacev, D. S., 'The legend of the calling in of the Varangians' in *Varangian problems; report on the first international symposium on the theme of the eastern connections of the Nordic peoples in the Viking period and early middle ages, Moesgaard, University of Aarhus, 7th–11th October 1968* (Copenhagen 1990), pp. 170–86

Liestøl, Aslak, 'The Maeshowe Runes: Some New Interpretations' in *Proceedings of the Fifth Viking Congress* (edited by Niclasen, Tórshavn 1968), (pp. 55–61)

Lindholm, Dan, *Stave Churches in Norway* (translated by Stella & Adam Bittleston, London 1969)

Lindquist, Sven-Olof (ed.), *Society and trade in the Baltic during the Viking Age* (Papers of the VIIth Visby Symposium held at Gotlands Fornsal, Gotland's Historical Museum, Visby, August 15–19th, 1983) (Visby 1985)

Line, Philip, *Kingship and State Formation in Sweden 1130–1290* (Leiden 2007)

Livingston, Michael (ed.), *The Battle of Brunanburh – A Casebook* (Exeter 2011)

Loe, Louise Boyle, Angela Webb, Helen & Score, David, *'Given to the Ground'*: *A Viking Mass Grave on Ridgeway Hill, Weymouth* (Oxford 2014)

Logan, F. Donald, *The Vikings in History* (London 2005)

Loyn, Henry R., *Anglo-Saxon England and the Norman Conquest* (London 1962)

Loyn, Henry R., *The Vikings in Wales, Dorothea Coke Memorial Lecture in Northern Studies, delivered at University College London, 2 March 1976* (Viking Society for Northern Research, London 1976)

Loyn, Henry R. & Percival, John, *The Reign of Charlemagne: Documents on Carolingian Government and Administration* (London 1975)

Lund, Niels (ed.), *Two Voyagers at the Court of King Alfred* (York 1984)

Lynnerup, N., *The Greenland Norse: A biological-anthropological study* (Copenhagen 1998)

McCormick, Michael, *Origins of the European Economy, Communications & Commerce AD 300–900* (Cambridge 2001)

McGhee, Robert, 'Contact between Native North Americans and the Medieval Norse: A Review of the Evidence' in *American Antiquity* 49.1 (1984), pp. 4–26

McGhee, Robert, *Ancient People of the Arctic* (Vancouver 2001)

McGhee, Robert, *The Last Imaginary Place: A Human History of the Arctic World* (Oxford 2006)

McGovern, T. H., 'Cows, Harp Seals and Churchbells: Adaptation and Extinction in Norse Greenland' in *Human Ecology* 89 (1980), pp. 245–75

McKinnon, James, 'The Emergence of Gregorian Chant in the Carolingian Era' in James McKinnon (ed.), *Antiquity and the Middle Ages* (London 1990)

McKitterick, Rosamond, *The Frankish Kingdoms under the Carolingians, 751–987* (Harlow 1983)

McLeod, Shane, *The Beginning of Scandinavian Settlement in England: The Viking Great Army and Early Settlers, c. 865–900* (Turnhout 2013)

McTurk, Rory (ed.), *A Companion to Old Norse-Icelandic Literature and Culture* (Oxford 2005)

McTurk, Rory, 'Kings and kingship in Viking Northumbria' in *The Fantastic in Old Norse Icelandic Literature, Preprint Papers of the 13th International Saga Conference, Durham and York, 6th–12th August 2006* (edited by John S. McKinnell, David Ashurst & Donata Kick, Durham 2006)

Mack Smith, Denis, *Medieval Sicily 800–1713* (London 1968)

MacNamidhe, Margaret, 'The "Buddha Bucket" from the Oseberg Find' in *The Irish Arts Review* (1989), pp. 77–82

Magnusson, Magnus, *Vikings!* (London, 1980)

Marcus, G. J., 'The Norse Emigration to the Faroe Islands' in *English Historical Review*, vol. lxxi (1956), pp. 56–61

Marsden, John, *The Fury of the Northmen: Saints, Shrines and Sea-Raiders in the Viking Age, AD 793–878* (London 1993)

Marsden, John, *Harold Hardrada, The Warrior's Way* (Stroud 2007)

Marstrande, Sverre, 'On the Gripping Beast Style and its Origin' in *Proceedings of the Fifth Viking Congress* (edited by Niclasen, Tórshavn 1968), pp. 141–50

Mason, Emma, *The House of Godwine, The History of a Dynasty* (London 2004)

Matthew, Donald, *The Norman Kingdom of Sicily* (Cambridge 1992)

Maund, K. L. (ed.), *Gruffudd ap Cynan: A Collaborative Biography* (Woodbridge 1996)

Mead, W. R., *An Historical Geography of Scandinavia* (London 1981)

Means, Philip, *The Newport Tower* (New York 1942)

Melnikova, E. A., *The Eastern World of the Vikings – Eight Essays about Scandinavia and Eastern Europe in the Early Middle Ages* (Gothenburg 1996)

Menzies, Gavin, *1421* (London 2002)

Mitchell, Stephen A., *Witchcraft & Magic in the Nordic Middle Ages* (Philadelphia 2011)

Mooney, John, 'Discovery of Relics in St Magnus Cathedral' in *Proceedings of the Orkney Antiquarian Society* 3 (1924–5)

Morawiec, Jakub, *Vikings Among the Slavs – Jomsborg and the Jomsvikings* (Vienna 2009)

Mowat, Farley, *Westviking: The ancient Norse in Greenland and North America* (London 1966)

Muir, Tom, *Orkney in the Sagas, The Story of the Earldom of Orkney as told in the Icelandic Sagas* (Kirkwall 2005)

Mundahl, Else, 'The Perception of the Saami and their religion in Old Norse sources' in *Shamanism and Northern Ecology* (edited by Juha Pentikäinen, New York 1996), pp. 97–117

Mundahl, Else, 'Co-existence of Saami and Norse culture – reflected in and interpreted by Old Norse Myths' in *Norse Myths, Literature and Society. Papers of the 11th International Saga Conference* (Sydney, 2000), pp. 346–55

Murillo, Stephen (ed.), *The Battle of Hastings, Sources and Interpretations* (Woodbridge 1996)

Murray, H. K., *Viking and Early Medieval Buildings in Dublin: A Study of the buildings excavated under the direction of A. B. O Riordain in High Street, Winetavern Street and Christchurch Place, Dublin, 1962–63, 1967–76*, BAR British Series 119 (Oxford 1983)

Nansen, Fridtjof (translated by Arthur G. Chater), *In Northern Mists: Arctic exploration in early times* (London 1911)

Nelson, Janet, *Charles the Bald* (Harlow 1992)

Niclasen, Bjarni (ed.), *Proceedings of the Fifth Viking Congress, Tórshavn July 1965* (Tórshavn 1968)

Nielsen, Richard & Wolter, Scott F., *The Kensington Rune Stone: Compelling New Evidence* (Madison, Wisconsin 2005)

Noonan, Thomas S., 'Ninth-century Dirham Hoards from European Russia, a preliminary analysis' in Blackburn & Metcalf (eds), *Viking Age Coinage in the Northern Lands*, BAR International Series 122 (Oxford 1981), pp. 47–118

Noonan, Thomas S., *The Islamic World, Russia and the Vikings, 750–900: The numismatic evidence* (Aldershot 1998)

Nordal, Sigurður, *The Historical Element in the Icelandic Family Sagas*, WP Kerr Memorial Lecture 15 (Glasgow 1957)

Nørlund, Poul, *Viking Settlers in Greenland (and their Descendants During Five Hundred Years)* (Cambridge 1936)

Norwich, John Julius, *The Normans in the South 1016–1130* (London 1967)

Nuttgens, Patrick, *The History of York from the Earliest Times to the year 2000* (Pickering 2007)

Ó'Cróinín, Dáibhí, *A New History of Ireland, volume 1: Prehistoric and Early Ireland* (Oxford 2005)

O'Donoghue, Rev. Denis, *St Brendan the Voyager* (London 1895)

O'Donoghue, Heather, *Old Norse-Icelandic Literature: A Short Introduction* (Oxford 2004)

Olausson, Lena Holmquist, 'The defence of Birka – this year's excavation at the Garrison' in *Viking Heritage* 5 (1998), pp. 6–8

Ó Ríordáin, Breandán, 'The High Street Excavations' in *Proceedings of the Seventh Viking Congress* (edited by Almqvist, Dublin 1976), pp. 135–9

Oxenstierna, Eric (translated and edited by Catherine Hunter), *The Norsemen* (New York 1985)

Page, R. I., *Reading the Past: Runes* (London 1987)

Page, R. I., *Chronicles of the Viking: Records, Memorials and Myths* (London 2000)

Pálsson, Gísli (ed.), *From Sagas to Society – Comparative Approaches to Early Iceland* (London 1992)

Partington, J. R., *A History of Greek Fire and Gunpowder* (Cambridge 1960)

Paskiewicz, Henryk, *The Origin of Russia* (London 1954)

Pestell, Tim & Ulmschneider, Katharina (eds), *Markets in Early Medieval Europe* (Macclesfield 2003)

Petts, David & Turner, Sam (eds), *Early Medieval Northumbria: Kingdoms and Communities, AD 450–1100* (Turnhout 2011)

Pierce, I., *Swords of the Viking Age* (Woodbridge 2003)

Pollard A. et al., '"Sprouting Like Cockle Amongst the Wheat": The St Brice's Day Massacre and the Isotopic Analysis of Human Bones from St John's College, Oxford' in *Oxford Journal of Archaeology*, 31 (1) (2012), pp. 83–102

Pollard, Justin, *Alfred the Great: The Man Who Made England* (London 2005)

Pollington, Stephen, *The Warrior's Way – England in the Viking Age* (London, 1989)

Pons-Sanz, Sara María, 'The Basque Country and the Vikings during the ninth century' in *Journal of the Society of Basque Studies in America* 21 (2001)

Pons-Sanz, Sara María, '"Whom did al-Ghazal meet?" An Exchange of Embassies Between the Arabs From al-Andalus and the Vikings' in *Saga Book of the Viking Society* 28 (2004), pp. 5–28

Power, Rosemary, 'Magnus Barelegs' Expeditions to the West' in *Scottish Historical Review*, vol. 65, no. 180, part 2 (October 1986), pp. 107–32

Price, Neil S., *The Vikings in Brittany*, Viking Society for Northern Research (London 1989)

Rafn, C. C., *Antiquitates Americanæ, sive Scriptores septentrionales rerum ante-Columbianarum in America* (Copenhagen 1837)

Rafn, C. C., 'Supplement to the Antiquitates Americanae' in *Mémoires de la Société Royale des Antiquaires du Nord* (Copenhagen 1838–9)

Randsborg, Klaus, *The Viking Age in Denmark: The Formation of a State* (London 1980)

Renaud, Jean, *Les Vikings en France* (Rennes 2000)

Renfrew, Colin, *The Prehistory of Orkney, 4000 BC–1000 AD* (Edinburgh 1985)

Reuter, Timothy, *Alfred the Great: Papers from the eleventh centenary conferences* (Aldershot 2003)

Rex, Peter, *Harold II: The Doomed Saxon King* (Stroud 2005)

Rex, Peter, *King & Saint: The Life of Edward the Confessor* (Stroud 2008)

Richards, Julian, *Viking Age England* (Stroud, 2000)

Richards, Julian, *The Blood of the Vikings* (London 2001)

Rink, Hans, *Tales and Traditions of the Eskimos* (London 1875)

Ritchie, Anna, *Viking Scotland* (London 2001)

Robinson, C. H., *Anskar, The Apostle of the North* (London 1921)

Roesdahl, Else (translated by Susan Margeson & Kirsten Williams), *Viking Age Denmark* (London 1982)

Roesdahl, Else, *The Vikings* (Harmondsworth 1991)

Rollason, David, *Northumbria 500–1100: Creation and Destruction of a Kingdom* (Cambridge 2003)

Rowley, Graham, 'The Dorset Culture of the Eastern Arctic' in *American Anthropologist*, new series, vol. 42 (1940), pp. 490–9

Rumble, Alexander R., *The Reign of Cnut, King of England, Denmark and Norway* (London 1994)

Sandvik, Gudmund & Sigurðsson, Jón Viðar, 'Laws' in Rory McTurk (ed.), *Old Norse-Icelandic Literature and Culture* (Oxford 2005)

Sawyer, Birgit, *The Viking-Age Rune-Stones; Custom and Commemoration in Early Medieval Scandinavia* (Oxford 2000)

Sawyer, Birgit & Sawyer, Peter, *Medieval Scandinavia: From Conversion to Reformation c.800–1500* (Minneapolis 1993)

Sawyer, Peter, *Kings and Vikings* (London 1982)

Sawyer, Peter, 'The Viking Expansion' in *The Cambridge History of Scandinavia*, vol. 1 (edited by Knut Helle, Cambridge 2003)

Sawyer, Peter (ed.), *The Oxford Illustrated History of the Vikings* (Oxford 2003)

Scott, G. et al., 'Dental conditions of medieval Norsemen in the North Atlantic' in *Acta Archaeologica* 62 (1991), pp. 183–207

Scragg, Donald (ed.), *The Battle of Maldon AD 991* (Oxford 1991)

Scragg, Donald, *The Return of the Vikings, The Battle of Maldon 991* (Stroud 2006)

Seaver, Kirsten, *The Frozen Echo: Greenland and the Exploration of North America ca. A.D. 1000–1500* (Stanford 1996)

Seaver, Kirsten, *Maps, Myths and Men: The Story of the Vinland Map* (Stanford 2004)

Seaver, Kirsten, *The Last Vikings* (London 2010)

Sheehan, John & Ó'Corráin, Donnchadh, *The Viking Age: Ireland and the West: Proceedings of the Fifteenth Viking Congress* (Dublin 2010)

Shepard, Jonathan, 'Some Problems of Russo-Byzantine Relations c. 860–c.1050' in *The Slavonic and East European Review* 52 (1974), pp. 10–33

Siddorn, J. Kim, *Viking Weapons and Warfare* (Stroud 2005)

Sigmundsson, Svavar (ed.), *Viking Settlement & Viking Society, Papers from the Proceedings of the Sixteenth Viking Congress* (Reykjavík 2011)

Silliman, Horace F., *The Newport Tower: The English Solution*, New England Antiquities Research Association (November 1979)

Simek, Rudolf & Engels, Ulrike (eds), *Vikings on the Rhine – Recent Research on Early Medieval Relations between the Rhineland and Scandinavia*, Studia Medievalia Septentrionalia 11 (Vienna 2004)

Sjøvold, Thorleif, *The Viking Ships in Oslo* (Oslo 1979)

Skelton, R. A. Thomas, Marston E. & Painter, George D., *The Vinland Map and the Tartar Relation* (New Haven, Conn. 1965)

Skre, Dagfinn (ed.), *Kaupang in Skiringssal*, Kaupang Excavation Project Publication Series, vol. 1 (Aarhus 2007)

Smith, Kevin P., 'Landnám: The Settlement of Iceland in Archaeological and Historical Perspective' in *World Archaeology* 26 (1995), pp. 319–47

Smith, Kevin P., Olafsson, Guðmundr & McGovern, Thomas H., 'Outlaws of Surtshellir Cave: The Underground Economy of Viking Age Iceland' in *Dynamics of Northern Societies* (edited by Jette Arneborg and Bjarni Grønnow, Copenhagen 2006)

Smith, Kevin P., Olafsson, Guðmundr & McGovern, Thomas H., *The Viking Age: Ireland and the West, Proceedings of the Fifteenth Viking Congress, Cork, 2005* (Dublin 2010)

Smyth, Alfred P., *Warlords and Holy Men, Scotland AD 80–1000* (London 1984)

Smyth, Alfred P., *King Alfred the Great* (Oxford 1995)

Smyth, Alfred P., *The Medieval Life of King Alfred the Great* (Basingstoke 2002)

Spurland, Terje (translated by Betsy van der Hoek), *Norwegian Runes and Runic Inscriptions* (Woodbridge 2005)

Stefanson, Vilhjamur, *Greenland* (London 1943)

Stenton, Sir Frank, *Anglo-Saxon England* (Oxford 1943)

Stumman Hansen, Steffen & Randsborg, Klaus (eds), *Vikings in the West, Acta Archaeologica*, vol. 71 (Copenhagen 2000)

Sutherland, P. D., 'The Norse and native North Americans' in Fitzhugh and Ward (eds), *Vikings: The North Atlantic Saga* (Washington 2000)

Swanton, M. J., 'Dane-Skins: Excoriation in Early England' in *Folklore*, vol. 87, no. 1 (1976), pp. 21–8

Thernstrom, Stefan (ed.), *Harvard Encyclopedia of American Ethnic Groups* (Harvard 1981)

Thomson, W. P. L., *The New History of Orkney* (Edinburgh 2008)

Thorpe, Lewis, *The Bayeux Tapestry and the Norman Invasion* (London 1973)

Thorson, Per, 'A New interpretation of Viking' in *Proceedings of the Sixth Viking Congress* (edited by Foote & Strömbäck, Viking Society for Northern Research 1971), pp. 33–7

Thorstenberg, Edward, *The Skeleton in Armour and the Frithiof Saga*, *Modern Language Notes*, vol. 25, No. 6 (June, 1910), pp. 189–192

Titlestad, Torgrim (translated Stephen R. Parsons), *Viking Norway, Personalities, Power and Politics* (Hafsfjord 2008)

Tornøe, J. Kristian, *Columbus in the Arctic?* (Oslo 1965)

Townend, Matthew (ed.), *Wulfstan, Archbishop of York, Proceedings of the Second Alcuin Conference* (Turnhout 2004)

Turville-Petre, E. O. G., *The Heroic Age of Scandinavia* (London 1951)

Turville-Petre, E. O. G., *Scaldic Poetry* (Oxford 1976)

Van Regteren, Altena H. H. & Heidinga, H. A., 'The North Sea region in the Early Medieval Period' in *Ex Horreo* (edited by B. van Beek, R.W. Brandt & W. Groenman-van Waateringe, Amsterdam 1977), pp. 47–67

Vernadsky, George, *The Origins of Russia* (Westport, Conn. 1975)

Wahlgren, Erik, *The Kensington Runestone: A Mystery Solved* (Madison, Wisconsin 1958)

Wahlgren, Erik, *The Vikings and America* (London 1986)

Wainwright, F. T., 'The Scandinavian settlement' in *The Northern Isles* (edited by F. T. Wainwright, London 1962), pp. 117–62

Wallace, Birgitta, 'L'Anse aux Meadows: gateway to Vinland' in *Acta Archeologica 61* (1990), pp. 166–97

Wallace, Birgitta, 'L'Anse aux Meadows, the Western Outpost' in *Viking Voyages to North America* (edited by B. L. Clausen, Roskilde 1993), pp. 30–42

Wallace, Birgitte, 'L'Anse aux Meadows: Different Disciplines, Divergent Views' in *Viking Settlement & Viking Society, Papers from the Proceedings of the Sixteenth Viking Congress* (edited by Svavar Sigmundsson, Reykjavík 2011), pp. 448–68

Wallace, Patrick F., 'The Archaeology of Ireland's Viking-age towns' in *A New History of Ireland, volume 1: Prehistoric and Early Ireland* (Oxford 2005)

Wallace Hadrill, J. M., *The Vikings in Francia* (Reading 1975)

Wallach, Luitpold, *Alcuin and Charlemagne: Studies in Carolingian History and Literature* (Ithaca 1959)

Walker, Ian W., *Harold, the Last Anglo-Saxon King* (Stroud 1997)

Walsh, A., *Scandinavian Relations with Ireland during the Viking Period* (Dublin 1922)

Wawn, Andrew, *The Vikings and the Victorians, Inventing the Old North in Nineteenth-Century Britain* (Cambridge 2000)

Wawn, Andrew & Sigurðardóttir, Þórunn (ed.), *Approaches to Vinland: 'Proceedings of a Conference on the Written and Archaeological Sources for the Norse Settlements in the North-Atlantic Region and Exploration of America. Held at the Nordic House, Reykjavik 9–11 August 1999* (Reyjkavík 2001)

Whitelock, Dorothy, 'Fact and Fiction in the Legend of St Edmund' in *Proceedings of the Suffolk Institute of Archaeology 31* (1968), p. 233

Whitelock, Dorothy, Douglas, David C., Lemmon, Charles H. & Barlow, Frank (eds), *The Norman Conquest, its setting and Impact* (London 1966)

Willemsen, A., *Vikings! Raids in the Rhine/Meuse Region 800–1000* (Utrecht 2004)

Williams, Anne, *Aethelred the Unready, The Ill-Counselled King* (London 2003)

Wilson, David M., *The Vikings and Their Origins: Scandinavia in the First Millennium* (London 1970)

Wilson, David M. (ed.), *The Northern World* (London 1980)

Wilson, David M., *The Vikings in the Isle of Man* (Aarhus 2008)

Webber, Nick, *The Evolution of Norman Identity (911–1154)* (Woodbridge 2005)

Wood, Ian & Loud, G. A. (eds), *Church and Chronicle in the Middle Ages: Essays Presented to John Taylor* (London 1991)

Woolf, Alex, *From Pictland to Alba 789–1070* (Edinburgh 2007)

Wormald, Patrick, 'Archbishop Wulfstan: State-Builder' in *Wulfstan of York, Proceedings of the Second Alcuin Conference* (edited by Matthew Townend, Turnhout 2004)

Yorke, Barbara (ed.), *Bishop Aethelwold: His career and influence* (Woodbridge 1988)

Yorke, Barbara, *Kings and Kingdoms of Early Anglo-Saxon England* (London 1990)

Zachrisson, Inger, 'The Sami and their interaction with the Nordic peoples' in *The Viking World* (edited by Stefan Brink, London 2010), pp. 32–9

Notes

Introduction

1. 'The Battle of Maldon Poem', translated by Kevin Crossley-Holland in *The Battle of Maldon and Other Old English Poems* (London 1965)
2. The exact words of the prayer are almost certainly apocryphal, as no medieval manuscript contains this precise formula.
3. The very first use of the word comes in the *Widsith*, a seventh-century Anglo-Saxon poem, which pre-dates the beginning of the Viking Age by more than a century. For a discussion of the various theories on the origin of the word Viking, see 'Who Were the Vikings?' in Stefan Brink (ed.), *The Viking World* (London 2008), pp. 4–7.
4. The main manuscript containing the *Elder* (or *Poetic*) *Edda* is the *Codex Regius*, an Icelandic manuscript dating from 1270. For an account of the theories on the provenance of the Eddic poems, see 'Eddic Poetry' by Terry Gunnell in *A Companion to Old Norse–Icelandic Literature and Culture* (edited by Rory McTurk, Oxford 2005), pp. 82–100.
5. We have the names of around 250 skalds, including picturesquely named characters such as Eyvind *skáldaspillir* ('the plagiarist') and Þorodd *dráput-stúfr* ('Poem-stump'), so named for his fondness for very short verses.
6. *Hávamál*, verse 77

Chapter 1: The Origins of the Vikings

1. What is commonly referred to as the *Anglo-Saxon Chronicle* in fact exists in seven manuscripts, all of them somewhat different in the dates that they cover. The 'Parker MS', held in Corpus Christi, Cambridge, was written by a single scribe up to 891 and then by a series of successors who seem to have been based in Winchester, providing a good general account up to 920, but after that date covering largely local events. The 'B' manuscript goes up to 977 and appears to share the same original source as the C version which carries the story up to 1056, with single additions for 1065 and 1066. Versions D and E seem to share material

from a set of northern annals (which were also used by Symeon of Durham in his *History of the Kings*), and the addition of other material of interest to the north of England has been interpreted as meaning that they were compiled in York (although the E manuscript seems to have made its way to Canterbury in the mid-eleventh century and was added to there and at Peterborough until 1155). The F manuscript was compiled by a scribe who used E as his main model, but also seems to have possessed a copy of A and to have used other sources, probably those available in the scriptorium at Christ Church, Canterbury. G was made in the early eleventh century and is a version of A, while H is a fragment that covers only the years 1113–14. *The Anglo-Saxon Chronicle: A Revised Translation*, edited by Dorothy Whitelock, David C. Douglas & Susie I. Tucker, (London 1965), pp. xi–xxiv.

2. The development (and authorship) of Symeon's chronicle is almost as complex as that of the *Anglo-Saxon Chronicle*. See Symeon of Durham, *Libellus de Exordio atque Procursu istius, hoc est Dunhelmensis, Ecclesie / Tract on the origins and progress of this the Church of Durham* (ed. David Rollason, Oxford 2000), pp. xvii–l for a detailed discussion.

3. Rollason, *Symeon of Durham*, pp. xxii, 89

4. Donald A. Bullough, *Alcuin: Achievement and Reputation* (Leiden 2004), p. 300. The monastic community of Lindisfarne was refounded by St Cuthbert, thirty years after the initial foundation by St Aidan in 635.

5. *English Historical Documents, Volume 1: c.500–1042*, no. 193, edited by Dorothy Whitelock (London 1979), p. 842

6. The *Chronicle* inserts the story under the year 789, but this is the year that Beorhtric married King Offa of Wessex's daughter, and the story of the murdered reeve is said to have happened 'in his days', without any further specification of the year.

7. Stefan Brink (ed.), *The Viking World* (London 2008), p. 342

8. Barbara Crawford, *Scandinavian Scotland* (Leicester 1987), p. 44

9. *Annals of Ulster, 795*. See *The Annals of Ulster (to AD 1131)*, (edited by Seán Mac Airt and Gearóid Mac Niocaill, Dublin 1983). The most probable location for *Rechru* is the island of Raithlin off the north-east coast of Ireland.

10. The term Francia is used for the Germanic kingdom that emerged in what had been Roman Gaul, to differentiate it from the medieval kingdom of France that emerged from the eleventh century onwards.

11. It was at this time that Godfred attacked the Abodrite trading centre of

Reric and forced its merchants to move to his own foundation at Hedeby. See p. 105 below.

12. *Frankish Royal Annals,* p. 810

13. See p. 47 below

14. The tree cover was so dense that in 1177 a group of Norwegians took seventy-seven days to travel from Malang in Dalarna to Storsjön in Jutland, a distance of just 170 miles. Birgit and Peter Sawyer, *Medieval Scandinavia: From Conversion to Reformation, c .800–1500* (Minneapolis 1993) p. 37

15. This was roughly the region that would be covered by the Gulathing Assembly and Law of c.900.

16. None of Pytheas's works have survived directly. What we have is excerpts quoted in later authors and digests, such as Strabo's *Geography* of the first century BC. For a detailed account of his voyage, see Barry Cunliffe, *The Extraordinary Voyage of Pytheas the Greek* (London 2001).

17. Knut Heller (ed.), *Cambridge History of Scandinavia, Volume 1: Prehistory to 1520* (Cambridge 2003), introduction by Knut Heller, p. 1

18. The sixth-century Byzantine historian Procopius had also actually visited the northern fringe of Europe (and found 'Thule' to be barren). He describes thirteen nations dwelling in Scandinavia, among them the Serithifnoi (possibly the Saami), who had the curious habit of abandoning their babies shortly after birth, leaving them with a morsel of food in their mouths on which to suck.

19. 'The chronology of the Vendel Graves' by Brigit Arrhenius in *Vendel Period Studies – Transactions of the Boat Grave Symposium in Stockholm, February 2–3 1981* (edited by J.P. Lamm & H.-Å. Nordström, Stockholm 1983), pp. 39–65

20. For an account of Norse religions, see p. 113 below.

21. For the misadventures of the Yngling kings, see *Ynglinga Saga* in Snorri Sturluson's *Heimskringla* (edited by Erling Momsen, translated by A.H. Smith, Cambridge 1932), pp. 1–35.

22. Although Nicolaysen recorded this, no nails were preserved in the collection of artefacts that he found, and it was only later excavation in 1989–91 that found remains of them. See 'The Royal Cemetery at Borre, Vestfold: A Norwegian centre in a European periphery' by Bjørn Myrhe in *The Age of Sutton Hoo: The Seventh Century in North-Western Europe* (edited by M.O.H. Carver, Woodbridge 1992), pp. 301–13.

23. See p. 135 below.

24. See p. 95 below.

25. See Helen Clarke and Björn Ambrosiani, *Towns in the Viking Age* (Leicester 1991), pp. 69–72.

26. Although the explanation also provided, that Dan had a brother called Angul, from whom the Angles took their name, suggests a suspicious neatness in the etymologies. Gwyn Jones, *A History of the Vikings* (revised edition, Oxford 1984), p. 44.

27. Gregory of Tours, *History of the Franks*, book III, chapter 3 (see translation by Lewis Thorpe, London 1974)

28. Knut Heller (ed.), *The Cambridge History of Scandinavia* (Cambridge 2003), p. 147

29. See p. 104 below.

30. Forming part of the Elder (or Verse) Edda. See p. 114 below.

31. There are dangers in looking to legal measures to assess when slavery ended in the Viking world. In Iceland, for example, there was never any formal abolition of the practice, but the last slave we know of (mentioned in literary sources) was Gilli, who was the slave of Thorsteinn Siðu-Hallsson shortly after 1050. Yet there are measures in the Grágás law-code which imply that there were still slaves in around 1117. In Norway there is also evidence that slavery was still practised into the twelfth century, while it did not end in Denmark until a century later and there may still have been slaves in Sweden into the early fourteenth century.

32. *Konungsbók 112* in Peter Foote, Andrew Dennis & Richard Perkins, *Laws of Early Iceland: Grágás, the Codex Regius of Grágás with Material from Other Manuscripts* (Winnipeg 1980–2000 in two volumes), pp. 172–3

33. For an account of Ohthere's journeys, see p. 96 below.

34. See 'The Perception of the Saami and their religion in Old Norse Sources' by Else Mundahl in *Shamanism and Northern Ecology* (edited by Juha Pentikäinen, New York 1996), pp. 97–117.

35. In the *Gull-Ásu-Þorðar-Páttr*. See Mundahl, 'The Perception of the Saami and their religion in Old Norse Sources', p. 105.

36. 'The Sami and their interaction with Nordic peoples' by Inger Zachrisson in *The Viking World* (edited by Stefan Brink), pp. 32–9

37. 'Co-existence of Saami and Norse culture – reflected in and interpreted by Old Norse Myths' by Else Mundahl, pp. 346–55

38. *Egil's Saga*, chapter 40

39. See J. Kim Siddorn, *Viking Weapons and Warfare* (Stroud 2005), for a detailed account of the techniques of Viking weapon production.

40. See p. 292 below.

41. See Paddy Griffith, *The Viking Art of War* (London 1995), p. 174.

42. See p. 307 below.

43. These were in fact present on helmets found in Scandinavia in the pre-Viking period, and also on Celtic helmets from the Iron Age, which may have influenced them. The horns became popularised during the nineteenth century when the rise of interest in native Scandinavian history as part of the nationalist movements in Norway and Sweden led to a general revival of things Viking and, for some reason, the horned helmet became part of the universally approved 'Viking costume'. It is also possible that horned helmets may have derived from Roman models. The helmet found in Valsgärde 7 grave in Sweden had horns with animal-headed terminals, while a late Roman regiment, the *Cornuti* ('horned ones'), is recorded in the *Notitia Dignitatum*, a fifth-century catalogue of Roman army units. *Vendel Period Studies – Transactions of the Boat-grave symposium in Stockholm, February 2–3 1981* (edited by J.P. Lamm & H.-Å. Nordström) – Museum of National Antiquities, Stockholm Studies 2 (Stockholm 1983), p. 15.

44. Paddy Griffith, *The Viking Art of War*, p. 137

45. *Anglo-Saxon Chronicle*, 896 in *English Historical Documents, vol. 1: c.500–1042*, ed. Dorothy Whitelock (London 1965)

46. Foote and Wilson, *The Viking Achievement*, p. 285

47. This massacre, at Verdun, had the opposite effect to that intended and initially stiffened Saxon resistance, before their final conquest in 797. Rosamond McKitterick, *The Frankish Kingdoms Under the Carolingians 751–987* (London 1983), pp. 61–3.

48. On the *Knútsdrápa*, see 'King Cnut in the verse of his skalds' by Roberta Frank in *The Reign of Cnut: King of England, Denmark and Norway* (edited by Alexander R. Rumble), pp. 106–24. There has been a lively debate about whether the blood-eagle should be taken as a literal description, or more figuratively in the sense of an eagle hovering. See Roberta Frank 'Viking atrocity and Skaldic verse: the rite of the blood eagle' in *English Historical Review* (1984), pp. 332–43; 'The blood eagle again' in *Saga-Book of the Viking Society for Northern Research*, vol. 22, pp. 287–9; and 'The blood eagle once more' by Bjarni Einarsson in *Saga-Book*, vol. 23, pp. 80–81.

49. See p. 10 below.

50. The *Chronicle's* chronology is slightly wrong here, and the battle seems actually to have taken place in 896.

51. See p. 58 below.

52. The exact size of the Great Army in particular has been a source of some debate, since Peter Sawyer first put it at just several hundred in 1958, and then revised his figure up to 1,000 in *The Age of the Vikings* (London 1960), p. 125. While Sawyer has received support from others, including David Sturdy in *Alfred the Great* (London 1995), p. 111, a counter-current argues that this figure is too low. See Simon Keynes, 'The Vikings in England, c. 790–1016' in P. Sawyer (ed.), *The Oxford Illustrated History of the Vikings* (Oxford 1999), pp. 48–82. Richard Abels in *Alfred the Great: War, Kingship and Culture in Anglo-Saxon England* (London 1998), p. 113, suggests that at its arrival (and before its various divisions) the Great Army may have consisted of more than 5,000 men. For an interesting discussion of how the Great Army managed to feed itself, see 'Feeding the *micel here* in England c. 865–878' by Shane McLeod in *Journal of the Australian Early Medieval Association*, vol. 2 (2006), pp. 141–56.

53. 'The Viking Expansion' by Peter Sawyer in *The Cambridge History of Scandinavia*, vol. 1, pp. 106–7

54. Adam of Bremen, *History of the Archbishops of Hamburg-Bremen* (translated by Francis J. Tschan, New York 1959), book four, p. i

55. Adam of Bremen, *History of the Archbishops of Hamburg-Bremen*, book four, p. vii

56. Else Roesdahl (translated by Susan Margeson & Kirsten Williams), *Viking Age Denmark* (London 1982), p. 17

57. Dudo of Saint-Quentin, *Historia Normannorum*, book 1, chapter 2

58. One of the coins in the Sutton Hoo burial in East Anglia, c. 625, carries the name *Quantia* as its place of minting, which presumably refers to Quentovic, while in 664 Theodore of Tarsus is said to have set sail from the port on his way to take up his position as Archbishop of Canterbury.

59. Michael McCormick, *Origins of the European Economy: Communications and Commerce AD 300–900* (Cambridge 2001), p. 607

60. McCormick, *Origins of the European Economy*, p. 609, note 115

61. P. H. Sawyer, *Kings and Vikings: Scandinavia and Europe AD 700–1100* (London 1982), p. 75

62. *Egil's Saga*, chapter 69

63. The Nydam Boat was the first of the important early Scandinavian vessels to be excavated, by Conrad Engelhardt in 1859–63. Originally two boats were found, but unfortunately one of them was cut up for firewood by troops during the Danish-German War in 1864.

64. The Vikings did not, however, themselves invent the sail, nor were they

the first pirates to raid the coastlines of north-western Europe. As early as AD 69–70 the Romans were fighting against a fleet controlled by the Chauci, a North Sea coastal tribe whose raids had plagued the Frisian coast for thirty years. The Bruges Boat (found in Belgium in 1899) dates to AD 180–250 and has a mast step, so it was clearly adapted for sail, while the Anglo-Saxons were definitely using sailing ships by the mid-seventh century, as the missionary St Wilfred returned from Gaul to England in one.

65. The carving's exact age is unknown, but it is dateable to sometime in the seventh century.

66. See p. 222.

67. See p. 232 below.

68. In fact, Harald's conquests may have taken place even later. The dating depends on the statement by the Icelandic historian Ari the Wise that his rule over all Norway began in 870, which is otherwise unsupported. Sverre Bagge, *From Viking Stronghold to Christian Kingdom: State Formation in Norway, c. 900–1350*, p. 24.

69. Such as that of Svein Forkbeard and Cnut to England in 1013. See p. 000 below.

Chapter 2: From Raids to Settlement

1. See Judith Nelson, *Charles the Bald* (London 1992), pp. 132–7, for a detailed discussion of the Verdun division.

2. St Philibert's relics were first moved in 836 after the initial Viking attack, when they were transferred to Déas, and then in 845 moved once more to Cunault on the banks of the Loire. In 865 they finally reached Messais in Poitou. There is, however, some evidence from charters that the monks had been preparing the site at Déas to receive St Philibert's relics since 819, so they had clearly been aware of the dangers posed by the Vikings even before their own monastery was raided for the first time. Ermentarius, *De Translationibus et Miraculis Sancti Filiberti* (edited by R. Poupardin, *Monuments de l'histoire des abbayes de Saint-Philibert*, Paris 1905).

3. Although sometimes the fleets based on these rivers operated outside their region; Nantes was sacked by the Seine Vikings in 853. See Rosamond McKitterick, *The Frankish Kingdoms under the Carolingians 751–987*, p. 237.

4. Pippin was Charles the Bald's nephew and was in revolt against the settlement that gave Aquitaine to Charles, rather than to him (his father,

Pippin I, had been King of Aquitaine). See Janet Nelson, *Charles the Bald* (London 1992), pp. 101–4, 139–44.

5. Janet Nelson, *Charles the Bald*, p. 170

6. Fortunately the threat was short-lived, as just three years later Salomon allied himself with Charles the Bald to attack the Loire Vikings. Unfortunately for him, the promised Frankish army never materialised, and he was left fighting Hasteinn's Vikings alone. Neil Price, *The Vikings in Brittany*, Viking Society for Northern Research (London 1989), pp. 32–4.

7. Who may or may not be the father of the leaders of the Great Heathen Army that attacked England in 865. See p. 51 below.

8. The *Translatio* is a peculiarly Viking-Age genre of religious writing prompted by the need to remove the relics of saints from monasteries that were exposed to Viking attack (or had actually been destroyed by them). The *Translatio* of a saint recounts the happenings as the remains are removed to their new sanctuary, often involving miracles at each new resting place. One of the more prolonged of the Translations was that of St Cuthbert in England, which began when his remains were removed from Lindisfarne in 895, finally ending up in Chester-le-Street for ninety-one years before their final interment in Durham Cathedral in 995. The monks of the monastery of St Philibert on Noirmoutier removed the bones of the saint every year from 839 to 876, before abandoning the monastery altogether and then moving further and further inland in search of sanctuary, until they finally came to rest at Tournus in Burgundy in 875 – an odyssey recounted in detail by Ermentarius, a member of the St Philibert community.

9. For the subsequent epic voyage of a section of this Viking group into the Mediterranean, see p. 82 below.

10. *Annals of St Bertin*, 869. See translation by Janet Nelson (Manchester 1991), p. 152.

11. Price, *The Vikings in Brittany*, p. 26

12. For more on this agreement, the Treaty of Saint-Clair-sur-Epte, see p. 276 below.

13. The leading Frankish magnate, two of whose sons, Odo and Robert, would become Kings of France; he was the ancestor of the Capetian kings who ruled the country from 987 to 1328.

14. Recent work, however, has suggested that these may in fact represent a Frankish element and are not Viking at all. Price, *The Vikings in Brittany*, p. 64.

15. See p. 124 below.

16. Price, *The Vikings in Brittany*, p. 71

17. See p. 57 below.

18. *Annals of St Vaast* (edited by B. von Simson, Hanover 1909)

19. Janet Nelson, *Charles the Bald*, pp. 255–6

20. Although Odo was elected king of the western part of the Frankish empire, the Carolingian empire fractured as another assembly elected Arnulf, the son of Carloman, to be king in the east. In Italy, Berengar of Friuli took the throne; Louis of Provence took much of the south; Rudolf, son of Conrad the Welf, held sway over Burgundy; while another petty king, Guy (or Wido), occupied part of Neustria (between the Seine and the Loire).

21. See p. 59 below.

22. Charles was crowned king in 893, but was unable to exert his authority effectively until Odo's death in 898.

23. For more on the development of the Duchy of Normandy, see p. 276 below.

24. See Jean Renaud, *Les Vikings en France* (Rennes 2000), p. 100, for artefacts found at Péran.

25. For a detailed account of the various Viking rulers of Frisia (including arguments for and against the two Haralds being the same person), see 'From poachers to gamekeepers: Scandinavian warlords and Carolingian kings' by Simon Coupland in *Early Medieval Europe*, vol. 7, no. 1 (1998), pp. 85–114.

26. 'Two Viking Hoards from the Former Island of Wieringen (The Netherlands): Viking Relations with Frisia in an Archaeological Perspective' by Jan Bestemanin in *Land, Sea and Home – Proceedings of a Conference on Viking-period settlement at Cardiff, July 2001* (edited by John Hines, Alan Lane & Mark Redknap, Leeds 2004), pp. 93–108

27. 'Frisia in Carolingian Times' by Egge Knol in *Viking Trade and Settlement in Continental Europe* (edited by Iben Skibsted Klaesøe, Copenhagen 2010), pp. 43–60

28. For a discussion of possible Frisian participation in the Viking Great Army of 865 (and the attack on York), see Shane McLeod, *The Beginning of Scandinavian Settlement in England: The Viking Great Army and Early Settlers, c. 865–900* (Turnhout 2013).

29. An unknown location, most likely somewhere in Surrey

30. The fact that the army was able to split up into several separate groups,

one of which was still able to engage in a major invasion of Wessex, argues for the initial *micel here*'s numbers being in excess of the high hundreds.

31. 'Kings and kingship in Viking Northumbria' by Rory McTurk, Thirteenth International Saga Conference (Durham & York 2006)

32. The identification of Ivar and his brothers as sons of Ragnar Loðbrok is a late one, coming principally from Icelandic sagas composed in the thirteenth and fourteenth centuries, notably *Ragnar's Saga*. It has been argued that the real Ragnar died of dysentery in 845 and that Loðbrok was a figure more legendary than real. 'Ragnar Loðbrok in the Irish Annals?' by Rory McTurk in *Proceedings of the Seventh Viking Congress (Dublin 15–21 August 1973)*, (edited by Bo Almqvist and David Greene, Dublin 1976), pp. 93–124.

33. See David Rollason, *Northumbria 500–1100, Creation and Destruction of a Kingdom* (Cambridge 2003), pp. 212–13.

34. A ritual dedication to Odin, by pulling the victim's lungs from his ribcage to create bloody 'wings'. For the authenticity of this rite, see p. 29 above.

35. The exact political situation in York is unclear for some time after 866. In 872 the Vikings expelled Egbert from York, but it is probable that they had installed him as a dependent king in the first place.

36. *Anglo-Saxon Chronicle* in English Historical Documents, vol. 1: c.500–1042, ed. Dorothy Whitelock (London 1979), p. 192

37. Written by Abbo of Fleury in the mid-980s

38. *Anglo-Saxon Chronicle* in *English Historical Documents*, vol. 1 (London 1979), p. 193.

39. Possibly Marten, 20 miles north of Wilton. Timothy Reuter (ed.), *Alfred the Great* (London 2003), p. 127

40. See *Asser's Life of Alfred*, translated by J.A. Giles in *Six Old English Chronicles* (London 1848), p. 56.

41. Burgred, who had previously been castigated by Pope John VIII for allowing nuns to marry, seems to have been well received at Rome, and lived in obscure retirement for the rest of his life. He was buried in the church of St Mary's in Saxia (Rome), which formed the focal point for the small Anglo-Saxon community, while his wife, Aethelswith, died in Pavia in 888, possibly while trying to return to England.

42. See 'Repton and the "great heathen army", 873–74' by Martin Biddle and Birthe Kjølbe-Biddle in *Vikings and the Danelaw – Select Papers from the Proceedings of the Thirteenth Viking Congress, Nottingham and York, 21–30*

August 1997 (edited by James Graham-Campbell, Richard Hall, Judith Jesch & David N. Parsons, Oxford 2001), pp. 45–96; and Richard Hall, *Exploring the World of the Vikings* (London 2007), pp. 83–5.

43. *Anglo-Saxon Chronicle 876* in *English Historical Documents*, vol. 1 (London 1979)

44. See Reuter, *Alfred the Great*, p. 155; Downham, *Viking Kings of Britain and Ireland*, p. 71.

45. See p. 60 below.

46. *Anglo-Saxon Chronicle* in *English Historical Documents*, vol. 1 (London 1979), p. 195. There are also some suggestions that he was actually deposed, at the behest of Archbishop Aethelred of Canterbury, in a deal that would have seen a Viking puppet king installed in Wessex, along the lines of Ceolwulf in Mercia or Egbert in Northumbria. See Reuter, *Alfred the Great*, pp. 156–67.

47. *Asser's Life of Alfred* in *Six Old English Chronicles* (translated by J.A. Giles, London 1848), p. 61

48. For a discussion on various versions of the legend of the burning of the cakes and its transmission into Renaissance, Victorian and modern histories, see David Horspool, *Why Alfred Burned the Cakes, A King and his Eleven-Hundred Year Afterlife* (London 2006), pp. 77–96.

49. Justin Pollard, *Alfred the Great* (London 2005), p. 183

50. *Asser's Life of Alfred*, translated by J.A. Giles, p. 62

51. For the Treaty, see 'The Treaty between Alfred and Guthrum' in Dorothy Whitelock (ed.), *English Historical Documents*, vol. 1, pp. 416–17. The future capital was 'occupied' by Alfred around 886, and so it is possible to argue that the treaty with Guthrum post-dates this, but there was probably some form of West Saxon control over London even before it.

52. A King Guthfrith is recorded by the chronicler Aethelweard as being buried at York Minster in 895, and as we have no record of any intervening ruler, it is presumed that this Guthfrith was Halfdan's immediate successor.

53. This document, which probably dates to about 911–14, in the reign of Alfred's son, Edward the Elder, lists thirty-three *burhs*, together with the number of hides (which amounted to 27,000 throughout the system) that are needed for the upkeep of their defences, with every four hides yielding four men, enough to man a 'pole' length of wall (around 5 yards). D. Hill and A.R. Rumble (eds), *The Defence of Wessex: The Burghal Hidage and Anglo-Saxon fortifications* (Manchester 1996), pp. 189–231.

54. Guthrum died in 890; although he was notionally a Christian after his baptism in 878, the chronicler Aethelweard unkindly remarks in his note on the Danish king's passing that 'he breathed his soul out to Orcus', the Roman god of the underworld.

55. *Anglo-Saxon Chronicle*, 892 in *English Historical Documents*, vol. 1 (London 1979). Once again, the number is suspiciously exact, but must indicate at the very least an unusually large fleet.

56. The site of this is not certainly identified, but may be Castle Toll, near Newenden (see Pollard, *Alfred the Great*, p. 274).

57. See p. 78 below.

58. A legal compilation made by Archbishop Wulfstan around 1002–8 refers to compensation payments to be made *on Deone lage* ('according to the Danish law'). An earlier law-code (IV Edgar issued in 962–3) mentions 'secular rights in force among the Danes', but not the Danelaw itself. The fifteen counties where the Danelaw was in force were Yorkshire, Nottinghamshire, Derbyshire, Leicestershire, Lincolnshire, Northamptonshire, Huntingdonshire, Cambridgeshire, Bedfordshire, Norfolk, Suffolk, Essex, Hertfordshire, Middlesex and Buckinghamshire. See 'Defining the Danelaw' by Katherine Holmes in *Vikings and the Danelaw – Select Papers from the Proceedings of the Thirteenth Viking Congress, Nottingham and York, 21–30 August 1997* (edited by James Graham-Campbell, Richard Hall, Judith Jesch & David N. Parsons, Oxford 2001), pp. 1–12.

59. See Julian D. Richards, *Viking Age England* (Stroud 2000), pp. 43–7, and Gillian Fellowes-Jensen's work, including 'The Vikings and their Victims: The Verdict of the Names', *Dorothea Coke Memorial Lecture in Northern Studies, delivered at University College, London, 21 February 1994, Viking Society for Northern Research* (London 1995).

60. There are various other Norse endings such as '–toft', meaning house-site, while studies of field names, which tend to be more conservative, have yielded more information about Danish settlements in areas where an examination of the place-names of larger units or settlements might not have indicated a significant Scandinavian population.

61. Richards, *Viking Age England*, p. 46

62. See p. 250 below.

63. It also, interestingly, recorded the names of those who owned the land at the time the survey was carried out, and those of the owner at the time of Edward the Confessor. Among the more obvious pattern of Anglo-Saxon ownership being replaced by Norman incomers, half of

the names listed in the Confessor's reign in Nottinghamshire and Cheshire are Scandinavian, as are 40 per cent of the names listed in Derbyshire.

64. Excluding the brief reoccupations by Harald Hardrada in 1066 and during the Northern Revolt in 1069–70.

65. Analysis of the 8-inch-long stool, which was found beneath Lloyds Bank in York, revealed that the intestines of the unfortunate 'owner' were riddled with worms.

66. Both of these kings are really only known from the appearance of their names on coins (including those found in the Cuerdale Hoard). It is possible that Sigfroth was the same as the Northumbrian Viking of the same name who attacked Wessex with a fleet in 893, and the *jarl*, also called Sigfroth, who was involved in fighting around Dublin in 893. Downham, *Viking Kings of Britain and Ireland*, pp. 78–9.

67. 'Some Archaeological Reflections on the Cuerdale Hoard' in *Coinage in Ninth-Century Northumbria: The Tenth Oxford Symposium on Coinage and Monetary History* (edited by Howard B. Clarke et al., Oxford 1987), pp. 329–54

68. *Anglo-Saxon Chronicle* in *English Historical Documents*, vol. 1 (London 1979), p. 209

69. The names are suspiciously close to a group of Viking leaders active in the 860s and 870s, and so could possibly simply have been transferred from accounts of earlier actions. Downham, *Viking Kings of Britain and Ireland*, p. 87.

70. The northern part of the old Northumbrian kingdom, around Bamburgh, had established a semi-autonomous position, free of direct control from the York Vikings.

71. See Sir Frank Stenton, *Anglo-Saxon England* (Oxford 1943), p. 329

72. Sihtric's coinage is found south of the Humber and it is possible that he reconquered the area between 921 and 924. Downham, *Viking Kings of Britain and Ireland*, pp. 97–8.

73. See Higham, *The Kingdom of Northumbria*, p. 193. See also Alistair Campbell, *The Battle of Brunanburh* (London 1938). Bromborough was historically in the county of Cheshire, although it now forms part of Merseyside.

74. *Anglo-Saxon Chronicle* 937 in *English Historical Documents, vol. 1* (London 1979), pp. 200–201

75. Stenton, *Anglo-Saxon England*, p. 357

76. For Eirik's period as King of Norway, see p. 98 below. The English sources

do not, surprisingly, make any mention of his former career in Norway. Even according to Scandinavian sources, such as the *Ágrip*, written about 1200, Eirik of Norway was granted the earldom of Northumbria, but was soon thrown out and died as a pirate in Spain. Downham argues that Eirik, King of York, was in fact a descendant of Ivar, whose deeds became assimilated with those of Eirik Bloodaxe of Norway through a confusion over the names. Downham, *Viking Kings of Britain and Ireland*, pp. 118–20.

77. There is some doubt over this, as it is based on a disputed reference in the *Life of St Cuthbert*. Downham, *Viking Kings of Britain and Ireland*, p. 113.

78. See p. 80 below.

79. It is not clear who this person was; it is possible that Olaf, his father, was either Olaf Gothrithsson or Olaf Sihtricsson, which would argue for Eirik being killed by one of the York Viking community, with a possible eye to replacing him. Stenton, *Anglo-Saxon England*, p. 362.

80. Svein Forkbeard and Cnut would later become kings of all England, but they did not re-establish the old Danelaw or rule from York.

81. Richard Hall, *Exploring the World of the Vikings* (London 2007), pp. 118–19

82. A further hoard from Kell may be from the late ninth or early tenth century, but the date is not confirmed. David Wilson, *The Vikings in the Isle of Man* (Aarhus 2008), p. 105.

83. For an account of the Battle of Clontarf and its background, see p. 323 below.

84. See p. 304 below.

85. There is some evidence suggesting that one of the skeletons buried in the Viking overwintering site at Repton in Derby may have been sacrificed. See M. Biddle & B. Kjølbe-Biddle, 'Repton and the "great heathen army", 873–4' in *Select Papers from the Proceeding of the 13th Viking Congress* (Oxford 2001), pp. 45–96.

86. Wilson, *The Vikings in Man*, p. 41

87. Andreas, 128

88. For more on Fenrir and Viking religious beliefs, see p. 113 below.

89. A claim that depends in part on the break in sessions of the Icelandic Althing between 1800 and 1844, see p. 157 below.

90. It first appears in a panegyric written in 297 in honour of the Roman emperor Constantius I for his recovery of Britain from a long-standing rebellion. It was long considered that this was penned by the rhetorician Eumenius, but this is probably not the case, and the author remains

anonymous. See C. E. V. Dixon and Barbara Saylor Rodgers, *In Praise of Later Roman Emperors* (Berkeley 1994), p. 104.

91. This is actually derived from the Old Norse form *Péttlandsfjörður*.

92. See James Graham-Campbell and Colleen E. Batey, *The Vikings in Scotland: An Archaeological Survey* (Edinburgh 1998), pp. 8–9.

93. See K. Jackson, 'The Pictish Language' in F.T. Wainwright, *The Problem of the Picts* (Edinburgh 1955), pp. 129–66.

94. By which is meant Christian hermits. *Historia Norwegiae, VI*, 1–5 (translated Peter Fisher, Copenhagen 2003).

95. A halfpenny of the English king Edmund (939–46) provides the date after which the burial must have taken place.

96. W. P. L. Thomson, *A New History of Orkney*, pp. 26–7.

97. Agreements of this nature in the sagas seem to have been more honoured in the breach than in the observance, and Magnus Erlendsson, a later Earl of Orkney (and saint), would similarly fall foul of his cousin Håkon's flagrant violation of the number of ships they were supposed to bring to a parlay on the Isle of Egilsay. See p. 272 below.

98. *Orkneyinga Saga*, chapter 6

99. A type of dwelling that is round, with a central hearth, with internal partitions which have the appearance of the spokes of a wheel, dividing the living space.

100. For more detail on the Jarlshof settlement, see James Graham-Campbell and Colleen E. Batey, *Vikings in Scotland: An Archaeological Survey* (Edinburgh 1996), pp. 155–60.

101. There are a number of others that survived. Hugh Marwick found around thirty toponyms with Celtic roots in Orkney; and Jakob Jakobsen, the Faroese philologist, concluded that between 5 and 10 per cent of Orkney place-names could be deemed of Celtic origin. But this still leaves more than 90 per cent of names with Norse roots. See Thomson, *New History of Orkney*, pp. 14–20.

102. This is a combination of the 'Myhre' hypothesis and the 'earldom' hypothesis, which are amongst the major interpretations of the early Viking period in the Northern Isles (along with the 'genocide' hypothesis). See Brink (ed.), *The Viking World*, pp. 419–21.

103. Callum G. Brown, *Up-helly-aa: Custom, culture and community in Shetland* (Manchester 1998), pp. 126–9

104. *Annals of St Bertin* (translated by Janet Nelson), p. 65

105. 'The Archaeology of Ireland's Viking-age towns' by Patrick F. Wallace

in *A New History of Ireland, volume 1: Prehistoric and Early Ireland* (Oxford 2005), pp. 814–16. On the exacavations at South Great George's Street that finally found the site of the *longphort*, see 'The first phase of Viking activity in Ireland: The archaeological evidence from Dublin' in *The Viking Age: Ireland and the West: Proceedings of the Fifteenth Viking Congress* (edited by John Sheehan & Donnchadh Ó'Corráin, Dublin 2010), pp. 418–29.

106. Wallace, 'The Archaeology of Ireland's Viking-age towns', in D. Ó Cróinín (ed.), *A New History of Ireland, volume 1: Prehistoric and Early Ireland* (Oxford 2005), pp. 820–21

107. The mound's appearance can only be recovered from seventeenth- and eighteenth-century descriptions of it, as it was later destroyed. There may also have been a *thing* near Wexford, commemorated in the name of Ting in Rathmacknee Parish; see Howard B. Clarke, Máire Ni Mahonaigh & Ragnhall Ó Floinn (eds), *Ireland and Scandinavia in the Early Viking Age* (Dublin 1998), p. 302.

108. The traditional view that the 'dark' or 'black' foreigners were Danes, probably from York, and that the 'fair' foreigners were instead Vikings from the Western Isles has been revised by David Dumville, 'Old Dubliners and New Dubliners in Ireland and Britain, a Viking-Age story' in Duffy S. (ed.), *Medieval Dublin VI*, pp. 78–93.

109. An unidentified kingdom, which may represent a Viking colony in western Scotland that was the source of the raids on Ireland in the 840s. Downham, *Viking Kings of Britain and Ireland*, p. 13. By the twelfth century the term, modified to *Lochlainn*, was used to refer to Norway; and so the term could instead refer to southern Norway as the source of the first raids.

110. See p. 53 above.

111. Sigfrith, confusingly, had the same name as Sihtric's brother, who had preceded him on the Dublin throne, ruling the city from 881 to 888.

112. *The Annals of Ulster*, 902 (edited by Seán Mac Airt and Gearóid Mac Niocaill, Dublin 1983), p. 353

113. Downham, *Viking Kings of Britain and Ireland*, p. 31

114. See p. 65 above.

115. See p. 67.

116. It seems to have been a fairly well-established trade. Merchants from

Verdun are reported as providing a constant flow of slaves from eastern Europe for sale in the slave markets of al-Andalus. See Richard Fletcher, *Moorish Spain* (London 1992), p. 42.

117. The word *majus* is also related to 'Magi', and this is probably related to the fire-veneration practices of the Zoroastrians, the leading main religion of pre-Islamic Persia (which the Muslims conquered between 642 and 644).

118. The account of the embassy is given by Ibn Dihya, a thirteenth-century writer from Valencia. See 'Whom did al-Ghazal meet?' in *Saga Book of the Viking Society*, 28 (2004), pp. 5–28. For more on Horik of Denmark, see p. 14.

119. One such is a tenth-century deer-antler box from León.

120. See Sara María Pons-Sanz, 'The Basque Country and the Vikings during the ninth century' in *Journal of the Society of Basque Studies in America* 21 (2001), pp. 48–58.

121. It was called Greek Fire from its use by the Byzantine armies, and the Arabs may have learnt the formula after facing it in the eastern Mediterranean. Those Vikings who operated in Russia and the Black Sea would have known the substance better (see p. 230 below.)

122. See Hugh Kennedy, *Muslim Spain and Portugal* (London 1996), p. 47.

123. Not in fact that Rome in the mid-ninth century could boast a fraction of the wealth it had contained when Alaric the Goth sacked it in 410. Although in its imperial heyday in the first century the population exceeded one million, by the ninth century it had declined to around 30,000.

124. See F. Donald Logan, *The Vikings in History*, p. 110.

125. This could be what is now Luna in Liguria, although already in the time of the Lombard king Liutprand (712–44) it was hardly more than a village and could scarcely have been mistaken for Rome, even by the most backwoods Vikings.

126. The Irish chronicler Duald Mac-Fuirbis later recorded that 'after that the Norsemen brought a great host of Moors in captivity with them to Ireland . . . long were these blue men in Ireland'. See Neil Price, 'The Vikings in Spain, North Africa and the Mediterranean' in *The Viking World* (edited by Stefan Brink), pp. 462–9.

Chapter 3: Chieftains, Myths and Ships

1. The method of wireless communication between handheld computerised devices that bears the Bluetooth name does indeed derive from the greatest of the Jelling dynasty, and the ubiquitous symbol for it is composed of the runic letters for 'H' and 'B', apparently chosen as a codename for the project for the way in which Harald united the Danes, just as Bluetooth is said to unite communication between computers. One of the early posters advertising Bluetooth even had a stylised image of Harald taken from the Jelling Stone, carrying a laptop in one hand and a mobile phone in the other.

2. Employing the younger *futhark* script then in use in Scandinavia. See p. 108 above.

3. Their names were Horied, Liafadag and Reginbrand. G. Turville-Petre, *The Heroic Age of Scandinavia* (London 1951), p. 92.

4. For a discussion of traditional Viking beliefs, see p. ooo above.

5. The church itself was built around 1125 and the bronzes added at the beginning of the thirteenth century.

6. *Vita Willibrordi* by Alcuin of York, chapter 10, translated by the Reverend Alexander Grieve in *Willibrord, Missionary in the Netherlands, 691–739* (London 1923)

7. See p. 101.

8. These pre-scientific excavations were not in fact undertaken through any desire to find what lay in the mound, but because the well that the Jelling villagers had dug at the top of it had run dry, and they were trying to excavate a deeper one to find a fresh source of water.

9. See p. 136 below.

10. *Saga of Grettir the Strong,* chapter XVIII (see translation by Denton Fox & Hermann Pálsson, Toronto 1974)

11. An additional piece of evidence is that the largest fort of all, Aggersborg, was built not at the western end of the Limsfjord, as easy access to the North Sea and raids against England would demand, but instead in a better position to control the land towards the Norwegian coast. Else Roesdahl, *Viking Age Denmark,* pp. 153–5.

12. Roesdahl, *Viking Age Denmark,* p. 47

13. From the *Hákonarmál,* a skaldic poem quoted in Snorri Sturluson's *Heimskringla,* book iv, chapter 32 (translated by Erling Monsen, Cambridge 1932).

14. A runestone found in Sønder Vissing church in Jutland reads: 'Tovi,

Mstivoj's daughter, wife of Harald the Good, Gorm's son, had this memorial made for her mother.' Her father, Mstivoj, the ruler of the Obodrites, turned out to be a less-than-reliable friend, as in 974 he allied himself with Emperor Otto II when the Germans invaded Denmark. See Jakub Morawiec, *Vikings Among the Slavs – Jomsborg and the Jomsvikings* (Vienna 2009), p. 13.

15. Interestingly, although two of the main historical sources, Saxo Grammaticus and the *Fagrskinna*, concur in this foundation story, the *Saga of the Jomsvikings* itself gives an alternative version in which it was established by Palnatoki, the *jarl* of Fyn island, and Burizleif, the King of the Slavs.

16. Who is one of the candidates for the noblewoman interred in the Oseberg ship. See p. 125 below.

17. Gwyn Jones, *History of the Vikings*, p. 89

18. See p. 71 above.

19. The total distance is about 1,100 miles, so he seems to have travelled just 35 miles in an average sailing day. See Niels Lund (ed.), translated by Christine E. Fell, *Two Voyagers at the Court of King Alfred*, p. 30.

20. See Gwyn Jones, *A History of the Vikings*, p. 110.

21. Lund (ed.), *Two Voyagers at the Court of King Alfred*, p. 22

22. See p. 68 above.

23. The inscription is, however, undated and could equally well date to 1036, or twelve years after the assembly at Moster, when Olaf Tryggvason declared that Norway was a Christian nation. Ferguson, *Hammer and the Cross*, pp. 264–5.

24. See Snorri Sturluson, *Heimskringla*, book IV, chapter 16–17.

25. See p. 93 above.

26. See p. 262 below.

27. See Brink (ed.), *The Viking World*, p. 668.

28. See p. 105 below.

29. Adam of Bremen, *History of the Archbishops of Hamburg-Bremen*, book 1, chapter xxiii

30. Adam of Bremen, book 2, chapter xxxviii

31. The origin of this nickname is rather obscure. *Skött* means 'treasure' or 'tax', and so *skötkonung* may either refer to the tribute that the Swedes paid to Denmark or possibly to Olof's position as the first Swedish monarch to mint his own currency.

32. See p. 259 below.

33. *Cambridge History of Scandinavia*, vol. 1 (Cambridge 2003), pp. 223–224

34. Adam of Bremen, book 4, chapters xxvi–xxvii

35. A date yielded by dendrochronology on the site. Helen Clarke and Björn Ambrosiani, *Towns in the Viking Age* (Leicester 1991), p. 52.

36. Brink (ed.), *The Viking World*, p. 129

37. In the form of thirty-three sunken buildings in the southern part of the settlement, in some of which raw materials and semi-finished objects were found, indicating the occurrence of some kind of manufacturing. Else Roesdahl (translated by Susan Margeson & Kirsten Williams), *Viking Age Denmark* (London 1982), pp. 73–5.

38. See p. 300 below.

39. The earliest extant version of the *Bjarkøyrett* is from the mid-thirteenth century, but it clearly derives from older antecedents. Brink (ed.), *The Viking World*, p. 88.

40. Clarke and Ambrosiani, *Towns in the Viking Age*, p. 76

41. One estimate has as many as two million coins being minted at Sigtuna during Olof's reign. Brink (ed.), *The Viking World*, p. 143.

42. See p. 96 above.

43. By the archaeologist Charlotte Blindheim. There were earlier attempts at excavation, including one beginning in 1867, by the antiquarian Nicolay Nicolaysen, who concentrated on the burial mounds at Kaupang, of which he dug into seventy-nine. Over half of them contained nothing and the rest, which were cremation burials, a set of grave-goods considerably poorer than the royal graves that Nicolaysen had hoped to find.

44. See p. 124 below.

45. See p. 118 below.

46. From the *Hávámal* ('Lay of the High One'), (London 1866), verse 141

47. Terje Spurkland (translated by Betsy van der Hoek), *Norwegian Runes and Runic Inscriptions* (Woodbridge 2005), pp. 3–4

48. See R. I. Page, *Reading the Past: Runes* (London 1987), p. 25

49. Including, for example, the loss of the initial 'j' in many words, so that the Scandinavian 'år' is represented in other Germanic languages by 'year' or 'Jahr'.

50. See p. 299 below.

51. See Birgit Sawyer, *The Viking-Age Rune-Stones: Custom and Commemoration in Early Medieval Scandinavia* (Oxford 2000), pp. 123–45.

52. Birgit Sawyer, *The Viking-Age Rune-Stones*, p. 26

53. See p. 238 below.

54. See p. 263 below.

55. See Michael P. Barnes, *The Runic Inscriptions of Maeshowe* (Uppsala 1994), pp. 39–41.

56. *Njal's Saga*, chapter 26, and Michael Barnes, *The Runic Inscriptions of Maeshowe*, p. 39

57. Spurkland, *Norwegian Runes and Runic Inscriptions*, pp. 172–3

58. See p. 208 below.

59. Wahlgren, *The Kensington Runestone*, p. 129

60. The most important manual to preserve the Poetic Edda is the *Codex Regius*, composed around 1270, though almost certainly copied from still earlier manuscripts. The *Codex* spent several centuries in Denmark before being repatriated to Iceland in 1971; see p. 149 below.

61. *Voluspá*, stanza 17. 'Ask' derives from the Old Norse word for an ash-tree, but the etymology of 'Embla' is more obscure.

62. There were also further subdivisions, with the Vanar having their own domain called Vanaheim, the giants dwelling in Jotunheim, the dwarves in Svartalfheim ('home of the dark elves') and, at the base of all, Hel, the land of the dead.

63. In one sense the Norns are superficially similar to the *Moirae*, the Greek Fates. Yet although there are three of them (Urth, Verthandi and Skuld), they do not appear individually to have a specific role in determining the past, present or future of a particular person (or of measuring and cutting the cloth of his life). There are, indeed, references to a multiplicity of Norns who visit a person at the time of his or her birth, and not just the three who made their homes in the shadow of Yggdrasil.

64. See p. 108 above.

65. H. R. Ellis-Davison, *Pagan Scandinavia* (London 1967), pp. 132–5

66. Christopher Abram, *Myths of the Pagan North: The Gods of the Norsemen* (London 2011), pp. 61–3

67. Abram, *Myths of the Pagan North*, p. 70, and Anne-Sofie Gräslund, 'The Material culture of the Old Norse religion' in *The Viking World* (edited by Stefan Brink), pp. 291–3

68. Where the *goði* combined the role of priest and chieftain (see p. 159 below)

69. The saga of the people of Eyri, which tells of the feud between Snorri *goði* and Arnkel *goði*, two members of the Icelandic priestly-aristocratic class.

70. Stephen A. Mitchell, *Witchcraft and Magic in the Nordic Middle Ages* (Philadelphia 2011), p. 21

71. *The Borgarthing Law of the Codex Tunsbergensis . . . Diplomatic edition, with an introduction on the paleography and the orthography* (edited by George T. Flom, Urbana 1925).

72. *Grettir's Saga*, chapters 18–19 (Kar the Old), 32–5 (Glam) (translated by George Ainslie Hight, London 1914)

73. Richard Frye, *Ibn Fadlan's Journey to Russia: A Tenth-Century Traveler from Baghdad to the Volga River* (Princeton 2005), pp. 66–7.

74. Frye, *Ibn Fadlan's Journey to Russia*, pp. 67–70.

75. P. Sawyer, *The Age of the Vikings* (London 1971), pp. 75–7

76. Thorleif Sjøvold, *The Viking Ships in Oslo* (Oslo 1985), p. 54

77. See p. 122 above.

78. 'The Oseberg Ship Burial, Norway: New Thoughts On the Skeletons From the Grave Mound' by Per Holck, in *European Journal of Archaeology*, vol. 9, nos 2–3 (August 2006), pp. 285–310

79. 'The "Buddha Bucket" from the Oseberg Find' by Margaret MacNamidhe in *The Irish Arts Review* (1989), pp. 77–82

80. *Encomium Emmae Reginae*, edited by Alistair Campbell, with a supplementary introduction by Simon Keynes (Cambridge 1998), book 2, chapter 5, p. 21

81. See Peder Lamm, *Stones, Ships and Symbols: The Picture Stones of Gotland from the Viking Age and Before* (Visby 1978), pp. 13–16.

82. Snorri Sturluson, *Heimskringla* (translated by Erling Monsen, Cambridge 1932), pp. 181–2

83. See p. 258 below.

84. Confusingly the numeration of the Skuldelev vessels goes up to six, despite there being only five ships. This is because at an early stage of the reconstruction Skuldelev 2 and 4 were believed to be two separate ships, although it is now known that those fragments both formed part of the same original boat (which is numbered as Skuldelev 2/4, or simply Skuldelev 2). The final ship at Skuldelev, numbered 6, is a smaller fishing vessel.

85. But which, unfortunately for the Greenlandic economy, often failed to do so. See p. 186 below.

86. See p. 63 above.

87. See p. 145 below.

88. See 'The Discovery of an Early Bearing Dial' by Carl B. Sölver in *Journal*

of the Institute of Navigation, VI, no. 3 (July 1953), pp. 294–6, and 'The Course for Greenland' by G. J. Marcus in *Saga-Book of the Viking Society*, vol. XIV (1953–7), pp. 12–35.

89. See p. 199 below.

90. The general classification of European styles of the Germanic Migration Age is into three broad styles: I, II and III (Salin, *Die altgermanische Thieroramentik*, Stockholm 1904). The last was further divided into three styles: C, which was in use in the seventh and early eighth centuries; D, which lasted for much of the eighth century; and E, which appeared around the start of the Viking raids at the end of the eighth century and endured into the ninth century.

91. For more details of the significance of the Borre mounds, see p. 19 above.

92. See p. 90 above.

93. The legend of Sigurd has proved one of the most enduringly popular of the Norse myths, from its appearance in the *Völsunga Saga* in the thirteenth century to its later adaptations in the German epic poem the *Nibelungenlied*, which formed the core of Richard Wagner's *Der Ring des Nibelungen* and, later, was remodelled by J. R. R. Tolkien into *The Legend of Sigurd and Gudrún*. In the original, the smith Regin forges Sigurd an enchanted sword, with which he avenges the death of his father and brother. In return Sigurd slays the dragon Fafnir (who is Regin's brother and has stolen a treasure given by the gods as payment for Loki's killing of their father). Regin asks Sigurd to roast Fafnir's heart and give it to him to eat, but as Sigurd is doing so, some of the blood drips onto his finger and he licks it off. He finds he can now understand the language of the birds, which are discussing how Regin intends to betray and kill Sigurd. Hearing this, Sigurd rides off, confronts Regin and strikes his head from his body. Sigurd then takes possession of the treasure (which will in turn lead to his own death in the end). Popular scenes portrayed on runestones and other carvings are the slaying of the dragon Fafnir, the forging of the sword by Regin and the cooking of Fafnir's heart.

94. Around 700 or 800 were originally built between the eleventh and thirteenth centuries, although only around twenty have survived the intervening centuries. Some of them contain runic carvings, including one at Stedje (in Sogn), which reads: 'I rode past this place on St Olav's Day. The Norns did me much harm as I rode by', indicating that awareness of (if not adherence to) traditional beliefs was still very much alive sometime after the official conversion to Christianity. For more on stave

churches, see Dan Lindholm, *Stave Churches in Norway* (translated by
Stella and Adam Bittleston, London 1969) and Anders Bugge, *Norwegian
Stave Churches* (translated by Ragnar Christophersen, Oslo 1953).

Chapter 4: Across the Atlantic

1. See Símun V. Arge, 'Vikings in the Faroe Islands' in Fitzhugh and Ward
   (ed.), *Vikings: The North Atlantic Saga*, p. 154.
2. *Dicuili, Liber de Mensura Orbis Terrae* (edited by J. J. Tierney, London 1967),
   chapters 14–15
3. As argued by Jóhannes Jóhannesson in 'Studies in the vegetational history
   of the Faroe and Shetland Islands' in *Annales Societatis Scientiarum
   Faroensis*, supplementum II (Tórshavn 1985). See also 'Peaceful Wars and
   Scientific Invaders: Irishmen, Vikings and palynological evidence for the
   earliest settlement of the Faroe Islands' by Kevin J. Edwards & Douglas
   B. Borthwick in *The Viking Age: Ireland and the West: Proceedings of the 15th
   Viking Congress* (edited by John Sheehan & Donnchadh Ó'Corráin, Dublin
   2010), pp. 66–79. The evidence for two possible pre-Viking phases of settlement (the earliest in the fourth to sixth centuries) has come from carbon
   dating of carbonised barley grains at the site of Á Sandum on Sandoy. See
   'The Vikings were not the first colonisers of the Faroe Islands' by Mike J.
   Church, Símon V. Arge et al in *Quaternary Science Reviews*, July 2013.
4. See p. 71 above.
5. See p. 68 above.
6. Olúva was the daughter of Aud's son, Thorstein the Red, by her husband,
   King Olaf the White of Dublin.
7. P.G. Foote, *On the Saga of the Faroe Islanders*, (London 1965), p. 10
8. There have been some suggestions that the Romans visited Thule/
   Iceland, largely on the basis of three Roman copper antoniniani dating
   from around AD 270–305 (one each from the reigns of Aurelian (270–74),
   Probus (276–82) and Diocletian (284–305) respectively), which were found
   in eastern Iceland (on two separate, though nearby, sites). They could
   have been brought there by Viking settlers (as antique curios rather than
   valuables, as they are made of copper, rather than silver or gold), who
   later lost them, by the elusive *papar* or even, according to some theories,
   by Romans either driven accidentally onto the shores of Iceland or on
   a deliberate voyage of exploration. The use of the word 'Thule' by such
   authors as the fifth-century Roman poet Claudian, who refers in his
   Against Rufinus to 'Thule which lies ice-bound the Pole Star', has been

taken as support for this theory. However, since the time of Virgil, Roman writers had used 'Thule' as a poetic synonym for the furthest part of the world (Virgil actually used the term *Ultima Thule*) and so references to it by Claudian and others cannot be taken literally. Whatever the means by which the coins reached Iceland – and it was most probably on a Viking ship – their presence cannot be taken to mean any substantial Roman exploration (let alone colonisation) of the island.

9. Dicuil's is not in fact the first mention in literature of an island that might be Iceland. The Greek geographer Pytheas, who lived in Marseilles in the fourth century BC, undertook a voyage through north-western Europe, which certainly took in the British Isles. We only know his work through its quotation by later authors, in particular from the compendious *Geography* of the Roman geographer Strabo in the first century BC. Pytheas describes a country that lay six days to the north of Britain, close to the point where the sea becomes frozen. His description of the sun staying above the horizon all night during the midsummer is sufficiently close to Dicuil's to raise questions as to whether the later Irish writer was simply repeating Pytheas's account.

10. See Jón Jóhannesson, *Íslendinga Saga, A History of the Old Icelandic Commonwealth* (Winnipeg 1974), p. 6.

11. See Geoffrey Ashe, *Land to the West – St Brendan's Voyage to America* (London 1962)

12. This and the other very early voyages to Iceland are recounted in the *Landnámabók* (translated by H. Pálsson & P. Edwards, Manitoba 1972)

13. See p. 141 above.

14. *Landnámabók,* chapter 6 (*The Book of Settlements,* translated by Hermann Pálsson & Paul Edwards, Winnipeg 1972)

15. The *Sturlubók*, an adaptation by Sturla Thórðarson (who died in 1284), which is relatively complete; the *Hauksbók*, named for Haukr Erlendsson (d. 1334), which is again mostly intact; and the fragmentary *Melabók,* which is believed to be the work of the fourteenth-century lawman Snorri Markússon (d. 1313). See Jóhannesson, *Íslendinga Saga,* p. 11.

16. For more on the tephrochronology of Iceland, see 'The tephrochronology of Iceland and the North Atlantic region during the Middle and Late Quaternary: a review' by Haflidi Haflidison et al. in *Journal of Quaternary Science* 15 (1) (2000), pp. 3–22.

17. There is also some evidence from radiocarbon dates at Herjólfsdalur on the Westmann Islands (off the west coast), which give a date in the seventh

century. The site has not yielded artefacts that would confirm this very early settlement, so uncertainty still remains about whether pre-872 settlement took place (and, if so, by whom). See Kevin P. Smith, *Landnám: The Settlement of Iceland in Archaeological and Historical Perspective* (1995).

18. See p. 166 below.

19. The *Flateyjarbók* contains the text of the *Saga of the Greenlanders*, as well as that of the *Orkneyinga Saga* and *Faereyinga Saga* (in both cases being the only surviving original copy of these in Icelandic), as well as sagas dealing with a number of Norwegian kings, including Olaf Tryggvason, Olaf Haraldsson (St Olaf), Magnus the Good and Harald Hardrada. The *Codex Regius* (or *Konungsbók*) contains the text of the Poetic Edda, which, without the survival of this manuscript, would be almost completely unknown. A leaf in the *Flateyjarbók* states that it was written in 1387, making it one of the few major Icelandic manuscripts that can be precisely dated. See Guðvarður Már Gunnlaugsson, 'Manuscripts and Palaeography' in *A Companion to Old Norse-Icelandic Literature and Culture* (edited by Rory McTurk, Oxford 2005). The *Codex Regius* is believed to have been written around 1270.

20. Which was needed in response to a terrible famine that had struck the country and reduced the population in 1703 to just 50,358.

21. Including some 300 in the Royal Library in Stockholm, 250 in the British Museum, 150 in Oxford University's Bodleian Library and 100 in the National Library of Scotland. See Jeanette Greenfield, *The Return of Cultural Treasures* (Cambridge 1996), p. 17.

22. Nordal was Iceland's ambassador to Denmark from 1951 to 1957. See his *The Historical Element in the Icelandic Family Sagas* (W. P. Kerr Memorial Lecture 15, Glasgow 1957).

23. The decree stipulated that the first fire was to be lit at sunrise and that the men should walk to each successive fire, which should be at a distance from the previous one that the smoke from it could still be seen. They could then continue until the sun was setting. Whether anyone actually carried out this procedure is unknown. See Jóhannesson, *Íslendinga Saga*, p. 30.

24. This has been disputed by some historians, such as Barði Guðmunsson, who pointed to strong differences in customs (such as cremation of the dead, which west Norwegians practised but Icelanders never did, and the higher status of women in Iceland) to theorise that the Icelandic settlers came instead from an eastern Scandinavian group that had settled

in western Norway. Barði Guðmunsson, *The Origins of the Icelanders* (Lincoln, Nebraska 1967).

25. See 'mtDNA and the Islands of the North Atlantic: Estimating the Proportions of Norse and Gaelic Ancestry' by Agnar Helgason et al. in *The American Journal of Human Genetics*, vol. 68, issue 3 (March 2001, pp. 727–31). This study showed that the Scandinavian component of mtDNA in the modern Icelandic population was only 37.5 per cent (as opposed to 35.5 per cent in the Orkneys).

26. Large quantities of driftwood still come ashore in western Iceland, often from logging in Siberia, where the cut trunks have made their way into the ocean and then been carried by the currents westwards into the Atlantic.

27. *Njál's Saga*, chapter 63 (translated by Magnus Magnusson & Hermann Pálsson, London 1964)

28. This literally means 'forest-going' and so harks back either to a time when there really were forests of a sort on Iceland, shortly after the first settlement, or is a name carried over from Scandinavia.

29. *Gisli's Saga*, chapter 12 (translated by George Webbe Dasent, London 1866)

30. See p. 118 above. The cave forms part of the Hallmundarhraun lava field and is basically one very long lava tube.

31. See 'Surtshellir: a fortified outlaw cave in West Iceland' by Kevin P. Smith, Guðmundr Olafsson & Thomas H. McGovern in *The Viking Age: Ireland and the West, Proceedings of the Fifteenth Viking Congress, Cork, 2005* (Dublin 2010).

32. See 'Outlaws of Surtshellir Cave: The Underground Economy of Viking Age Iceland' by Kevin P. Smith, Guðmundr Olafsson & Thomas H. McGovern in *Dynamics of Northern Societies* (edited by Jette Arneborg & Bjarni Grønnow, Copenhagen 2006).

33. See p. 167 above for more on Sighvatsson's role in the Icelandic civil wars.

34. See 'Laws' by Gudmund Sandvik & Jón Viðar Sigurðsson in Rory McTurk (ed.), *Old Norse-Icelandic Literature and Culture* (Oxford 2005), pp. 221–44.

35. The honour of being the oldest extant continuous parliament may then go to another Viking foundation, the Tynwald, the Isle of Man's parliament, which has been dated to 979. See p. 69 above.

36. *Njál's Saga*, chapters 117–24

37. One in every nine tax-paying farmers was legally obliged to attend. The census of these in 1095 revealed that there were 4,560, so at least 500 farmers must have come, meaning in all probability that there would have to have been at least 1,000 people at each annual gathering.

38. Jesse Byock, *Viking Age Iceland* (London 2001), p. 176. The office became hereditary in the family of the descendants of Ingólf Arnarson.

39. The laws were written down during the Lawspeakership of Bergthórr Hransson and were compiled at the farm belonging to Haflidi Másson, from which the document on which they were written came to be referred to as Haflidi's scroll. It was available for consultation by the Lawspeaker and legislators, but unfortunately updates to it were not properly policed and so by the late twelfth century there were a number of competing law scrolls in circulation. Jóhannesson, *Íslendinga Saga*, p. 91.

40. A lawsuit arose over the burning to death of Thorkell Blund-Ketilsson – disposing of enemies by burning down their farms seems to have been a frequent means of exacting revenge – and the two chieftains found themselves on opposing sides, leading to an armed confrontation at the Thingnes Assembly. The case was then referred to the Althing. Jóhannesson, *Íslendinga Saga*, p. 49.

41. A side-effect of the reforms was that the number of *godar* was set at thirty-nine, with three each being sent from the thirteen regional *várthing*. As this would have given an unfair advantage to the Northern Quarter, which had four *várthing* and so sent twelve *godar* rather than nine, the other three were allowed to send an additional three *godar*, making forty-eight in total.

42. Jesse Byock, *Viking Age Iceland*, p. 182

43. *Landnámabók*, chapter 218

44. Note that there must always have remained some Christians in Iceland, including the one who wrote the *Hafgerðingadrápa* poem on the voyage from Iceland to Greenland *c.* 985. See p. 260 below.

45. The law-code set out that a verse was to be taken 'as it is spoken' and not interpreted 'according to the language of poetry', thus preventing obscure interpretations of verses from being the excuse for lawsuits or violence. *Konungsbók* 237 in Foote et al., *Laws of Early Iceland*, vol. 2, p. 195.

46. This was known as the *fraendaskömm* ('kin-shame law').

47. Although even then Olaf kept hold of four hostages, one from each Quarter, in case the Christian chieftains reneged on their deal or the pagans refused to be convinced.

48. See Jóhannesson, *Íslendinga Saga*, p. 135.

49. For a detailed discussion of the 'under the cloak' incident, see Jón Hnefill Aðalsteinnson, *Under the Cloak: The Acceptance of Christianity in Iceland, with Particular Reference to the Religious Attitudes Prevailing at the Time*

(Studia Ethnologica Upsaliensia 4, Uppsala 1978), which concludes that parallels with incidents in Heligoland and Sweden suggest that Thorgeir was consulting the gods rather than merely thinking matters over (and that the muted reaction to the decision was because pagans were accustomed to entrusting important decisions to oracles).

50. See Charles Odhal, *Constantine and the Christian Roman Empire* (London 2005).

51. Baptism at the time was generally carried out by immersion, and so reluctance to be plunged into streams that were icy-cold, even at the height of summer, is understandable.

52. See p. 258 below for an account of the battle.

53. See Jóhannesson, *Íslendinga Saga*, p. 146.

54. Clerical marriage, although generally disapproved of by the Church, was not unheard of in the Middle Ages and only came to an end after a decree of the Second Lateran Council in 1123, which declared any marriage undertaken by clerics of the higher order to be invalid. Also, Gizur was born in 1042, fourteen years before his father became bishop.

55. Lund had become the archiepiscopal see for all of Scandinavia in 1104.

56. This reform largely stuck and although the first two days in modern Icelandic are Sunnudagur ('Sun-day') and Mánudagur ('Moon-Day'), the rest of the days bear satisfyingly non-pagan names: Þriðjudagur ('Third Day'), Miðvikudagur ('Midweek Day'), Fimmtudagu ('Fifth Day'), Föstudagur ('Care Day') and Laugardagur ('Washing' or 'Pool Day'), the last presumably an indication that laundry and personal ablutions were confined to one day a week.

57. Both bishops did, however, receive posthumous rewards as they were recognised as saints by the Althing, Thorlák in 1199 and Jón Ögmundarson the following year. As the 'canonisation' had not been sanctioned by the papacy, it was not regarded as valid, and Thorlák was only officially recognised as a saint by the Catholic Church in 1984, when Pope John Paul II canonised him (and declared him the patron saint of Iceland).

58. See Jóhannesson, *Íslendinga Saga*, pp. 251–3.

59. See Jóhannesson, *Íslendinga Saga*, p. 267.

60. There are in fact a number of reasons to believe that Harald Finehair's dynasty did not rule Norway in an unbroken line to 1387. The claims of descent from Harald to Olaf Tryggvason and Harald Hardrada (amongst others) may have been simply attempts to attribute dynastic legitimacy to what would otherwise have been considered a usurpation.

Chapter 5: The Colony that Vanished

1. Excluding Australia, which is usually counted as a continental landmass.

2. *Landnámabók*, chapter 2 (Time and Place). A more direct route from the coast of Norway took five to seven days' sail, according to Adam of Bremen, *History of the Archbishops of Hamburg*, xxxvii, 36 (translated by Francis Tschan, New York 1959).

3. Gwynn Jones, *The Norse Atlantic Saga*, p. 45; Finn Gad, *History of Greenland* (London 1970), vol. 1, p. 27

4. See Waldemar H. Lehn, 'Skerrylike mirages and the Discovery of Greenland' *in Applied Optics* 39, no. 21 (2000), pp. 3612–29.

5. *Landnámabók*, chapter 122 (translated by Pálsson & Edwards, 2007)

6. *Erik the Red's Saga*, chapter 2

7. For further details of types of Icelandic outlawry, see p. 154 above.

8. Finn Gad, *History of Greenland*, vol. 1 (London 1970), p. 29

9. See p. 179 below.

10. *Eirik the Red's Saga*, chapter 2

11. There were alternative theories about the name, such as that given by Adam of Bremen, who theorised that 'The people there are greenish from the salt water, whence too, that region gets its name'. Adam of Bremen, *History of the Archbishops of Hamburg*, xxxvii, 36 (translated by Francis Tschan), p. 218.

12. *Saga of the Greenlanders*, chapter 1

13. Possibly written sometime around 1250, this is in the form of a dialogue between father and son, with the father possibly being intended to be Håkon IV and the son his successor, Magnus VI. *The King's Mirror (Speculum Regale)*, (translated by Laurence Marcellus Larson, New York 1917), p. 135.

14. 'Hafgerdingar: A mystery from the King's Mirror explained' by Waldemar H. Lehn & Irmgard I. Schroeder in *Polar Record* 39 (210), (2003), pp. 211–17

15. The whole story is related in the *Story of Einar Sokkason*, contained in the *Flateyjarbók*.

16. There is some evidence that Eirik set up the first *thing* in Greenland at Brattahlid (there are remains of some structures, which may be *thing* booths), which became the principal assembly of the colony. At some point in the twelfth century, however, a *thing* was established at Garðar, which seems to have replaced that at Brattahlid as Greenland's supreme assembly.

17. One theory has it that Eirik cast his high-seat posts into the sea to deter-mine where he should settle (just as Ingólf had done in Iceland). As the Norse for these posts is *set-stokkar*, Stokkanes may indicate where they landed, although if this is true, then Eirik did not regard himself bound by the tradition, as he chose the superior land at Brattahlið for his farm-stead. Paul Nørlund, *Viking Settlers in Greenland* (Cambridge 1936), p. 22.

18. J. Kristian Tornøe, *Columbus in the Arctic?* (Oslo 1965)

19. N. Lynnerup, *The Greenland Norse: a biological-anthropological study* (Copenhagen 1998), p. 118.

20. 'The Early Medieval Warm Epoch and its Sequel' by H. H. Lamb in *Palaeogeography, Palaeoclimatology, Palaeoecology*, vol. 1 (1965), pp. 13 37

21. One estimate (for Iceland) calculated that each cow needed 12.5 kilos of hay per day, which might amount to 2,500 kilos of hay for a winter lasting 200 days. Nørlund, *Viking Settlers in Greenland* p. 69.

22. Or GUS, from the Danish *Gården under Sander*. A detailed discussion of the site is to be found in Jette Arneborg & Hans Christian Gulløv, *Man, Culture and Environment in Ancient Greenland* (Copenhagen 1998).

23. The action of the river was, indeed, threatening the integrity of the site, as it had undermined the layer of permafrost that protected the buildings and was causing the sand to collapse into the river. During the course of the actual excavations, a river flood caused the water level to surge almost 3 feet; the site miraculously survived the inundation. *Vikings: The North Atlantic Saga* (edited by William W. Fitzhugh & Elisabeth I. Ward, Washington 2000), pp 296–7.

24. Gad, *History of Greenland*, vol. 1, p. 138; Gwynn Jones, *North Atlantic Saga*, p. 48

25. While Rogation Day is fixed at 25 April, the Little Rogation Days are dependent on Easter Day, falling on the three days before Ascension Thursday (itself forty days after Easter). The earliest possible date for Easter is 22 March, giving Little Rogation Days of 28–30 April, and the latest is 25 April, which would mean Little Rogation at 1–3 June, but such early and late Easters are rare, and so the vast bulk of possible dates are in May.

26. Gad, *History of Greenland*, p. 138

27. See p. 202 below.

28. The Dorset did survive somewhat longer on the North American main-land, and it would have been possible for the Norsemen to encounter them there as late as 1300. See Robert McGhee, *Ancient People of the Arctic*

(2001), and Hans Christian Gulløv, 'Natives and Norse in Greenland' in Fitzhugh & Ward (eds), *Vikings: The North Atlantic Saga*, pp. 318–26.

29. McGhee, *The Last Imaginary Place*, pp. 116–24

30. *Vikings: The North Atlantic Saga* (edited by Fitzhugh & Ward), pp. 324–5. For the end of Viking Greenland, see p. 190 below.

31. Hans Rink, *Tales and Traditions of the Eskimos* (London 1875)

32. Which could just possibly be a corruption of the Norse Yngvar.

33. *Landnámabók,* chapter 93

34. See p. 200 below.

35. Knud Krogh, *Viking Greenland* (Copenhagen 1967), p. 42

36. His nickname may also have meant 'drip-nose'.

37. Bishop Eirik *does* appear on an inscription on the Vinland Map (see p. 211 below), where he is said to have gone on his journey in 1117, but the veracity of this text is very much in doubt.

38. *Vikings: The North Atlantic Saga* (edited by Fitzhugh & Ward), p. 313. By comparison the Archbishop of Nidaros's hall back in Norway was larger, at over 2,000 square feet, but this served as the centre of a major Scandinavian archdiocese.

39. See p. 174 above.

40. Smyrill is recorded as being in Iceland in 1202 and 1203 and also travelled to Norway and Rome, so at this stage the connections between Greenland (or at least the Church there) and Europe were functioning well.

41. A radiocarbon dating carried out in 1999 yielded a date of 1272, which would be too late for the deceased to have been Jon Smyrill, but would be consistent with one of the other bishops. Jette Arneborg et al., 'Change of diet of the Greenland Vikings determined from stable carbon isotope analysis and 14C dating of their bones', *Radiocarbon* 41 (2) (1999) pp. 157–68.

42. See p. 168 above.

43. These were 1326, 1350, 1355 and 1374. Gwynn Jones, *The North Atlantic Saga*, p. 67.

44. The account of this voyage has some significance for the history of the Vikings in North America, see p. 220 below.

45. Farm W54, *Vikings: The North Atlantic Saga* (edited by Fitzhugh & Ward), p. 337

46. Graeme Davis, *Vikings in America*, p. 55

47. He was Sigurd Kolbeinsson, who was *umboðsmaðr* for King Håkon VI of Norway. A letter from the king in July 1374 refers to Kolbeinsson's

confiscation of some land that had become alienated from the crown. Gad, *History of Greenland*, vol. 1, p. 149.

48. *Historia Norwegiae* I.12 (edited by Inger Ekrem & Lars Boje Mortensen, translated by Peter Fisher, Copenhagen 2003)

49. Gad, *History of Greenland*, vol. 1, p. 150, and Kirsten Seaver, *The Frozen Echo: Greenland and the Exploration of North America ca. A.D. 1000–1500* (Stanford 1996), pp. 148–50

50. T. H. McGovern, 'Cows, Harp Seals and Churchbells: Adaptation and Extinction in Norse Greenland' in *Human Ecology*, 89 (1980), pp. 245–75

51. Joel Berglund, 'The Decline of the Norse Settlements in Greenland' in *Arctic Anthropology*, vol. 23, nos 1/2 (1986), pp. 109–35

52. Berglund, 'The Decline of the Norse Settlements in Greenland', pp. 109–35

53. McGovern, 'Cows, Harp Seals and Churchbells', pp. 245–75

54. *Vikings: The North Atlantic Saga* (edited by Fitzhugh & Ward), p. 336

55. Paul Nørlund, *Viking Settlers in Greenland*, p. 132. The Norwegian *alen* or cubit was around 25 inches.

56. See Seaver, *The Frozen Echo*, pp. 230–1.

57. G. Scott et al., 'Dental conditions of medieval Norsemen in the North Atlantic', *Acta Archaeologica*, 62 (1992), pp. 183–207

58. Gad, *History of Greenland*, vol. 1, p. 156

59. Gad, *History of Greenland*, vol. 1, p. 158

60. See p. 200 below. Kirsten Seaver in *The Last Vikings* puts forward the idea that English traders persuaded the Norsemen of the Eastern Settlement to collaborate in a venture to set up a colony in North America and that they migrated en masse to this. The colony failed for some reason and the survivors disappeared, either dying or through migration to another (unknown) point. James Robert Enterline in *Viking America* (New York 1972) favours the theory that the remaining Norsemen penetrated the Canadian Arctic and North American interior further south and merged with the Inuit and Native American populations (although many of the finds cited, such as the Vérendrye Stone discovered in 1738, in an area of North Dakota inhabited by Mandan Native Americans and identified as having a Norse runic inscription, are unverified, discredited or – in the case of the Vérendrye Stone itself – lost).

61. Fridtjof Nansen, *In Northern Mists: Arctic Exploration in Early Times* (translated by Arthur G. C. Chater), vol. 2 (London 1911), pp. 101–3

62. 'mtDNA variation in Inuit populations of Greenland and Canada:

Migration history and population structure' by Agnar Helgason & Gisli Pálsson et al., *American Journal of Physical Anthropologists*, vol. 130, issue 1 (May 2006) pp. 123–34. The study also revealed that the Thule may have interbred with existing Dorset populations in Greenland and Canada rather than displacing them completely.

63. Seaver, *Maps, Myths and Men*, p. 84

64. Gad, *History of Greenland*, vol. 1, p. 180

65. Frobisher took the man's wife and infant back to Bristol. The luckless Inuit, named Calichough or Collichang, was exhibited in England as a native of 'Cathay' and demonstrated the art of kayaking and hunting birds with a spear. He died within a month from pneumonia, complicated by a broken rib that he had received during his capture. His wife died soon afterwards, and the infant was taken to London, but did not survive long and was buried at St Olave's Church.

66. Finn Gad, *History of Greenland*, vol. 11 (London 1973), pp. 45–51

67. For an account of these voyages, see Kirsten Seaver, *The Last Vikings*, pp. 199–201.

Chapter 6: The Search for Vinland the Good

1. See edition in *The Vinland Sagas* (translated by Keneva Kunz, London 1997).

2. See 'The Date of the Composition of the Saga of the Greenlanders' by Jón Jóhannesson (translated by Tryggvi J. Oleson) in the *Saga-Book of the Viking Society* XVI (1962–5), pp. 54–66. Using the dates of the Bishops of Hólar mentioned, the *Saga of the Greenlanders* must date from 1263 or earlier and the *Saga of Eirik the Red* from 1264 or later.

3. Bjarni's voyage must have taken place after the discovery of Greenland by Eirik the Red in 986, so can most likely be dated to 988 or 989.

4. It was in fact aboard the ship of Bjarni's father, Herjolf Bárðarson, that the Christian poet who wrote the *Hafgerðingadrápa* poem sailed. See p. 174 above.

5. See p. 157 above for details of the booths at the Althing.

6. Or from *eyktarstaðr* to *dagmálastaðr*

7. An alternative derivation, put forward by Helge Ingstad, the excavator of the site at L'Anse aux Meadows, has the name coming from *Vín*, an Old Norse word for 'meadow'. Generally, however, this interpretation has not been accepted. 'The Discovery of Vinland' by Birgitta Wallace in Brink (ed.), *The Viking World*, p. 604.

8. Leif is said to have gone to Norway sixteen years after the colonisation of Greenland, which would date his meeting with Olaf Tryggvason to 1002. Unfortunately Olaf had perished in 1000 at the Battle of Stiklestad and so either the chronology given by the saga is wrong or the meeting (and the order to evangelise Norway) cannot have taken place.

9. The monopods, a tribe who shade themselves from the sun with their single large foot, are first mentioned by the Greek historian Herodotus in the sixth century BC, and then by the Roman naturalist Pliny in the first century AD (*Natural History*, book 7, 2), who described them as being able to leap with surprising agility. The tradition was carried on by the encyclopaedist Isidore of Seville in his *Etmyologiae* in the seventh century (book XI, Iii, 21) and was still current in the fourteenth century, when it occurs in the *Travels* of John Mandeville. Doubtless the composer of the saga had some such reference in mind, rather than any direct observation of a genuine one-footed tribe.

10. The range of estimates is from 1005 to about 1013, but 1005 is surely too soon after the initial discovery of Vinland by Leif Eiriksson.

11. *Saga of the Greenlanders,* chapter 6

12. The word used in the saga is *búnyt,* which could refer to milk, although in this case the image of them devouring it makes less sense, so it must be something more solid, like butter or cheese.

13. After the collapse of the Vinland venture, Snorri Thorfinnsson is said to have been taken back to Iceland, where he inherited the family farm at Glaumbaer in Greenland after the deaths of Karlsefni and Guðrið, and had two children, a son named Thorgeir and a daughter named Hallfrid. His descendants were said to have included several of the early bishops of Iceland. The next recorded European child to be born in the Americas was Martín de Arguëlles in the Spanish colony at San Agustín, Florida, in 1566/7.

14. *Saga of the Greenlanders,* chapter 7

15. The Blessed Isles are said to be on the 'left side of Mauretania' close to where the sun sets, and the hill ridges are covered with grape vines, while, instead of weeds, the island spontaneously sprouts harvest crops and herbs. See *The Etymologies of Isidore of Seville*, book XIV, chapter vi.8 (translated by Stephen A. Barney, W. J. Lewis, J. A. Beach, Oliver Berghof, Cambridge 2006).

16. Anne-Stine Ingstad, *The Norse Discovery of America*, vol. 2, p. 220

17. The children's names are not given, although their mother's name is said

to be Vaetilldi and their father Uvaegi. Some attempts have been made to identify the *skraeling* language on the basis of this tenuous evidence. Gwyn Jones, *The Norse Atlantic Saga*, p. 212.

18. Birthe L. Clausen (ed.), *Viking Voyages to North America* (Roskilde 1993), p. 5. C.C. Rafn, *Antiquitates Americanæ, sive Scriptores septentrionales rerum ante-Columbianarum in America* (Copenhagen 1837).

19. See p. 178 above.

20. He was taking time out between his resignation from Bowdoin College, Brunswick, and his assumption of the post as Smith Professor of Modern Languages at Harvard.

21. Letter to Stephen Longfellow, 20 September 1835 (in *The Letters of Henry Wadsworth Longfellow*, edited by Andrew Hilen, Cambridge, Mass., 1966, p. 515)

22. See F. W. Putnam, Notes & News, *American Anthropologist*, new series, vol. 3, no. 2 (April–June 1901), pp. 387–96

23. 'Supplement to the Antiquitates Americanae' by C. C. Rafn in *Mémoires de la Société Royale des Antiquaires du Nord* (Copenhagen 1838–9), pp. 369–83

24. Benedict Arnold, who was governor of Rhode Island three times between 1663 and 1678, was the great-grandfather of the similarly named American Revolutionary general. A great storm destroyed Newport's wooden windmill in 1675, and it is supposed that Arnold built the Newport Tower in stone as a sturdier replacement. For a discussion of the origins of the Tower, see Philip Means, *The Newport Tower* (New York 1942). There is also a marginally earlier reference in a deed by Nathaniel Dickens (in which he transfers land for the building of a Jewish cemetery) mentioning 'the old stone mill', which could conceivably also refer to the Newport Tower. The date of this, February 1677 – as opposed to that of Arnold's will (December 1677) – does not, however, materially push back the known dates for the Tower's existence. Horace F. Silliman, *The Newport Tower: The English Solution*, New England Antiquities Research Association (November 1979). William S. Godfrey Jr in 'The Archaeology of the Old Stone Mill in Newport, Rhode Island', *American Antiquity*, vol. XVII (1951–2), pp. 120–9, concludes from artefacts found in the construction trenches of the tower that it must have been built no later than the mid-seventeenth century and was probably originally a watch-tower that was adapted by Arnold in 1675–7 as a mill.

25. The Chesterton structure was built in 1632, some three years before Benedict Arnold came to America, but it may only have been adapted for use as a mill after 1700. See Means, *The Newport Tower*, pp. 188–92.

26. 'True or False – fake traces of the Vikings in America' by Keld Hansen in Clausen, *Viking Voyages to North America*, pp. 83–9

27. There are, of course, stone buildings in Greenland (wood, except for driftwood, was almost unavailable as a building material), but the stone churches at Hvalsey and elsewhere, the stone feasting halls and barns are not paralleled by any large stone towers of the Newport type.

28. Although the full range is 1410–1930, the C-14 dating can be somewhat imprecise and the 1410 date cannot be taken as a firm one. Johannes Hertz, 'The History and Mystery of the Old Stone Mill' in *Journal of the Newport Historical Society*, vol. 68, part 2 (1997).

29. Two Venetian brothers, Nicoló and Antonio Zeno, are said to have set off on a voyage across the Atlantic around 1380. They are said to have been shipwrecked on an island named Frislanda, and Nicoló became a pilot for 'Zichmni', the ruler of the nearby kingdom of Porlanda. In a series of subsequent voyages with Zichmni, the brothers sailed west to Icaria, where the inhabitants would not let them land, and to Engrouelanda, where they did make landfall. The whole account is probably a conflation of other travellers' tales combined with real accounts of Iceland and the Northern Isles of Scotland. Unfortunately for the brothers' credibility, in 1394, at the selfsame time they were supposed to be exploring the western Atlantic, Nicoló was on trial for embezzlement in Venice. See Andrea di Robilant, *Venetian navigators: The voyages of the Zen brothers to the Far North* (London 2011).

30. Gavin Menzies, *1421* (London 2002)

31. In the 1880s more than 186,000 Norwegians and 475,000 Swedes came to the United States, so that by 1900 first-generation migrants from those countries represented 8.8 per cent of the population (as against 0.7 per cent fifty years earlier). *A Century of Population Growth: From the First Census of the United States to the Twelfth 1790–1900* (Department of Commerce and Labor, Bureau of the Census, Washington 1909) and *Harvard Encyclopedia of American Ethnic Groups* (Harvard 1981).

32. See p. 133 above for Viking ship replicas in general.

33. After a rather forlorn voyage to New Orleans following the end of the Fair, the *Viking* was returned to Illinois, where it was generally forgotten until its transfer to the Lincoln Memorial Park in 1920. There it languished,

with periodic renovations funded by the local Scandinavian-American community, but generally falling into a state of parlous disrepair, until in 1993 the authority responsible for Chicago's parks announced that a planned redevelopment of the Lincoln Park meant the ship's eviction. A rescue council was established and the *Viking* was transferred to Good Templar Park in Geneva, Illinois. However, attempts to have a proper museum set up for this unique ship foundered and there the vessel has remained.

34. Who held the chair of Comparative Linguistics and Old Norse at Christiania.

35. In fact the original says 'Goths', presumably referring to Gotland, culturally a part of Sweden. But to translate it as Goths invites additional confusion with the fourth- and fifth-century Germanic barbarian Goths (such as Alaric, the sacker of Rome).

36. Wahlgren, *The Kensington Stone: A Mystery Solved* (Madison, Wisconsin 1958). p. 3.

37. See p. 188 above.

38. See p. 111 above.

39. See Wahlgren, *The Kensington Stone*, p. 115.

40. The *Sveriges Historia* by Oskar Montelius. See Wahlgren, *The Kensington Stone*, p. 129.

41. At one point there were some twenty-four runic inscriptions from New England, West Virginia, Nova Scotia and Ontario, which were all said to be evidence of Viking activity in those areas. See 'True or False – fake traces of the Vikings in America' by Keld Hansen in Clausen, *Viking Voyages to North America*.

42. See Richard Nielsen & Scott F. Wolter, *The Kensington Rune Stone: Compelling New Evidence* (2005), which amongst other things also suggests a connection between the Kensington Runestone and the Templar crusading order.

43. See Seaver, *Maps, Myths and Men*, pp. 75–6.

44. R. A. Skelton, Thomas E. Marston & George D. Painter (eds), *The Vinland Map and the Tartar Relation* (New Haven, Conn. 1965), pp. 139–40

45. See p. 184 above.

46. Kirsten Seaver in *Maps, Myths and Men*, pp. 91–3, suggests this may have been the collection of Luís Fortuny Bieto, a Madrid bookseller.

47. Skelton, Master & Painter (eds), *The Vinland Map and the Tartar Relation*

48. For the type of script, see 'The Manuscript: History and Description'

by Thomas E. Marston in *The Vinland Map and the Tartar Relation*. For the anomalies in the script, see Seaver, *Maps, Myths and Men*, p. 172.

49. See 'Analysis of Pigmentary Materials on the Vinland Map and Tartar Relation by Raman Microprobe Spectroscopy' by Katherine L. Brown & Robin J. H. Clark in *Analytical Chemistry* (August 2002).

50. The circumnavigation was not achieved until 1997–2001 by an expedition led by Lonnie Dupré, which covered just over half the distance in dog-sledges and the rest using kayaks.

51. See Fitzhugh & Ward, *Vikings: The North Atlantic Saga*, p. 265.

52. Seaver, *The Frozen Echo*, p. 28

53. Possibly *Elymus virginicus*; Fitzhugh & Ward, *Vikings: The North Atlantic Saga*, p. 234

54. *Historia Norwegiae*, book I, chapter 12

55. See p. 179 above.

56. Steven L. Cox, 'Palaeo-Eskimo Occupations of the North Labrador Coast' in *Arctic Anthropology*, vol. 15, no. 2 (1978), and Anne Stine Ingstad, *The Norse Discovery of America*, vol. 2, p. 289

57. R. McGhee, 'Contact between Native North Americans and the Medieval Norse: A Review of the Evidence' in *American Antiquity* 49.1 (1984), pp. 4–26

58. 'The 1976 Excavations at L'Anse aux Meadows' in *Research Bulletin of Parks Canada*, no. 67 (1977)

59. See 'L'Anse aux Meadows, the Western Outpost' by Birgitta Linderoth Wallace in *Viking Voyages to North America*, pp. 30–42

60. See Fitzhugh & Ward, *Vikings: The North Atlantic Saga*, p. 214

61. Fitzhugh & Ward, *Vikings: The North Atlantic Saga*, p. 215, and 'The Discovery of Vinland' by Birgitta Wallace in *The Viking World* (edited by Stefan Brink), p. 610

62. See Niels Lynnerup, 'The Greenland Norse: A biological-anthropological study' in *Meddelelser om Grønland: Man & Society* 24, pp. 1–149

63. For a discussion of saga scholars' attempts to locate the Vinland settlements, see 'The Quest for Vinland in Saga Scholarship' by Gísli Sigurdsson in *Vikings: The North Atlantic Saga* (Washington 2000), pp. 232–7. See also Niels Vinding, *The Viking Discovery of America 950–1008* (translated by Birgitte Moye-Vinding, New York 2005), and Farley Mowat, *Westviking*, for St Paul's Bay, and Páll Bergthórsson, *Vinlándsgátan* (Reykjavik 1997).

64. See Erik Andersen & Claus Malmros, 'Ship's Parts Found in the Viking

Settlements in Greenland' in Clausen, *Viking Voyages to North America*, pp. 118–22.

65. See p. 178 above.

Chapter 7: Furthest East

1. See Heiki Balk, 'The Vikings and the Eastern Baltic' in *The Viking World* (edited by Stefan Brink, London 2008), pp. 485–95.

2. As recounted by Snorri Sturluson in the *Heimskringla*.

3. For a discussion of the various Normanist and anti-Normanist arguments and camps, see H. Paskiewicz, *The Origins of Russia* (London 1954), pp. 109–32, and 'The Varangian Problem: a brief history of the controversy' in *Varangian Problems* (Copenhagen 1970), pp. 7–20.

4. Signs of Scandinavian influence in Grobin include the finding of picture stones, similar to those produced on Gotland, which appear in graves, together with male belt-buckles and female brooches of Scandinavian type. The presence of the last in particular indicates that this was a fully fledged colony, as opposed to an ephemeral trading stop or fortified point inhabited exclusively by merchants or warriors.

5. See *The Annals of St-Bertin* (translated and edited by Janet Nelson, Manchester 1991), p. 44.

6. See H. R. Ellis Davidson, *The Viking Road to Byzantium* (London 1976), p. 59, and Simon Franklin & Jonathan Shepard, *The Emergence of Rus* (London 1996), p. 28.

7. Liutprand went on an embassy to the Byzantine emperor Constantine VII Porphyrogenitus in 949, when he would have had ample time to observe Vikings serving in the imperial army. He later wrote up his experiences in the *Relatio de Legatione Constantinopolitana*. The theory that the Rus were originally an Alan sub-group was put forward by George Vernadsky (see *The Origins of Russia* (Westport, Conn., 1975), p. 180). This group, according to Vernadsky, established the first Rus khaganate at Tmutorakan on the mouth of the Kuban River, and eventually moved northwards towards Kiev and merged with Vikings coming from Sweden, who took on the Rus name.

8. For the history of the Varangian Guard in Constantinople, see p. 291 below.

9. Blöndal, *The Varangians of Byzantium*, p. 7. The word has also been connected by Russian scholars to the Turkish word *varmak*, meaning walk (and hence 'wanderers').

10. Although probably not by Nestor, a monk from the Pechersk monastery at Kiev, to whom it was traditionally ascribed. The chronicle exists in various redactions, most notably the Laurentian and Hypatian. See *Russian Primary Chronicle*, Laurentian Text (translated and edited by Samuel Hazzard Cross & Olgerd P. Sherbowitz-Wetzor, Cambridge, Mass., 1953), pp. 5–15.

11. *Russian Primary Chronicle*, pp. 58–9.

12. See 'Ninth-century Dirham Hoards from European Russia, a preliminary analysis' by Thomas S. Noonan in M. A. S. Blackburn & D. M. Metcalf (eds), *Viking Age Coinage in the Northern Lands*, BAR International Series 122 (Oxford 1981), pp. 47–118.

13. Franklin & Shepard, *The Emergence of Rus*, pp. 101–3

14. Of around 1,000 graves, only sixty yielded artefacts that were certainly identified as Scandinavian, although in many, being cremation graves, organic material would have perished when burnt. A detailed examination of the evidence in *Viking Rus – Studies on the Presence of Scandinavians in Eastern Europe*, Wladyslaw Duczko (Brill 2004), pp. 160–80, suggests that items such as an equal-armed brooch of undoubted Norse provenance, pennanular brooches and a number of swords of Scandinavian type and bridle pieces attest to a very strong Scandinavian presence.

15. Although he may have based this on earlier sources. See Ellis Davison, *The Viking Road to Byzantium*, pp. 63–4.

16. Ibn Rusteh, see *Les Atours Précieux* (translated into French by Gaston Wiet, Cairo 1955), p. 163

17. The name of this king is given in Ibn Fadlan's account as Almish ibn Shilki Elteber. His kingdom was largely pagan, although there were some converts, and he may have sought to free himself from dependency on the Khazars by converting to Islam and so gaining a useful ally in the Baghdad caliphate. Frye, *Ibn Fadlan's Journey to Russia*, pp. 8–9.

18. Frye, *Ibn Fadlan's Journey to Russia*, p. 64

19. The *Russian Primary Chronicle* says this took place in 862, but as the attack on Constantinople (which is known from other sources to have occurred in 860) post-dates the brothers' death by four years, the date in the chronicle must be wrong.

20. It is quite likely the raid was actually launched from Gorodishche, as the archaeological record suggests that Kiev was not yet a significant centre for the Rus. Franklin & Shepard, *The Emergence of Rus*, p. 54.

21. *The Homilies of Photius, Patriarch of Constantinople*, Ar II 6 (translated by Cyril Mango, Cambridge, Mass., 1958)

22. *The Homilies of Photius, Patriarch of Constantinople*, Ar II 36

23. The Samanids were the first native Persian dynasty to come to power after the Arab invasion of Persia. Their initial power base was around Samarkand in the 860s, and they gradually expanded east of the Caspian until they occupied Bukhara and all of Khurasan by around 900. Their empire began to fragment in the mid-tenth century under pressure from the Karakhanids and Ghaznavids, until in 992 the Karakhanid ruler Bughra Khan captured Bukhara. See 'The Samanids' by R. N. Frye in *The Cambridge History of Iran*, vol. 4 (edited by R. N. Frye, Cambridge 1975), pp. 136–61.

24. See Ellis Davison, *Viking Road to Byzantium*, p. 123.

25. This was a common Byzantine stratagem for preventing ship-borne invaders from penetrating the city's defences. It was also in use at the time of Harald Hardrada's service in the Varangian Guard (see p. 296 below).

26. Ellis Davison, *Viking Road to Byzantium*, p. 126

27. The story of Oleg's death is suspiciously close to the demise of Arrow-Odd from Halogoland, whose death was predicted by a Lapp seeress. Odd had the horse referred to in the prophecy killed and buried. Many years later, Odd returned to his old farm and saw the skull of the horse on the ground. He poked at it with a spear, and a snake slithered out and bit him on the leg, causing it to swell up from the effects of the poison. Some days later, Odd died. His story is told in *Örvar-Odds Saga* (available in Seven Viking Romances, translated by Herman Pálsson & Paul Edwards, London 1985).

28. The Lombard historian Liutprand of Cremona gives a figure of 1,000, but even this is probably an exaggeration.

29. For a detailed account of its use and development by the Byzantines (and theories of its composition), see J. R. Partington, *A History of Greek Fire and Gunpowder* (Cambridge 1960).

30. Leo the Deacon, see Ellis Davison, *The Viking Road to Byzantium*, p. 131.

31. The bezant was a catch-all term for gold coins, and this probably equates to fifty Byzantine solidi (the gold solidus being the largest-value coin, almost 95 per cent pure gold in the mid-tenth century). Fifty solidi equated to roughly the sum needed to purchase eight Russian slaves in 944 (each one costing twenty nomismata, or around six and a half solidi). Angeliki

Laiou (ed.), *The Economic History of Byzantium*, vol. 2 (Dumbarton Oaks 2002), p. 847.

32. This was probably about 35–40 miles downstream from Kiev. The town is not mentioned in Russian sources, but could be the same as the Uvetichi referred to in the *Russian Primary Chronicle*. See *Constantine Porphyrogenitus: De Administrando Imperio*, vol. 11 (Commentary), edited by R. J. H. Jenkins (London 1962), pp. 37–8.

33. The island is a few miles from Zaporizhia, and was probably named for the Armenian saint, Gregory the Illuminator.

34. There were possibly earlier raids, including one between 864 and 884, referred to by a thirteenth-century writer from Merv, Ibn Isfandiya, and another in 910, described by the same author when a force of sixteen Viking ships reached the Caspian.

35. See N. K. Chadwick, *The Beginnings of Russian History: An Enquiry into Sources* (Cambridge 1946), pp. 50–1.

36. Leo the Deacon, *History*, book IX, 11 (translated by Alice-Mary Talbot & Denis F. Sullivan in *The History of Leo the Deacon: Byzantine Military Expansion in the Tenth Century*, Dumbarton Oaks 2005)

37. There were indications in fragments of a manuscript entitled 'Report of a Greek Toparch', which would give a date of 962–3, but these are now regarded as a forgery. Ellis Davison, *Viking Road to Byzantium*, p. 138.

38. See p. 230 above.

39. See above for the description of Svyatoslav that Leo the Deacon gave on this occasion. The apparition was believed by Byzantine writers to have been St Theodore.

40. See Ellis Davison, *Varangians in Russia*, pp. 148–9; Franklin and Shepard, *The Emergence of Rus*, pp. 152–5.

41. *Russian Primary Chronicle* (edited by Hazzard Cross & Sherbowitz-Wetzor), p. 111

42. See p. 235 above.

43. For an account of the later history of the Varangian Guard, see p. 296 below.

44. In 1015 (twice), in 1018 and again shortly thereafter, in 1019, 1024 and 1036. The only concrete number given is 1,000 for the second group recruited in 1015. See Franklin and Shepard, *The Emergence of Rus*, p. 203.

45. See *Yngvar's Saga*, chapters 5–7 (translated by Herman Pálsson & Paul Edwards in *Vikings in Russia: Yngvar's Saga and Eymund's Saga*, Edinburgh 1989).

Chapter 8: New Empires in Britain and Scandinavia

1. *Anglo-Saxon Chronicle* 978 in *English Historical Documents, vol.* 1 (London 1979)

2. Though not everyone went as far as the chronicler Henry of Huntingdon, who claimed that the queen had herself delivered the fatal blow to her stepson. Henry of Huntingdon, *Historia Anglorum*, book V.27 (see translation by Diana Greenway, Oxford 1996, p. 325).

3. It is also a pun on his name, Aethelred meaning 'of noble counsel', and did not in fact come into common use until the twelfth century, well after the king's death.

4. See p. 280 below for the evolving Norman policy towards Scandinavia.

5. As the *The Saga of Olaf Tryggvason* does, although this is unlikely in fact to have been the case, and the ancestry was 'manufactured' to give Olaf's claim to the Norwegian throne greater credibility.

6. See Donald Scragg, *The Return of the Vikings: The Battle of Maldon 991* (Stroud 2006), pp. 80–1. Colchester was inland up the River Colne and had strong defences, which might explain Olaf's decision to attack Maldon rather than the ostensibly richer prize.

7. There are a number of other islands in the Blackwater, some of which have causeways, such as Osea, which could conceivably be the site of the battle, but the balance of evidence suggests the traditional attribution, to Northey Island, is the correct one. See Scragg, *The Return of the Vikings*, pp. 131–2.

8. See Scragg, *Return of the Vikings*, p. 91.

9. As well as the *Anglo-Saxon Chronicle* and 'The Battle of Maldon' poem, there is the 'Winchester obit', written in a calendar by a monk at Winchester; a chronicle by John of Worcester, which gives the name of the Viking leader as Guthmund; the *Vita Oswaldi*, a life of St Oswald; and two twelfth-century monastic chronicles, the *Liber Eliensis*, written in Ely, and the *Chronicon Abbatiae Rameseinsis*, composed in Ramsay.

10. 'Battle of Maldon' poem, line 83

11. 'Battle of Maldon' poem, line 89

12. This was apparently still in place when the body was moved to the north wall of the abbey's choir in 1154. Scragg, *The Return of the Vikings*, p. 155.

13. See 'The Battle of Maldon: Fact or Fiction' by D. G. Scragg in *The Battle of Maldon, Fiction or Fact* (edited by Janet Cooper, London 1993), pp. 19–31.

14. Ann Williams, *Aethelred the Unready, the Ill-Counselled King* (London 2003),

p. 45. In revenge, Aethelred is said to have had Aelfric's son blinded the following year.

15. Ian Howard, *Svein Forkbeard's Invasions and the Danish Conquest of England 991–1017* (Woodbridge 2003), p. 9

16. See p. 258 for an account of the Battle of Svold.

17. See p. 280 below for how this marriage alliance ultimately led to William the Conqueror's claim to the English throne.

18. The skin (and another from Copford Church), when examined in 1973, showed some signs of having the same structure as human skin. The church, however, was founded by King Cnut of Denmark after his accession to the English throne in 1016, and it does not seem likely that he would countenance the skin of one of his dead compatriots being used as a door covering for his own ecclesiastical foundation. Another 'Dane-skin' at Westminster Abbey proved to be cowhide. See "Dane-Skins": Excoriation in Early England' by M. J. Swanton in *Folklore*, vol. 87, no. 1 (1976), pp. 21–28.

19. 'Sprouting Like Cockle Amongst the Wheat': The St Brice's Day Massacre and the Isotopic Analysis of Human Bones from St John's College, Oxford' by A. Pollard, P. Ditchfield, E. Piva, S. Wallis, C. Falys & S. Ford in *Oxford Journal of Archaeology*, 31 (1), (2012), pp. 83–102.

20. William of Malmesbury adds the detail that Svein's sister Gunnhild, who had married Pallig, an English count, was among the victims, but this probably relates to a later killing, around 1013. Anne Williams, *Aethelred the Unready*, p. 4.

21. The 'A' version of the *Anglo-Saxon Chronicle* is somewhat kinder, with its account showing the English putting up a stouter (if equally fruitless) resistance, and the portrayal of Ealdorman Ulfcytel of East Anglia's payment of tribute to the Vikings as a perfectly reasonable solution to the situation, rather than the base cowardice of which Aelfric is accused. Ann Williams, *Aethelred the Unready*, pp. 50–1.

22. Aelfhelm came from a Mercian family who rose to prominence in the 990s (his brother Wulfric founded Burton Abbey). He became Ealdorman of Northumbria in 993.

23. A hide was the unit of measurement denoting the amount of land that could be ploughed by a single ploughman. It varied between 60 and 240 acres, until it was standardised in the Domesday Book as 120 acres.

24. He later served under Cnut, and also drafted law-codes for his new master. See 'Archbishop Wulfstan: State-Builder' by Patrick Wormald in

Wulfstan of York, Proceedings of the Second Alcuin Conference (edited by Matthew Townend, Turnhout 2004), pp. 9–28.

25. See Anne Hill, *Aethelred the Unready*, p. 91. Thorkill is also said, in saga tradition, to have been one of the leaders of the Jomsvikings. See p. 93 above.

26. The exact date of the *Sermo* is unknown, and it may also date to the period after Svein Forkbeard's death and the recall of Aethelred to England, acting as a kind of manifesto for the way in which the restored king should rule.

27. The Saga of Olaf Haraldsson contains a skaldic verse by Ottar Svarte, which contains the lines 'London Bridge is broken down. Gold is won, and bright renown.'

28. Alistair Campbell (ed.), *Encomium Emmae Reginae*, book I.4 (Cambridge 1998)

29. Aethelred's three eldest sons were Aethelstan, Edmund and Eadred, whom he had with his first wife Aelgifu. By 1013 they were all in their mid-twenties and plausible candidates for the throne. By this time, however, Aethelred had two more sons by Emma, Alfred and Edward (who later became king as 'the Confessor'), who might in time pose a threat to their elder brothers in terms of the royal succession. By 1013 Aethelstan appears to have been sick with an unspecified illness and died sometime before 1015. His sickness probably explains the weakness of those who might have opposed Aethelred, but nonetheless wanted an English candidate on the throne.

30. Higham, *The Death of Anglo-Saxon England*, p. 60. Williams, *Aethelred the Unready*, p. 122, gives 3 February.

31. *Anglo-Saxon Chronicle*, 1014

32. The *witangemot* was an ad hoc group of royal advisers, containing notables such as the two archbishops, other leading bishops, the ealdormen and other important thegns. It met as and when required by the king (in Aethelred's time it gathered some twenty-three times between the first meeting at Kingston in 979 and the final one at Oxford in 1015). It also had an important role in potentially disrupted successions (such as that of Edmund or of Harald Godwinson in 1066) when its recognition of a candidate for the throne could be decisive.

33. The chronicler Thietmar of Merseburg records the date of Cnut's arrival as July; the May date is that given in the *Anglo-Saxon Chronicle*.

34. The precise location of the battle site is disputed, with the two main

candidates being Ashingdon in south-east Essex and Ashdon to the north-west. See Warwick Rodwell, 'The Battle of Assandun and its Memorial Church' in *The Battle of Maldon* (edited by Janet Cooper), pp 127–158.

35. *Anglo-Saxon Chronicle*, Winchester version, and also Higham, *Death of Anglo-Saxon England*, p. 78

36. He may have married Aelfgifu without Christian rites, and so the 'second' marriage was canonically acceptable. Harold Godwinson had a similar relationship with Edith Swan-neck – *more Danico* 'according to the Danish custom'.

37. This levy was referred to as *heregeld* ('army tax'), a tax first imposed in 1012 as an annual due to pay for defences against (and tribute payments to) the Danes. Previous sums raised to bribe the Viking armies were referred to as *gafol*. Only later did these two taxes become conflated and referred to as Danegeld. See 'The Collection of Danegeld and Heregeld in the Reigns of Aethelred II and Cnut' by M. K. Lawson in *The English Historical Review*, vol. 99, no. 393 (October, 1984), pp. 721–38.

38. Eadwig was buried at Tavistock in Devon, and although it is not certain that Cnut had him killed, it is most likely. See Higham, *The End of Anglo-Saxon England*, p. 89.

39. For an account of this battle, see p. 262 below.

40. For more on Godwine, see p. 283 below.

41. Although there was a campaign against the Welsh in 1039, in which Leofric's brother, Edwin, died in battle against Gruffudd ap Llywelyn, the ruler of Gwynedd.

42. *Anglo-Saxon Chronicle*, 1042

43. See p. 301 below.

44. Timothy Bolton, *The Empire of Cnut the Great, Conquest and the Consolidation of Power in Northern Europe in the Early Eleventh Century* (Brill 2009), pp. 136–50

45. He was the son of Cnut's sister, Estrid, and Ulf (who had rebelled against Cnut in 1027).

46. See p. 93 above.

47. See Torgrim Titlestad, *Viking Norway, Personalities, Power and Politics* (translated by Stephen R. Parsons, Hafsfjord 2008), pp 133–34.

48. The *Anglo-Saxon Chronicle* gives a figure of 16,000 pounds of silver, while the actual treaty with Aethelred specifies 22,000, which may include various regional gelds paid in addition to the initial sum.

49. See Titlestad, *Viking Norway*, p. 110.

50. Gwynn Jones, *History of the Vikings*, p. 133

51. See the account in Titlestad, *Viking Norway*, pp. 162–6. There are some indications that there was already a significant Christian presence in Vestland in the decades before 996.

52. Adam of Bremen, *History of the Archbishops of Hamburg Bremen*, book 2, chapter xl (translated by Francis J. Tschan)

53. *Historia Norwegiae*, book XVII, pp. 33–42

54. See p. 129 above for details of this vessel.

55. See Titlestad, *Viking Norway*, p. 245.

56. Snorri Sturluson, *Heimskringla, History of St Olav*, chapter 1

57. See *Heimskringla, History of St Olav*, chapters 3–4

58. According to a skaldic poem by Ottar the Black, Olaf ensured the 'return of tracts of land'.

59. According to Saxo Grammaticus, however, Olaf actually cooperated with Cnut initially, and the cause of the split between them was that the Danish king seduced Olaf's mistress Alfiva (see Titlestad, *Viking Norway*, p. 251), while yet another account (*The Saga of Olav the Holy*) related that Cnut asked for Olaf's help in taking London, and in return promised to support any attempt Olaf might make on the Norwegian throne.

60. *English Historical Documents*, vol. 1 (*c*.500–1042), edited by Dorothy Whitelock (London 1979), p. 338.

61. His wife, Astrid, was Yaroslav's sister-in-law. She was the daughter of Olof Skötkonung of Sweden, and her sister Ingegerd had married Yaroslav.

62. Whilst the saga tradition gives 29 July as the date, Snorri Sturluson also says that the battle coincided with a solar eclipse, and this can only have taken place on 31 August.

63. Phillip Line, *Kingship and State Formation in Sweden 1130–1290* (Brill 2007), pp. 370–1.

64. Line, *Kingship and State Formation in Sweden*, pp. 103–4

65. See p. 72 above.

66. Tom Muir, *Orkney in the Sagas, The Story of the Earldom of Orkney as told in the Icelandic Sagas* (Kirkwall 2005), p. 17

67. See p. 29 above for more on the ritual of the blood-eagle.

68. See William P. L. Thomson, *A New History of Orkney* (Edinburgh 2008), pp. 64–67, for a discussion.

69. See p. 823 below for an account of Clontarf.

70. See Muir, *Orkney in the Sagas*, pp. 23–4.

71. For an account of the battle, see p. 304 below.

72. See p. 325 for more details of Magnus's expedition.

73. The story of the exile at Henry's court appears only in the *Longer Magnus Saga*, a thirteenth-century expansion of the *Orkneyinga Saga*'s account of Magnus's life. *New History of Orkney*, pp. 92–3.

74. *Orkneyinga Saga*, chapter 50 (translated by Alexander Burt Taylor, London 1938).

75. Many of these are recorded in the Shetlands, where there was no such strong official opposition to Magnus's sainthood. Muir, *Orkney in the Sagas*, p. 72.

76. Rögnvald had only secured the earldom the year before, see p. 328.

77. For an account of the discovery of the relics and their analysis, see John Mooney, 'Discovery of Relics in St Magnus Cathedral' in *Proceedings of the Orkney Antiquarian Society* 3 (1924–5), p. 73.

Chapter 9: The Last Vikings

1. For a discussion of the theories about his origin (including an outlandish suggestion by Dudo of Saint-Quentin that he was the son of the 'King of Dacia'), see 'Rollo of Normandy' by D. C. Douglas in *The English Historical Review*, vol. 57, no. 228 (October, 1942), pp. 417–36.

2. David Bates, *Normandy before 1066* (London 1982), p. 8

3. Harper-Bill, *A Companion to the Anglo-Norman World*, p. 21

4. Dudo of Saint-Quentin, *Historia Normannorum*, book 2, chapter 6

5. Bates, *Normandy before 1066*, p. 9

6. See p. 15 above.

7. The first ruler of Normandy known to have used the title Duke was Richard III. Its earliest appearance is in a charter of the abbey of Fécamp, from 1006. However, the title of Duke (or *dux*) was still used alongside that of Count (or *comes*) until the reign of Henry I (1106–35), when duke became the exclusive title of the lords of Normandy. See Bates, *Normandy before 1066*, pp. 148–9.

8. Harper-Bill, *A Companion to the Anglo-Norman World*, p. 25

9. The leader of the family that would eventually displace the Carolingians in 988 and establish the Capetian dynasty, which, in one form or another, ruled France until the nineteenth century.

10. Bates, *Normandy before 1066*, pp. 18–19

11. 'Les relations entre la Normandie et les colonies scandinaves des îles britanniques à la lumière des noms de lieux' by Gillian Fellows-Jensen

in *Les fondations scadinaves en Occident et les débuts du duché Normandie: Colloque de Cerisy-la-Salle (25–29 septembre 2002)*, edited by Pierre Baudin (Caen 2005), pp. 215–39

12. Harper-Bill, *A Companion to the Anglo-Norman World*, p. 28

13. Bates, *Normandy before 1066*, p. 22

14. See p. 251 above.

15. William of Poitiers, *Gesta Guillelmi*, i.41

16. Higham, *The Death of Anglo-Saxon England*, pp. 156–8

17. There is an alternative theory, since the account by William of Poitiers is late, and not supported by any of the contemporary chroniclers. According to this theory, there may have been no envoy sent to Rome and no papal sanction for the invasion of England, but the visit of papal legates in 1070 marked an *ex post facto* recognition of William's right to the English throne (and enabled him to depose Archbishop Stigand, an unwelcome reminder of the pre-Conquest church hierarchy). Harriet Harvey Wood, *The Battle of Hastings* (London 2008), pp. 140–1.

18. See p. 286 below for the deposition of Tostig.

19. David C. Douglas, *William the Conqueror* (London 1964), pp. 194–5

20. See p. 304 below.

21. Emma Mason, *The House of Godwine: History of a Dynasty* (London 2004), p. 32

22. Higham, *The Death of Anglo-Saxon England*, p. 121

23. Svein was further in royal disfavour, having been exiled for kidnapping the Abbess of Leominster. He had slipped back to England in an effort to restore his position, and a failed attempt to get Beorn to intercede with Edward on his behalf led to the fatal kidnapping.

24. Higham, *The Death of Anglo-Saxon England*, p. 134

25. Aelfgar was exiled by the royal council in 1055. It is not exactly clear why, but most probably he was simply removed on trumped-up charges of treason to eliminate a potential rival to Harold. Higham, *The Death of Anglo-Saxon England*, p. 139, and Peter Rex, *Harold II: The Doomed Saxon King* (Stroud 2005), pp. 92–3.

26. Stigand's predecessor, Robert of Jumièges, was still alive and had not been removed by the Pope, so technically Stigand could not succeed him as archbishop. In addition, Stigand conjointly held the see of Winchester, which he did not relinquish – another infringement of canon law that led to his excommunication by successive popes, including Leo IX, Victor II and Stephen IX. As a result, Stigand did not receive the *pallium* (the

broad band worn around the archbishop's neck) that was the symbol of archiepiscopal authority and only got this from Benedict X, who was briefly Pope in 1058, before being deposed the next year (again casting doubt on Stigand's legitimacy).

27. *Vita Edwardi Regis*, book 1, chapter 7 (edited and translated by Frank Barlow in *The Life of King Edward who rests at Westminster*, Oxford 1992)

28. See p. 301 below.

29. *Vita Edwardi Regis*, book II, chapter 11 (translated by F. Barlow, Oxford 1992). The woman in question was Harold's mother Gytha, the daughter of Earl Godwine.

30. This appointment took place sometime between October 1065 and spring 1067, so might possibly have occurred during the reign of Edward the Confessor or even that of William the Conqueror.

31. Snorri Sturluson, *Heimskringla, History of St Olav*, chapter 76

32. See p. 262 above.

33. Olaf had mediated between Thorfinn and Brusi, two sons of Earl Sigurd of Orkney, and had given each of them one-third of the Orkneys to rule, retaining the final third for himself, which he then entrusted to Earl Brusi to govern as his regent. Olaf kept Brusi's young son, Rögnvald Brusason, as a hostage against his father's good behaviour. So it was that Rögnvald (to Harald Sigurdsson's great fortune) came to be at Olaf's court. See Barbara Crawford, *Scandinavian Scotland*, pp. 76–77, and p. 270 above, for the history of Orkney in the tenth and eleventh centuries.

34. There are indications that they may not have. John Marsden, *Harald Hardrada*, pp. 66–8, argues that Rögnvald's previous stay as part of Olaf Haraldsson's retinue in Novgorod made him a more familiar figure to the court and he may have fought as part of Yaroslav's *druzhina*, his personal retinue. Harald, instead, may have been attached to the forces commanded by Eilif Rögnvaldson, the son of Rögnvald Ulfsson, who had come to Russia as part of the escort bringing the Swedish princess Ingigerd to Yaroslav in 1019.

35. Sigfús Blöndal, *The Varangians of Byzantium: An Aspect of Byzantine military history* (translated, revised and rewritten by Benedikt S. Benedikz, Cambridge 1978), pp. 54–5

36. Marsden, *Harald Hardrada*, p. 70

37. They were finally dealt with by Yaroslav in 1036, when he raised a huge army (which was said to include Scandinavians) and crushed a Pecheneg

host that was attempting to besiege Kiev. The Pecheneg confederacy crumbled, but it was all to no avail, as before long they were replaced in their role as scourge of the steppelands by a new Turkic nomadic group, the Kipchaks (or Cumans).

38. See p. 231 above. The suggestion in the *Morkinskinna* version of *Harald's Saga* that he reached the Byzantine empire by making a wide arc in entirely the wrong direction, travelling via northern Germany and Lombardy in northern Italy, is probably a misreading of Harald's later role in putting down a Norman revolt in 1040 in southern Italy (which was also referred to as *Longobardia* or Lombardy, from the Lombard duchies that had been established there in the eighth century).

39. Quoted by Snorri Sturluson in the *Heimskringla, King Harald's Saga*, chapter 2.

40. Blöndal, *The Varangians of Byzantium*, p. 36

41. Or 1153 nomismata. In exchange for this fee, the guardsman received a *roga*, or fee, of 44 nomismata a year, meaning that it would take nearly twenty-seven years to recoup the initial investment. The *roga*, however, would have been supplemented by imperial gifts and the plunder from any expeditions in which the unit took part. Ellis Davidson, *Viking Road to Byzantium*, p. 181.

42. Vladimir also had to promise to convert to Christianity, a stipulation that he duly fulfilled. When Anna travelled to Kiev, she probably brought in her entourage Thorvald Far-Traveller, the former missionary bishop of Iceland, whose violent temper had got him expelled by the Icelanders in 981. See p. 160 above.

43. The rebellion was finally put down in 1018. Blöndal, *The Varangians of Byzantium*, p. 51

44. Ellis Davidson, *Viking Road to Byzantium*, p. 182

45. This work is incorporated in the larger *Strategicon* of Cecaumenos, which includes a great deal of advice to emperors and was probably written when Michael VII was emperor (1071–7).

46. Although this has sometimes been interpreted to mean a campaign in North Africa, it is more likely to mean the expedition to Asia Minor.

47. Blöndal, *The Varangians of Byzantium*, p. 66

48. See p. 318 below.

49. The story is later, however, and first appears in Geoffrey of Monmouth's *Historia Regum Britanniae* around 1140. For a detailed discussion of the genesis of this legend, see 'The Legend of the Incendiary Birds' by

Helen Cam in *English Historical Review*, vol. 31, no. 121 (January 1916), pp. 98–101.

50. See p. 83 above. For the various appearances of the bird and funeral story, see Blöndal, *The Varangians of Byzantium*, pp. 71–3.

51. Although the *Flateyjarbók* manuscript containing *Harald's Saga* says they were held in a tower, which later became a tourist attraction for visiting Scandinavians. Ellis Davidson, *Viking Road to Byzantium*, p. 222.

52. *Heimskringla, History of Harald Hardrada*, chapters 14–15

53. See Blöndal, *The Varangians of Byzantium*, p. 100, and Ellis Davidson, *Viking Road to Byzantium*, p. 228. There are also indications in Icelandic sources of priests who came to Iceland whose doctrines were enticingly more lax than those of the official missionaries sponsored by Archbishop Adalbert of Hamburg. The Icelandic law-code, the *Grágás*, also makes reference to bishops who did not know the Latin tongue, and who were probably either Armenian or Greek.

54. Blöndal, *The Varangians of Byzantium*, p. 110.

55. Geoffrey of Maleterre specifically states that there were English warriors on the Byzantine side, while a little later Anna Comnena refers to Varangians as having come from 'Thule', a place she says had formerly belonged to the Roman empire and which could mean Britain. Blöndel, *The Varangians of Byzantium*, p. 141.

56. Blöndal, *The Varangians of Byzantium*, p. 156

57. Blöndal, *The Varangians of Byzantium*, pp. 231–3

58. See John Marsden, *Harald Hardrada, The Warrior's Way* (Stroud 2004), p. 140

59. See p. 238 above.

60. For the Roskilde ships, see p. 132 above.

61. Harald had sailed with a larger fleet initially, but when Svein failed to turn up at the appointed battle site on the Gaut Elf River, the Norwegian presumed that his Danish adversary had reneged on their agreement and sent part of his own force home.

62. Marsden, *Harald Hardrada*, pp. 188–9

63. Snorri Sturluson, *Heimskringla, King Harald's Saga*, chapter 79

64. Vegetius, *Epitoma Re Militaris* 1.9. See Vegetius, *Epitome of Military Science* (translated by N. P. Milner, 2nd edition, Liverpool 1996).

65. *Heimskringla, King Harald's Saga* (translated by Magnus Magnusson & Hermann Pálsson, London 1976)

66. Snorri Sturluson, *Heimskringla, King Harald's Saga*, chapter 87

67. This banner, *Landeyðuna*, was Hardrada's most cherished possession, possibly acquired during his service in the Varangian Guard. After Harald fell on the battlefield of Stamford Bridge, the standard was taken up by Eystein Orri, who led a hopeless last stand. It is possible that the *Am Bratach Sidhe* ('Fairy Flag') held at Dunvegan Castle on the Isle of Skye by the Clan Macleod could be none other than 'Landwaster', though the stories that swirl around it tell of a gift from the fairy folk or, more prosaically, of it being brought back from a crusade. Yet the Clan Macleod traces its ancestry back to Helga, the sister of Godred Crovan, King of Man, who fought at Stamford Bridge and was one of those who survived. See John Marsden, *Harald Hardrada*, pp. 231–3.

68. Snorri Sturluson, *Heimskringla, King Harald's Saga*, chapter 91

69. For berserks, see p. 29 above. Snorri's *King Harald's Saga* says that the English retreat was a feint, whereas the versions of the saga in *Morkinskinna*, *Fagrskinna* and *Flateyjarbók* suggest that it was a counter-attack.

70. *Fagrskinna*, pp. 140–1

71. Recorded in Snorri Sturluson's *Heimskringla, The Saga of Harald Hardrada*

72. Ordericus Vitalis, *The Ecclesiastical History of England and Normandy*, book III, ii.144 (translated by Thomas Forrester, London 1854)

73. See William of Poitiers, *Gesta Guillelmi*, ii.10.

74. The *Anglo-Saxon Chronicle* E text says that Harold fought the Battle of Hastings before his army had been fully assembled, while William of Malmesbury claims that his refusal to share the booty won at Stamford Bridge led to many deserting the ranks.

75. Ordericus Vitalis, *The Ecclesiastical History of England and Normandy*, book III, chapter 14

76. On his mother's side. Odo was the son of William's mother Herleva and Herluin de Conteville, to whom she had been married once her position as Duke Robert's concubine was no longer convenient. He became Bishop of Bayeux at the tender (and distinctly uncanonical) age of eighteen, and in 1067 received the earldom of Kent, making him both an ecclesiastical and secular baron of great power.

77. Michael J. Lewis, *The Real World of the Bayeux Tapestry* (Stroud 2008), pp. 7–9

78. William of Poitiers, *Gesta Guillelmi*, ii.10

79. As William of Poitiers claims, in *Gesta Guillelmi*, ii.14.

80. See Lawson, *The Battle of Hastings*, p. 71. The event is referred to by Henry of Huntingdon, but also by William of Poitiers and the *Chanson*.

81. The scene in the Bayeux Tapestry which depicts the deaths of Gyrth and Leofwine is shown at about this point in the battle.

82. See Lawson, *The Battle of Hastings*, pp. 226–32.

83. See Lawson, *The Battle of Hastings*, p. 228. There is a yet further possibility, from stitch-holes on the back of the Tapestry, that the second figure also had an arrow in his skull. See Brooks & Walker in *The Study of the Bayeux Tapestry* (edited by Gameson), pp. 63–92.

84. The other three are said to have been Count Eustace of Boulogne, Hugh of Ponthieu and a certain Gilfard. Lawson, *The Battle of Hastings*, p. 225.

85. William of Poitiers, *Gesta Gullielmi*, ii.23

86. Ordericus Vitalis, *The Ecclesiastical History of England and Normandy*, book III, chapter 14. Ordericus says that 'almost 15,000' died, but he may be referring to the whole battle and not just this one incident.

87. William of Malmesbury disagreed and stated that William had in fact returned the corpse to Gytha (and had refused any payment) and that it was later buried at Holy Cross Church at Waltham.

88. Lawson, *The Battle of Hastings*, p. 244

89. That in the west was led by two of Harold Godwinson's sons, Godwine and Edmund, who had been lent ships by Diarmait mac Mail, King of Leinster. They were fairly easily seen off by Brian of Brittany and retreated to Ireland, where they died sometime in the 1080s. Another son, Ulf, was imprisoned by William and was only released on the king's death in 1087. He is said to have supported Robert Curthose's attempt to unseat William II Rufus in 1088, but thereafter his fate is unknown. One of Harold's daughters, Gytha, escaped to the court of Svein Estrithsson in Denmark and was subsequently married to Vladimir II Monomakh of Kiev. One of their descendants, Isabella of France, married King Edward II of England in 1308. Given that all subsequent monarchs of England have descended from them, the blood of both Harold Godwinson and William the Conqueror flows in the veins of the current British monarch, Elizabeth II.

Edgar the Atheling led a chequered career after the failure of the 1069 rising. He escaped to Scotland, where he was for a time sheltered by Malcolm III. But William's successful invasion of 1072 forced Malcolm to recognise his overlordship and one of the prices of peace was the expulsion of Edgar, who then took refuge at the court of Robert of Flanders, another long-term opponent of William. In 1074, he returned to Scotland, but while on a return trip to France (where Philip I had offered him some land) he was shipwrecked in England and surrendered to William's men. He lived for ten years as a pensioner of the man who had seized his throne, and then in 1086 he received William's permission to move to the new Norman principalities in southern Italy. After William's death in 1087, Edgar threw in his lot with Robert Curthose and, as a result of the defeat of the 1088 uprising, was deprived of most of his lands. Edgar went back to Normandy with Robert, but was restored by William to favour and in 1097 led an invading army into Scotland on William's behalf. He is said to have gone on a pilgrimage to the Holy Land in 1102, and by 1106 was back in Europe and was taken prisoner at the Battle of Tinchebrai, when Henry I of England finally defeated Robert Curthose. Henry pardoned him and he died around 1125.

Chapter 10: The End of the Viking Age and the Legacy of the Vikings

1. Although isolated outposts such as Rometta (near Messina) held out as late as 965. Denis Mack Smith, *Medieval Sicily 800–1713*, p. 5.

2. Harald Hardrada of Norway probably also took part in this expedition during his service in the Varangian Guard. See p. 293 above.

3. Nick Webber, *The Evolution of Norman Identity*, p. 64, implies that this took place in 1042/3 before William's death.

4. Edward Gibbon, *The Decline and Fall of the Roman Empire*, chapter LVI (edited by J. B. Bury, London 1912)

5. Anna Comnena, *The Alexiad*, book I, chapter X (translated by Elizabeth A. S. Dawes, London 1928)

6. We do not actually possess the original of Amatus's work, which was lost, but his history has been transmitted to us through a Norman-French version, the *Ystoire de li Normant* of the fourteenth century.

7. James William Barlow, *The Normans in Southern Europe* (London 1886), p. 129

8. The last to fall were Castrogiovanni in 1088 and Noto in 1091.

9. *The Annals of Ulster*, 980.1

10. He did not in fact last long, dying the following year (981).

11. The regalia were known as the Sword of Carlus and the Ring of Thor.

12. *Njal's Saga* portrays Brodir of Man as an apostate pagan, who used sorcery to defeat his enemies. The Irish Annals, on the other hand, refer to a Brodor of York, who died in the battle, and so Brodir may not have been from Man at all. Benjamin Hudson, *Viking Pirates and Christian Princes: Dynasty, Religion and Empire in the North Atlantic* (Oxford 2005), pp. 98–9.

13. 'High-kings with opposition' by Marie Therese Flanagan in *A New History of Ireland, Volume 1: Prehistoric and Early Ireland* (Oxford 2005), pp. 898–900

14. Although there are many other names of Viking origin, such as Waterford, Wexford, Wicklow, Carlingford and Limerick (not to mention Dublin itself).

15. Explanations for Magnus's curious nickname varied. Snorri Sturluson thought it was because the king had adopted a style of Gaelic dress that left the lower part of the legs bare, while Saxo Grammaticus believed it was because Magnus had once been forced to flee barefoot from an attack on him. See 'Magnus Barelegs' Expeditions to the West' by Rosemary Power in *Scottish Historical Review*, vol. 65, no. 180, part 2 (October 1986), pp. 107–32

16. For the subsequent bloody history of Håkon and Magnus, see p. 271 above.

17. It was during this battle that Magnus Erlendsson acquired his reputation for sanctity by refusing to fight, preferring instead to recite psalms. See p. 272 above.

18. *Orkneyinga Saga*, chapter 108 (translated by Alexander Burt Taylor, London 1938)

19. *Orkneyinga Saga*, chapter 66

20. See p. 272 above.

21. *Orkneyinga Saga*, chapter 75

22. *Orkneyinga Saga*, chapter 106

23. See Muir, *Orkney in the Sagas*, p. 126

24. Christian had become King of Norway as well in 1450 and so inherited the Norwegian claim to Orkney and Shetland.

25. See p. 279 above.

26. See Raymond I. Page, 'How Long did the Scandinavian Language Survive in England: The Epigraphical Evidence' in *Runes and Runic Inscriptions*, pp. 181–97.

27. See Michael P. Barnes, 'Scandinavian Languages in the Viking Age' in Stefan Brink (ed.), *The Viking World*, pp. 274–81

28. Michael P. Barnes, *The Norn Language of Orkney and Shetland* (Lerwick 1998), p. 3

29. See p. 111 above.

30. Barnes, *The Norn Language of Orkney and Shetland* (Lerwick 1998), p. 11

31. Which was only actually published in 1879.

32. Barnes, *The Norn Language of Orkney and Shetland* (Lerwick 1998), p. 17

33. J. J. Campbell, 'The Norse Language in Orkney in 1725' in *Scottish Historical Review* 33, p. 175

34. See Barnes, *The Norn Language of Orkney and Shetland*, p. 26

35. The *Historia de omnibus gothorum sveonumque regibus* (1554) by Johannes (1488–1544) and *Historia de gentibus septentrionalibus* (History of the Northern Peoples, 1555) by Olavus (1490–1557)

36. See p. 148 above.

37. Macpherson was best known for his 'discovery' in 1761 of a series of poems about the ancient Irish hero Fingal, allegedly penned by the poet Ossian. Macpherson provided 'translations' of these, but it soon became apparent (despite his many defenders) that the whole poetry cycle was his own forgery.

38. The journal was named after Iduna, the Norse goddess whose golden apples gave immortality to the gods.

39. *Viking Tales of the North: The Sagas of Thornstein, Viking's Son, and Fridthof the Bold* (translated by Rasmus Bjorn Anderson & Jon Bjarnason, Chicago 1876), canto XV, p. 291

40. Ian Bradley, *William Morris and His World* (New York 1978), p. 57

Chronology

c.12,000 BC Hamburg reindeer hunters penetrate southern Scandinavia

c.4,000 BC Agriculture reaches Scandinavia

500 BC Beginning of Iron Age in Scandinavia

500–1 BC pre-Roman Iron Age in Scandinavia

300 BC Greek traveller Pytheas mentions 'Thule', a possible reference to Iceland or Scandinavia

c.300 BC Hjortspring Boat shows evidence of clinker-built technique of shipbuilding

AD 1–400 Roman Iron Age period

AD 5 Roman fleet reaches the northern tip of Jutland

AD 200–500 Finds of weapons sacrificed in bogs in Denmark

310–320 Construction of the Nydam Boat

c.400 First carved picture stones on Gotland, Sweden

c.400–600 Occupation of trading and market site of Helgö in Sweden

AD 400–600 Migration period

AD 550–750 Vendel period in Sweden

c.515 Chochilaichus's attack on Francia shows evidence of pre-Viking era raids by Scandinavians

650 Foundation of Swedish colony at Grobina, Latvia

c.700 Building of the Kvalsund boat, showing development of true keel in Scandinavia

c.714 St Willibrord leads unsuccessful Christian mission to Scandinavia

c.710 Foundation of trading centre of Ribe

726 Digging of the Kanhave Canal on Danish island of Samsø

734 Eastern Frisia conquered by the Franks

737 Construction of the Danevirke begins

750 First evidence of settlement at Hedeby

c.750 Establishment of Staraya Ladoga in northern Russia, later to be Viking colony; beginning of settlement at Birka in Sweden

780 First Islamic dirhams appear in Scandinavian hoards

782 Charlemagne massacres 4,500 pagan Saxons after a revolt against Frankish rule

786–802 Reign of Beorhtric of Wessex, during which the Vikings attack Portland in Dorset

792 Offa of Mercia issues decree calling on men of Kent to defend themselves against 'pagan peoples'

793 First dated Viking raid in western Europe, against the Northumbrian monastery of Lindisfarne

794 Viking attack on the Hebrides

795 Viking raids commence against Ireland; Monastery of Iona off the west coast of Scotland raided

796 Viking attack on monastery at Jarrow beaten off

797 Franks complete conquest of Saxony, bringing their territory to the borders of Scandinavia

799 Vikings attack monastery of St-Philibert at Noirmoutier, first raid in Francia

c.800 Establishment of trading settlement at Kaupang in Sweden

806 Viking attack on the monastery of Iona kills 68 of the brethren

807 Vikings sack Inishmurray off Connaucht coast of Ireland

808 Godfred, king of the Danes, destroys the Abodrite settlement of Reric and moves its merchants to Hedeby

810 Ravaging of Frisia by the Danish king Godfred. He is assassinated and his nephew Hemming makes a treaty with the Franks

812 Vikings defeated in Ireland by the king of Loch Léin

814 Death of Charlemagne; Louis the Pious becomes Frankish ruler

815 Frankish attempt to restore Harald Klak to the Danish throne fails

819 Harald Klak becomes joint ruler of Denmark with Godfred's sons

819–36 Under constant threat of Viking attack, the monks of St-Philibert leave Noirmoutier

820 Viking fleet ravages the coast of Flanders and Aquitaine

822 Viking raid against Cork

822–23 Mission of Archbishop Ebbo of Rheims to Denmark

c.825 First minting of coins in Scandinavia, at Hedeby

c.825 Probable date of first Viking settlement in the Faroes

826 Baptism of Danish King Harald Klak at Mainz; beginning of Anskar's first mission to Denmark

827 Expulsion of Harald Klak from Denmark

829–31 Anskar's mission to Sweden

*c.*830–40 The Norwegian Nadod first sights Iceland

832 Vikings raid Armagh in Ireland three times in a single month

833 Harald Klak attacks Frisia, with the encouragement of Lothar, son of Louis the Pious

834–38 Series of Viking raids on the *emporia* of Dorestad and Quentovic in northern Francia

835 Vikings attack Sheppey in Kent

*c.*834 Oseberg ship burial in Sweden

837 Arrival of large-scale Viking fleets on the Boyne and Liffey in Ireland

839 Viking Rus first recorded as reaching Byzantine capital of Constantinople; Viking attack on the Picts

840 Civil war breaks out in Francia after death of Louis the Pious; Viking fleet overwinters in Ireland for the first time, on Lough Neagh

840 Viking attacks on Southampton and Portland

841 Lothar grants Walcheren as a fief to the Danish ruler Harald

841 Viking *longphorts* established at Dublin and elsewhere in Ireland

842 Vikings sack Quentovic

843 Treaty of Verdun partitioning the Carolingian empire between the children of Charles the Simple weakens Frankish resistance to the Vikings; Viking raids on Brittany commence with attack on Nantes

843 Aethelwulf of Wessex defeated by Viking fleet at Minehead

844 First major Viking raiding expedition in the Iberian Peninsula defeated at Seville in Spain; Viking attack on Toulouse

845 Viking army sacks Paris and is bought off with tribute of 7,000 pounds of silver

848 Vikings capture Bordeaux after a siege

*c.*850 Horik I of Denmark gives permission to Anskar to build churches in Hedeby and Ribe

*c.*850 Gokstad ship burial in Norway

851–52 Anskar returns on a new mission to Sweden

850 Viking fleet overwinters for first time in England, on the Isle of Thanet; Godrid Haraldsson and Rorik ravage Frisia

851 Conflict between the *Dubh-Gaill* ('Dark Vikings') and *Fin-Gaill* ('Fair Vikings') in Ireland

852 Battle of Carlingford Lough – the *Dubh-Gaill* defeat the *Fin-Gaill*

852 Vikings overwinter for the first time on the Seine

853 Vikings overwinter in the Loire valley; Irish Vikings accept Olaf, son of the king of *Laithlind*, as their leader

854 Viking fleet overwinters on the Isle of Sheppey

855 Rorik occupies Frisia (and holds it to at least 873)

857 Pippin II of Aquitaine defects to the Loire Vikings

859 'Varangians' (Vikings) recorded as imposing tribute on Slavic groups in Russia

859–62 Voyage of Bjorn and Hasteinn into the Mediterranean

860 Russian chronicle records invitation of the Slavs to Rurik and his brothers to rule them

860 Viking attack on Constantinople

860 Viking fleet sacks Winchester

c.860 Garðar Svarvarsson's voyage to Iceland

c.862 Rurik establishes himself in Novgorod; Askold and Dir seize Kiev

864 Olaf defeats and kills Conchobar, ruler of Meath

864 Pippin II of Aquitaine captured and killed, ending his rebellion

864 Charles the Bald orders campaign of construction of fortified bridges to contain Viking raids into Francia

865/870 Floki Vilgertharson visits Iceland

865 Danish 'Great Heathen Army' (or micel here) arrives in England

865 Death of Anskar, succeeded as archbishop of Hamburg-Bremen by Rimbert

866 Danish Vikings capture York; Loire Vikings sack Le Mans

866 Expedition of Olaf and Ásl to Pictland

867 Failed attempt by Osbert and Aelle, kings of the Northumbrians, to retake York leads to both their deaths; Vikings install Egbert as puppet king in York

868 Vikings attack Mercia, but return to overwinter in York

869 Vikings attack East Anglia and kill the East Anglian king, Edmund

c.870 Harald Finehair becomes ruler of Vestfold in Norway

c.870 Establishment of Viking earldom of Orkney under Earl Rögnvald of Møre

870 Irish Viking army captures Alt Clud (Dumbarton), capital of the British kingdom of Strathclyde

871 Danish Great Army's attempt to invade Wessex defeated at Ashdown by King Aethelred; Alfred becomes king of Wessex; Battle of Wilton: Vikings defeat Alfred, who has to pay tribute to get them to withdraw from Wessex

872 Vikings expel King Egbert from York

873 Death of Ivar, ruler of the Dublin Vikings, succeeded in turn by his three sons

873–914 'Forty Years Rest' from Viking raids in Ireland

874 Possible date of expedition of Harald Finehair of Norway to Orkney

874 Great Army deposes Burgred, King of Mercia, and sets a puppet ruler, Ceolwulf, on the Mercian throne; Great Army divides; one part returns to Northumbria under Halfdan; the other overwinters in Cambridge

874 Viking colony on Iceland established by Ingólf Arnason

875 Renewed Viking invasion of Wessex; Alfred makes peace with them

876 Northumbrian Vikings begin to settle down on the land

877 Vikings begin to settle in Mercia; Halfdan killed at Battle of Strangford Lough in Ireland

878 Viking army under Guthrum invades Wessex, Alfred flees into Athelney Marshes and gathers an army which defeats Guthrum at the Battle of Edington; Guthrum accepts baptism

879 Part of Great Army crosses from Fulham to the Meuse in Francia; Guthrum settles his army in East Anglia

879/880 Treaty between Alfred and Guthrum establishes the boundary of the Danelaw

c.880 Date given by *Saga of the Faroese* for settlement by Grim Kamban in the Faroes

c.880 Oleg of Novgorod occupies Kiev, uniting the two principalities

881 Vikings attack Liège, Utrecht and Aachen; Louis III of Francia defeats Vikings at Saucourt but dies soon after

882 Charles the Fat grants a fief in Frisia to Godfred

884 Charles the Fat becomes ruler of a united Frankish realm after a period of division; Vikings storm Pont de l'Arche defensive position on the Seine

885 Guthrum launches large-scale invasion of Wessex, which is defeated

885–86 Vikings unsuccessfully besiege Paris

c.885–90 Battle of Hafsfjord: Harald Finehair establishes himself as dominant king in Norway

886 Vikings overrun part of County of Nantes in Brittany

887 Charles the Fat deposed in favour of Odo, the defender of Paris during the 885 siege

c.890 Sigurd the Mighty attacks northern Scotland from Orkney

891 Battle of the Dyle; Arnulf, ruler of East Francia, defeats Viking army, whose remnants cross over to England

891 Death of Earl Sigurd of Orkney

892 Large Viking army crosses from Boulogne and lands in Kent

893 Viking army withdraws into Mercia

896   Viking army in England breaks up, some settle down, others return to Francia; Sihtric Ivarsson, leader of the Dublin Vikings, killed in a factional dispute

899   Death of Alfred the Great, succeeded by his son Edward the Elder; Edward's cousin Aethelwold is elected king of York by the Vikings

c.900   Norwegian Vikings begin to settle in north-western England

900/930   Gunnbjorn Ulf-Krakason discovers Gunnbjorn's skerries between Iceland and Greenland

902   Expulsion of the Vikings from Dublin

902   Battle of the Holme: Aethelwold defeated and killed by Edward the Elder

902/3   Viking attack on Anglesey

906   Treaty of Tiddingford between Edward the Elder and the East Anglian and Northumbrian Vikings

907   Treaty between the Viking Rus and Byzantine empire sets terms of trade between them

907   Oleg leads second Viking attack on Constantinople

910   Battle of Tettenhall: Danish raiders into Mercia badly defeated

911   Treaty of St Clair-sur-Epte between Rollo and Charles the Simple grants the Vikings land in Normandy

911   Second trading treaty between Byzantines and Vikings

912   Viking expedition raids around the Caspian Sea

912–20   Wessex conquers the Danelaw south of the Humber

912–36   Viking occupation of Brittany

913   Viking fleet attacks Waterford harbour

914   Death of Oleg, Viking ruler of Kiev; succeeded by Igor

917   New Viking fleet under Rögnvald and Sihtric arrives in Ireland and takes Dublin

918   Battle of Corbridge: Rögnvald Ivarsson defeats English-Scots alliance

919   Rögnvald crosses to England and becomes king of York; huge Viking fleet attacks Brittany

920   Rögnvald succeeded as king of York by Sihtric

921   Robert of Neustria cedes Nantes to Rögnvald, leader of the Vikings in Brittany

921   Arab traveller Ibn Fadlan takes part in an embassy to the khan of the Volga Bulgars and leaves account of Vikings he meets along the way

924   Edward the Elder of Wessex dies, succeeded by Athelstan

924   Land grants in Bessin and Hiémois increase size of Viking colony in Normandy

926 Battles of Carlingford and Strangford Lough, both defeats for the Dublin Vikings

927 Athelstan takes direct control of York after expelling Sihtric's brother Guthfrith

c.930 All land in Iceland is fully claimed

930 The *Althing* assembly is set up in Iceland

c.933 Harald Finehair dies, succeeded as king of Norway by Eirik Bloodaxe

934 Emperor Henry the Fowler of Germany invades Denmark

c.934 Eirik Bloodaxe deposed, Håkon the Good becomes king

934 Olaf Guthfrithsson becomes king of Dublin

935 Archbishop Unni of Hamburg sends mission to King Gorm the Old of Denmark

936 Alain Barbetorte recaptures Nantes from the Vikings

937 Battle of Brunanburh: defeat of Olaf Gothrithsson's alliance of Scots and Vikings by Athelstan of Wessex

939 Death of Athelstan of Wessex, succeeded by Edmund; Olaf Gothrithsson again becomes king of York; last force of Loire Vikings defeated in Brittany

940 Olaf Guthfrithsson invades Scotland, reaching as far as Dunbar; Edmund gives up land north of Watling Street to Olaf

941 Olaf Guthfrithsson dies, succeeded as ruler of York by Olaf Cuarán

941 Igor launches attack on Constantinople, which is driven off using Greek fire

943–44 Igor raids around the Caspian Sea

944 Igor attacks Constantinople again, agrees a new trading treaty with the Byzantines, less favourable to the Vikings than before

944 Congalach, overking of Brega, sacks Dublin, killing 400 Vikings

945 Edmund takes back control of York

948 Eirik Bloodaxe becomes king of York

948 Establishment of first bishoprics in Scandinavia (at Ribe, Århus and Schleswig)

949 Eirik Bloodaxe expelled from York, Olaf Cuarán restored

c.950 Harald Bluetooth builds additional fortifications along the Danevirke

c.950 Emergence of Mammen artistic style

951 Viking raids against Galicia

952 Eirik Bloodaxe restored to the throne of York; Olaf Cuarán returns to Dublin

954 Håkon the Good of Norway attacks Denmark

954 Eirik Bloodaxe, last Scandinavian king of York, killed at Stainmore in northern England

958 Death of Gorm the Old, Harald Bluetooth becomes king of Denmark

960 Svyatoslav of Kiev attacks the Khazar empire, sacking its capital Itil

960/965 Håkon the Good is defeated and fatally wounded in Battle of Fitjar against the sons of Eirik Bloodaxe

962 Iceland is divided into Quarters

964–71 Svyatoslav of Kiev conducts series of campaigns against Bulgars and Byzantines

965 Conversion to Christianity of Harald Bluetooth of Denmark

965/966 Further Viking raids in Galicia

972 Vikings attack the Algarve

972 Svyatoslav, Viking ruler of Kiev, killed by Pechenegs

973 Otto I of Germany occupies southern Jutland (to 983)

974 Harald Bluetooth defeats Harald Greycloak (son of Eirik Bloodaxe) at Battle of Limfjord, restoring Danish domination of Norway and leaving Håkon, *jarl* of Lade, to rule most of the country

974–81 German occupation of Hedeby

c.975 Foundation of Sigtuna (Sweden)

978 Construction of bridge at Ravning Enge in the Velje valley, Denmark

978 Battle of Belan: Olaf Cuarán of Dublin kills the king of Leinster

980 Viking raids against England resume

c.980 Olof Skötkonung becomes king of Sweden

980 Construction of Trelleborg fortresses by Harald Bluetooth

980 Earl Sigurd the Stout becomes ruler of Orkney (to 1014)

980 Battle of Tara: decisive defeat of Olaf Cuarán by Maél Sechnaill

982–85 Eirik the Red's first voyage to Greenland

986 Eirik the Red establishes Viking colony in Greenland

c.990 Bjarni Herjólfsson sights coast of mainland North America

986/7 Harald Bluetooth dies after an uprising against him by his son Svein Forkbeard

988 Establishment of the Varangian Guard by Byzantine emperor Basil II; conversion of Vladimir, prince of Kiev, to Orthodox Christianity

989 Sihtric Silkenbeard becomes king of Dublin

991 Battle of Maldon: Olaf Tryggvason defeats Byrhtnoth, ealdorman of Essex

991 Peace treaty between Wessex and Normandy aimed at preventing the latter harbouring Viking fleets for raids on southern England

994 Svein Forkbeard of Denmark embarks on joint attack on London with Olaf Tryggvason

995 Olaf Tryggvason baptised, leaves England and seizes control of Norway; Olof Skötkonung becomes king of united realm of Svear and Götar in Sweden

996 Chiefs of Vestland acknowledge Olaf Tryggvason as king at the Gula Thing

997 Máel Sechnaill of the southern Uí Néill and Brian Bóruma ally, with Brian overlord of Dublin

997–1002 Viking raids on England intensify, leading to payment of large tributes

c.998 Construction of the Long Serpent, the largest recorded Viking warship

999 Battle of Glenn Máma, Dublin Vikings' revolt is crushed by Brian and Máel Sechnaill

1000 Battle of Svöld: Death of Olaf Tryggvason in battle with Svein Estrithsson of Denmark and Olof Skötkonung of Norway

1000 Icelanders accept conversion to Christianity

c.1000 First Viking voyages to Vinland

c.1000 Beginning of Ringerike artistic style

1001 Aethelred of Wessex pays 24,000 pounds of silver in tribute to Viking fleet

1002 St Brice's Day Massacre of Danish settlers in England

1002 Marriage of Emma, sister of Duke Richard I of Normandy, and Aethelred of Wessex

1003–05 Campaigns of Svein Forkbeard in England

1005 Gilla Mochonna, overking of southern Brega, sacks Dublin

1006 Viking fleet in England extracts a tribute of 36,000 pounds of silver

1008 Olof Skötkonung of Sweden baptised

1009 Thorkell the Tall arrives in England with a new Viking fleet, sacks Oxford

c.1010 Colonising expedition of Guðrid and Thorfinn Karlsefni to Vinland

1012 Thorkell captures Canterbury and archbishop Aelfeah is killed, a tribute of 48,000 pounds is paid to the Vikings

1013 Conquest of England by Svein Forkbeard; Aethelred of Wessex, his wife Emma and their children flee to Normandy

1014 Battle of Clontarf: Viking-Irish coalition defeated by Brian Bóruma and his allies, but Brian is killed

1014 Svein Forkbeard dies and Aethelred regains the English throne. Svein's son, Cnut, returns to Denmark

1014 Thorfinn the Mighty becomes joint Earl of Orkney (to 1065), power of Orkney earldom is at its height

1015 Death of Vladimir of Kiev followed by a civil war between his sons

1015 Cnut launches new campaign against England

1016 Olaf Haraldsson becomes Norwegian king after Battle of Nesjar on the Oslofjord; Aethelred dies, and Cnut defeats his son Edmund Ironside at Assandun, who soon after dies; Cnut becomes king of England

1018 Cnut becomes king of Denmark after death of his brother Harald

1026 Olaf defeated at the Battle of the Holy River by Cnut

1027 Cnut undertakes a pilgrimage to Rome; in his absence a rebellion almost unseats him

1028 Olaf Haraldsson defeats his main Norwegian rival Erling at Sola, but his support then collapses and he flees Norway and finds refuge in Kiev

1030 Olaf Haraldsson returns to Norway; Battle of Stiklestad: Olaf defeated and killed by the men of Trøndelag; Harald Hardrada, who fought on Olaf's side, flees to Kiev

c.1030 Skuldelev 1 ship constructed in Norway

c.1030 Flow of Islamic dirhams into Viking lands virtually ceases

1034 Harald Hardrada begins service in the Byzantine Varangian Guard

1034 Rainulf Drengot granted fief at Aversa by Sergius IV, duke of Naples, beginning Norman settlement in southern Italy

1035 Cnut dies; succeeded in Denmark by Harthacnut and in England by Harold, his son by Aelfgifu

1035 Faroes become part of the Norwegian kingdom

1035 Death of Duke Robert of Normandy, succeeded by his seven-year-old son William

1036 Aethelred's sons Alfred and Edward return to England in bid to seize the throne; Alfred is killed, Edward flees back to Normandy

c.1040 Skuldelev 2 ship built, probably around Dublin

c. 1040 Expedition of Yngvar the Widefarer to the east of the Caspian Sea

1040–41 Harald Hardrada takes part in suppression of revolt in Bulgaria by Peter Deleanos

1042 Death of Harthacnut, end of Danish rule in England; Edward the Confessor becomes English king; Magnus of Norway elected king of Denmark

1045–46 Harald Hardrada goes to Sweden, allies himself with Svein Estrithsson and ravages Denmark

1046 Harald Hardrada becomes joint king of Norway with Magnus

1046 Drogo de Hauteville granted title of 'Count of all the Normans of all Apulia'

1047 Death of Magnus of Norway; Harald Hardrada becomes sole Norwegian king; Svein Estrithsson becomes king of Denmark

1047–66 Series of Viking raids around Santiago, Spain

1048 Foundation of new Norwegian royal capital at Oslo

1048 Earl Thorfinn of Orkney makes pilgrimage to Rome

c.1050 Emergence of Urnes artistic style

1051 Earl Godwine exiled by Edward the Confessor

1052 Earl Godwine returns to England, eclipse of the pro-Norman group at the English court

1053 Earl Godwine dies and Harold Godwineson becomes Earl of Wessex

1053 Battle of Civitate, Normans defeat Imperial army and become dominant force in southern Italy

1054 Normans defeat French army at Mortemer

1056 Ísleif becomes first Icelandic bishop

1060 Normans begin conquest of Sicily (complete by 1091)

1062 Harald Hardrada defeats Svein Estrithsson at naval Battle of Nissa

1064 Treaty between Denmark and Norway ends half a century of warfare

1064–5 Visit of Harold Godwineson to Normandy

1065 Revolt against Harold Godwineson's brother Tostig, earl of Northumbria, leads to his deposition and exile

1066 Edward the Confessor dies and Harold Godwineson is chosen to succeed him; invasions of England by Harald Hardrada of Norway with the assistance of Tostig and by William of Normandy; Battle of Fulford: Hardrada defeats northern English levies; Battle of Stamford Bridge, Harald Hardrada defeated and killed. Battle of Hastings, William of Normandy defeats Harold Godwineson and seizes English throne.

1066 Anti-Christian reaction in Sweden under King Stenkil

1069 Svein Estrithsson sends invasion fleet to England which joins forces with a northern uprising against William, but the revolt collapses

1070–71 Earl Morcar and Hereward the Wake continue resistance against William of Normandy in East Anglia

1076 Death of Svein Estrithsson

1079 Godred Crovan conquers the Isle of Man

1081 Battle of Dyrrachium: Norman army under Robert Guiscard defeats Byzantine emperor Alexius I

1084 King Inge of Sweden deposed by his brother-in-law Sven *blott* in another pagan reaction

1085 Planned invasion of England by Knut IV of Denmark aborted

1090   Destruction of the pagan cult centre at Uppsala

1095   Earliest census in Iceland shows there are 4,560 free farmers in the country

1098   Expedition of Magnus Barelegs of Norway to the Scottish Isles

1102–03   Magnus Barelegs campaigns in Ulster, but is killed as he prepares to return to Scandinavia

1103–04   First Scandinavian archbishopric established at Lund

1107–11   Expedition of King Sigurd of Norway to the Holy Land

1116   Murder of Earl Magnus Erlendsson of Orkney by his cousin Håkon. Magnus is subsequently canonised

1117–18   Icelandic laws written down for the first time

1121   Bishop Erik Gnuppson travels from Greenland to Vinland and disappears

1122–33   Ari Thorgilsson composes the *Íslendingabók*

1125   Wreck of two ships off Greenland coast leads to law-suit and feud between Norwegians and Greenlanders

1126   Arnald, first Greenlandic bishop, arrives and settles at Garðar

1151–53   Earl Rögnvald-Kali of Orkney goes on pilgrimage to the Holy Land

1153   Earl Harald Maddaðarson of Orkney shelters in a burial mound after a storm, possible date of runic carvings at Maeshowe

1156   Conquest of the southern Hebrides by Somerled

1164   Archbishopric established at Uppsala in Sweden

1180–1280   Main period of composition of Icelandic *konungasögur*

1202   Icelandic poet and historian Snorri Sturluson moves to Borg

1209   Battle at Hólar begins period of instability in Iceland

1236   Snorri Sturluson goes into exile in Norway after defeat of his party at the Battle of Baer

1237   First mention of the Tynwald assembly on the Isle of Man

1238   Defeat of the Sturlunga faction at Örlygsstaðir in Iceland, Sturla and Sighvat killed

1241   Murder of Snorri Sturluson at Reykholt

1246   Iceland's largest ever battle at Haugsnes

1250/1300   Date of runic carving at Kingitorssuaq in northern Greenland

1261   Greenland Norse colony accepts direct rule from Norway

1262   The Icelanders accept direct Norwegian rule; Battle of Largs, Scots defeat Håkon IV of Norway

1264   Men of the Eastern Quarter in Iceland agree to Norwegian rule

1266   Greenland Viking expedition finds traces of *skraeling* (or Inuit), native inhabitants

1266 Norwegian cession of the Hebrides and Man to Scotland

1271 Járnsiða law-code, modelled on that of Norway, issued for Iceland

1341 Western Settlement in Greenland abandoned

1341 Last mention of the Varangian Guard

1347 Last reported Viking voyage to North America, when a ship gathering timber in Markland is driven on to Iceland

1355 Danish crown appoints Poul Knudsson to lead an expedition to Greenland, but it probably does not set out

1368 Ivar Bardarson reports that the *skraelings* have captured the Western Settlement

1368 Bishop Alf, the last known bishop resident in Greenland, arrives to take up his see

1369 Regular voyages to Greenland end when the royal vessel carrying out the trade between Scandinavia and Greenland is wrecked and not replaced

1379 Greenland Viking settlements attacked by Inuit

1397 Union of Kalmar brings Denmark into personal union with Norway

1408 Wedding in Hvalsey is last written record of the Greenland Viking colony

1448 Pope Nicholas V orders Bishop of Skálholt in Iceland to send a priest to Greenland, but no expedition sets out

c.1450–75 Probable end of Viking Norse colony in Greenland

1469 Denmark cedes Orkney and Shetland to Scotland

1578 English explorer Martin Frobisher reaches Greenland

1723 First post-Viking European visitors find the ruins of the Western Settlement

Index

Entries in *italics* indicate maps.